Trevilian Station,
June 11–12, 1864

ALSO BY JOSEPH W. MCKINNEY

*Brandy Station, Virginia, June 9, 1863:
The Largest Cavalry Battle of the Civil War*
(McFarland, 2013 [2006])

Trevilian Station, June 11–12, 1864

Wade Hampton, Philip Sheridan and the Largest All-Cavalry Battle of the Civil War

Joseph W. McKinney

McFarland & Company, Inc., Publishers
Jefferson, North Carolina

LIBRARY OF CONGRESS CATALOGUING-IN-PUBLICATION DATA [new form]

Names: McKinney, Joseph W., 1948–
Title: Trevilian Station, June 11–12, 1864 : Wade Hampton, Philip Sheridan and the largest all-cavalry battle of the Civil War / Joseph W. McKinney.
Description: Jefferson, North Carolina : McFarland & Company, Inc., 2016. | Includes bibliographical references and index.
Identifiers: LCCN 2015046546 | ISBN 9780786499038 (softcover : acid free paper)
Subjects: LCSH: Trevilian Station, Battle of, Va., 1864. | Virginia—History—Civil War, 1861–1865—Cavalry operations. | United States—History—Civil War, 1861–1865—Cavalry operations.
Classification: LCC E476.6 .M35 2016 | DDC 973.7/455—dc23
LC record available at http://lccn.loc.gov/2015046546

ISBN (print) 978-0-7864-9903-8
ISBN (ebook) 978-1-4766-2320-7

BRITISH LIBRARY CATALOGUING DATA ARE AVAILABLE

© 2016 Joseph W. McKinney. All rights reserved

No part of this book may be reproduced or transmitted in any form or by any means, electronic or mechanical, including photocopying or recording, or by any information storage and retrieval system, without permission in writing from the publisher.

Front cover images: Wade Hampton, C.S.A., between 1860 and 1870; Major General Philip H. Sheridan, between 1855 and 1865; *Sheridan's final charge at Winchester*/Thulstrup, facsimile print by L. Prang & Co., c1886 (Library of Congress)

Printed in the United States of America

*McFarland & Company, Inc., Publishers
Box 611, Jefferson, North Carolina 28640
www.mcfarlandpub.com*

To the war horses lost on the Trevilian's Raid

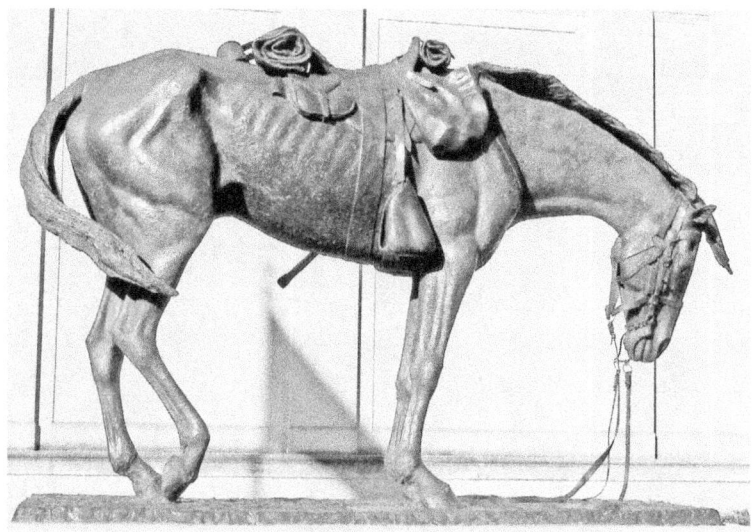

The War Horse was given to the Virginia Historical Society by Paul Mellon of Upperville, Virginia. The statue, designed by Tessa Pullan of Rutland, England, was unveiled on September 17, 1997. It stands in front of the Society's museum in Richmond (author's photograph).

Table of Contents

Preface	1
Introduction	3
1. "I had rather die than be whipped" The Battle at Yellow Tavern and the Death of J.E.B. Stuart	7
2. "Proper commanders. Where can they be obtained?" Lee Defers Selecting a Cavalry Commander	18
3. "Strike fast and strong" Evolution of the Cavalry Corps, Army of Northern Virginia	26
4. "When am I to get another horse?" Confederate Cavalry Regiments—New Commanders, Old Problems	32
5. The "New Issue" Reinforcements for Lee's Cavalry	41
6. "The Very Man I want" Philip Sheridan and His Senior Commanders	63
7. Veteran Volunteers Manning, Mounting, and Arming Union Cavalry	79
8. "I will not *fight* under the orders of a *Dutchman*" Changes in Composition of the Union Cavalry Corps	94
9. "Break up the railroad" Grant's Concept for a Cavalry Raid	104
10. "Thumping along" The March to Louisa County	115
11. "An exceedingly messed up affair" The Battle Opens on the Fredericksburg Road	122
12. "Where is the 9th N.Y.?" Union Momentum Builds on the Fredericksburg Road	134
13. "Pardonable zeal" Colonel Alger's Charge to Trevilian Station	139

14. "Where the hell is the rear?"
   Custer's First Last Stand 146

15. "Roll them up like a ribbon"
   Sheridan Prevails at Trevilian Station 159

16. "Too horrible to dwell upon"
   The Night of an Unfinished Battle 169

17. "A theatre of bloodshed"
   The Battle Continues on June 12 175

18. "Damn, damn, all the time"
   The Union Withdrawal 188

19. "The most disorderly retreat I have seen"
   Union Defeat at Samaria Church 200

20. "I regret my inability"
   Assessing the Outcome of the Trevilian's Battle and Raid 212

21. Old Soldiers Fade Away
   Lives After the Battle 223

Appendix A. Order of Battle and Casualties 259

Appendix B. West Pointers at Trevilian Station 267

Appendix C. Custer's Captured Wagons 271

Appendix D. Edward L. Wells and the Hampton vs. Fitz Lee Controversy ... 275

Chapter Notes 283

Bibliography 327

Index 339

Preface

The fighting at Trevilian Station on June 11 and 12, 1864, was confusing to both the participants and to historians since. My purpose in writing this book is twofold. First, to describe what happened on those two eventful days. Second, to explain why things happened as they did.

Among Civil War authors, I believe I am uniquely qualified to take on those tasks. I was a career army officer and like many of the principals in this book, am a member of West Point's "Long Gray Line." I served as an infantry platoon leader in Viet Nam, earned a master's degree in military arts and sciences, and was a tactics instructor on the faculty of the Army's Command and General Staff College at Fort Leavenworth, Kansas. Consequently, I believe I have a good understanding of both the visceral and intellectual dimensions of warfare at the tactical level. Additionally, I am an experienced horseman. For more than thirty years, I have owned, ridden, trained, and shod horses. I am probably among only a few authors who, like Sheridan's and Hampton's troopers, has experienced a wild gallop cross-country in a crowd of horses and riders. Having written a book about Brandy Station, the major cavalry battle of 1863, it seemed natural to follow-up with a book about Trevilian's.

In this book, I am critical of Philip Sheridan's performance at Trevilian Station. However, I think that Ulysses S. Grant, who directed the raid, can also be fairly criticized. While Grant's operational concept for the raid was sound, he underestimated the capability of Sheridan's cavalry to accomplish the assigned objectives. As a result, many men and horses were lost for little gain.

In preparing this book, I have relied upon the *Official Records*, soldiers' diaries and letters, and accounts in then many regimental histories that were prepared by veterans in the years after the war. I have also drawn from the considerable body of scholarly work produced by more recent authors and historians. That said, the opinions and conclusions contained in this book are mine.

Introduction

In 2006, shortly after I submitted the final manuscript on *Brandy Station, June 9, 1863: The Largest Cavalry Battle of the Civil War* to my publisher, my editor at McFarland asked if I had another book in mind. I told him that I did not, and that for the foreseeable future I intended to work on projects around my farm. However, in the course of my research on the battle at Brandy Station I made many "friends" in the cavalry of the Army of the Potomac and the Army of Northern Virginia, and I found it difficult to turn away from them. Consequently, I soon began thinking of writing another book. It seemed natural to explore the battle at Trevilian Station. That battle was fought on June 11–12, 1864, almost exactly a year after the battle at Brandy Station. While the battle at Brandy was the major cavalry fight of 1863, the fighting at Trevilian Station was the major cavalry battle of 1864. Brandy Station is generally considered the largest cavalry battle of the Civil War, while Trevilian Station is touted as the largest "all-cavalry" battle of the war (two Union infantry brigades played minor roles in the fighting at Brandy Station). There, similarities in the two battles end, in part a result of differences in the terrain, weapons, tactics, and—perhaps most significantly—the leaders at all echelons of command.

As a professional military officer, I believe it is important that readers are mindful of the factors that contribute to effectiveness in battle. In my research, I have found that most soldiers—both Union and Confederate—were brave when bravery was needed. Thus, it appears to me that individual valor—by itself—rarely secured the laurels of victory. In almost all armies, past and present, men are organized into units; and both the men and their units are trained and equipped to perform specific battlefield tasks. How well the men and units perform those tasks is largely dependent upon their discipline—which to a great degree, is a product of their training—and upon the quality of their leaders. Consequently, a significant portion of this book is devoted to the men, their organization, their weapons and horses, and their leaders (by this time in the war, little actual training was conducted). I apologize to those readers who might consider such material a digression from the account of the actual fighting.

At Brandy Station, J.E.B. Stuart commanded the Army of Northern Virginia's cavalry division, while Alfred Pleasonton led the Army of the Potomac's cavalry corps. Stuart was mortally wounded at Yellow Tavern in May 1864, and Wade Hampton exercised tactical command over both his cavalry division and that of Fitzhugh Lee at Trevilian's. Pleasonton had been relieved of his command in March 1864, replaced by Philip Sheridan. Additionally, below Hampton and Sheridan, a new crop of officers—Matthew C. Butler and George Custer among the more notable at Trevilian Station—had been promoted to fill vacancies in senior leadership positions.

Perhaps most contentious of the issues associated with command was the selection of a successor to J.E.B. Stuart following his mortal wounding at Yellow Tavern and death the following day. Instead of appointing a successor, Robert E. Lee elected to personally direct the activities of the three Confederate cavalry division commanders: Hampton, Fitz Lee, and Rooney Lee. It is well known that Robert E. Lee carefully evaluated officers who were considered for promotion to the more senior grades. Some officers were effective fighters but exhibited personal qualities that Lee considered disqualifying, while others were efficient managers but did not possess the intangible spark essential for achieving victory in battle. Although Lee kept his own counsel when deciding not to immediately appoint a successor to Stuart, I've explored in some detail the factors he may have considered.

In the intervening year between Brandy Station and Trevilian's, Federal cavalry had improved considerably. Sheridan, in his corps, commanded six more regiments than Pleasonton, and his regiments for the most part were filled with veteran troopers and led by seasoned officers. Always better equipped, some Union regiments were armed with repeating rifles and carbines which gave them a distinct technological advantage over their adversaries on the battlefield at Trevilian's. Finally, although complaints persisted, in the year between Brandy Station and Trevilian's, the Union War Department greatly improved their system for providing suitable horses in adequate quantities to mount the army's cavalry troopers.

Southern cavalry, while still a potent fighting force, had improved little—if at all—since it clashed with Union horsemen in the fields between Brandy Station and the Rappahannock River. In the summer of 1863, Stuart's cavalry division had approximately twenty-two regiments assigned. In the spring of 1864, the Cavalry Corps of the Army of Northern Virginia had roughly twenty-four regiments assigned to its three divisions.

In a more significant change, two veteran regiments from South Carolina had returned to their home state and been replaced in Virginia by fresh—but untested—units from the Palmetto State, Georgia, and Alabama. The "New Issue," as the fresh regiments were called, arrived in Virginia in late May and went almost immediately into battle. I believe that readers will find this topic interesting, particularly the efforts made by officials in South Carolina to oppose the swap and the manner in which the regiments made the move north.

Confederate cavalry continued to be equipped with a variety of weapons, and many troopers carried muzzle-loading rifles as their long arm. The Confederate system, under which enlisted men were required to provide their own mounts, resulted in more and more dismounted men being relegated to "Company Q" as the supply of horses throughout the South diminished.

All historians face a significant challenge when attempting to reconstruct a battle. As John Keegan wrote in *The Price of Admiralty*:

Yet the exact circumstances, let alone the rhythms and dynamics of land battle, defy easy reconstruction even by the expert visitor to Gettysburg or Waterloo. However precise his understanding of blackpowder tactics, however detailed his knowledge of Lee's or Wellington's regimental dispositions, he will never quite be able to place the people of the past in the time and place on the ground that he treads.[1]

Regarding the battle at Trevilian Station, I quickly found that understanding and then explaining what happened there was much more difficult than describing events at Brandy

Station. The key terrain in eastern Culpeper County is clear to even a casual student of tactics: fords through the Rappahannock River; high ground near Saint James Church and Hansbrough Ridge; and most significantly, Fleetwood Hill, which dominates the approaches to Brandy Station. In contrast, the terrain in northwest Louisa County is almost devoid of significant contour and drained by numerous small or intermittent streams. Observation and fields of fire are obscured now—as in 1864—by extensive coverage of scrub pine.

With good cause, Shelby Foote wrote in his *Civil War: A Narrative* that the battle at Trevilian's "was about as bewildering to one side as to the other, and was to be even more confusing to future students attempting to reconcile conflicting reports of the action."[2] In a similar vein, Douglas Southall Freeman in *Lee's Lieutenants* called the battle "as bewildering a fight as the Confederate Cavalry had ever waged."[3] In his more recent and thorough *Union Cavalry in the Civil War*, Stephen Z. Starr wrote, "The confused and confusing battle of Trevilian Station fought on June 11 is uncommonly difficult to describe."[4] Hopefully, with this book I have been able to bring order to some of the confusion regarding the events of June 11–12, 1864, although I make no claim to having precisely fixed events with respect to either time or place, or to even describing the action with complete accuracy.

I found that accurately describing the flow of the battle on June 11 and 12 was a difficult task. Like Foote, I, too, had difficulty "reconciling conflicting reports." However, a greater problem facing students of Trevilian's is that few official reports are available. Many commanders either failed to prepare reports, or their reports were lost. For example, on the Confederate side the only official reports are those of Wade Hampton and Fitzhugh Lee, and Lee's was written in December 1866, at the request of Robert E. Lee. If any of the Confederate brigade or regimental commanders prepared official reports, they were lost. While more Union commanders filed reports—including Sheridan, both division commanders, all brigade commanders, and several regimental commanders—few provided many details (the reports written by Torbert and his three brigade commanders were the most substantive). Sheridan devoted a single paragraph—albeit a lengthy one—to the fighting on June 11 and 12 in his original official report of the Trevilian's Raid. In May 1866, Sheridan did file a more comprehensive report of the Overland Campaign, with a few more details about the fighting at Trevilian's.

There are a goodly number of accounts of the fighting in letters, diaries, and post-war publications. However, the thick terrain in which much of the fighting took place made it difficult for both leaders and soldiers to see, and in turn, describe accurately what was occurring around them. Many accounts—such as those describing every charge being initiated with a shout and culminating with the enemy fleeing in disorder—must be taken with a grain of salt. Much of the Trevilian's fighting could be better characterized as a hard slog.

Because of the lack of accurate first-hand information, the nature of the terrain, and the continual challenge of sequencing actions by time, I on occasion drew upon my experiences as an infantry officer—and Trevilian's, with cavalry mostly fighting on foot, was basically an infantry fight—to flesh out events. On other occasions, I found it necessary to be vague. I have attempted to make clear my own opinions and assumptions as well as those facts—who, what, when, and where—that I simply could not discover.

As with Brandy Station, sorting out who won at Trevilian's also presented a challenge. Both Hampton and Sheridan claimed victory, with their claims supported by Southern and Northern newspapers, respectively. Even more recently, opinions continue to vary. Bruce

Catton, in perhaps his seminal work, *Grant Takes Command*, devoted about two sentences to Trevilian Station, noting that while Sheridan had a "hard fight and a hard march," he "had the better of Wade Hampton's Cavalry in a hard fight at Trevilian Station."[5] Taking an opposite view, Allan Nevins, in the sole sentence he devoted to the battle, wrote in *War for the Union* that "Sheridan was defeated by Wade Hampton's Southern cavalry at Trevilian Station and forced to call off his raid."[6] I've concluded that the laurels of victory belong to Hampton and his men.

Another lingering controversy about the Battle of Trevilian Station is the performance of Fitzhugh Lee. Some have speculated that Lee was not pleased to serve under Hampton, who was not a graduate of West Point and had less experience as a cavalry commander, and that consequently Lee did not provide his full support to Hampton during the first day of the battle. Because this issue lingers today, I've addressed its origins and provided my views in an appendix. Regarding this topic, I relied heavily on the scholarship of A. Wilson Greene in his introduction to the reprint edition of Edward Wells's *Hampton and His Cavalry in '64*.

As with many Civil War actions, this battle in central Louisa County came to be known by various names. Among locals at the time of the battle, the site of the fighting on June 11, 1864, was known simply as "Trevilian's" after Charles Trevilian, a wealthy local landowner. More formally, the site was referred to as "Trevilian's Station," a wood and water stop on the Virginia Central Railroad, later truncated to today's name, "Trevilian Station." For some unknown reason, George Washington Cullum, in his biographies of United States Military Academy graduates, added an extra "l," converting the location's name to "Trevillian Station." Other accounts occasionally feature alternative spellings for Trevilian—such as Trevelyan or Trevellion—thereby creating an inconvenience when conducting catalog searches and defeating computer softwares' "find" function. In the course of this book, I have generally referred to the site as Trevilian Station or Trevilian's and used those terms interchangeably.

As with my previous work, I've concluded this book with summaries of the post-war lives of some of the participants in the battle. For those who also fought at Brandy Station, I've attempted to avoid repeating information found in my earlier book.

Finally, I believe that it is important to remember that cavalry consists of both the men and their mounts. For the cavalry horse, the Trevilian's Raid was a sad story, to which I have tried to do justice.

1

"I had rather die than be whipped"
The Battle at Yellow Tavern and the Death of J.E.B. Stuart

In the spring of 1864, as in the previous two years of war, military campaigning began with a Union offensive. On May 4, the Army of the Potomac, marching from its camps in Culpeper County, crossed the Rapidan River into Orange County. There, in the Wilderness, a vast area of broken ground covered with a tangle of second-growth scrub, the blue-clad soldiers were met by Robert E. Lee's hard-marching, veteran infantrymen.[1] The new Union General-in-Chief, Ulysses S. Grant, received a tactical setback in the bloody encounter. Over the course of two days' fighting, the Army of the Potomac suffered 18,400 casualties against 11,400 Rebels killed, wounded, and captured.[2]

However, unlike in past years, this time the Federal army did not fall back across the Rappahannock to safety. Instead, Grant shifted his forces to the left, moving closer to Richmond and, again, drawing the Confederates into battle. As the infantry of both armies jockeyed for position near Spotsylvania Court House, an insignificant hamlet at a crossroads southwest of Fredericksburg, Grant sent his cavalry, commanded by a protégé, Major General Philip Sheridan, on a raid toward Richmond. The purpose of that movement was to engage and destroy Lee's cavalry, commanded

Major General Philip Sheridan, ordered east in March 1864 to take command of the Army of the Potomac's Cavalry Corps, brought with him a new objective. Throughout the Overland Campaign, Sheridan would relentlessly pursue the destruction of Robert E. Lee's cavalry (Library of Congress).

as it had been for the past two years, by Major General J.E.B. Stuart, the *beau sabreur* of the Confederacy. Any damage done to Confederate lines of communication and supplies during the raid would be an ancillary benefit to Grant's main effort: the destruction of Lee's army.

The impetus for the raid was an argument between Sheridan and his nominal commander, Major General George Meade, who, despite Grant's presence, remained in command of the Army of the Potomac. Upon taking command of the Army of the Potomac's cavalry corps in April 1864, Sheridan proposed to Meade that the primary purpose of his corps ought to be fighting Confederate Cavalry, and, to that end, the strength of his corps should be preserved, not frittered away on extended picket and escort duties. Meade, who remained skeptical of the fighting ability of cavalry, did not fully share Sheridan's views. Matters between the two commanders came to a head in the Wilderness on the evening of May 8 when Sheridan reported to Meade at his headquarters. Both generals were fatigued, and were frustrated with the army's lack of progress in defeating Lee. Meade criticized the performance of Sheridan's cavalry during an engagement near Todd's Tavern, claiming that cavalry blocking the road had impeded the movement of General Gouverneur Warren's 5th Corps. Sheridan took great umbrage, and strongly rejected Meade's criticism. At the conclusion of the heated argument—essentially a shouting match between the two generals—Sheridan asserted that if Meade turned him loose, he would "whip" J.E.B. Stuart.

Shortly thereafter, Meade reported Sheridan's near-insubordination to Grant. Instead of censuring Sheridan, as Meade had probably expected and hoped, Grant wisely advised Meade to turn Sheridan loose to try and fulfill his boast. Meade returned to his tent and wrote an order for Sheridan to "immediately concentrate [his] available mounted force, and with [his] ammunition trains and such supply trains as are filled (exclusive of ambulances) proceed against the enemy's cavalry."[3]

Sheridan's column, comprised of roughly ten thousand horsemen and six artillery batteries, moved south early on the morning on May 9, tearing up railroad tracks and burning Confederate supplies along the way. Sheridan set a leisurely pace for a raid, both to preserve his men's horses, and to ensure that he did not outrun Stuart. During each day's march, Sheridan made his way up and down

Major General George Gordon Meade, commander of the Army of the Potomac, reluctantly ordered Sheridan's raid on Richmond with the intent of drawing Stuart into battle (Library of Congress).

the long column, and the troopers became accustomed to seeing him, whether their regiment was in the vanguard or bringing up the rear.[4]

Meanwhile, Stuart rose to the bait. The Confederate cavalry commander split his forces, pursuing the Federals with one brigade commanded by Brigadier General James B. Gordon, while moving along a parallel route with Fitzhugh Lee's Division—two brigades with seven Virginia cavalry regiments—to overtake and block Sheridan's column. Stuart's total force among the three brigades numbered between four and five thousand men.[5]

On the evening of May 10, the Federal troopers were surprised when orders were passed down for them to unsaddle their horses and make camp for the night. In past raids, the horses had usually remained under saddle for the duration of the mission, much to their detriment. Additionally, the men, who had anticipated only an hour or two of fitful sleep while lying on the ground with their horses' reins wrapped about their hands, welcomed a good night's rest.[6] In contrast, by riding hard through most of the night Stuart, with Lee's Division, passed to the east of Sheridan's long column on the morning of May 11. Stuart directed Lee to take up defensive positions along the Telegraph Road at Yellow Tavern, a dilapidated hostelry on the outskirts of Richmond. Expecting Sheridan to approach from the west, along the Mountain Road from Louisa Court House, Stuart deployed his force in roughly a horizontal V, with Brigadier General Lunsford Lomax's Brigade arrayed to the east of the Telegraph Road north of its junction with the Brook Turnpike, and Brigadier General Williams Wickham's Brigade on high ground to the north of Turner's Run, a small stream running generally west to east between the two roads.[7] There, Stuart prepared to meet Sheridan's attack with his regiments dismounted—only the 1st Virginia Cavalry, a regiment in Wickham's Brigade, and Stuart's initial command of the war—remained mounted.

Prudently, Stuart sent his Assistant Adjutant General, the trusted Major Henry B. McClellan, to Richmond to confer with General Braxton Bragg, who commanded the Richmond garrison. McClellan was to find out whether or not Bragg could repel an attack by Sheridan, should the Union commander avoid Stuart and bypass Yellow Tavern. If Bragg's men could hold their fortifications, Stuart would have a free hand to fight Sheridan as he pleased. At the time, Bragg's attention was focused to the east where forces under the command of Major General Benjamin Butler were threatening Richmond by advancing up the south bank of the James River. Bragg was confident that he could repel Sheridan if need be with battalions comprised mostly of government office clerks, but to ensure success, he nonetheless ordered three brigades from Southside to meet the threat presented by the Federal raiders. McClellan set out toward Yellow Tavern with that news.[8]

In mid-morning, Sheridan's troopers approached, as expected, from the northwest along the Mountain Road. Upon detecting Stuart's defensive line to his front, the Union General immediately prepared to attack. As his objective was to destroy Stuart's forces, Sheridan dispensed with any elaborate and time-consuming maneuvers. He did not seek out an exposed flank to exploit, nor delay the action until all of his divisions were up and capable of launching a coordinated attack. Instead, Sheridan intended to quickly overwhelm the outnumbered Confederates with blunt force—a frontal assault by his lead division, commanded temporarily by Brigadier General Wesley Merritt (the division's commander, Major General A.T.A. Torbert was in Washington undergoing surgery on a cyst at the base of his spine).[9] However, Sheridan's minimal preparations still took some time, since the Federal column extended roughly thirteen miles up the Mountain Road. Merritt's trailing brigades were a mile or two back from the head of the column and had to move forward before he could launch his attack against Stuart's line on the Telegraph Road.

Awaiting the Union assault, Stuart ranged up and down the line of Lomax's Brigade, exhorting the outnumbered Virginians to stand firm once the battle began. Stopping at the 5th Virginia's position in the center of the line, Stuart spoke briefly with the regimental commander, Colonel Henry Clay Pate. Pate and Stuart had been at odds since the spring of 1862 when, at Stuart's urging, Thomas Rosser, an artillery officer, had been appointed colonel of the newly formed regiment over Pate, who had also raised several of the regiment's companies. Shortly afterward, in an embarrassing episode, Pate reported Rosser for being drunk on duty. Stuart, instead of thoroughly investigating Pate's charges, dismissed them after only a cursory review.[10] Rosser, most likely in retaliation, promptly arrested Pate for being absent from camp without authority (Pate, who thought he had received permission from Rosser, had left camp overnight to visit his wife who was staying with friends nearby). In March 1863, Pate was acquitted by courts-martial, but the bad feelings between Stuart and Pate endured, even after Pate was promoted and given command of the regiment upon Rosser's promotion to brigadier in the fall of 1863. Now, with Sheridan's assault looming, Stuart and Pate set their hard feelings aside and reconciled. Although the words between the two were not recorded, before Stuart rode on, Pate offered his hand, which Stuart shook warmly.[11]

Merritt delivered his attack about noon.[12] He advanced with three brigades abreast: Brigadier General George Custer's Brigade in the north; Colonel Thomas Devin's Brigade in the center; and Colonel Alfred Gibbs' Brigade in the south.[13] Consistent with the emerging style of cavalry fighting, Merritt's attack featured a mix of both mounted and dismounted men. As Merritt prepared to launch the attack, Sheridan rode forward and joined Custer's Michigan regiments, where he ordered his color bearer to shake out his battle flag, which was lying limp in the still air.[14] In that manner, the new Union cavalry commander displayed his presence on the field to the men as they prepared to move forward

Major General J.E.B. Stuart was in attitude perhaps more English cavalier than modern soldier. In this photograph he displayed the traditional symbols of a cavalry commander: frock coat, thigh-length boots, leather gauntlets, yellow sash, plumed hat, and saber (Library of Congress).

against Lomax's position. Sheridan, unlike his predecessor, Pleasonton, was not reluctant to lead from the front.[15]

Given the order to attack, Merritt's troopers advanced through the Confederate fire, pressing Lomax's men along the Telegraph Road and threatening to overrun their line. It soon became apparent that Lomax's outnumbered Brigade would be unable to hold its position to the east of the Telegraph Road, and consequently Stuart ordered Lomax to withdraw to his right rear and fall in to the left of Wickham's Brigade on the high ground north of Turner's Run. To cover the withdrawal of Lomax's flanking regiments, Stuart sent an aide de camp galloping to Pate with orders for the colonel to hold his position in the center of the line at all hazard—if the 5th Virginia were to be driven back, the flanks of the other regiments would be exposed as they withdrew north. At the time, Pate was still dismounted and fighting from the center of his line. There, the Telegraph Road, worn down by years of traffic, had "sunk" below the level of the bordering fields, thus offering some protection to Pate and his men from the Union fire. Despite the cover, Pate realized the mission from Stuart would be difficult to accomplish, and would likely lead to the destruction of his regiment.[16]

As the 6th Virginia and the 15th Virginia began to withdraw, the men of the 5th Virginia held their ground on the sunken road as the pressure against them increased. Encouraging his troopers to fight on, Pate turned to his men and shouted, "One more round boys, then we'll get to the hill." At that moment, he was shot through the right temple and killed instantly.[17] With Pate dead, resistance collapsed and the 5th Virginia was driven back in disorder, with many of the fleeing troopers captured by the advancing Yankees. Pate's orderly, sixteen-year-old "Little Jimmy" Moore, carried Pate's body under fire to the rear. With the help of the regimental adjutant, the two took Pate to the nearby residence of a Doctor Shepherd where he was laid on the floor of the sitting room. The adjutant wrote Pate's name and rank on a slip of paper and pinned it to Pate's chest before the two Confederates fled to safety.[18]

Meanwhile, as the 6th and 15th Virginia, along with the remnants of the 5th, withdrew across Turner's Run, the Union attack petered out, and Merritt pulled his brigades back to the Telegraph Road to regroup.

Although Lomax had been forced from his initial position and Lee's Division was obviously overmatched by Sheridan's corps, Stuart remained confident that he could hold his ground against further Federal attack. Additionally, McClellan finally arrived with good news: Bragg was confident that he could defend the fortifications of Richmond, and he had called for three brigades of infantry to be sent from Southside to further increase his strength in the northern trenches. Stuart, always optimistic, took heart. Sheridan would now probably attack from the south. Should Bragg's infantry sally from their trenches, they could fall upon Sheridan's rear, providing a new opportunity for Stuart to take the offense. Stuart believed that a concerted effort by his cavalry and Bragg's infantry could seriously damage Sheridan's force. To that end, at 3:00 p.m. Stuart sent a message to Bragg, informing him of Sheridan's dispositions, and advising that in a combined attack with Brigadier General Eppa Hunton's infantry brigade, he did not see how Sheridan could escape.[19] Unfortunately for Stuart, Bragg had neither capability, nor intention, of attacking that day. Stuart was left to fight on his own.

Sheridan, rightly concluding that Confederate infantry in the defenses of Richmond posed no threat to his rear, brought up additional troops from Gregg's and Wilson's divisions and attacked again about 4:00 p.m.[20] The second federal, attack, like that of the morning, was delivered with a mix of mounted and dismounted regiments. Custer, whom Sheridan selected to spearhead the attack with a mounted charge, invited Lieutenant Colonel Addison Preston and his 1st Vermont Cavalry to join in—the Vermonters, who had moved up on Custer's left flank, had served in Custer's brigade during the summer and fall campaigns the previous year. Preston readily agreed, but Colonel George Chapman, Preston's brigade commander and a "conceity little upstart" according to his former regimental surgeon, objected.[21] Custer appealed to Sheridan, who told Custer he could take any regiment in the charge whose commander wished to go along. Overruled, and thus placed in an awkward position by Sheridan, Chapman elected to accompany Preston and the 1st Vermont during the afternoon's attack.[22]

Sheridan launched the attack just as a thunderstorm broke, and the Union troopers advanced on horseback and on foot through a driving rain.[23] The Yankees, moving now from south to north, achieved initial success. Custer, with his Michigan Brigade and the 1st Vermont, penetrated the center of Stuart's line where it straddled the Telegraph Road, overrunning a battery of Stuart's artillery in the process. During the charge, Major Henry Granger, commanding the 7th Michigan fell dead, the result of two gunshot wounds and two saber blows.[24]

Stuart, as usual, was in the center of the fighting. Positioning himself with Wickham's Brigade near where the Telegraph Road passed through the Confederate line, Stuart rode up and down the line, setting a personal example for his men while exhorting them to beat back the attackers.[25] To blunt the Federal penetration, Stuart dispatched a courier to call up the 1st Virginia Cavalry, Fitzhugh Lee's reserve. As the Virginians rode forward, Stuart ordered them to dismount and urged them into the fight, shouting, "Boys, don't stop to count fours. Shoot them! Shoot them!"[26] The men of 1st Virginia responded and successfully, if only temporarily, contained the penetration. The Federal troopers began falling back.

As the Union soldiers began to withdraw from their salient in the center of the Confederate line, Stuart paused among a few privates of the 1st Virginia who were fighting dismounted from behind a fence along the Telegraph Road. With his horse's head and neck over

Henry Clay Pate, commander of the 5th Virginia Cavalry, shown in an engraving from his book extolling the virtues of Virginia and Virginians, fought with pro-slavery forces against John Brown in Kansas in 1856. Pate was killed at Yellow Tavern shortly after he and Stuart reconciled, setting aside their long-standing differences (*American Vade Mecum*).

the fence, Stuart encouraged the troopers to keep calm and "give it to them [the Yankees]!"[27] Stuart, himself, was caught up in the action. Drawing his pistol, Stuart took the Federals under fire. Holding his pistol in his right hand, Stuart steadied his aim with his left forearm, while grasping his horse's reins with his left hand.[28]

By chance, one of the Union troopers hustling to the rear on foot, Private John Huff of the 5th Michigan, turned and snapped off a shot at Stuart with his own pistol from a range of about forty yards. The ball from Huff's .44 caliber Colt struck Stuart in the abdomen, most likely penetrating his intestines and perhaps his liver.[29] Stuart, who thus far in the war had been unscathed, was known to remark that he "did not fear any bullet aimed at him—but stray bullets were dangerous." Private Huff's shot proved him wrong.[30]

In obvious pain and unable to continue in action, the Confederate commander was helped to ground by the nearby Virginians. Believing a resumption of the Federal attack was imminent, Captain Gus W. Dorsey, the commander of Company K, 1st Virginia, ordered his men to immediately take Stuart to safety. Since Stuart's horse had become excited and difficult to lead, Dorsey helped Stuart into the saddle of a quiet mount belonging to Private Fred Pitts.[31] At about the time Stuart was being helped onto Pitts' horse, Fitz Lee, having received word of Stuart's wounding, galloped up. Stuart wasted no time on commiseration. Instead, he sent his favorite subordinate back to duty with the assurance, "Go ahead, Fitz old fellow. I know you will do what is right!"[32]

Captain Dorsey led Stuart a short distance to the rear, an ambulance was brought up, and Stuart was transferred into it. Meanwhile, the Federal attack resumed. Stuart, spying a few of his men fleeing the fighting, shouted to them: "Go back! Go back! And do your duty as I have done mine, and our country will be safe. Go back! Go back! I had rather die than be whipped."[33] However, with Stuart down and the Federal attack renewed in greater strength, the Confederate defenses collapsed. Sheridan had fulfilled his pledge to Meade that he would whip J.E.B. Stuart.

After the fighting for the day ended, Sheridan and his column marched through the night to the east. Their movement was impeded by "torpedoes": artillery shells placed at the side of the road with friction primers attached to trip-wires stretched across the path of

George Armstrong Custer is shown here as a brigadier general. Shortly before leaving Culpeper at the start of the Overland Campaign, Custer shaved off his "imperial" goatee and mailed it to Elizabeth, his new bride, as a keepsake. One of Custer's men was credited with mortally wounding Stuart at Yellow Tavern (Library of Congress).

The Telegraph Road north of Yellow Tavern today runs through a residential suburb of Richmond and the Yellow Tavern battlefield is bisected by Interstate 295. A monument dedicated in 1888 marks the spot near where J.E.B. Stuart received his mortal wound on the afternoon of May 11, 1864 (author's photograph).

the tired Union troopers. After several horses were killed and a few men wounded by exploding shells, Sheridan ordered a party of prisoners to lead the column and search out the trip wires, an action that prevented any further Union casualties.[34] Delayed by destroyed bridges over the Chickahominy River, on May 13 Sheridan was forced to fight a contingent of Confederate infantry that had at last been sent out from the defenses of Richmond. These soldiers, not on a par with Robert E. Lee's veterans, were unable to defeat the Yankee raiders and soon withdrew to their trenches. On May 14, Sheridan and his men reached the James River, and there linked-up with forces under the command of Major General Benjamin Butler. After a pause of several days for rest, Sheridan began his march back to the Army of the Potomac, eventually reporting to General Meade at Chesterfield on May 22.[35]

As soon as they were clear of the fighting near Yellow Tavern, Stuart's attendants took their wounded commander by ambulance to the home of his brother-in-law, Dr. Charles Brewer, in Richmond where he arrived that evening. Brewer, a respected doctor, was serving in the office of the Surgeon General of the Confederacy. Before the war, Brewer had served as an army surgeon with the 1st U.S. Cavalry in Kansas. During the 1857 campaign against the Cheyenne, Brewer had treated Stuart after he was wounded—shot in the chest—during the Battle of Solomon Fork in July of that year.[36]

It was immediately apparent to the attending doctors—Stuart had been accompanied from the battlefield by Dr. John Fontaine—that the general's wound was mortal, and his wife, Flora, who with her children was staying near Beaver Dam Station at the home of Edmund Fontaine, the president of the Virginia Central Railroad, was summoned. With the telegraph lines cut by Sheridan's raiders, she did not receive the message until about noon the following day, May 12. Although Flora and her children left immediately for Richmond, they were much delayed—Sheridan's men had torn up the railroad tracks and destroyed the bridge over the Chickahominy River.

Throughout the day, Stuart's strength ebbed. Additionally, the wound caused Stuart much pain, which he tried to relieve by holding ice to it. Visitors, including President Jefferson Davis, called to pay respects. Major Heros von Borcke, a Prussian and favorite on the Cavalry Division staff who had been seriously wounded at Middleburg the previous June, stopped in and sat with Stuart for a time, as did a few other officers from Stuart's staff.[37] To those in attendance, Stuart generously praised the heroism of Colonel Henry Clay Pate, whose death further mitigated any bad feelings there had formerly been between the two.[38] Frequently, Stuart asked for word of his wife, and inquired if her arrival at his deathbed was imminent.[39]

Advised that death was near, Stuart said to Dr. Brewer, "I am resigned if it be God's will; but I would like to see my wife. But God's will be done."[40] Flora Stuart finally arrived in Richmond at 11:30 p.m. Her husband had died four hours earlier.

At the time of the fighting near Yellow Tavern, Robert E. Lee was fully engaged in managing his army's defense of the "mule shoe" near Spotsylvania Court House. On May 12, during the fighting for what became known as the "bloody angle," Lee was handed a telegram advising that Stuart had been mortally wounded. After composing himself for a moment, Lee turned to the officers present and announced: "Gentlemen. We have very bad news. General Stuart has been mortally wounded." After a brief pause, Lee exclaimed, "He never brought me a piece of false information."[41] Reportedly, upon receiving the news of Stuart's pending death, several of Lee's staff officers broke out in tears.[42]

In a letter to his wife written four days later, Lee wrote, "As I write I am expecting the

The wounded Stuart was taken to the home of his brother-in-law, Dr. Charles Brewer, where he died on May 12. Stuart had only been wounded once earlier in his career: shot in the chest by an Indian in 1857 in Kansas. Dr. Brewer—then an army surgeon—had treated Stuart for that wound as well. This is an early 1900s drawing of Brewer's home. Today the location is the site of the Richmond police department headquarters (*Life of J.E.B. Stuart*).

sound of the guns every moment. I grieve the loss of our gallant officers & men, & miss their aid & sympathy. A more zealous, ardent, brave & devoted soldier, than Stuart, the Confederacy cannot have."[43] On May 20, Lee followed his lamentation to his wife with a general order announcing Stuart's death.

> The commanding general announces to the army with heartfelt sorrow the death of Maj. Gen. J.E.B. Stuart, late commander of the Cavalry Corps of the Army of Northern Virginia. Among the gallant soldiers who have fallen in this war General Stuart was second to none in valor, in zeal, and in unfaltering devotion to his country. His achievements form a conspicuous part of the history of this army, with which his name and services will be forever associated. To military capacity of a high order and all the nobler virtues of the soldier he added the brighter graces of a pure life, guided and sustained by the Christian's faith and hope. The mysterious hand of an Allwise God has removed him from the scene of his usefulness and fame. His grateful countrymen will mourn his loss and cherish his memory. To his comrades in arms he has left the proud recollection of his deeds, and the inspiring influence of his example.[44]

The *Richmond Examiner*, which had eleven months earlier excoriated Stuart for being surprised by the Federal attack across the Rappahannock at Brandy Station, announced his death to the public in the May 14 edition. Setting aside any criticism, the paper wrote of Stuart's death: "No incident of mentality, since the fall of the great Jackson, has occasioned more

JEB Stuart was buried in Hollywood Cemetery, Richmond, on the evening of May 13, 1864. His simple headstone was later replaced by a more elaborate obelisk (Library of Congress).

painful regret than this. Major-General J.E.B. Stuart, the model of Virginia cavaliers and dashing chieftain, whose name was a terrour to the enemy, and familiar as a household word in two continents, is dead, struck down by a bullet from the dastardly foe, and the whole Confederacy mourns him. He breathed out his gallant spirit resignedly, and in the full possession of all his remarkable faculties of mind and body, at twenty two minutes to eight o'clock Thursday night."[45]

Stuart's funeral was held at St. James Episcopal Church in Richmond at 5:00 p.m. on May 13.[46] The church was crowded with mourners, including President Jefferson Davis, the few senior army officers present in the city, and a few members of Stuart's staff. After the service, the metal casket with the general's remains was placed in a hearse drawn by four white horses. In the rain, the funeral procession wound its way for a mile and a half through the streets of Richmond to Hollywood Cemetery. There, on the brow of a small hill, Stuart was buried, his grave marked by a simple headstone.[47] Because the garrison of Richmond was occupied with the defenses of the city, Stuart had neither military ceremony at his funeral, nor an honor guard to escort him on his final ride.[48] Always a showman, Stuart would probably have been disappointed with the lack of pomp.

On his deathbed, Stuart divested himself of the trappings of his position. He bequeathed his saber to his four-year-old son, J.E.B. Stuart, Jr. His gold spurs he ordered sent to a woman in Shepherdstown, West Virginia. Stuart gave his two horses to his most trusted staff officers.[49] However, the one thing Stuart could not bestow was his position as the commander of the Cavalry Corps of the Army of Northern Virginia. The appointment of Stuart's successor was the responsibility of Robert E. Lee.

2

"Proper commanders. Where can they be obtained?"
Lee Defers Selecting a Cavalry Commander

When notified of Stuart's death, Robert E. Lee was preoccupied with more pressing matters—his command was being hammered by the Army of the Potomac in Spotsylvania's "mule shoe." In that day's fighting, General Grant's forces succeeded in penetrating the Confederate position, overrunning some of Lee's artillery and capturing two Confederate generals while killing one and wounding two others.[1] Doubtless, however, upon receiving the news regarding the imminent death of his trusted cavalry commander, Lee thought to himself, "Who will replace Stuart ... can he truly be replaced?"[2]

Lee felt an enduring and supreme confidence in the in the ability of soldiers of his army, but the capabilities of his subordinate commanders were of continual concern. To that end, he wrote to Major General John Bell Hood shortly after Chancellorsville in May 1863: "I agree with you in believing that our army would be invincible if it could be properly organized and officered. There were never such men in an army before. They will go anywhere and do anything if properly led. But there is the difficulty—proper commanders. Where can they be obtained?"[3]

Lee, better than many senior officers both North and South, understood the importance of establishing a clearly defined chain of command. Military organizations—and many civilian organizations, as well—operate with greater efficiency when one person is in charge. In the military, that person, the commander, is vested with the authority to *order*—rather than merely recommend—actions; and conversely, the commander's subordinates are obligated by law and custom to *obey*. Further, the commander is responsible for the performance of both his subordinates and his organization, and he is held accountable for the failures of that organization, regardless of where the fault may lie. Lee realized that it was essential to carefully select commanders who possessed the right qualities. Many officers, though energetic and efficient, were not temperamentally suited to lead men in battle. To an even greater extent, throughout the war both Union and Confederate armies in all theaters had been plagued by senior officers who were simply unwilling or unable to perform their duties fully and effectively. In many cases, commanders found wanting—those who were not killed or disabled by wounds—resigned from the service of their own volition. Other marginal commanders, perhaps less aware of their own shortcomings, were forced to resign. In some cases, Lee

2. "Proper commanders. Where can they be obtained?" 19

This photograph, taken under the back porch of Robert E. Lee's home in Richmond shortly after the war, shows Lee between his eldest son, George Washington Custis Lee, on his right and one of his staff officers, Lieutenant Colonel Walter Taylor, on his left. Stuart communicated his reservations about Wade Hampton to his West Point classmate Custis Lee, but it is not known if Lee passed those concerns to either his father or Jefferson Davis (Library of Congress).

arranged for commanders who failed to meet his high standards to be transferred of to less important duties, frequently in a different theater of war.

Obviously, the top contenders to succeed J.E.B. Stuart in command of the cavalry corps were Stuart's two senior subordinates: Major General Wade Hampton and Lee's nephew, Major General Fitzhugh Lee. Hampton was senior to Fitz Lee, but only by the narrowest of margins. The wealthy South Carolinian had two months seniority in grade as a brigadier, but both he and Lee had been promoted to Major General on the same day—August 3, 1863— and on the same promotion order.[4] Thus, Hampton was officially the senior of the two generals by virtue of his seniority as a brigadier. The third major general of cavalry in the Army of Northern Virginia, W.H.F. "Rooney" Lee, the commanding general's second son, was far junior to Hampton and his cousin, Fitz, and less experienced as well. Rooney, who had spent nine months as a Union prisoner of war after being wounded at Brandy Station, had missed much of the hard campaigning in 1863. Most significantly, he had not been promoted to major general and assigned to divisional command until April 24, 1864; thus, he had less than one month's tenure in that grade.

At the time he recommended Hampton and Fitz Lee for advancement to Major General, Lee hinted that Hampton was the more deserving of the two brigadiers, although he made no clear recommendation for one over the other. In his August 1863 recommendation to Jefferson Davis regarding the reorganization of Stuart's cavalry, Lee wrote: "I further propose to your consideration the promotion of Generals Hampton and Fitzhugh Lee to the rank of major-general. General Hampton, I think, deserves it both from his services and his gallantry; of Fitz Lee I do not wish to speak so positively, but I do not know any other officer in the cavalry who has done better service. I should admire both more if they were more rigid in their disci-

According to Manly Wade Wellman, Wade Hampton's biographer, this photograph shows Wade Hampton as a major general in 1864. However, the uniform coat is not that of a general officer and the shoulder straps are not the standard Confederate insignia of rank. Consequently, it is more likely this photograph was taken early in the war (Library of Congress).

pline, but I know how difficult it is to establish rigid discipline in our armies, and therefore make allowances."[5]

Thus far in the course of the war, Hampton had demonstrated that he was a courageous, skillful, and tenacious fighter. Further, he had earned the full confidence and devotion of his men. However, because Hampton had effectively led a brigade, and then a division, in battle did not necessarily mean that he was the best choice to command the army's cavalry corps.

Prior to the war, Hampton had no military experience. Unlike many senior officers in Confederate service, he had not attended West Point, had not fought in Mexico, and had not campaigned on the Plains or in the West. Instead, he had lived a life of ease as a wealthy planter, managing vast estates in South Carolina and Mississippi. An outsider to the military, he did not display the easy comradery—developed over years assigned to isolated outposts on the frontier—found among many senior commanders. Like many Southern "gentlemen," Hampton was quick to perceive a slight and to take offense.

In August 1863, Robert E. Lee relented and recommended the War Department approve J.E.B. Stuart's proposal that the Army of Northern Virginia's cavalry division be reorganized as a cavalry corps, thus creating the major general's billets for Hampton and Fitz Lee. Hampton, convalescing from his Gettysburg wound in South Carolina at the time, welcomed the promotion. However, he found out that along with Fitz Lee, Jefferson Davis also planned to promote Cadmus Wilcox and Stephen D. Lee to major general, and, furthermore, that the effective dates of promotion for Wilcox and Stephen D. Lee would precede those of Fitz Lee and himself. Because Stephen D. Lee had begun the war as the artillery battery commander in Hampton's Legion, Hampton considered the promotion scheme an insult, and complained to his confidant, Senator Louis Wigfall, a fellow South Carolinian, former Confederate brigadier general, former U.S. Senator from Texas, and, like Hampton, a graduate of South Carolina College.[6] Perhaps after being informed by Wigfall of Hampton's displeasure, Jefferson Davis amended the promotion scheme and promoted all four brigadiers with the same effective date, allowing their date of rank at brigadier general to establish seniority among them.[7]

In February 1863, Brigadier General William Nelson Pendleton, Lee's chief of artillery, recommended a comprehensive reorganization of the artillery of the Army of Northern Virginia. The crux of Pendleton's plan was that artillery could be more effectively and efficiently managed under centralized command. To that end, he recommended that the army's artillery batteries be grouped into battalions commanded by artillery officers. Robert E. Lee, seeing the merits in Pendleton's proposal, recommended its approval. On March 7, 1863, Hampton wrote to Lee, and among other things, apparently complained of the official transfer of Hart's Battery from his cavalry brigade to the Stuart Horse Artillery Battalion. Hampton reminded Lee that when the battery was formed in 1861 as part of the Hampton Legion, that he had purchased its Blakely guns with his personal funds. Lee responded tactfully on March 31. "[I] think you deserve the thanks of the country for the importation of the rifled Blakely guns you mention. In my own behalf, I cordially give you mine." Lee, while expressing his support for Pendleton's reorganization plan, added, "It will give me pleasure to assign to you all the guns that you have imported whenever practicable."[8] This somewhat ambiguous response apparently put the issue to rest. The battery—Hart's—with Hampton Blakely guns was assigned to the Stuart Horse Artillery Battalion then under the command of Major John Pelham. However, Hart's Battery habitually supported Hampton's Brigade.

Other factors also weighed against Hampton. While he had performed well while serving under Stuart, Hampton had not had much opportunity to exercise independent command. Also, on occasion, particularly in the winter of 1862–1863, Hampton had great difficulty maintaining the fighting strength of the regiments assigned to his brigade—perhaps hinting to Lee that the South Carolinian failed to pay sufficient attention to discipline and the administrative aspects of command.[9] Additionally, Hampton, at forty-six years of age, was much older than the other two major generals (Fitz Lee was twenty-eight and Rooney was just shy of his twenty-seventh birthday), and most of the cavalry brigadiers as well.[10] Lee may well have been concerned that Hampton would be unable to withstand the more arduous duty incumbent with cavalry corps command, and that it might be best to leave mounted service to younger men.

Perhaps of greatest concern to Lee was Hampton's personality. Hampton had not been content during his service with the Army of Northern Virginia. Hampton's ire, for the most part, stemmed from his belief that his superiors, both Robert E. Lee and J.E.B. Stuart, were biased against him and other non–Virginians. Hampton felt that under Lee and Stuart, officers born in Virginia were selected for promotion ahead of equally (or perhaps even more) qualified officers from other states. Similarly, and with some justification, Hampton believed that West Pointers were also unfairly favored for promotion. Furthermore, within the cavalry corps, Hampton perceived that Virginia regiments were assigned less arduous duties than regiments from the Carolinas, Georgia, and Mississippi. Adding to Hampton's distaste for Virginians was his closely-held belief that Virginians—specifically those assigned to the 4th Virginia Cavalry—were responsible for the death of his younger brother, Frank. Lieutenant Colonel Frank Hampton had been mortally wounded at the outskirts of Stevensburg on June 9, 1863, after the 4th Virginia ignominiously fled the field, leaving Frank Hampton and two dozen troopers of the 2nd South Carolina to face an assault by three Union regiments. Frank Hampton was shot in the abdomen during the ensuing melee and died of his wound that evening.[11]

Wade Hampton's actions reflected his attitude. Hampton initially made a name for himself commanding infantry before accepting a brigadier's commission and command of a cavalry brigade. Hampton later remarked that he regretted his move from the infantry to the cavalry, perhaps because that arm of service was more predominately Virginian than the infantry assigned to the Army of Northern Virginia.[12] On more than one occasion, Hampton attempted to obtain a transfer to another theater, moves that were thwarted by Lee, who had high regard for Hampton's abilities.

Nonetheless, almost certainly Robert E. Lee found Hampton's attitude troubling. Hampton's personal beliefs could have been easily overlooked had he kept his views private. However, Hampton did not keep his opinions to himself—they were common knowledge among subordinates in his brigade, and were shared by many of his non–Virginian officers. In March 1864, matters came to a head when Hampton openly challenged Stuart's authority. At the time, Stuart, with the approval of both Lee and the War Department, was organizing a third cavalry division to be commanded by Rooney Lee, who had just been released from Union captivity. To man the division, Stuart ordered both Fitz Lee and Hampton to give up several of their regiments. Hampton wrote through Stuart to Robert E. Lee in protest of the pending transfers. Lee met with Hampton to discuss the issue. During that session, Lee, perhaps in frustration, remarked: "I would not care if you went back to South Carolina with your whole division." Hampton, who was unused to being rebuked, had his feelings hurt. Fortunately for both Lee and Hampton, and the Army of Northern Virginia, the intensity of the issue faded with time.¹³

There may have been another reason that Lee was reluctant to appoint Hampton to command: the recommendation of Stuart, privately delivered. In the spring of 1864, Stuart, unable to obtain promotion to lieutenant general in the Army of Northern Virginia, considered requesting transfer to a vacancy in the Trans-Mississippi. To help his chances, Stuart on April 9 wrote to his friend and West Point classmate, Brigadier General George Washington Custis Lee. At the time Custis Lee, the eldest son of Robert E. Lee, was serving as a military assistant to the Jefferson Davis. In the self-serving missive, Stuart offered himself for reassignment to the West or to the command of an infantry corps should an opening in the Army of Northern Virginia become available. He concluded his letter with comments regarding his possible replacement as cavalry corps commander. Stuart wrote, "Hampton is not the man for such a command.... Hampton is a gallant officer, a nice Gentleman, and has done meritorious service, but there you *must stop*." Stuart went on to observe that Hampton had frequently expressed a desire to serve in Mississippi, and that if Stuart could be promoted, it would serve the public interest to transfer Hampton there.¹⁴ There is no evidence that Custis Lee interceded with Davis on Stuart's behalf. However, it is possible that Custis Lee conferred with his father on the matter of succession of command either before or after Stuart's death.

Fitzhugh Lee, the other most likely successor to Stuart, was almost the opposite of Hampton in personality and background. A Virginian from a prestigious family, Lee attended West Point, graduating in 1856. Upon commissioning, the young officer was posted to Texas for duty with the newly formed 2nd U.S. Cavalry. There he distinguished himself as a hard fighter. He was severely wounded on an expedition to the Washita in 1859, but just a few days after returning to duty he was involved in a skirmish in which he chased down and fought an Indian in

Major General Fitzhugh Lee was Stuart's favorite subordinate. Well after the war, Wade Hampton faulted Lee's performance on the first day at Trevilian's. Some speculated that Lee was unhappy at having to serve under the more senior Hampton during the operation to thwart Sheridan's raid (USMA Library).

hand-to-hand combat.¹⁵ After resigning from the regular army in 1861 to serve his state, Lee followed in Stuart's footsteps, rising to command of the 1st Virginia Cavalry before being promoted to brigadier in 1862 and then major general in 1863. Stuart's favorite, Fitz Lee was thought by some to be a frivolous officer, more interested in charades and song than the serious business of warfare. But Lee's disposition merely masked his competence. He had participated in most of the major operations of the war, and had generally performed well. Outnumbered by more than two-to-one, he had stymied his friend from West Point days, Union brigadier William Woods Averell's foray into Culpeper County at the Battle of Kelly's Ford on March 17, 1863. At Chancellorsville, Lee and his men discovered Hooker's unprotected flank and guided Jackson and his corps into position for the devastating attack against the Union XI Corps on May 2, 1863.

Additionally, Fitz Lee was well known by his uncle, the commanding general. During Fitz Lee's first three years as a cadet, Robert E. Lee served as the academy's superintendent. On two occasions, Lee was involved in disciplining his nephew. In December 1853, Fitz, then a third-classman, left the academy grounds after dark with several other cadets for a bout of drinking at Benny Havens, a local tavern. He and the others were caught, and upon the recommendation of the elder Lee they were court-martialed. While serving his punishment—restriction to the academy grounds—the following summer, Fitz again visited Benny Havens, was again caught, and faced almost certain dismissal from the academy. However, Fitz, though lacking in self-discipline and not studious, was well liked by his peers. His classmates unanimously pledged to not leave the academy grounds without authority for the coming academic year if the charges against Fitz were dropped. Lee recommended approval of the cadets' proposal, and it was accepted by the Secretary of War, Jefferson Davis, thus preserving a future for the wayward cadet.¹⁶

Robert E. Lee also had ample opportunity to gauge the qualities of his young nephew as a junior officer. In 1855, the elder Lee transferred from the Engineers, the branch of service in which he had served for twenty-six years, to the cavalry. He was posted to Texas as the Lieutenant Colonel of the newly formed 2nd Cavalry. Although frequently away from his regiment on leave or courts-martial duty, Lee certainly kept abreast of developments in his nephew's career.

Despite the availability of two seemingly qualified officers, Robert E. Lee deferred his decision on selecting a replacement for Stuart. In General Order Number 14, dated May 14, 1864, Lee directed that the three cavalry divisions would report directly to and receive orders directly from the Headquarters of the Army of Northern Virginia. In the same order, the officers of the cavalry corps headquarters were distributed to the cavalry divisions or returned to their respective departments. Lee also directed General William Nelson Pendleton, his Chief of Artillery, to distribute the horse artillery batteries among the three cavalry divisions in a manner to best serve the interest of the army.¹⁷

Lee's decision to defer selecting a successor for Stuart led to speculation that he preferred his nephew, Fitz, but could not select him without offending Hampton (and perhaps being forced to finally approve a transfer for the South Carolinian). It is more likely, however, that Lee's decision was driven more by operational considerations.

Since the beginning of the spring campaign, the nature of the war had changed. Instead of fighting a pitched battle, followed by a lull as the armies regrouped to go at each other again, the Federals and Confederates fought in the Wilderness, and immediately afterward at Spotsylvania Courthouse. As the order was being drafted, Lee anticipated another shift to his right toward the North Anna River and another battle. In this type of warfare, Lee probably felt little need for a cavalry corps headquarters. In fact, when using one cavalry division on the army's right flank and a second on the left—leaving one division in reserve—an intermediate headquarters between the army and the divisions might prove more an impediment than a benefit. Looking ahead, Lee may have simply felt that he would have little opportunity to launch large-scale, independent cavalry operations and that as his army fell back toward Richmond, the threat from Federal raiders would diminish.[18]

Lee certainly did not anticipate that his decision to personally exercise control of the Army of Northern Virginia's three cavalry divisions would remain an issue lingering to this day.

3

"Strike fast and strong"
Evolution of the Cavalry Corps, Army of Northern Virginia

The conditions leading to Lee's dilemma regarding selection of a cavalry corps commander evolved over the previous year, during which Stuart's cavalry division was reorganized as a corps of two divisions, and then expanded to a corps of three divisions.

Since the early spring of 1863, J.E.B. Stuart had advocated converting his division into a cavalry corps of two or three divisions, believing that more brigades—each with three regiments instead of five or six—would be more effective in battle. Additionally, such reorganization would create more general officers positions, allowing deserving colonels to be rewarded for their service with promotion to brigadier. Robert E. Lee, noting the small size of many of Stuart's cavalry regiments, did not feel that a brigade of only three regiments warranted a general officer as commander, and consequently he had not approved Stuart's proposal.[1]

However, shortly after the Gettysburg Campaign, Lee acceded to Stuart's long-standing request to form a cavalry corps, apparently accepting Stuart's logic that smaller brigades would be more manageable on the battlefield. On August 1, 1863, Lee recommended to President Jefferson Davis that Stuart's division of five brigades be split into two divisions, each with three brigades, and that Wade Hampton and Fitzhugh Lee both be promoted to major general and appointed to divisional command.[2] Davis readily accepted Lee's proposal, and it was quickly implemented by the War Department, although at the time, Hampton was absent while recovering from the wounds he received at Gettysburg. (Please refer to Table 1: Evolution of the Cavalry Corps, Army of Northern Virginia, at the end of this chapter for further information.)

The reorganization created the opportunity for promoting several proven and talented colonels to brigadier general. Matthew Calbraith Butler, commander of the 2nd South Carolina, was promoted to take command of what had been Hampton's Brigade.[3] At the time Butler was in South Carolina recovering from the loss of his foot at Stevensburg on June 9. Williams Wickham, commander of the 4th Virginia, was promoted to fill the vacancy created by the promotion of Fitzhugh Lee.[4] Finally, Colonel Lunsford Lomax, commander of the 11th Virginia, was promoted to brigadier and given command of a newly-formed brigade consisting of the 5th Virginia, the 6th Virginia, and the 15th Virginia.

As part of the reorganization, the 1st North Carolina from Hampton's Brigade and the

2nd North Carolina from William Henry Fitzhugh "Rooney" Lee's Brigade were combined with the 4th and 5th North Carolina which had been in a "demi-brigade" commanded by Brigadier General Beverly Robertson. Brigadier General Robertson, whose lack of aggressiveness at Brandy Station was criticized by Stuart, had performed equally poorly through the duration of the Gettysburg Campaign. After returning to Virginia, Robertson requested reassignment, claiming, "I consider it injustice to myself and the service to remain longer in my present position" since he only commanded two regiments (three regiments of the brigade he had commanded in North Carolina had not made the move to Virginia).[5] After forming the North Carolina Brigade with its four North Carolina regiments, Lee accommodated Robertson's request, concluding his letter to Davis by writing: "You will perceive that by classifying the four North Carolina Regiments under Colonel [Laurence] Baker, it deprives General Robertson of his command, consisting of the Fifty-ninth and Sixty-third North Carolina Regiments [the 4th and 5th North Carolina Cavalry Regiments]. General Robertson has more than once applied to be relieved of the command of these regiments and ordered to the rest of his brigade in North Carolina. The promotion of Colonel Baker will enable you to gratify him." Robertson was quickly shipped off to the command of a district in South Carolina.[6]

Brigadier General Beverly Robertson's performance had been disappointing at Brandy Station and throughout the Gettysburg Campaign. Reorganization of the cavalry corps facilitated Robertson's transfer to South Carolina, a move approved by both Stuart and Robert E. Lee (Library of Congress).

Upon Robertson's departure, Colonel Laurence Baker, commander of the 1st North Carolina, was promoted and appointed to the command of the North Carolina Brigade. Unfortunately, almost immediately after assuming command of the North Carolina Brigade, Baker was seriously wounded at Brandy Station on August 1, 1863. He never returned to field duty with the Army of Northern Virginia.[7]

In a change to prior practice, the War Department authorized the promotion of several colonels who had been tapped for temporary brigade command in place of absent incumbents. Pierce Manning Butler Young, commander of the Cobb's Legion Cavalry, was promoted to brigadier general to fill Matthew Calbraith Butler's billet. James B. Gordon, newly promoted colonel of the 1st North Carolina, was promoted as a temporary replacement for Laurence Baker. Finally, in December 1863, John Chambliss, the colonel of the 13th Virginia who had been commanding William Henry Fitzhugh "Rooney" Lee's Brigade since Lee had been captured shortly after being wounded at Brandy Station, was promoted to brigadier.

In September 1863, the bad feelings between Brigadier General William E. "Grumble" Jones and J.E.B. Stuart finally came to a head, resulting in Stuart arresting Jones and referring court-martial charges against him for disrespect. The court-martial board acquitted Jones on two charges, but convicted him of a third. However, because of the trivial nature of the offense, the board recommended that Jones's punishment be only a private reprimand from Robert E. Lee. Lee administered the reprimand, but was reluctantly forced to transfer Jones to the command of a brigade in the Department of Southwestern Virginia and East Tennessee.[8] Jones, despite his acerbic personality, was a highly talented commander and his transfer was a loss to the Army of Northern Virginia. With the departure of Jones, Stuart arranged the promotion of Thomas Rosser, the commander of the 5th Virginia. Rosser—who coveted a general's stars perhaps more than he deserved them—took command of Jones's Brigade which later became known as the Laurel Brigade.[9]

In March 1864, Brigadier General "Rooney" Lee, Robert E. Lee's second son, returned from captivity. His exchange and return to duty prompted additional changes in the organization of the cavalry corps. Consistent with his recommendations of the spring of 1863, on March 23, 1864, Stuart urged the formation of a third cavalry division and the promotion of Rooney Lee as its commander.[10] The following day, Robert E. Lee concurred with Stuart's proposal and forwarded it to the War Department for its approval. Rooney Lee received his second star a month later, on April 23, 1864. A month shy of his twenty-seventh birthday, Lee became the youngest major general in Confederate service. The following day, Robert E. Lee, who was contemplating the coming campaign and had not received word of the War Department action, wrote to his son: "To resist the powerful Combination now forming against us, will require every man at his place.... I have not heard what action has been taken by the [War] Dept in reference to my recommendations Concerning the organization of the Cavy. But we have no time to wait &

Upon his return from ten months in Union captivity, William Henry Fitzhugh "Rooney" Lee, Robert E. Lee's second son, was promoted to major general and appointed to command of a newly organized cavalry division (Library of Congress).

you had better join your brigade. This week will in a probability bring us active work & we must strike fast and strong."[11]

On April 30, 1864, the War Department published Special Order No. 118, transferring Chambliss's and Gordon's brigades to the newly formed cavalry division commanded by Rooney Lee.[12] Fitzhugh Lee quickly complied, transferring Chambliss's Brigade, which had formerly been commanded by Rooney Lee, to his cousin's command. However, Hampton, who had been in South Carolina during much of the time the reorganization was being considered, did not favor transferring any regiments from his division.[13] However, he reluctantly complied with the order on May 5. On that day Hampton's adjutant wrote to Brigadier General James B. Gordon with instructions to without delay report to Stuart for further orders. The adjutant added, "I am directed by Major-General Hampton, in communicating the above orders, to express to you, and through you to your whole brigade, the surprise with which he has received the orders [to transfer the brigade], and the pain it causes him to execute them. He indulges the hope that his wishes may be consulted, and that a new assignment may be made as soon as the present emergency shall have passed, which will return your brigade to his division and give him back the troops to whom he has become so attached and whom he has learned to trust in times of danger and trial."[14] Such a public disagreement with a directive from his superiors could easily have been construed as insubordinate conduct. However, no action in response was taken by Stuart, who had more pressing matters at hand.

Despite having secured promotions for three of his brigadiers to the grade of major general and the advancement of eight colonels to brigadier, Stuart was unable to obtain promotion for himself. In the Confederate Army, the authorized grade for a corps commander was lieutenant general, and Stuart strongly believed that he well deserved promotion to that grade. In September 1863, he was optimistic regarding his promotion, writing to his wife, Flora, that rumors were "rife" that he had already been promoted. He went on to express the wish that Flora could personally hand him his new commission as she had with his previous two advancements in grade. However, a week later his hopes had begun to fade and he advised Flora that he had not been promoted, that he and General Lee had not spoken about a promotion for him, and that he was "not sanguine" for the prospect of receiving a third star.[15] Stuart's sensing of his prospects proved correct.

Some historians speculate that Lee's decision to not promote Stuart reflects the army commander's dissatisfaction with Stuart's performance during the Gettysburg Campaign.[16] However, in the absence of any evidence to support that supposition, it seems more likely that Lee's decision reflected his opinion that command of the cavalry corps was not as great a responsibility as command of an infantry corps.[17] A hint to Lee's thinking on the relative weight of cavalry command versus infantry command is found in Lee's response to Stuart's initial request—made in May 1863—to reorganize his division into a corps. In a letter dated May 30 of that year, Lee disapproved Stuart's proposal, writing, "With the depleted regiments which you now have, a brigade of three regiments would be a very small command for a general officer." Later in that same letter, Lee added, "It would give me great pleasure to see brigadiers and colonels promoted who have served the country long and well, but nothing is accomplished by their promotion unless they can get enlarged commands with it."[18] Clearly, Lee equated the size of a command with the authorized grade of its commander. Stuart's cavalry corps, like his division before, on a good day could muster roughly 8,000 sabers. Lee's three infantry corps, commanded by Lieutenant Generals Longstreet, Ewell, and Hill, generally mustered between 20,000 and 30,000 muskets.[19] Consequently, it is not surprising that Lee did not arrange a promotion for his cavalry commander.

From an operational perspective, the changes made to the organization of the Army of Northern Virginia's cavalry in the year since Brandy Station made sense. It is generally accepted that smaller formations can maneuver with greater agility than larger, more cumbersome formations. In theory a commander can more rapidly maneuver a brigade of three regiments than a brigade of five regiments. Additionally, management of units in battle is made easier by reducing commanders' "span of control"—the number of subordinates that each must direct and supervise. Finally, increasing the number of divisions from one to three and the number of brigades from five to seven provided the army or corps commander greater flexibility when employing the cavalry against an enemy that had both the initiative and superiority in strength.[20]

However, the organizational changes would provide little benefit in battle had Robert E. Lee not had proven leaders to command the organization. The general officer positions at both brigade and division level were filled by seasoned officers who had demonstrated their bravery and their competence repeatedly in battle. And despite J.E.B. Stuart's failure to attain the rank of lieutenant general, Robert E. Lee's cavalry corps was commanded by the most experienced cavalry officer in either the Union or Confederate armies.

Table 1

Evolution of the Cavalry Corps
Army of Northern Virginia
Stuart's Division

BRANDY STATION—JUNE 1863

Hampton's Brigade	Fitz. Lee's Brigade	Robertson's Brigade	W.H.F. Lee's Brigade	Jones's Brigade
1st South Carolina	1st Virginia	4th North Carolina	2nd North Carolina	6th Virginia
2nd South Carolina	2nd Virginia	5th North Carolina	9th Virginia	7th Virginia
1st North Carolina	3rd Virginia		10th Virginia	11th Virginia
Cobb's Legion	4th Virginia		13th Virginia	12th Virginia
Phillips Legion	5th Virginia		15th Virginia	35th Bn. Virginia
Jeff Davis Legion				

Stuart's Corps

SEPTEMBER 1863

Hampton's Division			Fitz Lee's Division		
Butler's Brigade	Jones's Brigade	Baker's Brigade	W.H.F. Lee's Brigade	Lomax's Brigade	Wickham's Brigade
1st S. Carolina	7th Virginia	1st N. Carolina	9th Virginia	5th Virginia	1st Virginia
2nd S. Carolina	11th Virginia	2nd N. Carolina	10th Virginia	6th Virginia	2nd Virginia
Cobb's Legion	12th Virginia	4th N. Carolina	13th Virginia	15th Virginia	3rd Virginia
Phillips Legion	35th Bn. Va.	5th N. Carolina			4th Virginia
Jeff Davis Leg.					

3. "Strike fast and strong"

Stuart's Corps
May 1864

Hampton's Division

Butler's Brigade
4th South Carolina
5th South Carolina
6th South Carolina

Young's Brigade
7th Georgia
20th Bn. Georgia
Cobb's Legion
Phillips Legion
Jeff Davis Legion
4th Bn. Alabama

Rosser's Brigade
7th Virginia
11th Virginia
12th Virginia
35th Bn. Virginia
1st Maryland

Fitz Lee's Division

Lomax's Brigade
5th Virginia
6th Virginia
15th Virginia

Wickham's Brigade
1st Virginia
2nd Virginia
3rd Virginia
4th Virginia

W.H.F. Lee's Division

Chambliss's Brigade
9th Virginia
10th Virginia
13th Virginia

Gordon's Brigade
1st North Carolina
2nd North Carolina
5th North Carolina

4

"When am I to get another horse?"
Confederate Cavalry Regiments—
New Commanders, Old Problems

The promotions cited in the previous chapter, combined with battle losses, resulted in the turnover of commanders in many of the cavalry regiments of the Army of Northern Virginia. Fortunately, as in the Army of the Potomac, there were abundant field grade officers who were both capable and battle-tested, and were prepared to assume command.

In Wickham's Brigade of Fitz Lee's Division, Richard Welby Carter, a farmer from Fauquier County, succeeded James Drake in command of the 1st Virginia. Drake had been killed in July 1863. Carter, who had attended VMI for two years, began the war as captain of Company H, 1st Virginia, and had served with the regiment ever since.[1] William H.F. Payne, who began the war as the commander of Fauquier County's Black Horse Troop, was promoted to colonel of the 4th Virginia upon Williams Wickham's promotion to brigadier general. Unfortunately, Payne had been captured at Hanover, Pennsylvania, on June 30, 1863, and would remain a prisoner until exchanged on May 8, 1864. In Payne's absence, the regiment was commanded by Lieutenant Colonel Robert Lee Randolph, also of Fauquier County.[2] The other two regiments in Wickham's Brigade did not undergo changes of command. Colonel Thomas T. Munford, who had been recommended for promotion to brigadier on two occasions, only to be passed over in favor of other officers, remained in command of the 2nd Virginia. Colonel Thomas Owen remained in command of the 3rd Virginia. In Owens's lengthy absence on leave and court-martial duty, the regiment had been ably commanded by Lieutenant Colonel William R. Carter, a lawyer from Nottoway County. Carter was considered a highly capable cavalry commander by both the men of his regiment and his superiors.[3]

In Lunsford Lomax's Brigade, chains of command within all three regiments had undergone changes since Brandy Station. In the 5th Virginia, Henry Clay Pate, the former "Border Ruffian" from Missouri, was promoted into the vacancy created by Thomas Rosser's promotion. As previously discussed, Pate, whose battalion had formed the nucleus of the 5th when the regiment was organized in June 1862, had been court-martialed by Rosser for disobedience of orders, but was acquitted in April 1863 after a lengthy trial. Afterward, Pate remained on uneasy terms with both Rosser and J.E.B. Stuart, who had arranged for Rosser's appointment to command of the regiment when it was organized.[4] Pate had missed ten months of campaigning in 1862–1863 while under arrest. In June 1863, he had been injured in a fall when his horse was killed at Aldie and missed much of the Gettysburg Campaign.[5] Consequently,

Pate was among the least experienced of Stuart's regimental commanders. In the 6th Virginia, the War Department had granted an exception to policy allowing a former commander of the regiment, Julien Harrison, to be reappointed to command. Harrison, who had commanded the regiment for several months in 1862, had resigned his commission because of a severe case of hemorrhoids.[6] On October 11, 1863, just a few days after returning to the regiment, Harrison was severely wounded at Stevensburg in one of the opening encounters of the Bristoe Campaign. Lieutenant Colonel John Shackelford Green, who a month earlier had been acquitted of charges preferred against him by Grumble Jones in May 1863, assumed command in Harrison's absence. In April 1864, Green resigned from the army for the good of the service. Major Cabel Flournoy, who while in temporary command of the regiment at Brandy Station led the impetuous charge that disrupted Brigadier General John Buford's advance up the Beverly Ford Road, again assumed command of the regiment. Flournoy was promoted to lieutenant colonel to fill the vacancy created by Green's resignation (the colonel's billet continued to be encumbered by the wounded Harrison).[7] In the 15th Virginia, Colonel

Colonel Thomas T. Munford was a VMI graduate and a reliable regimental commander. He had been recommended for promotion to brigadier general in October 1862 to replace Jones, who was not in Stuart's favor. That promotion was not approved and Munford remained a colonel in command of the 2nd Virginia, passed over by both Wickham and Rosser (Library of Congress).

William Ball, who had been absent due to illness since December 1862, resigned his commission in January 1864. This allowed the promotion of Major Charles R. Collins, who had exercised command of the regiment since April 1863, to be promoted to colonel. Collins, a brave and capable officer, was promoted over the regiment's lieutenant colonel, John R. Critcher, who had been captured in May 1863 and was unavailable for duty until exchanged in March 1864.[8]

In Chambliss's Brigade of Rooney Lee's Division, the only regiment that had changed commanders was the 13th Virginia. When Chambliss was promoted to brigadier, his lieutenant colonel, Jefferson Phillips, who had been severely wounded in the melee on Yew Ridge, was promoted to fill the vacancy.[9] Colonel R.L.T. Beale, a highly competent officer who assumed command of the 9th Virginia when Rooney Lee was promoted to brigadier in September 1862, remained in command of that regiment.[10] Colonel James Lucius Davis, who had been appointed to command of the 10th Virginia when the regiment was formed in May 1862, continued in command. However, Davis had been captured at Hagerstown, Maryland, on July 6, 1863, and was not exchanged until March 10, 1864. In his absence, the regiment had been ably commanded by Lieutenant Colonel Robert Caskie, who before the war had worked as a tobacco merchant in Richmond.[11]

The North Carolina Brigade of Rooney Lee's Division, commanded by James B. Gordon, had been created from regiments assigned to other brigades at the time of the battle at Brandy Station. The turnover of commanders among those regiments was greater than in any other brigade of the corps.

Colonel Solomon Williams, the commander of the 2nd North Carolina, had been shot and killed at Brandy Station, just two weeks after returning from a lengthy detail on court-martial duty. Lieutenant Colonel W.H.F Payne, of the 4th Virginia—who had commanded the 2nd North Carolina during Williams's absence—was again placed in temporary command of the regiment, much to the dissatisfaction of some officers who resented being commanded by a Virginian. At Hanover, Pennsylvania, on June 30, Payne's horse was killed and he was captured. Through the remainder of the Gettysburg Campaign the regiment was commanded by one of its captains.[12] In July 1863, Lieutenant Colonel William G. Robinson, who had been captured in April 1862, was exchanged, took command of the regiment, and was promoted to colonel. However, Robinson was frequently absent, leaving day-to-day command to Major Clinton M. Andrews. Robinson resigned his commission in May 1864 upon being detailed to the Confederate Navy, and Andrews, who had six days earlier had been promoted to lieutenant colonel, was promoted to colonel to fill the vacancy. Andrews had mustered-in to the regiment in 1861 as the commander of Company B, had been promoted to major in September 1862, and had seen extensive service with the regiment in both North Carolina and Virginia.[13]

The commander of the 5th North Carolina, Colonel Peter Evans, was mortally wounded and captured while leading

Colonel Richard Lee Turberville Beale, a University of Virginia graduate and lawyer, took command of the 9th Virginia upon Rooney Lee's promotion to brigadier and was himself promoted to brigadier general in February 1865. Beale served two terms in the U.S. Congress: 1847–1849 and 1879–1881 (Library of Congress).

a charge through the streets of Upperville, Virginia, on June 21, 1863. He died a month later in Washington. Upon Evans's wounding, Stuart placed Lieutenant Colonel James B. Gordon, of the 1st North Carolina, in command of the 5th North Carolina.[14] Gordon commanded the regiment through the Gettysburg Campaign and for some time thereafter. In August, with the formation of the North Carolina Brigade, Gordon was promoted and assigned to the command of the 1st North Carolina and command of the 5th devolved upon the regiment's lieutenant colonel, Stephen B. Evans (no relation to Peter Evans). Stephen Evans was apparently in poor health, and the major of the regiment, James H. McNeil, was promoted to colonel over him in November 1864. Before the war McNeil had served as a Presbyterian clergyman and was the secretary of the American Bible Society. He was commissioned as a captain in the regiment in June 1862, and had been wounded at Middleburg in June 1863.[15]

The 1st North Carolina had been commanded by Laurence Baker on June 9, 1863. Upon Baker's promotion, James B. Gordon assumed command of the regiment. Shortly afterward, Gordon was promoted to brigadier and elevated to command of the brigade as a result of Baker's wounding. Colonel Thomas Ruffin followed Gordon in command of the 1st North Carolina. On the morning of October 14, 1863, just two weeks after being promoted to colonel, Ruffin was mortally wounded leading an early-morning charge against Union infantry at Auburn, Virginia. Ruffin's charge, while costly, allowed Stuart to extricate his forces from encirclement by Major General Gouverneur Warren's Corps. W.H. Cheek, who began the war as captain of Company E, succeeded Ruffin in command.[16]

The 4th North Carolina was commanded at Brandy Station by Colonel Dennis Ferebee, who continued in command of the regiment. Ferebee was shot in the right foot during the Bristoe Campaign and was absent convalescing until April 1864.[17] On January 25, 1864, the regiment was ordered from Virginia to Woodville, North Carolina, where its horses could find better grazing. In late April, the 4th was reassigned from Gordon's Brigade to a newly formed brigade under the command of Brigadier General James Dearing. In May Dearing's Brigade returned to Virginia and was assigned to Beauregard's command defending Richmond. On June 18, after the bulk of Robert E. Lee's army had crossed to the south side of the James River, Dearing's Brigade was assigned to Rooney Lee's Division.[18]

In the spring of 1864 as the time for active campaigning neared, two of the brigades in Hampton's Division were undergoing significant change. In February 1863, Hampton proposed sending his regiments from South Carolina and the Deep South back to their home states to be replaced by cavalry regiments then serving in that part of the Confederacy. The proposal had some merit. Several of Hampton's non–Virginia regiments were severely depleted with many horses unfit for active service and with the men unable to obtain remounts. Additionally, there were several cavalry regiments in South Carolina and Georgia that were at or above full strength, and had seen only light duty since their formation earlier in the war. The replacement of Hampton's veterans with a "New Issue" will be discussed in the following chapter.

Rosser's Brigade of Hampton's Division, formerly commanded by Brigadier General William E. Jones, consisted of the 7th, 11th, and 12th Virginia Cavalry, and the 35th Battalion Virginia Cavalry. The 7th Virginia continued under the command of Colonel Richard Dulany, who during the Battle of Brandy Station had been convalescing at the Confederate hospital in Charlottesville. Dulany had received a gunshot wound to his left arm at Greenland Gap, West Virginia, on April 25, 1863. After several furloughs and additional hospitalizations,

Dulany returned to duty with his regiment in October 1863.[19] In July 1863, Oliver R. Funsten, the popular lieutenant colonel of the 11th Virginia, was promoted to colonel to fill the vacancy created by Lomax's promotion to brigadier. Earlier in that year, Funsten submitted his resignation, unhappy that Lomax, who had not served with the regiment, had had been brought into the regiment and appointed over him. Robert E. Lee, however, did not accept Funsten's resignation and he remained on duty. Funsten, who had been born in 1817, was older than many of his contemporaries, and also larger than most—his men affectionately referred to him as "our big colonel."[20] Colonel Asher Harmon, commander of the 12th Virginia, was wounded—saber blow to the neck—during the Battle of Brandy Station. He was captured in July 1863 almost immediately after returning to duty from a convalescent leave of absence. Harmon remained a prisoner until February 1865 when he was paroled to await exchange. In Harmon's absence, the regiment was commanded by Lieutenant Colonel Thomas Massie. Massie, a farmer from Warren County, had received a commission as first lieutenant in March 1862 and was promoted to captain of Company G the following month. He was promoted to major in June 1862 and to lieutenant colonel in April 1863.[21] The 35th Virginia Cavalry, a six-company battalion, continued under the command of Lieutenant Colonel Elijah White. In January 1862, White recruited a company, White's Rebels, for border service along the Potomac in Loudoun County. In the fall of 1862 the battalion was organized with White elected as its commander, although he was convalescing from a gunshot wound to the shoulder at the time. Since recovering from his wound, White had led the battalion without interruption.[22]

Young's Brigade of Hampton's Division had seen relatively little turnover among its regimental commanders. The Jeff Davis Legion, a battalion of six companies from Georgia, Mississippi and Alabama, remained under the command of Lieutenant Colonel J. Frederick Waring who began the war as the commander of the Georgia Hussars, a militia company from Savannah that became Company F of the Jeff Davis Legion.[23] The Phillips Legion, a battalion of six companies from Georgia, remained under the command of Lieutenant Colonel William W. Rich. Rich, a planter and assistant U.S. marshal from Cass County, Georgia, had first seen military service as an officer in a company of mounted infantry during the Mexican War. At the outbreak of the Civil War, he was elected captain of Company B in the Phillips Legion Cavalry. He had been appointed commander of the legion's cavalry battalion and promoted to lieutenant colonel in summer of 1862. In January 1863, the infantry and cavalry of the Phillips Legion were split, and the cavalry, under the command of Rich, was assigned to Stuart's cavalry division.[24] Pierce M.B. Young, who had commanded the Cobb's Legion at Brandy Station, was wounded—shot in the chest—in another fight at Brandy Station on August 1, 1863. In October 1863, shortly after returning to duty from convalescence, Young was promoted to brigadier general and placed in temporary command of Butler's Brigade since Butler was still in South Carolina recovering from his wound.[25] With Young's promotion, Lieutenant Colonel William G. Deloney commanded the Cobb's Legion. At Jack's Shop on September 22, 1863, Deloney was wounded and captured. He died ten days later in Washington, D.C.[26] Upon the death of Deloney, Gilbert J. "Gid" Wright was appointed to command of the Cobb's Legion and promoted to colonel (unlike the Phillips and the Jeff Davis Legions, the Cobb's Legion had ten companies and was thus authorized a colonel in command). Wright had served as a private in the 1st Georgia Infantry during the Mexican War and been wounded in the neck; he suffered from stiffness in the neck for the remainder of his life. After the Mexican War, Wright read law and practiced as an attorney in Albany, Georgia. At the beginning of the Civil War, he served initially as a lieutenant in Company D of the Legion. He was promoted to captain in 1862 and made major on June 9, 1863. He was conspicuous on the battlefield for his "bulldog courage" and his "stentorian voice," and had been wounded at least twice prior to his promotion to colonel.[27]

While the cavalry of the Army of Northern Virginia was well-led, as in past years, arming and mounting Confederate cavalry remained problematic.[28] With regard to weapons, the Southern states simply lacked the industrial capacity to produce arms in the quantity and quality needed to equip a large, modern army. Prior to the actual outbreak of hostilities, the South had armed many of its newly formed units with the roughly 200,000 weapons—mostly obsolete—that were seized from federal arsenals.[29] While the Confederate War Department established several armories and arsenals—even moving machinery from Harpers Ferry to Fayetteville, North Carolina—it was able to only manufacture approximately 100 weapons per day.[30] Consequently, the Confederacy met most of its weapons requirements by importing arms from Europe, heavily supplemented by the distribution of weapons captured from the Union or scavenged on battlefields.[31]

The Confederacy's problems with weaponry affected the cavalry in two ways. Most significantly, many troopers were armed with muzzle-loading rifles or carbines, not the preferred breech-loaders. Certainly muzzle-loading weapons were more cumbersome to use while in the saddle. However, when fighting dismounted, the advantages of breech-loaders were not as significant. Also, reliance upon captured or scavenged weapons resulted in regiments with men carrying different models of rifles, carbines, and pistols, which usually fired different ammunition. For example, only several thousand Sharps model carbines were manufactured at the Richmond Arsenal which was totally insufficient to entirely arm Stuart's cavalry corps. Consequently, within a regiment some men might be armed with the Richmond Sharps and others with captured Union Sharps, which featured a different priming system. Other soldiers might be armed with captured Burnside or Maynard carbines which differed in caliber and naturally fired different ammunition.[32] While today this mix of weaponry would be a logistician's nightmare, Confederate troopers seemed to have adapted to the problem, or at least coped with it reasonably well.

As in previous years, the Confederate War Department was unable to provide adequate subsistence—for both men and horses—to its cavalry regiments during the winter of 1863–1864. In response, Robert E. Lee dispersed much of J.E.B. Stuart's cavalry to places where the horses might graze. Several regiments of Lee's division were moved to Albemarle County, near Charlottesville, which had not yet been fought over by large armies. Rosser's Brigade returned to the Shenandoah Valley, which had seen relatively little action over the past year, for much of the winter. Lee, surprisingly, as noted above, allowed the North Carolina regiments to return to their home state for much of the winter. Additionally, the men of several Virginia regiments—at least those whose companies had been raised in counties not occupied by Union forces—were furloughed for the winter. The men were allowed to return home with the understanding that they would assemble every few days, would return to duty when called upon, and that they would recruit their friends and neighbors to the ranks. With the cavalry dispersed, the burden of providing security for the army fell mainly on the regiments from South Carolina and the Deep South. Because of the distances involved, it was simply impractical to send the men of those regiments home for the winter. The War Department's solution, was to essentially recreate Butler's Brigade from scratch and to bring north fresh troops for the three legions. That effort will be discussed in the following chapter.

In the North, the Federal government had expended great effort and resources in improving its system for purchasing and distributing horses to the army's cavalry. By contrast, in the South the Confederate War Department continued to place responsibility for mounting its cavalrymen squarely upon the troopers themselves. The policy of requiring the men to provide their own mounts had been expedient, but quickly proved inefficient. If a cavalry horse was lost to lameness or disease, the soldier, alone, bore the burden of procuring a remount. Upon enlistment, a soldier's horse was appraised, and should the horse be lost as a result of battle, the soldier was to be reimbursed for that loss at the appraised value. However, in practice, many horses' appraised values were quickly outstripped by inflation. As the war progressed into its fourth year, the supply of horses—particularly in Virginia—diminished. Additionally, Confederate currency steadily lost value, causing the price of all goods and services—including horses—to rise. At the beginning of the war, the appraised value for a good mount might be $150. By 1864, it was not unusual for the purchase price of a good horse to run to several thousand dollars. Consequently, soldiers found it difficult to purchase remounts, particularly on a private's salary of twelve dollars per month.[33] The cavalrymen who were able to travel home on a "horse pass" and bring back a remount from the family farm were fortunate indeed.

Cavalrymen without horses created a significant problem within regiments. Generally dismounted men were assigned to an ad hoc "Company Q" until they could secure a remount. As dismounted men became more numerous, some brigade commanders aggregated their regiments' Company Qs into dismounted battalions. In theory, the dismounted men were to be assigned suitable duties or to fight essentially as infantrymen. However, the Company Qs or dismounted battalions were unable to keep up with their regiments when on the move. Also, it is important to realize that every dismounted man, although considered present for duty, was absent from the mounted company to which he was assigned. In regiments with

In August 1863, Colonel John Chambliss wrote a scathing critique of the Confederate War Department's efforts to man, equip and mount Southern cavalry. The critique—sent via "back channel" to the War Department—resulted in no substantive improvements. Chambliss, promoted to brigadier general, was killed on the Charles City Road on August 16, 1864 (*Photographic History of the Civil War*).

large numbers of dismounts the burden of fighting, as well as other duties such as picketing, fell more heavily on those with horses. This both reduced the regiments' combat effectiveness and contributed to morale problems among the men.[34]

In August 1863, Colonel John Chambliss, then in command of Rooney Lee's Brigade, sent a letter to Colonel Alexander R. Boteler, a volunteer aide de camp on J.E.B. Stuart's staff. In the letter, shown below, Chambliss provided a comprehensive, first-hand description of problems affecting the operational efficiency of Confederate cavalry. Additionally, Chambliss recommended solutions to address and resolve those problems. The letter is provided below in its entirety.[35]

> COLONEL: In compliance with your request, I will briefly touch upon those points which in my opinion demand the consideration of our authorities in advancing, recuperating, and promoting the efficiency of the cavalry service, and call attention to the causes that have produced the difference which now exists between its present condition and that of a few months ago. A great disparity exists between the effective cavalry force of the enemy and ours. Especially, in view of the probability that their advantages in this respect may be vastly increased, it is most important that our cavalry be placed upon an equality with theirs. Should it be deemed compatible with the public interest, there is no doubt that at this time, particularly under a proper recruiting system projected in the different counties of our State especially, many valuable acquisitions to our now shattered ranks would accrue to us. Hundreds of details have been made from the cavalry of men to easy places in quartermaster's, commissary, or medical departments, and no orders can force or invoke these detailed men to their commands when their employers declare it incompatible with the public service that they should be ordered back. Their places can be easily supplied by competent, crippled or otherwise, disabled soldiers.
>
> The superiority of the enemy's cavalry armament, coupled with their better ammunition, is a point demanding prompt attention. It is accorded that no arm for mounted service can be compared to the breech-loading carbine. Dismounted fighting with the carbine on the part of the enemy has become very popular, and comprises the best share of their fighting. The inferiority of our armament and ammunition tends to inspire the one not at all and to make bolder the other. It would seem that not a very high degree of mechanical skill is required in perfecting the present Richmond carbine made after Sharps patent, or that it is not impossible to provide a sufficiency of such arms put up in the very best style of manufacture abroad. Encouragement to inventors and experimentalists in perfecting and putting up not only such arms but fixed ammunition, with a view to its preservation in wet weather and under rough handling, will go far toward arresting the wholesale waste and destruction of powder and lead.
>
> The sabers issued by the Department are miserably inferior weapons, estimated at so low a value by the soldier, and really of so little account, that they are soon lost or cast away as worthless. The soldier will prize a good weapon, the quality of which will inspire him with pride for its good keeping and confidence when in contact with his foeman's steel.
>
> The saddles issued by the Ordnance Department are dreaded, ridiculed, and avoided by officers and men, and are used only through necessity, seldom without proving ruinous to the backs of horses. Though samples of the best approved saddles can be had anywhere, it is strange that no trees can be manufactured comparable to the McClellan saddles, when as much time and material is consumed in constructing the miserable apologies issued to the cavalry in imitation of the above-named saddles. It would seem that a board of suitable and enterprising officers would take pleasure in instituting inquiry on this subject and in arresting the useless waste of material in the manufacture of these Confederate saddles.
>
> Other parts of the cavalry soldiers' equipments furnished by the Government might be greatly improved, but are of inferior moment to those already mentioned. Above all other considerations rises the question now causing much dissatisfaction and disorganization in the cavalry, "When am I to get another horse, and how can I buy one at the present prices after I have lost so many without any compensation from the Government?" The provisions of the bill passed by Congress

allow payment for those horses only killed in action. I know that a majority of my most efficient men have lost from one to five horses, broken down by the hardships of the service, and a small minority of horses lost in the service are killed in action. It is with great reluctance that an officer can exchange or part with an accomplished and experienced cavalry soldier whom he finds dismounted through such circumstances, and is pecuniarily unable to provide himself forever and ever with horses. The good soldier of this dismounted class of two or more years' experience is too valuable to be parted with, and some provision should be made to supply such men. Although there are many in this service who for various reasons should be transferred to other branches of the service, and there are many infantrymen who are applying for transfers to the cavalry, and such transfers would greatly recruit and strengthen us, still the objections raised by company and field officers of the infantry render such exchange nigh to an impossibility. I would suggest that you call attention not only to the foregoing matter of this paragraph relative to the providing payment for horses lost by being disabled, broken down, exhausted, and left within the enemy's lines, &c., but also to rendering exchange a matter easier to be effected. There is a crying want of veterinary surgeons to be attached to and to accompany the cavalry to provide medicines and proper treatment in the field and camp for such horses. The establishment of a veterinary hospital in some locality secure from cavalry raids, convenient and accessible to the main railroad communications, where cheap sheds or coverings for the winter season might be erected, where surgeons and farriers might be appointed, with the labor of hired negroes to attend to the horses, would greatly enhance the efficiency of the service; would put a stop to straggling and lurking behind with the shadow of an excuse, and effectually hush the discontent arising from the necessity of having to retain invalid horses in the field and of making worthy cavalry soldiers involuntary members of the foot battalion for any length of time.

The chief and main cause of the present dismembered and shattered state of our ranks has been the want of horseshoes and horseshoe nails, forges, and transportation therefor. Provide every soldier with shoe pouches and shoes to put in them, and fewer dismounted men will harass the service. A greater number of blacksmiths should be retained and employed in each regiment.

Drilling is indispensably necessary to rendering troops thoroughly efficient. The force of cavalry now confronting the enemy is so small that every man is on picket or outpost duty for a majority of the time, and the horses are so constantly employed that a horseback drill is dreaded. With increased numbers we would be more upon an equal footing with the enemy and be enabled to withstand the various shocks incident to a service having so small an effective force of cavalry. During the late expedition into the enemy's country many valuable horses were lost owing mainly to the want of shoes, which failed to arrive and be provided before the start. Men became dismounted, separated from their commands, and thus left behind from the impossibility of keeping a pace with the mounted men [had] to find places of safety and to congregate in masses of "Qs." I have hastily drawn attention to the main causes of disorganization and dismemberment in this branch of the service, and in view of the vastly superior resources of the enemy and their superior strength, prompt remedies are imperatively demanded.

JNO. R. CHAMBLISS, JR.
Colonel, Commanding Lee's Cavalry Brigade[36]

Colonel Boteler forwarded Chambliss's letter directly to Secretary of War James Seddon without going through either Stuart or Robert E. Lee, and he apologized for "transgress[ing] any rule of the service or conventional propriety." Seddon forwarded the letter to Colonel Josiah Gorgas, the Chief of Ordnance, who provided a brief reply in which he agreed to begin using the McClellan saddle since "the general testimony of officers has lately been decidedly in favor of it."[37]

Unfortunately for soldiers in the Confederate cavalry, and for their mounts, more substantive action with regard to Chambliss's observations was not taken.

5

The "New Issue"
Reinforcements for Lee's Cavalry

In early 1864, two circumstances led to the most significant changes in the composition of the cavalry of the Army of Northern Virginia since the formation of J.E.B. Stuart's division in the summer of 1862. The formation of over-strength and underused regiments in the Deep South, coupled with Wade Hampton's desire to relieve his South Carolina regiments from their long and arduous duty in Virginia that the men might return to their home state, resulted in the Confederate War Department ordering to Virginia four regiments and two battalions of cavalry—the "New Issue" as they were called by Stuart's veterans—from South Carolina, Georgia, and Alabama to Virginia.

In early 1864, Robert E. Lee began preparing for the coming campaign, which would inevitably begin once good weather returned in the spring. One of Lee's major concerns was the condition of his cavalry, particularly among the regiments from South Carolina, Georgia, and Mississippi. All those regiments were under strength, and suffered from a shortage of horses. On January 13, Lee wrote to Colonel J.S. Preston, the Superintendant of the Bureau of Conscription, complaining that the privilege of volunteering for military service was being abused. As an example, he cited a company, the Rutledge Cavalry of South Carolina. The Rutledge Cavalry had accepted volunteers well beyond its authorization of about 100 men, resulting in its division into two—and then four—separate companies. Lee recommended that men who were excess to the authorization for their companies be sent to the armies in the field. In his letter, Lee wrote, "Upon the vigilant and strict execution of the conscript law depends in a great measure the issue of the coming campaign, and no effort should be spared to bring out the recruits at once, that they may be prepared by the opening of the spring." In this communication, Lee implicitly indicated the importance of ensuring that recruits from the Deep South—who had not seen much action—were adequately trained for the hard fighting he anticipated in Virginia. Lee closed his letter by offering Colonel Preston some officers from the Army of Northern Virginia to assist his "enrolling officers" with collecting conscripts.[1]

A week later, on January 19, Lee wrote to Jefferson Davis, apprising him of the difficulty in maintaining the regiments from states in the Deep South. Specifically, Lee complained that men, after being conscripted by the Confederate War Department, were then allowed to "volunteer" for service in regiments assigned to duty in their home state. Lee advised the President that "the South Carolina Regiments in this Army are much reduced by hard service, and it has been found impossible to recruit them, principally, if not entirely, on account of the encouragement given to men to volunteer in regiments engaged in the defense of the Department of South Carolina, Georgia, and Florida, and the measures adopted in that department to retain conscripts." To emphasize his point, Lee noted that four cavalry regiments serving in South Carolina, which had seen very little active service, had a combined strength of 4,550 men: the 3rd South Carolina Cavalry—about 1,100; the 4th—1,350; the 5th—1,200; the 6th—1,000. In contrast, Butler's Brigade of Hampton's Division, comprised of two regiments from South Carolina, one regiment from Georgia, and a battalion each from Georgia and Mississippi, could mount, at best, 500 men. As he had done in his letter to Colonel Preston, Lee advised Davis that "it is a matter of great moment that the recruits for this army should reach it in full time for the coming campaign, and whatever is to be done to bring them out should be done without delay."[2]

Jefferson Davis promptly held a meeting with Colonel Preston, during which he read aloud Lee's letter of January 19. On January 22, Preston gave President Davis documents revealing the conscription abuses his bureau had encountered in South Carolina. That day, Davis wrote to Secretary of War James A. Seddon offering his guidance. "The illegal organization of new companies composed of conscripts is to be remedied by the enrollment of the men and their assignment to companies as provided by law and regulations. Whenever a company exceeds the maximum the excess should be transferred. Another remedy seems appropriate, which is to exchange the full regiments which have not seen service for the skeletons reduced by campaigns and battles. In the cavalry of Virginia there is need of both men and horses; that of the army of South Carolina is represented to be full. The present is a favorable period for the correction of the abuses referred to within and noted in similar communications."[3] Secretary Seddon forwarded President Davis' correspondence to the army's Adjutant General, General Samuel A. Cooper, for corrective action.[4] Cooper forwarded Davis' guidance regarding abuses of the conscription system to General P.G.T. Beauregard, who commanded the Depart-

In response to complaints from Robert E. Lee regarding abuses in the conscription system, on January 22, 1864, President Jefferson Davis recommended bringing fresh regiments from the Deep South to replace "skeleton" cavalry regiments depleted by hard service in Virginia. Unfortunately, because of red tape and resistance by officials in South Carolina, the replacement regiments did not arrive in Virginia until late May (Library of Congress).

ment of South Carolina, Georgia, and Florida. Unfortunately, neither the War Department nor the Adjutant General's office took immediate action on Davis' recommendation to swap fresh regiments for "skeletons." Had they done so, they would have ameliorated some of the tension developing in the relationships between Wade Hampton and his immediate superiors, J.E.B. Stuart and Robert E. Lee. Moreover, prompt attention to Davis' recommendation would have strengthened Stuart's cavalry corps before active combat operations began in the spring, as had been desired by Robert E. Lee.[5]

In compliance with Davis' guidance regarding over-strength companies, Beauregard's chief of staff, Brigadier General Thomas Jordan, issued General Order Number 25 dated February 20, 1864. In the order, Jordan directed district commanders to reduce the size of their cavalry companies to 5 sergeants, 4 corporals, 1 farrier, 1 blacksmith, 2 musicians, and 80 privates, for a composite strength of 93 enlisted men. Excess men who were dismounted and unable to obtain remounts were to be transferred to infantry and artillery companies. District commanders were also directed to appoint boards of officers to distribute between old and new companies on a pro-rata basis men who were chronically sick or disabled. Distribution was to be made "in a spirit of harmony and regard for the good of the service." District commanders were directed to implement the special order within thirty days.[6]

Meanwhile, problems with the strength of Stuart's non–Virginia cavalry regiments remained unaddressed. In a letter to Secretary Seddon dated January 23, 1864, Robert E. Lee, anticipating hard fighting when spring began, again expressed his concerns regarding the cavalry of the Army of Northern Virginia. He prefaced his remarks by noting that his cavalry, particularly the two "southern" brigades, were worn down by hard service and the lack of forage over the winter and that the Union, which had already fielded cavalry greatly superior in numbers, would largely replenish their divisions before campaigning began. In response to the projected disparity in cavalry forces, Lee recommended that "some portion of the cavalry in South Carolina and Southwestern Virginia be sent to [the Army of Northern Virginia] so soon as the grass begins to grow." He went on to also recommend that companies from Georgia be brought north to bring the Phillips Legion and the Jeff Davis Legion—each a battalion of six companies—up to regimental strength of ten companies each. Further, Lee recommended that Brigadier General M.C. Butler, then recuperating in South Carolina, be authorized to recruit men for the two South Carolina regiments in the Army of Northern Virginia from those who were excess to cavalry regiments and companies on duty in that state. Lee acknowledged to Seddon that commanders in Southwestern Virginia, South Carolina, and Georgia would object to his proposals.[7]

Somewhat belatedly, J.E.B. Stuart on January 28 wrote General Cooper stating that "the strong arm of authority is absolutely necessary to secure to the regiments of this command from South Carolina and Georgia the recruits which they absolutely need." Stuart recommended that General Butler be empowered to inspect the units in South Carolina, and to "take from their numbers by lot or other fair process a sufficient number to increase the First and Second South Carolina Cavalry Regiments, now on duty with this command, to their proper proportions." He went on to recommend that Major Barrington S. King of the Cobb's Legion, who was on leave in Georgia at the time, be directed to do the same as Butler to bring the Georgia cavalry units up to strength.[8]

Concurrently, Wade Hampton had become increasingly concerned, frustrated, and then angry over the condition of his cavalry, particularly the regiments from South Carolina, Georgia, and Mississippi. Within a month after recovering from his wounds at Gettysburg and returning to duty, Hampton wrote to Robert E. Lee with his concerns. In a letter dated December 7, 1863, he advised Lee that "owing to the great distance from their home, the men in these brigades find great difficulty in keeping themselves well mounted, and horses have reached such prices that I greatly fear many of my best men will be forced into the infantry."[9] Hampton recommended that his two brigades with regiments not from Virginia, if they could be spared, be sent for the winter to Weldon, North Carolina, where there was ample forage for the horses, and that Rosser's Brigade of Virginia regiments be sent to the Shenandoah Valley where they could better subsist during the winter. Hampton also urged Lee to arrange for units to be transferred to his division from Georgia. Adding a battalion and four separate companies would bring the Phillips and Jeff Davis Legions up to regimental strength. Hampton further recommended that the 5th Georgia Cavalry be brought north to provide sufficient regiments to form a new brigade for P.M.B. Young, a Georgian who was temporarily commanding Butler's Brigade.[10] Hampton also advised Lee that he had heard of several cavalry companies in South Carolina that were to be disbanded, and recommended that the soldiers be sent to his two South Carolina regiments as individual replacements. Hampton concluded his letter by asking, should his recommendations regarding the disposition of his brigades be accepted, that he be sent to Mississippi for the winter. Hampton owned vast estates in Mississippi and believed his knowledge of the country would allow him to be of immediate service to General Joseph Johnston who was in command there.[11]

Hampton did not receive a formal response to his memorandum from Lee, although some of his recommendations were eventually implemented. Rosser's Brigade was sent to the Shenandoah Valley where it took part on raids into West Virginia before going into camp for the winter. As mentioned earlier, later in the winter, the bulk of Gordon's North Carolina Brigade returned to their home state where both the men and their horses could better subsist.

After conducting a lengthy raid into West Virginia, most of Fitzhugh Lee's division, comprised entirely of Virginia regiments, was essentially furloughed for roughly two months. Wherever possible, Lee's men were permitted to return to their homes so they could better feed themselves and their horses while encouraging others to enlist. This left Hampton with Butler's Brigade—under the command of Young—to pull the bulk of the picket duty along the lower Rappahannock River for the Army of Northern Virginia. This disparate division of labor between the men of Lee's Division and Hampton's Division helped feed Hampton's personal view that the cavalry regiments from Virginia received preferential treatment. From his camp south of Fredericksburg, Hampton, on January 5, 1864, wrote a letter to his sister in which he frankly expressed his opinions. "Stuart has not replied to my letter proposing that my two southern Brigades should be sent to N.C. and I suppose that he intends to keep us here. If he does, my command will be unfit for duty next spring, and in this event, I shall ask to be transferred to some other army, or I will resign. I am thoroughly disgusted with the way things are managed here, and I have no doubt but that Yankee cavalry will be better next spring, than ours. No care is taken of ours, and they are made to perform very hard, and very useless work."[12]

Throughout the winter, Hampton attempted to ease the burdens which duty imposed upon his men. On January 13, 1864, Hampton wrote to Stuart recommending that most of his pickets along the Rappahannock be replaced by infantry. As justification, he explained that some of the pickets were required to travel forty miles from their camps to their posts, and that there was no forage available along the river. Stuart forwarded Hampton's proposal to Robert E. Lee recommending its approval. Lee, however, did not concur with the views of his two senior cavalry officers. In his endorsement, Lee wrote: "I very much regret that the picket duty comes so heavy on the cavalry, and I wish I could relieve them. Small infantry pickets, as proposed, could easily be cut off. Nothing less than two [infantry] brigades would be safe such a distance from support."[13] Consequently, Hampton's men continued to pull duty far from the relative comfort of their camps.

Lee and Stuart did what they could to help supply Hampton. Extra wagons and teams were sent to Hampton to improve his ability to distribute corn and forage to his regiments, and Stuart recommended that Hampton use the railroad to transport corn to his units and use the extra wagons to haul forage. Hampton wrote to Stuart again on February 1, complaining of the lack of forage. Hampton concluded the letter recounting the dismal condition of Butler's Brigade: "Within the last twelve months upward of 2,000 horses have been brought on to this brigade, besides those which were captured, and now not 500 men can be mounted on serviceable horses."[14]

Things began to come to a head regarding the condition of Hampton's cavalry in February 1864. On February 10, Brigadier General P.M.B. Young, commanding Butler's Brigade, wrote to Stuart requesting that the brigade be relieved with "four full regiments from the coast of Georgia and South Carolina." He stated that two-thirds of his men were dismounted and unable to obtain remounts in Virginia, that many companies were depleted by casualties and below their effective minimum strengths, and went on to warn, "Something must be done, and done soon, or at the beginning of the spring campaign this brigade will not put as many men in the field for duty as ought to constitute one regiment." Young, anticipating that commanders in Georgia and South Carolina would be reluctant to support his proposal, opined that his regiments, if serving near their homes, would be up to strength within a month of returning to their home state.[15]

Hampton approved and forwarded

In February 1864, Brigadier General Pierce Manning Butler Young, in temporary command of Butler's Brigade, recommended that four fresh regiments be brought to Virginia from Georgia and South Carolina. Later, Young was sent to South Carolina to help expedite the movement of replacement regiments. Unfortunately, Young was seriously wounded on May 30 and was unable to command the fresh regiments in their initial actions (Library of Congress).

Young's proposal. In his endorsement, Hampton added that if three regiments from South Carolina and two from Georgia were ordered to Virginia, they would bring 5,000 fresh horses onto the field in the spring. Stuart, in his endorsement dated February 13, forwarded Young's proposal to Robert E. Lee. Stuart "heartily approve[d] the immediate and preemptive transfer" of four regiments from the Deep South. However, Stuart did not concur with the proposal to send the depleted regiments back to their home states since his cavalry "was already inadequate for the work to be done."[16]

Robert E. Lee, on February 15, forwarded Young's proposal to the Adjutant General, Samuel Cooper. In his artfully worded endorsement, Lee wrote: "We have not now, nor have we ever had, a sufficiency of cavalry in this army for the service required of it. I cannot recommend the transfer of any from this army unless its place is supplied by that from other departments, and request to know the regiments to be sent here before these are removed."[17]

As Young's letter was making its way through channels, Hampton on February 12 wrote to the Secretary of War on the matter. In his letter, Hampton proposed that his two South Carolina regiments be immediately sent home and at the same time two regiments from South Carolina be ordered to Virginia. Upon the arrival of the two fresh regiments, the remaining regiments of the brigade would be sent south to be replaced by other regiments. That plan would, in Hampton's view, keep a sufficient force of cavalry in Virginia as well as along the southern Atlantic coast. By such a proposal, Hampton was perhaps hoping to satisfy Stuart and overcome anticipated objections from Beauregard. However, in his endorsement dated February 15, Stuart curtly dismissed Hampton's idea opining, "This is an unpropitious time for marching cavalry as much reduced as this [cavalry] is so far." In some relief to Hampton, Stuart did note that arrangements had been made to send Butler's Brigade in March to Matthews or Middlesex counties for thirty days, and that the brigade would be provided with twenty-five extra wagons to haul hay.[18] Middlesex and Matthews counties, at the tip of Virginia's "middle peninsula" between the Rappahannock and York rivers, had seen little fighting and had not been significantly occupied by either the Union or Confederate armies. Presumably, Stuart believed that there Butler's Brigade could obtain adequate forage for the horses and with a month's rest recover much of its fighting strength.

General Samuel Cooper considered the missives from Young and Hampton, along with Stuart and Lee's endorsements. On February 19, Cooper recommended that Secretary of War Seddon approve the transfer "as suggested" by Lee. Seddon responded to Cooper that day with one sentence: "You will select a proper regiment in South Carolina, full in numbers, and exchange."[19]

Hampton, apparently unaware that action was underway to relieve his depleted regiments, continued to fume over their poor condition, as well as over plans to reorganize his division to create a new brigade for Young upon Butler's return to duty. On March 12, Hampton wrote a letter through Stuart to Lee that was clearly insubordinate. Regarding the positioning of Butler's Brigade, which was assigned to picket the lower Rappahannock, Hampton wrote: "As I regard the location selected by General [Lee?] unsuitable and dangerous, it is due to myself to declare that I cannot hold myself responsible either for the condition or safety of the brigade if it is placed there." Regarding Stuart's decision to allocate the Georgia units of Butler's Brigade to a new brigade for Young, Hampton informed Lee that he had told Stuart: "I cannot consent to the division of Butler's Brigade until the other regiments are brought on." Further, Hampton concluded: "I have received no orders from competent authority to break up one of my brigades, and until such orders come I shall not divide Butler's Brigade. I respectfully request the commanding general not to authorize any change in my command without at least consulting my wishes on the subject."[20]

The *Official Records* contains no response to Hampton from either Stuart or Lee, who were both likely shocked by the tone of Hampton's letter, as well as by his open disagreement with the directives of his superiors and his flat refusal to obey orders. It is possible that Lee discussed the letter with Jefferson Davis, prompting Lee's verbal rebuke of Hampton after Hampton had personally intervened with Davis as discussed earlier. Fortunately for the three generals and the Cavalry Corps of the Army of Northern Virginia, five days later this controversy was overcome by events.

Meanwhile, upon receiving Seddon's one-sentence decision of February 19, General Cooper had set to work preparing for the transfer of the units between Virginia and the Deep South. On March 17, he sent General P.G.T. Beauregard, commander of the Department of South Carolina, Georgia, and Florida, a telegram: "The First South Carolina Cavalry and Second South Carolina Cavalry have been ordered to South Carolina. The Fourth South Carolina Cavalry, Colonel Rutledge, the Fifth South Cavalry, Colonel Dunovant, the Sixth South Carolina Cavalry, Colonel Aiken, the Seventh Georgia Cavalry, Colonel White, the remaining companies of Colonel Millen's (Georgia) battalion, and the cavalry companies of Captains Tucker, Wallace, Boykin, Trenholm, and McGee have been ordered to Virginia. Prepare them for movement without delay in light marching order with their wagon trains; the heavy baggage will come by railroad. Orders sent by mail. General Hampton will superintend the movement."[21] Hampton, taking advantage of the lull in the fighting, had planned to take leave to visit his home in Columbia, South Carolina, and was thus available to prepare the regiments for the move and start them on their way to Virginia.

Naturally, the Confederate War Department would try to restrict the information regarding the swap of the regiments to prevent its disclosure to the Union army. Today, the information would be classified and details of the plan would be disseminated on a "need to know" basis. We do not know what security measures were taken by the Confederate War Department. However, we do know that any such measures taken were not particularly effective. On March 18, the day after Cooper notified Beauregard of the plan, Captain Leonard Williams of the 2nd South Carolina wrote to his wife informing her, "There is at present a rumor and general impression that the 1st and 2nd regiment[s] will be ordered to S.C. and 2 or 3 fresh regiments brought out here in our stead. I think myself the thing is very probably." The following day, Williams further advised his wife that "we have not yet recd orders but it is known that orders have been issued by the Sec. of War to send our regiment and the 1st South Carolina. I expect we will start for S.C. about the 1st April. Everybody is jubilant at the prospect and many sent off telegrams to their wives to look for them early in April."[22] At the time, the 2nd South Carolina was performing picket duty along the south bank of the Rappahannock River and despite the apparent common knowledge of the plan among the soldiers of the regiment, there is no indication that Union scouts or spies learned of the plan.

Despite Captain Williams's comment to his wife, not everyone was pleased with the word that the two regiments would be ordered back to South Carolina. The 1st South Carolina was—like many other regiments in Hampton's Division—in poor shape as the winter drew to a close. According to Colonel John Logan Black, the regimental commander, at the time the 1st South Carolina had on hand only twenty-seven "first class serviceable horses." However, the regiment also had about 250 horses on pasture at the recruiting camp with a detachment of 65 remounts en route from South Carolina. Colonel Black later wrote that he "resented being ordered back to South Carolina from an active to an inactive field. But my rule was to obey & do so promptly." Despite believing that he would be able to muster between 550 to 600 mounted men when campaigning began, Black took a day's leave to go to Richmond and without complaint made arrangements for the movement of his regiment and its horses to Columbia.[23]

As anticipated, the directive to send the equivalent of five regiments of cavalry to Virginia was not favorably received. When Cooper's telegram was sent to Charleston, Beauregard was in Florida. Beauregard's chief of staff, General Thomas Jordan, advised Beauregard of Cooper's orders via telegram on March 18: "You are ordered by General Cooper to send to Virginia Rutledge's, Dunovant's, and Aiken's regiments, and five other companies, including Trenholm's (South Carolina) cavalry, and White's new regiment, and the rest of Millen's companies, Georgia Cavalry, and in their place will receive First and Second Regiments South Carolina Cavalry from Virginia." Jordan concluded his telegram with a cryptic question: "Can't you guess source of this raid on your cavalry."[24] It is likely that Jordan suspected General Braxton Bragg, Davis's military advisor, was behind the swap of regiments between the two departments.

Beauregard received Jordan's message and responded directly to Cooper by telegram the following day: "Cavalry ordered to Virginia will be sent at once, although considered indispensible to guard country and railroad from Charleston to Savannah and to defend military department. Scouts near Jacksonville report enemy's forces reinforced by 2,500 men on 16th and 17th instant."[25] Also on March 19, Jordan sent Beauregard a second telegram hinting at local opposition to the War Department orders: "I telegraphed you last night of orders received from Richmond of sweeping away four regiments and eight companies of cavalry from your department. It will be needless to apply, then for delay of Millen's battalion. Some prominent Carolinians will interpose, but I doubt their success." Beauregard, in response, directed that Jordan "send to Virginia cavalry ordered by General Cooper, and make best disposition of remaining troops to meet present emergencies."[26] Although Beauregard was verbally compliant with Cooper's orders, his later actions would prove to be less accommodating.

As Jordan and Beauregard exchanged telegrams, the Adjutant General's office published Special Order Number 65, which formalized Cooper's directive to Beauregard and provided additional instructions. The baggage trains to accompany the regiments as they marched north were to carry only cooking utensils. The 4th, 5th, and 6th South Carolina Cavalry Regiments, upon arrival in Virginia, would be formed into a brigade under the command of Brigadier General Butler. The individual companies cited in Cooper's directive—commanded by Tucker, Wallace, Boykin, Trenholm, and McGee—were to be assigned to the Holcomb Legion, which would be renamed the 7th South Carolina Cavalry.[27]

Also that day, Jordan sent Beauregard a third telegram in which he mentioned the order to transfer the cavalry to Virginia, adding, "I recognize Bragg's work in this. I am not wrong." Jordan's estimate of General Braxton Bragg's role was clearly in error, although Bragg, who was serving as Jefferson Davis's principal military advisor, was certainly consulted by Davis on the plan.[28]

Brigadier General Jordan apparently shared the content of Special Orders Number 65 with one or more prominent citizens of Charleston. Those citizens sent a telegram to their representative in the Confederate Congress, William Porcher Miles, apparently expressing their dissatisfaction with the War Department plan. Unfortunately for Jordan, he was required to personally approve the transmission of the telegram since it contained military information. Miles, in Richmond, delivered the telegram to Secretary of War Seddon. Since the transfer of the regiments had been approved by President Davis, Seddon forwarded the telegram to Bragg. On March 25, Seddon responded in writing to Miles, advising the congressman of Bragg's comments. Specifically, Seddon wrote that the order to transfer the cavalry had come from President Davis after due deliberation, and that Bragg approved the "policy and justice of putting into active service those troops which have been long stationed near their homes, without hardship or much exposure, and replacing them with veterans, worn and exhausted." He also informed Miles that Bragg believed that Beauregard would have sufficient cavalry for the defense of his department if they were to be "properly posted and judiciously used." Seddon concluded his letter with a rebuke from Bragg: "I am requested to mention as extraordinary that the President's order to the movement of troops should have been furnished to citizens who had no knowledge of the necessities of the service or the reasons operating, and their remonstrance forwarded and approved by the chief of staff of a military department through a member of Congress. Such a course is thought to be injudicious and calculated to demoralize the troops."[29]

The following day, Congressman Miles sent a lengthy letter to Seddon in rebuttal to some of Bragg's comments. He explained that Jordan had not actually "approved" of the content of the citizens' telegram, but that since the telegram included military matters, it was submitted to Beauregard's headquarters for authorization to be transmitted. Miles also claimed that the inference that the president's orders were shared with civilians was "too hastily drawn" because as the men made preparations, their pending movement would be "very speedily known to intelligent citizens in the immediate locality."[30] Jordan, who had been quickly informed of the government's negative response to the citizens' inquiry and to the allusion of poor judgment on his part, sent a telegram to Seddon on March 27. In his telegram, Jordan stated that he "conceived he had no right to prevent communication between the principal citizens of community and their member of Congress" and that the telegram was sent after the order directing the troops to prepare for movement had been disseminated.[31]

On March 31, in an endorsement to Congressman Miles' letter, Bragg provided his final opinion on the matter: "Both Mr. Miles and General Jordan fail to meet the main objection to the course of action pursued in this matter. By the official action at department headquarters, information most valuable to the enemy, and which the [War Department] would have not entrusted to the telegraph except in cipher, has gone forth to the enemy with official sanction. They are virtually invited to take advantage of it. I cannot agree with Mr. Miles that the public good may thus be jeopardized that the private interests of constituents may be represented."[32]

Meanwhile, upon arriving in Columbia on his leave of absence from Virginia, Hampton discovered that moving cavalry from South Carolina to Virginia might prove as difficult as arranging for the transfer of the regiments from Butler's Brigade from Virginia to South Carolina.

On March 29, Hampton wrote to General Cooper—the new regiments were not yet assigned to Lee's Army of Northern Virginia—with the status of the transfer. Hampton opened his letter his letter with bad news: "I find most of the cavalry so badly equipped here that there will be some delay in moving them."[33] Hampton, who estimated that he could have most of the regiments on the move by April 15, also informed Cooper that he was encountering interference from officials in the department and that efforts were being made to keep the 4th South Carolina near Charleston, despite the regimental commander's support for the move. Hampton, apparently unaware of the what had transpired earlier regarding conscription abuse that prompted Beauregard's General Orders Number 25, also complained that the Department had issued orders to reduce the size of companies in the regiments moving north to 80 men, although regulations permitted companies to carry up to 125 men on their rolls. Despite past conscription abuses, Hampton correctly observed that the excess men "are needed far more in Virginia than here."[34]

The following day, Hampton traveled to Charleston to confer with General Beauregard regarding the transfer of the units. If Hampton was expecting his conference with the department commander to easily resolve the problems associated with transferring the regiments to Virginia, he was most likely disappointed. The session between the two generals began badly. Hampton's purpose for the meeting was to determine the dates the regiments could be relieved from their present duties so that he could schedule their movement. Beauregard, as described above, had received the War Department's order, but he did not agree with it. He informed Hampton that "if this cavalry were taken away, the whole State between Charleston and Savannah would be left entirely open." Petulantly, Beauregard offered that since the regiments were under Hampton's orders he "could take them at any time."[35] Hampton corrected Beauregard—his superior by two grades—by explaining that his orders were "to take charge of the movement" and that Beauregard must choose which units he could release first. In response, Beauregard ordered the 5th South Carolina relieved from its duties on the coast, but refused to release the other regiments until the 1st and 2nd South Carolina arrived from Virginia.

Also while in Charleston, Hampton found the situation regarding the transfer of excess men from the designated regiments worse than he had described earlier. Hampton learned that company strengths were to be capped at eighty privates, and that a "fair proportion" of the men on the company rolls would be those who were dismounted, sick, or otherwise absent. Consequently, the companies moving to Virginia would take with them less than eighty men, and some of the men making the move would be unfit for duty, at least initially. In what he considered an egregious example of the department's transfer policy, Hampton found that the district commander in Charleston, Colonel Alfred M. Rhett, had removed a soldier from a cavalry company so that the soldier could serve as Rhett's orderly. The company commander, who had protested the transfer of his soldier, had been threatened with court-martial.[36] Hampton discussed the orderly issue with Brigadier General Jordan, who asserted that he, Jordan, had "the right to transfer men, not only without but even against the consent of their commanding officers."[37] While Jordan was perhaps correct with respect to his authority, he appears to have lost sight of the "spirit of harmony and regard for the good of the service" mentioned in Special Order Number 25.

In an effort to obtain the quick release of the 4th and 6th South Carolina, Hampton sent a formal memorandum to General Jordan on April 1: "By Special Orders No. 65, from War Department, I am charged with the prompt movement of the cavalry from this department to the Army of Northern Virginia. In accordance with these instructions to me, I have the honor to request that the general commanding will order the troops embraced in the order mentioned above to rendezvous at Columbia as soon as he can relieve them from duty in his department." Hampton's memorandum perhaps prompted second thoughts. General

Jordan informed Hampton that "under the order he had received from Richmond, he thought these regiments should move at once, and that he would therefore order them to rendezvous [in Columbia] at once."[38]

Upon arriving back in Columbia, Hampton wrote a lengthy letter to General Cooper on April 4, apprising him of the situation he had encountered in Charleston. Regarding the transfer of men from the regiments, Hampton recommended that Cooper should "allow the captains to select the men to go with them to Virginia, and order all left behind sent at once to the conscript camp, [thus] an efficient body of men will be carried on [to Virginia], a great abuse will be broken up here, and the men who are now trying to shirk their duty will be punished."[39]

Upon receipt of Hampton's telegram, Cooper directed his staff to "stop this interference of General Jordan with regard to transfers, and have the orders heretofore given carried strictly out in the name of the President." Cooper's staff immediately sent a letter to that effect to Beauregard.[40] By mid–April, departmental orders were at last issued to implement the War Department's plans, and the regiments began moving to Columbia to make final preparations for the march to Virginia. However, the month's delay between when the War Department issued its orders and when those orders were executed ensured that the "New Issue," as they became known among the veterans in Virginia, would miss the opening rounds of the coming campaign.

Hampton, an experienced combat commander, prepared the regiments as best he could for the move to Virginia and the coming campaign. Upon arrival in Columbia, the regiments were inspected. As he mentioned in his message to Cooper, the most significant deficiency uncovered was the condition of many of the saddles, which had to be condemned. After enlisting, many of the men had continued riding their horses with their personal saddles, which while adequate for light duty, were unsuitable for long marches and extended campaigning. The most important part of a saddle is its "tree," upon which the leather seat and skirts are affixed. The tree of Civil War era saddles consisted of two broad wooden slats which were connected at each end so that they were rigid and parallel (modern saddles may have trees fashioned from wood, steel, or plastics). The tree ideally distributes the weight of the rider across a broad area on the horse's back, while keeping pressure off the horse's withers and spine. The preferred saddle of the Civil War was the McClellan, the standard saddle for the Union Army. The McClellan, which was based on a Prussian saddle, had been designed by George B. McClellan while serving as a captain in 1856. The standard Confederate saddle was the Jenifer, developed by Walter Jenifer, a noted horseman and a colonel in the Confederate army.[41] Unfortunately, Jenifer's saddle caused some horses to develop saddle sores as they lost weight when undergoing hard use, although the saddle's problems may have been more a result of poor manufacturing than poor design. Consequently, many Southern cavalrymen rode with McClellan saddles, either captured from Union troopers or manufactured in the South.[42]

Hampton also arranged for all the horses to be freshly shod before beginning the march north. Periodic shoeing is necessary because horses' hooves grow and iron shoes wear down. The rate of hoof growth varies from horse to horse and with changes in diet. Generally, horses require shoeing roughly every six to eight weeks. When shoeing a horse, the farrier or blacksmith removes the old shoes, trims the horse's hooves to the proper length, and then nails new shoes—shaped to fit the horse's hooves—to the freshly trimmed hooves. The nails, which penetrate through the outer hoof wall, are "clinched" so that the shoe is held securely to the bottom of the hoof. Thus shoeing five thousand horses was a significant, but necessary, undertaking. Freshly shod horses were less likely to lose, or "cast," shoes during the march to Virginia, a situation that could lead to damage to the hoof and cause lameness for the horse.[43]

Most cavalry leaders as well as ordnance department officials, North and South, had long recognized the advantages of providing cavalry with breech-loading long arms. As described later in Chapter 7, the Union army was well along in equipping its troopers, who had been almost universally armed with breech-loaders, with repeaters. Unfortunately for the men being ordered to Virginia, the Confederacy was incapable of either manufacturing or procuring modern carbines in sufficient quantities to equip them.[44] Consequently, the men of Hampton's fresh regiments were armed with muzzle-loading Enfield rifles, imported from Britain. Many of the men initially were scornful of the long weapons, considering them inappropriate for a true cavalryman to carry. When the Charleston Light Dragoons were issued their Enfields in May 1862, several men openly showed their contempt: one man rode his new rifle like a child on a broomstick; another shouldered his rifle upside-down and hung his cartridge box around his neck like a necklace; a third dragged his rifle behind him like a log.[45]

The regiments were also reviewed while in Columbia. This provided Hampton an opportunity to observe the men of the regiments as individuals—their uniforms, arms and accoutrement, horses, and demeanor—and to gauge the readiness of the regiments as organizations. As a regiment's squadrons passed in review and performed various turning movements and maneuvers, Hampton could observe the unit's proficiency at drill and draw inferences with regard to whether the officers could effectively train the men for combat, and most importantly, impose discipline. Reviews generally concluded with the regiment simulating a charge, which allowed Hampton to observe the men's horsemanship and their élan. It was quite common for a few troopers to be thrown from their horses while charging, adding some excitement for both the participants and the spectators alike.

Naturally, the officers and men did their best to appear soldierly and proficient when reviewed, thereby making a good impression on their new commander. Joseph McAllister, commanding the 7th Georgia, wrote of a "grand" review—a review having more than one regiment participating—that was held May 9.[46] "We had a grand review yesterday—and a charge and although we are the youngest regt, not a man was thrown—and I had my men rallied and coursed a line of battle and ready for a[nother] charge ere the other commands have their men rallied and they have a dozen or more flung."[47]

Finally, reviews also gave the men in the regiments opportunity to observe their new commander as well. Men, in their letters to family and loved ones, commented on Hampton's military bearing. A trooper in the Charleston Light Dragoons recalled seeing Hampton inspecting the 4th South Carolina. "When the General galloped down the lines, looking every inch a chieftain, the air rang with the shouts of the soldiers..."[48]

Not all the soldiers' time in Columbia was devoted to work. The people of the community acted as proper hosts for the men now heading off to war. There were a series of dinners and fetes, the largest being held on the grounds of the state asylum on April 22. That grand affair, described in detail in a special edition to Columbia's *Daily South Carolinian*, was held to honor the men of the 1st and 2nd South Carolina who had returned from Virginia, but "soldiers one and all were gladly welcomed without restraint." Three tables, each from two to three hundred feet in length, were set up to accommodate the crowd of soldiers and civilians who dined on "pies and patties, pigs and poultry, chocolate, coffee, cakes and custards, salads, syllabubs and sausages, blanc mange, bread and butter, pies, pickles, and preserves." Flowers and Confederate flags were everywhere. The battle flag of the Hampton Legion was unfurled over the speaker's podium, from which Dr. Benjamin Palmer, a minister, gave a patriotic address. At the close of Palmer's speech, the crowd chanted, "Hampton, Hampton, Hampton."[49] It is interesting to speculate whether the veterans of the 1st and 2nd South Carolina, while mingling at the fete, told the New Issue what they could expect upon arrival in Virginia. If so, it might have put a damper on the festive mood for some.

Hampton left Columbia for Richmond by train on the evening of April 27, leaving behind M.C. Butler, who had completed his convalescence, and P.M.B. Young, who had recently arrived from Virginia, to complete the preparations for the movement of the regiments. Shortly after Hampton's departure, the "New Issue" regiments begin the march north, with a regiment departing every few days. One-half to two-thirds of the men in each regiment were fur-

Matthew Calbraith Butler, having completed his convalescence resulting from the loss of a foot at Brandy Station, oversaw the preparation for the movement of "New Issue" regiments South Carolina to Virginia. This image appears to be a composite with a photograph of Butler's head superimposed on a drawn torso and background (*Butler and His Calvary*).

loughed for roughly two weeks and allowed to return home. After returning from furlough, they traveled by train to Richmond. The remaining men made their way to Richmond riding one horse and leading one or two others. By alternating horses each day, the men were able to conserve the strength of their regiments' mounts.[50] The regiments generally followed the direct line between Columbia and Richmond—Charlotte, North Carolina, to Greensboro to Danville—although each had a slightly different route. This was done to ensure that the quartermasters, who traveled a day or two ahead of the main body of their regiments, could arrange for fresh camp sites with adequate pasture.

The regiments and battalions beginning their movement north, while at full strength with fresh horses, had only limited combat experience. For the most part, both the soldiers and their leaders were untested in battle.

The 4th South Carolina was formed in December 1862 by combining the 10th and 12th Battalions South Carolina Cavalry into a regiment.[51] Until the 4th moved to Virginia sixteen months later, it served continuously along the coast of South Carolina and northeastern Georgia. Although portions of the regiment had participated in several small engagements, most of the officers and men had little or no combat experience.

The commander of the regiment, Benjamin Huger Rutledge, was born in 1829 in Statesburg, South Carolina. Rutledge graduated from Yale University and took up the practice of law in Charleston, was elected to the state legislature, and served as a delegate to the South Carolina's Secession Convention. Rutledge also commanded an exclusive militia company, the Charleston Light Dragoons. Upon the outbreak of the war, he continued in command of the "Drags" until the regiment was formed, whereupon he was appointed its colonel.[52]

The regiment left Columbia on April 29; Butler and Rutledge ordered a hasty departure to avoid receiving orders to further reduce the size of the companies and to take back some of the dismounted men who had been transferred from the regiment.[53] After two days marching, the regiment stopped in Camden, South Carolina, for two days to complete shoeing the horses. Once all the horses were freshly shod, the mounted detachment of the regiment resumed marching north under the command of Major William Stokes. Colonel Rutledge and some of the furloughed men later joined the mounted detachment in Greensboro. During the march between Greensboro and Richmond, the regiment was alerted that Union cavalry raiders were close by. Rutledge deployed a detachment to meet the threat, but the alarm proved to be false. It was fortunate that Union forces were not active in strength along the route of march since, among them, the men of the 4th carried roughly 250 sabers and pistols. The regiment's rifles had been sent to Richmond by train so that the men would be less encumbered during the march. The 4th South Carolina reached Richmond on May 24, one day behind schedule.[54]

The 5th South Carolina Cavalry was created in January 1863 when the War Department combined the 14th and 17th Battalions South Carolina Cavalry and two independent cavalry companies.[55] The regiment served continuously on the South Carolina coast until ordered to Virginia, except for two companies that were detached for duty in North Carolina from July 1863 until May 1864. The men of the regiment had seen almost no combat.

The initial commander of the 5th South Carolina was Colonel Samuel W. Ferguson, an 1857 graduate of West Point. Ferguson—whose family spelled their name "Fergusson"—was a capable and well-connected officer. At the time of his appointment, Ferguson was assigned to cavalry duty in Mississippi.[56] Before he was able to join the regiment, he received a brigadier general's commission and command of a cavalry brigade under Joseph

Colonel John Dunovant, a Mexican War veteran, was dismissed for drunkenness from Confederate service in June 1862 while in command of an infantry regiment. In a remarkable career turnaround, Dunovant was appointed to command of the 5th South Carolina, and in August 1864 promoted to brigadier general. Dunovant was killed in the fighting around Fort Harrison near Petersburg on October 1, 1864 (Library of Congress).

Wheeler in Tennessee.⁵⁷ After Ferguson's reassignment, the regiment was temporarily commanded by its lieutenant colonel, Robert Jeffords.

In June 1864, John Dunovant was appointed to command of the regiment. Dunovant—unlike the other regimental commanders moving north—had extensive military experience. He fought in the Mexican War as a sergeant in the Palmetto Regiment, and afterward obtained a commission in the regular army. Serving mostly in the West, he rose to the grade of captain in the 10th Infantry before resigning after the secession of South Carolina in 1861. Almost immediately, Dunovant was given command of a South Carolina infantry regiment, but he was cashiered in the summer of 1862 for drunkenness. Apparently Governor Pickens arranged Dunovant's reinstatement as a colonel and appointment to command of the 5th South Carolina.⁵⁸

Private James M. Barr—known as "the Major" in recognition of his pre-war position in the State Militia—left Columbia on April 16 as part of the advance party of the 5th South Carolina. Traveling ahead of the regiment had several advantages. The small party could move more rapidly than a long column of men and horses, and the men and horses were less plagued by dust. Also, the advance party usually spent their nights in villages and towns where they could find shelter for themselves and stabling for their horses.

Shortly after the orders for the move to Virginia were announced, Barr obtained a new horse from his brother. The horse, named Jeff Davis, was a fine mount. Barr's brother claimed that "his equals are few, *his superiors—there are none.*"⁵⁹ However, Jeff Davis was a young horse and quickly began to suffer from the rigors of the long march. From Rock Hill, South Carolina, on April 19, Barr wrote to his wife: "I have only one blanket with me and wish I had some of my clothing home. I have too many for my horse to tote. I have too many drawers. Will have to throw some away. I wish now I had my gray horse. Yes, Jeff Davis is too young for this trip and it is a pity to kill a young horse. Yet he is no better than I am and I have to go."⁶⁰ Experienced cavalry officers believed that horses younger than six years of age were unsuitable for cavalry service. Unfortunately, in the third year of the war, it was necessary to press young fillies and colts into cavalry service in both the Union and Confederate armies.

One squadron of the 5th South Carolina had an easy march to Virginia. Companies B and K had been on detached service in southeastern North Carolina since September 1863. Life in North Carolina proved pleasant for the soldiers of the two companies—the men faced almost no enemy action and living conditions were comfortable. The commander of Company B, Alfred B. Mulligan, wrote to his mother and sisters in March 1864, "We have here in our camp almost a little village. Several good pine log cabbins well covered with boards, all neatly fitted up & the cracks stopped with clay to keep out the winter winds…. Have small cabbins for servants. Have some eight or less foul [sic] coops & we have ourselves much more poultry than half the neighborhood can produce. I have five fat shoats in pen worth some $50 each &c. Then we have fine stables for [the] many horse[s] in camp, all well covered and enclosed with good fences. A large mule yard with good shed for our teams of mules. A good tack house, fodder house, &c, &c." Mulligan, who was unmarried, went on to add, "And last but not least, we enjoy good socials among the young ladies here."⁶¹

Mulligan received word of the move to Virginia during the first week of April. Writing again to his mother and sisters on April 5, Mulligan informed them, "When we all [the four regiments] get together in Virginia we will form a glorious phonomial of strength and we will make the Yankees quail." In a letter five days later he assured his relatives that he would be safe in Virginia: "I am not sorry that we are going [to Virginia]. I will do better, I think, in many respects in Virginia than I could either here or in South Carolina. The cavalry are not so much exposed in Va. as infantry and artillery [are].... My Dear Mother, I know that you dislike the idea of my going to Virginia but I must beg you not to be anxious or uneasy about me. Cavalry is detached service like I am and have been out of danger when in a large army."[62]

On May 6, the two companies, delayed for two weeks by Union activity along the North Carolina coast, began their march to Richmond under the command of Lieutenant Colonel Jeffords. Captain Mulligan was nicely outfitted for the march, having a cart for his personal belongings, three saddle horses, and the assistance of his servant, Simon. The troopers had a pleasant march through Goldsboro and Weldon before crossing into Virginia. The small column arrived in Petersburg on the night of May 13, and instead of continuing on to Richmond, the two companies were attached to Brigadier General James Dearing's brigade and deployed east of Petersburg to check Major General Benjamin Butler's advance up the south side of the James River.[63]

Over the next few days, Mulligan learned that conditions in Virginia were much different than he expected. He immediately discovered that it was difficult to maintain a single horse on the feed provided, let alone three. Consequently, Mulligan sold one of his horses on May 15 and sold a second a week later. Fortunately for the newly-arrived captain, cavalry mounts were in great demand in Virginia and prices were high—the two horses fetched $7,750.[64] Mulligan sent most of the money home with instructions to his family to spend it buying anything they might need for the winter including shoes for all the servants. He admonished his mother and sisters: "REMEMBER THIS; I make it a rule to never keep Confederate money on hand. If we gain our independence soon the money will be repudiated. If we do not whip the Yankees soon it will take $10,000 to purchase a pound of tea."[65] A few days later, Mulligan sent Simon to Richmond to deposit for safe keeping his trunk, mess chest, and cooking gear at either the South Carolina Soldiers Home or the Spotswood Hotel. To make up for the absence of his gear, Mulligan purchased "the most convenient little cooking utensil at Richmond that you ever saw. It is a frying pan, a plate so arranged that I can strap it to my saddle and carry it without any inconvenience."[66] Thus relieved of his impedimenta, Mulligan rejoined the rest of his regiment near Hanover Junction on May 25.

In January 1863, the War Department authorized the 16th Battalion South Carolina Cavalry, also known as Aiken's Partisan Rangers, to reorganize as the 6th cavalry regiment from the state.[67] During the reorganization, the 16th grew from seven companies to ten. Like the other South Carolina cavalry regiments, the 6th had served continuously along the estuaries and rivers of the South Carolina coast. While the coast was under the threat of ship-borne Federal forces, actual incursions in significant strength were rare. For example, the only mentionable engagement for the 6th South Carolina occurred on July 10, 1863, when two Union gunboats and a steamer sailed up the Pon Pon River (today the Edisto River). Several companies of the 6th supported by two sections of light artillery engaged the Union forces at Willstown Bluff and drove them back down the river with the loss of one ship that had been hit by artillery and caught fire. Union casualties were unknown. The Confederates lost two men wounded, one of whom was captured. Also, one courier was reported missing.[68]

The 6th was commanded by Colonel Hugh K. Aiken, who had previously commanded the partisan ranger battalion. Aiken, a planter and cotton factor, had long been active in the militia before the war, serving at the grades of both brigadier and major general. At the beginning of the war, Aiken raised the 16th Battalion and had served with it continuously as its lieutenant colonel until formation of the regiment. Aiken's father-in-law was the governor of Alabama, and his brother-in-law was Colonel Josiah Gorgas, the Chief of Ordnance for the Confederacy.[69]

Aiken first received orders to move the 6th to Columbia on April 1, but those orders were almost immediately countermanded by Beauregard. Eventually, after Aiken interceded with Hampton, the regiment was relieved from its costal defense duties on April 16 and ordered to move to Columbia. The bulk of the regiment arrived in Columbia on the evening of April 22 having covered 110 miles, averaging about 18 miles per day.[70] By the time Aiken and his men arrived in Columbia, the available blacksmiths were busy shoeing the horses of other regiments. The shoeing of the horses of the 6th South Carolina did not begin until May 3. After having new shoes put only on the front hooves of the regiment's horses—hind shoes generally wear more slowly than front shoes—the 6th left Columbia on May 5, marching shorter distances for the first few days as the regiment's blacksmiths finished shoeing the hind hooves.

Aiken did not travel to Richmond with his men. The mounted detachment traveled under the command of the regiment's major, T.B. Ferguson. The detachment of 360 dismounted men, after their furloughs, traveled by train to Richmond under the direction of the regiment's lieutenant colonel, L.P. Miller. They arrived in the Confederate capital on May 23.[71] Upon his arrival in Richmond on May 22, Aiken stayed at the residence of his sister and brother-in-law.

The 7th Georgia Cavalry was created in February 1864 when the War Department issued orders combining the 21st Battalion Georgia Cavalry, the 24th Battalion Georgia Cavalry, and a two-company squadron named the Hardwick Mounted Rifles.[72] The process of organizing the regiment had begun five months earlier, in October 1863, when the commander of 5th Georgia Cavalry, Colonel Robert H. Anderson, who was likely hoping to secure a brigadier general's billet for himself, proposed that various small cavalry units of the district be grouped into regiments and brigaded in the interest of efficiency and effectiveness.[73] The three affected commanders, Lieutenant Colonel William P. White, Major Edward C. Anderson, Jr., and Captain Joseph L. McAllister, resisted the consolidation of their units out of reluctance to lose their independence and over questions of seniority. Nonetheless, the regiment was eventually formed with White as its colonel, McAllister as its lieutenant colonel, and Anderson as its major.[74]

The companies of the new regiment, which had a combined strength of 868 men on the rolls in January 1864, had seen little action.[75] Some of the men had fought in minor engagements against waterborne incursions by Federal soldiers and sailors along the rivers and estuaries of the South Carolina and Georgia coasts. The companies had lost one man killed in action. In contrast, three troopers died from accidental gunshot wounds, one was struck by lightning and killed, while thirty-seven died from disease.[76]

Colonel William P. White, the first commander of the 7th Georgia, was born in Savannah in 1812. For most of his adult life he practiced law, although for several years he held the position of customs appraiser for the Port of Savannah. For more than thirty years, White was active in the Georgia militia, and he had risen to the grade of brigadier general in command of a brigade. At the beginning of the war, White, who was reported to be the best horseman Georgia, raised three companies of cavalry that was known as White's Battalion, which became the 21st Battalion Georgia Cavalry.[77]

White's tenure as commander of the 7th Georgia was brief. Less than a month after the regiment was ordered formed, and before the two battalions and the squadron that comprised the regiment had consolidated, White was shot by a soldier of his battalion. The incident took place about ten p.m. on the evening of March 6, 1864. White was sitting in a frame house near Georgetown, South Carolina that was being used as his headquarters. Sergeant Eli Grimes shot White through the wall of the building, the bullet striking White in the left knee. Grimes was soon apprehended and confessed, claiming he was coerced into shooting White by a former captain in the 21st, C.C. Bowen. White developed gangrene and died on April 6. Neither Grimes nor Bowen were convicted of the crime.[78]

Upon White's death, Joseph L. McAllister assumed command of the regiment. McAllister was born at Strathy Hall, the family plantation south of Savannah. McAllister studied at Amherst College from 1837 until 1840, but did not graduate. After leaving Amherst, he toured Europe and then returned home to manage the plantation with his father, who died in 1850. At the beginning of the war, McAllister urged the construction of Fort McAllister on his family property. The earthwork fort, named for McAllister's father, prevented Union ships from traveling up the Great Ogeechee River. In April 1862, McAllister raised a cavalry company, the Hardwick Mounted Rifles, which eventually grew into a two-company squadron. The Hardwick Mounted Rifles was stationed much of the time at Fort McAllister, which was unsuccessfully attacked several times by Union gunboats.[79]

The 7th Georgia assembled at Savannah in late April and departed from there for Columbia, South Carolina via Augusta. The march between Augusta and Columbia—eighty miles—was particularly grueling. Colonel McAllister, in a letter to his sister, recorded: "[S]uch dust I never saw. Stifling to horse and man—our column extended over a mile and a half and the whole extent was just one Cloud. Such a dirty crowd you never saw, but we have stood it well and the men are in fine spirits." The regiment arrived in Columbia on May 6, and remained there until the morning of May 12. Like the other regiments, McAllister furloughed half his men, and the remaining troopers rode out of Columbia riding one horse and leading at least one other horse. Unlike the march to Columbia, the men were now plagued by uninterrupted rain. Swollen streams and rivers slowed the pace of the march, and the 7th was delayed two days at Rock Hill, South Carolina, while the horses were ferried across the Catawba River. After leaving Charlotte, McAllister increased the pace of the march, traveling thirty to forty miles on most days, to make up for lost time.

McAllister wrote regularly to his sister Emma, and his observations provide a personal perspective of the march from South Carolina to Virginia.

- Rock Hill, South Carolina, May 15. "We have had a miserable time of it since we left [Columbia] and uninterrupted rain. No one has had a dry thing day or night.... Today I am delayed as I have to ferry my horses over the Catawba, and the flat only carries 12 horses at a time, and can make but 3 trips an hour.... You must not worry about me—exposure seems to agree with us. I eat beans three times a day and never hear of dyspepsia." Regarding Major Anderson, his second in command, McAllister wrote, "I get along very well with him. He is terribly conceited [but] outside of that he is a very pleasant companion."
- Salisbury, North Carolina, May 20. "I am making long marches to make up for lost time crossing the Catawba—in hopes to have some hand in the glorious fights going on.... I have not seen anything of this town—for they have the small-pox here. As we marched into the first camp ground selected a nurse came out and informed us the pest house was on that lot. So we left that at the double-quick. We then marched to another grove—sent one of the men to inquire if any smallpox

was there, answer three cases—marched again and after selecting another point a mile out of town was informed that the next lot had 150 cases buried on it but as I am not afraid of even small pox ghosts—shall sleep quietly."
- Greensboro, North Carolina, May 22. "It was excessively hot—three horses died and one of the mules. We found water but twice on the road for our horses, they suffered very much.... Tonight we go to bed supperless and blanketless but it is a bright clean moonlight night so that is no hardship."
- Christianville, Virginia, May 25. "One cannot but be struck by the difference between N.C. & Virginia. We knew the instant we crossed the line—from the difference in the people—the air of neatness and—so much better looking—even the poorest, they meet us on the roadside with flowers and pails of water and milk—and express so kindly their regrets at having nothing better to offer us—." Along the route, young women presented the troopers with bouquets, prompting an observation from McAllister: "Some *funny* notes attached to the bokets. They all seem to think that the matrimonial chances are daily lessening—and every note wants you to write—these as a matter of course are plain country girls just from school. Some pretty some ugly."
- Burkesville, Virginia, May 30. "I find a telegraph here to march from this point to Richmond in two days, so will have to make forced marches of 40 miles a day.... Keep up your spirits—to take care of me if I get a bullet in me—which I trust will not be the case—still we must all do our duty in this struggle and while I shall not foolishly expose myself, I will not disgrace our names."[80]

The 7th Georgia arrived in Richmond on the evening of June 2 as battle began at Cold Harbor and McAllister received orders to hold his men in readiness to move throughout the night should Union cavalry approach. On June 4, McAllister, who had led his regiment out in support of the army, wrote to his sister that "I have never seen dead bodies lay so thick."[81] With that experience, McAllister and his men probably began to fully understand the difference between the war in Virginia and what, for them, had passed for war along the Georgia coast.

The 20th Battalion Georgia Cavalry was commanded by Lieutenant Colonel John M. Millen. Millen's initial service was as 1st Lieutenant of Company K, 10th Georgia Infantry, a company that was converted to the Pulaski Light Artillery. Millen resigned his commission in March 1862 and returned to Georgia from Virginia to raise a battalion of partisan rangers. Initially Millen raised three companies—officially designated the 20th Battalion Georgia Partisan Rangers—which he commanded in the grade of major. Raising another three companies earned Millen promotion to lieutenant colonel. Millen's battalion, like the 7th Georgia, was assigned to protect the Georgia coast and had seen almost no action. In January 1864, its reported strength was 480 men.[82]

The 20th Georgia left its camp at Blackshears, a small village near Waycross, on March 9, and eventually arrived in Richmond on May 24. On June 4 the battalion joined Young's Brigade north of Richmond.[83]

Finally, by separate directive, the War Department ordered three companies of the 4th Battalion Alabama Cavalry to join Lee's Army in Virginia, leaving two companies on duty in their home state. The battalion, also known as Love's Battalion after its commander, Captain Andrew P. Love, had been had been organized in the spring of 1863 in southeastern Alabama. Thus far, the men of the battalion had seen little service, spending most of their time searching for and apprehending deserters. The battalion left Montgomery for Richmond on April 1, 1864.[84]

The men made the long ride to Virginia in good order, crossing into the Old Dominion at Danville on May 12. A Confederate ordnance officer at Danville noted that the battalion of three companies totaled 160 men who were well mounted but had no weapons. After arrival in Richmond, the three companies of the battalion were initially attached to the Phillips Legion.[85]

As with the other units moving to Virginia, some of the men of Love's Battalion traveled north by rail. William H. Locke, writing to his wife from Greensboro, North Carolina described some of the challenges with rail travel in 1864. "We have had a perfect scramble for seats ever Since We left Macon Ga (but some how I have for Most of the time been fortunate enough to obtain Seat in the Ladys Car—Owing I think altogether to my good look—Don't you think so?"[86] Three days later from Richmond, Locke wrote that he had endured "lying over thirty six hours on the route" from Greensboro.[87]

Upon arrival in Virginia, the companies of Love's battalion were temporarily attached to the Phillips Legion of Georgia so their tactical deployment was determined by Lieutenant Colonel William W. Rich, the commander of the Phillips Legion.[88] Almost immediately after linking up with the Phillips Legion, the men of Love's battalion found themselves in action.

William Locke experienced his first combat in Virginia on the afternoon of May 28, just hours after writing to his wife about the trip from Greensboro. The 4th Alabama, after marching about ten miles toward the front, was sent forward as dismounted pickets, the men's horses being considered untrained for combat. Union infantry advanced and threatened to cut off the men of the 4th Alabama and the battalion was ordered to fall back in a hurry. Locke's movement to the rear—after remounting his horse—was memorable:

> The Yankees were Coming through a skirt of Woods Making for a lane that we were Compelled to go through to Keep from being Captured and I assure you we lost no time because about the time we got to the Skirt Woods they commenced firing—every body was going on full speed and about that time My Horse fell down Heels over Head in a big Mud hole and rolled over Threw me off—and muddied Me and everything I had—those behind me Came verry Near running over Me—but fortunately I Come out all right unhurt but Just about as Muddy a White Man as You ever saw.[89]

Locke also told his wife that in this action, the men of his battalion "did not fire a gun," a practice that would significantly change in the coming two weeks.[90]

Upon his arrival in Richmond, P.M.B. Young was directed to take charge of the fresh cavalry as it arrived and prepare them "as rapidly as possible for active field service." However, Young was given little time to accomplish that task. On May 27, the Adjutant General's office directed him to "immediately proceed with the cavalry under his command, belonging to the Army of Northern Virginia, to Hanover Junction, Va. And report to General R.E. Lee, commanding, &c, for assignment."[91] Doubtless, little training or other preparation could be accomplished in less than a week.

Additionally, while the move to Virginia had been made without serious incident, authorities in Richmond were dissatisfied that the transfer of the units had not been completed within the time envisioned. On May 23, General Bragg directed the fresh regimental and battalion commanders to provide detailed reports of the process by which their units made the move from South Carolina and Georgia to Virginia. Adding additional emphasis, General Butler informed his subordinate commanders that their units had been "very much censured for the delay" in their arrival.

On May 30, Colonel Aiken submitted his report to Colonel John B. Sale, Bragg's military secretary. Accompanying the report were itineraries from Major Thomas Ferguson providing

Table 2

March of the 6th South Carolina Cavalry

Date (May)	Location	Miles Marched
5	Columbia	
6	Near Winnsborough	15
7	Winnsborough	15
8	Black Stock	16
9	Chester	13
10	Rock Hill	23
11	Charlotte	27
12	Concord	21
13	Salisbury	21
	Lay-Over Crossing The Yadkin River.	
16	Lexington	15
17	High Point	17
18	Greensboro	16
19	Reidsville	25
20	Danville	25
21	Laurel Grove	17
22	New's Ferry	16
23	Clark's Ferry	27
24	Crossing Staunton River	5
25	Keysville	23
26	Burkeville	20
27	Amelia Courthouse	20
28	Winterpock	23
29	Richmond	25

Total Miles: 475

the details of the 6th South Carolina's march north and from Lieutenant Colonel L.P. Miller with details of the march of the regiment from the South Carolina coast to Columbia and movement of 360 men from Columbia to Richmond by rail, respectively. For information, Ferguson's report is provided in the accompanying table. As an aside, even experienced horsemen will likely be surprised at the details of the 6th South Carolina's march. That type of sustained riding is rarely done today.

If the other regimental and battalion commanders prepared similar reports, they were lost. There is no indication that any corrective action was taken by Bragg or other senior commanders as a result of the delays. Most likely, this issue was simply overcome by events with the 4th and 5th South Carolina and the 20th Georgia going into battle at Haw's Shop on May 28.[92]

In Virginia, the new arrivals from the Deep South were easily recognizable. The cloth of their uniforms was a mixture of cotton and wool, called "jeans," while the regiments that had been serving in Virginia wore uniforms made from much better quality gray cloth. Also, the new arrivals carried long muzzle-loading Enfield rifles, while many—if not most—of the Virginia veterans carried Sharps carbines, many of which had been captured from Union soldiers. The South Carolinians and Georgians also noticed that J.E.B. Stuart's veterans had a "jaunty air" as they rode along.[93]

By the first week of June the equivalent of five regiments of fresh cavalry had joined Hampton's Division. Unfortunately, because of delays at the War Department in issuing orders, obstruction on the part of military officials in South Carolina, and the normal "frictions" associated with military movements, the regiments were not available to participate in the fighting during the first month of the campaign. However, contrary to the earlier concerns of some of the officers and men, plenty of hard fighting remained ahead.

6

"The Very Man I want"
Philip Sheridan and His Senior Commanders

Alfred Pleasonton, who had been promoted to Major General shortly after Brandy Station, had remained in command of the Cavalry Corps until the end of March 1864. Despite having opposed Kilpatrick's raid to Richmond, Pleasonton shared in the blame for the failure of what became more commonly known as the "Dahlgren Raid." The utter failure of the raid weakened any support Pleasonton may have had in the War Department. Additionally, in early March Pleasonton had been called to Washington testify before the Joint Committee on the Conduct of the War. Before the members of the committee, Pleasonton expounded on—in his view—the failures of his superior, Major General George Meade, during the Gettysburg Campaign. Specifically, Pleasonton opined that Meade had allowed Robert E. Lee's army to escape to Virginia by failing to aggressively pursue the Confederates after the Union victory on July 3, 1863. Although there was some validity to Pleasonton's observations, Meade, understandably, was furious at receiving public criticism from a subordinate. In a letter to his wife dated March 9, 1864, Meade wrote of the ongoing hearings before the Committee. "[Major General David B.] Birney and Pleasonton have appeared in the hostile ranks. The latter's course is the meanest and blackest ingratitude; for I can prove but for my intercession he would have been relieved long since."[1]

Shortly after providing his testimony, Pleasonton was relieved of command of the Army of the Potomac's cavalry corps. Meade informed his wife of the relief on March 24, claiming that while he did not instigate the action, it may have been brought about when he advised Secretary of War Stanton that he no longer had any opposition to his cavalry commander's removal. Meade informed his wife that Stanton had long wished to remove Pleasonton from command but had deferred to Meade's opposition. With Meade no longer supporting Pleasonton's retention, the cavalry commander was summarily relieved and posted to duty in Missouri.[2] In any event, Pleasonton's tenure with the cavalry corps was about to end since the army's new general-in-chief, Ulysses S. Grant, was of the opinion that in the past the Army of the Potomac's cavalry had not accomplished all that it could have, and that a new commander was needed.[3]

Alfred Pleasonton, once dubbed a "newspaper humbug" by a subordinate, had shown himself to be a passive combat commander, generally content to issue orders, then to allow his subordinates fight the enemy without his personal intervention. At Brandy Station he

Major General Alfred Pleasonton, show here in Warrenton, Virginia, in October 1863, was relieved of command of the Cavalry Corps in March 1864, opening the way for the appointment of Major General Philip Sheridan. Pleasonton spent the remainder of the war in Missouri and Kansas (Library of Congress).

exercised virtually no control over events once the battle began. During the march to Gettysburg, Pleasonton's reports to General Hooker regarding the activities of Lee's army were notoriously inaccurate. After Meade took command of the Army of the Potomac, Pleasonton's position as a field commander was further diminished. In Meade's view, cavalry's primary role was scouting and security, and consequently Meade considered Pleasonton more a staff officer than tactical commander. At Gettysburg, Pleasonton remained at his headquarters, which was adjacent to Meade's, while his division commanders fought their engagements on their own. For few days, Pleasonton acted as a de facto chief of staff before Meade appointed Brigadier General A.A. Humphreys to that position.[4] While both Meade and, apparently,

Pleasonton were comfortable with the limited role of the Cavalry Corps commander during field operations, Pleasonton's replacement, Major General Philip Sheridan, was not.

The origins of Philip Sheridan, brought from Tennessee by Grant to replace Pleasonton, are unclear. At different times in his life, he stated that he was born in 1830, 1831, or 1832, and placed his birth in Massachusetts, New York, or Ohio. By other accounts, Sheridan was born aboard ship as his immigrant parents traveled to the United States. It seems more likely that Sheridan was born in Ireland before his parents booked their passage.[5] Sheridan grew up in Somerset, Ohio, and entered West Point with the class of 1852 after his congressman's first choice for appointment failed his entrance examination.

As a cadet, Sheridan's academic performance was average, and he was perhaps best known as a young man with a quick temper. In September 1851, nine months before Sheridan's scheduled graduation, a cadet sergeant, William Terrill, ordered Sheridan to "dress" in formation, meaning that Sheridan was to align himself with the cadet on his right. Sheridan believed he was properly dressed, and that, further, Terrill used an improper tone of voice when giving the order. Sheridan, aggrieved, lowered his musket and bayonet from his shoulder, and advanced threateningly toward Terrill. However, thinking better of his action, Sheridan broke off the attack and returned to his position in the ranks. Nonetheless, Terrill reported Sheridan for his indiscipline. Still angry, the following day Sheridan confronted Terrill in front of the barracks, and a bout of "fisticuffs" ensued. Academy officials, correctly judging that Sheridan was clearly in the wrong, suspended Sheridan from the academy until August 1852, at which time he was readmitted as a "turn-back" to the class of 1853.[6]

After graduating in June 1853, ranking thirty-fourth out of his class of fifty-two, Sheridan was commissioned as a brevet second lieutenant in the 1st U.S. Infantry and posted to Texas. After a little more than a year, he received a commission as a second lieutenant in the 4th U.S. Infantry which was stationed in the Pacific Northwest. Joining his new regiment, Sheridan served in Northern California, Oregon and Washington until the outbreak of the Civil War.[7] His duties were mostly mundane, with the occasional excitement of an encounter with hostile Indians.

Following the outbreak of the Civil War, Sheridan initially saw wartime service in Missouri as a quartermaster. However, after a falling out with his commander, he was detailed as an agent charged with purchasing horses. Fortunately, Sheridan was soon able to secure a position on General Henry Halleck's staff which helped lead to his appointment at the end of May 1862, as colonel of the 2nd Michigan Cavalry. While with his regiment in northern Mississippi, one of Sheridan's officers gave him a horse that the officer suspected might be a difficult mount. Sheridan named the horse, a three-year-old, 16-hand Morgan, "Rienzi," after a nearby town. The horse quickly became Sheridan's favorite and, later, most famous horse.[8]

In July 1862, Sheridan was appointed brigadier general of volunteers. He spent the following twenty months in Kentucky and Tennessee commanding first an infantry brigade, then an infantry division. The high point of this service came at Chattanooga on November 15, 1863, when his division, while making a limited advance, continued forward and swept General Braxton Bragg's Confederates from Missionary Ridge. That event brought Sheridan to General Grant's attention—Grant, newly arrived at Chattanooga, was observing the battle—and established Sheridan's reputation throughout the army.

In March 1864, General Grant came east to assume the duties of general-in-chief. Grant correctly determined that the Army of the Potomac's cavalry could accomplish more if commanded by an aggressive officer. Grant's first choice to replace Pleasonton as Cavalry Corps commander was his West Point classmate, William B. Franklin. Franklin graduated first in the class of 1843, while Grant graduated twenty-first among the thirty-nine members of the class. Franklin, however had been politically out of favor since the debacle at Fredericksburg in December 1862. In a meeting with President Lincoln, General Henry Halleck suggested that Grant bring Sheridan east to command the Army of the Potomac's cavalry. Grant readily acceded to Halleck's recommendation, later writing that he replied to Halleck by saying that Sheridan was "the Very Man I want."[9]

One of the few officers Sheridan brought with him from Tennessee was Captain James W. Forsyth, who ably served as the Cavalry Corps chief of staff. Sheridan's biographical sketch in Cullum's *Biographical Register* says of Forsyth: "In all the practical and laborious duties of administration and command he [Sheridan] was most ably and efficiently seconded by his 'dear friend' and chief of staff, the clear headed, methodical, and accomplished James W. Forsyth, also a graduate of the Military Academy" (Library of Congress).

Sheridan made the move from Tennessee and arrived at his new headquarters in Culpeper on the evening of April 5, 1864, where he was greeted with some suspicion by his new subordinates. Sheridan was an outsider from a western theater of operations and he was not known to be a cavalryman. Other senior officers—most notably Major General John Pope—had succeeded in the West only to fail miserably in the East. Additionally, cavalry officers were only too aware that many infantry commanders held their arm of service in disdain.

Sheridan worked quickly to overcome his subordinates' misgivings and to establish himself as their leader. His entourage consisted of only three officers: Captain James Forsyth, his chief of staff, and two aides de camp, Lieutenants T.W.C. Moore and M.V. Sheridan, his younger brother.[10] In a popular move, Sheridan retained the officers on Pleasonton's staff as his own. Concurrently, Sheridan began a series of inspections and reviews to gauge the readiness of his new command to take the field. Also, while Sheridan was unable to fully gain George Meade's acceptance for his views regarding the primary role for cavalry in the coming campaign— that of fighting J.E.B. Stuart's cavalry—he was able to convince Meade to relieve many of his regiments from picket duty, a welcome change for both the officers and men of the cavalry corps.

In contrast to Pleasonton, Sheridan brought a more active style of command to the cavalry corps of the Army of the Potomac. Unlike Pleasonton, Sheridan did not shy away from fighting. At Antietam, Pleasonton reportedly sent his regiments into battle, then sat behind an embankment, protected from enemy fire, and read a newspaper. In contrast, when his division attacked Missionary Ridge, Sheridan, advancing with his line of infantrymen, rode his horse into an entrenchment. There, he personally accepted the surrender of a few Confederates who had not had time to flee.[11] Pleasonton was known for the quality of his uniforms and the sophistication of his mess. With respect to the latter, in early 1864 George Custer's new bride, Elizabeth, recorded that Pleasonton served six-course meals, accompanied by various wines.[12] Sheridan wore a plain major-general's uniform, his only distinctive feature his unusual hat. In his dealings with others, Sheridan was direct and blunt, and he showed little tolerance for those who were slow moving or slow witted. Not known for his gentility, over the years Sheridan had established a reputation for hard drinking and profanity, punctuating his orders with oaths.[13]

Sheridan was complemented by a cohort of seasoned commanders, although many were of limited tenure in their positions. Of the ten officers, in addition to Pleasonton, who held general officer billets at Brandy Station, only three—Brigadier General David McMurtrie Gregg, his cousin, Colonel John Irvin Gregg, and Colonel Thomas Casimer Devin—remained in their positions.

Colonel Benjamin Franklin "Grimes" Davis, in brigade command at Brandy Station, had been shot and killed on the Beverly Ford Road as the fighting began on June 9. Brigadier General John Buford, stricken by typhoid, had succumbed to that disease in December 1863. Colonel Luigi di Cesnola, captured at Aldie and held for ten months in Libby Prison, was now relegated to the command of his regiment, the 4th New York Cavalry.

The other five officers had been transferred from the Army of the Potomac. Colonel Sir Percy Wyndham, the flamboyant Englishman and Italian knight who was wounded on Fleetwood Hill on June 9, had been sent to Washington to recuperate and then remained in the capital as the officer in charge of the remount depot at Giesboro. Wyndham returned to the cavalry corps in September, but on October 2, 1863, the War Department relieved him from duty without explanation.[14] Immediately after Brandy Station, Major Charles Whiting, the senior officer present with the Reserve Brigade at Brandy Station, was detailed to recruiting duty at Portland, Maine, his home state. While there, he was cashiered for making disrespectful remarks about President Lincoln.[15] Two days after Brandy Station, Colonel Alfred Napoleon Duffié, despite his pending promotion to brigadier, reverted to command of his regiment, the 1st Rhode Island Cavalry, when General Pleasonton reorganized the cavalry corps, reducing the number of divisions from three divisions to two and thereby eliminating Duffié's billet. A week later, Duffié's regiment was virtually destroyed when surrounded by Confederates at Middleburg. Despite that embarrassment, the natty Frenchman, who barely escaped capture himself, received his promotion to brigadier with reassignment to duty in the Department of Western Virginia.[16] Colonel Judson Kilpatrick, despite his questionable character and lack of demonstrated ability, was promoted to brigadier on June 14, 1863. While commanding a cavalry brigade, and then a division, he continued to actively promote himself as a hard-fighting leader. However, he justly received much of the blame for the disastrous outcome of the

Dahlgren Raid on Richmond in March 1864 and was subsequently removed from command and transferred to Sherman's army in Tennessee.[17]

Of the departed senior leaders, only the loss of Buford and Davis could be considered seriously detrimental to the operations and efficiency of the cavalry corps. Both were seasoned veterans, and both had displayed competence leading men in battle. The value of the others to the Union war effort was only marginal.

The departure of Kilpatrick was certainly no loss to the cavalry corps. He had consistently mismanaged his command in combat, starting at Fleetwood Hill where he fed his regiments into the fight piecemeal and was soundly thrashed by Wade Hampton. Kilpatrick's judgment and fighting skills did not improve with experience, as evidenced by his equivocating leadership on the disastrous Dahlgren Raid. Simply stated, Kilpatrick's performance as a combat leader consistently bordered on incompetence.

Cesnola's value is more difficult to judge. The dapper Italian was personally brave—in 1897 he would receive the Medal of Honor for his valor at Aldie on June 17, 1863—but his tenure as a brigade commander had lasted less than three weeks.[18] Further, Cesnola's regiment, the 4th New York, was one of the most inefficient regiments in the Cavalry Corps. Filled with immigrants, many of whom did not speak English, the regiment was considered unreliable. The low point for the regiment had come on September 16, 1863, in Culpeper when one of its squadrons was captured without much of a fight. In a show of his displeasure, the following day General Pleasonton prohibited the regiment from carrying its colors or guidons.[19] After Cesnola's return from captivity, the regiment's efficiency improved. In an inspection conducted after Sheridan assumed command, an inspector general noted that the horses of the 4th New York "were especially good and evince[d] care and good treatment." The inspector also noted that "the men are clean and wear the pro-scribed [sic] uniform."[20]

Brigadier General David McMurtrie Gregg, commander of the 2nd Cavalry Division since the formation of the Cavalry Corps in February 1863, was Sheridan's most experienced subordinate. His division was mauled by Hampton at Samaria Church, but saved the large wagon train Sheridan was escorting to the James River. A steady and capable officer, Gregg unexpectedly resigned his commission in February 1865 (Library of Congress).

Duffié, another foreign-born officer, was a talented trainer and personally brave, but lacked the judgment desired in a senior commander. At Brandy Station, he became lost with his division en route to Kelly's Ford, delaying Gregg's attack for two hours and throwing off the plan for the battle. Later that same day, he failed to move promptly to Gregg's assistance and was consequently blamed for Gregg's failure to secure Fleetwood Hill. A week later at Middleburg, his stubborn adherence to orders as the tactical situation dramatically changed cost him his regiment.

Wyndham, the third foreign-born brigade commander at Brandy Station, had shown himself to be an energetic and efficient officer who inspired loyalty among his subordinates. Also, he had performed reasonably well while in brigade command, although he had misjudged the situation at Fleetwood Hill, mistaking a single cannon and a few couriers as a strong defense. However, by most standards, the British officer was as capable than many of his contemporaries.

Despite the loss of senior leaders through attrition or transfer during the past year, Sheridan was fortunate to have for the most part a solid team of division and brigade commanders who were experienced and aggressive.

Among Sheridan's subordinate senior officers, the most experienced

Major General A.T.A. Torbert commanded infantry units during the first three years of the war. Having undergone surgery, he was absent during the opening weeks of the Overland Campaign. Trevilian's was his first cavalry raid and his first experience commanding cavalry in a large battle (Library of Congress).

was Brigadier General David McMurtrie Gregg, who had commanded his cavalry division since December 1862.[21] Gregg had graduated from West Point with the class of 1855, been commissioned in the dragoons, and served in New Mexico, California, and the Pacific Northwest until the eve of the Civil War. Coming to the East, he received a captain's commission in the newly formed 6th U.S. Cavalry before accepting appointment as colonel of the 8th Pennsylvania Cavalry in January 1862. Since that time, Gregg had participated in virtually all the campaigns of the Army of the Potomac.[22] He had developed a well-deserved reputation as a capable and steady—if not brilliant—cavalry commander.

Newly promoted Brigadier General James Wilson, an engineer officer who served on Grant's staff, had never commanded troops in combat before being appointed to command of the 3rd Cavalry Division. In June 1864 he led the Wilson-Kautz Raid against the rail lines south of Richmond during which he was thoroughly drubbed by Fitz Lee (Library of Congress).

Brigadier General Alfred T.A. Torbert commanded Sheridan's 1st Cavalry Division. Like Gregg, Torbert graduated from West Point in 1855. Unlike Gregg, however, Torbert received his commission in the infantry, with which he served in Texas, Florida, the expedition to Utah, and New Mexico. Torbert's home state was Delaware, a slave state, and the Confederate congress confirmed a commission for Torbert as a first lieutenant of artillery in the Confederate army. While he may have briefly considered the Confederate government's offer, Torbert remained loyal to the Union.[23] Upon the outbreak of hostilities, the army posted Torbert, who had been at home on a leave of absence, to New Jersey to muster-in soldiers who had enlisted in volunteer regiments. While there, Torbert accepted appointment as colonel of the 1st New Jersey Infantry. Commanding either his regiment or his brigade, Torbert fought in campaigns of the Army of the Potomac through 1862. During the first six months of 1863, Torbert was on a leave of absence ostensibly due to a recurrence of malaria. However, during his absence he devoted considerable effort to securing his promotion to brigadier general, an endeavor in which he succeeded: he was promoted in February 1863, effective November 29, 1862, the same date of rank as classmate and fellow commander, David McM. Gregg.[24]

In April 1864, Torbert transferred from the infantry to the cavalry, assuming command of the 1st Division of the Cavalry Corps which had formerly been commanded by Buford. The exact process by which Torbert made the relatively uncommon move from infantry to cavalry remains unclear. According to one post-war account Meade arranged the move, while according to another account, Sheridan requested Torbert, whom he had known at the military academy.[25] With regard to the former, it is not clear why Meade would have taken an interest in Torbert. Torbert, who served in Sedgwick's VI Corps, not in Meade's V Corps, was not one of Meade's close and trusted subordinates.[26] Sheridan's role is equally unlikely. While the two were undoubtedly acquainted while cadets at West Point, it is implausible they were close friends since Sheridan was two—and initially three—classes ahead of Torbert. It seems more likely that the transfer was arranged by Pleasonton at the request of Torbert. The two may have met in Florida where both had served during the campaigns against the Seminoles in 1856–1857. At the time, Torbert was a lieutenant in the 5th U.S. Infantry while Pleasonton served as the acting assistant adjutant general of the Department of Florida. During the Army of the Potomac's winter encampment at Brandy Station, Torbert's brigade camped on the Wellford Farm—today Farley—less than a mile from Pleasonton's Cavalry Corps Headquarters on the adjacent Green Farm. It is possible that Torbert, who was known for his sociability, and Pleasonton renewed their acquaintance there.

Brigadier General Wesley Merritt, an 1860 graduate of West Point and one of Pleasonton's "boy generals," commanded the Reserve Brigade in Torbert's Division. A highly capable officer, Merritt demonstrated superlative leadership, courage, and organizational skills throughout his forty-year career (Library of Congress).

As commander of the 3rd Division of the cavalry corps, Grant selected a former staff officer from the west, Brigadier General James Harrison Wilson. Wilson, a "boy general," graduated from West Point sixth in his class of forty-one in 1860, whereupon he was commissioned as a lieutenant in the topographical engineers. Prior to the Civil War, Wilson served at Fort Vancouver on the Columbia River in Washington, before coming east after the outbreak of hostilities. Wilson served initially along the coast of the South Carolina and Georgia performing mostly engineer duties. After a brief stint as George McClellan's aide de camp during the Antietam Campaign, Wilson moved west to assume duties as the chief topographical engineer for Grant. After Vicksburg, Wilson accompanied Grant to Chattanooga, continuing to serve on the staff as an engineer, and earning promotion to brigadier general of volunteers in that capacity. In February 1864, Wilson's organizational abilities were recognized with a brief detail to Washington to head the newly formed Cavalry Bureau, a position he held for only six weeks before moving to Culpeper to rejoin Grant and assume command of his cavalry division. Wilson, to this point in the war had never served with the cavalry, and had never commanded troops in battle.[27]

Grant's selection of James Wilson as a cavalry division commander created some problems within the cavalry corps. Wilson, who was promoted to brigadier effective October 1863, was junior in that grade to the two brigade commanders of his division: George Custer and Henry Davies, who had been promoted in June and September of 1863, respectively. To resolve that problem, in mid–April—a few days before Wilson assumed command of his division—Davies was transferred to the 2nd Division and replaced by a more junior officer. At the same time, Custer—a Michigan man with a Michigan brigade—was transferred with his brigade to the 1st Division. A brigade from the 1st Division with a commander junior to Wilson was sent to the 3rd Division.[28]

Perhaps Pleasonton's most significant legacy to the cavalry corps was the promotion of two of his favorites: Wesley Merritt and George Custer, both of whom on the eve of the 1864 campaign commanded brigades in Torbert's division.[29] When Pleasonton took command of the cavalry corps in May 1863, both were junior officers—Merritt a captain and Custer a first lieutenant. Both had served on Pleasonton's staff: Merritt, briefly, as ordnance officer; and Custer as an aide de camp. At the time of their promotions, both had

Brigadier General Henry Davies, a New York lawyer, followed Judson Kilpatrick up the promotion ladder, succeeding Kilpatrick in command of the 2nd New York and at brigade level. Unlike Kilpatrick, however, Davies had performed competently at all levels of command thus far in the war (Library of Congress).

limited experience. Merritt's sole experience leading men in battle came at the head of the 2nd U.S. Cavalry at Yew Ridge on June 9, 1863. Custer had only twice commanded men in battle—he saw limited action at First Manassas and led a company in a charge against a few Confederate pickets at Catlett in March 1862—although he had been under fire many times as an aide or a staff officer.[30] Both Merritt and Custer were promoted at Pleasonton's behest on June 29, 1863. Since then, both had shown themselves to be talented combat leaders at Gettysburg, and in the campaigns that followed: Merritt in command of the Reserve Brigade, and Custer in command of the so-called "Michigan Brigade" of cavalry.[31] Of the two, Custer was the most flamboyant, aggressive, and well known. Merritt, whose star perhaps did not shine as brightly as Custer's, was more consistent, and probably more competent.

Additionally, Pleasonton arranged the promotion of a lesser-known but highly capable officer, Colonel Henry E. Davies, Jr., to brigadier. Davies, a lawyer from New York City, began the war in an infantry regiment before securing an appointment as major of the 2nd New York Cavalry, the Harris Light. As a lieutenant colonel, Davies commanded the regiment at Brandy Station. Promoted to colonel in June, he continued in command of the Harris Light

Before the war, Colonel Thomas Devin was a house-painter in New York City. Because of his long service in the New York militia, he was initially mustered into federal service as a captain in the 1st New York Cavalry and in November 1861 was appointed to command of the 6th New York Cavalry. Devin, who was highly respected by his men, was elevated to brigade command upon the formation of the Cavalry Corps in early 1863. However, Devin did not receive a commensurate promotion to brigadier general until March 1865 (Library of Congress).

through the campaigns of the summer of 1863. In September 1863, Davies was promoted to brigadier and appointed to command of a brigade in Kilpatrick's division. Shortly afterward, on October 19, 1863, he was routed by Stuart in the "Buckland Races," an event that proved to be Stuart's last victory while in tactical command on a field of battle.[32] With the Spring 1864 reorganization of the Cavalry Corps, Davies, who was senior to Wilson, took command of the 1st Brigade in Gregg's division.

Experienced colonels commanded the remaining four brigades in Sheridan's Cavalry Corps. In Torbert's 1st Division, Colonel Thomas Devin commanded the 2nd Brigade, while Brigadier Generals Custer and Merritt commanded the 1st Brigade and Reserve Brigade, respectively. Devin, a house painter from New York City, had spent many years in the New York militia, rising to the grade of lieutenant colonel before the war. He was appointed colonel of the 6th New York Cavalry, a billet he still filled, when that regiment was formed in December 1861. Upon formation of the Cavalry Corps in February 1863, Devin was appointed to command of his brigade, a position he had held since, while encumbering the colonel's billet in his regiment.[33] Devin had demonstrated that he was a competent cavalry commander who instilled confidence in his men. Upon the death of Colonel "Grimes" Davis early in the morning of June 9, 1863, Buford had ordered Devin to take charge of the 1st Cavalry Division, an indication of the esteem in which superiors held the New Yorker. Devin fought the division during most of the day-long battle of Brandy Station.

While David McM. Gregg's 1st brigade was commanded by Brigadier General Henry Davies, his second brigade was commanded by his cousin and fellow Pennsylvanian, Colonel John Irvin Gregg. Colonel Gregg had extensive pre-war military experience. He had enlisted as a private during the Mexican War and rose to the grade of captain before the end of hostilities. Afterward, he remained active in the Pennsylvania Militia, over the years earning promotions to lieutenant colonel. At the outbreak of the Civil War, Gregg obtained a commission as a captain in the 6th U.S. Cavalry, a new regiment which was raised during the summer of 1861 at Pittsburgh. After serving with the regiment during the Peninsular Campaign, Second Manassas, and Antietam, Gregg accepted a volunteer commission as colonel of the 16th Pennsylvania Cavalry. The 1863 Saint Patrick's Day fight at Kelly's Ford was Gregg's only experience leading a regiment in combat. Afterward, he was appointed to brigade command, initially in Duffié's division, while still filling the colonel's billet in the 16th Pennsylvania. He led the brigade throughout the campaigns of the summer and fall of 1863, and spent most of the winter of 1863–1864 in Washington undergoing medical treatment.[34]

To accommodate Wilson's lack of seniority, both brigades in his division were commanded by colonels. Initially, Timothy Bryan, an 1855 West Point classmate of Generals Gregg and Torbert, commanded the 1st Brigade. Bryan, who had resigned his regular commission in 1857, began the war as a lieutenant colonel in a Massachusetts infantry regiment before accepting appointment as colonel of the 18th Pennsylvania Cavalry in December

A highly regarded and experienced officer, Colonel John B. McIntosh commanded Wilson's 1st Brigade. McIntosh's older brother, a Confederate brigadier, was killed at Pea Ridge, Arkansas, in March 1862. This photograph was taken later in war, after McIntosh lost his leg as a result of wounds at Winchester in September 1864. By the end of the war, McIntosh had been brevetted to major general in both regular and volunteer services (Library of Congress).

1864. However, Bryan was almost immediately replaced as brigade commander by a more senior officer, Colonel John B. McIntosh, who had been absent recuperating from injuries received when he fell from his horse.[35] McIntosh had been born in 1829 in Tampa, Florida, where his father was serving as an army officer. McIntosh desired to attend West Point, but consistent with the practice of the time, he was unable to obtain an appointment to the academy because his older brother was already a cadet. Instead, during the Mexican War McIntosh entered the navy as a midshipman, an endeavor from which he resigned after two years. Upon the outbreak of the Civil War, McIntosh, whose brother entered Confederate service only to be killed as a brigadier at Pea Ridge in March 1862, received a commission as second lieutenant in the 5th U.S. Cavalry. In September 1862, the Governor of Pennsylvania appointed McIntosh colonel of the 3rd Pennsylvania Cavalry. In volunteer service, McIntosh had distinguished himself, earning regular army brevets to major and lieutenant colonel, while for most of the time commanding a cavalry brigade.[36]

Colonel George H. Chapman, 3rd Indiana Cavalry, commanded Wilson's 2nd Brigade. Like McIntosh, Chapman served as a midshipman during the Mexican War. After three years in the navy, Chapman returned to Indiana and became an attorney. In October 1861, he was appointed major of the 3rd Indiana Cavalry and earned steady promotions to lieutenant colonel and colonel.[37] The regimental surgeon referred to Chapman as "conceity little upstart," but acknowledged that the former sailor ran a well-managed regiment and that he would fight.[38] Chapman—on leave at the time—missed the battle at Brandy Station on June 9, 1863. However, as part of William Gamble's Brigade, his troopers were among the first to face Confederate Major General Henry Heth's infantrymen on McPherson's Ridge west of Gettysburg on July 1, 1863. In late fall 1863, Chapman took command of the brigade in the absence of Colonel Gamble.[39]

It is interesting to compare the leaders serving at Brandy Station to those in place during the campaign of 1864. Although Sheridan had only limited experience with the cavalry, he had been an aggressive and highly capable infantry commander. Further, he had shown an eagerness to personally take charge in battle: to lead, as well as to direct. In contrast, Pleasonton had been a passive corps commander, willing to let his subordinates fight their battles. Additionally, Pleasonton was apparently content to remain at his headquarters, well away from the scene of the action.

Within the 1st Cavalry Division, the changes among senior leaders were mixed. Buford, experienced and capable, was greatly missed. Torbert, although he had rendered good service as an infantry brigade commander, had no experience leading mounted troops. Additionally, Torbert had taken several long leaves of absence from his regiment and brigade as a result of illness, raising questions regarding his fitness for the rigors of cavalry service.[40] George Custer, now in command of the division's first brigade, certainly possessed more flair than Benjamin F. "Grimes" Davis, who had been shot dead on the Beverly Ford Road early in the morning on June 9, 1863. Custer, the youngest "boy general," with flowing blond hair, outlandish uniforms, and bold leadership, had gained fame among the public. More significantly, he had earned the respect and loyal support of his men. However, Davis, although not flamboyant, had been considered by some to be the best cavalry officer in the army at the time of his death.[41] Colonel Thomas Devin, still in command of the 2nd Brigade, was an experienced and capable commander, known as a leader "who knew how to take his men into action and how to bring them out."[42] Commanding the Reserve Brigade, now the 3rd Brigade of the 1st

George H. Chapman commanded Wilson's 2d Brigade. He served credibly throughout the war in the grades of major through brevet major general while commanding a cavalry regiment, brigade, and, in late 1864, a division. After the war he served as a judge in Marion County, Indiana, and was elected to one term in the Indiana Senate (Library of Congress).

6. "The Very Man I want" 77

Division, Wesley Merritt had exhibited a high degree of competence. He was certainly a more effective brigade commander than Charles Whiting. To be fair, however, Whiting commanded the Reserve Brigade for less than a month in the spring of 1863, and as a major he could not act with the authority of a general officer.

David McMurtrie Gregg, the most experienced senior cavalry officer present in 1864, commanded the 2nd Cavalry Division. Almost all sources—both contemporaneous to the present—consider Gregg a far superior leader to Alexander Duffié, who commanded the 2nd Division at Brandy Station. In the eight months he had commanded the division's 1st Brigade, Henry Davies had performed proficiently. While his brigade had been routed by Stuart at the Buckland Races on October 19, 1863, that debacle is more reflective of Kilpatrick's lack of judgment than Davies's tactical and leadership skills. It is difficult to compare Davies' abilities to those of Luigi di Cesnola, who commanded the brigade on June 9, 1863. As previously mentioned, Cesnola served in brigade command for roughly three weeks. Colonel John Irvin Gregg—a solid performer—continued in command of the division's 2nd Brigade.

The 3rd Division, which with David McM. Gregg had been commanded by the general officer with the most cavalry experience, was with James Wilson commanded by the officer with the least experience. By all measures except one, Wilson was unqualified for cavalry division command. However, Wilson's one qualification—he had the trust and confidence of U.S. Grant—trumped all others. As a staff officer and as chief of the Cavalry Bureau, Wilson

This photograph, from an unpublished biography of General Gregg, shows Sheridan and several of his key subordinates in a casual pose. From the left are Henry Davies, David McM. Gregg, James Wilson, A.T.A. Torbert, an unidentified officer, Sheridan, and Wesley Merritt. Surprisingly, Custer is absent (Library of Congress).

had exhibited intelligence and energy. However, those traits, while important, do not necessarily predict how an officer will perform in combat—George B. McClellan's failure, despite his initial promise, comes to mind. Fortunately, the reorganization of the Cavalry Corps provided Wilson with two junior, but capable, subordinate commanders: Colonels John McIntosh and George Chapman in the 1st and 2nd Brigades, respectively. Undoubtedly, McIntosh was a more skilled combat leader than Judson Kilpatrick who had earlier commanded the brigade, despite Kilpatrick's reputation among the public as a hard fighter. At the time, it would have been more difficult to predict whether Chapman was an improvement over the flamboyant Sir Percy Wyndham, who led the 2nd Brigade at Brandy Station. However, since Wyndham had fallen out of favor it is doubtful that he could have continued to serve effectively in a position of responsibility with the Army of the Potomac.[43]

All-in-all, at the senior levels of command, the Army of the Potomac's Cavalry Corps was led by officers who had demonstrated competence thus far in the war. Led by Sheridan, as the campaigns of 1864 began, both Grant and Meade had reason to feel confident that the mounted arm of their army would fight hard and fight well.

7

Veteran Volunteers
Manning, Mounting, and Arming Union Cavalry

Senior commanders throughout history have acknowledged that having experienced veterans in the ranks is a critical element in the combat effectiveness of military organizations from company through army level. Despite this understanding and the resulting efforts to maintain unit strengths, personnel issues continued to challenge both tactical leaders and officials at the War Department as the Civil War entered its third year.

Most regiments—both cavalry and infantry—in the Eastern Theater were severely under strength, operating with between 300 and 400 men—or even fewer—instead of at the authorized strength of more than 1,000. Additionally, many regiments had been raised during the second half of 1861, with the men enlisting for a three-year term of service. Those terms of service were set to expire during the campaign season of 1864.

Throughout the war, the predominate Union response to shortfalls in manpower was to task the states with raising additional regiments. Experience had shown that it was generally easier to induce men to enlist in a new regiment than to induce them to enlist as individual replacements for existing regiments already serving with the army. Also, additional officers' billets came with new regiments, and governors readily rewarded those who were politically loyal with appointment to company and field grade positions. In part to meet the requirements for individual replacements, the Federal government first enacted a conscription act in 1862, followed by a more effective conscription act in March 1863.[1] The ensuing 1863 draft, while necessary for the war effort, was immensely unpopular and sparked riots in New York City; Troy, New York; and Boston.

As early as the summer of 1863, Federal officials began to address the problem of an anticipated 1864 exodus of the most experienced soldiers in the army. To induce veterans in the army to reenlist, on June 25, 1863, the War Department issued General Order Number 191. The order authorized all men who had served for at least nine months to immediately reenlist for an additional three years or the duration of the war. As an inducement, men reenlisting, henceforth known as "veteran volunteers," would be entitled to a federal bounty of $402, and after the expiration of their original enlistments, each would be authorized a thirty-day furlough, military situation permitting. Additionally, each veteran volunteer would be presented a "service chevron" to be worn on the uniform as a "badge of honorable distinction."[2]

This initial effort to induce soldiers to reenlist was not particularly successful, in part because the men were skeptical of the army's promise that they would receive furloughs at some distant time in the future. As a practical matter, it may have occurred to many veterans that they might not survive to obtain the promised furloughs. In response to lagging reenlistments, on November 21, 1863, the War Department issued General Order Number 376. This order specified that soldiers who reenlisted would receive their thirty-day furloughs before the expiration of their original terms of service. It also provided an incentive for the men to reenlist en masse. Each regiment or company in which seventy-five percent of the men assigned reenlisted would be furloughed as a body, ostensibly for the purpose of reorganizing and recruiting in the men's home state.[3] Additionally, regiments in which seventy-five percent of the men eligible reenlisted would have the word "Veteran" appended to their designation. Thus the 6th New York Volunteer Cavalry would become the 6th New York Veteran Volunteer Cavalry.

The prospect of an immediate group-furlough proved enticing to many of the soldiers in their winter camps in Culpeper, and beginning in December, successful reenlistment drives were undertaken in many regiments, both infantry and cavalry. With the new year, regiments and companies began departing for home on their furloughs, with transportation costs paid by the government. Soldiers who were not eligible to reenlist because they lacked sufficient time in service, or who declined to reenlist, remained behind in camp.

As of January 2, 1864, General Meade reported to Washington that 16,189 men—about one in eight of his soldiers—had reenlisted, and that two regiments and fifteen companies of cavalry were among the units that had departed on their thirty-day furloughs.[4] The unit furloughs were problematic for cavalry because of the need to care for the unit's horses while the men were away. In some cavalry units the men were required to turn their mounts into the quartermaster department before departing. Upon returning from furlough, those units initially reported to the Cavalry Bureau's depot at Giesboro, near Washington, for remounting before returning to duty with the Army of the Potomac. Consequently, some furloughed cavalry units might be unable to take the field for two or three months after departing on their furloughs.[5] In other cavalry units, the men who remained behind in camp cared for the horses of those on furlough. Naturally, with some regiments on furlough, the burden of scouting and picket duty fell heavier upon the units that remained behind in Culpeper.

The army's efforts to retain veterans, and the incentives to induce soldiers to extend their enlistments, created emotional conflicts for many men. Many soldiers felt a patriotic desire to see the war through to a victorious conclusion. At the same time, many believed that while they had been serving, others at home had been shirking—and it was now the shirkers' turn to step forward and take up the fight. Other men were tempted by the offer of generous reenlistment bonuses. Bonuses were paid by the federal government, as well as state, county and municipal authorities. A reenlisting veteran could receive between $500 and $800—equivalent of up to five years' pay—although the bonuses were not all paid in an up-front lump sum.[6] Of course, in the back of every soldier's mind was the knowledge that he might not live to receive his promised bonus in full. Finally, there were strong bonds of camaraderie within the companies and regiments. These men had served together for nearly three years. Together they had endured—and survived—hardship and danger in many camps and on many battlefields. While most men naturally wished to rejoin their wives and sweethearts at home, they were at the same time reluctant to abandon their friends and mess-mates.

As men reached their decisions on whether or not to reenlist, a certain amount of turmoil ensued. Generally, reenlisting veterans were transferred to several companies within their regiments before departing on their furloughs. Men who declined to reenlist were aggregated in other companies and remained behind. Those latter companies would muster out during the summer and fall of 1864, perhaps degrading the efficiency of the regiments at that time.

Private William C.H. Reeder, 20th Indiana Infantry, was a soldier who elected not to reenlist. On December 28, 1863, he wrote to his parents at some length about the army's efforts to retain its veterans. Reeder took issue with the use of furloughs and bonuses as inducements, writing: "I will not sell myself for three years to get thirty-days' furlough and a few dollars in money. I did not come for money, and I will not start now for a few paltry dollars." Reeder concluded his letter with a sentiment held by many who chose not to reenlist: "I think this, if I served my three years and the war is not closed, then let some other young stout man come in my place and try it for awhile."[7] The 20th Indiana made the seventy-five percent threshold and departed on furlough at the end of February. Those who chose not to reenlist—including Reeder—were organized into two provisional companies and remained behind.

On the other hand, the efforts to retain veterans were considered militarily necessary by nearly all officers and many enlisted men as well. As Daniel Peck, a corporal in the 9th New York Cavalry—who chose not to reenlist—observed in a letter to his sister written in February 1864: "But I am glad so many are re-enlisting. One of them are worth four new soldiers. They are acclimated & know how to fight."[8] In the coming campaign, senior cavalry leaders would look to their veterans—those who "know how to fight"—to carry the heaviest burden in battle.

Throughout the early years of the conflict—and the later years as well—the War Department experienced significant difficulty providing horses in sufficient quantity to mount the army's cavalry regiments. Field commanders frequently complained to the army's Quartermaster General, Montgomery Meigs, whose bureau was responsible for purchasing and distributing horses, about both the quality and quantity of the mounts received.[9] Meigs, with much justification, frequently responded that practices in the field contributed greatly to the problem. He pointed out that senior commanders overused their cavalry, and that troopers—either ill-disciplined or poorly trained—did not take proper care of their mounts.[10]

From the departmental perspective, however, the issue was cost. In a supplemental report to the Secretary of War dated November 15, 1863, General-in-Chief Henry Halleck wrote, "The waste and destruction of cavalry horses in our service has proved an evil of such magnitude as to require an immediate and efficient remedy." To support that assertion, Halleck wrote that the strength of the cavalry of the Army of the Potomac averaged 10,000 to 14,000 men over the past six months, and that during that period the cavalry had been issued 35,078 horses—the equivalent of a remount for every man every two months.[11] With the cost of horses varying between $125 and $145 per head, the expense of mounting the Army of the Potomac, alone, approached $5 million for the period.[12]

After the Gettysburg Campaign, the War Department created a Cavalry Bureau to address the problems associated with the purchase and distribution of horses, and to raise the efficiency of cavalry regiments.[13] As the Cavalry Bureau's first chief, the Secretary of War appointed Major General George Stoneman, Alfred Pleasonton's predecessor in command of the Cavalry Corps.[14] At the time, Stoneman, who had been replaced by Pleasonton after the Chancellorsville Campaign, was in Washington convalescing from a severe case of hemorrhoids.

The specific responsibilities of the Cavalry Bureau were set forth in General Order

Number 236, dated July 28, 1863, and lay in four areas:

- The Cavalry Bureau was in charge of the organization and equipment for the cavalry forces of the army, and for the provision for the force's mounts and remounts.
- While the Quartermaster Department would continue to purchase horses for cavalry service, those purchases would be made under the direction of the Chief, Cavalry Bureau.
- The bureau was placed in general charge of a system of remount depots. The depots would be established for the "reception, organization and discipline of cavalry recruits and new regiments, and for the collection, care, and training of cavalry horses."
- The bureau was also empowered to call for inspection reports and returns from cavalry units at any time.

The general order concluded with a statement emphasizing the need to improve the management and care of cavalry horses and promising punishment for those who failed to comply. "Great neglects of duty in this connection are to be attributed to officers in command of cavalry troops. It is the design of the War Department to correct such neglects by dismissing from the service officers whose inefficiency and inattention result in deterioration and loss of public animals under their charge."[15]

Major General George Stoneman was removed from command of the Cavalry Corps after the Chancellorsville Campaign in May 1863. Assigned to Washington as the chief of the newly-created Cavalry Bureau, Stoneman struggled with the problems of mounting, arming, and training the Union cavalry arm, an endeavor in which he achieved little success. In January 1864, Stoneman returned to duty with troops in Tennessee, much to both his relief and the satisfaction of Secretary of War Stanton (Library of Congress).

Concurrent with the establishment of the Cavalry Bureau, the War Department in true bureaucratic fashion implemented a reporting system that field commanders must have considered a nightmare. By General Order Number 237, also dated July 28, 1863, the War Department directed that every cavalry regiment be inspected at the end of every month, with the reports of inspection forwarded to the Cavalry Bureau "without delay." The reports were to include:

- The condition of the inspected unit in general, with particular attention on the condition of the unit's mounts;
- The service performed by the unit since the last report, including both the miles the horses had traveled and the character and circumstances of the service performed;

- The care taken of the mounts (veterinary treatment, shoeing, forage provided);
- Any other information which the commander believed should be brought to the attention of the Bureau.

Finally, each regimental commander was to provide an assessment of the status of his regiment's horses, dividing them into four categories: horses to be condemned as unfit for any military purpose; horses permanently unfit for cavalry service that might be used to haul guns in artillery batteries or as draft animals; horses that were presently unfit for cavalry service, but with "timely care and treatment in depots" would be restored to satisfactory condition and could then be reissued to the cavalry; and, finally, horses that were serviceable as cavalry mounts.[16]

One can imagine the frustration felt by regimental commanders charged with inspecting their units and preparing the lengthy and detailed reports while on active campaign. Naturally, compliance with the reporting requirement was sketchy at best.[17]

Unfortunately, the functional responsibilities of the Cavalry Bureau were in potential conflict with the responsibilities of other, long-established bureaus, and in some cases impinged upon the traditional responsibilities of field commanders. For example, as cited above, the Quartermaster Department would continue to purchase cavalry mounts, but do so under the direction of the chief of the Cavalry Bureau. Also with regard to horses, the Cavalry Bureau was charged with issuing horses to cavalry units, formerly a process conducted by the Quartermaster Department.[18] Similarly, the Cavalry Bureau was assigned responsibility for equipping cavalry forces while the Ordnance Bureau retained responsibility for procuring the weapons with which the regiments would be armed. Also, the Cavalry Bureau was charged with training and disciplining cavalry recruits and regiments, responsibilities that had heretofore been exercised by line commanders, not departmental bureaus.

Despite the bureaucratic frictions, General Stoneman plunged ahead in an effort to improve the organization and management of the Union's mounted arm. In this, he and his successors met with much disappointment and only limited success.

By October 1863, the War Department detailed ten quartermaster officers—nine captains and one lieutenant—to the Cavalry Bureau to purchase cavalry mounts under the supervision of Stoneman. Additionally, the War Department assigned eleven experienced cavalry officers—three lieutenants, six captains, one major, and one colonel—to the Cavalry Bureau as inspectors. Their duty was to examine horses being purchased by the quartermaster officers to ensure that the animals selected were suitable for cavalry service.[19] The senior inspector, Colonel William Gamble, was a highly qualified and well-respected officer. He had served from 1839 to 1843 as an enlisted man in the 1st Dragoons, and as colonel of the 8th Illinois Cavalry had commanded a brigade with distinction during the Gettysburg Campaign.[20]

In addition to problems associated with efficiently providing quality remounts to the cavalry, outright fraud had plagued the War Department's purchase of horses and mules since the beginning of the war. As an example, in August 1863 Colonel Henry S. Olcott was sent to Ohio to examine irregularities in Quartermaster Bureau purchases. He wrote, "Thus I discovered within forty-eight hours that by a corrupt conspiracy between a government purchasing agent, an inspector, a Cincinnati contractor, and an Indianapolis horse dealer, and a Republican politician, the United States had been systematically robbed of one million dollars in the purchase of horses and mules, at the Cincinnati corral, during the preceding year."[21]

Olcott went on to add that in the Department of the Ohio, fraud in the purchase of

The federal cavalry depot at Giesboro, near Washington, had a capacity of 32,000 horses. Note the expanse of wooden stables for horses in the background, while cavalrymen sent to the depot for remounting are billeted in tents at the foreground (Library of Congress).

horses and mules had also been perpetrated in Louisville, leading to the court-martial of an assistant quartermaster purchasing officer.[22]

In compliance with General Order Number 236, the War Department transferred the Quartermaster Bureau's remount depot at St. Louis to the Cavalry Bureau, while Stoneman set to work establishing a cavalry remount depot at Giesboro Point in Washington to support the cavalry forces in the Eastern Theater.[23] Eventually, six remount depots would be established, of which Giesboro was the largest.

The Giesboro Depot was designed to initially have a capacity of 16,000 horses with an adjacent "dismounted camp" where "all new regiments ... can be sent to be mounted, armed, accoutered, and equipped, and to which men of old regiments are sent to be refitted and again sent to the field." The Giesboro Depot featured a horse hospital with stalls for 2,500 horses and 32 stables capable of housing 6,000 horses. Open-air corrals eventually increased the depot's capacity to 32,000 horses, although the maximum number on hand at any one time was 21,000. Supporting structures included horse shoeing shops (the depot employed 100 blacksmiths), barns for hay and grain storage, wharves allowing three steamers to load or unload horses and supplies simultaneously, a grist mill, barracks, mess halls, and a chapel.[24]

Giesboro Depot, with its large capacity, helped the War Department meet the Army of the Potomac's almost insatiable requirement for remounts. Perhaps most significantly, the depot provided a facility where malnourished, broken-down, lame, or ill horses could rest and recuperate. Many horses recovered sufficiently to return to cavalry service, while others were converted to alternative military uses or sold out of the service altogether. Unfortunately, many horses died at the depot while others were destroyed.[25]

Despite efforts to rehabilitate horses and return them to service, thousands of horses died or were destroyed at Giesboro. Disposal of their carcasses was necessary. The caption by artist Alfred Waud reads, "disabled horses shot at the top of the slide, and slid down into barges below." While the disposition of the carcasses is not given, they were likely sold to renderers (Library of Congress).

However, Giesboro and other remount depots never operated as envisioned. Little, if any, training for horses, troopers, or organizations was conducted at the depots. Horses, riders and regiments continued to be sent to the army in the field with only minimal training.[26] Additionally, many field commanders vigorously opposed the concept of dismounted camps to which their soldiers would be sent for refitting or remounting.

Following the Bristoe Campaign in the fall of 1863, Judson Kilpatrick advised General Pleasonton that "the men of my command have learned to appreciate the easy life offered them at the Dismounted Camp, and take every opportunity to get there. They neglect their horses, lose their equipments, knowing that in either case they will be sent there to refit."[27] Both Pleasonton and General Meade concurred with Kilpatrick's observations.

At about the same time, George Custer, commanding one of Kilpatrick's brigades, reported that a detachment of forty men of the 7th Michigan Cavalry left the dismounted camp in Washington to rejoin their regiment with new horses. Only twenty-three troopers reported to the regiment because the horses of seventeen men were unable to complete the journey. Custer went on to opine, "So far as my experience and observation extend, my command suffers about as much from the influences and effects of the Dismounted Camp as it does from the weapons of the enemy." Pleasonton forwarded Custer's report to Stoneman who endorsed and returned it. In his endorsement, Stoneman asserted that Kilpatrick's division had been remounted with the best horses the government could provide, and added, "I have understood that Custer's brigade are great horse-killers, and it is very likely that the 17 horses were used up as stated, though they were considered serviceable when they left the depot."[28]

Unaddressed in both Kilpatrick's and Custer's criticisms of the remount depot was the issue of the responsibility for imposing discipline. Ensuring that men do not neglect their horses or lose their equipment as a means for shirking duty is squarely the responsibility of company officers and noncommissioned officers—a fact seemingly misunderstood by Kilpatrick. Moreover, as a standard practice, detachments from regiments were sent to the remount depot under the charge of regimental officers or sergeants who presumably were responsible for ensuring that the enlisted men's time at the depot was used productively. The experience of the Reserve Brigade, which was sent to Giesboro from August until October 1863 for complete remounting, provides an interesting contrast. Wesley Merritt, writing after the war, expressed the view that it was "exceeding doubtful" if the time the brigade spent at the depot "was an advantage to it in any way." However, Merritt added: "I would not be understood as insinuating that there was any neglect while the brigade was at Giesborough. On the contrary, everything was done that was possible. Officers and men labored incessantly. But the time which it was possible to allow for refitting was short, and a great deal was necessary to be done."[29]

However, General Pleasonton persisted with his criticism of the remount depots. On November 5, he again officially complained about the support provided to his corps by the Cavalry Bureau. In this instance, however, he proposed that the problems be resolved by transferring the responsibility for remounting cavalry to the army commander.

> I would therefore respectfully suggest that the entire business of fitting out the cavalry of this army be placed under the orders and control of the commanding general; that depots be established (within the actual limits of the army where practicable) where men who have lost horses or equipments can be rapidly re-equipped for the field instead of, as at present, lying sometimes for months together in a Dismounted Camp over which he has no control, where it is reputed there is no discipline or order, and which both officers and soldiers have learned to look to as a comfortable escape from the performance of duty in the field. Depots thus established could receive the attention of the corps commander in an equal degree, with any other portion of his command, being under his immediate-eye and for the advantage solely of his own troops, suitable officers could and would be selected for their charge, and any evils could and would be promptly checked. Under the present system, although horses of a generally poorer quality than ever before received are furnished the command, although a very large number of officers and men are absent at Dismounted Camp, without the limits of this army, who properly belong to it, and whose services could be usefully employed in the field, I have no power to apply the least remedy.[30]

It appears that General Meade may not have fully ascribed to Pleasonton's views, and it is likely he did not wish to take on additional responsibilities for establishing and operating remount depots. Meade forwarded Pleasonton's memorandum to General Henry Halleck simply for information, making no recommendations regarding Pleasonton's proposals. Halleck forwarded Pleasonton's memorandum to Stoneman, inviting him to comment on the proposal.

On November 12, Stoneman provided his comments to General Halleck. Stoneman acknowledged that some of the horses issued to the Army of the Potomac were unsuitable for cavalry service because they were "too young, unbroken, and unsound," but that every effort was being made to resolve that problem. Stoneman noted that the Cavalry Bureau had 17,000 horses on hand in October, many of which had been sent to the depot for recuperation. He informed Halleck that most newly procured horses were sent to other armies or newly-formed regiments, while the Army of the Potomac was mostly being issued horses considered fit following their recuperation. Horses issued to the Army of the Potomac which were found to be unfit, were replaced. Stoneman explained that this system was being used to "make the most" of the 17,000 horses on hand. Stoneman acknowledged that instead of sending men to the remount depots for horses, the horses could be sent to army in the field. He opined that General Halleck should be the judge of which method to follow and promised "hearty cooperation" with whichever decision was made. Stoneman concluded his memorandum with a jab at General Pleasonton.

> General Pleasonton's opinions in regard to the discipline of the Dismounted Camp, and also in regard to the quality of the horses issued by the Cavalry Bureau, might possibly have more weight had they been founded in either case upon personal observation and inspection. The plan he proposes of having his own depots under his own supervision and within the actual limits of the army necessarily indicates that he contemplates that in future the Army of the Potomac shall remain stationary to protect them from Stuart, or that his depots shall be of a portable character and capable of being transported and taken with the army in its various and uncertain movements.[31]

General Halleck's response to Stoneman's memorandum is not known. However, no official action was taken with regard to Pleasonton's proposals. This is not surprising since Halleck had expressed the view that the principal cause of the problem with keeping the cavalry mounted was the poor treatment of their horses by cavalry soldiers. He had earlier recommended "the transfer to the infantry service [of] every man whose horse is, through his own fault or neglect, rendered unfit for service."[32]

General Stoneman, during the six months he headed the Cavalry Bureau, was unable to satisfy the expectations of his supervisor, Secretary of War Edwin Stanton. Undoubtedly, Stoneman felt a great sense of relief when at the end of January 1864, he left Washington to assume command of an infantry corps in Tennessee.[33] Stoneman's replacement was Brigadier General Kenner Garrard, an 1851 graduate of West Point who had spent most of his pre-war career with the dragoons in the West. Garrard also proved a disappointment. He left the Cavalry Bureau at his own request after only three weeks to assume command of the 2nd Cavalry Division in the Army of the Cumberland.[34]

Perhaps desperate for an effective manager, Assistant Secretary of War Charles Dana, on January 17, 1864, telegraphed General U.S. Grant in Tennessee, requesting that Grant detail the young Brigadier General James H. Wilson, a trusted and competent assistant, to the Cavalry Bureau for sixty days. Dana wrote that Wilson was needed to impose "order and honesty" on the Bureau and went on to add, "It is a question of saving millions of money and rendering the cavalry arm everywhere efficient." Naturally Grant acceded to the request, replying by telegraph on the following day, "I will order General Wilson at once. No more efficient or better appointment could be made for the place."[35] By special orders dated January 26, 1864, Wilson was assigned to the charge of the Cavalry Bureau and directed to relieve General Gerrard "without delay."[36] Somewhat ironically, three weeks later Grant notified Wilson, now in Washington, that his command in Tennessee required that 12,000 horses be sent to Nashville.[37]

Wilson went about his new duties with his customary efficiency. He organized horse inspection teams—one regular officer, one volunteer officer, and one local civilian—for each of the Cavalry Bureau depots. He also began branding horses that the teams rejected with an "R" that they might not be later sold to the government. Wilson discovered that fraud and mismanagement, such as had been uncovered by Colonel Alcott, persisted. After the first contracts for horses were awarded with Wilson as chief of the bureau, Wilson ordered five of the six contractors arrested for defaulting on the agreed-upon terms for the delivery of remounts. Wilson noted that afterward, the supply of horses to the government "became much more regular and the quality greatly improved."[38]

In early 1864, the War Department encountered difficulty in finding suitable officers to serve as Chief of the Cavalry Bureau. In April, one week after Brigadier General James Wilson returned to duty with the Army of the Potomac, Major General Henry Halleck, the Army Chief of Staff, assumed personal responsibility for the functioning of the Cavalry Bureau and the officers of the Bureau were ordered to report directly to him. (Library of Congress).

In late March, mindful that he had been promised Wilson's return before campaigning began, General Grant wrote to General Halleck and, among other things, recommended that Wilson be posted to the Army of the Potomac. A week later, on April 6, Grant again wrote Halleck, informing him that he wanted Wilson to command a cavalry division, and asking that the Secretary of War make a decision regarding Wilson's release so that necessary arrangements could be made.[39] The following day the War Department cut orders relieving Wilson of his duties at the Cavalry Bureau, and directing that Wilson report to General Grant for assignment.[40]

Officials in Washington were apparently concerned about ensuring the effective management of the Cavalry Bureau after the departure of Wilson. On April 14, a week after Wilson's reassignment, the War Department issued General Order Number 162 which reorganized the Bureau and redefined responsibilities within the organization. Most significantly, the Bureau was placed under the direct command of Major General Henry Halleck, the chief of the army staff, "who shall perform the duties of the chief of the Cavalry Bureau prescribed by existing orders, and the officers of that Bureau respectively will report to him." The general order specified that duties relating to organization, equipment, and inspection of cavalry were to be performed by a cavalry officer while "the duties in relation to purchase and inspection of horses, [and] the subsistence and transportation of horses purchased" were to be performed by an officer of the Quartermaster's Department appointed to that duty. The order assigned those duties to Lieutenant Colonel James A. Ekin, a quartermaster officer.[41] A day earlier, on April 13, the Secretary of War ordered Ekin to "proceed in person to various points where horses are being purchased" to expedite the delivery of mounts for the armies in the Eastern Theater.[42]

General Halleck, before General Grant's promotion to lieutenant general, had served as the general in chief in Washington where he devoted much of his energy toward raising manpower and other administrative details. Obviously, Halleck would be unable to devote his full attention to the Cavalry Bureau or to manage the day-to-day activities of the Bureau. However, having Halleck "dual-hatted" as both chief of staff and chief of the Cavalry Bureau should—in theory—improve the process by which horses were provided to commanders in the field. Halleck was senior to all serving regular officers with the exception of Grant, Major General John C. Fremont, and Major General George B. McClellan.[43] In a hierarchical organization like the army, Halleck's seniority would dampen criticism from many far more junior general officers, such as Alfred Pleasonton, and perhaps even some army commanders as well. Additionally, with his senior grade and long experience at the departmental level, Halleck could be expected to more effectively cut through the red tape of the headquarters bureaucracy.

For the final year of the war, Colonel James A. Ekin, a quartermaster officer, was responsible for the procurement of all cavalry horses for the Union army, a duty that he efficiently carried out. Ekin later served on the board of officers that tried the Lincoln assassins (Library of Congress).

The reorganization also better defined the relationship between the Quartermaster Department and the Cavalry Bureau. The previous arrangement—having the Quartermaster General responsible for purchasing horses, but doing so under the supervision of the Chief of the Cavalry Bureau was probably not the best way to ensure that quality horses in sufficient quality were purchased for cavalry service. Such shared responsibilities frequently result in a lack of accountability by all parties. General Order Number 162 clearly affixed the responsibility for procuring suitable cavalry horses with the Quartermaster Department. Given the Quartermaster Department's long experience with the procurement of horses and other supplies, the change was probably for the best.

At the time, Wilson's deputy at the Cavalry Bureau was Colonel August Kautz, an 1852 graduate of West Point who at the beginning of the war had served as a captain in the 6th U.S. Cavalry. The War Department had apparently planned for Kautz to assume increased responsibility within the Cavalry Bureau upon Wilson's departure. However, concurrently Major General Benjamin Butler, commanding the Army of the James, had been clamoring for a suitable officer to command his army's cavalry. On April 12, Butler, apparently not aware that Wilson had been transferred back to the Army of the Potomac, asked Grant to assign Wilson to the command of the cavalry of the Army of the James. As discussed above, Grant had other plans for Wilson, but he promised to provide Butler a suitable cavalry commander if one were available.

On the evening of April 15, Grant asked Halleck to arrange for Kautz's appointment as a brigadier general and his reassignment to Butler's army. Shortly after noon the following day, Halleck advised Grant the he would comply, if Grant thought Kautz more needed by Butler than at the Cavalry Bureau. He cautioned Grant that there was no competent replacement for Kautz, and that the difficulty in obtaining horses was increasing. Grant, responding that same evening, informed Halleck that Butler was "absolutely without a cavalry commander" and went on to add that he could "think of no one available equal to Kautz." Grant also questioned whether another cavalry officer, Brigadier General John W. Davidson, or an officer of lesser grade could fill Kautz's position at the bureau, now that the responsibilities of the Cavalry Bureau had been modified.[44] On April 20, General Kautz's appointment as Butler's chief of cavalry was announced.[45]

While the remount situation had improved following establishment of the Cavalry Bureau and the construction of remount depots, problems still persisted despite the increased attention and effort on the part of the War Department. For example, On January 20, 1864, Colonel Edward Sawyer, the commander of the 1st Vermont Cavalry, reported that his 943 men in camp had 112 serviceable horses and 230 unserviceable horses, with 601 men having no horses at all. Earlier in the war, Sawyer had resorted to sending the lieutenant colonel of his regiment home to Vermont to procure suitable horses and avoid the inferior mounts provided by the Quartermaster Bureau.[46]

Although problems mounting the Union's cavalry—eventually numbering 272 regiments, 45 separate battalions, and 78 separate companies—persisted, improvements in the process for purchasing horses and the efficiency of the depot system helped. Ekin, promoted to colonel and eventually brevetted to brigadier, remained with the Cavalry Bureau for the remainder of the war, bringing needed continuity to the organization. In the coming campaign, the more efficient process for purchasing horses and the capacity of the Giesboro Depot would help meet the Army of the Potomac's requirement for remounts. However, little had been done to correct what many saw as the underlying problem plaguing the cavalry: individual soldiers who neglected their horses and officers who failed to enforce proper standards of care for the mounts.

Throughout the war, the Union cavalry trooper was generally better equipped than his Southern counterpart. As the war progressed, the Northern advantage with respect to weaponry increased dramatically beginning in mid–1863 with the initial fielding of repeating rifles and carbines. In the North, innovative manufacturers developed "repeating" rifles in which ammunition was fed into the breech from a pre-loaded magazine. During the war, the most successful repeater design was developed by Christopher M. Spencer. The Spencer, patented in 1860, featured a seven-round magazine which was inserted through the rifle's stock. The magazine could hold seven metallic rimfire cartridges, or "rounds."[47] In a rimfire cartridge, the ammunition's primer is placed in the rim of the cartridge instead in a separate percussion cap. Eliminating the need for the firer to seat a percussion cap on its nipple made the Spencer even easier to fire. To operate the weapon, a soldier ejected a spent round and moved a fresh round from the magazine into the breech by rotating the hinged trigger guard downward and then back to its closed position. That motion also cocked the weapon's hammer, making the weapon ready to fire again.

In the spring of 1861, Spencer offered his weapon to the U.S. Navy for testing. Later that year, a few officers in the army became interested in the weapon and arranged limited trials. However, the bureaucracy of the army was not particularly enamored with the new firearm. In a December 1861 memorandum to Simon Cameron, Lincoln's Secretary of War at the time, the Army Chief of Ordnance, Brigadier General James Ripley, found fault with the Spencer's need for special ammunition and the weapon's weight when loaded. He also questioned whether ammunition could be safely carried in the Spencer's magazine. Finally, Ripley opined that the Spencer did not offer any advantage over other breech-loading carbines, such as the Sharps, because the rate of fire for other carbines was adequate.[48]

Despite the objections of the army's Chief of Ordnance, on the day after Christmas 1861, the army offered Spencer and his associates a contract for the purchase of 10,000 repeating rifles.[49] The army's contract required deliveries to begin in March 1862 on a schedule—roughly 1,000 per month—that proved impossible since at the time Christopher Spencer had no factory in which to produce the weapons. The first 1,000 Spencers were finally shipped to the Columbus, Ohio, arsenal in January 1863, and from there were issued to four independent companies of Ohio Sharpshooters. The first regiment in the Cavalry Corps of the Army of the Potomac to receive Spencers was the 5th Michigan, which was issued 479 of the weapons shortly before the battle of Gettysburg.

During the remainder of 1863 and 1864, Spencer rifles and carbines replaced many of the Sharps, Burnsides, and various other carbines in the Cavalry Corps as the army eventually issued more than 57,000 Spencer repeaters to Union soldiers. The army purchased roughly 107,000 Spencers, but deliveries of the 1865 model of the weapon did not begin until April 1865 and consequently very few were issued to the troops.[50] The repeaters were distributed throughout the Union army with the Army of the Potomac receiving its fair share. By August 1864, sixteen of Sheridan's regiments were fully armed with Spencers and three regiments were partially armed with Spencers.[51]

The Spencer met with immediate approval from soldiers and combat commanders, who almost universally praised the effectiveness of the weapon. References to Spencer repeaters in the *Official Records* generally fall into two categories: testimonials to the improved combat effectiveness of units armed with Spencers and requests that the Ordnance Department issue Spencers to units—both infantry and cavalry—equipped with muzzle loading or breech loading weapons. One of the more interesting comment regarding Spencers was made on April 4, 1865, by Colonel E.D. Osband, who commanded a cavalry brigade in the District of West Tennessee. Regarding a recent skirmish along the Memphis and Charleston Railroad, Osband wrote: "I do not understand how thirty men armed with Spencer carbines could be driven by about sixty rebels armed with Enfield rifles." Osband went on to demand an investigation of the incident.[52]

The army's most ardent proponent of the Spencer was Brigadier General Wilson, who while chief of the Cavalry Bureau strongly urged that the repeaters be issued to mounted troops. Later in the war, while commanding the cavalry corps of the Department of Mississippi, he wrote to the Chief of Ordnance: "… permit me to observe that all carbines are bad by comparison with the Spencer, and that the troops of this army will receive no other without protest. There is no doubt that the Spencer carbine is the best fire-arm yet put into the hands of the soldier, both for economy of ammunition and maximum effect, physical and moral. Our best officers estimate one man armed with it [is] equivalent to three with any other arm. I have never seen anything else like the confidence inspired by it in the regiments or brigades which have it."[53]

Although quantitative data regarding the performance of Spencer repeaters in battle is lacking, it is generally accepted that Spencers provided three distinct advantages over the weapons they replaced:

- First, a soldier equipped with a Spencer could fire far more rapidly than a soldier armed with most other rifles or carbines. A trained soldier could fire a muzzle-loading weapon approximately three times per minute, and could fire slightly faster with a breech-loading carbine. A soldier armed with a Spencer could fire seven shots in a matter of seconds. Reloading the Spencer's magazine required less than a minute.[54] Units with soldiers armed with Spencers could quickly achieve what today is called "fire superiority" meaning that once in contact, they could fire more, and more effectively, than their enemy.
- Second, as mentioned above the Spencer used metal rimfire cartridges, while most earlier-developed weapons used paper or linen cartridges with the powder ignited by percussion caps. The Spencer's metallic cartridges were essentially impervious to water. They could be reliably loaded and fired in a driving rain, or immediately after being immersed in a river. For the first time soldiers—at least those armed with Spencers—need not worry about keeping their powder dry.[55]
- Third, soldiers lying prone could easily reload their Spencers, a task that was difficult for soldiers armed with muzzle-loading weapons. Fighting from a prone position provided two advantages. First, a soldier lying on the ground presented a much smaller target to the enemy than a soldier standing upright. Second, while lying prone with elbows on the ground, a soldier could steady his aim and fire more accurately, particularly at longer ranges.

Perhaps more important was an intangible advantage of the Spencer alluded to by Wilson. Troopers armed with the modern repeater felt more confident, and thus more willing to fight aggressively, even when outnumbered.

Much to the frustration of commanders and their men, distribution of the Spencers was sporadic. The popular repeater was in demand in all theaters, and that demand far surpassed the capability of the manufacturer to produce the weapons and the Ordnance Department to distribute them. In response to limited supplies, innovative distribution schemes were implemented. Usually, Spencers were issued first to veteran regiments, which were considered deserving of the more modern weapons. On occasion, when there were insufficient Spencers for all troopers, the repeaters were issued to a regiment's two "flanker" companies—companies habitually positioned on the right and left of the regimental line—or to individual marksmen. On several occasions, commanders arranged for Spencers to be transferred between regiments to better equip soldiers for important missions.[56]

While Spencers were appreciated by soldiers who carried them, and were envied by those who did not, the question remained: Would the Spencers prove decisive in the battles to come?

Although much had been undertaken to improve the combat capabilities of Union cavalry, problems—although somewhat ameliorated—persisted. During the second week of April 1864, Captain Frederick C. Newhall, an officer of the 6th Pennsylvania Cavalry detailed to the corps staff as an assistant inspector general, inspected the regiments of the 1st and 3rd Cavalry Divisions.[57] In the 1st Brigade, 3rd Division, he noted "large deficiencies of carbines and pistols in all regiments but one." However, the one satisfactory regiment was the 1st Connecticut Cavalry which was armed with Smith carbines, which were reported as "entirely unreliable." Additionally, the 1st Connecticut had another, potentially more serious, problem. Assigned to the regiment were eighty-five men who had deserted from the Confederate cavalry and taken the oath of allegiance to the Union. The regimental commander had no confidence that the deserters would fight, and recommended that they be sent to the rear. Newhall concurred with that assessment.

The 2nd Brigade, 3rd Division had "very large deficiencies of arms and horses" and the brigade "had become considerably disorganized during the winter from the effects of General Kilpatrick's raid and too frequent changes of commanders." The 1st Brigade, 1st Division was reported as "very small with about 250 dismounted men." The Reserve Brigade's "horses are used up, and are in a deplorable condition for active duty in the field." Newhall also noted that the men of the 1st New York Dragoons were armed with Joslyn carbines which were "unreliable and worthless." He recommended that the weapons be turned in and the regiment rearmed, finding, "It is rather unaccountable that this has not been done before." Colonel Devin's brigade, the 2nd of the 1st Division, fared the best. Although Newhall found "large deficiencies of horses and arms," he reported that Devin's brigade had the best horses in either division. Overall, Newhall noted that the regiments were in no condition to "perform active duty with credit, on account of the condition of the horses" which had resulted from "heavy outpost duty in all sorts of weather, and almost no long forage." Newhall went on to opine that "paper reports give no idea of the state of these commands. I am convinced that both divisions cannot put into line of battle 5,000 efficient cavalry at the present time."[58]

While Newhall recommended that the two divisions' regiments be relieved of duty and devote their "whole attention to reorganizing," little time remained to fully correct many of the deficiencies he documented.

8

"I will not fight under the orders of a Dutchman*"*
Changes in the Composition of the Union Cavalry Corps

Of the twenty-five Union regiments assigned to the Cavalry Corps of the Army of the Potomac when Alfred Pleasonton attacked J.E.B. Stuart at Brandy Station in June 1863, twenty-one remained with the Army of the Potomac a year later.[1] Of those twenty-one regiments, three continued under the command of the same officers who had led them a year earlier: Major William Stedman of the 6th Ohio had been promoted to colonel of his regiment; Colonel Luigi di Cesnola, who had briefly served as a brigade commander in May-June 1863 and been captured at Aldie, had returned to the command of his regiment, the 4th New York, after ten months in Libby Prison; and Colonel John Taylor, who led the 1st Pennsylvania in its charge up Fleetwood Hill, remained in command of that regiment.

In all military organizations, a certain amount of turnover among commanders can be expected. Deserving officers, such as Wesley Merritt and Henry Davies, were promoted, making way for the advancement of their subordinates. Further, in wartime, combat leaders are under almost constant threat of being killed or wounded, and casualties among commanding officers created more opportunity for junior officers to advance in grade. Calvin Douty, colonel of the 1st Maine, was killed at Aldie and his highly capable deputy, Lieutenant Colonel Charles Smith, took command of the regiment and was, in time, promoted to colonel. A more complex sequence occurred in the 1st New Jersey. Colonel Percy Wyndham, the regiment's colonel who was in brigade command on June 9, was shot in the leg on Fleetwood Hill and subsequently transferred to the cavalry remount depot in Washington. The lieutenant colonel of the regiment, Virgil Broderick, who led the New Jersey men in the fighting that day, was killed on Fleetwood Hill. The senior major of the regiment, John Shelmire, was shot and killed during the withdrawal from the Fleetwood Hill. Although he recovered quickly from his wound, Wyndham only returned to duty with the cavalry for several weeks in September 1863.[2] During that time, in an unusual move, Wyndham recommended that the governor of New Jersey promote Captain John Kester over the regiment's two other majors to fill the position made vacant by Broderick's death. The governor complied, and upon Wyndham's discharge in July 1864, Kester was promoted to colonel of the regiment.[3]

Changes in command were also brought about by other, more mundane, reasons. For

8. *"I will not fight under the orders of a Dutchman"*

example, Colonel Josiah Kellogg, 17th Pennsylvania, was on extended sick leave from April 29, 1864, until November 1, 1864. After briefly returning to duty, Kellogg resigned his volunteer commission on December 27, 1864, and was detailed to a board of officers in Springfield, Massachusetts, examining breech loading arms. As campaigning began in 1864, the regiment was under the command of Lieutenant Colonel James Q. Anderson, a civil engineer who had recruited Company A and been commissioned as its first lieutenant when the regiment was formed in October 1862.[4] Lieutenant Colonel William Doster, 4th Pennsylvania Cavalry, contracted malaria and resigned his commission in October 1863. Major George Covode was promoted to fill Doster's position, and then promoted to colonel in May 1864.[5] A more complex set of circumstances altered the chain of command in the 3rd Indiana. George Chapman, the 3rd Indiana's colonel, was acting in brigade command. The regiment's lieutenant colonel was assigned with four of the regiment's companies on duty in Tennessee. William McClure, the major of that portion of the regiment assigned to the Army of the Potomac, was discharged that he might accept appointment as the colonel of the newly formed 9th Indiana Cavalry. Upon McClure's resignation, Captain William Patton was promoted in his stead. Since the regiment's colonel and lieutenant colonel billets were both encumbered, day-to-day command of the 3rd Indiana with the Army of the Potomac devolved upon Major Patton. Patton had begun his military service as first lieutenant of the regiment's Company A when the company mustered-in in August 1861.[6]

Despite the heavy—roughly eighty percent—turnover, the quality of the leadership among the Army of the Potomac's cavalry regiments had improved in the year since Brandy Station. The officers appointed to regimental command had, for the most part, joined their regiments at the beginning of the war and had served with the colors since. While during the first two years of the war the cavalry arm had been misused, the Army of the Potomac's mounted regiments had seen much hard service in the summer and fall of 1863. Beginning at Kelly's Ford in March, the blue-clad horsemen had gone up against their Southern counterparts in head-to-head combat on many occasions. The officers had learned their leadership skills while on-the-job at Brandy Station, Aldie, Upperville, Hanover, Gettysburg, and in many other raids, skirmishes, engagements, and battles.

Of typical experience was Colonel Charles H. Smith, who assumed command of the 1st Maine Cavalry after Colonel Calvin Douty's death. Smith, a thirty-three-year-old teacher from Eastport, Maine, had enlisted in September 1861 and was quickly appointed captain of Company D. He served with the regiment at Cedar Mountain and Second Manassas before being detailed as provost marshal of Frederick, Maryland, during the Antietam Campaign. In February 1863, after five months of maintaining order in Frederick, Smith returned to the regiment to be promoted to major, and, a month later, to lieutenant colonel. As Douty's second in command, he accompanied the regiment on Stoneman's Raid. On June 9, with Douty temporarily separated from the regiment, Smith took charge and extricated the 1st Maine from Rebel lines after its charge at Fleetwood Hill. After Douty was killed at Aldie, Smith led the 1st Maine through the summer and fall campaigns in Maryland, Pennsylvania, and the Virginia Piedmont.[7] By all standards, Smith was a seasoned combat leader and fully qualified to command a regiment.

The new commander of the 4th Pennsylvania Cavalry, Colonel George Covode, had similar military experience. At the outbreak of the war, Covode had enlisted as a private in what became Company D, 4th Pennsylvania Cavalry. Shortly afterward, Covode, the son of an influential member of the U.S. Congress, was elected first lieutenant of the company, promoted to captain of the company, and then in March 1862, promoted to major. Upon the departure of Lieutenant Colonel Doster in the fall of 1863, Covode moved up in grade. Some in the regiment believed that Covode's father orchestrated Doster's departure and that Covode thus obtained his promotion through "a little wire-pulling and political chicanery." In reality, as either a captain or a major, the twenty-eight-year-old Covode had participated in most of the campaigns of the Army of the Potomac, frequently acting in command of the 4th Pennsylvania while Doster was ill. Despite some suspicions regarding the legitimacy of his promotion, Covode was acknowledged by his men to be a "reliable and efficient officer" and was soon promoted to colonel of the regiment.[8]

One area which continued to be problematic within the Union army was the appointment of commanders for the regiments of the regular army. By regulation, regular regiments were commanded by the senior regular officer present for duty with the regiment. Many regular officers, particularly those holding field grade commissions, had transferred to the ranks of the volunteers as either colonels or generals. With the regular field grade billets thus encumbered by absentees, the regular regiments were usually commanded by company grade officers. As at Brandy Station, in the spring of 1864, all four regular regiments in Sheridan's cavalry corps were commanded by captains. These officers may have served faithfully and well, and they may have even had greater experience than their counterparts in volunteer regiments. Nonetheless, army regulations prohibited their promotion, and they could thus not receive the greater authority, prestige, and pay that came with wearing eagles on their epaulets.

The 1st U.S. Cavalry was commanded by Captain Nelson Sweitzer. An 1853 graduate of West Point, Sweitzer spent the first two years of the war as an aide de camp to Major General McClellan. He returned to duty with the regiment in August 1863 and as the senior officer present assumed command.[9] The 5th U.S. was commanded by Abraham Arnold, an 1859 academy graduate. Arnold served with the regiment during the first year of the war and was severely wounded at Gaines Mill in June 1862. After three months convalescent leave, he was detailed to recruiting duty for a year. He then returned to the cavalry corps and assumed command of the regiment in September 1863.[10] Captain Ira Claflin graduated from West Point in 1857 and was commissioned as a lieutenant in the Regiment of Mounted Rifles. He spent most of his early career in New Mexico. In February and April 1862, he commanded a company in the battles at Val Verde and Peralta and was brevetted captain for his service.[11] Returning to the East, Claflin served with the 6th U.S. from the summer of 1862 and was wounded during the Gettysburg campaign, earning a brevet to major. After recovering, he returned to the regiment and assumed command in September 1863.[12] Unlike the other commanders of regular regiments, Theophilus Rodenbough was commissioned in the 2nd U.S. from civilian life in March 1861. He participated with the regiment during the Peninsula Campaign commanding a company. At Second Manassas he was captured and held briefly before being exchanged. He served with the regiment during the campaigns of 1863, and in the absence of more senior officers, had commanded the regiment during the Battle of Gettysburg. Rodenbough again took command in the spring of 1864 when a more senior captain, George A. Gordon, left the regiment to serve as aide de camp to Major General Torbert.[13]

In the spring of 1864, most regimental commanders were supported by experienced field grade and company grade officers, and a cadre of now-veteran noncommissioned officers.

8. "*I will not fight under the orders of a* Dutchman"

Further, the soldierly qualities of the men in the ranks had been vastly improved by the hard campaigning during the summer and fall of 1863.

As noted at the beginning of this chapter, numerous changes had occurred in the composition of the Cavalry Corps between the summer of 1863 and the beginning of campaigning in 1864. Of the twenty-five regiments assigned to the Cavalry Corps at the Battle of Brandy Station, four had been reassigned to other commands, and one—the 3rd Pennsylvania Cavalry—had left the Cavalry Corps for duty with the provost guard at the Army of the Potomac's headquarters.[14] The four regiments that left the Army of the Potomac were the 8th and 12th Illinois, the 1st Maryland, and the 1st Rhode Island. During those eleven intervening months between June 1863 and May 1864, however, fourteen cavalry regiments had been added to the Army of the Potomac—ten with the Cavalry Corps and four with Major General Ambrose Burnside's IX Corps.[15] Thus Major General Philip Sheridan had under his command thirty-one regiments as campaigning began in the spring of 1864.[16] These changes in the organization of the cavalry corps are summarized below. Please refer to Table 3 at the end of this chapter for a summary of the major changes to the Army of the Potomac's cavalry corps.

The 8th Illinois had departed for Chicago on its veterans' furlough in January 1864. Upon returning to the East in late February, the regiment was sent to Giesboro for remounting and was then assigned to provost guard duties in the District of Columbia. Grant, at the urging of Sheridan, had requested that the regiment be immediately returned to duty with the Army of Potomac. Somewhat surprisingly, Halleck informed Grant that the 8th Illinois could not be spared. Sheridan continued to press the issue, prompting John A. Rawlins, Grant's chief of staff, to tersely advise the cavalry commander, "The general [Grant] has asked twice to have the Eighth Illinois Cavalry ordered here, but has been answered both times that it cannot be spared from Washington, hence it has not been returned to you."[17] For the remainder of the war, the bulk of the regiment performed duties associated with defense of the capital, including fighting in Maryland during Early's summer 1864 incursion, and against Mosby in Northern Virginia. However, five companies of the regiment rejoined the Army of the Potomac on May 15, 1864, and initially performed security duties at Belle Plain, Virginia.[18]

The 12th Illinois Cavalry, which did not participate in the battle at Brandy Station, left the Army of the Potomac in November 1863, en route to Chicago and furlough for its reenlisted veterans. In February 1864, the regiment was ordered to Louisiana and fought there and in Mississippi until the end of the war.[19]

In February 1864, the War Department transferred the 1st Maryland Cavalry to a separate cavalry brigade headquartered in Baltimore. The regiment remained in Baltimore until May 1864, when it was dismounted and reorganized as infantry. The new foot-soldiers were then assigned to Major General Benjamin Butler's Army of the James.[20]

In January 1864, the War Department transferred the 1st Rhode Island Cavalry to duty in the defenses of Washington. After brief service providing security at Belle Plain during the summer of 1864, the regiment returned to duty with the Cavalry Corps.[21]

While four regiments had left the Army of the Potomac, during the course of the year ten additional regiments had been assigned to that army's Cavalry Corps. The cavalry corps gained most of the new regiments during the Gettysburg Campaign when, after much urging by Alfred Pleasonton, the War Department transferred General Julius Stahel's cavalry division, which had previously been deployed in defense of Washington, from the XXII Corps. Stahel had been born in Hungary and Pleasonton was known to be prejudiced against foreign-born officers. When lobbying for control of the division, Pleasonton had written to a confidant, Congressman John Farnsworth, "Tell the President from me that I will sacrifice my life to support his Government & save the country, but that I will not *fight* under the orders of a *Dutchman* [emphasis in original]."[22] Since Stahel, as a major general was senior to Pleasonton, a brigadier, it was necessary for the War Department to relieve Stahel from command when the division was transferred to the cavalry corps.

Of the nine regiments joining the Cavalry Corps during the Gettysburg Campaign, half belonged to what became known as the "Michigan Brigade," which, as the name indicates, consisted of regiments from the State of Michigan.

The 5th Michigan was raised in Detroit over the summer of 1862. It mustered into the service in August of that year and left for Washington in December. The 6th Michigan mustered into service in October 1862 in Grand Rapids, and, like the 5th Michigan, traveled to Washington in December of that year. State officials began raising the 7th Michigan in October 1862, with the final companies being assigned to the organization in June 1863. The first battalion of the 7th Michigan moved to Washington in late February 1863.[23]

In Washington, the three Michigan Regiments were initially assigned to a provisional cavalry brigade in Brigadier General Silas Casey's infantry division. In March, the provisional brigade was re-designated the 1st Brigade of the Cavalry Division—the division commanded by Major General Stahel—of the XXII Corps. The brigade was commanded by Brigadier General Joseph T. Copeland. Copeland had initially served as the lieutenant colonel of the 1st Michigan Cavalry before being commissioned colonel of the 5th Michigan when that regiment was organized.[24]

Joseph T. Copeland, who as a colonel commanded the 5th Michigan, was promoted to brigadier general in November 1862 and appointed to command of what became known as the Michigan Brigade. In June 1863, Copeland's regiments were assigned to the Cavalry Corps and placed under the command of newly-promoted George Custer. Through the remainder of the war, Copeland commanded draft depots at Annapolis and Pittsburg and the military prison at Alton, Illinois (Library of Congress).

Once in the Capital, the men of the three Michigan regiments spent most of their time at drill. Although Francis W. Kellogg, who represented Grand Rapids in the U.S. Congress, boasted to Presi-

8. "I will not fight *under the orders of a* Dutchman"   99

dent Lincoln that the "wolverines" would pursue and capture J.E.B. Stuart, the three regiments saw almost no service in the field while serving under Casey and Stahel.[25]

The 1st Michigan Cavalry was mustered into service at Detroit in September 1861. It spent the winter of 1861–1862 along the upper Potomac, and in the spring of 1862 fought in the Shenandoah Valley under Major General Nathaniel Banks.[26] In the summer or 1862, the regiment served with the Army of Virginia under Major General John Pope. At Second Manassas, the regiment was severely mauled, losing 7 killed, 18 wounded, 7 known captured, and 106 missing. Among casualties was the regimental commander, Colonel Thornton R. Brodhead, who was shot leading a charge and died the following week.[27] Afterward, the War Department detailed the 1st Michigan to the defenses of Washington. Unlike the other Michigan Regiments, the 1st was assigned to the 2nd Brigade of Stahel's Division.

On June 27, 1863, as the Union army moved toward Gettysburg, General Stahel's division was assigned to the Cavalry Corps of the Army of the Potomac. Stahel, who was senior to Pleasonton, and his two brigade commanders were relieved of their duties. Pleasonton assigned Judson Kilpatrick to command of the division, and two days later the newly-promoted Brigadier General George Custer assumed command of the Michigan Brigade. As part of that reorganization, the 1st Michigan joined the other Michigan regiments in Custer's command.

As campaigning began in the spring of 1864, the 1st Michigan was commanded by Lieutenant Colonel Peter Stagg since the regiment's colonel, Charles H. Town, was in Michigan on extended convalescent leave. Stagg's first appointment had been as second lieutenant of Company K when the regiment was formed, and he had served with the regiment ever since.[28] The 5th Michigan was commanded by Colonel Russell Alger. Alger began the war as a Captain in the 2nd Michigan Cavalry where he had served briefly under Sheridan in Missouri, and been wounded and captured in an engagement at Boonesville, Mississippi. In October 1862, Alger

Major General Julius Stahel, a Hungarian by birth, was forced from division command in June 1863 so that his division could be transferred to the Cavalry Corps, which was commanded by Brigadier General Alfred Pleasonton (Pleasonton was junior to Stahel). Stahel was later appointed to command of a cavalry division under Hunter and was seriously wounded at Piedmont on June 5, 1864. In 1893, Stahel was awarded the Medal of Honor for his actions that day (Library of Congress).

was exchanged and assigned as Lieutenant Colonel of the 6th Michigan. Six months later he was appointed to command of the 5th Michigan. Alger had received a second wound during the Gettysburg Campaign.[29] George Gray, the colonel of the 6th Michigan, had been on either convalescent leave—chronic lumbar pain—or court-martial duty since September 1863. The regiment's lieutenant colonel was also absent, detailed to conscription duty in Michigan. Consequently, the regiment began the campaign under the command of Major James H. Kidd. Kidd, from Ionia, had been a student at the University of Michigan at the outbreak of the War and delayed joining the colors until October 1862, when he mustered-in as captain of Company E of the 6th.[30] In May 1864, the 7th Michigan began the campaign under the command of Major Henry W. Granger since the regiment's colonel, William D. Mann, and a more senior major had recently resigned their commissions. Granger, an experienced and well-respected officer, became one of Custer's favorite subordinates.

In addition to the Michigan regiments, at Gettysburg the 5th New York, 2nd Pennsylvania, 18th Pennsylvania, and 1st Vermont joined the Cavalry Corps.

The 5th New York had been recruited and organized in New York City in the fall of 1861. It had seen service in the Shenandoah Valley and in Pope's Army of Virginia before being assigned to the defenses of Washington in September 1862.[31] The commander of the regiment as campaigning began in 1864 was Lieutenant Colonel John Hammond who in September 1861 began his service with the regiment as captain of Company H. Hammond had commanded the regiment since the summer of 1863.[32]

The 2nd Pennsylvania had been raised in April 1862, with most of the companies recruited from the Philadelphia area. After moving to Washington, the regiment was assigned to Pope's Army of Virginia. The first major action in which the regiment fought was the battle of Chantilly at the close of the Second Manassas Campaign. During the Gettysburg Campaign, the regiment was detailed to policing stragglers and guarding prisoners, and it thus saw little action. After Gettysburg, the regiment was assigned to the 2nd Brigade of Gregg's division.[33] In 1864, the regimental commander, Colonel Richard B. Price, disgruntled that he was not selected for promotion, sought service on a military commission in Washington, leaving the regiment under the command of Lieutenant Colonel Joseph P. Brinton.[34]

The 18th Pennsylvania was raised in the fall of 1862. In December it moved to Bladensburg, Maryland, and in January 1863 deployed to Northern Virginia as part of Wyndham's brigade. For the following six months the regiment participated in fruitless searches for partisan leader John Mosby. Initially the men were armed only with sabers, making them essentially ineffective. Reportedly, Mosby wrote a note to Federal authorities complaining that the men of the 18th Pennsylvania were so poorly equipped that they were not worth capturing. In the reorganization of the cavalry during the Gettysburg Campaign, the 18th Pennsylvania was assigned to the 1st Brigade—commanded by newly promoted Brigadier General Elon Farnsworth—of Kilpatrick's Division which was later commanded by James Wilson.[35] For much of the time the brigade was commanded by the regiment's colonel, Thomas Bryan, leaving the regiment under the command of Lieutenant Colonel William P. Brinton, whose younger brother, Joseph, was the lieutenant colonel of the 2nd Pennsylvania.[36]

The 1st Vermont Cavalry, the sole cavalry regiment from that state, was mustered into service in November 1861. The regiment had seen service in the Valley with Nathaniel Banks, and at Second Manassas before being transferred to the defenses of Washington. The colonel of the Regiment was Edward Sawyer, a lawyer by profession before the beginning of the war.

Sawyer had been frequently absent from the regiment either convalescing from injury or recruiting in Vermont. After performing poorly in acting brigade command during the Dahlgren raid, Sawyer resigned his commission on April 29, 1864. He was replaced in command by Lieutenant Colonel Addison W. Preston, a change that was welcomed by most of the men of the regiment. Preston had frequently acted in command of the regiment in Sawyer's absence, and had been wounded twice.[37]

Finally, the 1st West Virginia Cavalry had been organized in the summer and fall of 1861. It had briefly been assigned to the Army of the Potomac in early 1862, but before the Peninsula Campaign had been sent to the Valley and then assigned to Pope's Army of Virginia. After Antietam the regiment had been assigned to the defenses of Washington and eventually placed under the command of Stahel. In December 1863, the regiment left the Army of the Potomac and returned to West Virginia for duty.[38]

Two regiments, the 1st Connecticut Cavalry and the 19th New York Cavalry, joined the Cavalry after the Gettysburg Campaign.

The 1st Connecticut Cavalry had been initially organized as a battalion in November 1862. It had seen brief service with the Army of the Potomac in late 1862, but had spent most of its service in West Virginia and in the defense of Baltimore. In January 1864, the War Department authorized the battalion to be brought up to regimental strength, and two months later the regiment joined the Cavalry Corps at Brandy Station. The Colonel of the regiment, William Fish, had been court-martialed and dismissed from the service and the lieutenant colonel, Charles Farnsworth, resigned his commission following his exchange after six month confinement in Libby Prison. In the absence of more senior officers, command devolved upon Major Erastus Blakeslee who had served with the regiment since its organization.[39] Blakeslee had established a reputation within the 1st Connecticut as a talented and efficient officer.

Perhaps the most unique new regiment in the cavalry corps was the 19th New York Cavalry, which was better known as the 1st New York Dragoons. The regiment had originally been organized at Portage, New York, in August 1862 as the 130th New York Volunteer Infantry. Its commander was a dragoon in the "old army," Colonel Alfred Gibbs, an 1846 West Point graduate and Mexican War veteran. The War Department initially posted the regiment to Suffolk, Virginia, where its men saw little action during their first year of service. In part responding to persistent requests from Colonel Gibbs, the War Department in the summer of 1863 ordered the regiment converted from infantry to cavalry, and the men went into camp near Manassas to be reequipped, mounted, and retrained.[40]

Like most men of the time, many of the former infantrymen of the 1st New York Dragoons knew how to ride horses. However, they needed much training to become proficient cavalrymen. As part of that training, the men received "lessons by the hour" on the proper method for mounting their horses. Colonel Gibbs, a stickler for discipline, was not satisfied until the men's movements at the commands "prepare to mount" and "mount" were conducted with precision, and in complete unison. After two months of training—interrupted by frequent raids from Mosby's guerrillas—the regiment joined the Reserve Brigade for the September 1863 advance through Culpeper to the Rapidan River.[41]

Despite losing a few regiments, in the ten months since Brandy Station, the cavalry of the Army of the Potomac had been considerably strengthened. In the spring of 1863, General Joseph Hooker had available twenty-five cavalry regiments with which to "disperse and destroy" J.E.B. Stuart's cavalry division on the fields of eastern Culpeper County. General

Grant, as he began the Overland Campaign, had available thirty-five regiments, including his headquarters provost guard and regiments in Burnside's corps. General Alfred Pleasonton could place roughly eight thousand sabers on the field at Brandy Station. As campaigning began in May 1864, Sheridan, with the thirty regiments of the cavalry corps, could probably mount in excess of 12,000 troopers. Less tangible, but no less important, both officers and men had much greater confidence in their ability to take the fight to J.E.B. Stuart's horsemen than they felt in the spring of 1863.

Table 3

Transition of the AoP Cavalry Corps

BRANDY STATION—JUNE 9, 1863

1st Division		2nd Division		3rd Division	
1st Brigade	**2nd Brigade**	**1st Brigade**	**2nd Brigade**	**1st Brigade**	**2nd Brigade**
8th New York	6th New York	1st Mass.	3rd Penn.	1st Maine	1st New Jersey
8th Illinois	17th Penn.	6th Ohio	4th Penn.	2nd New York	1st Maryland
9th New York		1st Rhode Island	16th Penn.	10th New York	1st Penn.
3rd Indiana		4th New York			12th Illinois

Reserve Brigade

1st U.S.	6th U.S.
2nd U.S.	6th Penn.
5th U.S.	

GETTYSBURG, JULY 1-3, 1863

1st Division			2nd Division		
1st Brigade	**2nd Brigade**	**Reserve Brigade**	**1st Brigade**	**2nd Brigade**	**3rd Brigade**
8th New York	6th New York	1st U.S.	1st New Jersey	2nd New York	1st Maine
8th Illinois	9th New York	2nd U.S.	1st Maryland	4th New York	10th New York
12th Illinois	17th Penn	5th U.S.	1st Mass.	6th Ohio	4th Penn.
3rd Indiana	6th U.S.	1st Penn.	8th Penn.	16th Penn.	
		6th Penn.	3rd Penn.	1st Rhode Island	

3rd Division

1st Brigade		2nd Brigade
5th New York	18th Penn.	1st Michigan
2nd Penn	1st Vermont	5th Michigan
1st West Virginia		6th Michigan
		7th Michigan

8. *"I will not fight under the orders of a* Dutchman*"*

OVERLAND CAMPAIGN—MAY, 1864
6th U.S. – Headquarters Escort

1st Division		*2nd Division*		*3rd Division*	
1st Brigade	**2nd Brigade**	**1st Brigade**	**2nd Brigade**	**1st Brigade**	**2nd Brigade**
1st Michigan	4th New York	1st New Jersey	1st Maine	1st Conn.	1st Vermont
5th Michigan	6th New York	1st Mass.	2nd Penn.	2nd New York	3rd Indiana
6th Michigan	9th New York	1st Penn.	4th Penn.	5th New York	8th New York
7th Michigan	17th Penn.	6th Ohio	8th Penn.	18th Penn.	
			16th Penn.		
			10th New York		

Reserve Brigade

1st U.S.	2nd U.S.	5th U.S.	19th New York	6th Penn.

NOT SHOWN: four regiments (3rd New Jersey; 22nd New York; 2nd Ohio; 13th Penn.) assigned to IX Corps. On May 26, the 13th Pennsylvania was reassigned to the 2nd Brigade, 2nd Division of the Cavalry Corps.

9

"Break up the railroad"
Grant's Concept for a Cavalry Raid

The four weeks since the Army of the Potomac crossed the Rapidan River, and began what later became known as the Overland Campaign, had been frustrating for the newly-appointed general-in-chief, Ulysses S. Grant. Grant had hoped to quickly draw Robert E. Lee's Army of Northern Virginia into decisive battle and destroy it, and thus far the two armies had fought three pitched battles during the campaign. The opening battle in the Wilderness area of Spotsylvania County had been bloody, but indecisive. The second battle, near a country hamlet named Spotsylvania Courthouse, was equally bloody, but a Union victory. However, Lee's army, although defeated at Spotsylvania, had not been destroyed. Grant, undeterred, continued moving to his left—called "sidling"—to threaten Richmond and thereby force Lee to fight again. Lee, using interior lines, kept his veterans between the Union army and Richmond and offered battle when advantageous to the Southern cause. On June 3, the two armies clashed again at Cold Harbor. This time the Army of the Potomac was bloodily repulsed.[1] Unable to threaten Richmond by marching further to his left, and faced with a weakened, but still potent adversary, Grant changed his operational plan.

While Grant's initial operational objective had been to destroy Lee's army north of Richmond, after the defeat at Cold Harbor, Grant decided that the best path to victory was to sever the supply lines leading from Richmond to the west and south. Grant surmised that without a steady supply of food and for both men and horses—delivered almost entirely by rail to Richmond and from there to the army—Lee would be unable to remain around Richmond and would thus be forced to withdraw toward southwestern Virginia or into the Carolinas. In Grant's view, he would have better opportunity to destroy Lee's army during that withdrawal than if he continued to threaten Richmond from the north and east. Additionally, the abandonment of Richmond by the Confederate government would be a strategic blow to the South.

Executing this plan, however, would require the Army of the Potomac to shift from the north side of the James River to the south, a movement fraught with risk. The James River was a significant obstacle, and Lee, with bridges in Richmond at his disposal might attack either north or south of the river while the Army of the Potomac was in the midst of crossing on ferry boats and pontoon bridges. A year earlier, President Lincoln had cautioned Major General Joseph Hooker that an army crossing a river was like an ox caught on a fence: unable to either gore to the front or kick-out behind. However, if Lincoln held similar reservations about Grant's plan, he kept them to himself.[2]

9. "Break up the railroad"

This photograph, dated June 4, 1864, shows General Ulysses S. Grant with his horse, Cincinnati. Note Cincinnati's height at its withers, and that Grant has a "horse pistol" affixed to the pommel of his saddle (Library of Congress).

The first hint of the pending shift in Grant's operational focus appeared on June 4, the day after the debacle at Cold Harbor, when the Army of the Potomac's quartermaster, Brigadier General Rufus Ingalls telegraphed Major General Montgomery Meigs, the army's Quartermaster General in Washington: "Lt Gen Grant wishes to receive a Lot of Implements to be used by our Cavalry in the Destruction of Rail Roads. Gen Haupt had several Kinds at Alexandria. Will you please have as many as can be procured and sent by Express to Capt P.P. Pitkin at White House & inform me by telegraph of what we may Expect."[3] Brigadier General Herman Haupt was in charge of the Federal military railroad system. Captain P.P. Pitkin was the quartermaster officer in charge of the Army of the Potomac's supply depot at White House on the Pamunkey River.

The following day, June 5, Grant began issuing the orders necessary to execute his new plan. He first telegraphed the army's Chief of Staff, Major General Henry Halleck, in Washington with an outline of the plan and his rationale for why it was necessary.

A full survey of all the ground satisfies me that it would not be practicable to hold a line northeast of Richmond that would protect the Fredericksburg railroad, to enable us to use it for supplying the army. To do so would give us a long vulnerable line of road to protect, exhausting much of our strength in guarding it, and would leave open to the enemy all of his lines of communication on the south side of the James. My idea from the start has been to beat Lee's army, if possible, north of Richmond, then, after destroying his lines of communication north of the James River, to transfer the army to the south side and besiege Lee in Richmond, or follow him south if he should retreat. I now find, after more than thirty days of trial, that the enemy deems it of the first importance to run no risks with the armies they now have. They act purely on the defensive, behind breast-works, or feebly on the offensive immediately in front of them, and where in case of repulse they can instantly retire behind them. Without a greater sacrifice of human life than I am willing to make, all cannot be accomplished that I had designed outside of the city. I have, therefore, resolved upon the following plan: I will continue to hold substantially the ground now occupied by the Army of the Potomac, taking advantage of any favorable circumstance that may present itself, until the cavalry can be sent west to destroy the Virginia Central Railroad from about Beaver Dam for some 25 or 30 miles west. When this is effected, I will move the army to the south side of James River, either by crossing the Chickahominy and marching near to City Point, or by going to the mouth of the Chickahominy on the north side and crossing there. To provide for this last and most probable contingency six or more ferry-boats of the largest class ought to be immediately provided. Once on the south side of the James River I can cut off all sources of supply to the enemy, except what is furnished by the canal. If Hunter succeeds in reaching Lynchburg that will be lost to him also. Should Hunter not succeed I will still make the effort to destroy the canal by sending cavalry up the south side of the river with a pontoon train to cross wherever they can. The feeling of the two armies now seems to be that the rebels can protect themselves only by strong intrenchments, while our army is not only confident of protecting itself without intrenchments, but that it can beat and drive the enemy wherever and whenever he can be found without this protection.[4]

That afternoon, Grant, through Meade, directed Sheridan to hold two divisions in readiness to carry out a raid against the Virginia Central Railroad. Specifically, on the morning of June 7, Sheridan and his men were to march on Charlottesville, destroy the bridge over the Rivanna River, and then, falling back, destroy the rail line from the bridge to Gordonsville, and destroy the rail line from Gordonsville to Hanover Junction if practicable.[5] The Virginia Central was the only rail line linking Richmond to western Virginia that lay north of the James and, as a practical matter, destroying it first—before the army shifted south of the James—made sense.

On reflection, Grant later that day modified his concept for Sheridan's raid. As commander of the armies of the United States, not just the Army of the Potomac, Grant was free to coordinate operations among the various armies, departments, and theaters. General David Hunter, then in command of the Department of West Virginia, had that day near Waynesboro defeated a small Confederate force under the command of Brigadier General William E. "Grumble" Jones, and during the battle Jones had been killed. Grant, although not yet aware of that victory, correctly believed Hunter to be near Staunton and moving toward Lynchburg. Grant anticipated that the Confederates would defend Lynchburg, and that Hunter might be defeated by them. So, Grant ordered Hunter to instead move east of the Blue Ridge, intersect the Orange and Alexandria between Lynchburg and Charlottesville, and to destroy the Orange & Alexandria between that point and Charlottesville. In Charlottesville, Hunter was to link-up with Sheridan and accompany the cavalry on its march east to rejoin the Army of the Potomac. Accordingly, the following order was sent by Grant through Meade to Sheridan 8:00 p.m. on June 5:

The object of the cavalry expedition to Charlottesville and Gordonsville is to effectually break up the railroad connection between Richmond and the Shenandoah Valley and Lynchburg. To secure this end they should go as far as Charlottesville, and work upon the Lynchburg branch and main line to Staunton for several miles beyond the junction. This done they could work back this way to where the road is already destroyed, or until driven off by a superior force. It is desirable that every rail on the road destroyed should be so bent or twisted as to make it impossible to repair the road without supplying new rails. After the work is accomplished, herein directed, the cavalry will rejoin the main army, keeping north of the Pamunkey until the position of the army is known to them. It maybe found necessary to keep on the north side as far down as West Point. Instructions will be sent to General Hunter by the cavalry expedition. He will be required to join his force to General Sheridan's and return with him to the Army of the Potomac. If it is found practicable, whilst the cavalry is at the most westerly point reached by it, to detach a brigade or more to go over to the James River and destroy the canal, it will be a service well repaying for three or four days' detention.[6]

Major General David Hunter graduated from West Point in 1822. Selected for promotion to major general early in the war by President Lincoln, Hunter was the army's fourth ranking volunteer officer. As a secondary objective of the raid, Hunter and his army were to link up with Sheridan at Charlottesville and return with the raiders to join the Army of the Potomac (Library of Congress).

In his implementing instructions accompanying Grant's order, Meade informed his cavalry commander that the operation would begin on the morning of June 7, leaving one full day for preparation. Meade's specific instructions to Sheridan were that the objective of the raid was to destroy the bridge over the Rivanna, to "thoroughly" destroy the railroad from that point to Gordonsville, and to destroy the railroad from Gordonsville toward Hanover Junction, and to Hanover Junction, "if practicable." Meade also advised that the army's chief engineer would provide Sheridan a pontoon train of eight boats.[7] All totaled, Sheridan was to thoroughly destroy about twelve miles of track on the Orange & Alexandria, and, if practicable, to destroy about fifty-five miles of the Virginia Central, not counting track from the Rivanna Bridge to the railroad junction in Charlottesville and beyond.

Grant sent implementing orders to Hunter, via Washington, on June 6.[8] From the content of Grant's communications with Halleck, Hunter, and Meade, as well as Meade's communications with Sheridan, it is clear that the primary objective of this raid was the destruction of the railroads supplying Richmond and Lee's Army of Northern Virginia.

The Virginia Central Railroad was chartered in 1836. It ran from Richmond to Jackson's River in the upper Shenandoah Valley, a distance of 195 miles. Major stations along the route were: Hanover Junction where it intersected with the Richmond, Fredericksburg, & Potomac railroad; Gordonsville, a junction with the Orange & Alexandria Railroad from the north; Charlottesville, where the Orange and Alexandria branched off to the south toward its Lynchburg terminus; and Staunton. Two dozen other, less significant stations were scattered every few miles along the route to serve passengers, freight, and to provide water and wood for the railroad's locomotives. At the beginning of the war, the Virginia Central owned 27 locomotives, 23 passenger cars, 11 mail cars, 188 box and flat cars, and 22 sand, coal, and gravel cars. An average train might consist of an engine pulling ten or fifteen cars carrying 150 to 200 tons of cargo. The railroad also owned several hundred slaves who were primarily employed cutting and hauling wood to fuel the locomotives.[9]

Henry D. Witcomb, a northerner, served as superintendent of the line and was responsible for managing its day-to-day operations. The president of the line was Edmund Fontaine, a wealthy planter, who had served in that capacity since the railroad was chartered.[10] Fontaine lived near Beaver Dam Station, a stop on the line forty miles from Richmond. During his pursuit of Sheridan in May, J.E.B. Stuart stopped briefly at Fontaine's home to see his wife and children, who were staying there as houseguests. In his haste—Sheridan's raiders had burned a Confederate supply depot at the station just hours earlier—Stuart did not take time to dismount from his horse on what was to be the last occasion he saw his family.[11]

The Virginia Central's iron rails with hardwood ties were usually laid directly upon the ground with little gravel or rock added as ballast. Consequently, both the speed of trains along the line and the cargo capacity of their cars were limited. By posted schedule, trains averaged roughly fifteen miles per hour. However, by mid–1864, conditions on Virginia's railroads had deteriorated significantly. Before the war, most rails had been bought in the North or imported from Britain. During the Civil War, the Confederacy produced no rails—Southern foundries and iron-works were devoted almost exclusively to producing ordnance. Consequently, the rails were severely worn. Replacement rails, when needed, were obtained by removing track from less important lines. In this regard, the Virginia Central was in better condition at the beginning of the war than many Southern railroads. In February 1861, it had purchased enough iron rails to replace ten miles of track.[12]

Another problem plaguing Southern railroads was the condition of locomotives. Most engines on Virginia rail lines, including the Virginia Central, had been manufactured in the North and during wartime were difficult to maintain. Those that were damaged during Federal raids could not easily be repaired. Other rolling stock had fallen into disrepair as well. Thus, while a train could theoretically travel at a speed of fifteen miles per hour, a speed of eight to ten miles per hour was more the norm. Halts for fuel and water, and lay-overs on sidings, further reduced the average speed of train traffic. By 1864, under the best conditions, trains on the Virginia Central and other lines in Virginia averaged between five to eight miles per hour.[13]

The Virginia Central had been a target for federal destruction earlier in the war. General George Stoneman, whose mission during the Chancellorsville Campaign was to destroy Confederate lines of communication between Lee's army, then in Spotsylvania County, and Richmond, reported afterward that for eighteen miles between Gordonsville and Louisa, his men had destroyed "all the railroad bridges, trains, cars, depots of provisions, lines of telegraphic communication, &c."[14] General John Buford, who commanded the Reserve Brigade during the campaign, reported that at Trevilian's, his men had destroyed the pumps and water tanks, 2 hand carts, a large supply of subsistence stores, and 2 wagons loaded with ammunition and arms. He added that his men had burned cordwood and ties, and that they had destroyed the telegraph by cutting down large sections of wire.[15] However, the damages had been quickly repaired and the line put back into service with no longstanding effect on the Virginia Central's capacity to move men or freight.

Since Grant's infantry had arrived at Cold Harbor on June 2, Sheridan's cavalry, with the exception of Wilson's division, had remained relatively inactive. After a small skirmish that day at Bottoms Bridge on the Pamunkey, Gregg's division had remained camped near Bottoms Bridge until June 5. Torbert's division camped near Bottoms Bridge on June 2 and 3, and then marched to Old Church on June 4, and on to Haw's Shop on June 5. On June 2, Wilson's division marched from Hanover County to a farm on the Totopotomy belonging to a Mr. Linney. On June 3, the division skirmished with Confederate cavalry and infantry near Haw's Shop. For the next two days, Wilson's division had the opportunity to rest, having gone into camp at New Castle Ferry on the Pamunkey River.[16]

Upon receipt of his initial orders for the raid, Sheridan selected Torbert's and Gregg's divisions for the operation, and designated Wilson's division to remain behind and support the infantry corps of the Army of the Potomac as they prepared to withdraw from their positions at Cold Harbor and cross the James. In Sheridan's absence on the raid, Wilson would receive his orders directly from Army of the Potomac Headquarters.[17]

Sheridan's most immediate need was horses. Since the beginning of May, many of his troopers' mounts had been killed or had broken down due to hard use. In May, the Cavalry Bureau had provided 6,683

Brigadier General Henry Hunt, shown in this photograph as a colonel, served as the Army of the Potomac's Chief of Artillery. He disagreed with Grant's plan to reorganize the army's artillery and eliminate its artillery reserve (Library of Congress).

horses to the Cavalry Corps, and an additional 1,000 were shipped during the first week of June.[18] However, those replacement mounts were insufficient. On June 4, Sheridan directed General Gregg immediately dismount the 13th Ohio Mounted Infantry Regiment, which was to report to the 2nd Division the next day, and distribute its horses to the dismounted veterans in his division.[19] Additionally, individual replacements for the various regiments of the Cavalry Corps were dismounted upon their arrival and their horses distributed to veterans.[20]

In the few hours available to them, there was little Sheridan's men could do to prepare for the pending raid, other than rest themselves, and, more importantly, rest their horses. Unfortunately, the terrain northeast of Richmond was poorly suited for recuperation of cavalry. Grass was scarce and of poor quality. Also, although drained by several rivers, sources of fresh water were limited.

While most of the cavalry rested, the horse artillery batteries which supported the Cavalry Corps were busy reorganizing. Two weeks into the Overland Campaign, General Grant concluded that the all of the artillery assigned to the Army of the Potomac was not needed. Each infantry corps was assigned one brigade of artillery, and three brigades of artillery were assigned to the Army of the Potomac's "Artillery Reserve." During the battles in the Wilderness and at Spotsylvania, the batteries of the Artillery Reserve were not employed, and in Grant's view, they merely impeded traffic over already-clogged roads. On May 16, Grant ordered the Artillery Reserve disbanded and the batteries sent to Belle Plain for further assignment.[21]

Brigadier General Henry J. Hunt, the Army of the Potomac's Chief of Artillery, did not agree with Grant's decision. Hunt convinced Grant it would be better to retain all the army's batteries, and instead downsize six-gun batteries to four guns each. Consequently, General Meade issued a special order reducing the size of many of the army's batteries. In addition, Meade disbanded the Artillery Reserve and distributed its batteries among the infantry corps. Batteries, however, were directed to retain all their ammunition caissons and all serviceable horses. Horse artillery batteries, organized and equipped to support cavalry, were initially excluded from Meade's order.[22]

At the beginning of the Overland Campaign, the Army of the Potomac had twelve horse artillery batteries organized into two brigades of six batteries each. One brigade, commanded by Captain James M. Robertson, was attached to the Cavalry Corps. The second brigade was attached to the army's Artillery Reserve. Four of the batteries were equipped with four 12-pound smooth-bore Napoleons, seven batteries were equipped with six 3-inch Ordnance Rifles, and the final battery was equipped with four 3-inch rifles. The ordnance for the horse artillery thus totaled 16 Napoleons and 46 rifled guns.[23]

On May 31, General Meade issued orders that brought horse artillery batteries generally into line with the rest of his army's artillery. He directed that the horse artillery be reorganized as a single brigade of eight batteries, and that each battery be equipped with a section of two Napoleons and a section of two Ordnance Rifles, for a total within the brigade of sixteen Napoleons and sixteen rifled guns.[24] Meade's decision to mix the ordnance in the horse artillery batteries probably reflected the belief held by many artillery officers that smooth-bore cannons performed better than rifled guns when firing canister.

The eight horse artillery batteries remaining with the Army of the Potomac were placed under the command of Captain James M. Robertson and his brigade remained attached to the Cavalry Corps. The four excess batteries, after giving up their serviceable horses and caissons to other batteries, were sent to Washington for further assignment.[25] Five of Robertson's horse batteries, one in support of each cavalry brigade, would participate in the raid. All five were from the 1st and 2nd U.S. Artillery Regiments, were led by regular officers, and had seen much action during the course of the war.

Details regarding the implementation of Meade's directive to reorganize the horse artillery are lacking. However, it seems likely that the four batteries selected to participate on the Trevilian's Raid would have reorganized during the week between the issuance of the order and the departure on the raid. First, Sheridan's cavalry and its supporting artillery were relatively inactive for several days prior to the raid. Second, the reorganization was relatively simple for each of the four batteries, consisting of swapping Ordnance Rifles and Napoleons and turning-in excess pieces. Doubtless, the batteries would retain their own caissons and serviceable horses.

The four-piece batteries would certainly have been easier to support than six-piece batteries: fewer pieces, caissons, and wagons to maintain; less ammunition to supply; fewer horses to shoe and feed. Also, the smaller batteries would have been easier for their commanders to control, and perhaps easier to maneuver. However, those benefits were gained at great cost as each battery's firepower was reduced by fifty percent. It is not recorded whether Sheridan, or any other senior cavalry commander, opposed the reorganization of the horse artillery.

On June 5, the engineer bridge train allocated to the cavalry corps reported for duty at New Castle Ferry, and Sheridan promptly put them to work. On June 6, Captain W.W. Folwell and his men laid a 150-foot pontoon bridge across the Pamunkey River.[26] Later that day, Torbert's and Gregg's divisions moved to New Castle Ferry. Gregg's division crossed the Pamunkey

Bridging pontoons were made with a collapsible wooden frame covered with canvas. For display purposes, this pontoon has been erected and is ready to be put in the water. Note the deck planking on the wagons in the rear (Library of Congress).

on the bridge and went into camp on the north side of the river while Torbert's division went into camp on the south side of the river.

Once in camp, the units made final preparations for the raid. The men drew three days' rations—intended to last for five days—and two days' grain for their horses. The troopers were to carry their rations in their haversacks and attach the grain for their horses to the pommels of their saddles. In addition, each man drew forty rounds of ammunition which was to be carried in his ammunition pouch. Another sixty rounds per man were carried in the ordnance trains. One medical wagon and eight ambulances supported the raiders.

Throughout history, tactical commanders have striven to reduce the size of the logistical "tail" that follows along behind their fighting forces, and senior commanders during the Civil War continued in that tradition. On August 10, 1862, General McClellan issued General Orders No. 153 which limited the number of wagons allowed to various headquarters and placed restriction on what could be carried in those wagons.[27] During Stoneman's Raid in May 1863, the Army of the Potomac attempted to improve the mobility of its Cavalry Corps by providing pack mules to carry supplies and ammunition instead of wagons. This experiment was unsuccessful. The Corps had insufficient men trained in loading and managing pack animals, and the pack trains—requiring one man for two mules—were a drain of the fighting force. As the quartermaster of the Cavalry Corps pointed out, the load carried by twenty-five pack mules could be carried in two wagons drawn by twelve mules managed by just two teamsters.[28] On November 5, 1863, General Meade revisited the issue of transporta-

This photograph shows a pontoon bridge laid by the 50th New York Engineers across the North Anna River at Jericho Mills in May 1864. Captain Folwell's bridge at New Castle Ferry would have looked much the same (Library of Congress).

tion during field operations by publishing General Order No. 100. The order set forth wagon allowances in three categories: baggage wagons, which carried personal items such as clothing, tentage, and mess equipment; the supply train, which carried subsistence, forage, and other quartermaster stores; and the ammunition train, which carried artillery and small arms ammunition.[29] Significantly, the general order also established a daily "marching ration" for horses and mules of ten pounds grain. This was considerably less than the standard horse's daily ration of fourteen pounds of hay and twelve pounds of oats, corn, or barley set forth in army regulations.[30] By applying the allocation factors in General Order No. 100 to the force selected by Sheridan for the Trevilian's Raid, the two divisions were allowed between 275 and 300 wagons, with about 45 in the ammunition train, 150 in the supply train, and about 90 baggage wagons accompanying the various headquarters, regiments, and artillery batteries.

To illustrate the challenges in logistically supporting a cavalry raid, one may note that Meade allocated thirty wagons to each cavalry division to carry grain for the division's mounts. An army wagon drawn by a team of six horses could carry on average one ton of cargo. Thus, the thirty wagons could carry 6,000 daily marching rations which would feed the mounts in a 3,000-man division for two days (not counting the 120 pounds of grain needed to feed each wagon's team).

According to one newspaper report, Sheridan's train consisted of 125 wagons, not counting Captain Folwell's pontoon train.[31] If that report is accurate, Sheridan severely limited the rolling stock in the trains. However, the choices he made when doing so are for the most part unknown. In his orders, Sheridan limited each division and brigade headquarters to one baggage wagon, which was actually only a net reduction of two wagons to those headquarters' allowance under Meade's general order. Whether Sheridan also eliminated nine wagons, allowed the division and brigade headquarters as part of the supply train for carrying "stores not provided hereto," is not known. Sheridan recorded that the he was furnished one medical wagon for the raid and eight ambulances, leaving unclear whether the twelve wagons allowed for carrying hospital supplies were included in the supply train.[32] Also, it is also not clear whether Sheridan curtailed the number of wagons allowed the regiments for carrying baggage and camp equipage. Those wagons traveled with the regiments or brigades, not as part of the corps trains.

If Sheridan did not direct that the number of regimental baggage wagons be reduced for the raid—and there is no indication that he did—he may have reduced the size of the ammunition and supply trains by about 75 to conform to the 125 figure quoted in the newspaper. This would amount to roughly a forty percent reduction in the number of ammunition and supply wagons. Alternatively, Sheridan could have chosen some other mix of wagons, perhaps electing to carry a full allowance of ammunition with a greater reduction in food and forage. It is quite likely that since the raid was being conducted in late spring, Sheridan anticipated finding some grazing for the horses along the route.

On June 6 at Newcastle Ferry, the regiments were directed to inspect their horses and those deemed unfit to withstand a "severe ten days' march" were culled out. Those horses and newly dismounted troopers, along with any wagons not accompanying the raiding party, were dispatched to the depot Sheridan had established at White House.[33] Meanwhile, the officers—who purchased their rations from the quartermaster or on the civilian market—were recommended to "lay in stores sufficient to last them for twelve days and relieve themselves of all unnecessary encumbrances." At the same time, the men were cautioned that they "need not expect to find themselves near any depot or resting place until the expiration of that period."[34]

Not everyone was occupied full-time making final preparations for the raid. While waiting for the raid to begin, Brigadier General George Custer took time to visit Courtland, the home of the Winston family in eastern Hanover County, roughly two miles from New Castle Ferry. On May 28, 1863, then–Colonel Thomas Rosser had married Betty Winston at Courtland, so Custer took the opportunity of the lull before the raid to pay a call on the wife of his closest friend at West Point. During the visit, Custer told Betty that that he believed he had engaged every Confederate cavalry brigade—save Rosser's—in hand-to-hand combat, that in all those engagements he had come out victorious, and would be happy to meet his old friend Rosser and his brigade. Doubtless, Custer did not foresee his wish being granted within the week.[35]

Just after first light the following morning, the men of Gregg's division began moving to the north as Torbert's division, followed by "a small number of wagons containing the requisite supplies and ammunition," began crossing the Pamunkey.[36] Setting an easy pace, the column—according to Sheridan roughly 6,000 strong—marched away from the north bank of the river and the Army of the Potomac. Sheridan's second raid had begun.

10

"Thumping along"
The March to Louisa County

Shortly after first light on June 7, the troopers of Brigadier General David McMurtrie Gregg's 2nd Cavalry Division left their camps on the north side of the Pamunkey River and headed generally north through King William County. Gregg's division would lead the march for three days, after which Torbert's division would take over the van. Once the north bank had cleared, Torbert's troopers had crossed the Pamunkey and followed Gregg. Afterward, Captain Folwell and his engineers recovered their bridge on the north bank of the river, collapsed their pontoons, loaded their wagons, and followed the cavalry north. For the engineers, it would be a long, hot, and mostly uneventful, march.[1]

Sheridan, to conserve the strength of the horses, ordered that the movement be made at a leisurely pace. The lead regiment proceeded at a walk, which was—by regulation—roughly four miles per hour.[2] Cavalry regulations also specified that "the preservation of the distances [between units] being the most essential point of the march in column, everything else should yield to it." Lieutenants were charged with the responsibility of maintaining the distance between units, and regulations cautioned that should gaps develop, they were to be "repaired gradually and with steadiness."[3] Despite such regulatory emphasis, an "accordion effect"—the bane of marching soldiers throughout history—was a problem for Sheridan's troopers. As the long column moved north, the leading regiments moved at a generally steady pace. However, troopers in the middle and toward the rear frequently encountered prolonged halts as they waited for the road ahead to clear. Invariably, after those halts the men would be forced to take up lengthy trots to close the gaps that had developed.[4] The changes in pace were tiring for both the men and their mounts.

Regarding the experience of riding on a large cavalry raid, Lieutenant Asa Isham, of the 7th Michigan, wrote:

> There is nothing particularly exciting or delightful in thumping along at a trot in a cavalry column. The clouds of dust, sent up by the thousands of hoof-beats, fill the eyes, nose, and air passages, give external surfaces a uniform, dirty gray color, and form such an impenetrable veil, that, for many minutes together, you cannot see even your hand before you. Apparently, just at the point of impending suffocation, a gentle sigh of wind makes a rift, and a free breath is inspired. Dust and horse-hairs penetrate every-where. Working under the clothing to the skin, and fixed by the sweat, the sensation is as though one was covered by a creeping mass of insects. Accumulations occur in the pockets; the rations come in for their full share, and with the bacon, particularly, so thoroughly do dirt and horse-hairs become incorporated, that no process of cleansing can remove

them. But there is no better appetizer than horseback jolting, and a little squeamishness with genuine hunger. A hunk of dirty, raw bacon, with "hard tack," on a campaign, are partaken of with keener relish and enjoyment than "a good square meal," when engaged in less arduous duty.[5]

During the first day's march, the column traveled generally north for roughly sixteen miles and camped for the night on Herring Creek near Aylett, a small hamlet on the Mattaponi River. The following day, Sheridan and his men swung to their left and marched west for about eighteen miles, passing through Pole Cat Station on the Richmond, Fredericksburg and Potomac Railroad before going into camp near Athens. On June 9, the column continued west through Chilesburg and New Market before going into camp in the southeastern corner of Spotsylvania County near Young's Mill on Northeast Creek, a distance of seventeen miles. On June 10, Torbert's division took up the lead as the long column continued west, striking the Fredericksburg-Louisa Courthouse Road at Good Hope Church. At that point, the 17th Pennsylvania of Devin's brigade was sent to the north to investigate reports of a Confederate hospital in the vicinity of Spotsylvania Courthouse.[6] The rest of the force crossed the road and continued west for a few miles. After entering Orange County, the long column turned to the south to cross the North Anna River at Carpenter's Ford. Once in Louisa County, the troopers continued south for several miles before going into camp. The distance marched that day was twenty-one miles, for a four-day total of about eighty miles.[7]

The route selected by Sheridan—having the Pamunkey and then the North Anna rivers on his left flank—offered some protection to his command. The counties north of the North Anna had been essentially abandoned by Confederate forces after the battles in the Wilderness and at Spotsylvania Court House. The Pamunkey and North Anna rivers were significant obstacles to north-south movement; crossing was limited to a few ferries and fords between New Castle Ferry and Gordonsville. Most of the bridges over the two rivers had been burned by Federal forces during Stoneman's Raid in May 1863, and had not been rebuilt.[8] Conse-

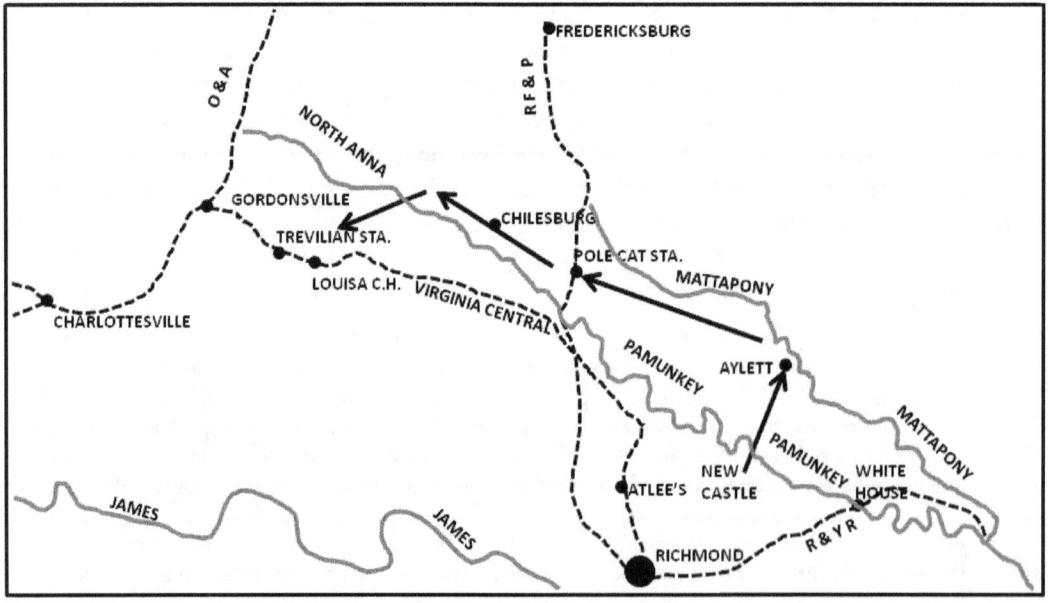

Sheridan's March to Trevilian's

quently, Sheridan's column proceeded without any significant opposition from Confederate forces—no formations of Confederate cavalry operated north of the rivers. That did not mean that the Union raiders could operate with complete impunity. A few individual Confederate soldiers—stragglers, men in search of horses, and those on "French Leave"—as well as small bands of Rebels harassed the raiders as opportunity arose. Additionally, some civilians took up arms to defend their families and their property.

Almost as soon as the march began, Sheridan's men began scouring the countryside to the right and left of the long column, looking for anything that the local populace might have that would be of use—most commonly food. Sheridan ordered that no horses leave the column, but that constraint did little to reduce the urge of the men to forage. Each morning parties from almost every company would set out on foot into the countryside in search of plunder. In the evening, the parties would make their way back into camp with flour, corn meal, bacon, hams, chickens, hogs, and sheep; provender that was much more pleasurable than salt pork, bacon, and hardtack. A lucky foraging party might even discover a cart and a horse or mule to carry the fruits of their endeavors. In a letter written immediately after returning from the raid, the chaplain of the 1st New York Dragoons wrote, that the men "lived like kings." He went on to add, "We have had flour and meal for pancakes, ham and bacon in any quantity, chickens, pigs, and sheep, together with various knickknacks in the shape of honey, apple-butter, preserves, butter, and cheese."[9]

Alternatively, writing well after the War, Captain Noble Preston, 10th New York recalled that the march was made through a "parched and cheerless country" and that "little or no foraging was done, which was probably due to the fact that there was nothing in the country through which we were marching to make it an object for the keen-scented cavalrymen to incur any extra risk for."[10]

However, foraging was not without some risk. An unlucky forager might fall into the hands of the few Confederates north of the North Anna, or even be shot by "bushwhackers" in a skirmish, although few such instances are documented.

After the war, several Union soldiers wrote that during the Trevilian raid, they saw Union "foragers"—more commonly characterized as "looters" by Virginians—hung from trees along the route of march. One Union officer wrote, "[I]t was no uncommon sight to see our dead comrades suspended conspicuously from the limbs of trees along our line of march, and labeled 'Such will be the fate of every forager caught!'" He went on to add that he recognized several of the dead foragers as "well remembered soldiers of our command."[11] However, such reports should be treated with a healthy degree of skepticism. First, those whom were reportedly hung remain unnamed, so the supposed first-hand post-war accounts are incomplete. Second, the hangings were not documented in official reports of the raid, although it seems highly likely that commanders, particularly aggressive officers like Sheridan and Custer, would draw attention to such events had they occurred. Finally, hanging a Union soldier in a tree along Sheridan's route of march would certainly be met with immediate, violent retaliation. Southerners fought and killed Union foragers when the opportunity arose, but only the most imprudent Rebel would invite reprisals against the local civilian population.[12]

On occasion, the men did not have to go afield to forage. On the evening of June 9 near New Market in Spotsylvania County, the 1st Maine was assigned to picket duty. After the picket posts were established, the men of the regiment not on post were permitted to unsaddle and make camp. As the troopers were busy making supper, shots rang out from the nearby picket line. The regimental commander, Colonel Charles Smith, ordered the regiment to prepare for action and a flurry of activity ensued. The troopers ran for their horses and began throwing on saddles. As the first men began to mount, an orderly rode up to Smith with a message, after which Smith turned to the regiment and issued an unusual and cryptic order. In a loud and official tone, Smith directed his troopers to "go on with your Apple sauce." As it turned out, the officer in charge of the pickets had come across several fat cattle which he decided to shoot and butcher. He sent his orderly to Smith to advise the colonel that there would be some gunfire, and after waiting what he thought was a suitable amount of time, ordered his men to open fire on the cattle. Unfortunately, the orderly had become lost en route to the regiment and failed to deliver the message before the shooting began. Afterward, the men of the regiment would joke with each other about Smith's directive for them to "go on with your applesauce."[13]

During the march, the forces of nature were more of an impediment to Sheridan's men than the Confederates. Two days into the march the heat and humidity, lack of forage, and level of work over the past six weeks began to take a toll on the horses. Many horses became worn down to the point that they would simply refuse to continue the march, despite the efforts of their riders to keep them moving. The prescribed practice when a horse gave out was for the rider to dismount, remove his saddle and bridle, and dispatch the horse with a bullet through the brain to ensure that the horse could not be of use to the Confederates. The soldier would then keep up with the column the best he could on foot, hopefully finding a baggage wagon to carry his saddle. Sheridan directed that a guard detail bring up the rear of the column with orders to kill all horses whose riders had found that duty too distasteful to carry out.[14] Captain Noble Preston explained the rationale for destroying the horses: "These horses were, in many cases, the best in the command, and a few hours' rest would render them as good as ever. It, therefore, became necessary to shoot the faithful creatures as soon as they 'played out' and had to be abandoned."[15]

Unfortunately for Sheridan and his men, the departure of the two Union divisions and their march to the west was almost immediately detected by Confederate scouts. However, the Confederates were unable to react to Sheridan's foray for two days.

As Sheridan's divisions began crossing the Pamunkey at New Castle Ferry, a party of three of Hampton's scouts, led by E.C. Moncure of the 9th Virginia approached the river from the north. Seeing the movement of the cavalry toward Aylett's, Moncure and his men—civilian scouts named Ashby and Liverman—took up a concealed position to observe, counting the units and artillery as they passed. From the amount of cavalry and the twelve artillery pieces they observed, they determined that Sheridan's entire corps was on the move. Liverman left to report to Hampton that Sheridan was on the move, which he did the next day. Moncure and Ashby continued to follow Sheridan's column. Two days later, after Liverman had returned, the three made a faux charge on the column's rear guard, galloping up the road shouting and firing their pistols. The three had planned to halt forty yards from the Yankees and fall back from there, but were gratified when the Union squadron wheeled about and fled.[16]

Also on June 7, two of Hampton's scouts, Hugh Scott and Dolf Kennedy, crossed the Pamunkey in search of a remount for Scott. By chance, the two encountered Sheridan's column and were able to observe its size and composition without being detected. That night, a woman living in the area told the two scouts that she had heard that Sheridan was en route to the Shenandoah Valley with 10,000 men, each of whom carried six days' cooked rations.

10. "Thumping along"

Scott sent Kennedy to report the news to Hampton while he continued to observe the Union force to determine the direction it was headed. The following day Scott, having confirmed that the column was heading west, returned through Confederate lines. Meanwhile, after riding about thirty-five miles through the night, Kennedy arrived at Hampton's headquarters near Atlee's Station on the morning of June 8 and informed the general of the Union troop movement.[17]

At about the same time, Captain Thomas Conrad, the chaplain of the 3rd Virginia who—unlikely as it may seem—was detached to the army's intelligence service as a scout, came across a mulatto man who, wearing a blue Union uniform jacket, was wandering through a field. The man said he had escaped from Sheridan's camp where he was a servant, and that earlier in the war he had been a servant for General Rosser. The man claimed he had important information regarding the Union raid and asked to be taken to Rosser. Conrad had the mulatto man mount behind him and rode to Rosser's camp. Rosser remembered the man, who had been his valet in 1861 when Rosser served as a captain in the Washington Artillery. The former valet "in a clear and straight forward manner related all that had occurred in Sheridan's camp preparatory for this expedition." Rosser sent the man to Hampton and later opined that the information "was of great service to us."[18]

Hampton, upon being apprised that a large body of cavalry and artillery had crossed the river, immediately sent word to Robert E. Lee requesting that he be allowed to pursue the Federals. Lee approved Hampton's request and ordered Hampton, accompanied by his and Fitz Lee's Divisions, to go after Sheridan while Rooney Lee's Division remain in support of Lee's infantry.[19] Hampton, as the senior general, commanded the two-division expedition.

The remainder of the day was spent making preparations for the movement. The men of the two divisions were issued three-day's rations consisting of about one half pound bacon and one and one half pounds hardtack per man. Many of the men cooked their rations. Others simply packed their crackers and raw bacon into their haversacks and ate their bacon raw while in the saddle. Quartermasters also distributed a fairly generous ration of corn for the horses and the troopers tied the bags of corn to their saddles.[20] Early on the morning of June 9, the Confederates began their march to the west generally following the Virginia Central Railroad through Hanover and Louisa Counties. Hampton's Division led, followed at some distance by Lee's.

By coincidence, on June 6, Captain John Esten Cooke, an Assistant Inspector General, had inspected Major Roger Chew's battalion of artillery which was assigned to the support of Hampton's Division. Cooke found that "The general condition of the batteries is very good; [Captain James W.] Thomson's especially. Great care has been taken of his horses by this active and efficient officer, and they are in excellent order. [Captain James F.] Hart's are not so good, but are fit for active e service.... The losses in these batteries since my last report have been inconsiderable, and the companies are full Thomson has 98 men for duty, and Hart about 112. The ordnance wagons are well supplied with ammunition, except Blakely. The limber chests and caissons are full and the ammunition properly packed." Cooke went on to inform Brigadier General William Nelson Pendleton, Robert E. Lee's artillery commander, that he would inspect the batteries supporting Fitz Lee's Division on either June 9 or 10.[21] The departure of the cavalry in pursuit of Sheridan precluded that inspection.

Although Sheridan had a two-day head start, Hampton was able to overcome that disadvantage. Hampton set a more rapid pace than Sheridan, and the heat, dust, and lack of water along the route added to the discomfort of both his men and their mounts. Because of the pace, the horses had little opportunity to graze. On the night of June 9, the two divisions halted near Beaver Dam Station for only three or four hours with the men lying on the ground holding their horses' reins in expectation of orders to move. Consequently, the horses subsisted mainly on the corn that they carried.

Just as in Sheridan's column, the Southern troopers were plagued by the accordion effect. Lieutenant Colonel J. Frederick Waring, commander of the Cobb's Legion, noted that the 7th Georgia, the least experienced regiment in the two divisions, marched very badly, observing that "they gallop too much." Waring also wrote that the two senior officers in the regiment, Colonel Joseph McAlister and Lieutenant Colonel Edward "Ned" Anderson were "determined to do something with them."[22]

Fortunately, Hampton's route was more direct than Sheridan's line of march—about forty-five miles to Sheridan's eighty. By the evening of June 10, the Confederates had drawn abreast of the Union forces. Fitz Lee's Division camped for the night near Louisa Courthouse. Hampton's Division was farther west, with Butler's Brigade near Trevilian Station, Young's Brigade under Colonel Gid Wright's command east of Trevilian's, and Rosser's Brigade several miles further toward Gordonsville near the Green Spring Valley section of Louisa County.[23] Hampton established his headquarters on the grounds of the Netherland home and tavern just east of Trevilian Station.[24]

Late in the afternoon on June 10, Sheridan's forces crossed the North Anna at Carpenter's Ford and after moving several miles south into Louisa County went into camp for the evening.

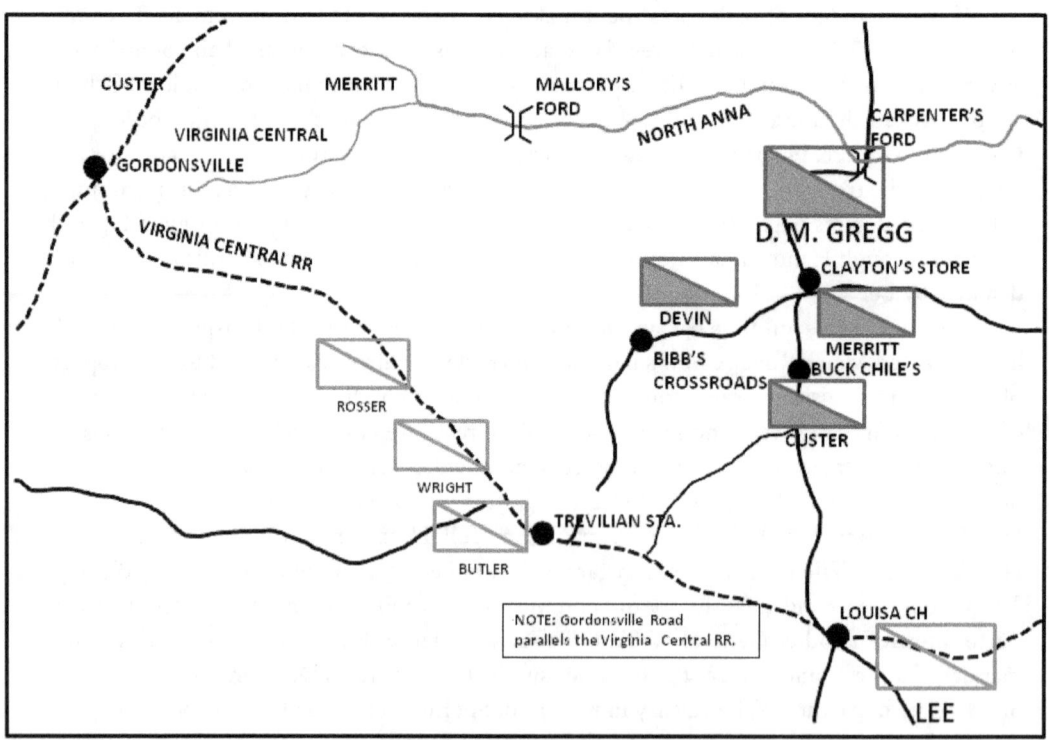

Disposition of Forces, Evening of June 10

Sheridan established his headquarters at Woodlawn, a farm north of Clayton's Store. Torbert's division was centered on Clayton's Store with Merritt's brigade just to the south near Buck Chile's farm. Devin's brigade was about a mile to the west at Woolfolk's farm, roughly about halfway between Clayton's Store and Bibb's Crossroads. Custer's brigade had advanced about a mile beyond Buck Chile's on the Marquis Road before going into camp.[25] John Irwin Gregg's brigade of Gregg's division camped between Clayton's Store and the North Anna, while Davies's brigade camped on the North Anna.[26] Torbert's division was thus well positioned to advance on the Central Virginia Railroad at both Louisa Courthouse and Trevilian Station with Gregg's division following as a reserve.

Later that evening, Sheridan sent a message to General Gregg informing him of his plans. During the night he anticipated that Torbert's men would "break" the railroad at Trevilian's, and at Cuffy's Creek and South Fork Creek near Gordonsville. At 5:00 a.m. the next morning, Torbert was to march to Gordonsville on the Old Stage Road via Trevilian's, Newark and Mechanicsville. Gregg's division was to follow Torbert with one brigade leading, the subsistence train and the engineer pontoon train, followed by Gregg's second brigade.[27] Presumably, Sheridan and Torbert had earlier conferred face-to-face regarding plans for the following day.

Unfortunately for Sheridan, the presence of Wade Hampton with his and Fitzhugh Lee's divisions—a presence apparently unknown to the Union commander—would prevent Torbert from marching to Gordonsville.

11

"An exceedingly messed up affair"
The Battle Opens on the Fredericksburg Road

As the regiments of Brigadier General A.T.A. Torbert's division were moving into their camps south of Clayton's Store, a general store once owned by Louisa County sheriff Arthur Clayton just north of the intersection of the Marquis Road and the Fredericksburg Road, a Confederate scouting party of ten or twelve men attacked the head of his column.[1] No casualties were incurred and the Rebels quickly withdrew as darkness began to fall. However, damage to the Union effort had been done: Hampton was quickly informed that Sheridan's raiders had crossed the North Anna into Louisa County; but despite this contact, Sheridan still had no firm knowledge of Hampton's whereabouts, or even that he had been pursued by the bulk of Robert E. Lee's cavalry.[2]

Hampton, now knowing the position of Sheridan's forward-most units, made his plans for the following morning, June 11. Hampton decided to attack Sheridan at daylight and sent orders for Fitzhugh Lee to advance his division on the Marquis Road, the road leading from Louisa Courthouse to Clayton's Store, while Hampton with his division advanced north on the Fredericksburg Road which led from Trevilian's to Clayton's store.[3] Hampton hoped that during the move Lee's division would be able cover his right flank, while his division covered Lee's left flank. Hampton also hoped to "conceal [his] real design, which was to strike [Sheridan] at Clayton's Store after uniting his two divisions."[4] With luck, both divisions might simultaneously fall unexpectedly upon Sheridan's regiments in their camps, and overwhelm all or part of the Union force before Sheridan could react. In a Confederate best case scenario, Sheridan's force might be pinned against the North Anna River and destroyed.

However, when executing this plan, Hampton would be accepting a certain level of risk. As they were camped for the night, Lee and Hampton were out of "supporting distance" of one another; meaning that were one division attacked, it could be defeated before the other division could come to its assistance. As Lee and Hampton moved north upon their separate axes of advance, they would move into supporting distance as the Marquis and Fredericksburg Roads converged. However, if either division made contact early in the movement toward Clayton's Store, it was likely that the division would fight alone.[5]

At this point, it is useful to explain the problems faced by a Civil War commander when conducting operations with dispersed forces. Today, commanders are linked by almost instant, secure communications and so it is easy to grossly underestimate the amount of time required to launch an attack such as that envisioned by Hampton.

To transmit his orders to Lee, it is likely that Hampton explained his plan to a staff officer and then dispatched the officer to Lee's headquarters. Finding a suitable staff officer, explaining the plan, and sending the officer on his way may have required twenty minutes or more.[6] The staff officer most likely took approximately an hour to ride the five miles from Trevilian's to Louisa Courthouse. Horses have a tendency to "spook" at shadows when alone in the dark, and it was a dark night with only thirty-three percent of the moon for illumination and with the moon-set at 11:32 p.m.[7] Additionally, the staff officer probably rode very cautiously along the road to Louisa to avoid meeting roving Union patrols which might be about, or being mistaken as a Union patrol by Confederate pickets.

Nearing Louisa Courthouse, and still in the dark, the staff the staff officer had to find Lee's headquarters. This would be done by asking those Confederates he met along the way as to Lee's whereabouts—and not all whom he met would know Lee's location, a task that would be much simpler today with a system of map coordinates and a global positioning device. A Civil War staff officer might require thirty to forty minutes—with stops at two or three regiments—before finding Lee. Then a few more minutes passed as the officer briefed Lee on Hampton's plan.

So, likely more than two hours would have elapsed before Lee received his orders.[8] He then had to devise his own plan—fortunately Hampton's plan was simple—and issue his own orders to his brigade commanders. Wickham and Lomax, in turn, had to issue orders to their regimental commanders. Regimental commanders, who were more responsible for executing orders than planning operations, were probably told simply to have their men ready to move at a designated time and location. The regimental commanders would issue the necessary orders to have the men "standing to horse" at the appointed time. It is likely that the orders were issued verbally to avoid alerting any nearby enemy with bugle calls. These "troop leading procedures" within Lee's division might require an additional hour or more before Lee's regiments were ready to execute Hampton's orders to move north along the Marquis Road toward Clayton's Store and battle.[9]

Similarly, in Hampton's Division, the orders for the coming day would have to be disseminated to Butler, Rosser, and Wright. Most likely, Hampton's orders to his subordinates were simple. Butler recalled that his only orders were to have his command mounted and ready for action at daylight the next morning.[10] However, as one of Hampton soldiers observed, "You may be sure staff and couriers had all they could do that night. The division was mounted on time, ammunition distributed, rifles slung ready for the fray. We waited in this attitude until about sunrise."[11]

About daylight on June 11, Brigadier General Thomas Rosser, who was anxious to learn what actually was planned for the day, left his brigade near the Green Spring Valley and rode toward Trevilian's.[12] Arriving at Matthew C. Butler's camp, Rosser greeted his fellow brigadier, "Butler, what is Hampton going to do here today?" "Damned if I know," Butler replied. "We've been up and mounted since daylight and my men and horses are being worsted by nonaction." With that news, Rosser suggested, "Let's ride down and enquire what Hampton's plans are." Butler ordered his men to dismount, and the two brigadiers rode together to find their commander.[13]

Arriving at Netherland's, a tavern and nearby house at the intersection of the Gordonsville Road and the Fredericksburg Road east of Trevilian Station, they found Hampton lying fully clothed on a wooden table in a horse-pen at the front of the house. As they

This 1935 photograph—captioned "farmhouse"—shows the Netherland Tavern. Wade Hampton spent the night before the battle sleeping on a wooden table in a nearby horse pen (Library of Congress).

11. "An exceedingly messed up affair"

approached, Hampton arose and greeted them. Rosser asked his commander, "General, what do you propose to do today, if I might enquire." "I propose to fight," replied Hampton. He went on to explain that he intended to "form a junction" with Lee's division at Clayton's Store and there engage Sheridan.[14] With that news, Rosser hurried back to the Green Spring Valley to prepare his brigade for movement while, at Butler's suggestion, Butler and Hampton rode out to reconnoiter through the woods north of the railroad.[15] Meanwhile, the advance elements of Fitz Lee's Division had made an early start. A courier arrived and informed Hampton that Lee's Virginians had begun moving north from their camps east of Louisa Courthouse at about 3:00 a.m.[16]

Together, Butler and Hampton rode north on the Fredericksburg Road. Immediately to the north of the rail line to the west of the Fredericksburg Road were several large fields where over the years timber had been cut to provide ties for the rails and fuel for the locomotives. Between one and two miles north of the tracks, the road entered a band of woods with thick undergrowth. The woods extended for roughly a mile, almost to Bibb's Crossroads, where the Fredericksburg Road turned east toward Clayton's Store.

As Butler and Hampton approached the band of woods, they encountered Butler's pickets, a squadron of the 5th South Carolina commanded by Captain A.B. Mulligan, which was falling back after making contact with advancing Federals.[17] Hampton ordered Butler to bring up his brigade and attack immediately. Butler sent word back for his regiments to advance from their camps. The first regiment of Butler's Brigade to arrive was the 4th South Carolina. Butler ordered the regimental commander, Colonel Hugh Rutledge, to have his leading squadron, commanded by Captain S.J. Snowden, move forward and immediately charge any enemy he encountered. By responding aggressively, Butler hoped that he would be able to quickly learn whether he was facing a determined push by Sheridan or merely a picket line or a reconnaissance in limited strength.[18]

Snowden's men, riding in a column of fours on the road leading to Bibb's Crossroads, soon encountered federal skirmishers advancing through the woods. Snowden put his men to the gallop and they charged up the road. The skirmishers, instead of meeting the charge, melted into the woods on the right and left allowing the saber-wielding Confederates to pass by. As soon as the charging Rebels could stop their horses, Snowden reformed his squadron and withdrew at the gallop, passing again through the Yankee skirmishers. Snowden's men, upon rejoining the regiment, were "quite satisfied to have escaped the bullets" fired at them as they ineffectually rode back and forth through the Union skirmish line.[19]

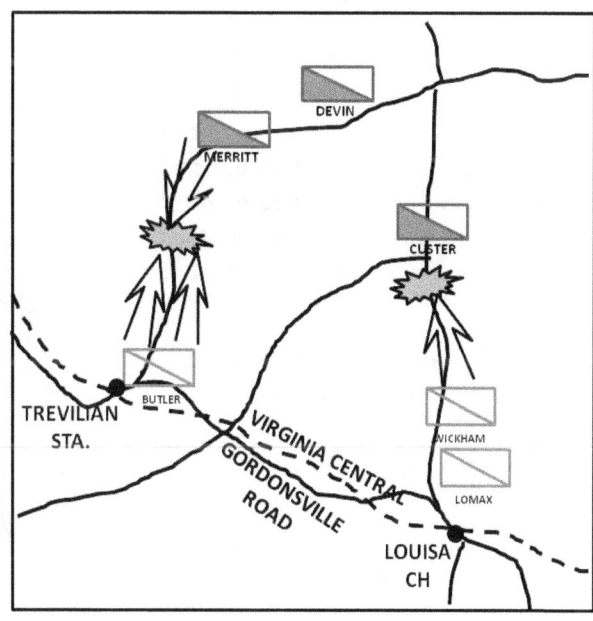

Opening Moves—Early Morning, June 11

Stephen Palmer, one of the soldiers in the 4th South Carolina, described the charge up the road through the woods in more detail.

> We charged under a pretty heavy fire from the enemy, who maintained their position until we got within twenty-five yards of them; they then wheeled and dashed back as fast as they possibly could, throwing away their overcoats, &c, as they ran. Being eager to overtake them, I dashed forward at full speed and passed the main portion of our command, four or five still being ahead of me at the time. I soon overtook and passed them. Finding I could not reach the flying enemy with my sword, I endeavored to draw my pistol, but it had slipped too far behind me. I continued the pursuit until I reached their reserve force of about a hundred men, and drawing my pistol, before I could fire, felt my foot sting as if struck by a stick. Finding myself cut off from my command, I fired five shots into the crowd, wheeled and dashed for the road, passing several of the Federals, who kept up a lively fire on me from the time I started until I got out of reach. One man, as I passed, swung his gun and struck at me, but fortunately missed me. One shot passed through the neck of the horse I rode, but did not seriously hurt him. I then went to the rear and had my foot examined, and it was found that a pistol ball had entered just below the ankle, passed around the foot, and come out at the heel.

Palmer, who although sick that morning had remained in the ranks, was placed in an ambulance and taken toward Trevilian's where a field hospital had been established.[20]

Butler then ordered a squadron of the 4th South Carolina to dismount and advance into the woods. Colonel Rutledge, on foot, accompanied the squadron, leaving his adjutant, Second Lieutenant Gabriel Manigault behind with Butler. In short order, Butler ordered all but one of the remaining squadrons of the 4th to dismount and sent them forward on the flanks of the leading squadron. Butler kept the squadron commanded by Captain John C. Calhoun in the saddle as his reserve.[21] The general, whose white mare had been killed earlier in the month, was mounted on a "beautiful bay mare" belonging to a soldier in the 4th South Carolina who had been wounded at Haw's Shop. On horseback, apparently unhampered by his wooden leg, Butler directed his troops from the Fredericksburg Road which bisected his line. A bend in the road gave him some shelter from enemy bullets whistling by. As his remaining two regiments came up,

Alfred Gibbs, a Mexican War veteran and dragoon in the regular army, as a volunteer commanded the 130th New York Infantry. Because of Gibbs's persistence, the War Department converted his regiment to cavalry. It became the 19th New York Cavalry, but was better known as the 1st New York Dragoons. On the morning of June 11, the men of the 1st New York Dragoons moved into battle following an unconventional order from Gibbs: "Hey there you men! Climb on them horses damn quick!" (Library of Congress).

Butler sent them forward to the right, extending his line in the woods to the east. Manigault, observing Butler directing the disposition of troops into battle, later recalled, "This he did admirably, and he never appeared to me to greater advantage than this forenoon."[22] As Butler was directing his regiments forward, a few Yankees who had apparently advanced through the woods undetected, emerged from the trees directly to Butler's front. U.R. Brooks, one of Butler's couriers, heard Butler shout, "You damn rascals, if you don't turn back, I'll murder the last damn one of you."[23] Whether deterred by Butler's admonition or by Confederates advancing up the road, the Yankees turned about and withdrew into the trees without uttering a word.

Meanwhile, Hampton had ordered Colonel Gilbert "Gid" Wright to bring up Young's Brigade, and the troops from Georgia, Mississippi, and Alabama began to arrive in the rear of Butler's South Carolinians.

Unbeknownst to Hampton, roughly five miles to the north his Union adversaries had made an early start that morning. During the night, as Brigadier General Torbert prepared his plans for the day, he "could get no accurate information in regard to the enemy" and was thus unaware that Confederates were in strength to his front.

Based upon his limited knowledge of the roads in the area, Torbert ordered Merritt with the Reserve Brigade to advance down the Fredericksburg Road from their camps south of Clayton's Store commencing at 5:00 a.m. Devin's brigade was ordered to follow Merritt. Tor-

As shown in this photograph, east of the Fredericksburg Road the ground slopes gently down to a small stream. The dense vegetation to both the east and west of the Fredericksburg Road hindered the ability of commanders to control their men and the ability of the men to engage the enemy (author's photograph).

bert did not explain why he chose to have Merritt pass through Devin to lead the advance instead of just leading with Devin, whose regiments were about a mile closer to Trevilian's than Merritt's.

Torbert ordered Custer's Michigan Brigade, which was camped a short distance down the Marquis Road, to move south toward Louisa Courthouse also at 5:00 a.m. Custer was further directed to turn right onto a "county road" which branched off the Marquis Road about a mile south of his camps. This narrow track intersected the Gordonsville Road, which paralleled the railroad tracks between Louisa Court-House and Trevilian Station, about 700 yards east of the station. Torbert further advised Custer to communicate with either Merritt or Devin when he approached Trevilian's.[24]

Merritt's forces began moving promptly at 5:00 a.m. with the 2nd U.S. Cavalry—Merritt's own regiment—leading the way. The regiment passed through the division's line of pickets and continued south at the trot. Very shortly afterward, the men of the 2nd U.S. encountered Butler's pickets and drove them back. At the time, Colonel Alfred Gibbs of the 1st New York Dragoons was still eating breakfast with Torbert at division headquarters. At the sound of gunfire he rushed back to his regiment and emerged from the woods found his men waiting—as they had been trained to do—for the proper commands to assemble, stand to horse and mount. As he galloped past on his horse, Old Blue, Gibbs instead shouted, "Hey there you men! Climb on them horses damn quick!"[25] In short order the men clambered into their saddles and the regiment began moving toward the sound of the firing.

At the van, the men of the 2nd U.S. encountered Confederates skirmishers in the stretch of thick woods. The regimental commander, Captain Theophilus Rodenbough, rode forward on the road supervising the deployment of his squadrons as they dismounted and moved off to the right and left. Without warning, a band of mounted Confederates appeared around a bend in the road and immediately charged. On young rebel galloped up to Rodenbough and shot him at close range.[26] Rodenbough, seriously wounded in his arm, was taken to the rear and command devolved upon Captain David S. Gordon, the next senior officer.

Meanwhile, Merritt brought his other regiments forward, sending the 1st New York Dragoons and the 6th Pennsylvania to the right of the 2nd U.S. and the 1st U.S. to the left. Merritt retained the 5th U.S.—with only six companies on the field—in the rear to support Lieutenant Edward Williston's Battery D, 2nd U.S. Artillery.[27]

As the battle developed, the nature of the terrain proved extremely challenging for the men and their commanders, both North and South. The trees and undergrowth were so thick that it was almost impossible to see a man at a distance of more than a few yards. Both Union and Confederate soldiers recalled that they could clearly hear enemy officers giving commands, but could not see them. In the woods a fair number of men from both sides were captured by inadvertently approaching an enemy who was invisible to them. Officers could see only a handful of their men, and likewise, only few men could see their officers, making command and control difficult. Officers also found it difficult to find the flanks of adjacent units and ensure that no gaps developed that could be exploited by the enemy. Finally, the dense woods and undergrowth added a psychological aspect to the fighting that morning. In most small units soldiers draw strength from their comrades and fight more effectively as a group than as individuals. Historically, when soldiers are isolated from one another, unit cohesion suffers and soldiers are more likely to panic.[28]

Shortly after Rodenbough was wounded, Captain Charles Leoser, commanding a squadron of the 2nd U.S., inadvertently wandered into Confederate lines and was captured. Leoser, on foot leading his horse, made his way to the Confederate rear to formerly surrender himself to the commanding officer on the field. He quickly came upon General Butler, who politely relieved the captain of his sword. Butler then took Leoser's poncho, which was in good condition, and offered to send his own well-worn poncho to Leoser later in the day. Taken farther to the rear, Hampton's chief of artillery exchanged his worn boots for Leoser's, giving Leoser no choice but to agree the swap. Eventually Leoser's escort turned him over to the provost guard and the Union captain was there relieved of his horse.[29]

As the Union and Confederate lines closed with one another, the firing in the woods became more intense. Hearing the 4th South Carolina moving about to his left front, Butler sent Lieutenant Manigault to find Colonel Rutledge and tell him to have his men move more quietly. Manigault rode into the woods, delivered the message, and returned to Butler leading a stray horse he had found among the trees.

General Butler, with his three regiments abreast in the woods felt confident that Colonel Aiken with the 6th South Carolina could hold his own on the right. However, Butler sensed that pressure on his left was increasing and perhaps threatening Colonel Rutledge and the 4th South Carolina. About that time a courier arrived from Rutledge advising Butler that his regiment was being flanked and he needed reinforcements. Butler turned to the courier and said, "Give my compliments to Colonel Rutledge and tell him to flank back."[30] The courier hurried off to deliver the order to Rutledge. Despite ordering Rutledge to fend for himself, Butler sent word to the rear for Colonel Gid Wright to bring forward Young's Brigade to support his South Carolinians.

The 7th Georgia, under the command of Lieutenant Colonel Joseph McAllister, had earlier dismounted, and leaving their led horses near the railroad, moved forward on foot accompanied by the 20th Battalion Georgia Cavalry. The 20th was commanded by Major Samuel Spencer, replacing Lieutenant Colonel John Millen who had been killed at Haw's Shop. As the Georgians closed on the rear of the 5th South Carolina in the center of Butler's line, Butler directed them to deploy to the left of the 4th South Carolina extending the Confederate line to the west and relieve the pressure on Rutledge's exposed flank.[31] McAllister moved off to the left and into the woods with his reinforced regiment and quickly ran into difficulty finding his position on Rutledge's flank because of the trees and undergrowth.

Under such conditions, several problems can occur when deploying into line. Since leaders are unable to see the units already deployed and fighting, gaps frequently develop between squadrons or regiments. Large gaps, which are subject to exploitation by advancing enemy soldiers, create a vulnerable point in a defensive line. Also, it is quite possible for units in thick woods to deploy one behind the other instead of falling in abreast. Men positioned behind friendly troops cannot effectively engage the enemy, and the possibility of friendly-fire casualties is increased. Finally, in thick woods it is easy for units to deploy facing the wrong direction. Terrain features such as streams and slopes effect how units deploy, particularly when leaders are unable to observe an enemy to their front. Unless care is taken, men tend to deploy along a contour facing down-slope, which may not be the direction toward the enemy.

An example of the problems encountered when fighting in thickly wooded terrain is provided by the account of Captain John Bauskett, who commanded Company B, 6th South Carolina on Butler's right.

We moved on, halted, moved again, halted, then a squadron dismounted and marched towards the firing line in a heavy oak and Chinkapin woods.

After a while our turn. (2nd Squadron Co's "B&F"). came and [we] dismounted to fight. We marched into the thicket and touched our right to the left of the other fellows. Then began the 'sushay': we moved a few yards by the right flank, then, an order to the left flank. All this time bullets were zipping over us, through us, and under us. Mose Humphrey, Captain of Company "H" in command [Moses Humphrey was actually in command of Company F, the Cadet Rangers]—and most of our men [were] raw troops never under fire before, and when the next command of right or left flank would come, the men would obey it, of course but in doing so would echelon to the rear. Noticing this I told Humphrey to put us [into the fight], get us to where the men could see the enemy. And in short if they didn't, they'd run directly. He agreed, and on his orders we moved forward and got to shooting, and then the men were alright. There is nothing more demoralizing to troops even old troops than to be shot at and not be allowed to shoot back. Of course, it's worse for raw soldiers it isn't fair.

Directly we got moving again. First toward one flank, then the other in those thick woods until we got lost.... I found myself and six men, separated from everybody, with firing all around; and we moved forward up to where some Yanks were sending their bullets toward us....

Increasing we were surrounded; not only us but all of Hampton's men. Now to get out; climb trees or hide seemed to be our best resources for all the trials of war, the worst being taken prisoner so I kept the best lookouts I could. Finally I heard some troops coning up in our rear. My heart was in my mouth for fear they were Yanks and we hadn't climbed the trees yet. But it was Capt. McGuire of our regiment with his squadron (two companies). He and his squadron were lost [and] we were glad to see each other the fire in the circle around us going on.[32]

McGuire's squadron initially took up positions directly in the rear of Bauskett's six men, but shortly afterward Major Thomas B. Ferguson arrived on the scene and moved McGuire's men up on Bauskett's left flank. Under Ferguson's direction, the men moved forward along a cow path and "got right into the fracas." They had not been fighting long when a major from Butler's staff crawled up on all fours with orders to quietly fall back, remount, and report to Hampton.[33]

As the remaining regiments of Young's Brigade moved forward, for the most part dismounted, Butler directed them into line. There is little information on the disposition of Wright's Regiments. It would have been preferable for Butler to have deployed all of Wright's regiments to left, thereby making it easier for Wright to exercise control over his force. However, due to federal pressure throughout the length of his front, Butler apparently was forced to send some squadrons into the line piecemeal on the right of the road.[34]

As the Georgians deployed extending the lines of battle, Butler continued to be concerned about the vulnerability of his flanks. Hearing gunfire through the woods off to his right front, Butler directed Lieutenant Manigault to find Colonel Hugh Aiken, whose 6th South Carolina was positioned on the right of his line. Butler instructed Manigault to warn the colonel to be alert for enemy movement around his flank. As Manigault began to ride forward, Butler advised him to leave his horse behind. Manigault dismounted, handed his reins to a near-by private and set off on foot. Advancing up the road about fifty yards, Manigault climbed over a rail fence at the edge of the road and began making his way to the right. He passed Captain Mulligan, whose company was now fighting dismounting against an enemy who could not be seen through the trees and undergrowth. Manigault observed that Mulligan's men "were doing effective work with their rifles" and that Mulligan was "encouraging [them] with much exposure of his own person." Proceeding a little further, Manigault came upon a lieutenant and asked him of Aiken's location. The lieutenant, a Georgian who knew nothing of Aiken, was busy at the time keeping his men from falling to the rear, leading Manigault to surmise that the line could not be defended much longer.[35]

Manigault considered turning back, but instead he continued skirting to the right and asking after Aiken. When almost to the end of the Confederate line, Manigault was told that Aiken was only a few yards farther, and with several of his men was holding a position from the protection of a rail fence. Heading toward Aiken's position, Manigault crossed a small clearing at the edge of which he saw the tops of two blue hats. He assumed the hats were worn by Confederates since many South Carolinians wore captured Union garments. However, when the two men raised their heads, Manigault could see they were the enemy. Instead of immediately fleeing into the woods and safety, Manigault hesitated momentarily and was left with no choice but to surrender as the two men raised their carbines toward him.

The two Union privates seemed very eager to search their new prisoner and perhaps thereby gain a windfall of money or a watch. However, their commander, a Lieutenant named Hunt, said that the men were "regulars" and that Manigault would not have to undergo the indignity of a search. Relieved, Manigault turned over his pistol to Lieutenant Hunt and, guarded by one of the men, was marched to the rear.[36]

On his way to the rear, Manigault observed the regulars, and found it "unusual" that he had the opportunity of "seeing two sides of a murderous conflict in the span of about ten minutes." Moving north on the road, Manigault came upon a group of regulars huddled behind some trees at a bend in the road. As a man was ready to fire, he would advance in the road until he could spot a target. He would then fire once, or at most twice, before falling back rapidly to the safety of the trees. Then another man would move forward to fire. Manigault also saw that the led horses, lined up in fours, were only a short distance behind the firing line. The fours were backed up into the trees, keeping the road clear for movement. At Haw's Shop, Manigault observed that many men of the 4th South Carolina were overrun and captured because the regiment's led horses were positioned too far in the rear. Contrasting the regulars to the "disorder and confusion among our horse holders at the Haw's Shop fight," Manigault concluded that "the federal cavalry had the advantage over ours in more attention having been paid to these small details which contribute much to the better management of a battle."[37]

Once out of range of Confederate fire, Manigault was turned over to Torbert's provost guard and escorted farther to the rear. During a short halt, a federal staff officer approached and asked to which command Manigault belonged. He replied, "Butler's Brigade," to which the staff officer responded that Butler's men were "not cavalry, but mounted infantry." Manigault took this as a compliment because "the cavalry under Stuart had made a bad name for themselves by the way in which they usually 'hauled out of a fight' and left the heavy work to be done by the infantry." Manigault acknowledged that the fact that Butler's Brigade was armed with muzzle loading rifles was another reason for the staff officer's observation. The staff officer then questioned Manigault about the strength of Butler's Brigade, but having been cautioned about disclosing such information, he replied that he was not at liberty to say.[38]

The Confederate prisoners were eventually collected into a larger group and moved from place to place in the Union rear as the battle developed. Among the prisoners was a very seriously wounded and unconscious lieutenant. In their affection for their officer, several of his men were carrying his body in a blanket, which significantly interfered with the movement of the group. The men were finally forced to abandon the "almost inanimate body" of their lieutenant at the side of the road.[39]

Meanwhile, the 1st New York Dragoons had moved up to the rear of the 2nd U.S. and Colonel Gibbs ordered his men to dismount and take position to the right of the regulars. Almost immediately, the New Yorkers were met by Confederates advancing toward them through the woods. In a letter to a local newspaper, one of the New Yorkers described the scene of the fighting.

> In this battle the men were deployed only a few feet apart, and as far as possible kept in line as we advanced. But we had some rough ground to go over, creeks to cross, and woods with thick underbrush to pass through. Then bear in mind there were a lot of ugly rebs in our front inclined to dispute our way by shooting in our faces, charging, and taking every possible advantage to discomfit us. Thus you will understand it was often a difficult thing to keep our alignment. Both hostile lines were ablaze, and bullets flew like hailstones, cannon on either side were throwing their missiles of death, and the air was sulphurous with smoke, our artillery often shooting over our heads and dropping their shells in the ranks of the enemy.

He went on to add, "Perhaps the generals understood the situation, but to the rank and file it was an exceedingly messed up affair."[40]

In the first few minutes of fighting, the 1st New York Dragoons received a "warm reception" during which several men were killed, wounded, or taken prisoners. Among those falling into Confederate hands were the regiment's lieutenant colonel, Thomas J. Thorp.[41] Although strongly resisted by the Confederates, the New Yorkers made progress through the woods. On occasion the order would be passed verbally along the line, "Forward, double-quick, charge." According to one account, as the bugles would sound the charge, the men would "set up a yell, like so many devils, rushing forward regardless of shot and shell; and then the scene became terrific beyond description as both sides contended for mastery in the sanguinary struggle."[42] In reality, however, not much substantial gain was initially made through the woods.

As the 1st New York Dragoons moved into the fight on the far right of Merritt's line, the 6th Pennsylvania Cavalry, commonly known as Rush's Lancers, moved up on Merritt's orders taking position between the dragoons and the regulars of the 2nd U.S.[43] Leading the regiment was Captain Joseph Hinckley Clark, who had assumed command two weeks earlier when the then-acting commander, Captain Charles Leiper was wounded at Old Church.[44]

Following the 6th Pennsylvania, the 1st U.S. Cavalry moved into position to the left of the 2nd U.S. The 1st U.S. was commanded by the senior captain present, Nelson B. Sweitzer, a West Point classmate of Philip Sheridan. Before the war, Sweitzer had extensive experience fighting Indians with the dragoons in the Southwest and Pacific Northwest. Earlier in the war he had served as an aide de camp to General George B. McClellan in the temporary grade of lieutenant colonel. After McClellan was relieved in November 1862, Sweitzer accompanied the general to New York to assist him in preparing his reports. Sweitzer returned to the Army of the Potomac in May 1863 and assumed command of his regiment in August of that year.[45]

Merritt kept his final regiment, the 5th U.S. in the rear, supporting Captain Edward Williston's Battery D, 2nd U.S. Artillery. The 5th U.S. had only six companies present on the field.

At this point in the battle, Merritt had deployed forty-five companies of cavalry while holding six companies in support of his artillery. Butler had deployed his thirty companies which were being reinforced by most of Wright's forty-two companies. Although the Confederates had an advantage in strength, the terrain and vegetation greatly hindered maneuver and was favorable to defensive fighting. Consequently, neither commander was able to gain an upper hand and drive his opponent from the field. As frequently happens at such a juncture, the opposing commanders, Torbert and Hampton, decided—apparently without much thought to alternative courses of action—to feed more forces into the fight in the woods.

12

"Where is the 9th N.Y.?"
Union Momentum Builds on the Fredericksburg Road

With Merritt's advance toward Trevilian Station stalled and Custer's disposition on the Marquis Road unknown, General Torbert called for his remaining brigade, that of Colonel Thomas C. Devin, to move forward. Devin, the colonel of the 6th New York, was a veteran of all of the campaigns of the Army of the Potomac's Cavalry Corps. For more than a year he had served in brigade command, demonstrating fine tactical judgment and calmness under fire. His men affectionately referred to him as "Old Tom" or "Old War Horse." Devin, who also happened to much older than the other senior commanders in Torbert's division, was admired as an officer "who knew how to take his men into action and also how to bring them out."[1]

On the morning of June 11, Devin had available three New York regiments: the 4th, the 6th, and the 9th. His remaining regiment, the 17th Pennsylvania, had the previous day been diverted to find a suspected Confederate hospital in Spotsylvania County and had not yet reported back from that mission.[2] As Devin's column moved forward, Merritt began repositioning his regiments, shifting to his right to extend the Union line to the west. Torbert intended for Devin to fall in line to Merritt's left, thereby extending the Union line to the east.[3] It is likely that Torbert wished to extend his line beyond both of Butler's flanks and thereby create an opportunity turn the Confederates out of their positions in the woods.

The 9th New York led Devin's column out of their camps and south on the Fredericksburg Road. As it moved up to the rear of Merritt's line about half way to Trevilian's, the regiment deployed to right of the Fredericksburg Road, tying in to the left flank of the 1st New York Dragoons. On the left of the 9th New York, a detachment of about thirty men from the 2nd U.S. was posted to block the road itself. The 9th New York, under the command of Colonel William Sackett, mustered about 220 officers and men after leaving one in four in the rear with the horses.[4]

Under orders from Torbert, Devin sent the 4th New York, which was following the 9th, to the left of the Fredericksburg Road, tying-in with the 1st U.S. on its right. The 1st U.S. had been immediately to the left of the detachment of the 2nd U.S. which was positioned on the road. Shortly after the 4th New York took up its positions, however, the 1st U.S. and the detachment of the 2nd U.S. were withdrawn, and Devin ordered the 4th New York to extend its line to the right while the 9th New York extended its line to the left, resulting in one of

12. "Where is the 9th N.Y.?"

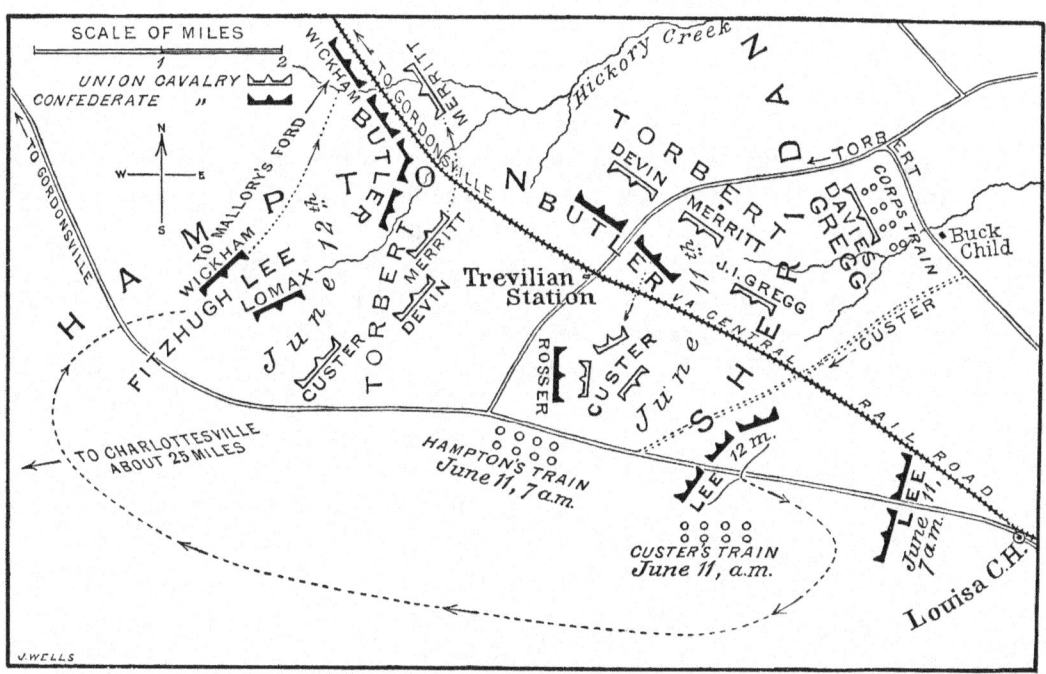

MAP OF THE BATTLE OF TREVILIAN STATION. FOR SHERIDAN'S ROUTE DURING THE RAID, SEE MAP, P. 190.

This map was prepared to accompany Theodore Rodenbough's article on the Battle of Trevilian Station in *Battles and Leaders of the Civil War*. It shows Devin's brigade attacking to the left of Merritt's brigade which is contrary to Devin's official report. Devin wrote that the 4th New York was to the left of the main road and the 9th New York was to the road's right, with Merritt's brigade to the right of the 9th New York. Many modern maps of the battle incorrectly conform to Rodenbough's (*Battles and Leaders*).

Devin's regiments being posted on each side of the road, thereby blocking the main avenue of approach from the south.[5]

Devin then brought Heaton's battery forward and posted it on his extreme left flank and ordered three squadrons of the 6th New York to support the guns. One squadron of the 6th was dispatched to the east to find and communicate with Custer's brigade, while one squadron remained with the division's baggage train to provide its security. Devin had previously detailed one company of the 6th—his own regiment—to his headquarters to provide security and serve as couriers.[6]

At this point, with two of Devin's regiments deployed abreast of Merritt, there was approximate parity between the opposing forces. The Confederates had seventy-two companies committed to the fight in the woods while the Union had committed sixty-eight.

Having deployed his forces, Devin positioned himself on the road between the 9th New York and the 4th New York. Almost immediately afterward, General Torbert arrived. Torbert, formerly an infantry brigade commander, likely felt at home with the dismounted troopers fighting in the woods. Accompanied by Devin, Torbert made his way forward to join the skirmishers and observe the action.

To the right and left of the road, fighting in the woods continued without either side gaining a clear upper hand. On Butler's far right, Colonel Hugh Aiken continued to maintain contact with the enemy, pushing his troops of the 6th South Carolina forward through the brush toward a rail fence which he intended to occupy as a breastwork. Unbeknownst to Aiken, Devin's New Yorkers were approaching the fence from the opposite direction with the same intention. As Aiken stooped to pass under a chinquapin bush, he was struck in the collarbone by a bullet. The ball passed downward through the left side of his chest and exited under his shoulder blade. Although the wound was thought to be mortal, Aiken's men carried their colonel to the rear where a field hospital had been established. With Aiken wounded, Major Thomas Ferguson assumed command of the regiment.[7]

Also fighting in the woods with the 5th South Carolina was Private James Barr. His horse, Jeff Davis, had suffered much on the march to Virginia and the in the initial fighting east and north of Richmond. In a letter to his wife on June 5, Barr wrote, "My horse is poor and does not look like himself.... I hope Wesley will come and bring me Jim or Old Pete. You may not think they will do, but we don't want fine horses here. All we want is a horse that will not fall down. It don't make any difference how ugly he is."[8] Despite his poor condition, Jeff Davis had made the march to Trevilian's and was in the rear with the led horses.

Barr, kneeling under the trees, was shot in the right leg about one and one-half inches below his kneecap. The ball struck the bone in his leg without shattering it, and then exited through the calf. Unable to walk, Barr lay on the field for about an hour before two men "toted [him] off to a hollow," and then carried him by litter farther back to an ambulance. As the ambulance took Barr and other wounded to the rear it was almost captured by Yankees.[9]

Shortly after Devin began deploying his regiments, General Sheridan arrived at the rear of Old Tom's brigade to see the fighting first-hand. Sheridan's presence at the front was always certain to arouse the ardor of the men in the ranks. Unfortunately, on the Fredericksburg Road with woods close on both the right and left, the commanding general was not visible to most of the men skirmishing in the brush and trees. The trees also obscured Sheridan's view of the front lines. However, Sheridan was an experienced commander and likely could tell from the sounds of gunfire—both

Colonel William Sackett, commanding the 9th New York Cavalry, was mortally wounded on the morning of June 11. He died in a Confederate field hospital on June 14. A month later, Sackett's wife, passing through the lines under a flag of truce, recovered her husband's remains and returned them to his home town for burial (Library of Congress).

its volume and direction—that Torbert's men were facing stiff opposition and having difficulty making headway. Noting the physical conditions of the battlefield and the apparent parity between the opposing forces, Sheridan sent to orders to the rear for General David McM. Gregg to send forward his second brigade, under the command of Gregg's cousin, Colonel James Irwin Gregg, to reinforce Torbert.

At this point, the battle essentially became Torbert's to win or lose. Sheridan had available five brigades of cavalry and five batteries of artillery. Of that force, he had now allocated four brigades of cavalry and four batteries of artillery—Randol's battery accompanied Gregg's brigade—to Torbert. David McM. Gregg—the most experienced senior Union cavalry officer on the field—was left with only one brigade under his command, and shortly later in the afternoon Sheridan directed Gregg to send an additional cavalry regiment, the 10th New York, to Torbert. For most of the day, the bulk of Davies's brigade, which remained under David McM. Gregg's control, guarded the expedition's trains west of the intersection of the Fredericksburg and Marquis Roads north of Buck Child's.[10]

As Colonel Gregg's five Pennsylvania regiments—the 2nd, 4th, 8th, 13th, and 16th—arrived in Torbert's rear, Torbert suspended his attack—such as it was—to complete the redeployment of his forces. Torbert ordered Gregg's regiments to fall in on his left thereby extending his line to the east as Merritt had extended the line to west. By overlapping the Confederate lines in the woods, Torbert intended to turn the Confederate left flank to the west of the Fredericksburg Road. In addition, he perhaps could make contact to the east with Custer, whose position and situation was still unknown.

Gregg, the colonel of the 16th Pennsylvania, was an experienced officer. He had served as a lieutenant and captain in the 11th U.S. Infantry during the Mexican War. Afterward he was active in the Pennsylvania militia, rising to the grade of lieutenant colonel. Upon the outbreak of the war he was commissioned as a captain in the newly-formed 6th U.S. Cavalry and served with that regiment until he was appointed commander of the 16th Pennsylvania in January 1863. Since Brandy Station, Gregg had been in command of the brigade and he could be relied upon to skillfully manage his regiments as they moved forward into the fight. However, neither Torbert nor Gregg recorded the disposition of the Pennsylvania regiments as they moved up into lin.[11] Gregg directed his sixth regiment, the 1st Maine, to support Randol's battery, 1st U.S. H&I.[12]

As the regiments moved into their new positions, the sound of fighting could be heard from the direction of Louisa Courthouse, Custer having advanced into the Confederate rear well east of Trevilian Station.[13]

At this point, conditions in the woods were turning to the favor of the Union. Attacking from the north, Torbert had available 129 cavalry companies supported by three batteries of artillery. Butler had available seventy-two cavalry companies supported by two batteries.[14] More importantly, Custer with forty-six companies and one battery had come into action in Butler's right rear, placing Hampton's Division at a severe tactical disadvantage.

Perhaps frustrated by Torbert's apparent lack of progress, aware of the sound of heavy firing in Hampton's rear, and anxious to get the attack moving, Sheridan went to Devin and inquired if he had a regiment that could break through the Confederate defensive line in the woods. Devin replied immediately, "Yes, I have. Where is the 9th N.Y.?" Devin, finding commander of the 9th New York, Colonel William Sackett, with his regiment skirmishing on the right of the road, ordered Sackett to advance his regiment, but advised him to proceed cautiously. Sackett gave the command, "Forward," and he and his 220 men aggressively plunged forward through the brush. Unable to see their enemy, the New Yorkers immediately came under heavy fire with Sackett among the first to fall, seriously wounded. About forty other officers and men were also killed or wounded during the first few moments of their attack, but despite their losses, the New Yorkers continued their advance in the Union center. They drove the Confederates back across an open field and through a wooded ravine. Once through the ravine, the advancing men came to the edge of a large field, offering a view to the railroad station near which Butler's led horses could be seen.[15]

At about the same time, Gregg's men begin to move into action, advancing on the left of the line. With the Confederates falling back under pressure from their line in the woods straddling the Fredericksburg Road, the stalemate in the woods along the Fredericksburg Road had begun to break. Although the regulars, Pennsylvanians, and New Yorkers were unaware, their successes were largely a result of the unexpected appearance of George Custer and his Wolverines in the rear of Hampton's Division.

13

"Pardonable zeal"
Colonel Alger's Charge to Trevilian Station

In accordance with Hampton's orders for the morning of June 11, Fitz Lee's Division made an early start from its camps east of Louisa Courthouse and proceeded north on the Marquis Road. Wickham's Brigade, with the 1st, 2nd, 3rd, and 4th Virginia Cavalry Regiments, led the march followed by Lomax's Brigade with the 5th, 6th, and 15th Virginia Regiments.

Making good progress against no opposition, the Virginians moved toward Clayton's Store where—if things went as planned—they would join with Hampton's Division and together attack Sheridan's force. Meanwhile, about half-way between Louisa Courthouse and Clayton's Store, the men of the 7th Michigan—Major Melvin Brewer commanding—of Custer's Brigade, Torbert's Division, were just beginning to brew their coffee and cook their breakfast of bacon and flapjacks.[1] At daylight, after advancing about three miles, Wickham's men made contact with Brewer's picket line. Wickham immediately launched an attack in regimental strength against the Union line, forcing Brewer's men to abandon their cook-fires to reinforce the men on picket duty. Wickham's attack stalled and he was not successful in overwhelming the Union security screen and driving it to the rear.

It is not clear how many regiments

Williams Wickham's Brigade of Virginians initiated the day's action, making contact with Custer's men along the Marquis Road south of Buck Chile's. However, Wickham did not press his attack, allowing Custer to move via a track through the woods into Hampton's rear (Library of Congress).

Wickham deployed after making contact, but the action was not particularly hard fought. In his memoir, Lieutenant Robert T. Hubard, Jr., 3rd Virginia Cavalry, recorded the events after making initial contact with Brewer's pickets early that morning:

> Coming now upon a larger body, we deployed skirmishers, halted to reconnoiter, brought up and planted some two or three pieces of artillery and somehow or other lost two or three hours.
>
> The clover in the field where we stood dismounted being fine, our horses were biting at it very vigorously and in this way Captain William Boyd's [squadron of] "A" and I [companies], having gotten some twenty-five yards in front of the line, were reclining in the grass and allowing our horses to bait. Mine being white attracted the attention of a Yankee sharpshooter who could not have been nearer that eight hundred yards. He fired at times and the ball fell about five feet short but it was a line shot. On loading, he fired again, the ball this time striking the ground about six inches of[f] the hind feet of my horse. Our guns now opened on their skirmishers who fell back somewhat.[2]

One may question why Lee, with seven regiments available, did not immediately bring up additional forces to drive in Custer's pickets and then continue his movement toward Clayton's Store. It is possible Lee was concerned that he had progressed farther than Hampton's Division, and might thus bring on a general engagement with Hampton unable to support him. At the time, Butler's Brigade had not yet made contact with Merritt's men on the Fredericksburg Road several miles to the west.

Custer, reacting quickly to the Confederate advance, sent the 1st Michigan, commanded by Lieutenant Colonel Peter Stagg, forward to support the 7th, which would have further impeded any progress that might have been attempted by Lee. Union and Confederate forces skirmished inconclusively along the road for roughly an hour. Since Lee failed to commit additional regiments to the protracted engagement, Custer retained the freedom to act as he wished. Consequently, in accordance with his orders from Torbert, Custer began his movement on the narrow road leading off to the right of the Marquis Road and through the woods toward Trevilian Station.[3] Sometime after Custer began his march, Lee ordered his dismounted men to advance at the quick time. According to Hubbard, the men moved forward "smartly," and found that "no force of consequence was upon our front."[4]

Coming into the open east of the station, Custer ordered Colonel Russell Alger to charge with the 5th Michigan. This portrait is marked "Alger" on its reverse. The facial features appear similar to Alger's (Library of Congress).

13. "Pardonable zeal"

Custer's column was led by Colonel Russell Alger and the 5th Michigan, with a battalion of four companies commanded by Major H.S. Hastings as the advance guard. Custer, with his color bearer and aides de camp, rode immediately behind Hastings's battalion. Alger and the main body of his regiment followed Custer, and Captain Alexander Pennington's four guns of Battery M, 2nd U.S. Artillery, followed Alger. Major James H. Kidd and the 6th Michigan followed Pennington.[5] After the 6th Michigan got underway, the 7th Michigan withdrew from the picket line and fell in behind the 6th, a movement that was conducted with a certain amount of confusion. Lieutenant Harmon Smith, commanding Company F, had dismounted with his pickets and was almost left behind. "Following up the rebels I almost forgot the rear of my own command, and upon looking about I saw the whole force in rapid motion going away from us and in the direction of the Station, my horse with the lot. By almost superhuman effort I gained the column and my horse."[6] As the 7th moved into the woods, the 1st Michigan fell-in at the rear of the column, acting as the brigade's rear guard.[7] Although not documented in the records, Custer's ambulances and wagons likely were between the 7th Michigan and the 1st Michigan in the march column.

That morning, Major Kidd, in command of the 6th Michigan, had made a foolish error in judgment. Another officer in the regiment had asked if Kidd would ride his "spirited and

This photograph shows the Trevilian depot in 2015 looking toward the west. During the Civil War, the depot stood on the north side of the track, not the south side as it does today. Perhaps contrary to Custer's orders, Alger and his men swept past the depot and overran Hampton's led horses and trains. However, surrounded by Confederates, the 5th Michigan suffered heavy losses including 136 men captured (author's photograph).

nervous black horse.... 'To take the ginger out of him.'" Kidd, not knowing that there would be fighting that day, had acceded to the request and found himself riding toward battle atop an excitable horse while seated in saddle such as a jockey might use in a race instead of a standard-issue McClellan saddle with its substantial pommel and cantle.[8]

The route Custer's brigade took through the woods toward Trevilian Station was more of a track than a road, and the regiments were unable to move in a column of fours which was the preferred formation for marching. Instead, the men were forced to move in a file, which greatly extended the length of the column and increased the time it would take for the regiments to deploy when it became necessary to do so.[9]

Torbert, when forming his plan for the day, believed that the track on which Custer's brigade was moving intersected the Central Virginia Railroad and the Gordonsville Road—which paralleled the railroad on its south side—near Trevilian Station. Actually, the track intersected the railroad and Gordonsville Road more than a mile to the east of the station, about one-third of the distance between Louisa Courthouse and Trevilian's. As the track neared the railroad, it entered a broad clearing where over the years the trees had been felled to provide ties for the rails and fuel for the locomotives. Major Hastings and his men, after crossing the railroad tracks and reaching the intersection of the track with the Gordonsville Road, were able to see across the clearing and were presented with a view to stir the heart of any cavalryman. Drawn up in the field to their front, unprotected, was Wade Hampton's baggage train. Custer, close behind Hastings, sent one of his aides, Lieutenant F. Stewart Stranahan, to Colonel Alger with orders to immediately charge with the 5th Michigan.[10]

Alger quickly moved his regiment—numbering about three hundred men—into the open field, closed ranks, and ordered the charge. Alger's Wolverines, galloping in a column up the Gordonsville Road, easily overran the baggage train while driving off any mounted Confederates in their path. James Hart's Battery which had been supporting Butler's Brigade, was also almost overrun and captured by Alger's men. However, Lieutenant E. Lindsay Halsey—Hart was ill that morning and had remained in camp—was able to withdraw his guns to a nearby hill where although hard pressed, they "opened on the enemy in all directions."[11]

Alger then sent Lieutenant Stranahan, who had accompanied him in the charge, back to Custer with word of the 5th Michigan's success.[12]

Custer later reported that he had directed Alger to halt at the station to allow the main body of the brigade to close-up, but in the heat of battle and "acting under the impulse of pardonable zeal," Alger continued his attack for roughly a mile past the station where his men captured about 800

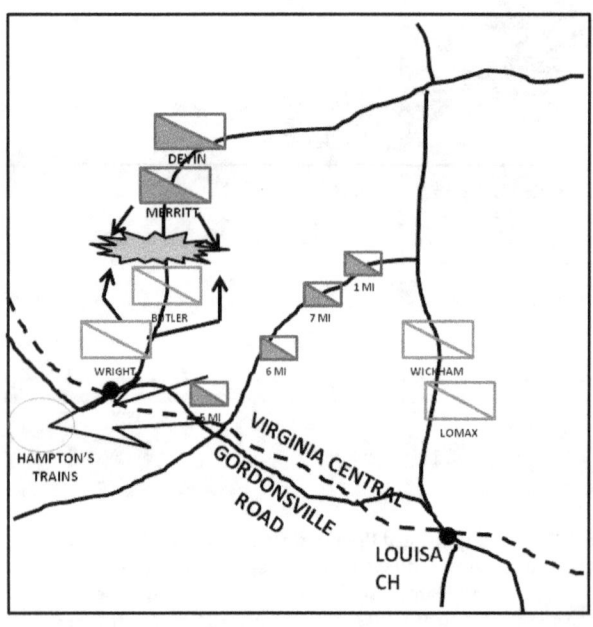

Alger's Charge at Trevilian's

horses from Butler's Brigade, along with several spare caissons belonging to Hampton's artillery.[13]

Sergeant Wiley Howard, of Company C, Cobb's Legion, being ill that morning, was detailed to remain with the led horses of Wright's Brigade and thus was in the path of Custer's brigade as it attacked toward the station. Howard described what it was like to be on the receiving end of Alger's charge as the led horses stampeded.

> Mounted on the horse of one of our dead comrades, I did what I could to stay the rush; but the Seventh Georgia being driven back on us, a general fall-back and reforming of the lines was necessary and in the melee I was chased for a mile by fifty or more Yankees. I jumped my horse over a pile of shells spilled in the road by a disabled caisson. Finally, my horse, descending a slant, stumbled and fell. I caught on my hands, tearing the hide from my hand and exposing the leaders. As I ran, a Yankee overtook me, shooting and shouting 'Surrender,' but I did not. I scrambled over the fence and heard a ball hit the rail behind me. I made time across the field while the whole pack practiced on me as a target. Strange to say, I was not hit and soon gained the cover of a wood, worn down and panting.

Next, Howard encountered a trooper from the Jeff Davis Legion who was also hiding in the woods. Evading the Yankees, the two made their way back to Confederate lines where they came upon Hampton's provost marshal with a detail guarding prisoners. Howard, who had bandaged his injured hand, remounted on a horse taken from a captured Union lieutenant colonel and spent the rest of the day acting as a courier for General Hampton.[14]

Once Alger launched his charge into the clearing, Custer sent one of his staff officers back with orders for Kidd to "take the gallop and pass the battery," referring to Pennington's guns. Unfortunately, Kidd, himself, had just reached the edge of the clearing, and his regiment was strung out in a file through the woods to the rear. Kidd, who had no knowledge of the situation to his front, commanded his leading squadron to "form fours, gallop, march." Kidd put his spurs to the excitable black horse and immediately found himself "flying to the front" with the men of his leading squadron catching up as best they could. Kidd had also detailed one of his staff officers to remain at the edge of the clearing and relay the order to form fours and take up the gallop to the trailing squadrons as they came forward in succession.[15] Thus, instead of entering the fight with his regiment, Kidd found himself at the front of a long column of widely separated squadrons.

As he neared the intersection of the track and the Gordonsville Road, Kidd saw Custer and his staff exchanging pistol fire with Confederates to their front. As Kidd approached, he noticed that Custer, "Who never lost his nerve under any circumstances," was this day "unmistakably excited." As he rode up, Custer "laconically" ordered Kidd to "charge them," and repeated the order for emphasis. Glancing to the rear and finding his leading squadron "pretty well closed up," Kidd commanded his men to "draw sabers." Without forming into line or waiting for the arrival of the bulk of his regiment, Kidd and the black horse led the squadron, still in what was a most likely ragged column of fours, into the fight.[16]

The Confederates scattered to the right and left as Kidd and his men continued their charge at "breakneck speed" for perhaps 500 yards. With no enemy in sight, Kidd holstered his pistol to free both hands for use on his reins, as the black horse, now with its blood up, was difficult to control. As the squadron commander, Captain Harvey Vinton, came alongside, Kidd ordered a halt. Vinton apparently did not hear the command and with his squadron continued the charge up the road as the black horse—by now completely out of control—

swerved off to the right and into some woods before Kidd could bring it to a halt. Hearing hoof beats behind him, Kidd thought that his men were returning, but next he heard a command for him to surrender "uttered in imperious tones." Looking over his shoulder, Kidd discovered a "sturdy" Confederate officer accompanied by several men, carbines at the ready. With no other recourse, Kidd surrendered, giving up the black horse and the jockey-style saddle and "glad to be rid of them on most any terms."[17]

Four Confederates were detailed to escort Kidd and a second prisoner to the rear and they set out, the Rebels mounted and the Yankees on foot. Fortunately, Custer had ordered a trailing squadron of the 6th Michigan, commanded by Captain Manning D. Birge, to charge after Kidd and Captain Vinton's squadron, who by then had ridden out of sight to the west. The sound of Birge's approach distracted the four guards, and the two prisoners made a break through the woods as the guards fled. Seeing four Confederates fleeing out of the woods, Birge led a portion of his squadron into the trees rescuing Kidd. Kidd, who had been a prisoner "for about ten minutes," later wrote, "I can see and freely acknowledge that to no man on this earth am I under greater obligation than to Manning D. Birge."[18] Birge and his men continued toward the depot as Kidd made his way on foot back toward Custer and the main body of the brigade.

Meanwhile, after advancing at the gallop for between three to four miles, Alger began consolidating his gains in expectation of a Confederate counterattack. Many of his men had been left along the route to guard the prisoners, horses, and wagons that had been captured.[19] Concerned about being isolated, Alger sent Captain Brewster, the regiment's commissary of subsistence, to the rear to ask for support. Brewster soon returned and informed Alger that the Confederates were in heavy force between the regiment and the main body of the brigade and that they were attacking the men who had been left behind as guards to secure the captured horses, men, and equipment.[20]

Alger began withdrawing, but was soon struck on the right flank by a large body of Confederates. The Confederates captured many of Alger's men and then turned to engage the main body of the brigade, effectively cutting off Alger's route of withdrawal. With about forty men and half-dozen officers, Alger withdrew to his right to take cover in a narrow strip of woods. Once they were concealed in the trees, columns of mounted Confederates passed by the men of the 5th Michigan on both the right and left. At one point, a Confederate officer, spotting the Wolverines, entered the woods and asked which command they belonged to. One of Alger's officers, thinking quickly, replied, "Hampton's," and the Rebel officer returned to his unit.[21]

Cautiously picking their way east, Alger and his small party encountered another column of Confederate cavalry blocking their route of escape. Alger ordered a charge to break through the column, but more than half of his men were cut-off and left behind, hiding in the woods under the charge of commissary sergeant Henry Avery.[22] Alger and the few men still with him made their way east almost to Louisa Courthouse. They then headed to the north and reentered Federal lines near where they had camped the night before, covering about twenty miles during the day.

Thus far in the morning, Custer and his men had enjoyed unexpected success. With relative ease they had captured Wade Hampton's baggage train and many of his division's led horses. However, several aspects of the situation were troubling. The 5th Michigan was disorganized and although few men had been killed or wounded, a large number—including the commander—were either captured or evading capture. The commander of the 6th Michigan had been captured and one-third of that regiment was scattered. The 7th Michigan and the 1st Michigan were still moving forward through the woods. While Custer was not yet heavily engaged, bodies of Confederate cavalry—although uncoordinated—had begun to respond to the incursion in their rear. However, it is likely that Custer did not fully realize the true gravity of his situation. To his north were two brigades of Confederate cavalry—those of Butler and Wright—which although decisively engaged were capable of deploying some amount of force against the Michigan Brigade. To the west was Rosser's Brigade which had not yet been committed to battle. To the northeast lay Fitz Lee's Division which within one to two hours could commit two brigades against Custer's rear. There was a distinct possibility that over the next few hours, Custer's Brigade might be engaged by superior forces from the north, the west, and the east, and be destroyed.

14

"Where the hell is the rear?"
Custer's First Last Stand

While George Custer, with his brigade near the railroad depot surrounded by Confederate forces, faced challenges, Wade Hampton found himself under equally difficult circumstances. Two of his brigades, mostly dismounted and dispersed in the woods to the right and left of the Fredericksburg Road, were fighting three dismounted Union brigades. To his rear, he was threatened by a fresh Union incursion in significant strength, although Hampton may or may not have known that the threat was Custer's Brigade. Hampton's only uncommitted force was Thomas Rosser's Brigade, held in reserve about two miles west of Trevilian Station on the Gordonsville Road.[1] Rosser's "Laurel Brigade" had considerable strength, consisting of the 7th, 11th, and 12th Virginia Regiments and the 35th Virginia, a six-company battalion. Additionally, Rosser's Brigade was augmented with the 1st Maryland Cavalry, also a six-company battalion.

While Hampton may not initially have been aware that an enemy brigade had gained his rear, or that his baggage train, artillery caissons, and led horses had been taken, once he understood that the threat was significant he reacted quickly. Immediately, Hampton sent orders to Butler to withdraw his regiments from contact and remount. Later, Butler observed that this order was "easier said than done."[2] His regiments, dismounted and deployed in the thick woods, were aligned with the 4th South Carolina on the left, the 5th South Carolina in the center, and the 6th South Carolina on the right, and all were under heavy pressure on their front from dismounted Union cavalry. Regiments assigned to Young's Brigade, under the command of Colonel "Gid" Wright, were intermixed with Butler's regiments making a coordinated withdrawal even more difficult. Butler was unaware of the location of his subordinate commanders and perhaps also unaware that Colonel Aiken, commanding the 6th, had been seriously wounded. At the time, Butler had only one squadron in the saddle and capable of reacting quickly, that being commanded by Captain John Calhoun of the 4th South Carolina. On receiving his orders, Butler reportedly told Hampton's courier, "Say to General Hampton it is hell to hold on and hell to let go." Butler went on to explain to the courier, "If I withdraw my entire line at once the blue coats will run over us, and that the best I can do is to mount one regiment at a time and gradually retire."[3] As the courier hurried off to Hampton with that information, Butler began slowly withdrawing his brigade one regiment at a time as he had advised, mounting each on "such horses as we could reach."[4]

As Butler's forces began disengaging, Torbert pushed his regiments forward, maintaining contact and intending to turn Hampton's right flank with Gregg's Brigade. Although about this time Torbert could hear Custer's guns from the vicinity of the Trevilian's depot, he believed that the Confederate withdrawal was more a result of pressure from Merritt's and Devin's Brigades than a response to a threat in the Confederate rear.[5]

Meanwhile, to the west awaiting orders, Rosser sent out scouts toward Gordonsville to determine if Union forces were attempting to move around Butler's left flank to attack the railroad at that important junction. He also sent scouts to the rear of his brigade to ensure he was not being enveloped by the enemy. However, before his scouts returned, a soldier assigned to Young's Brigade came galloping up the road from Trevilian Station. The trooper, who was without his hat and had suffered a saber cut across his face, reported that Union cavalry was in the rear of Butler's and Young's Brigades, and that the enemy had captured Hampton's wagon train and the two brigades' led horses. Rosser ordered a company to mount up and move east to confirm the report, but before the company could get underway, several more Confederates came galloping up at full speed shouting, "Yankees! Yankees!" Rosser immediately ordered his brigade to mount and led his men forward at the trot.[6]

At West Point, Thomas Rosser and George Custer had been close friends. At Trevilian's, they fought each other for the first time. Wounded late in the day, Rosser advised his next-in-command, "... fight with the men mounted. Let the other Cav. fight as infantry" (*Battles and Leaders*).

At the crossroads east of the depot, Custer was busy attempting to bring order to his disorganized brigade and establish a coherent defense until Merritt's and Devin's Brigades could link-up with him. Colonel Alger and the 5th Michigan had charged well past the depot and were out of sight to the east. Major Kidd, as ordered, had followed the 5th with one or two of his squadrons of the 6th Michigan and Confederates had closed-in behind them, blocking the road to the depot and threatening Custer's main body. In response, Custer dismounted a portion of the 7th Michigan and sent them forward to counter that threat and very quickly the Rebels withdrew.

At about this time, Major Kidd, who had just escaped from his very short period of captivity, made his way back to rejoin Custer. Kidd found that Custer had thrown up a barricade across the road and had posted two mounted squadrons in the woods at the side of the road to repel any further incursions that might be made against the brigade by the Rebels. After a few minutes, Sergeant Martin Avery, who had participated in the charge led by Captain Birge, also returned through the Union line. Avery brought with him a very well-mounted Confederate—the Confederate riding ahead with Avery following, his pistol drawn and

Thomas Rosser, shown waving his hat at center left, charged Custer with his brigade on the morning of June 11, initiating what some have since called "Custer's first last stand." Custer, on the right center, saved his battle flag after Sergeant Mitchell Belloir, his color bearer, was mortally wounded (*The Confederate Soldier in the Civil*).

cocked. Upon being ordered, the Confederate dismounted and according to Kidd "gave the horse a caress and with something very like a tear in his eye said: 'That is the best horse in the Seventh Georgia Cavalry.'"[7] The horse, with Avery's permission, was turned over to Kidd as a replacement for the black horse that had been taken from him earlier. For the price of a few minutes' captivity, Kidd thus obtained a fine horse he would ride until it succumbed to severe weather in the Shenandoah Valley during the coming winter.[8]

Thus far, Custer's opposition appears to have been mainly companies and squadrons from Wright's brigade that had not yet dismounted and deployed into the woods to take up the fight against Merritt, Devin, and Gregg. The Confederates were not in great strength, nor were their actions coordinated. Nonetheless, the Rebels reacted swiftly and aggressively, aided by the fact that the bulk of two of Custer's regiments were at the time strung out to the rear on the track through the woods. Although the Confederates could not initially generate sufficient strength to defeat Custer's Brigade, as Hampton withdrew Butler's and Young's Brigades from contact in the woods, more pressure could be brought to bear on Custer from the north.

Once the enemy to his front had withdrawn, Custer shifted his command about a mile to the west, perhaps hoping to regain contact with Alger and the 5th Michigan. However, at the depot Custer discovered a large body of Confederate cavalry supported by a battery of artillery on the road to his front. Custer deployed his men near the depot, called forward a section from Pennington's battery to go into action at the depot, and ordered the 7th Michigan to draw sabers and charge the Rebels as soon as Pennington's guns opened fire. Custer then sent word to the rear for the 1st Michigan, to move forward as rapidly as possible. Custer intended to conduct a coordinated attack against the Confederates to his front with the 7th charging the enemy frontally and the 1st Michigan against a flank. However, Custer was unable to execute the plan because he learned that the 1st Michigan was "fully employed in holding the enemy, who were making a vigorous assault on our rear."[9]

Meanwhile, as he rode briskly east toward the sound of the fighting, the dense growth of scrub oaks on each side of the Gordonsville Road reminded Rosser of his home in east Texas and he described the vegetation as "almost a chaparral." The road was crooked with frequent turns which limited Rosser's visibility to his front. Rounding a bend well west of Trevilian's depot, he was surprised to come upon a party from Custer's brigade drawn up on the road. Custer's men, apparently not expecting Confederates to approach from the west, had not sent out pickets to provide early warning, and they appeared to Rosser to be as surprised as he was at the unexpected contact. The Yankees apparently believed that Rosser and his men were likely a scouting party and wheeled about to prepare and meet the Confederates while Rosser ordered his bugler to sound the charge. Rosser then led his regiments at the gallop toward the Yankees. In Rosser's words, "I was too quick and too strong for him [Custer] and as I went crashing into him, breaking up and scattering his squadrons, he made a gallant and manly effort to resist me."[10]

Leading with Elijah White's 35th Battalion, known as "The Comanches," on the left of the road and the 11th Virginia on the right of the road, Rosser launched a furious assault on Custer's front. In response, Custer charged west on the road from the station with those men he could gather to blunt this latest Confederate foray. Rosser and Custer had been very close friends at West Point, and through the smoke and dust of the battle, Rosser spied his comrade from their academy years.[11] Rosser later lauded Custer's leadership that day: "Sitting on his horse in the center of his advanced platoons, and near enough to be easily recognized by me, he encouraged and inspired his men by

Lieutenant Colonel Elijah White and his "Comanches" led Rosser's charge. In the confusion afterward, several of White's men dismounted to fill their canteens from a barrel of applejack that had fallen from a wagon. Alert Union artillerymen dropped a shell into their midst, killing two men and wounding five others (Library of Congress).

appeal as well as by example." According to Rosser, in the melee his acting assistant adjutant general, Major Holmes Conrad, who while perhaps shooting at Custer, instead hit Custer's color bearer, Sergeant Mitchell Belloir. Belloir, although mortally wounded, remained in the fight until the Union lines began to waver. He then made his way to Custer and told him, "General, they have killed me. Take the flag." Custer tore his battle flag from its staff and stuffed it inside his uniform jacket for safe-keeping.[12]

In the confused fighting, Lieutenant Colonel White pressed ahead with his Comanches, as Custer's troopers fell back and sought safety in the woods. Seeing an unsupported artillery battery, White began deploying men toward it to offer it protection. Fortunately, at that moment Hampton rode up and shouted, "Colonel White, what are you going to do?" White replied, "Going to support that battery." At that, Hampton ordered, "Get away from here, Colonel, it's a Yankee battery." As White quickly began repositioning his troops away from the enemy battery, several men stopped at a wrecked wagon which had lost its load—including a barrel of apple-jack—in the road. Three dismounted men were wrestling with the barrel to open the bung and a few riders stopped with the intent of filling their canteens. The small group in the road was too tempting a target for the nearby artillery, which dropped a shell into their midst. One man was killed outright, one was mortally wounded, and five were seriously wounded, one of whom lost a leg. The shell also killed one horse and wounded a second.[13]

Facing pressure heavy pressure from Confederates to his west, and increasing pressure from the north and east, Custer withdrew his regiments into a circular perimeter—described by some as more triangular in shape—enabling him to defend against attacks from any direction. Interior lines within the perimeter allowed Custer to rapidly shift men from one side to the other to counter Confederate incursions as they arose. As one of Custer's officers characterized the fight for the perimeter, "We had been fighting in an irregular circle extending over a large territory, a circle the boundaries of which were continually changing. The enemy was energetically and constantly contracting it, at all points, while we were as industriously engaged in expanding it here, there, and everywhere; and there was no place of safety anywhere."[14]

However, withdrawing into a perimeter also had its disadvantages. Custer wrote that "The smallness of my force compelled me to adopt very contracted lines. From the nature of the ground and the character of the attacks that were made upon me our lines resembled very nearly a circle. The space over which we fought was so limited that there was actually no place that could be called under cover, or in other words, the entire ground was in range of the enemy's guns."[15]

Another problem confronting Custer that was made more difficult by

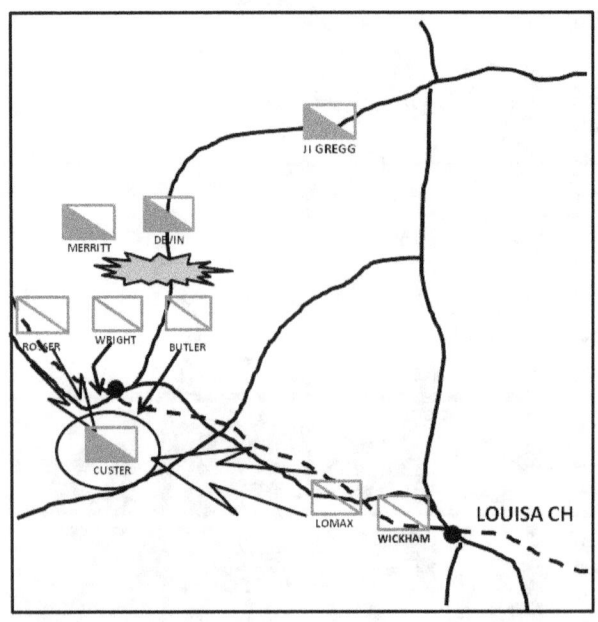

Custer's First Last Stand

the size of the perimeter was the management of the fruits of Alger's headlong charge past the station and deep into Hampton's rear. According to Custer, Alger's 5th Michigan had taken "a large number of wagons, ambulances, caissons, and about 800 led horses, these being the horses of the force engaging General Merritt and Colonel Devin."[16] Additionally Custer's wagon train had come forward with the trailing regiments of the brigade. Within the perimeter there was insufficient space to assemble and secure the captured horses and wagons together with Custer's own led horses and wagons. Additionally, and perhaps more importantly, Custer needed all of his men—and more—to fight the Rebels pressing his position initially from the west and the north, and later from the east.

As Custer was shifting forces to form his perimeter, a decision was made to move the captured horses and material, and Custer's wagon train, which was also within the perimeter. Lieutenant Harmon Smith, who was commanding Company F of the 7th Michigan, recalled that it was his "fortune to be near Genl. Custer, and of course in the middle of the fray," when up came "one officer [who] was so muddled that he asked Custer if it would not be better for safety to move certain things to the rear. The General said 'Yes, By all means,' and then added, 'Where the hell is the rear?'"[17] Smith did not identify the "muddled" officer, who presumably left to move the captures and the trains to west or south.

In his official report of the battle Custer gave a different account of the matter, writing that the situation in the perimeter caused the unidentified officer, "who had assumed charge of the pack trains, caissons, headquarters wagons, and all the property we had captured, to seek without orders a place of safety. In doing so he conducted them into the lines of the enemy where they were captured. In causing this mishap he acted on his own responsibility, impelled by fear alone, and I might add that for his conduct on this occasion the President of the United States has dismissed him from the service for cowardice and treachery."[18]

It seems likely the unidentified officer was Captain Daniel Powers, the commander of Company B, 6th Michigan, who had been detailed with his company to secure the baggage train and the captures. Powers, himself, was captured during the fighting that day. In December 1864, while being held as a prisoner in Columbia, South Carolina, Powers learned that he had been dismissed from the service on July 5, 1864, for cowardice and treachery. Nonetheless, Powers, despite officially being a civilian, continued to be held until his exchange on March 8, 1865.[19]

Additionally, withdrawing into a small perimeter made it difficult for Custer to safely and effectively employ Pennington's four guns. Artillery can generally be most effectively employed at long range. A 3-Inch Ordnance Rifle had an effective range of just more than a mile—roughly four times the effective range of a rifle musket—while the range of a twelve-pound "Light Napoleon" was slightly less than a mile. At range, artillery can engage targets while remaining impervious to either infantry or cavalry small arms fire. Within Custer's perimeter, Captain Pennington's guns were continually under small arms fire and subject to the threat of direct Confederate attack. For example, as mentioned previously, relatively early in the fighting Custer ordered Pennington to bring a section of guns forward to the depot. Pennington found Custer and his staff mounted and standing behind a board fence. Custer directed the captain to place one gun on the road and put the second gun into action behind the fence. The crews positioned their pieces and unlimbered. At the fence, one of the crewmen got an ax to knock down the boards to clear the gun's field for fire. About the time the gunner raised his ax, a line of dismounted Confederates began climbing over a split rail fence about one hundred yards to right. Custer succinctly ordered everyone to "get out of there." According to Pennington, his gun crew "lost no time" in complying.[20]

After breaking contact with Rosser and withdrawing to the east toward the depot, Custer began to come under increasing pressure from Butler and Young's Brigades on his north. Fortunately for Custer—and unfortunately for Hampton—the offensive actions by Butler and Wright were not executed in sufficient strength to overrun Custer's perimeter and defeat the Michigan Brigade. Over the next few hours, elements of Butler's and Young's Brigades launched at least five charges against Custer, none in greater than regimental strength.

John C. Calhoun's squadron of the 4th South Carolina remained mounted as the other squadrons dismounted and deployed into the woods early that morning. Thus Calhoun and his troopers were prepared to rapidly react to the threat posed by Custer's Brigade. In a letter written in November 1908, Calhoun described the events. As Alger's regiment charged—stampeding the horse holders and capturing the led horses and the wagons—Hampton emerged from some trees, jumped his horse over a fence, and galloped up to Calhoun. He ordered Calhoun to form into a column of fours and charge south on the Fredericksburg Road and attack the Union cavalry in the rear. In response, Calhoun's squadron struck Alger's men, "completely routing them" and earning a compliment from Hampton on the field. In his diary entry for June 11, Calhoun provided additional details of the charge: "I charged through the enemies' line of skirmishers throwing them in great confusion; went some two hundred yards to the rear of their line and drove off a squadron of cavalry and charged back through the lines, and occupied my original position." Later that day Calhoun made a second charge. By that time, a number of his men had been detailed to other duties, reducing the strength of his squadron to about sixty-five men. Despite his limited strength, Calhoun charged to the north through Sheridan's lines against a force estimated at two regiments, which he claimed was thrown into confusion.[21]

Also, fairly early in the day Hampton ordered Lieutenant Colonel J. Frederick Waring, commanding the Jeff Davis Legion, to take a small body of his men—likely all that remained mounted—to the rear and charge the Yankees who were at the time capturing the wagons and led

Lieutenant Lucius Carver was lucky on June 11. He and Hampton emptied their pistols at one another over an abandoned artillery piece. Both rode away unscathed. During the fighting on June 11, Hampton—a crack shot—killed two Union soldiers with his pistol. Unfortunately, Carver was killed two months later at Front Royal (*Seventh Regiment Mich. Vol. Cav.*).

horses. Waring led his men south, charged Custer's men, and was in turn charged by them. Waring ordered his men to fall back to his right—the west—and re-crossed the railroad tracks looking for Hampton. Instead he found Major Roger Preston Chew and Chew's Battery, which was under the command of Captain James W. Thomson since Chew's promotion and appointment to battalion command. Since Chew had no cavalry to support the battery, Waring stayed with the guns and watched as the Yankees made off with the trains and horses.[22]

Wade Hampton himself perhaps led the most well-known charge of the day. Hart's Battery, on a small hill in no-man's land between Butler and Custer, was unsupported by Confederate cavalry and threatened with being overrun by Union Cavalry. When Hampton learned of this situation, he rode up to Major Thomas Ferguson, then in command of the 6th South Carolina, and ordered Ferguson to mount his men and follow him. In the lead—directly behind Hampton—was Captain Moses Humphrey's Company F, the Cadet Rangers, many of whom had attended the Citadel before enlisting in the Confederate service.[23] Lieutenant John Bauskett's Company B followed the Cadet Rangers. It is not clear which other companies of the regiment—if any—were able to mount and join the attack. Coming within

Shown from left are four horse artillery officers: Lieut. Robert Clarke, Capt. Charles Tidball, Lieut. W. Neil Dennison, and Capt. Alexander C. M. Pennington. Dennison, the son of the governor of Ohio, commanded Battery A, 2nd U.S., which supported Davies's brigade. Pennington's Battery M, 2nd U.S., supported Custer's Brigade and suffered heavy casualties—2 killed, 5 wounded, and 37 missing—on June 11 (Library of Congress).

sight of Hart's Battery, Hampton ordered a charge and the men spurred their horses into the gallop. In the confusion, Hart's gunners briefly took their fellow-Carolinians under fire, but Hampton pressed ahead. He galloped up to a Union lieutenant, Lucius Carver of the 7th Michigan, and the general and the lieutenant emptied their pistols at each other over one of the guns at a range of ten feet. That neither man was hit was surprising, especially since Hampton was an acknowledged marksman who emptied two Union saddles during the fighting that day.

At about that time, an unidentified Michigan squadron launched a counterattack into Hampton's flank. To meet the attack, Humphrey and Bauskett's men wheeled about, rode down into and up out of a deep railway cut, then jumped a small rail fence before they could get at the Yankees. In the ensuing melee, Lieutenant Bauskett shot the Union officer leading the charge and the man next him, and the Union force fell back. With the defeat of the Union counterattack, Hart's guns were saved.[24]

Later in the day at a field hospital to the rear of Butler's line in the woods, Butler and Hampton met for the first time since fighting had commenced early that morning. Hampton remained concerned about Custer's brigade in his rear and ordered Butler to take a detachment from the Phillips Legion, which was lined up in a column of fours nearby, and attack a large body of Union troopers near the railroad. It is likely that only a squadron or two of the Phillips Legion was available since Lieutenant Colonel Rich, the commander of the Phillips Legion, was not present. Instead, at the head of the column of Georgians was Lieutenant Hugh Buchanan, the commander of Company D. Butler deployed a line of mounted skirmishers and moved out to the south. Upon approaching the railroad, the Confederates came under fire and Lieutenant Buchanan was wounded in the chest and carried from the field. Butler ordered a charge, and the men of Phillips Legion drove the Union troopers back from the tracks.[25]

From high ground near the railroad, Butler could see most of Custer's brigade and concluded that it was being hard-pressed from several directions. Butler sent a staff officer, Captain Andrew Pickens Butler to Hampton with a request for artillery.[26] But instead of receiving artillery, a courier from Hampton arrived with orders for Butler to return to the field hospital as quickly as possible since the defensive line at that location was threatened by Yankees advancing from the north.

Meanwhile to the east, Fitzhugh Lee, alerted by the sound of heavy fighting off to his west, had ordered his regiments to remount and begin moving south toward Louisa Courthouse. Presently, a courier from Hampton arrived and informed Lee that Butler's Brigade was engaged and had suffered heavy losses. In response, Lee picked up the pace and upon reaching Louisa Courthouse turned west on the road to Gordonsville toward the sound of the fighting.[27] Lomax's Brigade, which had trailed Wickham's Brigade on the early-morning march toward Clayton's Store, was now leading the movement with the 15th Virginia at the front. About the time the division began moving that morning, an unexpected event occurred. General Lomax, in the presence of the regiment, relieved Lieutenant Colonel John Critcher from command of the 15th Virginia.

Critcher, a lawyer from Westmoreland County who was not highly regarded by his superiors, had seen little duty in the past year.[28] Captured in May 1863, he was exchanged in March 1864 after ten months' imprisonment at Johnson Island. However, he did not return to duty with the regiment until mid–May.[29] Lomax, upon observing Critcher in the field quickly formed the opinion that the lieutenant colonel was unsuitable for regimental command. Lomax consulted with Fitz Lee on the matter, and Lee apparently agreed with Lomax's assessment. However, the relief itself was delayed because of the tempo of operations in late May through early June, including the rapid march to Louisa County. Although changes in command can be disruptive, Lomax obviously thought it imperative to replace Critcher with a more capable officer before the regiment went into battle on June 11. To that end, Lomax and Lee had previously arranged to replace Critcher with a highly regarded major, Robert Mason, a cousin to Fitz Lee who was serving as Lee's divisional quartermaster. It is likely that Lomax's decision to bring in Mason that morning was also influenced by the fact that the 15th Virginia had no field grade officers—other than Critcher—and only three captains present for duty at the time.[30]

Advancing to the west from Louisa Courthouse along the Gordonsville Road with the 15th Virginia in the lead, the sound of gunfire and artillery to their front told Lomax's veterans that they were approaching an intense fight. Doubtless, the men of the advance guard were surprised when they unexpectedly came upon Custer's brigade trains—baggage wagons, ambulances, and artillery caissons—pulled off at the side of road.[31] Very quickly the Virginians overran and captured Custer's trains, which was not too significant a gain, other than the caissons. Of most interest then—as now—was the fact that Lomax's men also captured Custer's headquarters wagon with his correspondence and personal belongings, as well as Custer's cook, Eliza Brown, a former slave from near Amissville in Culpeper County.[32] Private B.K. Whittle, 2nd Virginia, wrote of the event in a letter to his father. "We captured all of Custer's baggage & a negro woman who claimed to be his wife, but she lies I expect."[33]

Eliza, who because of her tart personality was called "The Queen of Sheba" by Custer's headquarters staff, traveled in a dilapidated carriage that had been taken from its Southern owners sometime earlier in the war. When the trains were overrun by the Confederates, Eliza fled on foot carrying both her valise and Custer's. She was quickly apprehended, and her captors relieved her of Custer's bag. One of the Rebels ordered Eliza to get up behind him on his horse and she refused, prompting the Rebel to remark, "Ain't she damned impudent." Somehow, Eliza—after being escorted about two miles to the rear—escaped and made her way back to rejoin Custer that evening.[34] Unfortunately, while Custer got his cook back, he permanently lost three of his horses, his uniforms, bedding, underclothing, field desk, and his commission, leaving him with only his toothbrush. He also lost all of his personal correspondence.[35] The implications of this loss are covered in detail in Appendix C: "Custer's Captured Wagons."

At about the same time as Lomax's men, supported by Munford's 2nd Virginia, were overrunning Custer's trains, they encountered and recaptured most of Hampton's led horses, wagons, and caissons that had not been retaken earlier by Rosser. They also freed many of the Confederates who had been taken prisoner by Custer's men. The military significance of recovering the men and horses was likely much greater than that of denying Custer his baggage and Pennington a few caissons.

Advancing rapidly to west with the 15th Virginia in the lead, Lomax's Brigade passed the Trevilian's depot and deployed into a line running generally north-south. The 3rd Virginia, Wickham's Brigade, dismounted and moved forward to support Lomax. Lieutenant Colonel William Carter's Virginians took up a defensive position in Lomax's rear on the south side of the railroad tracks behind a wooden fence running south from the station. The 4th Virginia moved up to the right of the 3rd Virginia and took up a defensive position oriented to the north along the south side of the Fredericksburg Road. The 3rd and 4th Virginia's lines thus formed a right angle with the apex near the depot. The 1st and 2nd Virginia, under Munford, were sent forward on the far left to make contact with Butler and to close the gap between Lee's Division and Hampton's Division.

Like many regiments on June 11, the 3rd Virginia captured its share of prisoners during the confused fighting. Thomas Conrad, the chaplain-scout of the 3rd Virginia, had accompanied his regiment in the pursuit of Sheridan. Near the station, Conrad came upon a Union cavalryman in a skirt of woods by the road. The cavalryman quickly surrendered, and informed Conrad that a number of non-combatants were scattered in the woods and would surrender if they were protected from harm. From a short distance away, Conrad called over George Zimmerman, the chaplain of the 12th Virginia, and artillery battery commander Captain James Thomson. Together, the three rode into the woods. Thomson rose in his stirrups and called in a loud voice, "If you Yankees will come forward and surrender like men you shall not [sic] be treated as prisoners of war. But if not, we will blow you to hell in five minutes." In short order, twenty men—quartermaster and commissary sergeants, teamsters, blacksmiths, a chaplain, and stragglers—came forward and gave themselves up. They brought with them forty horses and mules. Afterward Conrad advised Zimmerman that if he were asked how they had almost single-handedly captured twenty men, he should quote "an Irishman" who after capturing five men explained: "Faith and BeJasus. I surrounded them."[36]

Captain Reuben Boston, who after the death of Pate at Yellow Tavern assumed command of the 5th Virginia, had a more difficult encounter during the back-and-forth fighting against Custer's brigade. Mistaking a group of wagons as Confederate, he rode up to them, was captured, and then placed under the charge of a Union sergeant. As the two were riding to the rear, the sergeant proposed a smoke and Boston suggested they try some of his "old Virginia weed," which was superior to the tobacco offered by the Yankee. The two men filled their pipes and lit up. As the two rode along, side by side smoking, the sergeant relaxed and holstered his pistol. At that instant, Boston put his spurs to his horse, galloping across a field and out of captivity.[37]

As Lomax continued to advance to the west, an incident occurred that demonstrates the difficulty in piecing together battlefield events. As Lomax's men approached Custer's defensive perimeter from the east, they passed through a belt of woods and came to the edge of a large field full of broom sedge. As they emerged from the woods, they were taken under fire from guns of Pennington's battery, situated on a small hill about 500 or 600 yards ahead. On Lomax's orders, Captain Daniel Grimsley, commanding the 6th Virginia, took a squadron from his regiment entered the field and immediately encountered a swampy area with difficult footing for the horses. Under fire, the forty or so men picked their way through the swamp in single file. Once on firm ground, Grimsley aligned his men, and attacked. As the Virginians charged across the broom sedge field in good order, the gunners fled, abandoning their piece. Grimsley led his men over the hill and down the opposite side in pursuit of Pennington's gunners. As they galloped down the hill, a line of dismounted men appeared out of the broom sedge and scrub pines to their front, weapons at the ready. Grimsley and his men continued their charge as the dismounted Union troopers took them under fire, emptying a few saddles. As the Virginians pressed their charge home, the dismounted men to their front began to waver. However, at that moment a party of Union cavalry emerged from woods and struck Grimsley's flank. The outnumbered Confederates broke and fled to the rear, losing many men.[38]

14. "Where the hell is the rear?"

The near-capture of one of Pennington's guns was also described from the Union perspective. The gun—in a forward position on the eastern edge of the perimeter—was overrun by a Confederate charge. The crew managed to escape with the limber, but the piece was left behind. Pennington reported the loss to Custer and informed him that the Confederates apparently intended to drag the piece off. The general's immediate response was, "I'll be damned if they do!" Custer gathered about thirty men and led them forward to attempt the recovery of the gun, which was then being man-handled to the rear by the Confederates. Determining that his small party was insufficient for the task at hand, Custer rode to a nearby group of horse-holders, each man mounted while holding three led horses. Custer ordered the horse-holders to double-up, resulting in half the men holding six horses each. Thus freeing about thirty mounted men, Custer, accompanied by Pennington, led his personal staff and his newly formed-from-scratch squadron in a charge that succeeded driving back the Confederates and retaking the piece.[39]

An article in the *New York Herald* offered a similar but slightly simpler version of the recapture of the gun. According to the *Herald,* Pennington reported to Custer, "General, they have taken one of my guns." Custer responded, "No! damned if they have; come on." Custer, followed by Pennington and a few men charged "with the utmost fury" and retook the piece.[40]

Lieutenant Harmon Smith, in command of Company F, 7th Michigan, later wrote a thrilling, but perhaps exaggerated, account of the recovery of Pennington's gun. "[A] force of seventy-five to one hundred of our boys made a saber charge, one of the sharpest hand-to-hand contests I ever witnessed and recaptured it [the gun]. The Commander of the Battery stood gallantly by his gun. One of the Johnnies stunned him by a saber stroke. It was my privilege to take after this chap, a Johnnie took after me. Lieutenant Lyon after the Johnnie, another Johnnie after Lyon, and another Yankee after him. This all happened in a moment's time, but we held the gun and as the Rebels got out the Artillery boys sailed into them, letting the Johnnies have three shots. Boom, Bang, Bang. As the smoke cleared away there were five of our men and fifteen Johnnies lying dead. I never knew what became as to all in the race farther than the fellow ahead of me went down, and Lyon said the one after me followed suit. He was no good with the saber, as he gave me five blows on the back, any of which with a well directed point would have run me through."[41]

In his official report, Custer offers only a terse account of the travails of Pennington's gun. Custer mentioned only one gun being threatened during the day's fighting, commenting, "About this time the enemy charged one of my guns, but before he could get if from the field the Seventh Michigan, led by Majors Brewer and Walker, charging them, killing and wounding quite a number. Twice the enemy charged this gun, but was unsuccessful in its capture."[42] Although Custer made no mention—perhaps out of modesty—of his own role in the recapture of Pennington's gun, Torbert cited Custer for his energy and gallantry: "The enemy captured one gun, but it was immediately recaptured in a charge led by General Custer in person."[43] As an indication of how hard-pressed Pennington's guns had been that day, the battery, alone, suffered forty-four casualties, thirty-seven of whom were missing and likely captured.

For several hours, Custer had been fighting alone. From the sound of the fighting, Torbert and his subordinate commanders were fully aware that Custer was heavily engaged in Hampton's rear. By the same token, Custer could hear fighting in the woods to the north and likely anticipated Merritt or Devin coming to his relief at any moment. Publicly Custer kept his feelings to himself, but privately to Libbie, he expressed criticism: "I carried out instructions to the letter, but the others [Merritt and Devin] were three hours behind time.... Had the others been prompt, we would have struck the greatest blow inflicted by our cavalry." Custer went on to blame the loss of the captured horses and Confederate materiel on a lack of support from the rest of his division.[44]

During the morning, Tolbert, on several occasions had sent staff officers forward to attempt to penetrate the Confederate lines and make contact with the embattled Michigan Brigade. None succeeded. Shortly after noon, however, Torbert's assistant adjutant general, Captain Amasa E. Dana, picked his way through his way through enemy lines and made contact with Custer. Dana found Custer's troopers hard-pressed in their perimeter. According to a report in the *New York Herald*, "The first portion he came to was facing in one direction, and their seven shooters going crack, crack, crack, in the most lively manner. Reaching the center, he found that, facing in exactly opposite course, the same weapons discoursing the same music there. Again the other wing was facing in a third front and just as fiercely engaged as the rest."[45]

While Dana's appearance did not alter the balance of forces between Custer and his Confederate opponents, it did raise hope that relief might arrive sooner rather than later, and it encouraged the Wolverines to fight on despite the odds against them. Of greater significance, unbeknownst to both Union and Confederate soldiers and their leaders, the situation in the woods north of the Trevilian's depot was about to change dramatically.

15

"Roll them up like a ribbon"
Sheridan Prevails at Trevilian Station

After conferring with Custer, Captain Amasa Dana left the Michigan perimeter and made his way north back through Confederate lines. Reaching the safety of the Union forward positions, he reported to Torbert, apprising him of the situation facing Custer. That Dana had twice successfully traversed the mile or so between Merritt's and Custer's regiments perhaps indicated to Torbert that Hampton had thinned out his defensive line and that the time was ripe for a concerted effort to relieve Custer's embattled brigade.

Torbert, with Colonel John Irwin Gregg's brigade from Gregg's division moving into position on his left, had spent part of the morning repositioning his forces, extending his right to turn Hampton's left while Devin held his ground in the center. Now Torbert ordered a general advance intending for Merritt's Reserve Brigade to fall upon the Confederate left as Devin's 2nd Brigade advanced south toward Trevilian's Station while straddling the Fredericksburg Road with the 9th New York to its right and the 4th New York on the left of the road. Having issued the orders, Torbert moved forward to skirmish line where he could directly observe and influence the action.[1]

In the woods on the right, the 1st U.S. had been fighting most of the day in close contact with the Rebels—so close that the men could hear every enemy voice command as distinctly as the orders coming from their own leaders. About noon the Confederates began to give way and were driven back some distance. However, the men of the 1st U.S. had expended virtually all of their ammunition, so before advancing further is was necessary to withdraw the regiment a short distance to allow the men to refill their cartridge cases from reserve ordnance stores.

Once the ammunition had been replenished, the regiment moved forward again through an almost tranquil setting. Captain George B. Sanford, who commanded a battalion of the regiment, described the scene: "We moved down a steep hill and across a little valley through which ran a small stream bordered by willows. On the other side of the stream the ground rose again in high hills, on the crest of which was a large brick house and several farm buildings and a good sized orchard. Along the edge of the hill ran a stone wall." Unfortunately, as the regulars advanced to the stream, the tranquility was broken as concealed Confederates rose from behind the stone wall and began sending volleys of fire into the Union line. Sanford noted that his enemy was "well protected and we had nothing bigger than a blade of grass" as cover. Sanford ordered his men—all on foot—to continue to push forward up the hill. The Confederates, likely outnumbered, fell back and Sanford's regulars advanced beyond the stone wall, working their way to the brick house.

From the brick house, Sanford's men could engage the Rebels' exposed left flank, causing the Confederates to withdraw even farther. However, the rest of the 1st U.S. did not move up abreast of Sanford's battalion and, instead, took up positions on the north side of the stone wall where the men would be better protected from enemy fire. Finding himself and his men exposed and in danger of being cut off should the Confederates discover the situation, Sanford ordered his battalion to withdraw to the stone wall and there fall in with the bulk of the 1st. U.S. Sanford recalled that the Confederates "made it very hot" for the regulars as they withdrew through the open field to the wall.[2]

Upon reaching the wall, Sanford climbed over it and took shelter by lying down. Almost immediately, he received news that during the advance through the valley his friend and regimental adjutant, Lieutenant Frederick C. Ogden, had been shot between the eyes and killed instantly. Sanford and Ogden had been speaking to each other just before the 1st U.S. launched its attack an hour or so earlier and Ogden had then moved off down the line of troops to find Captain Nelson Sweitzer, the regimental commander. Ogden, who graduated from Yale in the class of 1860, was a popular officer and his death was a heavy blow to the other officers of the regiment. Regarding Ogden's death, Sanford recalled, "The regiment never seemed quite the same afterward to me."[3]

The push toward Trevilian's in the center of Torbert's line did not begin auspiciously. Devin ordered the 4th New York and the 9th New York to advance together. Colonel William Sackett led about 220 men of the 9th New York into the woods and the men quickly came under heavy fire from concealed Rebels. Sackett, who had earlier been told to advance cautiously, apparently did not heed that warning. At the front of his regiment, Sackett was shot and severely wounded. Lieutenant Colonel George S. Nichols assumed command of the regiment and continued to push forward. However, moving through the trees and without visible landmarks to guide upon, the regiment began to drift to the right, opening a gap between it and the 4th New York.

Nichols and his men eventually emerged from the trees into a large field. Immediately to their front, they could see a body of Confederates occupying a ridge lying about three-quarters of a mile north of the Trevilian's depot. The center of the Confederate line was anchored on a farm house and orchard. Devin, who was with the 9th New York, ordered the regiment to charge and seize the house and orchard. The men, likely relieved to be out of the trees and underbrush, gave a cheer and surged forward. The New Yorkers quickly drove the Rebels back and occupied their objective, taking a number of prisoners in the process.

In attacking the ridge, the gap between the 4th New York and the 9th New York was further widened, and Torbert, who was on the scene, ordered the advance halted on the crest of the ridge until he could realign his front.[4]

In the meantime, a regiment from Gregg's brigade which had also become misdirected and passed to the rear of the 4th New York, crossed the Fredericksburg Road and entered the field in the gap between the 4th New York and the 9th New York. Devin, taking advantage of the unexpected reinforcements, immediately ordered the regiment to occupy the ridge between the two New York regiments, whereupon Torbert ordered the advance to resume.[5]

Also, at about that time, Devin sent word to the rear for the 6th New York—then in support of Heaton's battery—to come forward to join the fighting. Upon arriving, Devin placed the 6th into line on the flank of the 9th New York.⁶

The three New York regiments resumed the movement to the south toward the railroad line against lessening Confederate resistance.⁷ Meanwhile, General Butler, responding to Hampton's orders, arrived back at the threatened Confederate field hospital just north of the railroad. There he found a body of Union soldiers—likely from Devin's brigade—advancing from the north in line of battle. The Confederates, although outnumbered and at a tactical disadvantage with Merritt and Devin to their north and Custer to their south, were not without some bite left.

Lieutenant Long, of the 6th South Carolina, was acting as Hampton's provost marshal and thus had command of the headquarters escort of roughly thirty mounted men. The men of the escort were in-hand at the field hospital and ready for action. Ordered by Butler to check the enemy advance, Long led his men forward and launched an unexpected saber charge against the much larger enemy force. Several men of the escort were killed, but Long's audacious attack delayed the surprised Yankees until the Confederate dead and wounded could be loaded onto ambulances and evacuated through a railroad cut to the immediate rear and then to the southwest and safety.⁸

Meanwhile, to the east of the Fredericksburg Road, Colonel Luigi di Cesnola's 4th New York was making better progress than it had made earlier in the day. After about three hours spent skirmishing in the woods without much gain, Cesnola's men finally emerged into the large open fields to the north of the railroad and initiated a series of dismounted charges against the weakened Confederates to their front. Capturing eighty-five Rebels and twenty-three horses, Cesnola's regiment took possession of the railroad station where they found a wagon loaded with mail, a supply of Richmond newspapers, and two large barrels of sherry wine. This last was much enjoyed by the officers and men of the regiment's 1st and 2nd Squadrons. Cesnola's losses up to that point in the battle were light: seven men killed and wounded, and one officer wounded. The wounded officer was Captain John Hall, the commander of Company L, who lost a leg.⁹

Cesnola's men were soon joined at the station by those of the 9th New York, who found several reams of writing paper inside the station which they distributed as souvenirs. On further examining the mail

Major Henry Avery and his 10th New York were ordered by Gregg to attack the Confederates' flank in support of Gregg's other regiments. Avery, concerned that his attack would fail, hesitated in giving the order to charge (*History of the Tenth New York Cavalry*).

wagon, they also discovered a box of "eatables" that had been sent to a Confederate soldier from his home. It is likely that in addition to sampling the food from home, they joined in drinking the sherry if any had been left by Cesnola's men. The men of the 9th New York also captured a loaded ammunition wagon belonging to the 5th South Carolina. The wagon, with its team of four mules in harness standing calmly, had apparently been abandoned by its driver as the Union soldiers advanced. In the wagon, the men also found a Confederate battle flag.[10]

Louisa County civilians were also caught up in the battle. As the fighting intensified around the station, Lucy Dettor Hughson and her baby son, Otis, were forced to make what the family later called a "Sprint with Death." At the time of the battle, Lucy was living in what had been the home of James Trevilian, a few hundred yards to the west of the Trevilian's depot. During the day, the house came under fire several times, initially during the morning fighting between Custer's and Rosser's Brigades.

A Union soldier, seeing Lucy looking anxiously from an upstairs window, rode to the house and told Lucy to get back inside. "Where should I go?" she asked. "Into the cellar," he replied, to which she answered, "But we don't have a cellar." "Well then, one place is as good as another!" shouted the soldier before riding off. After a few minutes, an artillery projectile passed through the walls of the house, just above the baby's crib.

Lucy grabbed the baby and dashed out of the house headed for her sister-in-law's who lived down the road to the southwest. As Lucy ran across the field with shells crashing and bullets whizzing nearby, shouts arose from soldiers on both sides. A Union captain galloped out into the field, lifted the baby into his arms, and with Lucy holding on to his stirrup, escorted the two non-combatants about one-half mile to the rear. From there, Lucy made her way to her sister-in-law's house where she and Otis spent the night.

The next morning Lucy returned to her home. In the yard she found the dead horse of the soldier who had told her to take cover in the cellar. Barrels of flour had been taken from the house and fed to horses, and she discovered that her bedding had been taken to the station to be used as bandages.[11]

The 10th New York, although assigned to Davies's Brigade, fought this day under the command of Colonel John I. Gregg. About 9:30 that morning, the regimental commander, Major M. Henry Avery, received orders to guard the division trains.[12] As the brigade moved forward, the regiment remained in the rear to await the arrival of the wagons which were toward the tail end of the column. As the men waited, a courier rode up with other orders: Avery was to report with his regiment to General Torbert, presumably to go into action. Avery formed his men into column and took up the march to the southwest where he expected Torbert could be found. About the time Avery closed on the rear of Cesnola's and Sackett's regiments, a staff officer galloped up with new orders. The 10th was instead to report to Colonel Gregg, whose brigade was fighting on the far left. The staff officer guided Avery and his men to Gregg, and the colonel briefed Avery on the disposition of the enemy and his plans. Gregg's regiments were on the right of a road in a band of woods while the Rebels occupied a band of trees on the left side of the road. Gregg ordered Avery to take his regiment to the far left of the Union line, dismount and occupy a rail fence running generally in a right angle to the road. Once Gregg's brigade launched its attack and had begun driving the Rebels from their positions, Avery was to attack, falling upon the enemy right flank. As Gregg rode off to rejoin his main body, Avery and his men dismounted and advanced to the rail fence without drawing the attention of the Confederates.¹³ To their front was a plowed field extending about 150 yards beyond which Confederates could be seen occupying a band of woods.

Riding with Avery was Lieutenant Noble D. Preston, who was assigned as the regimental commissary officer and had been detailed as the acting commissary of subsistence to Davies's brigade. Preston had made the march to Louisa County with the brigade trains and was tired of the dull routine and the heavy dust that plagued those with the wagons in the rear of the column. With action imminent and few official duties looming, he sought and obtained permission to rejoin his regiment.

Shortly after the men of the 10th had taken their positions behind the rail fence, Gregg's men launched their attack. To the men of the 10th New York, who could hear the action on their right but see little, it seemed as if Gregg's attack may have failed to drive the enemy from their positions, and Avery hesitated in issuing the order for his men to climb over the fence and charge. About that time, Captain H.C. Weir, Brigadier General Gregg's assistant adjutant general, ran out from the woods on the right, swinging his saber in the air and shouting for the 10th New York to charge. Major Avery, who may have not seen Weir's signal, hesitated, being reluctant to commit his regiment to an attack that might fail.

Lieutenant Preston, however, read the situation differently. Referring to the Confederates, he advised Avery, "We are right across their flank and would roll them up like a ribbon. Besides, they are all broken up now. But if anything is done, it must be done at once, or they'll be in shape to receive us. We won't get another such a chance to make a record for the regiment." Avery, acceding to Preston, agreed to make the attack and Preston quickly made his way to the center of the 10th New York's line passing the word, "All ready for a charge boys," as he went down the line of troops.¹⁴

Once in the center of the line, Lieutenant Preston shouted for the men to charge. He then climbed over the fence and started across the field under fire with the men following. Unfortunately, among the first casualties was Preston, who was shot in the hip and incapacitated. Avery stopped for a moment to assist Preston as New Yorkers continued forward across the plowed field.¹⁵

Under fire, the New Yorkers closed on the Confederates in the band of trees, many of whom surrendered as other fled. Those who surrendered were disarmed and sent to the rear as the New Yorkers continued their attack. After advancing roughly 200 more yards across another open field, the men reached the railroad which at that point ran through a deep cut. The New Yorkers made their way down into the cut, across the tracks, and up the opposite bank, then continued forward up a

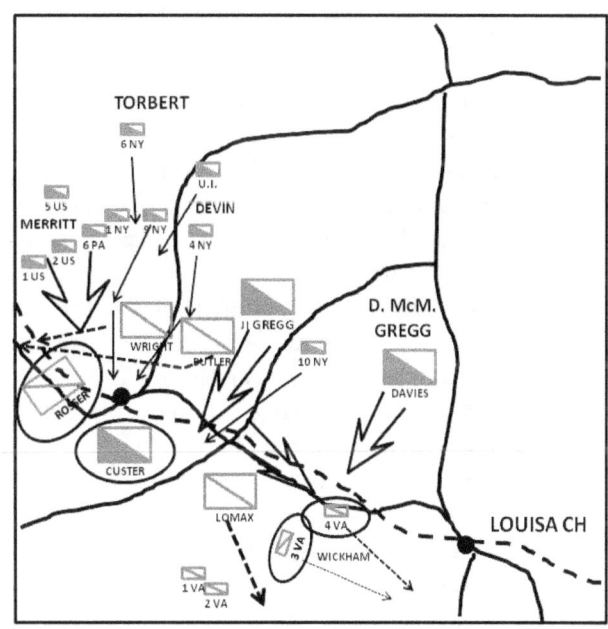

The Union Prevails at Trevilian Station

small incline toward the main Confederate position. As the men advanced across the field under fire, Corporal Kimball Pearsons was walking next to his company commander, Captain George Vanderbilt. At that point, Pearsons was shot through the body. He turned to Vanderbilt and said, "Captain, here is my diary; send it to my sister and tell her I am not sorry I enlisted." Pearsons then sank to the ground. Recalling the event, Vanderbilt wrote of Pearsons: *"Noble Boy."*[16] Closing with the Confederates, the New Yorkers overran the main enemy position, capturing many more prisoners in the process.

The Confederates opposing the 10th New York, while not specifically identified, were possibly from the 7th Georgia. During the day, the regiment had been repositioned to the right of Hampton's line, east of the railroad depot. In its fight with the 10th New York, the 7th Georgia lost heavily, particularly among its leaders. Lieutenant Colonel Joseph McAllister, in command of the regiment, was killed as the regiment was overrun. Reportedly, McAllister, who had been slightly wounded in the arm earlier in the day, was ordered to surrender but instead continued to fire his pistol until he was shot down—struck once in the body and once through the neck. Major Ned Anderson, who with a detachment was separated from the 7th's main body, was slightly wounded and captured.[17] Also, the regiment's acting major, Captain Whiteford Russell, was mortally wounded while one company commander, Captain John Hines, was killed.[18] Under heavy pressure from the 10th New York, a veteran regiment, and with all of its senior leadership dead, wounded, or missing, active resistance by the men of the 7th Georgia essentially ceased. The troopers either surrendered—a total of 181 were taken prisoner—or fled. Among those captured were four captains commanding companies.[19] Private Noble Brooks of the Cobb's Legion, which was positioned to the rear of the 7th, recorded in his diary that "we were suddenly surprised by a stampede of a portion of the 7th Ga. Cavalry who was charged upon and hotly pursued by a party of Yankees. We mounted in stanter [sic] and tried to stop them but could not. Capt. Bostie drew his saber and threaten to cut them into [sic], but it did no good."[20] Unfortunately for Brooks, two of the fleeing Georgians ran up against his horse, forcing him to drop his weapon. As Brooks dismounted to retrieve the gun, a party of Yankees charged, firing their pistols. Brooks's horse became excited and Brooks was unable to remount. Brooks turned his horse loose and dashed into the railway cut for cover as the Yankees charged past. As the Yankees charged past the cut, he heard one of them shout, "We are giving them fits now." After just a few minutes, the Yankees ran into a larger party of Confederates and came retreating back past Brooks, galloping just as fast as when they had advanced. Brooks was amused by the turn of the tables.[21]

Once the 10th New York had taken control on the small rise, the men of the regiment remained under fire from Confederates to their front and flanks. Unexpectedly, a Union artillery battery went into position to the north, mistakenly took the New Yorkers for Confederates, and brought them under fire. Major Avery called for a volunteer to go back and advise whoever was in charge that the artillery should either cease fire or elevate their pieces to increase their range and thereby fire over the friendly troops.[22] Sergeant Hubert E. Farnsworth, the regimental sergeant major, volunteered to carry the message and strode off briskly across the knoll while under small arms fire. Making his way back to the woods where the regiment's attack began, he found his horse, remounted, and delivered the message to General David McM. Gregg, who notified the battery.[23]

Perhaps the men of the 1st Maine Cavalry experienced the most frustrating day of those assigned to Gregg's brigade. In the words of the regiment's historian, June 11 "was a hard day's work for the command, while the Maine boys considered it one of the hardest days in their experience, for the amount of actual fighting they had to do. The regiment prepared to fight on foot half a dozen times in as many positions without firing a shot. It moved all along the Union lines, taking up various positions, only to leave them without getting into action. In short it was moving round and getting ready during most of the engagement, a great part of the time supporting a battery which could not seem to get where it wanted to."[24] The only action occurred late in the day when Randol's battery, which the 1st Maine was supporting at the time, came under heavy Confederate artillery fire with many of the projectiles exploding in and around the men from Maine. Colonel Charles Smith, the Regimental Commander, calmly ordered his men to mount and move in a column of fours to a safer position. After getting out of the impact zone of the artillery fire, Smith rode along his line of troops to ascertain his casualties. Surprisingly, only three or four men and two horses were wounded. Smith rode back to his position at the front of his regiment shaking his head and muttering, "I cannot understand it. I cannot understand how they can throw so much of that stuff in amongst us and not hurt more of us; I cannot understand it."[25] Although perplexed, Smith was doubtless pleased that his regiment had emerged relatively unscathed.

One of the men from Maine who might have taken issue with Colonel's Smith's assessment of the ineffectiveness of the Confederate artillery fire was Private Thomas Trask, Company B. He was struck in the arm by a fragment of an artillery shell and severely wounded. Trask was evacuated to a field hospital where doctors determined that the arm needed to be amputated. The private disagreed with that prognosis, sneaked away, and returned to his company where his arm was treated by the regimental surgeon. Trask was later admitted to a hospital established at West Point and after six weeks' hospitalization, he was returned to duty with the regiment, his arm intact.[26]

The situation had become increasingly difficult for Hampton's Division. By this time, Torbert had committed 225 cavalry companies to the battle. Hampton's entire division of 124 cavalry companies was under pressure on its front, flanks, and rear. To the east, Lee, with sixty of his companies was thus far less heavily engaged. Hampton's commanders attempting to extricate their units from the fighting north

Colonel Charles Smith and the men of the 1st Maine had a tedious day on June 11. The regiment, assigned to support an artillery battery, moved frequently but saw almost no action. The regiment came under artillery fire once late in the day (History of the First Maine).

of the railroad faced a quandary. Custer's Brigade, although pressed mainly from the west and east, still occupied its perimeter southwest of the station. Additionally, Gregg's Brigade was enjoying success in its attack from north to south to the east of the station. Consequently, Butler and Wright's regiments were required to withdraw to the south to break contact with Merritt's and Devin's forces, and then shift to the west to avoid becoming engaged with Custer.

Despite the precarious situation with Custer in the rear and Merritt and Devin making headway from the north, Butler's regiments continued to fall back to the southwest in relatively good order, although as some men withdrew they encountered Custer's Brigade and were captured. Some Confederates were taken individually, others in small groups. An officer from the 7th Georgia unwittingly led a dozen of his men into the picket line of the 6th Michigan. Major Kidd, himself a prisoner earlier in the day, received the officer's pistol, which was "a very fine shooting arm of an English make."[27]

Butler, moving with the ambulances rescued from the field hospital, briefly halted south of the railroad to organize a hasty defensive line which checked Merritt long enough to enable a gun from Hart's Battery to limber-up and withdraw. Shortly afterward, Butler's forces linked up with Rosser's regiments. The two generals established a cohesive line of battle and advanced their men to try and check the Union advance. Passing through a small peach orchard, Rosser was shot in the right knee and incapacitated. As he was being carried to the rear, Rosser turned over command of his brigade to Colonel Richard Dulany, 7th Virginia Cavalry. Rosser's final order to Dulany was: "Col[onel] fight with the men mounted. Let the other Cav. Fight as infantry."[28] As it turned out, that was not an order that Dulany could obey.

About three o'clock that afternoon, Fitz Lee's Division began coming under increasing pressure from the north as Torbert's Division, reinforced with Gregg's brigade, drove off Butler's and Wright's Brigades. Lee's position south of the railroad and east of the station was not particularly strong. A single regiment, the 4th Virginia, was deployed in a line stretching west to east facing Torbert's forces. A second regiment, the 3rd Virginia, was deployed in a line stretching from north to south. The two regiments were supported by a section of guns from Shoemaker's Battery and a section from Johnston's Battery, both fighting under the direct command of Major James Breathed. Breathed had been conspicuous in the action that day. His gunners recalled that when Pennington's fire would drop close to Breathed's guns, he would shout, "Move up closer; they have got the

Major James Breathed commanded the artillery supporting Lee's Division. Always in the thick of the action, Breathed was heard to encourage his men by shouting, "Move up closer; they have got the range boys" (Brandy Station Foundation).

range boys."²⁹ Wickham's other two regiments, the 1st and 2nd Virginia, had been sent off to the southwest to make contact with Rosser's Brigade. Meanwhile, the bulk of Lomax's Brigade was engaged with Custer's Brigade about a mile to the west. Recognizing that the situation was precarious, Wickham directed that should the 4th Virginia be driven back, Lieutenant Colonel Carter was to withdraw to his right to deny his flank to the enemy.

Concealed by a large thicket, Union soldiers advanced undetected to within a short distance of the 4th Virginia's line. Emerging into the open and firing their Spencers, the Union troopers advanced rapidly on foot. The men of the 4th fired several volleys with little effect and began falling back. Carter, moving behind his line, issued the orders for his men to swing back so they would be facing the imminent threat on their right flank. At that moment, Carter was shot through the right knee and several men close to him also went down.

With its right flank open, the Union attack gained the rear of the 3rd Virginia as confusion—and then panic—set in. Initially the Virginians, individually and in small groups dashed to the rear to find their horses and remount. After fleeing for several hundred yards to the east, the men found they were not being hotly pursued and their officers began to rally them, establishing a new defensive line running north-south across the Gordonsville Road. Carter, who was left on the field, was taken to a Union hospital where surgeons were optimistic that he would recover from his wound. Major Henry Carrington, Jr., assumed command of the regiment.³⁰

Late in the day, Sheridan ordered a final push against Fitz Lee on the extreme left of the Union line. This provided an opportunity for Brigadier General David McM. Gregg to get a part of Davies's brigade into action for the first time that day. Gregg reported that the men fought "a severe contest of about twenty minutes' duration before Lee's men were 'routed.'" Colonel John Kester of the 1st New Jersey reported that Major Hugh Janeway found an opportunity to lead the regiment's 3rd Battalion "in a dashing charge on the enemy's rear, which was managed so cleverly that it excited the admiration of all who saw it." In the charge, Janeway lost one man killed, one lieutenant wounded, one man mortally wounded and one man lightly wounded.³¹ One might question how heavy a blow was actually struck against Lee by Davies's Brigade. In both days's fighting, Davies's Brigade—less the 10th New York—lost one killed, four wounded, and six missing, which is not indicative of intense combat during the Civil War.

Wickham's men of the 3rd and 4th Virginia held their second position generally unmolested by the enemy until near nightfall, when Fitz Lee withdrew his division toward Louisa and went into camp well south of the railroad.

With Hampton's regiments driven back to the south and west toward Gordonsville, and Lee's regiments pushed back toward Louisa Courthouse, the threat against Custer's Brigade, which had spent several hours cut off to the southwest of the station, was diminished. Custer's last action of the afternoon was to lead the 7th Michigan in a thrust toward Louisa to try and recover his wagons. Custer and his men came upon the rear of the rear of the trains which were being driven to the east by Lee's men. The Wolverines were able to recover two caissons, three ambulances and a few wagons, but because of the Confederate strength, Custer broke off the action and fell back toward the main body of his brigade. In the foray, Custer failed to recover his personal baggage wagon, which would have repercussions in the future. Upon returning to his brigade, Custer found that his perimeter was now "connected with the other brigades of the division."³²

During the day, virtually all of the fighting had been done by General Torbert's Division supported by John Irvin Gregg's Brigade. In his report Torbert summarized the results. "This day the Reserve Brigade captured 150 officers and men; the First Brigade, 8 officers and 133 men; the Second Brigade, 10 officers and 136 men. The enemy in his flight destroyed one caisson and one Wagon with hospital and commissary stores. Their loss in killed and wounded was very heavy. Our loss was quite heavy as the accompanying lists will show, but the enemy was more severely punished."[33] Torbert praised his three brigade commanders, noting, "Much credit is due General Custer for saving his command under such trying circumstances" and that Merritt and Devin "distinguished themselves for bravery and coolness in action."[34]

Unfortunately, Torbert did not account for his casualties during the day's fighting, nor did he apparently attempt to tally the Confederate casualties left on the field. However, there was no doubt that Torbert's division had a successful day and that his assessment of the performance of his three brigade commanders was accurate.

16

"Too horrible to dwell upon"
The Night of an Unfinished Battle

As night fell on June 11 and the day's fighting subsided, most men—both Yankees and Rebels—would naturally have preferred to settle down for a full night's sleep. Unfortunately, for many that was simply not possible.

Many of the units were scattered after the fighting in the woods, and the first task for commanders was to assemble their men. This was most difficult for the regiments of Hampton's Division which—wedged between Merritt and Devin on the north and Custer on the south—had to fight as they withdrew to the south and west. Complicating matters was the fact that most of the fighting had been dismounted. Other than in Custer's brigade, when the fighting ended most of the horses of Union regiments were being held well north of the railroad and commanders had to either bring the horses to the men or march the men to the horses. Reuniting the men with their horses was also a challenge for Hampton's subordinate commanders since many of the led horses had been captured by Custer and then recaptured by Rosser and Lee earlier in the day. One can appreciate that many men in Butler's and Wright's brigades had a very difficult time finding their mounts after night fell.

In many battles "stragglers" are a problem. Rarely, however, had so many men become separated from their units as occurred on the first day at Trevilian's. While there is no official tally, it is possible—if not likely—that at the end of the day several hundred men found themselves separated from their companies.

Day or night, within military organizations there are always duties to be performed. Most are routine and consequently not well documented in regimental histories and soldiers' diaries and letters. In companies, after battle first sergeants counted the men to determine the day's casualties and the number of those remaining present and fit for duty. Regimental officers and staff consolidated information and prepared status reports to be sent up the chain of command. Within the regiments, ordnance sergeants distributed ammunition and replacement weapons for those that may have been lost or become unserviceable. Conversely, the ordnance sergeants would also try to collect the weapons of the men who had been killed. Quartermaster officers were charged with accounting for and redistributing captured horses, although many men who were fortunate enough to capture a replacement mount did not bother to report their gain, a transgression that was frequently overlooked by the chain of command. Commissary officers and sergeants might issue rations to the companies. However, since both Sheridan's and Hampton's forces had traveled light, there was perhaps little food distributed on the night of June 11. After battle, it was common to send out parties of men to gather the wounded and recover the dead. Additionally, Southern commanders habitually sent parties out on the battlefield to scavenge for weapons and other needed equipment. It was also customary within regiments to post "police guards." Soldiers would be detailed to watch over the colonel's tent and to prevent men from leaving or entering the camp without a proper authority. Finally, it was usually necessary for commanders to establish security measures, such as placing out pickets to provide early warning and prevent the force from being surprised by the enemy.

After a day's battle, an infantryman can generally care for himself. However, a cavalryman's first responsibility was to his horse. After a hard day's work, horses were to be unsaddled, groomed, watered and fed. Afterward, if the enemy was near, horses were to be re-saddled, but left with their girths loose. However, when actively engaged, it was common for horses to not be unsaddled and groomed for days at a time either a result of neglect on the part of the officers and men, or because of the demands of the tactical situation. For example, the 6th New York's horses remained saddled all night after the first day's fighting because the regiment was assigned to picket duty. Reportedly, some of the horses in Hampton's Division were not unsaddled for eight days.[1]

Watering could be problematic in terrain such as that around Trevilian's because there were few free-flowing streams or ponds that could satisfy the thirst of thousands of horses and mules. Even when sources of water were available, watering was a time-consuming chore. Usually several men would be detailed to lead their company's horses to a source of water, allow the horses to drink, and then return with them to camp. Frequently, not all horses would be able to drink at once, causing queues to form.[2] It was also difficult to ensure the horses were adequately fed. The corn that had been carried by the men when leaving New Castle Ferry was long gone. While in theory, wagons would be brought from the supply train to the regiments and the men issued several days' ration of corn, in practice that was not always possible. Consequently, the horses' nourishment might be limited to several hours of overnight grazing if a field of grass or clover was handy.[3]

Many soldiers on both sides were hungry that night. Most men had consumed all the rations they were issued before setting off for Trevilian's, and many men had nothing to eat on June 11. Many of Hampton's men had last eaten on June 10.[4] A few regiments were fortunate to be issued rations from the supply train during the night. One was the 1st Maine, which after a long, tiring, and frustrating day with little fighting, settled into camp in a field near the artillery battery which it had spent the day supporting. Two squadrons of the regiment were soon dispatched to establish a picket line on the road leading to Louisa Courthouse. Instead of resting, the men left in camp spent much of the night drawing several days' rations, which according to the unit historian was a "service the men were generally most ready to perform, but they would have preferred some other time than the night after a hard day's work."[5]

One soldier who did not go hungry that evening was Private J.V. Baxley, 6th South Carolina. He had been captured on the morning of June 11 and was quickly relieved of his horse which he characterized as "a very fine charger." That afternoon, as the prisoners were being marched to the rear, the Union guards were charged by a company of the 1st Maryland of Rosser's Brigade. With the Confederates now in control, Baxley demanded "a fine horse on which rode a big bucksom german." Once mounted, Baxley found that with the horse he had obtained "a nice pair of blankets, a nice Yankee overcoat, a fine pistol and a carbine, a frying pan, a coffee pot, a big country ham, coffee and sugar." After the Union prisoners were turned over to Hampton's provost guard, Baxley and the other freed Confederates set out to find their regiments. Unsuccessful in finding the 6th South Carolina, after dark Baxley and a few other men set up camp and enjoyed a "real royal feast" of ham before being almost drowned by a heavy downpour. The next morning, Baxley rejoined his regiment as its men were preparing for Sunday's action.[6]

Some Confederates were able to obtain food from nearby farms relying upon the good will of local residents, and doubtless some Union soldiers were successful foraging for their meals. However, many men on both sides—unlike Private Baxley—went hungry that night.

While Sheridan's forces camped on the battlefield, Hampton's and Lee's divisions withdrew, and the Confederates generally enjoyed a more restful night than their Union counterparts. Hampton marched his division several miles west to the Green Spring Valley of Louisa County, an area noted for its beauty and prosperous farms. There Hampton's men reportedly "found an abundance of water for man and beast" before going to sleep on their arms.

As he was moving his division to the Green Spring Valley, Hampton's thoughts were on the events for the following day. Hampton believed that the next morning Sheridan would continue his advance toward Gordonsville. Consequently, he evaluated the terrain as he went along, looking for a defensible position where he could await Sheridan. About two miles west of Trevilian's, Hampton found his spot: where the Charlottesville Road branched off to the southwest from the Gordonsville Road, the intersection of the two roads created an angle with its apex toward the east which was suitable for defense. The angle was further strengthened by the railroad which paralleled the Gordonsville Road immediately to its north.

Fitz Lee withdrew his division to the east until he was out of contact with Torbert and Gregg. He then marched south of the Louisa-Gordonsville Road for a mile or two before going into camp and spending the night unmolested by Union forces.[7]

The men, hungry and tired, were further discomfited by the weather that evening. During the middle of the night it rained heavily and the temperature dropped. Captain Joseph H. Bradley, the well-respected chaplain of the 10th New York, remembered the night after the fighting at Trevilian Station as one of the most miserable in his military service, if not his entire life.

> That June night after the fight at Trevillian I think I came nearer to freezing to death than ever in my life. The Regiment bivouacked on a slope of ground and the rain began falling. It seemed to enter to and chill the very marrow in the bones. We built fires and laid ourselves so close to them that the one side of the body almost roasted while the other froze. The enemy, seeing our fires, shelled the position, and in the black darkness and with considerable confusion we vacated that place. I imagine everybody felt altogether miserable and wretched.... Take that whole night through and I would put it down as the worst spent one of my whole army life. About midnight I managed to find room in the partial shelter of what I believe was a half-full corn-crib along with a miscellaneous company of others, where rank and previous conditions seemed to count for little. The farm-house and barn, etc., constituted a sort of universal headquarters for all ranks and departments of the service, a large number of officers and men being mixed up in the same conditions of deplorable difficulties."[8]

For the local population, many of whom spent the day sheltering in their cellars, the night was also busy. Union Surgeons took over many residences on or near the battlefield to establish field hospitals. Casualties—both Union and Confederate—were collected. What would today be termed "triage" was performed. Those considered so severely wounded that they were likely to die were placed aside, made as comfortable as possible, and left to hopefully pass quietly away. Treatment of soldiers with only slight wounds was deferred, allowing the surgeons to concentrate their efforts on those with serious—but not fatal—wounds who would most benefit from immediate treatment. Today, when one thinks of Civil War medicine, amputations come immediately to mind, for amputation was frequently the only effective available treatment for a gunshot wound to a limb.[9]

However, many other wounds were equally or even more horrific than those requiring amputation. James Bowen, of the 1st New York Dragoons, described a visit to a field hospital at Trevilian's.

> Here were bare-armed surgeons, with their bloody instruments, amputating the mutilated arms and legs of the poor, groaning sufferers, or bandaging some ghastly wound of the face or body. I assisted in carrying one poor boy who had been shot through both cheeks, nearly cutting off his tongue, besides having his shoulder shattered. One man was struck by a piece of shell which tore away his chin and lower jaw, some with shocking wounds were stretched upon the ground in the last stages of life, while swarms of flies reveled upon their gashes. Some were shot through the lungs or bowels, and were groaning in their agony of suffering. But such things are too horrible to dwell upon.[10]

Captain Noble Preston, shot in the hip when he led the men of the 10th New York over a rail fence as the regiment began its charge, found himself on the ground and unable to move. Several men passing by lifted him back over the fence and laid him on the ground on the side opposite the enemy. Shortly afterward, a few other men carried him farther to the rear and laid him in the shade of a tree. The regimental surgeon, Dr. Henry K. Clarke, passed by, examined Preston's wound, and gave him a few encouraging words and drink from a canteen before continuing forward. However, Clarke did not dress Preston's wound and shortly afterward told Major Henry Avery, the regimental commander, that Preston would probably die shortly, a prognosis that proved in error.

Artillery fire began to fall near the trees where Preston and several other wounded had been congregated, but fortunately General Gregg passed by and ordered the wounded moved to a safer location. Shortly after being moved, Preston lost consciousness and did not awaken until after dark to find Aaron, his black servant, looking over him with great concern. Preston sent Aaron for assistance and the servant soon returned with two men who placed the incapacitated officer on a litter and carried him to a nearby house that was being used as a field hospital. The men placed Preston in "an old rickety bedstead, on which was a straw mattress." Preston vividly described the scene. "The room presented a weird appearance. There were, perhaps, 20 wounded and dead soldiers, Confederate and Union, lying around the room. A burning fagot in the fireplace ever and anon blazed up, lighting up the wretched place, and then dying down would make the gloom seem more intense than before."

Among the wounded who were brought into the room was a Confederate major who was placed in the bed next to Preston. "He was pale and weak, but, clothed in a new uniform of regulation gray, he was a handsome fellow. His countenance bore an unusual intellectual cast. In a husky voice that clearly indicated his near approach to death," the major, whose name was Russell, explained that he had been shot through the hip and that the ball had penetrated his spine. Major Russell also told Preston that most of his regiment had also been killed or taken prisoner that afternoon. Russell, of the 7th Georgia, asked to speak to an officer of his regiment who had been captured, and the unidentified officer was brought into the house

On the night of June 11, local homes were commandeered into service as hospitals, headquarters, and to provide shelter from the weather. George Custer established his headquarters at the home of Charles Trevilian which stood near the railroad station. Custer and his staff limited their activities to the front porch so as not disturb Trevilian's daughter who was suffering from typhoid (author's photograph).

under guard. Russell was able to convey to the officer his last words for his loved ones before dying at about midnight.[11]

Other Louisa County residents were inconvenienced as various commanders set up their headquarters in homes around the battlefield. After the fighting ended on June 11, Custer established his headquarters in the home of Charles Goddall Trevilian, a major landowner for whom the railroad station was named. At the time of the battle, Trevilian's daughter was seriously ill with typhoid fever. Trevilian went to Custer and asked that it be kept as quiet as possible around the home so that his daughter might rest. Custer reportedly replied, "I can only do so by making the house my headquarters," and Trevilian happily agreed. Considerately, Custer limited his headquarters activity to the house's front porch and had his surgeon leave medicine for the daughter when they left the next day.[12]

Next to the wounded, the prisoners—who were herded into fields where they could be more easily guarded—probably suffered the most that night.

During the afternoon, Captain Charles McK. Leoser, after being relieved of his sword, poncho, overcoat, horse, and boots, was handed over to Hampton's provost marshal guard. Admonished that he would be shot if he should he cross a line which was pointed out on the ground, Leoser was turned out into a field with the other prisoners. No supper was provided to the prisoners that evening, and after dark the severe thunderstorm stuck. Unfortunately, General Butler had not fulfilled his promise to send Leoser his well-worn poncho as a replacement for the new poncho that Butler had taken from Union captain that morning. Consequently, Leoser, both hungry and wet, found a "comfortable furrow" and went to bed.[13] Perhaps Leoser was more accustomed to hardship than Chaplain Bradley.

As previously described, the adjutant of the 4th South Carolina, Lieutenant Gabriel Manigault, was also captured on June 11. Showing great initiative, Manigault prepared a roster of the fifty-seven soldiers of the regiment who had been also captured that day, adding a note that there were other prisoners who were wounded and in hospital whose names he had not obtained. Manigault left the list of names with one of the wounded men who was recovered by the Confederates after the battle. The list of names was eventually published in the *Charleston Daily Courier*.[14] Like other prisoners, Manigault recalled that it was cold on the first night in captivity. After being marched back and forth the men were halted in a corn field where they were to spend the night. As their names were being recorded, Manigault asked a guard who had a "pleasant and sympathetic face" for a blanket. Surprisingly, the guard, who had two blankets, gave up one to Manigault. Manigault, with two Confederates on each side of him, spent the night under the blanket in relative comfort.[15]

Private Samuel Rucker, Sr., 6th Virginia, also spent the night as a prisoner. Rucker was captured by a "Dutchman" who immediately took Rucker's new hat and gave Rucker his old hat which had been split across the top. Being taken to the rear, Rucker passed through a field upon which lay a number of Union dead and wounded. The wounded cursed the Confederate prisoners "for all they could think of." That night, like Leoser, Rucker lay in a corn furrow and was soaked by the rain. He happened be held near a Union headquarters with couriers coming and going throughout the night, and was amused when one of the couriers was thrown by his horse and landed head-first on the ground.[16]

Sergeant James H. Avery, with about twenty men of the 5th Michigan and several captured Confederates whose escape had been cut off after Colonel Alger's charge past the station, had remained hidden in the woods while the battle swirled around them during the remainder of the day. Late that afternoon, the Michigan men began debating the best route of escape without arriving at a decision. Fortuitously, a black man attempting to liberate himself from slavery stumbled upon them. The black man, who was familiar with the area, offered to guide them through Confederate lines.

After dark, the men, hiding their sabers under logs and tying their horses to trees, made their way on foot through the thick woods. Stopping frequently to listen, the small band headed north and according to their guide, passed through Confederate lines near the railroad station. Afterward they made better progress before laying-up before daylight in the thickest brush they could find.[17] Avery and the men of his party were probably unaware that they had also passed to the north of Union lines, and they would have a lengthy journey to safety.

During the night, most men, although hungry, wet, and tired, anticipated more hard fighting when the sun rose on Sunday morning. For most, that expectation would be fulfilled.

17

"A theatre of bloodshed"
The Battle Continues on June 12

All was peaceful around Trevilian's as the sun rose on the morning of Sunday, June 12, 1864. No opposing units were in contact and thus no gunshots rang out to break the stillness. However, the calm was not to last the day. As one Confederate later recalled, "This morning the first rays of the sun fell on a peaceful vale where nature with all its beauty was reposing in peaceful solitude.... But alas; that paradise was soon to be made a theatre of bloodshed."[1]

Instead of fighting, many of the men of Sheridan's corps began the day with laborious—although less dangerous—duty than on the previous day. Instead of immediately taking up the march to the Rivanna Bridge, his objective near Charlottesville, the Union general directed his two division commanders to begin destroying the Virginia Central between Trevilian's and Louisa Courthouse.[2]

Lieutenant Samuel Cormany, 16th Pennsylvania, recorded in his diary the technique employed by Gregg's troopers.

> P.M. all hands tearing up R.R. track, or turning it upside-down—the process is rather simple—A joint is first broken on one side. Men stand shoulder-to-shoulder—say one thousand abreast along the rail—a few with fence rails and chunks, pry the rail and ties up for 100 or more feet, underpinning the one side—the the height of several feet—Now, at the word of command, every man lifts harder and harder, and soon the men at the broken joint have the ties in perpendicular position while those next are nearly so. Continuing the lift and tearing up, while now the ties and rail at the break are beyond perpendicular and so bear down and at the same time remaining spiked to the ties—help in the overturning process—so once fairly started the R.R. track is turned upside down with considerable speed and extreme strain and twist, of the turning over mass, twists and otherwise damages nearly every rail.[3]

After the rails were torn from the ground and their ties, the raiders piled up ties, telegraph poles, cordage and other pieces of wood. They then laid the rails atop the piles and ignited the wood. The intense heat of the fires softened the iron rails, causing them to droop under their own weight. For good measure, the men then twisted some of the rails around nearby trees, creating what have come to be known as "Sherman's neckties."[4]

Sheridan's men destroyed several miles of track between Trevilian's and Louisa Courthouse. They also tore down the telegraph line that paralleled the tracks and burned the Trevilian's station, its water tank and several train cars that they found abandoned on a siding next to the water tank.[5]

Not all Union effort was devoted to destruction that morning. At about 11:00, the officers

This sketch depicts the men of Wilson's division destroying track on the Weldon Railroad south of Richmond in July 1864. The activities of Sheridan's raiders at Trevilian's would have been very similar. Note the horses lined up neatly as the men are at work dismounted (Library of Congress).

of the 1st U.S. Cavalry retrieved the body of Lieutenant Frederick Ogden from the house where they had laid it the previous evening. They buried Ogden in the house's yard and marked the grave with a wooden board at its head. Chaplain Joseph H. Bradley of the 10th New York read the Episcopal funeral service which was attended by all the men of the regiment who could be spared from duty.[6]

As previously mentioned, to the west Hampton had chosen the ground on which he would fight that day should the enemy advance towards Gordonsville. About three miles west of Trevilian's, the road leading through Mechanicsville and then on to Charlottesville branched off from the Gordonsville Road at about a sixty-degree angle. Within the angle, the railroad tracks on the left provided some cover, while positions within the "V" between the tracks and he road offered clear fields of fire toward the east. At about daylight, Hampton's troopers began moving from their camps into the angle. Sergeant Charles Hansell, 20th Georgia, rather wryly recorded the start of the day for Hampton's men.

> The next morning, Sunday, June 12, '64, we rose pretty early, and after making our toilets, which consisted of pulling our shoes out from under our heads and putting them on our feet and then putting on our coats, we proceeded to clean our house by rolling up our blankets and strapping them to our saddles and we were ready to vacate the premises. We were soon mounted and rode back to a point where a road left the pike going northward, and we turned into this and went a short distance up it and were ordered to halt and dismount.[7]

Hampton ordered his brigades into position with Rosser's Brigade, under the command of Colonel Richard Dulany, on the right; Young's Brigade, under the command of Colonel Gilbert Wright, in the center; and Butler's Brigade on the left.

17. "A theatre of bloodshed" 177

This is a close-up of destroyed track on the Orange & Alexandria near Bristoe. There were no secret techniques for destroying railroads. The work shown in this photograph was performed by Confederates (Library of Congress).

Once in the angle, Hampton's men went to work fortifying their positions. Not having shovels or other tools suitable for digging impeded their efforts, but rail fences were plentiful nearby. The men tore down the fences and used the rails to construct parapets along their forward line. As one of Hampton's men recounted, they relatively quickly had constructed "such temporary defenses as lay in their power using rails, logs, brush and what earth could be scooped up without spade or shovel." While the parapets were low and would not likely have met with an infantryman's approval, they did offer some cover from the fires of an enemy advancing up the road from the east.[8]

In his diary, Sergeant Hansel described his company's position in some detail.

> I took charge of the nine men constituting Company E and three or four from Company D, and went to a house between this road and the woods beyond the house…. Along side of [an outbuilding] we built a rail pile, but not as good or as high as it ought to have been; but it was hot and the men were tired, so we quit with that about 2 or 2 ½ feet high, then an opening 3 or 4

inches wide to shoot through, and a rail above to protect our heads while fighting. In front of us the ground sloped downward for about half or more of the distance, some 300 yards or more between us and a rail fence that bounded the open field, and back of the fence was a thick oak woods; to our left and front the same open field continued to a point where it reached the R.R. at a little two story white house.[9]

From the description, Hansel and his small band occupied a fairly defensible position. They would be fighting from behind hasty fortifications with a 300-yard field of fire to their front.[10]

Butler's Brigade, at the apex of the angle, held the critical position in Hampton's line with the 5th and 6th South Carolina facing east and the 4th South Carolina positioned parallel to the railroad facing generally northeast. Thus positioned, Butler's South Carolinians could expect to bear the brunt of an enemy attack.

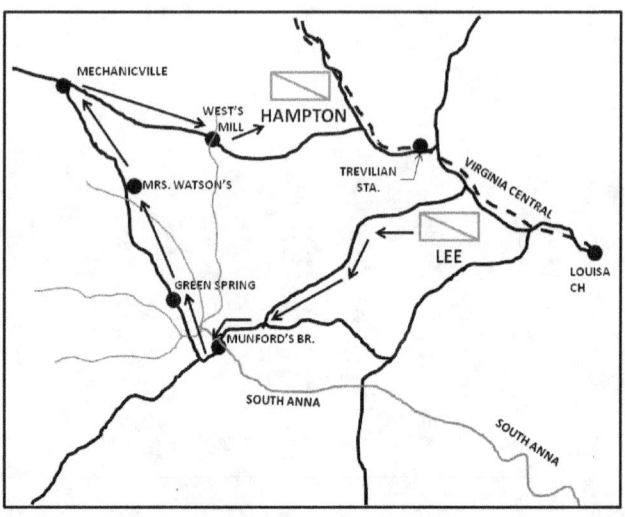

Lee Joins Hampton—Morning, June 12

This photograph is taken from the apex of the angle in Hampton's defensive line looking south with the Ogg House in the center of the field. From this point the 6th and 5th south Carolina would have been arrayed along the right border of the photograph facing east with Wright's and Dulany's forces beyond. Custer's regiments attacked from left to right (author's photograph).

Hampton, anticipating the arrival of Fitz Lee, placed Butler in command of his division. This freed Hampton to concentrate on exercising command over the entire force. Colonel Hugh Rutledge—with both Colonels Dunovant and Aiken wounded—assumed command of Butler's Brigade.[11]

Overnight, Fitz Lee's regiments had camped well south of the railroad about midway between Trevilian's and Louisa Courthouse. Early on the morning of June 12, Lee's regiments left their camps and began a march to join Hampton. Lee's Division took a circuitous route to avoid any chance of contact with the federals, and his movement was apparently not initially detected. The division moved south on the road leading to Munford's Bridge over the South Anna River. After crossing the river, the division marched northwest passing through Mrs. Watson's farm. From there the division headed north, and then east after striking the road through Mechanicsville. Crossing back to the north side of the South Anna at West's Mill, the division arrived at Hampton's position shortly before noon.[12] Hampton initially placed Lee's division to the rear of Butler's Division where, acting as a reserve, it could reinforce Butler's line or respond to threats arising on either flank.[13]

Back at Trevilian's, at about 3:00 p.m. Sheridan ordered Torbert with his division—reinforced by Davies's Brigade from Gregg's Division—to advance toward Gordonsville and attack Confederate forces who were believed to have taken up position five miles east of that town. Torbert began his movement about 4:00 p.m. with Custer's Brigade in the lead followed by Merritt's Reserve Brigade, then Devin's brigade, with Davies bringing up the rear.[14]

This photograph is taken from the apex of the angle in Hampton's line facing southeast. The slight cut along the rail line is visible. Over the years the ballast under the tracks has built up. During the war, the rails would have been laid at ground level (author's photograph).

The 6th Michigan was in the van of Custer's brigade. Custer, anticipating contact with the Confederates, designated a spot along the route where he thought the Confederates would be located. He directed Major Kidd to halt before reaching that spot so that the division might close up and deploy before going into battle.[15] However, after marching just a mile or two, Kidd's advance guard reported that entrenched Confederates were immediately to the front and blocking the way. As skirmishing began—the Confederate commanders had placed out pickets forward of their defensive line—Kidd deployed a squadron and sent the trusted Sergeant Avery forward through a band of trees to determine what was lying to the front. Within about ten minutes, Avery returned and reported that the entrenchments were "thoroughly manned" and that he had seen a column of about 1,000 Rebels moving into entrenchments on the enemy's south.[16]

Kidd sent Avery back to report his information on the enemy strength and disposition to Custer. Custer, upon hearing from Avery, immediately rode forward to join Kidd, and ordered the major to dismount his entire regiment to fight on foot. Kidd's troopers dismounted and formed for battle on the left of the railroad. Within a few minutes, the 7th Michigan moved up adjacent to the 6th on the right of the railroad and also dismounted. Custer initially kept the 1st and 5th Michigan in reserve in the rear of the rear of the 6th and 7th Michigan.[17]

As the two deployed Michigan regiments moved forward and began exchanging fire with the Confederates to their front—but before any significant fighting began—Custer could see that more forces would be required to drive the Confederates out of their field fortifications. He ordered the 1st and the 5th Michigan forward to "reinforce" the 6th and 7th. The men of the 1st and 5th Michigan dismounted and deployed to the left of the 6th. Meanwhile, the rest of the division was continuing to close up.[18]

One of Custer's officers described the nature of the fighting south of the railroad. "Our men crawled up on their hands and knees to the rail fence that ran along the edge of the woods, when we opened on the enemy, the most of us lying flat on the ground behind trees and logs. We fought Indian style, every man to suit himself. Our foes were in easy range, and every time we saw one we fired, and the way they poured lead at us was terrible."[19]

Sergeant Hansel described the fighting from the Southern perspective. Fighting from behind their parapet of rails, one of Hansel's men, William Baggs, had been shot in the knee. While being taken to the rear, Baggs was shot again, and this time mortally wounded.

> Soon after Baggs left us our Adjt. Thos. G. Pond, came over to see us to see how we were getting along. He had no arms but his pistol and I told him to go on back that we did not need him. He knelt down behind our little breastwork built of rails, in just the same place Baggs had occupied. I told him he had better get away from there or that fellow [the Union marksman] would get him. Our pile was a space between the main pile of rails and the top rail. The Adjt. rested his head against the top rail and looked through the opening for a minute or two when a ball came along and cut a piece out of the top rail almost touching his head. I again told him to get away; but had hardly said so, when another cut out another piece of the same rail just a little closer to his head. He then decided I was right and left. A few minutes later Leonard Sims, a man about the same age and size of Baggs, from East Point, Ga., moved into this place and in a few minutes a ball struck him between the collar bone and the neck. We saw he was done for, but to do what we could for him. The four of us took him up and carried him back to the chimney of the Kitchen and there gave him water and did what we could for him.[20]

With fighting having broken out to the front, Torbert ordered Merritt to move his brigade up on the right of Custer's brigade to attack the rebel left flank. Merritt deployed his regiments to the north of the railroad with the 6th Pennsylvania on his extreme right with his other regiments extending to the south to form a juncture with the 7th Michigan on Custer's right. Merritt retained one squadron of the 2nd U.S. in the saddle to support Williston's Battery D, 2nd U.S. Artillery.[21]

At about that time, Torbert ordered a "general advance," intending for Custer's Brigade to fix the Confederates while turning the enemy's left flank with Merritt's Brigade.[22] Custer, whose four regiments had been fighting for some time without making much headway, determined that the Confederate positions were too "formidable" to be taken and instead fell back to a position nearer the road junction.[23] Merritt's men attacked "vigorously" but it "was slow work." In Merritt's assessment, "as the enemy was not pressed [by Custer] on the left he concentrated his forces on the brigade." Merritt's regiments advanced more rapidly on the right—where there was less Rebel opposition—than on the left, and his line "so swung round as to be exposed to attack on its wing."[24]

As Merritt's attack was underway, Lee proposed to Hampton that he move his division north of the railroad, form a right angle with Butler, and attack to the southeast against the Union right flank with both of his brigades. Hampton, knowing that the 4th South Carolina was threatened, instead directed that Wickham's Brigade dismount and take up positions to the left of Butler's line. This would counter a potential attack by Merritt's Reserve Brigade against Butler's exposed flank. Wickham's Brigade began to move toward its designated position accompanied by Captain Phillip Johnston's battery of horse artillery. This left Lee with Lomax's Brigade to execute the flanking movement that he had proposed.[25]

As Wickham's Brigade moved north across the rear of Hampton's line, the men could hear heavy firing off to their right. Passing through a stretch of woods, several Virginians were struck by stray bullets. Entering a broad open field—"ploughed beautifully by cannon and minie balls"—the regiments deployed and advanced toward the railroad. Munford, as the senior regimental commander, could have demanded the position of honor on the right of the line for the 2nd Virginia, and in past engagements he has asserted that prerogative. However, on this day Munford demurred. Since his regiment was second in the column, Munford claimed that too much time would be lost in bringing the 2nd Virginia forward. Instead, the 3rd Virginia led the brigade forward and to the right across the field toward the railroad where it fell in on the left of the 4th South Carolina.[26]

Climbing over a rail fence, the men of the 3rd Virginia pressed forward to the railroad, hoping to take cover behind the cuts and fills along the track. However, once there they came under enfilading fire from Merritt's men and casualties began to mount. The fire was so intense that the Virginians were unable to carry off their wounded comrades without risking death. Among the wounded was the regimental adjutant, Robert Hubard, Jr., who was struck in the right hip with what would have likely been a mortal wound had his holstered pistol not taken the force of the bullet. Instead, Hubard suffered only a serious contusion. At about that time the Yankees launched an attack on Wickham's lines but were repulsed with heavy losses.[27]

On the Union side, Private George Stockweather, Company F, 1st New York Dragoons, was shot through the face. The ball destroyed his teeth and left ear before passing out the back of his neck. As the regiment withdrew, the men left Stockweather behind, presuming him dead. However, as the line of New Yorkers fell back, Stockweather called out, "Boys! Boys! Don't leave me!" However, because of the heavy fire, the men were unable to retrieve Stockweather and left him and their other wounded comrades on the field.[28]

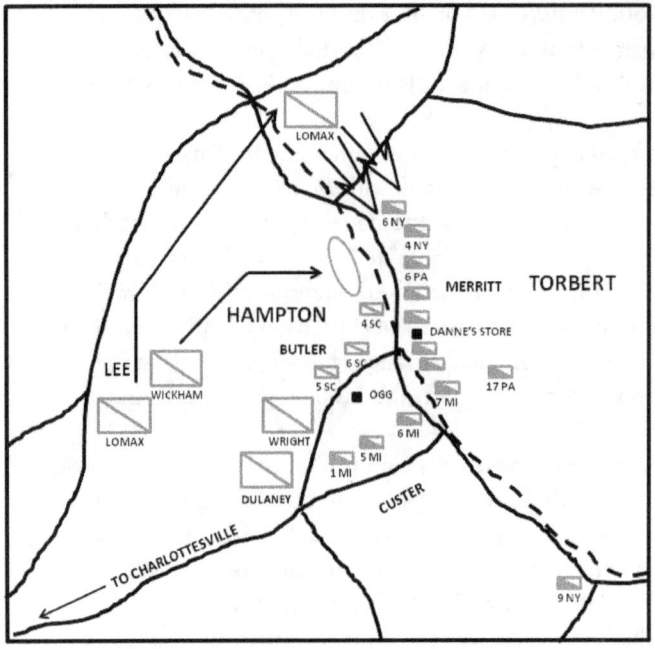

The Fight at the Angle, Late Afternoon

As Wickham's troops deployed, Devin's Brigade had closed on the rear of Custer's Brigade. Initially Torbert, apparently concerned that Hampton might launch a counterattack into his rear, ordered Devin to hold the road leading to Munford's Bridge on the South Anna River. Elements of Hampton's force were detected making a demonstration on the road, so Devin dispatched the 9th New York to drive them off.

As Wickham's Brigade completed its deployment along the railroad, it apparently became clear to Torbert that Hampton's line south of the railroad would overlap Merritt's line north of the railroad. In response, Torbert directed Devin to dismount one regiment on the north side of the railroad as a reserve near the junction between Merritt and Custer, and to send two regiments to report to Merritt for further orders.

Devin sent the 17th Pennsylvania, which after its mission to the Confederate hospital in Spotsylvania County had missed the first day's fighting, to the north side of the railroad. Devin sent one of his staff officers, Lieutenant Cating, with the regiment to assist with its deployment. Devin also dispatched the 6th New York and the 4th New York to Merritt, accompanied by Captain Wright of Torbert's Staff. Devin remained with the 9th New York and Heaton's battery near the intersection of the Gordonsville Road and the road leading to Munford's Bridge.[29]

Meanwhile, as Wickham's trailing regiments moved up into line, they brought increasing pressure on the 6th Pennsylvania, Merritt's right flank regiment. Merritt detected that the Confederates "were not slow to take advantage" of the situation with his "exposed" right flank and that they had launched an attack against it. Merritt ordered a squadron of the 2nd U.S., his only mounted reserve, to move up on the right of the 6th Pennsylvania and charge, which they did "nobly" and "though few in numbers, by the impetuosity of their onslaught, drove the enemy back."[30]

The charge of the mounted squadron of the 2nd U.S. bought enough time for Merritt to move the two New York regiments into position with Colonel Cesnola dismounting the men of the 4th on the right of the 6th Pennsylvania and Lieutenant Colonel Crocker dismounting the 6th New York to the right of Cesnola.

During the day's fighting, artillery played a major role for both Union and Confederate forces. For most of the day, guns on both sides were positioned well forward—within 400 or 500 yards or less of enemy marksmen. This placed the guns on both sides within easy

Lieutenant Edward Williston's guns, D Battery of the 2nd U.S., performed good service on June 12, turning back a Confederate attack against Merritt's brigade. Merritt effusively praised Williston's performance, and Williston was later awarded the Medal of Honor (Library of Congress).

range of their targets—and within canister range should the enemy expose themselves in an assault. However, the guns were also within small arms range of the enemy. While dismounted cavalrymen mostly fought from behind cover, it was necessary for the gunners to stand to man their pieces. The situation was particularly difficult for Thomson's Battery which in support of Butler's Brigade was positioned within the apex of the angle and thus subject to fire from both its right and left front.[31]

Sergeant George Neese recorded the nature of the fighting that day in his diary. "Three times the enemy charged from the woods and the railroad cut, firing as they came, and were repulsed each time. As the assaulting lines came dashing out of the woods and over the field we opened on them with canister, firing as rapidly as possible, breaking their line every time and hurling it back into the woods, while our cavalry poured a heavy fire into the Yanks until their broken line slipped into the woods."[32]

Neese recalled that as the federals attacked, their bullets "zipped and whizzed and thudded around our guns as thick as hail." In the lulls between the assaults, he observed that men from both sides "stood and fired at each other like animated targets."[33]

Meanwhile, the crew of the second gun in the section was in more difficult straits. Thompson had deployed that gun well forward. To the left of the gun at a distance of about 100 yards, a railroad cut was filled with Yankees who immediately took Thomson's men under fire. "Jap" Pierce, Major Chew's color bearer, stayed in the saddle displaying his flag and was the first man to go down—reportedly shot six times and severely wounded. Corporal Frank Reily, Thomson's cousin, was in the act of loading the gun when he was shot through the chest and killed. Another member of gun crew, George Nicewander, was shot through the wrist. Observing the deadly effect of the Union fire, Butler ordered Thomson to withdraw the crew to cover, and the canoneers ran about twenty paces to the rear and took shelter behind an abandoned building.[34]

Thomson, however, was unwilling to abandon the gun and sent orders back to his second section to have three men sent forward to replace the dead and wounded. Among the three volunteer replacements was Charles McVicar, a twenty-three-year-old private from Winchester. The three volunteers rode rapidly forward, but before reaching the gun they were stopped and told to take their horses to the rear and run on foot to the building where the surviving members of the gun crew was taking cover. Once the three had linked up with the gun crew, Thomson ordered McVicar to take six men and drag the gun off by hand. The small party dashed forward and began manhandling the piece. As they raised the trails, Anthony Beale Burgess was shot through the head and killed instantly. Reuben Phillips took Burgess's place at the trails, was wounded, but able to continue the work. Corporal Carthage Kendall was hit—perhaps by a fragment of a shell fired by Pennington's battery—and dazed. As the crew was pulling the gun to safety, Cal Miller was shot in the back, John Hare was shot in the thigh, and James Crawford had his little finger shot off. McVicar was the only member of the party of six to make it unscathed it to safety behind the old house.[35]

As the gun was being recovered, Thomson summoned Sergeant Neese from the section's number one gun to replace the gunner of the number two gun. Instead of trying to dash across 300 yards of open field, Neese fell to the rear and made his way through the woods. As he was climbing over a fence at the western edge of the field, a Union artillery projectile crashed through the fence directly below him. Neese rather stoically observed, "but once more a miss was as good as a mile."[36]

Upon reaching the number two gun, Neese noticed that Union sharpshooters on the second floor of a nearby farmhouse were "now and then dropping a cavalryman dead in his tracks" with their long range rifles. However, the priority for the artillery was to engage "close game" so he fired eight or ten shells at the line of Union dismounted men. General Butler rode up, instantly assessed the situation, and tersely ordered Neese, "Fire that house." Neese and his crew wheeled the gun about and struck the house with their first shell, setting it alight. For good measure, they put another shell into the house and as smoke began to rise the crew had the satisfaction of seeing "a nice little stream of Yankee sharpshooters rolling out below."[37]

Meanwhile, north of the railroad tracks, as the 2nd and 4th New York moved into line Merritt ordered Williston to take his battery forward to where his guns could more effectively engage the Confederate cavalry behind their breastworks on the south side of the railroad. Williston—not shy about getting into the fight—immediately complied. As Merritt described the action, "Right gallantly did the battery come up in the midst of a heavy musketry fire, we being at that time so close to the enemy that their shells all flew far over us. Planting three guns of the battery in this position, where it dealt the enemy heavy blows, Lieutenant Williston moved one of his brass 12-pounders onto the skirmish line. In fact, the [skirmish] line was moved to the front to allow him to get an eligible position, where he remained with his gun, in the face of a strengthened enemy (who advanced to its very muzzle), dealing death and destruction in their ranks with double loads of canister." As darkness began to fall, Colonel Cesnola mistakenly withdrew the 4th New York, leaving Williston's guns unsupported. Williston maintained his position, directing his fire "by the overheard commands of the Rebels and by the flashes of their muskets." Summarizing the battery's action that day, Merritt wrote, "I cannot speak too highly of the battery on this occasion. The light 12's were magnificent."[38]

After a few charges by the Union troopers, both sides settled down to prolonged fighting along the railroad line. With the heavy firing from covered positions, ammunition began to run low on both sides, while in Butler's Brigade many of the men had expended all of their bullets and—according to one trooper—were preparing to repel the next assault with rocks. At that moment, a two-horse wagon with its team at the gallop came speeding down the rear of Butler's line. In the back of the wagon, Ordnance Sergeant Nealy Grant was busily pitching cases of rifle cartridges over the side to the waiting troopers. Amazingly, Grant and the wagon driver were unscathed by the hail of fire through which they had driven, while the wagon was bullet-ridden.[39]

Unbeknownst to Torbert and his subordinate brigade commanders, Fitzhugh Lee had withdrawn Lomax's Brigade to where it could cross the road and railroad without its movement being detected. Lomax's cavalry was accompanied by Captain John Shoemaker's battery.[40] After crossing the road and railroad, Lomax brought his regiments into line perpendicular to Wickham's line and across Merritt's right flank. Just before nightfall, Lomax's Virginians dismounted and began to move forward through the trees toward the unsuspecting federals.

Lee's attack was to fall initially—and most heavily—on the two regiments of Devin's Brigade, the 6th New York and the 4th New York. Those regiments were among the last of Torbert's Division to deploy, getting into action about 5:00 p.m. in accordance with Merritt's orders to advance "toward the setting sun."[41]

Cesnola, commanding the 4th New York, was not pleased with the situation in which his regiment was placed. He found it inexplicable that Hampton had been given the morning to concentrate his forces and prepare defenses, later writing to the father of an officer who was killed that day, "my regiment was sent to help General Merritt who was hardly pressed by an enemy who had been allowed stupidly the day before (after being defeated) to concentrate himself and throw up any amount of breastwork." Cesnola was also unhappy with the positioning of his regiment. "The enemy was behind breastworks made of rails, trees, etc. and we were ordered to form line of battle on the crest of a hill completely without timber and not 100 yards from the rebels. The enemy could pick out man by man of my command, while I could scarcely see them behind the breastwork. In short we were obliged to ly down flat on the ground and from that reclining position to fire and advance like snakes." Despite those disadvantages Cesnola claimed that the rebels—with ten times his strength—charged his regiment with a shout, but were "gallantly repulsed over and over again."[42]

Initially, the 6th New York enjoyed success on the far right of Merritt's line. Making contact as they moved up the tracks in the direction of Gordonsville, they drove the Rebels back with one New Yorker noting that at close range their breech loading carbines were superior to muzzle-loading rifles. However, those Confederates had withdrawn across a field and into a stand of woods about the time Lee launched his attack from the right. Running his artillery forward, Shoemaker's gunners opened on the men of the 6th New York at close range "with great rapidity and accuracy." Simultaneously, the dismounted Virginians emerged from trees and fell on the New Yorkers' exposed flank. Private John C. Donohoe, Company K, 6th Virginia, recorded in his diary that the attack was "one of those sublime spectacles sometimes witnessed on the battlefield. Amid the surrounding gloom could be seen a constant stream of fire from our lines as we advanced with victorious shouts upon the bewildered foe. Again the air was illuminated by the flash of opposing batteries as they belched forth their terrible thunders at each other while screaming shells traced firecy arches through the air and bursting, scattering fire and death around."[43]

The action was similarly described by a member of the 6th New York. "For a short time after sunset the fighting was fierce, their larger numbers giving us volley after volley, when a heavy movement on our right, and an enfilading fire from one of their batteries, caused us to fall back, placing our whole division in a critical position, being followed by a heavy force. But a longer stand was impossible against such odds and a general retreat of the whole line was necessary. At eight o'clock we got a good position on a hill a mile back from our battle line, and held it until eleven o'clock, during which time the enemy amused us by throwing numerous shells along our line—appearing like a celebration with skyrockets, but doing us no damage. About eleven o'clock we fell back to our lead horses, mounted and rode back two miles and halted to rest."[44]

As the 6th New York began to fall back under pressure from Lomax, Colonel Cesnola's 4th New York felt the brunt of the Rebel attack. "At last our line was without ammunitions since about 3/4 of an hour none could be procured, the whole of the rebel line then advanced, their artillery throwing grape and canister into our led horses creating a great stampede as the horses belonging to the Regulars to the 6th N.Y. and to my regiment were all running over the country. Then the entire line of Genl. Merritt command fell back (a very polite word) and the enemy would have pursued us farther if the night had not close upon that scene."[45]

Lee summed up the action in his report, writing that "the enemy, surprised, offered slight resistance—their right gave way, and they were driven back in confusion. Night and the thickness of the country put an end to the pursuit." In any event, had the pursuit continued, Merritt had fresh regiments—the 10th New York and the 17th Pennsylvania—in position to impede further advances by Lomax's Brigade.[46]

At about dusk—and after several hours of fighting—Torbert had concluded that he would be unable to drive the Confederates from their prepared positions within the angle. In Torbert's view, to carry Hampton's lines would require a larger force than he had available and could only be accomplished with heavy losses. Further, Torbert believed that Hampton had been reinforced by one or two regiments of infantry that had been sent out from Gordonsville. As a result, fighting began to taper off. At about nightfall, Sheridan ordered Torbert to suspend his attack, and after darkness fell, Torbert received orders to withdraw his division to Trevilian Station.[47]

However, the end of the battle did not spell the complete termination of contact between the opposing forces that day. Well after dark, Lieutenant Colonel William Rich, commanding the Phillips Legion, led a detachment onto the battlefield in keeping with the standard Confederate practice of scavenging for horses, weapons, and other materiel. The Georgians soon came upon a Union lieutenant and five men who had become separated from their regiment and were out of ammunition. Rich ordered the lieutenant to surrender. Instead, the lieutenant had his men draw sabers and told Rich that he heard Confederates were afraid to fight with only cold steel. Rich called the lieutenant's bluff and ordered his men to holster their pistols, draw their sabers, and advance. The lieutenant quickly surrendered "with great pomp and arrogance" according to Rich. Rich ordered the Yankees to dismount, lay their weapons on the ground, and remove their boots. He then told the lieutenant that he and his men were free to go. Rich advised the lieutenant that "Richmond was full," and "we don't need any more Union prisoners." As Rich and his men rode off with the weapons, horses, and boots, they could see the Yankees "in their stocking feet running through the woods, where they would most assuredly be captured again within the hour."[48]

Looking back on June 12, 1864, one of Custer's troopers ruefully observed: "Thus ended the two days' terrible battle at Trevilian Station, of which history has not much to say."[49]

18

"Damn, damn, all the time"
The Union Withdrawal

During the afternoon of June 12, Sheridan made the decision to curtail his raid well short of his objective, to withdraw from Trevilian's, and to rejoin the Army of the Potomac. This decision was likely made after Torbert's division had become decisively engaged with Hampton's forces, which, although beaten the day before, had demonstrated that they were both resilient and prepared to contest any further advances by Sheridan.[1] In reaching his decision to withdraw, Sheridan claimed to have been influenced by prisoners and local citizens who reported that Major General George Pickett's division—or part of it—was moving to Gordonsville to defend that important rail junction. The presence of infantry across his path would make it very difficult—if not impossible—for Sheridan to reach and destroy the Rivanna Bridge at Charlottesville. It is quite possible that Confederate prisoners and local residents falsely reported the movement of Confederate infantry to confuse and deceive the Union raiders. However, it is fair—since there was no deployment of Confederate infantry in response to the raid—to fault Sheridan for failing to seek independent, reliable confirmation of those reports.[2]

Factors other than Confederate opposition that afternoon coupled with the possibility of Confederate reinforcements also influenced Sheridan's decision: Sheridan was very concerned about the combat effectiveness of his command. His men had expended much of their ammunition and resupply was not possible. His two divisions had suffered heavy casualties, his ability to provide medical treatment to the wounded was limited, and evacuation of the wounded without a sizeable escort was not an option. The federals had also captured roughly 400 Confederates who, having to be guarded and fed, would hamper any further movement. Also many of Sheridan's men had consumed all of their rations and opportunities for foraging were limited. Finally, by that Sunday afternoon it must have become clear to Sheridan that his command's horses could not stand up to much more marching and fighting. Regarding the lack of rations for the men and forage for the horses, Sheridan succinctly concluded, "Living off the country was a failure." Consequently, after dark on that Sunday, Sheridan issued the orders for his two divisions to begin the withdrawal.[3]

Much work was needed to prepare the command for the movement, particularly with regard to the evacuation of the wounded. The surgeons evaluated their patients to determine those whose condition precluded their movement by wagon, and made arrangements to care for those who would of necessity be left behind. Providing medical care for wounded during a cavalry operation was always particularly challenging. Elias J. Marsh, the Surgeon-in-Chief of Gregg's Division, summarized the problems he and other surgeons faced in his report of operations from July to December 1864.

> ... the many differences between the cavalry and infantry branches of the service must be borne in mind. Cavalry operations are always quickly done, and their movements rapid, having generally the character of reconnaissances. When before the enemy we seldom remain one day in the same locality, and many of our battles are running fights. Moreover, we are always limited as to transportation, and during my connection with the division in not a single instance has an army wagon been allowed to accompany the troops. Hence, our supplies are extremely limited, and we are obliged to restrict them to tent-flies, food, blankets, and dressings, that may be carried in the Autenreith [sic] wagon or ambulances. Also a small number of ambulances only is allowed. In one case it was limited to five for the division. Under these circumstances the proper care of the wounded becomes extremely difficult, and our field hospitals are necessarily of the most temporary nature. The wounded are often placed in ambulances with temporary dressings and carried along for miles, perhaps till evening, before they can be properly examined and operated on. We are unable to establish hospitals in the rear, because the column would soon pass on and leave them unprotected.[4]

As pointed out by Surgeon Marsh, at Trevilian's the number of wounded who could withstand the move—a total of 317—far exceeded the capacity of the eight ambulances which had accompanied the raiding force.[5] Consequently it was necessary to allocate ammunition and supply wagons to the surgeons to transport the wounded. In addition, to augment military transport, parties scoured the local countryside confiscating farm wagons, buggies, and carriages along with their teams, if the horses could be found.

Sheridan was forced to leave behind three hospitals with about forty Confederate wounded and ninety-two of his own who were too seriously wounded to be moved. Several surgeons and assistant surgeons—aided by volunteers from the ranks—remained to care for those left behind. Sheridan ensured that the hospitals were well stocked with "medicines, liquors, some hard-bread, coffee and sugar." Unfortunately, after daylight on June 13, advancing Confederates appropriated much of the hospital stocks that had been provided.[6]

Some soldiers—those most severely wounded—generally had no option but to accept their fate of being left behind. Others, however, protested the decisions of the surgeons.

Lieutenant Noble Preston, who had been shot in the hip on Saturday as he climbed over a rail fence leading the charge of the 10th New York, was visited by the regimental surgeon, Robert W. Pease. Pease informed Preston that he was to be left behind, and that the regiment's assistant surgeon, Peter E. Sickler, was also to remain behind to care for the wounded. Upon receiving that news, Preston insisted that he "would not voluntarily surrender himself to a lingering death in rebel prisons. If I was to die, I was determined it should be in an attempt to get away." Pease, apparently impressed by Preston's attitude, promised to provide transportation for the wounded officer, although he believed Preston would not survive two hours' movement.[7]

The next morning Preston was "suddenly seized by two men, taken to the door, and thrown into an ambulance; an officer standing by, meantime urging the men to 'hurry up; get these wounded out, quick!' The driver applied the whip to the team and the ambulance took off at a 'fearful pace'" over the rough roads. Although Preston's wound began to bleed, "I experienced a feeling of positive cheerfulness in the knowledge that I was not abandoned to the enemy. It was a fair example of the triumph of mind over matter."[8]

When the Cavalry Corps began its withdrawal at about midnight on June 12, it was also necessary to begin moving the 400 or so prisoners to prevent their possible recapture. As the corps began its movement to the northeast, many of the prisoners had been "obliged to almost run for several miles" to get them beyond Hampton's reach. When the column finally halted, some of the prisoners were "completely used up," and Lieutenant Gabriel Manigault later recalled that he "simply lay down in the dirt to rest myself, so exhausted was I."[9]

That night, the Cavalry Corps withdrew from Louisa County by the way it came two days earlier, re-crossing the North Anna River at Carpenter's Ford. Once in Orange County, Sheridan halted so that the men could unsaddle and graze their famished horses for a few hours.

Hampton did not begin an immediate pursuit of the federals. As the sun rose, details of men were sent out to bury the dead and collect the wounded who had not already been brought into field hospitals. Among the wounded were those seriously wounded Confederate and Union soldiers who had been left behind by Sheridan. Hampton's medical staff made arrangements to evacuate to Gordonsville and Charlottesville those who could be moved. Also, before he could begin a pursuit, Hampton also had to arrange for the several hundred prisoners his men had taken to be marched off into captivity.[10]

On the morning of June 13, the captured Union soldiers began the march to Richmond and prison. Arriving in Charlottesville that night, the prisoners were confined in an old tobacco warehouse which was a slight improvement over sleeping on the ground during the previous night or two. After the first day, on which they received wheat flour, the prisoners' rations consisted predominately of corn meal, causing Captain Charles Leoser to quip that the rebellious nation should be called the "Corn-federacy."[11]

On the morning of June 17, the prisoners left Charlottesville at about daybreak under the guard of Confederate infantry and marched until about 9:00 p.m. The worn out boots that Hampton's artillery officer had "swapped" for Captain Leoser's newer boots immediately after Leoser's capture on Saturday morning did not fit. To try and accommodate the boots to his feet, Leoser trimmed off the uppers and cut holes in the boots at various other places. Despite Leoser's best effort, the sharp edges of stiff leather painfully cut into his feet. The next day, Leoser found himself unable to continue walking so he dropped out of the column and sat down at the side of the road. The private guarding Leoser's group called a sergeant, and the sergeant threatened summary execution, specifically offering to blow Leoser's brains out. Fortunately, before carrying out his sentence on the Union captain, the sergeant summoned a lieutenant. The lieutenant examined Leoser's feet, called for a wagon, and had Leoser loaded in with "some very dirty blankets and haversacks, some muskets, and one or two private soldiers in much the same condition as the blankets."[12] Leoser rode in the wagon for the remainder of the day.

As the column trudged along to the southeast, women along the route came out to greet the Confederate guards with flowers, bread and milk, and to gawk at the Yankee prisoners as they passed by. Leoser, from his perch in the wagon, observed that as the column reached the James River and its canal, "the troops and their prisoners were swallowed up in a happy throng of enthusiastic girls, and the day was one of general and unalloyed rejoicing for the fair ladies of Fluvanna County." That evening the prisoners were loaded on canal boats for the final leg of the journey to Richmond and prison.[13]

Not all of Hampton's regiments left Trevilian's that day to take after Sheridan's raiders. Colonel Bradley Johnson, commanding the 1st Maryland, proposed to Hampton that he take his battalion on a raid through Maryland to Washington for the purpose of capturing President Lincoln at the Soldiers Home, where he spent many summer evenings. Hampton approved the plan and Johnson moved the battalion to Gordonsville to arrange for his horses to be reshod in preparation for the raid. About that time, Lieutenant General Jubal Early passed through with his corps en route to Lynchburg. Johnson disclosed his plan to Early, and—probably to Johnson's surprise—the general disapproved it. Instead Early directed Johnson to march to Waynesboro and to wait there until Early had defeated Hunter. Afterwards, as Early moved up the Shenandoah Valley, Johnson and the 1st Maryland would join his corps.[14]

Also heading west that day were several Southerners with a solemn duty. On Monday morning, the men of Thomson's Battery made wooden coffins for their three comrades who had been killed on Sunday. Before closing the remains in the wooden boxes, the artillerymen went through the pockets of the dead men's clothing to recover any possessions that might be of importance to the families. They then loaded the three coffins onto an ambulance and a detail of three men set out to find a suitable burying place. The small party headed west and after traveling about fifteen miles they selected a gravesite. Charles McVicar recorded in his diary that they selected a spot "in a small cedar grove on a high hill, half mile from the pike leading to Madison Courthouse and in front of Mr. Barton Haxall's house on his farm. We buried the bodies with feet toward sunrise. Magruder north; Riley in the middle and Burgess, south. The officers had us do all for them possible." McVicar also drew a sketch map to record the location of the burial site. After spending the night, the party with the ambulance traveled about forty miles on Tuesday and rejoined their battery near the North Anna River.[15]

On Monday afternoon, Hampton began his movement to the east, with Fitz Lee's Division in the lead, following Sheridan. As the Confederates passed over Sunday's battlefield, Private Noble Brooks, Cobb's Legion, observed "a great many dead—most shot in the head or breast and been stript by our men a very barbarous act." About a mile past Trevilian Station,

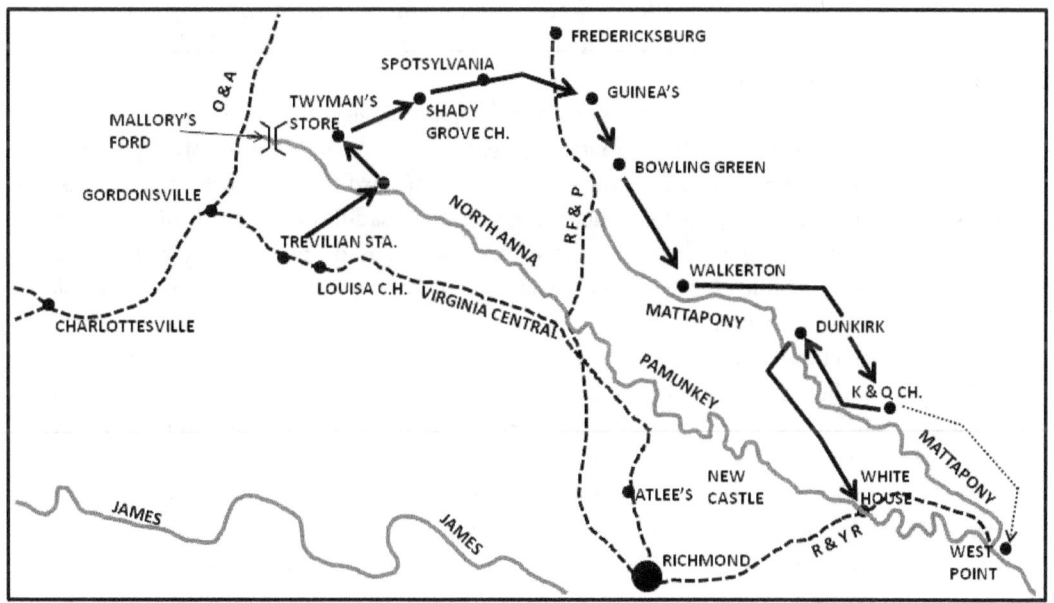

Sheridan's Withdrawal

Brooks recorded that he "saw Col. McAllister of the 7th GA Cav. lying by the road dead and a squad of men digging his grave."[16]

Hampton sent Fitz Lee across the North Anna River to follow Sheridan, while he marched down the south bank of the river, essentially paralleling route he had taken to Trevilian's the previous week. By doing so, Hampton kept his division between Sheridan and the Army of the Potomac, creating a situation that would hopefully force Sheridan into battle. However, although Hampton "constantly offered battle," it was "studiously declined" by Sheridan.[17]

On his return from Trevilian's, Sheridan followed a circuitous route that some of his men found puzzling. Unknown to them, Grant had specified the general route for Sheridan to follow in his instructions to Meade. "After the work [destruction of the railroad] is accomplished, herein directed, the cavalry will rejoin the main army, keeping north of the Pamunkey until the position of the army is known to them. It may be found necessary to keep on the north side as far down as West Point."[18]

Later on the afternoon of June 13, Sheridan's Cavalry Corps marched to Twyman's Store at a road junction several miles north of the river. There, the regiments went into camp for the night. During the day the withdrawing Union column marched essentially unmolested by the Confederates, although a small party of Rebels made contact with Sheridan's rear guard but were easily driven off. Concurrently, on the night of June 13, Sergeant James Avery and his band of about twenty men from the 5th Michigan and their prisoners continued north until about midnight when they stopped to rest. Early the next morning, the Yankees and Rebels together held a consultation. Avery proposed releasing the prisoners since there was not sufficient food to feed them. The prisoners said that they would abide by the decision of the Union soldiers and pledged that—if released—on their honor as Southern soldiers they would not betray their captors. With that, the men shook hands all around and parted ways as friends with the Michigan men and their Negro guide at last daring to move by daylight.[19] Meanwhile that day, the long Union column continued north. Upon reaching the Catharpin Road, Sheridan turned to the east and marched several miles before going into camp at Shady Grove Church.[20]

As Sheridan's long column made its way through Orange and Spotsylvania Counties, it must have presented a distinctly un-martial appearance. Of the 6,000 or so cavalry troopers, roughly 1,500 were unhorsed, trudging along on foot toward the rear of the column, some who were unable to find space in a wagon carrying their saddles on their shoulders. In the middle of the column were the 500 or so prisoners, mostly on foot, with guards on their flanks. Also in the middle of the column one would find the wounded, carried on a procession of ambulances, army wagons, and various farm wagons, buggies, carts and carriages. Bringing up the rear was a throng of slaves seeking liberation: men and women, young and old; children; even babies in their mothers' arms, with many carrying their possessions in bundles on their shoulders. The throng increased as the march progressed, finally totaling about 2,000 slaves when passing through King and Queen County.

During the march, Sheridan earned the respect and appreciation of his wounded. He realized that they were suffering greatly as the various wagons and carts bumped along, and their condition was made worse by the intense summer heat and the clouds of dust that plagued the column. Sheridan halted the march frequently each day to allow the surgeons to dress wounds and refresh the wounded as much as possible. Despite those efforts to help the

18. "Damn, damn, all the time"

wounded, however, Sheridan admitted that "our means for mitigating their distress were limited," but he observed that "the fortitude and cheerfulness of the poor fellows under such conditions were remarkable, for no word of complaint was heard." Sheridan added, "I saw on the line of march men with wounded legs driving, while those with one disabled arm were using the other to whip up the animals."[21] Lieutenant Noble Preston provided the perspective of a patient: "The efforts of General Sheridan to take the wounded with him were appreciated. Men who were clinging to the sides of the grave gratefully accepted the chances of a place in the hard, uncomfortable government wagons in which they were some cases packed-in crosswise. The march was continued from day to day, through oppressive heat and stifling dust, with scarcely a murmur from these noble fellows. On the completion of a day's march, after the train had parked, a detail passed along and removed those who had died during the day. But they met their fates bravely."[22]

About this time—the mid-point in the return march—the condition of the prisoners began to impede Sheridan's progress. In the hot, dry weather, many of the prisoners found it difficult to keep up the pace of the march on foot. Doubtless, the condition of the prisoners was adversely affected by the lack of adequate rations and insufficient rest since June 8 when Hampton and Lee had begun their march to overtake Sheridan's raiders.[23] Sheridan's solution to the weakened state of the prisoners probably did not meet with much favor from his troopers.

In that regard, Lieutenant Manigault recalled, "Towards the third or fourth days our progress as prisoners, which was as rapid as the cavalry, was exhausting us to such a degree, that it was found necessary to dismount certain regiments of federal cavalry and allow the prisoners to ride the horses. The federal privates were most indignant at this on the first occasion, and as they stood by looking at the miserable collection of hungry and fatigued rebels who were now going to use their horses, they assailed us with the vilest of epithets. None of us replied, as there was nothing to say, and each man of us got on a horse without further ado."[24]

Private Samuel Burns Rucker, Sr., 6th Virginia, had a somewhat different experience. He recalled, "They mounted one half of our 350 men at a time, and at midday they dismounted

UNHORSED TROOPERS RETIRING FROM SHERIDAN'S RAID.

This engraving depicts Sheridan's men returning from a raid. On Sheridan's orders, horses that broke down were shot to prevent them from falling into Confederate hands. Union troopers, left afoot, were frequently forced to carry their saddles until they could find a wagon (*Battles & Leaders of the Civil War*).

another like number of their cavalry. Those that rode in the morning were expected to walk in the evening." However, because of the slip-shod way the prisoners were counted when changing over, Rucker was lucky enough to be chosen to ride in both the morning and afternoon that day. He recalled, "As I started to mount a Yankee horse, three Yankees came running to me and wanted me to ride their horse. I never knew why they did that unless that I was quite slender and would not be very heavy on their horse."[25]

The following day the raiders crossed over the battlefield at Spotsylvania Courthouse, where a halt was called to bury many of both Union and Confederate dead whose remains lay in the open. A number of wounded from both sides were found in houses near the battlefield, and Union wounded who could travel were loaded onto wagons and taken with the Cavalry Corps when it resumed its march that afternoon.[26]

Many men were shocked at the conditions they observed on the battlefield. A soldier from the 6th Pennsylvania later wrote, "The debris of the battle strewed the ground; large trees were seen cut nearly in two, scarred and shattered by shot, shell, and musket-balls, while heavy lines of earthworks marked where the severest charges were made and resisted. The graves of those who fell on this terrible field were on every hand." An officer in the 4th Pennsylvania recorded that:

> We witnessed, too, many sad and revolting sights during the day. Here were myriad graves of soldiers, so shallow it seemed the sod had just been lifted to receive them. Thirty or forty bodies had been consigned to this hasty sepulcher and one time and in one place. Hands, feet, and portions of the head sometimes protruded from the ground. Locks of hair were seen exposed, the winds tossing them at their own reckless caprice. Sometimes a portion of the tattered uniform could be seen, through openings in the ground. A hand now and then was clearly visible, from which the flesh had been devoured or decomposed—a skeleton hand without, attached still to the bloated and decaying flesh of the body within the tomb.

A captain in the 1st Massachusetts recorded, "Such a scene of devastation! Everything had the gloom of death for miles, and everywhere were mounds where men lay in their last resting places. I tell you, it was a sad sight. Not one human being did we see all the time. I never want to go there again."[27] Later that afternoon, the march continued to Guinea's Station, near which the regiments went into camp. On June 16, the long column passed through Bowling Green and continued several miles farther before going into camp on the Mattaponi River.

While moving through Orange and Spotsylvania Counties, the successive days of hard work, little rest, and grossly inadequate grain and forage began to tell on the Cavalry Corps' horses. For many Confederates, and perhaps quite a few Union troopers, the defining feature of Sheridan's withdrawal was the destruction of hundreds of Union cavalry mounts.

The historian of the 1st Maine Cavalry recorded the problem. "From the fifteenth to the twenty-first were days of most tiresome marching. The sun was extremely hot, the roads extremely dusty, the men tired, worn, and, for the most part, hungry (as foraging was hard and not over-profitable), and decidedly cross, and the horses were worn out and half starved, which made riding much harder. Very many of the horses were played entirely out, and the rear guard had a large number of such to shoot before starting out each morning, so that they might not be recuperated and furnish aid to the enemy."[28] In a similar vein, a captain in the 1st Massachusetts wrote, "It was nothing but damn, damn, all the time, all tired out, and half starved, the horses playing out every minute, the men getting sick; it was rough indeed. A thousand fresh cavalry could have knocked us all to pieces easy."[29]

The Confederates took particular notice of the destruction of Union mounts. U.R. Brooks, in his account of Trevilian's, wrote, "When Sheridan started on his retreat from Trevillian Station on Sunday evening about 9 p.m. the 12th of June, 1864, we hounded him night and day through the hottest, dustiest, driest country at that time on the continent. It was not an infrequent thing for us to pass five or six or eight of Sheridan's horses lying dead on the line of march. These horses had no doubt broken down, were tied together, and shot in their tracks, no doubt to prevent their falling into our hands." Brooks commented further: "Sheridan's retreat was so precipitate that he could not wait for horses that showed signs of fatigue, but had them shot at once, and Colonel Zimmerman Davis [then a Captain in the 5th South Carolina] counted over two thousand dead horses with bullet holes in their heads, in the one hundred miles (averaging over twenty to the mile) from Trevillian to White House on the Pamunkey."[30]

Other estimates were more conservative. Captain Frank Myers, 35th Virginia, wrote, "It was estimated that in his retreat of one hundred miles his army left, on an average, twelve dead horses to the mile; that besides his losses in horse-flesh at the battle, twelve hundred were shot, by his order, on his retreat; but he took quite that number from the citizens along his route, and in a manner that no other man than a Sheridan or a Sherman would have done."[31]

William Locke, 4th Alabama, wrote of the march to his wife. "This fight is said to be the hardest cavalry fight that ever occurred in Virginia. While the Yanks were retreating they would blockade the road by cutting down trees &c. In pursuing them I am quite certain that we passed at least five hundred dead horses they killed Hundreds of saddles Bridles Guns &c. I was fortunate to pick up on the battlefield a very fine 'Spencer' repeating rifle that shoots seven times also a very fine pair of Bridle belts." Locke would probably have preferred to capture a Yankee horse, since his mount, having had no corn for three or four days, "gave out" as the Confederates began the march after Sheridan and Locke had to leave the animal behind. Fortunately, Locke was able to ride a mule belonging to a wounded man in his battalion.[32]

In his official report, Fitz Lee, whose division was following in Sheridan's tracks, simply wrote: "His trail was strewn with dead horses, which, as fast as they gave out, were shot."[33]

The Union Cavalry's destruction of horses surfaced again in 1910 upon the publication of U.R. Brooks's book, *Butler and His Cavalry*. Theophilus Rodenbough, then the editor of the *Journal of Military Service*, wrote a critical review of the book, prompting Brooks to write a lengthy rebuttal, concluding his "screed" with, "If Sheridan was not routed at Trevillian on June 12, 1864, why did he shoot to death two thousand of his cavalry horses to keep our cavalry from getting them? It really seems that the little general should have been punished for cruelty to animals, if he was not afraid of what he called the 'Rebel Cavalry.'" Rodenbough, in his reply, explained that "shooting of a large number of disabled horses on the return march to the Army of the Potomac was our custom on all our expeditions, to prevent their falling into enemy hands after recuperation." He went on to point out, "By the way, is it not stated in your book (page 380) that after Trevillian 'many hundred horses of Hampton's command were unfit for service?'" Brooks, however, got in the last word. "Yes, we had several hundred horses unfit for service after the Trevilian fight, but I don't recall that we shot any of them. Such cruelty was never our practice."[34]

The issue of destroying the horses to prevent their use by the enemy is perhaps more a reflection of the changing nature of modern warfare than of cruelty. Cavalry horses were considered war materiel and preventing war materiel from being taken and put to use by the enemy was an accepted practice. Both sides destroyed quartermaster stocks and ammunition on many occasions throughout the war to preclude their falling into enemy hands. However, horses were different.

In the Union army, most horses were owned by the government and commanders when necessary ordered their men to kill lame or broken down horses to prevent their capture. Earlier in the war, soldiers frequently would abandon their worn out or disabled horses to avoid the task of killing them, which many found personally distasteful. Sheridan simply brought discipline and efficiency to the practice, charging the rear guard with the responsibility of destroying all horses that could not keep up with the march and were abandoned.

Such orders could not be given in the Southern cavalry, and if they had been given, they likely would not have been obeyed because almost all cavalry mounts were the personal property of the individual troopers. Understandably, many Southern cavalrymen had close, emotional attachments to their horses, feelings that are documented in numerous letters, diaries, and memoirs. Consequently, accommodations were made to provide opportunity for worn out, lame, or diseased horses to recover their strength.

Butler established a "recruiting camp," commonly referred to by his men as the "deadline" for horses that could travel but were unfit for active service.[35] The camp was at Dover Mills, twenty miles upstream from Richmond on the James River. The dismounted men were organized into a battalion which fought on foot as their horses recovered. As horses were deemed serviceable, they were taken forward and reunited with their owners who could then leave the dismounted battalion and rejoin their regiments.[36] J.E.B. Stuart established what was sometimes called a "horse hospital" near Charlottesville where unsound or broken down horses could be rested and turned out to graze. Upon arriving in Louisa County, the horse belonging to Private Rufus Peck, 2nd Virginia, began suffering from a swollen and sore back. Peck was ordered to take his horse and two others that were condemned as unfit to the horse hospital—called the "horse pasture" by Peck—in Albemarle County.[37] Thus, on the eve of battle Fitz Lee gave up a man and three horses that the horses might be rehabilitated.

On the march to Louisa County, Sheridan had imposed constraints on foraging, although some men were not able to resist the lure of fresh meat or produce. In Louisa County and during the march from Louisa back to the Army of the Potomac, rations had for the most part been consumed and foraging of necessity increased so that the men might eat.

On June 21, Susan Leigh Blackford, a resident of Lynchburg, wrote to her husband, a captain serving as a judge advocate on Longstreet's staff. In her letter she described the destruction in Louisa County. "The soldiers who came up with Early give the most distressing accounts of the condition of affairs in Louisa County where the yankee raids have done so much harm to the unprotected. They say the desolation is so great that as they marched through women and children flocked to the road begging for something to eat, and would grasp eagerly the bit of cold corn-bread they could spare from their own haversacks. Is it not horrible to think of?"[38]

During Sheridan's withdrawal from Louisa County, his long column was harried by parties of Confederates acting as irregulars. On Sheridan's march to Trevilian's, Captain Thomas Conrad, the chaplain-scout, spent most of his time observing the Union column and reporting intelligence back to Hampton and Lee. On Sheridan's return march, Conrad and his comrades took a more active role against the Yankee raiders, particularly those caught foraging. Conrad recalled that while passing through King William County, he with three other scouts were "hanging on the flanks of Sheridan's column capturing and killing the stragglers who left the main line for the purpose of plundering defenseless citizens." Riding into the back yard of a mansion in a beautiful grove, Conrad found several horses tied to the fence. He asked an old Negro who the horses belonged to and "the old rascal" replied "our people," meaning Southerners. However, Conrad could tell from glancing at the saddles and tack that the horses belonged to Yankees. Two of the scouts dismounted and ran around to the back of the house, while Conrad and the other scout rode to the front. Moments later there was a pistol-shot from the back of the house and two Yankees ran out the front door and were shot down by Conrad and the other scout. The two dismounted and rushed through the front door "and as fast as a Yankee showed himself one of us shot him, until of the seven all but one was killed or mortally wounded. It was all done within five minutes." The lady of the house, who was the mother of an officer in Wickham's Brigade, threw her arms around Conrad thanking him for delivering her house from the "vile Yankees."[39]

The next day Conrad came upon a lone Yankee forager—a "plunderer" in Conrad's terms—on the road. According to Conrad, the Union trooper's horse was "strung with chickens, hams, ducks, and turkeys from its head to its tail." Conrad shot the forager, took his feet out of his stirrups, and dropped his body onto the road. He then concealed the horse in a

White House on the Pamunkey had been the home of Martha Custis before her marriage to George Washington. In 1857 the plantation was bequeathed to Rooney Lee. Since the river was navigable up to White House and a railroad was nearby, the Union established supply depots at White House in 1862 and 1864. As McClellan withdrew from the Peninsula in the summer of 1862, Union troops burned the home and its outbuildings (Library of Congress).

thicket until he could return after dark and retrieve it. Conrad did not record the disposition of the chickens, hams, ducks, and turkeys. However, he traded the horse for another horse named "Old Whitie."[40]

Most foragers, however, were not caught or killed by Confederate scouts. Nor were they deterred from foraging because if that threat. The men needed food, and their only feasible course of action was to take as much as they could from the civilian population. While certainly there were instances of wanton destruction and looting, most Union efforts were directed toward gathering food. Nonetheless, the civilians in areas not recently or heavily fought-over—Louisa, Carolina, King and Queen, and King William counties, for example—suffered greatly.

Private William Wilson, 12th Virginia, was from Jefferson County, Virginia, today West Virginia. However, he had relatives in King and Queen County. On June 27, 1864, Wilson wrote to his mother.

> I was fortunate enough to get to Uncle Richard's last week where I rested five days and had my clothes washed and mended. The terrible Yankees had been all thro' that country and stripped the people of everything they had. They took all his corn & bacon, poultry, molasses, a good deal of tobacco, 2 mules, 2 fine milch cows, 16 sheep, hogs, nearly ruined his growing crop of wheat besides doing various other damage and insulting his family. His neighbors fared even worse than he. Mrs. Smith lost everything Dr. Fleet, Mrs. Council, Mr. Temple Gwathmey, Hill and persons all through the Bruington and Stevensville neighborhood fared in this way. Uncle R lost only two of his negroes.... The Yankees burned the Walkerton Mills and Mr. Wm. _____ware's fine house with everything it contained.

Having apparently heard of Chaplain Conrad's encounter with the "plunderers," Wilson added, "Some of our scouts caught seven at Mrs. Capt. Haynes' plundering the property. They killed three of them—one in her parlor—I have no news to write."[41]

The activity of Rebel scouts directed against Union foragers apparently did not go unnoticed. On June 18, Sheridan ordered General Gregg, whose division was marching in the lead that day, to arrest all male citizens capable of bearing arms. The following day, Sheridan—perhaps in retaliation for Rebel actions—sent Gregg orders to have the mill at Walkerton burned, as mentioned by Wilson in his letter. For emphasis, Sheridan instructed Gregg to "send an officer in charge of the party to see that the order is executed."[42]

As Sheridan was marching through King & Queen County, Sergeant Avery and his men made their way to the Rapidan, crossing at Germanna Ford into Culpeper. Having wintered near Stevensburg, they were very familiar with the area and crossed the Rappahannock at Ellis's Ford. Once in Stafford County, the men followed a wagon road east to the banks of the Potomac, reaching the river on the morning of June 18. Shortly after daylight they were picked up by a Union gunboat and taken to Alexandria where they arrived that night, beating Sheridan's return to Union lines. At Alexandria, their Negro guide obtained a position with the army quartermaster department, "a good place with good pay," and the men of the 5th Michigan were sent through Washington to Giesboro Depot for remounting, where initially they had "nothing to do except to cook and eat."[43]

Sheridan was in somewhat of a quandary, not knowing exactly the status of Grant's army and its former supply bases at West Point and White House. Also, encumbered as he was with prisoners, wounded, and contrabands, Sheridan did not believe it prudent to cross the Mattaponi River and continue south between the Pamunkey and the Mattaponi where he might be attacked by Hampton with an obstacle to his back. Consequently, in compliance with his instructions, Sheridan continued toward White House.

On June 17 and June 18, Sheridan's long column made its way slowly through King & Queen County. On June 18, Sheridan learned that the depot at White House on the Pamunkey was still operating. So the following day, Sheridan sent the prisoners, wounded, and contrabands—accompanied by two regiments of cavalry—on to West Point on the York River. He then reversed course and marched north to Dunkirk. There, two squadrons of cavalry swam their horses across the Mattaponi to secure the far bank and Captain Folwell's engineers went to work laying a bridge. On June 20, the cavalry crossed the bridge and marched south through King William county, leaving the 4th New York behind to escort the engineers after they had recovered their bridge. After passing King William Courthouse, the two divisions went into camp on the north bank of the Pamunkey opposite White House.[44] Finally, much welcomed feed for the horses and food for the men was provided. However, Sheridan and his fatigued officers and men still had roughly twenty miles of hostile territory to traverse, three rivers to cross, and two Confederate Cavalry divisions to evade or fight before rejoining the Army of the Potomac.

19

"The most disorderly retreat I have seen"
Union Defeat at Samaria Church

Although the cavalry corps had reached the federal depot at White House and received some much welcome rations, there would be no rest for Sheridan's weary men and their mounts.[1] Upon hearing of Sheridan's arrival, Meade issued orders for Sheridan to move his command to City Point, crossing the James via a pontoon bridge at Deep Bottom. If unable to cross at Deep Bottom, Sheridan was to proceed to Douthat's Landing and cross the river on ferry boats.

At the time, the chain of command at the White House depot was in a state of flux. On June 20, Brigadier General J.J. Abercrombie, who had commanded the depot for several weeks, was replaced by Brigadier General G.W. Getty. On his first day in command, Getty received orders from Meade directing that as soon as Sheridan left for City Point, Getty was to break up the depot, send the Veteran Reserve units detailed to White House as a security force to Washington, and "bring the balance of your command and all public property to City Point." Concurrently, Meade dispatched Major George Forsyth, an officer of the 8th Illinois detailed to Sheridan's staff, with a letter of instruction for Sheridan, including guidance that all wagons and animals from the depot would accompany Sheridan on the march to City Point.[2]

Sheridan was not happy that his corps had been

As Sheridan arrived at White House, Brigadier General George Washington Getty was placed in command of the depot. His orders were to break up the depot and accompany Sheridan to the James. Moving the depot stores would add roughly 800 wagons to Sheridan's already-long column (Library of Congress).

tasked with the responsibility of escorting the supplies from the depot, writing later of "the immense train—which ought never to have been left for the cavalry to escort after a fatiguing expedition of three weeks."³ However, from the army perspective, it made sense to give the mission to Sheridan. Sheridan was at the depot, while it would take time to dispatch sufficient force—perhaps an infantry brigade or division augmented by two or three regiments of cavalry with supporting artillery—from City Point to carry out the mission. Also, it is unlikely that Meade was fully aware of the poor condition of Sheridan's two divisions.

As Sheridan had been in the last stage of his march to White House, Fitz Lee had crossed the Pamunkey rejoining Hampton, who planned to attack the Union Depot. Hampton considered charging the depot with the 5th South Carolina before Sheridan's arrival, but thought better of the plan and instead ordered Butler to forego any aggressive movements. In Lee's words, "A close reconnaissance discovered the garrison protected by gunboats and strong earthworks. It was, therefore, deemed impractical and the orders for the attack were countermanded."⁴ Thus Sheridan, upon arriving at the river, found the Confederates holding the bluffs around the now-destroyed White House farm and the depot, but not making any overt offensive actions.

Even though a general attack was not launched, some fighting took place at White House, characterized by one participant as "a desultory skirmish [that] was kept up for some time but all efforts to make an assault on the fort were abandoned and we withdrew to the adjoining hills." At the same time, Fitz Lee's Division, in position on Butler's right, came under fire from

In the early morning hours of June 21, the men of Gregg's division crossed the Pamunkey on a bridge constructed by Union engineers. At that point the river was deep enough for ship and barge traffic, but shallow enough for the engineers to use pilings rather than pontoons to support the roadbed. Note the ships—one with a locomotive on board—tied up behind the bridge (Library of Congress).

gunboats in the river. The men called the large projectiles "flour barrels," and when "they hit the ground and exploded, they would shake the earth and make holes in the ground large and deep enough to hide a small-sized horse."[5] A trooper in the 9th New York observed a Confederate artillery battery take up a position in an open field on the bluffs, whereupon a Union gunboat threw a "big shell" into their midst, "and men, horses, and guns flew in every direction." When the smoke and dust had cleared, the New Yorker reported that the battery "was nowhere in sight."[6]

Sheridan determined that to comply with his orders it was necessary to first drive the Confederates back from the bluffs. Consequently, at 2:00 a.m. on June 21, the men of Gregg's division began crossing the bridge over the Pamunkey followed by Torbert's division. The bulk of Gregg's division made the move on foot while Torbert's division was mounted. As the Union divisions deployed on the south side of the river, they found that the Confederates had obliged them by withdrawing from the bluffs without offering battle. Colonel Henry Davies's brigade reversed, and withdrew across the river, arriving in their camps at about 10:00 a.m. After eating breakfast, Davies's men mounted their horses and advanced back across the bridge to the south side of the Pamunkey. Meanwhile, Colonel John I. Gregg's brigade and Torbert's division brigade pushed out from the depot to regain contact with the Confederates.[7]

On the right, Gregg's brigade of Gregg's division moved generally east along the Richmond & York River Railroad toward Tunstall's Station

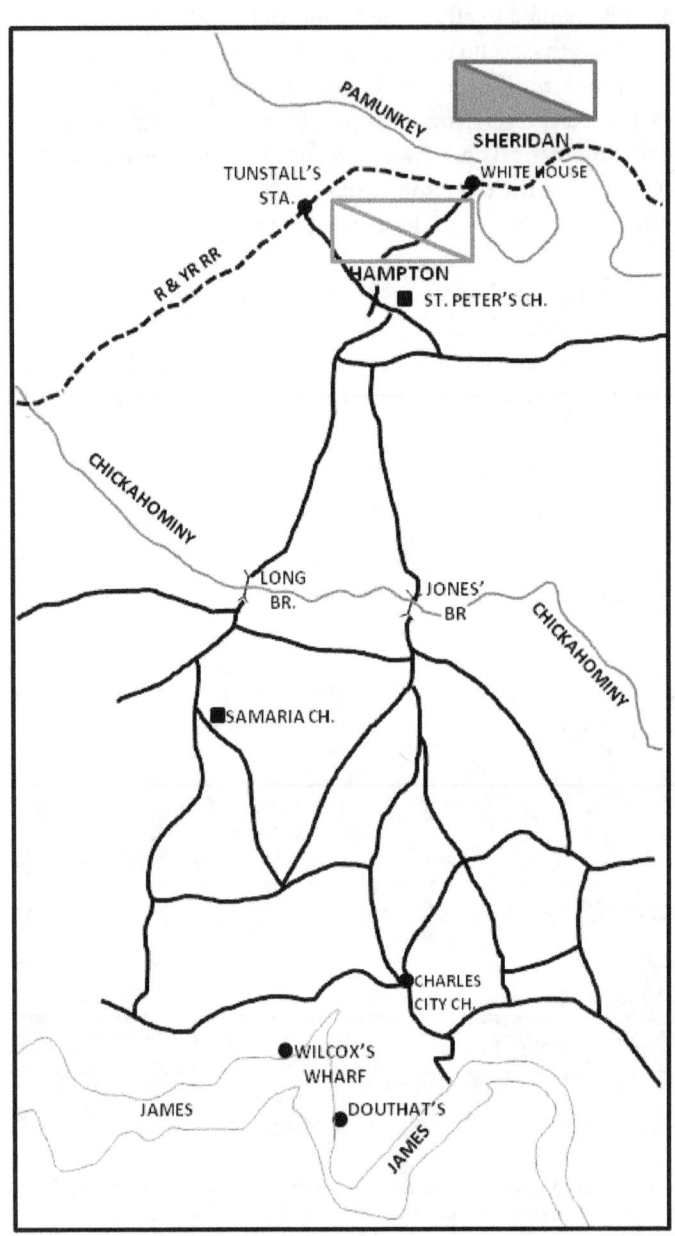

White House to the James River

with Merritt's brigade following in support. In the center, Devin's Brigade moved generally south toward Baltimore Cross Roads and Saint Peter's Church. On the right Custer's brigade marched generally to the southeast along the road to Cumberland Landing, the site of another Union supply base.[8]

After advancing a short distance, Devin's men in the center made contact with skirmishers from Wickham's Brigade. Devin advanced for about a mile, and then met increased resistance as he approached the Confederates' main defensive line just forward of the road leading from Saint Peter's Church to Tunstall's Station. Since the 17th Pennsylvania was low on ammunition, Devin brought up and dismounted the 9th New York in the center of his line. Observing heavy columns of dust moving from across his front, Devin determined that the Confederates were preparing to attack his left flank. In response he sent a squadron of the 6th New York to hold his left. As the squadron moved out, they came under a "hot fire" from dismounted Confederate skirmishers advancing down a hill toward them. In response, Devin dispatched the remaining squadrons of the 6th New York who succeeded in driving the Rebels back.

With the 17th Pennsylvania's ammunition replenished, Devin was prepared to make a general advance with all of his regiments, but instead he received orders from Torbert to hold his position. However, upon receiving word that the Confederates were withdrawing from his front, Devin—on his own initiative—pushed forward and occupied the Church and nearby road junction without further opposition. At the end of the day, Devin left the 9th New York to hold the church and crossroads and withdrew his other regiments about two miles and went into camp. Devin's casualties, all in the 9th New York and the 17th Pennsylvania, were six killed and eighteen wounded.[9]

On the right, Gregg's division made contact with Confederates on the west side of Black Creek, which runs south-north and crosses the road and railroad just east of Tunstall's Station. The Confederates advanced, in Gregg's estimation with the intent of reestablishing their positions on the bluffs overlooking White House. Gregg's men repulsed the attack, although intermittent fighting continued.[10] At about the time the Confederate attack began, Colonel Charles Smith, commanding the 1st Maine, along with the regiment's major, Jonathan Cilley, and Captain Paul Chadbourne, the commander of Company I, sat down for dinner. The three opened a box of sardines that had been hoarded during the march to Trevilian's and back. As they took their first bites, a volley of musketry caused them—and the men near them—to beat a hasty retreat. Instead of enjoying their meal, the three officers turned their attention to reforming the regiment's line. They never forgave the Confederates for the untimely attack that spoiled their meal.[11]

As the fighting subsided, the 1st Pennsylvania, which had been in reserve, was called forward and directed to drive off a Rebel artillery piece that had been harassing the Union skirmish line. The Pennsylvanians dismounted and, supported by one mounted squadron of the 1st New Jersey, advanced about one-half mile across a strip of cleared land with woods on each side. As the men of the 1st Pennsylvania reached the end of the clearing, they were struck on both flanks by Confederates concealed in the woods. In the words of the regimental historian, the regiment was "fairly entrapped," and their only course of action was "To retrace our steps, and precipitously too." In his official report, Colonel Davies wrote that the 1st Pennsylvania "had a severe fight, in a bad position, and were obliged to fall back a short distance."[12]

With Gregg's division blocking their way, the Confederates broke off the attack and withdrew during the night. Gregg's casualties were four killed, thirty-four wounded, and twenty-two missing. All of the missing and twenty-eight of the wounded were in the 1st Pennsylvania.[13]

On the left, Custer's brigade had a fairly easy day and he spent part of his time penning a letter to Libbie. Informing her of the action on June 21, Custer wrote, "We have been fighting all day." However, Custer reported no casualties in his brigade during the day's engagement which is known variously as Tunstall's Station, Black Creek, or Saint Peter's Church.[14]

During the fighting on June 21, William Locke, 4th Alabama, continued to experience difficulties with his mounts. Before the Trevilian's Raid, he had been thrown into a mud hole, after the fighting on June 12 his horse had played out, and on June 21 he was now riding a mule. In a letter to his wife on June 22, he described his part in the action. "Yesterday our regiment was going at full speed when our cannons commenced firing. My mule got frightened ran away with me fell in a ditch throwing me off and fell on top of me—and to my utter astonishment never hurt me at all. Today I have exchanged him for a horse."[15]

While Sheridan was engaged with Hampton, Meade sent a message to Grant, opining that with Hampton still north of the James and in a position to attack Sheridan, it was not likely that Sheridan could get to Deep Bottom to cross the James on the bridge unless Sheridan was first able to give Hampton "a severe and serious defeat." Meade also wrote to Grant that since Hampton was north of the James, it was safe to send Brigadier General Wilson's division on a raid to destroy the Southside Railroad leading to Lynchburg and Richmond and Danville Railroad at their junction in Burkeville. Meade, indicating that he had little understanding of the depleted condition of Sheridan's command, closed by adding, "If Sheridan were here there would be no doubt, I think, of he and Wilson going to Lynchburg."[16]

On the morning of June 22, Sheridan informed General Grant that Hampton's forces had retired toward Richmond, crossing the Chickahominy at Bottom's Bridge. Sheridan directed that Torbert advance with his division to Jones' Bridge, about ten miles east of Bottom's Bridge, and that Gregg send one of his brigades to support Torbert if needed. Gregg, in turn, tasked Davies to advance several miles to Baltimore Store and from there communicate with Torbert, assisting him as needed.[17]

On the night of June 22, Brigadier General Getty began moving of all the depot materiel to the south in a column of 800 wagons. Combined with the trains of the Cavalry Corps, Sheridan was responsible for escorting a train of approximately 900 wagons, which would extend for more than six miles.[18]

Also moving south from the White House were several combat units that had been assigned to the depot for its security: 28th U.S. Colored Troops; a battery from the 3rd New Jersey Light Artillery; and the 67th Pennsylvania Volunteers. Also included with Getty's command were two regiments of dismounted cavalry, the 13th Ohio and the 25th New York, which had been left at the depot as Sheridan prepared for his raid earlier in the month. The total strength among those units was reported at 51 officers and 1,365 enlisted men.[19]

At about the same time, Hampton received some much-needed reinforcements. As the Army of Northern Virginia shifted to Petersburg, Robert E. Lee had left Brigadier General John Chambliss's Brigade of W.H.F. "Rooney" Lee's Division on the north side of the James to assist Hampton in interdicting Sheridan as he attempted to rejoin the Army of the Potomac.[20] Chambliss's Brigade consisted of three Virginia Regiments, the 9th, 10th, and 13th.

19. "The most disorderly retreat I have seen" 205

June 23 was a day devoted principally to movement. At 4:00 a.m. Sheridan notified Grant that Torbert had secured a crossing on the Chickahominy at Jones' Bridge, and that the supplies had departed from the depot leaving behind only the rear guard. Before abandoning the depot, General Gregg's men destroyed the bridge across the Pamunkey and the wharf built to accommodate supply ships and barges.[21] As Torbert and the trains moved toward the James, Gregg moved into position to protect Sheridan's right flank. Hampton approached the long Union column from the west, seeking an opportunity to engage and hopefully destroy Sheridan before he could reach the James and come under the cover of gunboats on the river. However, the day was not without some fighting.

On the night of June 22, Devin's brigade, leading Torbert's division, had camped along the road leading from Long Bridge over the Chickahominy to Charles City Courthouse via Samaria Church (frequently shown as St. Mary's Church on Union maps). On the morning of June 23, Devin dispatched the 9th New York to Charles City Courthouse to patrol the road leading from there to Wilcox's Landing, one of the locations designated for Sheridan to cross the James. Shortly after the 9th moved off, Chambliss's Brigade launched an attack against the 6th New York, driving that regiment's pickets for about 500 yards back toward the east. Devin quickly reformed his line, bringing up the 4th New York and the 17th Pennsylvania. General Getty offered the 28th U.S.C.T., and the black soldiers also entered the fight. Devin observed that "the colored soldiers behaved well enough at first, but their officers could not be found, and they were soon in hopeless confusion."[22] In response, Devin repositioned the 17th Pennsylvania to bolster the 28th U.S.C.T. and ordered the 4th New York to attack on his right. Cesnola and his New Yorkers drove the Virginians back to a position from which—although hastily barricaded—they "retired with precipitation." At the conclusion of the fighting, Devin reestablished his pickets and withdrew the main body of his brigade back to their camp which controlled the road leading south.[23]

Meanwhile, Gregg, with his division, crossed the Chickahominy at Jones' Bridge. Davies's brigade continued south to within about three miles of Charles City Courthouse and went into camp. Gregg's Brigade went into camp after crossing the river.[24] That afternoon Torbert's division, followed by the wagons, continued moving south to Charles City Courthouse.

Hampton, knowing that the bulk of Sheridan's force had crossed the Chickahominy, pushed south toward Westover, placing the Confederates between Charles City Courthouse and Deep Bottom with its pontoon bridge.

At 3:30 in the morning on June 24, Sheridan sent orders to General Gregg informing him that the trains were moving east through Charles City Courthouse toward Deep Bottom, and that he was to move his division to Samaria Church and report once he had arrived there. Also that morning, Sheridan directed Torbert to move west from Charles City Courthouse on the River Road. Before reaching Westover, however, Torbert's advance guard encountered Lomax's Brigade blocking the route. Now knowing that without a major fight he would be unable to use the bridge at Deep Bottom, Sheridan ordered the trains to halt "at convenient points on the road" and for Torbert to move his entire division west to prevent the Confederates from attacking the wagons. Sheridan also sent instructions to Gregg to hold his position until all the wagons could pass east through Charles City Courthouse toward Wilcox's Landing.[25] Later that day, Sheridan received a message from Grant directing that he "drop down to where the army crossed the James River [at Wilson's Wharf], and directing General Ingalls to furnish transportation to cross his command."[26]

Initially, Sheridan was directed to cross the James on a pontoon bridge at Deep Bottom, shown in this photograph. However, Hampton positioned his two divisions between Sheridan and Deep Bottom, which forced Sheridan to withdraw to Douthat's and cross the river on barges. Note how the engineers had excavated the bank of the James to allow wagons easy access to the bridge (Library of Congress).

That morning, as Gregg's regiments were moving into positions near Samaria Church they encountered Confederate pickets, which they drove west beyond Nance's Shop. During the skirmishing, an officer of the 1st Massachusetts had an unfortunate—and likely embarrassing—accident. He was emptying his pistol at the fleeing Rebels when his horse threw up his head and the officer shot the horse through the neck. Fortunately for both the officer and the mount, the wound was not severe and the horse recovered.[27]

Now knowing that the federals had occupied the terrain around Samaria Church in some strength, Hampton determined to strike them with a heavy blow.

Earlier that morning, Brigadier General Martin Gary's Brigade, assigned to the defenses of Richmond, arrived to support Hampton.[28] Hampton and Gary knew each other well. Gary, a highly experienced officer, had served under Hampton early in the war. Later he had commanded the Hampton Legion Infantry, which since 1862 had seen hard service in Tennessee.[29] In March 1864, by the same order directing the 4th, 5th and 6th South Carolina to Virginia, the War Department ordered the Hampton Legion Infantry to be mounted and assigned to the defenses of Richmond, whereupon the regiment was designated the Hampton Legion Mounted Infantry.[30] Also in Gary's Brigade was the 24th Virginia which had been formed by combining two Virginia cavalry battalions and two Georgia cavalry companies. The 24th was commanded by Colonel William T. Robins, who had enlisted as a private in the 9th Virginia Cavalry. He rose to sergeant-major of the regiment before receiving a commission. Afterward, he served in a variety of assignments before being promoted to colonel and assigned to command of the regiment effective June 14, 1864.[31]

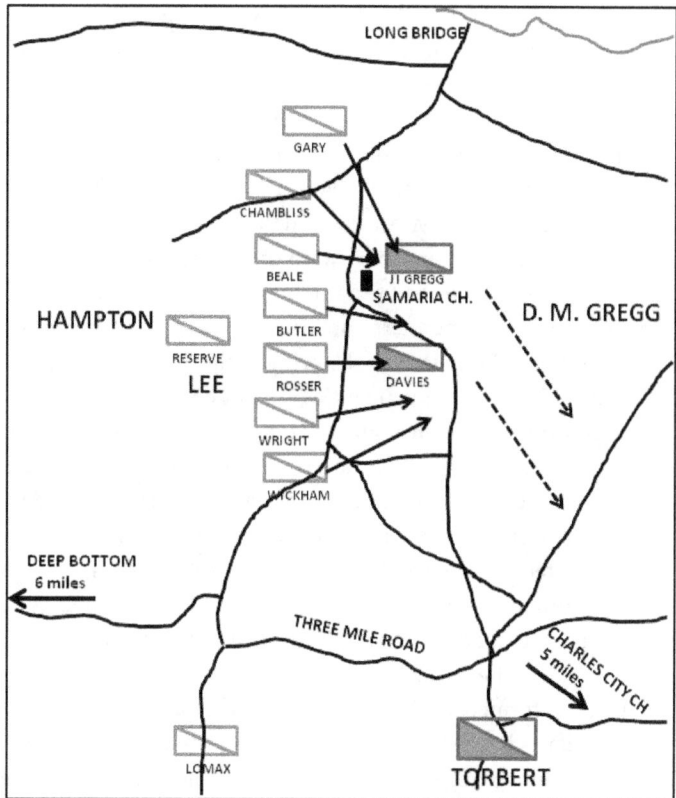

Samaria Church, June 24

Hampton's plan for the attack, while not particularly complicated, called for the enemy to be struck at several locations across a frontage of more than a mile. It also required significant repositioning of forces. Gary was ordered to move his Hampton Legion Mounted Infantry from Salem Church, where Hampton had his headquarters, through Smith's Store. From there he was to fall upon right flank of Gregg's division attacking from the north to south toward Samaria Church. Chambliss, with the 13th Virginia, was also sent north to participate in the attack on the Union right. Meanwhile, Colonel R.L.T. Beale, 9th Virginia moved his regiment and 10th Virginia, the other two regiments of Chambliss's Brigade into position to the west of Samaria Church, forming the north end of Hampton's line of battle. Hampton ordered Butler's, Rosser's and Young's Brigades, the latter two under the command of Colonels Dulany and Wright, respectively, to move into position on the right of Chambliss's Brigade, forming the center of his line.[32] Wickham was directed to bring his brigade forward on the right of Young's Brigade on the south end of Hampton's main line, while Lomax's Brigade protected the left flank from positions astride the River Road several miles to the south. Hampton positioned a mounted reserve consisting of the 12th Virginia, 24th Virginia, Phillips Legion and Jeff Davis Legion to the rear of the center of his line. While Hampton exercised overall command, he placed Fitz Lee in charge of his line of battle. For his main and flanking attack, Hampton had brought into position 147 cavalry companies with a mounted reserve of 35 companies.

Anticipating an attack, Gregg's troopers began preparing hasty fortifications, much as

Hampton's men had done almost two weeks earlier on the Gordonsville Road. On this day, while Hampton's men marched, Gregg's men constructed breastworks with fence rails, logs, and other materials at hand. Gregg placed John I. Gregg's brigade on the right of his line while Davies' brigade occupied the left. Gregg positioned his two artillery batteries in "commanding positions."[33] In his 11 regiments, Gregg had available 127 cavalry companies.

Hampton's repositioning and deployment took time, and "in the slow process of execution the morning hours wore away and the June sun flared down with sweltering heat on the exposed men."[34] Gregg's men were aware of the movement of enemy forces in the vicinity. However, because of the wooded terrain, they did not discern the deployment to their immediate west. About 3:00 that the afternoon, when all was ready, Chambliss and Gary advanced against Gregg's right flank. Upon hearing the firing to the north, Lee gave the order for a general advance. The men of Hampton's main battle line surged forward through the trees on foot. Soon the sound of gunfire echoed through the woods as skirmishers encountered Union pickets.

When the attack began, the commander of the 4th Pennsylvania, Lieutenant Colonel George Covode was well-forward with his skirmishers. As the skirmishers were being driven back toward the prepared positions, Covode was shot and seriously wounded. His men attempted to evacuate him from the battlefield on a makeshift litter, but—pressed hard by the Confederates—they were forced to abandon their commander at the side of the road. A few moments later, General Butler, following his advancing men, passed by and noticed Covode, whom he described as "a large man with red side whiskers" lying on the litter.[35] Upon being informed of Butler's identity, Covode, referring to himself, said, "This is the fate of Sheridan's Raiders, but General, I have the consolation of knowing I have done nothing dishonorable during this raid." Butler, ever the Southern gentleman, replied, "However that may be, sir, I certainly would not remind you of it under present conditions."[36] Butler then inquired about Covode's wound, and Covode replied that his arm had been shattered by a ball. Butler called for his surgeon, Dr. B.W. Taylor, to examine Covode, and the physician found that Covode had also been shot in the back. Butler later speculated that the Pennsylvanian had not mentioned the second wound because he was ashamed of having turned his back toward the enemy. The Confederates took Covode to a nearby field hospital for treatment, but he died of his wounds the following day.[37]

Lieutenant Colonel George Covode, 4th Pennsylvania, was mortally wounded at Samaria Church and was left on the field where he died on June 25. At the beginning of July, Covode's father, a member of Congress, traveled to Virginia and urged that his son's body be recovered. A party of men from the regiment crossed the James, found Covode's grave, and retrieved his remains which were reinterred in Ligonier, Pennsylvania (Library of Congress)

As the pickets fell back, the advancing Confederates emerged from the trees and came upon a line of works less than 100 yards to their front. Although taking heavy casualties, the Rebels charged and quickly drove the Yankees from their initial positions. While going over the breastworks, Lieutenant Cecil Baker, Company B, 9th Virginia was killed by a freak shot. A bullet struck a tree branch above the works and was directed downward, striking Baker from above and entering his heart. Nonetheless, without pause, Colonel Beale led the 9th and 10th Virginia forward.

The main line continued its advance to the east and soon came upon a second line of breastworks from behind which the defenders were firing at a tremendous rate. Stopping briefly to reform their line, the Confederates charged again and were rewarded by seeing the Yankees falling back with some confusion in their rear. Led by Major William Clement, the 10th Virginia drove the Yankees from the line of works. Lieutenant J. Lucius Davis, Jr., the son of the regimental commander, leaped upon the works to cheer the men on and was shot through the chest and mortally wounded.[38]

Meanwhile, to capitalize on the success that had been achieved so far, as the men approached the second, line of works, Hampton ordered his mounted reserve forward. Colonel Robins brought the 24th Virginia up, mounted, in support as General Chambliss and the 13th Virginia arrived on the field having succeeded in driving back the Union flank.

Having cleared the second line of works, Hampton's men continued the attack. Unfortunately for Hampton, at about this time problems began to arise as a result of unanticipated success. Ideally, with the federals driven from their prepared positions and falling back in disorder, the Confederates would have mounted their horses and transitioned from attack to pursuit, attempting to cut off Gregg's forces and force their surrender. However, the horse holders had not kept close upon the rear of the dismounted line as it advanced. Consequently, the bulk of Hampton's men were forced to chase after the Yankees on foot. As DeWitt Clinton Gallaher, a private in the 1st Virginia who served as a scout for both J.E.B. Stuart and Fitz Lee, recalled the assault that day:

> It was very warm, burning hot, and just before the charge was ordered we were at the edge of some woods and under fire of artillery and small arms, a piece of shell—called shrapnel now—struck my left boot and as I nearly fell, some of the boys (Jim Kerr and Phil Coiner) wanted to carry me off, supposing my leg was broken. When ordered to advance and charge the enemy there, we crossing an open field running as fast as we could, the Yankees began to "Skedaddle" and flee! I got up close to a General, or a bunch of officers, trying to rally their fleeing men, and took deliberate aim at him and can never understand why he did not fall as he galloped away. He may have been only wounded. We followed them on foot for three or four miles in a blazing sun. I was never so tired in my life carrying my carbine pistol and ammunition, but the excitement kept me up. We drove them until it was too dark to follow. They ran clean away in the night. Oh How glad I was to again mount my faithful horse and go into camp for the night!

The following day, Gallaher was so stiff and sore that he could hardly saddle and mount his horse.[39]

Within Gregg's regiments, the men were experiencing circumstances similar to those encountered by the Confederates. As Hampton's attack succeeded in driving the Union troopers from their positions, many of the Union horse holders had fallen far back to stay out of the line of fire. Consequently, most of the men in the defensive line were unable to remount and were forced to withdraw on foot. A trooper in the 1st Massachusetts commented on the "skedaddle" from the Union perspective.

The Road was full of led horses and artillery, all mixed up with pack mules, and men mounted and dismounted, all shouting and cursing. It was the most disorderly retreat I have seen since I have been in the service. If the rebels had pushed hard just then they would have gobbled the whole thing. The day was awfully hot, and the men had had no water all day, and had been fighting two hours against an overwhelming force,—the last part without ammunition, darkness coming on, and we all played out with marching, heat, hunger, and fighting day and night for the past eighteen days continuously. You can imagine what it must have been. The rebels captured a good many of the dismounted men in the lines, and while trying to get to their horses, as it was. They were so completely used up that they could not run. They would go a few rods, and then, if their feet touched the least obstacle, they would pitch head over heels, and lie there. We told them the rebels were right after them, then they would get up with great effort and try again, but it was no use; they had not the strength, poor fellows![40]

In his report of the battle, Gregg rather understated the circumstances of his withdrawal, writing, "The movement toward Charles City Courthouse was made in the best possible order, without confusion or disorder."[41]

Although Hampton claimed that the pursuit of the federals was continued until 10:00 p.m. it appears from other reports that the fighting tapered off in the late afternoon, probably as a consequence of exhaustion on both sides. At that time Gregg began withdrawing his wounded for whom there was transportation, wagons, caissons, and led horses to the southeast on the road leading to Charles City Courthouse. After dark, his main body retired on foot with some mounted detachments covering their movement. Gregg reported that his division began arriving at Charles City Courthouse about 8:00 p.m. where it went into camp.

In the fighting at Samaria Church, Gregg's division and its supporting artillery reportedly lost 29 killed, 188 wounded, and 122 missing for a total of 339. Hampton reported the losses in his division of 6 killed and 59 wounded. Richmond newspapers reported the casualties in the brigades commanded by Wickham, Chambliss, and Gary as 29 killed, 106 wounded, and 5 missing.[42] Thus it appears that at Samaria Church Union and Confederate losses—other than missing/captured—were approximately equal.

While Gregg was heavily engaged at Samaria Church, Sheridan claimed to be unaware of his predicament. He later wrote that Gregg "sent message after message to me concerning the situation, but the messengers never arrived, being either killed or captured, and I remained in total ignorance until dark of the strait his division was in."[43] However, at some time on June 24, Sheridan became aware of Gregg's situation and sent an officer to Grant with a verbal report which apparently overstated Gregg's losses. At 1:00 a.m. on June 25, Grant advised Major General Benjamin Butler that Sheridan had "been attacked this evening, and with great difficulty and with heavy loss of men has saved his train so far." Grant directed Butler to send 1,000–1,500 infantry to Douthat's Wharf before daylight to thwart an expected Rebel attack.[44] Later on June 25, Brigadier General Rufus Ingalls, the Army of the Potomac Quartermaster, arrived at Douthat's Landing and reported to Grant that Sheridan was there with his command, that the trains were there without loss and in good condition, and that Gregg's losses at Samaria Church were less than had been reported earlier that morning. Ingalls concluded that it would take several days to ferry the command across the river.

Without further hindrance from the Confederates, Sheridan's command assembled at Douthat's Wharf in preparation for ferrying across the James. The trains arrived at Douthat's on June 25, and began crossing as soon as ferries were available. The last of the trains crossed on the afternoon of June 27. On June 25, Gregg's division marched from Charles City Courthouse to Douthat's Wharf where it remained until the afternoon of June 27. The division was engaged in crossing the river the entire night of June 27–28. On June 26, Torbert's division marched to Douthat's and remained in camp for two days, and finally began finally crossing the James on June 28. On June 29, at 2:30 p.m. General Ingalls reported to General Grant that "the last of General Sheridan's crossed the James River at 11 a.m."[45] The Trevilian's Raid was over.

20

"I regret my inability"
Assessing the Outcome of the Trevilian's Battle and Raid

In assessing the outcome of the Trevilian's Raid, it is important to determine which side—if either—was victorious, including to what degree either side accomplished its mission. As part of that process it is necessary to critically evaluate the various claims made by participants regarding the outcome of the battle. Also, it is fair to critique the opposing commanders, although one must be cautious of second-guessing their decisions with the benefit of hindsight. There are a few issues—the strength of Sheridan's force and the advantage of the Union's superior weaponry—that also warrant review. Also, when assessing the raid, it is necessary to evaluate Grant's decision to conduct the operation in the first place.

As occurred after the battle at Brandy Station a year earlier, both sides claimed victory at Trevilian Station. Additionally, there are several similarities in the claims made by Sheridan and his predecessor in command of the cavalry corps, Alfred Pleasonton. While returning from the Trevilian's Raid, Sheridan penned a brief report to General Meade on June 16. In it, he claimed that his troops thoroughly destroyed the Virginia Central Railroad between Trevilian Station and Louisa Courthouse, with the ties burned and the rails "rendered unserviceable." Sheridan characterized the first day's engagement as a "complete rout" of the enemy who left his dead and nearly all his wounded in Union hands.

Of the fighting on the second day, June 12, Sheridan claimed that Hampton's cavalry had been reinforced during the night by infantry, and that although his men had carried part of the Confederate defensive works twice, they were in each case driven back by Rebel foot soldiers. All-in-all, Sheridan concluded that the battle was "by far the most brilliant of the present campaign."

Regarding his decision to withdraw short of his objective, Sheridan explained that his ammunition was running low, he had only one day's ration remaining for the men and almost no forage for the horses, and he had received reports that portions of Pickett's infantry division were arriving by train to prevent any further Union advance. Regarding his mission to destroy the bridge over the Rivanna River, link up with Hunter, and destroy the Virginia Central between Charlottesville and Gordonsville, Sheridan wrote, "I regret my inability to carry out your instructions."[1]

While Sheridan promised to provide Meade with a more detailed report, events interceded. On July 31, Grant, in response to Jubal Early's incursion toward Washington, appointed

Sheridan to independent command in the Shenandoah Valley, a position he held until almost the end of the war.

Hampton provided his views on the fighting at Trevilian Station in a report to Robert E. Lee dated July 9, 1863. Hampton glossed over the debacle on June 11, blandly informing Lee that the enemy which got into his rear "forced me to withdraw in front and take up a new line." He added that later Custer's brigade was "severely punished" when it was charged by Rosser and "driven back against General [Fitzhugh] Lee" and many prisoners were captured. Hampton informed Lee that the led horses, caissons, and wagons that Custer had captured earlier, were all recaptured by Rosser and Fitzhugh Lee.[2]

Regarding June 12, Hampton wrote that the enemy "who had been heavily punished in front, when attacked on his flank fell back in confusion, leaving his dead and a portion of his wounded on the field." Hampton summed up the raid overall by writing that "Sheridan was defeated at Trevilian, punished in the skirmishes at White House and Forge Bridge, and was routed at Samaria Church."[3]

In applying the standards of the time, one can easily conclude that Hampton had better claim to victory than Sheridan. Hampton suffered fewer casualties and held the field as Sheridan withdrew on the evening of June 12. Additionally, although it was not publicly known at the time, Sheridan had failed in his mission. As summarized by Grant in his report on the campaign, Sheridan was sent to Charlottesville and Gordonsville to "effectually break up the railroad connection between Richmond and the Shenandoah Valley and Lynchburg." That was not done.[4]

At Brandy Station, Joseph Hooker had sent Alfred Pleasonton into Culpeper on June 9, 1863, to "disperse and destroy" J.E.B. Stuart's cavalry division. Over time, however, Union participants and some historians accepted Pleasonton's false assertion that he was to merely conduct a reconnaissance of force into Culpeper.[5] Similarly, at Trevilian Station Sheridan's mission evolved over time.

In May 1866, Sheridan, then commanding the Department of the Gulf in New Orleans, finally submitted his detailed report of the operations of the cavalry corps from May through July of 1864. In that report, Sheridan postulated that in addition to breaking the Virginia Central Railroad and uniting with Hunter, the Trevilian's Raid was to serve another, and perhaps more important, purpose. He wrote, "There also appeared to be another object, viz, to remove the enemy's cavalry from the south side of the Chickahominy, as, in case we attempted to cross to the James River, this large cavalry force could make such resistance at the difficult crossings as to give the enemy time to transfer his force to oppose the movement."[6] Sheridan concluded his report by listing the accomplishments of his cavalry corps, including the claim that "we removed the enemy's cavalry from the south side of the Chickahominy by the Trevilian raid, and thereby materially assisted the army in its successful march to the James River and Petersburg."[7]

Sheridan's 1866 report differed from his 1864 report on several other points. In the 1864 report, Sheridan wrote that on June 12, he directed Torbert to advance toward Gordonsville and attack the enemy, which Torbert did. In the 1866 version, Sheridan wrote that he directed Torbert to "make a reconnaissance up the Gordonsville Road to secure a by-road leading over Mallory's Ford, on the North Anna," over which he planned to withdraw.[8] In the 1864 report, Sheridan wrote that the Confederates had been reinforced with infantry, noting that "trains of cars," ostensibly with Confederate reinforcements, arrived after the fighting on June 12, and prisoners and civilians reported that Major General George Pickett's division, or a part of it, was en route to prevent Union forces from seizing Gordonsville.[9] Two years later, Sheridan wrote that he learned that Ewell's Corps was advancing up the south side of the James toward Lynchburg, and that General John C. Breckinridge was either in Charlottesville or Gordonsville.[10] Finally, in his first report, Sheridan wrote that he could get no definite information regarding Hunter's location, although reports placed him near Staunton. In the later report, Sheridan wrote that from prisoners he learned that Hunter was "at or near Lexington, moving apparently on Lynchburg."[11]

Sheridan's account of the raid in his memoirs, published in 1888, closely conforms to his 1866 report. However, in his memoirs, Sheridan elaborated on his notion regarding the unstated objective of the Trevilian Raid first discussed twenty-two years earlier. Noting the difficulties facing Grant in shifting to the south side of the James River—swamps, thick underbrush, and Lee with interior lines—Sheridan asserted that "it became necessary to draw off the bulk of the cavalry while the movement to the James was in the process of execution, and General Meade determined to do this by requiring me to proceed with two divisions as far as Charlottesville to destroy the railroad bridge over the Rivanna River near that town, the railroad itself from the Rivanna to Gordonsville, and, if practicable, from Gordonsville back to Hanover Junction as well."[12] Thus, what first appeared to be merely a benefit of the raid, over the intervening years became the primary objective of the operation.

The genesis for Sheridan's assertion that the objective of the Trevilian's Raid was to draw off Confederate cavalry may been a contemporary newspaper commentary. Sheridan's June 16 report of the battle at Trevilian's appeared in *The New York Times* on June 19. The following day, *The Times* staff wrote an opinion regarding Grant's generalship in moving the Army of the Potomac to the south side of the James. The opinion stated in part:

> But even had it been necessary to enlarge the record in favor of the Lieutenant-General and his noble army, there was sufficient to be said without going a single step into the realms of fancy. We see now, for instance, on reading SHERIDAN'S report, how brilliantly conceived that expedition was, viewed merely as a diversion in favor of the movement of the main army. That LEE was effectually deceived as to the scope of SHERIDAN'S advance, is apparent in various ways—first in SHERIDAN'S report of the strong infantry force he found brought to within five miles of Gordonsville, and occupying a strongly entrenched position—second, in the fact of LEE having failed to press as he might, and with terrible effect, upon GRANT'S right flank, in the long roundabout march from Cold Harbor to the James—and third, the weakness of BEAUREGARD'S force when SMITH attacked his entrenchments on Wednesday northeast of Petersburg.[13]

There is no indication that the staff of *The New York Times* had knowledge of Grant's orders to Sheridan regarding the raid.[14] Additionally, as discussed, Sheridan did not encounter a "strong infantry force" between Trevilian Station and Gordonsville. Nonetheless, a linkage between the Trevilian's Raid and the movement of the Army of the Potomac to the south side of the James River had been claimed for the first time—a claim that persists to the present.

In evaluating whether the drawing off of Confederate cavalry was a mission actually imposed by Grant, it is interesting to review Grant's orders—issued through Meade—for his cavalry commander. Grant, in particular, was remarkably precise in describing what he wanted Sheridan to accomplish. Specifically, as mentioned earlier, the orders given to Sheridan began with the definitive statement: "The object of the cavalry expedition to Charlottesville and Gordonsville is to effectually break up the railroad connection between Richmond and the

Shenandoah Valley and Lynchburg." Grant went into great detail regarding what he wanted done: "go as far as Charlottesville, and work upon the Lynchburg branch and main line to Staunton.... It is desirable that every rail on the road destroyed should be so bent or twisted as to make it impossible to repair the road without supplying new rails."[15] Given the detail in Grant's instructions to Sheridan, it is inconsistent that Grant would leave undocumented an important task such as diverting two Confederate divisions. It also appears that the tasks directed by Grant and the implied mission of drawing off the Confederate cavalry are incompatible: Could Grant realistically expect Sheridan to penetrate beyond Charlottesville and destroy dozens of miles of track while simultaneously fighting Robert E. Lee's cavalry?

Sheridan, in his memoirs, mentions a face-to-face meeting with Grant before he embarked on the raid.[16] Thus, it is possible that Grant verbally expressed a desire to divert Lee's cavalry as the Army of the Potomac began its movement to the James. However, had Grant or Meade felt it essential that Sheridan lure Robert E. Lee's cavalry away from the Chickahominy, they would almost certainly have specified it in writing in their orders. Further, in their post-war writings, neither Grant nor Meade made mention of the need for such a diversion. While drawing off Hampton's and Fitz Lee's Divisions was surely helpful, it was apparently not considered particularly important—even in hindsight—by Sheridan's superiors. Consequently, one is led to conclude that the objective of drawing off Lee's cavalry was fabricated by Sheridan to provide a measure of success for the Trevilian Raid.

In June 1863, both General Gregg and General Pleasonton in part justified the decision to break off the battle at Brandy Station because "cars loaded with infantry were brought there from Culpeper."[17] In reality, no Confederate infantry were committed to that battle, although Robert E. Lee dispatched two of Ewell's brigades on foot toward Brandy Station in case Stuart needed support. Sheridan, in his three accounts—his two reports and his memoir—also claimed that his decisions were influenced by the arrival of Confederate infantry. However, no trains brought Confederate reinforcements to Louisa County on the two days of the battle or the day following. Breckinridge was not at Charlottesville or Gordonsville; at the time he was on the Blue Ridge near Rockfish Gap. Early with his division did not leave the Richmond area for the Valley until June 13, passing through the Trevilian battlefield on June 16.[18] Lee did not at any time dispatch Pickett's division to prevent the loss of Gordonsville. While it is quite likely that Sheridan's knowledge of the movement of Confederate forces was limited, it is difficult to excuse his decision making which appears to have been based more upon conjecture than on fact. However, it is also possible that Sheridan was knowingly misrepresenting the threat of Confederate infantry to better justify his decision to withdraw.

Moving beyond inconsistencies between Sheridan's reports and events, it is necessary to evaluate the actual conduct of the raid and Hampton's response to it.

All-in-all, Sheridan's decision to advance toward Gordonsville on the north side of the North Anna River was prudent as it protected his left flank from attack by Confederates who might wish to interdict his movement. However, the circuitous route added between twenty to thirty miles to the march from New Castle Ferry to Trevilian's. This extra mileage almost certainly contributed to the loss of horses throughout the course of the raid. Additionally, and significantly, Sheridan surrendered interior lines to Hampton, whose camp at Atlee's was roughly fifty miles from Trevilian's.[19]

Sheridan was apparently satisfied with his security north of the river and as far as can be determined failed to conduct any reconnaissance south of the North Anna during the march to Louisa County. Consequently, Sheridan was not aware that he was being pursued by two Confederate cavalry divisions. Nor was he aware that those divisions had overtaken him and were prepared to offer battle early in the morning on June 11. Consequently, Sheridan and his subordinate commanders were surprised to find Hampton blocking their movement south toward the railroad.[20]

Unlike Sheridan, Hampton's scouts ranged north of the river, monitoring Sheridan's movements, tallying his forces, and reporting his progress back to Hampton. Hampton was aware that Sheridan had crossed into Louisa County on the afternoon of June 10, and could thus anticipate that Sheridan would attempt to interdict the railroad on the following day. Further, while not explicitly stated, it appears that Hampton was confident that Sheridan was unaware of the Confederate presence. Unfortunately, Hampton did not fully take advantage of his knowledge and Sheridan's lack of intelligence.

As previously discussed, according to Hampton's plan, his division and Fitz Lee's Division were to advance on separate routes to jointly engage the Federals somewhere around Clayton's Store. Initially the two divisions would be out of supporting distance of one another, although if contact were made near the Union camps, the two divisions would be able to provide mutual support. However, as it turned out, both Hampton's Division and Fitz Lee's Division each encountered the enemy well south of Clayton's Store, unhinging the plan.

One may fairly question why Hampton did not make an earlier start on the morning of June 11. Even if the account of Butler and Rosser finding Hampton asleep in a horse pen at the Netherland's tavern and house is much embellished, it is well established that General Merritt's regiments were on the march toward the railroad before Butler began deploying his regiments to right and left of the Fredericksburg Road. Had Butler—followed by Wright—began moving north an hour or two earlier, the fighting in the woods would have certainly begun much closer to Sheridan's camps and possibly might have had a different outcome.

The defining event of the first day's fighting was Custer's movement by woodland track into Hampton's rear and Colonel Alger's impetuous charge past the station resulting in the capture of Hampton's wagons and led horses. It is difficult to overstate the significance of those events and had they not occurred, the flow of the June 11 fighting and its outcome likely would have been far different.

Instead of a defeat for Hampton on June 11—which it was, despite Hampton's verbiage in his official report—had the charge not been made, the first day's fighting might have ended inconclusively with both sides withdrawing after struggling with each other blindly in the woods with roughly equal odds for several hours. Should that have been the day's outcome, it is difficult to predict what might have taken place on June 12. For example, Sheridan might have elected recross the North Anna and then moved west to strike Gordonsville.

Custer's movement into Hampton's rear was pursuant to his orders from Torbert, which makes it difficult to fault Custer for becoming surrounded. However, in precipitously ordering Alger to charge with his regiment, Custer dispersed his forces and increased his exposure to counterattack. Whether Custer placed restrictions on Alger—restrictions which Alger may have exceeded due to "unpardonable zeal"—is difficult if not impossible to determine. In battle, it is easy for leaders to lose control of events, and that is what happened at Trevilian Station on June 11, 1864. Of greater significance is what happened next.

As a feat of arms, Custer's first last stand was possibly his best day as a combat commander. Only infrequently do cavalry charges result in prolonged, pitched combat as occurred on Fleetwood Hill at Brandy Station and with Custer's brigade at Trevilian Station. Simply stated, on June 11, Custer, through his courage, energy, and skill, saved his brigade. Custer was able to shift his forces to meet unexpected threats to his perimeter, and to organize local counterattacks to drive back the enemy when necessary. Observers, including Rosser, praised Custer's leadership that day. Custer was also lucky that Hampton, pressed from both the north and south, was unable to generate and mass sufficient combat power to overrun Custer's perimeter.

The fighting on June 12 is much easier to understand than the fighting on the first day at Trevilian: the positions of the opposing forces are reasonably well documented and the accounts of the fighting are generally consistent. However, the fighting on June 12, when compared to the official reports, raises questions regarding Sheridan's intent on that day.

In his first report, Sheridan wrote that he sent Torbert toward Gordonsville to "attack the enemy." However, Torbert, in his own report, wrote that he was dispatched to "reconnoiter the enemy's position on the Charlottesville and Gordonsville Roads." As previously mentioned, in his 1866 report and his memoirs, Sheridan wrote that he dispatched Torbert to make a reconnaissance to "secure a by-road leading over Mallory's Ford."[21]

Regardless of what orders he might have received, Torbert's actions on the afternoon of June 12 are perfectly clear: upon making contact with Hampton, he immediately deployed his brigades, launched an attack, became decisively engaged, and fought for approximately four hours before receiving orders from Sheridan to withdraw. It is doubtful that anybody engaged in that fight—from Torbert down to the lowest private in the ranks—considered themselves to be participating in a reconnaissance.

One may fairly question why Sheridan—if he intended for Torbert to conduct a reconnaissance—did not intervene to curtail the fighting. In his memoirs, Sheridan wrote about his plans for the day in some detail, but did not address that key question. From the memoirs, it appears that he made his decision to withdraw on the night of June 11, determining to do so "by leisurely marches, which would keep Hampton's cavalry away from Lee while Grant was crossing the James River." Sheridan hints that the purpose for the day's prolonged fighting was to secure the by-road Mallory's Ford. Specifically, he wrote that "although I brought up one of Gregg's brigades to Torbert's assistance, yet the by-road I coveted was still held by the enemy when night closed in."[22]

All-in-all, Sheridan's explanation for the events of June 12 makes little sense. From a practical standpoint, if a commander plans to withdraw to the east, why would he begin by advancing approximately eight miles to the northwest, particularly when the enemy is known to be in that direction? Also, when conducting a withdrawal, commanders generally attempt to avoid decisive contact with the enemy. In this instance, Torbert—without known objection from Sheridan—sought decisive engagement. From a review of available information, it is possible to draw two conclusions: Either Sheridan was not candid in his May 1866 report and his memoirs regarding his intentions on June 12, or he exhibited poor tactical judgment by allowing his force to be unnecessarily mauled.

As discussed earlier, the Union cavalry, armed with either breach loaders or repeaters, was better armed than the Confederates, particularly Hampton's Division in which many men were armed with muzzle loading rifle muskets. Surprisingly, there is little evidence that the quality of arms played a role in the outcome of the battle. On June 11, Butler's and Wright's brigades fought the brigades of Merritt, Davies, and Gregg mostly in the woods along the Fredericksburg Road. It appears that the trees and thick brush nullified any advantage of the Union's weaponry. The success that Torbert achieved later in the day seems more a result of Hampton withdrawing his regiments and weakening his line than of superior Union firepower.

The men of Custer's brigade were armed with Spencers. Although evidence is lacking, it is quite possible that the firepower of the repeaters did materially aid the Wolverines in beating back attacks against Custer's perimeter, particularly since in many instances his men were fighting outnumbered and at relatively close ranges with goods fields of fire.

On June 12, the character of the fighting was entirely different. For most of the day, Rebels and Yankees fired at each other from covered positions at moderate ranges. Some Union participants claimed that the Confederates with their rifle muskets had an advantage. One Union officer wrote that "Butler's rebel troopers were armed with 'long toms' which they used with deadly effect, being able to drop our boys before the latter were able to get within carbine-range of the Confederates. In this fight the rebels had great advantages over the Federals. One brigade armed with Enfield rifles and posted behind breastworks ought to be a match at any time for more than an entire division of dismounted cavalry."[23] While interesting, and perhaps commonly believed at the time, this is certainly an overstatement of the advantage of the rifle muskets in Confederate hands at Trevilian's. On June 12, much of the shooting took place at ranges of three hundred yards more or less, which is well within the effective range of breach loaders and repeaters. The fighting for the angle simply reflects the inherent advantage held by a defender in a prepared position. Cold Harbor, fought less than two weeks earlier, is another such example that comes to mind.

The relative strength of Sheridan's force to Hampton's has also been a perplexing issue over the years, and Sheridan's assertion that his two divisions numbered about 6,000 men has been repeatedly challenged.[24]

In his memoirs, Sheridan wrote, "Owing to the hard service of the preceding month, we had lost many horses, so the number of dismounted men was large; and my strength had also been much reduced by killed and wounded during the same period of activity."[25] Over the years since, Sheridan's strength figure has been questioned, and generally considered low. Two articles on the Trevilian's Raid appeared in *Century Magazine*. Theophilus Rodenbough, formerly a captain in the 2nd U.S., estimated Sheridan's strength "exclusive of noncombatants, at about eight thousand men." General M.C. Butler gave Sheridan's strength at 10,337 officers and men, based upon federal strength returns. In 1906, Butler wrote to the War Department asking for the strength of Sheridan's force at Trevilian's. The War Department referred Butler to the Army of the Potomac's field strength return for June 1, 1864, showing that Sheridan had an aggregate present for duty strength of 12,420 within all three of his divisions and supporting horse artillery. The War Department concluded, "As already stated, the number of men carried into action on June 11 and 12, 1864, has not been found of record, nor is there any return of strength on file bearing data between June 1 and June 11, 1864." More modern estimates of Sheridan's strength range from Jerry Meyers, who determined that Sheridan had 10,200 cavalry and 500 artillerymen at Trevilian's, to Bruce A. Suderow's figure of 9,286.[26]

One might suspect that in his memoirs Sheridan would provide a low estimate of his strength to mitigate criticism arising from his failure to accomplish his mission. However, it seems unlikely that Sheridan would understate his strength by more than 40 percent (10,200 versus 6,000). Unfortunately, many personnel records and reports do not always fully reflect the operational status of a unit. Men who have no horses, or have lame horses, may be carried as present for duty, as may many men who are temporarily placed on detail. Additionally, fifteen cavalry companies assigned to the regiments of Torbert's and Gregg's divisions were on duty elsewhere. Consequently, while one may suspect Sheridan's stated strength, it is difficult to accurately determine the number of men he took into battle on June 11.

In examining the Trevilian's Raid, it is also necessary to evaluate the decision by General Ulysses S. Grant to order the operation. Grant conceived the Trevilian's Raid as a complement to his plans to shift his army to the south side of the James River. In directing the raid, he foresaw two primary goals. First, he believed that the thorough destruction of the Virginia Central Railroad would isolate Richmond and make it more difficult for the Confederacy to resupply Robert E. Lee's army as it defended the Confederate capital.[27] Second, the raid would provide an opportunity to move Major General David Hunter's small army from the Shenandoah Valley to Richmond where it could be better used.[28] However, in ordering the raid, Grant made one error in judgment: he completely overestimated the capability of his cavalry.

Sheridan's cavalry had seen hard use since the Overland Campaign began on May 4, and by the time the raid begin on June 6, the long marches and short rations had greatly degraded the condition of the cavalry's horses. Also, despite policies to the contrary, many horses suffered from neglect on the part of their riders, a problem that plagued Union cavalry throughout the war. Sheridan was well aware that his horses lacked stamina and had taken steps to mitigate that problem. Horses that were considered unfit for the raid were culled out before leaving New Castle Ferry.

On Sheridan's orders, once the raid began horses that could not keep up were destroyed. While no official record regarding the number of horses destroyed was maintained, the number destroyed on the march out was small compared to that on the march back. Confederate sources estimated that during the withdrawal from Trevilian to White House from 500 to 2,000 horses were killed to keep them from falling into Confederate hands. The actual number will never be known.

As previously discussed, Sheridan's force marched march approximately eighty miles to Trevilian's before withdrawing. However, Sheridan's orders were to proceed to Gordonsville, another nine miles, and from there to the Rivanna River Bridge at Charlottesville, another nineteen miles. From the Rivanna Bridge, Sheridan's force was to destroy the railroad lines leading to Staunton and Lynchburg, roughly another ten miles. Finally, "if practical," Sheridan was to dispatch a brigade or two to the James River to destroy the James River Canal. From the Rivanna Bridge, the closest point on the James River is at Scottsdale, a distance of about twenty miles. Once at Scottsdale, raiders would be required to range up and downstream for several miles in each direction to destroy the canal where it bypassed rapids.

Sheridan's force, therefore, advanced 80 miles in a raid that conceivably required an outbound movement of about 140 miles, or only 60 percent of the required distance. Had Sheridan pressed on to Charlottesville and the James River, it is possible that his entire command would have been dismounted on the return march because of the demands placed on the horses, and a not a result of enemy action.

There is little doubt that Sheridan's Richmond raid, which resulted in the Confederate defeat at Yellow Tavern and death of J.E.B. Stuart, was worth the cost. However, the same might not be said regarding the Trevilian's Raid.

As had occurred after the battle at Brandy Station a year earlier, and despite the best efforts of Hampton, Lee, and their men at Trevilian's, the editors of *The Richmond Examiner* could not resist again criticizing the cavalry of the Army of Northern Virginia. In an editorial on June 27, they wrote, "The activity of the enemy's cavalry has, from the beginning, annoyed and injured the people of Virginia beyond measure, and the general impunity with which it has cut railroads, burnt bridges and farm-houses, devastated the fields, and outraged the female and aged inhabitants, has thrown much and just discredit upon [that same] arm of our own service, which should have met and checked it here as FORREST, and MORGAN, and STEPHEN D. LEE have done in the West." However, the editors went on to add that they could "not recall a single instance in which the operations of the Confederate army have been prevented or delayed by a cavalry raid." and that any damages done to railroads by raiders were quickly repaired.[29]

After Trevilian's, some officers in the Union cavalry were also becoming disillusioned with the concept of raiding. An officer in the 1st Massachusetts, writing to a wounded comrade who missed the raid, summed up the operation. "The whole expedition lasted from the 6th of June until the 25th, and it was hell…. All lost heavily, and the loss in horses was very great, while those left were all used up—living skeletons." The officer concluded, "I don't think these great raids amount to much."[30] Captain Benjamin Crowninshield, also of the 1st Massachusetts, confirmed the observations of the editors of the *Richmond Examiner* in his history of the regiment.

> There is no instance during the war of a cavalry raid making any interruption of communication which was not soon repaired. While it temporarily disarranged connections, yet no army was forced to abandon its position on account of such interruption. Still, these raids brought the cavalry of both sides together, and furnished opportunity for a good many lively battles. In those occasioned by General Wilson's raid, his cavalry got decidedly the worst of it, and rejoined Grant's army in a demoralized and almost disorganized condition…. Sheridan's raid to Trevilian's Station was another instance of the same thing. His battles were on a larger scale, and more successful; yet the Trevilian Station raid can hardly be considered a brilliant success. The fighting was severe and the honors about [even]. The losses of men were great, and the horses, immense.[31]

Offering a Southern view on the Union attitude toward raiding, a captain in the Phillips Legion writing to his wife observed that "I think Hampton has convinced them [the Yankees] that raiding is an unprofitable investment."[32]

Clearly, at Trevilian's the cost to both Sheridan and Hampton was heavy, but for Sheridan and the Army of the Potomac, there was little gain. But despite the misgivings of some, cavalry raiding continued until the end of the war. Perhaps the Union's most successful cavalry raid was its last, Wilson's Selma raid in March and April 1865, but by then the Confederacy was in state of collapse and unable to resist such incursions.

Finally, the battle at Trevilian Station, coming just a month after the death of J.E.B. Stuart, invites comparison of the fighting ability of Hampton and his predecessor, the Confederacy's great cavalier. Naturally, many men of the "New Issue" were proud of their performance and attributed much of their success to Hampton's leadership. Further, they enjoyed their reputation for fighting dismounted and many considered themselves mounted infantry.[33]

Many Virginians also held a favorable opinion of Hampton. In a letter to his father dated September 5, 1864, Colonel Richard Dulany compared Hampton and Stuart: "Hampton I think is superior to Stuart in prudence, good judgment, and military [illegible] not the extreme dash (sometimes costly as at Dranesville) and perseverance for which Genl. Stuart was remarkable."[34]

Writing well after the war, First Sergeant Jerry Haden, Company E, 1st Virginia, recounted:

> I will state here that the question has frequently been asked me as to my idea of the generalship of Generals Stuart and Hampton. My reply has generally been that what General Stuart was going to do, he would do before General Hampton got ready. But when Hampton got ready he was there. Stuart did his work with a rush, while Hampton never made an attack until he had made thorough preparation, and consequently, was generally successful, unless he was contending with overwhelming numbers. And while their modes of fighting were very different, I am unable to say which, in my judgment, would have accomplished the most in the end.

Referring specifically to Trevilian Station, Haden went on "My idea is, that when the enemy left Trevilians, General Stuart would have been on them like a duck on a June bug. And while he would have harassed them, and retarded their movements to some extent, I don't suppose that much could have been accomplished by the pursuit as they would have selected their position whenever they stopped to engage us: thus having the advantage in every instance."[35]

Major Frank Myers of the 35th Battalion Virginia Cavalry, White's Comanches, formed a favorable opinion of Hampton after first observing him in action at Haw's Shop on May 28.

> Up to this time the Cavalry Corps had not learned the style of their new commander, but now they discovered a vast difference between the old and the new, for while General Stuart would attempt his work with whatever force he had at hand, and often seemed to try to accomplish a given result with the smallest possible number of men, Gen. Hampton always endeavored to carry every available man to his point of operation, and the larger his force, the better he liked it. The advantage of this style of generalship was soon apparent, for while under Stuart stampedes were frequent, with Hampton they were unknown, and the men of his corps soon had the same unwavering confidence in him that the "Stonewall Brigade" entertained for *their* General.[36]

Perhaps the most insightful assessment of Hampton versus Stuart was provided years later by Douglas Southall Freeman. "All that had been said of the differences between [Hampton] and Stuart was being confirmed. The South Carolinian lacked the glamour the Virginian had in the eyes of the hard-riding young troopers of 1862, but Hampton appealed more strongly to the temper of 1864. If Stuart had the admiration of new soldiers, Hampton had the respect of veterans. The operations in Spotsylvania, the contest at Haw's Shop, the Battle of Trevilian Station—these and all the minor clashes of reconnaissance and patrol had been handled without blunder." Freeman went on to conclude that Hampton's performance at Samaria Church "confirmed belief that the discretion of Hampton could be trusted."[37]

While Hampton earned the admiration and respect from his soldiers, by his performance at Trevilian's he also gained the confidence and trust of Robert E. Lee. On July 2, 1864, Lee wrote to Jefferson Davis regarding command of the cavalry of the Army of Northern Virginia.

Lee confirmed his belief in the necessity of unity of command, stating, "I am convinced that the cavalry service will be benefitted by having one officer to control its operations, and to be responsible for its condition." Regarding the current situation where each division commander reported directly to army headquarters and that when two divisions operated together, the senior commander was placed in charge, he added, "The disadvantage of this arrangement in my opinion is that he [the senior commander] neither feels nor exercises that authority which is required by the responsibility of his position. It is taken up one day and laid aside the next, and is not as effective as if exercised by one who is permanently and solely responsible." Regarding Hampton, Lee advised,

> You know the high opinion I entertain of Genl Hampton, and my appreciation of his character and services. In his late expedition he displayed both energy and good conduct, and although I have feared that he might not have that activity and endurance so necessary in a cavalry commander, and so eminently possessed by Genl Stuart, yet should you be unable to assign anyone to the command of the cavalry in this army who you deemed possessed of higher qualifications, I request authority to place him in command.[38]

Davis apparently knew of no one more highly qualified, and on August 11, Robert E. Lee issued Special Order Number 189 appointing Hampton to command of the cavalry of the Army of Northern Virginia and directing that cavalry division commanders report to him instead of to army headquarters. By the same order, Lee appointed nine officers to serve on Hampton's corps staff. All nine had served J.E.B. Stuart in the same capacity at the time of his death.[39]

21

Old Soldiers Fade Away
Lives After the Battle

Shortly after Trevilian's, General U.S. Grant ordered Sheridan to the Shenandoah Valley with the bulk of his cavalry. There, Sheridan continued to achieve success against Confederate forces—both cavalry under Rosser and infantry commanded by Jubal Early. Perhaps Sheridan's most significant exploit, and definitely his most famous, was his "ride" from Winchester to Cedar Creek on October 19, 1863. Waving his hat and rallying his troops as he rode to the front, Sheridan obtained a victory from what had seemed a certain defeat. His actions that day were celebrated in paintings, poems, sculpture, and song. The ride earned Sheridan's horse, Rienzi, a new name—Winchester—and a place in the Smithsonian Institution.[1]

After participating in the final battles about Richmond and the pursuit of Robert E. Lee's army to Appomattox, Grant sent Sheridan west to restore Union control throughout Louisiana and Texas. Sheridan, unhappily, missed the honor of leading his troopers in the Grand Review through the streets of Washington on May 23, 1865. However, unlike most of his contemporaries, he retained the rank of major general during the ensuing drawdown and reorganization of the army.[2]

After two and one half years of controversial and frustrating reconstruction duty, Sheridan was posted to Fort Leavenworth, Kansas, to take command of the Department of the Missouri. When Grant became President in 1869, Sheridan was promoted to lieutenant general and moved to Chicago in command of the Division of the Missouri. While at both Leavenworth and Chicago, Sheridan was responsible for mounting campaigns against hostile Indians, mostly on the northern plains.[3] During a peace conference at Fort Cobb, Colorado, in January 1869, one of the Indian chiefs attending informed Sheridan that he was a "good Indian." Sheridan, perhaps in an attempt at humor, quipped: "The only good Indians I ever saw were dead." The quip is now remembered as "the only good Indian is a dead Indian," bringing Sheridan a certain degree of perhaps undeserved opprobrium.[4] In 1884 William Sherman retired from the army, and Sheridan succeeded him as commanding general in the grade of lieutenant general.

High-living after the Civil War was hard on Sheridan. When he took command of the Cavalry Corps in Culpeper in April 1864, he carried 115 pounds on his five-foot four-inch frame. As commanding general of the army, he became excessively fat and his health began to fail. In November 1887 Sheridan was diagnosed with heart disease, and in May 1888, he suffered a massive heart attack that left him incapacitated.[5]

This 1883 photograph shows Sheridan, then Commander of the Division of the Missouri, escorting President Chester A. Arthur to Yellowstone Park. Sheridan is third from the left, seated, while the President is sixth from the left, seated. Sheridan's brother, Michael, his aide de camp, is standing second from the left. Todd Lincoln is seated, second from the right (Library of Congress).

At the end of June 1888, Sheridan with his family and aides traveled to Nonquitt, Massachusetts. Sheridan and his wife had visited Nonquitt the year before, liked the setting, and had arranged for the construction of a modest vacation home. Sheridan died there from another heart attack on the evening of August 5. It was his only visit to his vacation home.[6]

In view of Sheridan's long and distinguished career, it is understandable that the government would honor him. Immediately following his heart attack in May 1888, Congress, reinstated the rank of full general so that Sheridan could have the honor of a final promotion before his death. Sheridan received his fourth star on June 1, 1888. His only official action in that capacity was to promote his brother and two captains who had served as his aides de camp.[7] Also in 1888, President Cleveland named a new army post north of Chicago, the construction of which Sheridan strongly supported, after the general. The army closed Fort Sheridan in 1993 as a cost cutting measure.[8] In the 1960s, the army named a new light tank, the M551, after Sheridan. The tank's main armament was a controversial and ill-conceived gun/missile launcher (the missile was named the Shillelagh, perhaps in-part as recognition of Sheridan's Irish heritage). The quirky tank was difficult to maintain, unpopular, and of limited usefulness.[9] It is not likely that Sheridan—a no-nonsense fighter—would have been pleased with his namesake tank.

Perhaps the best and most enduring honor to Sheridan is Gutzon Borglum's bronze statue of Sheridan on Rienzi—together making their famous ride to Cedar Creek. The statue

21. Old Soldiers Fade Away

In Washington, Sheridan's service is commemorated by Sheridan Circle, within which stands a Gutzon Borglum statue of Sheridan and Rienzi making their famous ride at Cedar Creek. Sheridan is buried in Arlington National Cemetery and Rienzi—stuffed—is on display at the Smithsonian (Library of Congress).

was dedicated in Washington, D.C. in 1908 and still stands in Sheridan Circle at Massachusetts Avenue and 23rd Street. Sheridan's widow and their three daughters later took up residence near the statue and the daughters reportedly began each day by going to a window and greeting the statue with, "Good morning, Papa!"[10]

Serving in the Shenandoah Valley under Sheridan, A.T.A. Torbert fell into his superior's disfavor. Sheridan, writing in his memoirs, noted that Torbert had "disappointed" him on two occasions and that, consequently, he distrusted Torbert's "ability to conduct any operation requiring much self-reliance."[11] Significantly, when Sheridan returned to the Army of the Potomac for the war's final campaign, he left Torbert in the Shenandoah Valley as chief of the small cavalry force remaining there.

Perhaps as a consequence of Sheridan's ire, as the army drew down in size after the war—although it remained significantly larger than the pre-war force—Torbert found himself an odd-man-out. Calling in political influence from his home state, Delaware, and from New Jersey, whose volunteers he had commanded, Torbert advised the War Department that he wished to remain in the service, hopefully with a colonel's commission. The War Department responded by offering Torbert a billet as a captain—his current regular grade—in an infantry regiment. Understandably, Torbert was not satisfied with that offer, which would place him far junior to officers who had served under him during the war, including Wesley Merritt, George Custer, Thomas Devin, and John Irvin Gregg, all of whom were posted to cavalry regiments as lieutenant colonels. Instead of submitting to the indignity of reverting to company grade, Torbert resigned.[12]

Almost as soon as he became a civilian, Torbert married Mary Elizabeth Currey, a woman from Delaware, his home state, with Generals Meade and Wilson present at the ceremony. Then, in 1868, he ran unsuccessfully for Congress. Upon Grant's election as President, Torbert solicited from him an appointment to the consular service. Although he asked to be sent to Lisbon, the Grant administration initially posted Torbert to El Salvador, and then to Cuba, before sending him to Paris in December 1873 as the United States Consul General to France. Torbert remained in Paris until he was replaced after President Rutherford Hays came into office in 1878.[13]

General A.T.A. Torbert, who commanded Sheridan's 1st Division at Trevilians, later fell into disfavor with his commander and left the army after the war. In 1880 Torbert drowned when the ship on which he had booked passage to Mexico sank in a hurricane off the Florida coast. Although serving as U.S. Consul to France at the time of this engraving, Torbert, as was customary among many former senior officers, wore his uniform as a major general of volunteers (USMA Library).

In August 1880, at the suggestion of Grant, Torbert booked passage for Mexico, there to establish a railroad and mining venture with the Mexican government. Torbert's ship, the *Vera Cruz*, was caught in a hurricane, and on August 31 it sank off Florida's east coast. Torbert was one of the 68—out of a total of 79—passengers and crew who drowned when the ship broke apart and sank.[14] An account of the disaster in the *New York Times*, hailed Torbert as a hero. According to Torbert's business partner, who had also booked passage on the ship, as the *Vera Cruz* began to break apart, Torbert circulated among the passengers "like a sunbeam," encouraging and assisting them in the effort to abandon the ship. As a result of the publicity, Torbert's body, which had washed ashore and been hastily buried in Florida, was taken to New York City to lie in state in the city hall. As an additional honor to Torbert, flags in the city were flown at half-staff. George B. McClellan, "Baldy" Smith, and Daniel Sickles were among the dignitaries who served as honorary pallbearers in the procession that escorted Torbert's remains from city hall to Trinity Church for services, and then to a ferry on the Hudson. From there, Torbert's remains were taken to Philadelphia for a second memorial service. The following day, September 30, Torbert's body was taken to Milford, Delaware, for burial.[15] In his death, Torbert received the respect and recognition that the War Department denied him in life.[16]

Torbert's West Point classmate and fellow cavalry division commander, David McMurtrie Gregg, earned a brevet to major general in August 1864 for his distinguished conduct during the campaigns of that spring and summer. When Sheridan moved to the Valley, Gregg with his division remained with Grant at Petersburg. Inexplicably, Gregg resigned his commission on February 3, 1865, and took up farming near Milford, Delaware.[17]

In February 1874, President Grant appointed Gregg United States Consul to Prague, but Gregg found the duties "uncongenial" and resigned his post after six months. From Prague, Gregg returned to his home state, Pennsylvania, and settled in Reading. In 1891, he successfully ran for election as Auditor General of Pennsylvania. After his term, Gregg returned to private life. He remained active in veterans' activities, serving as chief of his commandery of the Military Order of the Loyal Legion, a Union veterans' organization, from 1886 until 1904. He held the position of commander in chief of the Order from October 1903 until October 1905. Gregg died in Reading on August 7, 1916.[18]

As the Trevilian's Raid drew to a close, Brigadier General James Wilson, with his division and that of August Kautz, embarked on a raid to sever the railroads linking Richmond and Petersburg with the Carolinas. After ten days and 325 miles, the raiders returned through Federal lines, having suffered many casualties and ruining many horses. Wilson and his division were sent by boat to Washington, remounted, and then sent to the Shenandoah Valley to rejoin Sheridan.[19]

In October 1864, at the request of Sherman, Grant sent Wilson to Atlanta where he organized and took command of Sherman's cavalry corps. In that capacity, Wilson served essentially as Sheridan's cavalry counterpart in the west. When Sherman set off on his march to the sea with Judson Kilpatrick's cavalry division, Wilson with the remainder of his cavalry, supported Major General George Thomas against John Bell Hood's incursion into Tennessee. After Hood's defeat at Nashville, Wilson reorganized his cavalry and augmented his horsemen with mounted infantry. In March 1865, he launched a massive raid into Alabama with the intent of defeating Nathan Bedford Forrest. After whipping Forrest at Selma, Alabama, Wilson continued his advance into Georgia, capturing Columbus and Macon before hostilities ended. Wilson's raid culminated near Irwinville, Georgia, on the morning of May 10, 1865, when two of his regiments charged into the camp occupied by Jefferson Davis and his party. In the early morning light, the troopers captured the fleeing Confederate president. The only casualties in the foray were two Union soldiers killed and four wounded, all a result of friendly fire.[20]

In the reorganizations after the war, Wilson returned to engineer duties in the mid–West while holding a commission as lieutenant colonel of the 35th Infantry. However, not content with post-war service, Wilson requested a discharge from the army which was granted in 1870. While earning his living as a railroad executive, Wilson authored books and articles on the Civil War and other subjects, and traveled extensively abroad, including an extended visit to China in 1885–1886.

During the Spanish-American War, Wilson was brought back into the army as a major general of volunteers. He commanded a division during the invasion of Puerto Rico, and after hostilities served as the military governor of two provinces in Cuba. In 1900, in responding to the Boxer Rebellion, the War Department sent Wilson a telegram requesting that he serve as the deputy commander of United States forces in the multi-national expedition to relieve the foreign legations under siege in Peking. Wilson immediately arranged for the movement of his horses via Galveston to San Francisco, then booked passage for himself and his aides de camp to New York. From New York, the small party traveled five days by express train to San Francisco, then by Japanese steamer to Nagasaki, Japan. There, Wilson and his aides boarded a U.S. naval cargo ship for the voyage to the Chinese coast. Thirty-seven days after receiving the telegram from the War Department, the sixty-three-year-old general landed in China.[21]

Despite his haste, Wilson found that "all semblance of actual war had been over for three weeks and a state of perfect calm prevail[ed]."²² Wilson traveled on to Peking and assumed command of American troops in the city.²³ In December 1900, Wilson returned to the United States and the following year he was retired in the grade of brigadier general.²⁴

In his later years, Wilson remained active in the affairs of his alma mater, serving as the president of West Point's Association of Graduates in 1908–1909. In 1915, he was promoted to major general on the retired list. Until his death in death in 1925, he was the last surviving member of the class of 1860.²⁵

The careers of Wesley Merritt and George Custer, who had both been promoted from captain to brigadier general of volunteers on June 29, 1863, continued on parallel tracks. Both were brevetted to major general of volunteers effective October 19, 1864, for action at the battles of Winchester and Fisher's Hill. The end of the war found each serving in command of a cavalry division, and each was promoted to major general of volunteers in April 1865. After the war, each reverted to the grade of lieutenant colonel in regular service, Custer in the 7th Cavalry, and Merritt in—at the time—the less-prestigious 9th Cavalry, one of the two regular cavalry regiments of black soldiers.²⁶

In the following years, Merritt participated in numerous campaigns in the west against hostile Indians. In 1876, he was assigned to the 5th Cavalry, Custer's old regiment, and promoted to colonel. In the 1880s, he served for five years as superintendent at West Point. While in departmental command at Fort Leavenworth, Kansas, he supervised the "Oklahoma Land Rush," of April 22, 1889, during which a portion of the Indian Territories was first opened to white settlers. In September of that year, Merritt organized the army's first field training exercise during which 1700 officers and men maneuvered across the rolling hills of what is today north central Oklahoma. In April 1895 Merritt was again promoted to major general, thirty years after first achieving that grade as a volunteer officer

Wesley Merritt had a long and distinguished career after the war. He was a highly effective Indian fighter, conducted the army's first major field training exercise, supervised the Oklahoma Land Rush, and commanded the army forces that occupied Manila during the Spanish American War. At the time of his retirement in 1900, Merritt was the second ranking officer in the army. He died in 1910 and is buried at West Point (Library of Congress).

George Custer's remains were moved from the Little Bighorn and reinterred in the West Point Cemetery in October 1877. In 1879, the Academy dedicated a statue overlooking the Hudson River to the fallen general. Custer's widow, Libbie, hated the statue's portrayal of her husband, and vigorously protested its display to West Point's superintendent, to General Sherman, and to the Secretary of War. In 1884, the statue was quietly removed and placed in storage. Today, its whereabouts are unknown (1880 Class Album, Special Collection, USMA Library).

in Virginia. During the Spanish-American War, Merritt commanded the expedition that captured Manila in August 1898, after which he remained in the Philippines as the island's governor general.[27]

On the way across the county en route to the Philippines, Merritt stopped briefly in Chicago to become engaged to Miss Laura Williams, the daughter of a prominent Chicago businessman. At the time, the general was sixty-two years old while his fiancé was just twenty (Merritt's first wife died in 1893). Miss Williams was described as "a tall and pretty blonde, very fond of outdoor exercise, and is popular in society."[28] Merritt and Miss Williams were married in London in October 1898 as Merritt was traveling to Paris to attend the peace conference that settled the war.[29]

Merritt retired from the army in June 1900 shortly after his return from the Philippines. In his last few years, Merritt's health began to fail and he suffered from senility. He died on December 3, 1910, at a spa in Natural Bridge, in Virginia's Shenandoah Valley. Three days later he was buried at West Point. A severe snow storm struck on the day of his funeral, delaying by several hours the train carrying Merritt's casket up the Hudson to the academy. Because of the delay, services at the academy chapel were cancelled, and Merritt's funeral procession proceeded from the train station directly to the academy cemetery. Merritt's cortege, escorted by the Corps of Cadets, made its way through the dark, the way lighted by lanterns, as cannons boomed. Once at the cemetery, Merritt was buried next to his first wife, a simple tombstone marking the spot.[30]

George Custer's post-war career on the Plains, ending with his death at the Little Bighorn in 1876, is well documented in numerous books and articles and need not be repeated here. Custer was initially buried on what is today known as "Custer Hill," where he and many of his men fell. A year later, in July 1877, an army detail returned to the Little Bighorn, exhumed the remains of the officers who had been killed, and shipped them east for reburial. Custer's wife, Libbie, arranged for her husband to be reburied at West Point. The ceremony, with full military honors, was conducted on October 10, 1877.

Two years later, officials at the Academy dedicated a monument to Custer. The statue showed Custer standing as if going into battle, saber at the ready in his right hand and pistol in his left. Unfortunately for those who proposed the statue, Libbie hated the way it portrayed her husband and began a vigorous campaign to have the statue removed. In a January 1882 letter to General Sherman, the army's commanding general, she wrote, "I can no longer endure the idea that our whole country, all our foreign tourists, who invariably visit West Point—besides generations of cadets will receive their impressions of General Custer from this frightful libel on his character." She went on to list several specific objections, stating that the depiction was of a "bloodthirsty ... Wild Bill type" and that "the face is that of an old man of seventy."[31] Sherman spoke with the Secretary of War, who informed the Superintendent at West Point that based upon that discussion, "I have no doubt that the statue be very bad," and that if it were to be removed from view, it should be done so quietly.[32] The bureaucracy at the academy ground on slowly, but in 1884, the statue was without fanfare removed from the cemetery and placed into storage in what had earlier been a stable. The superintendent at the time was Wesley Merritt.

Years later, academy officials considered removing the head from the statue and displaying it merely as a bust, and in 1905 the statue was shipped to Stanford White, a noted designer in New York City for the work to be done. Libbie, when informed of the proposed conversion, supported it. In a letter to the Superintendent of the academy she wrote, "I want to ask if you will give the order before you leave [your position] to have the head and shoulders cut from the statue of my husband. I am so afraid that someone may sometime, when I am no longer here, attempt to erect the figure on another pedestal."[33] The Superintendent assured Libbie that the statue had already been dismembered. Unfortunately—or perhaps fortunately, depending upon one's outlook—the bust was never completed. Stanford White was murdered—shot at a dinner party by the husband of his former mistress—and the pieces of the statue, including its head, were misplaced and never found.[34] The original base for the statue, now capped with a simple obelisk, marks Custer's grave in the West Point cemetery. Libbie Custer, who died in 1933, is buried with her husband.

Colonel Thomas C. Devin continued to serve with the cavalry corps until the end of the war, during which he would fight in seventy-two battles and engagements. He was promoted to brigadier general, to date from the battle of Cedar Creek. During the Appomattox Campaign, he commanded the 1st Cavalry Division and was brevetted to major general of volunteers after hostilities had ceased. In 1866, upon the reorganization of the army, Devin was commissioned lieutenant colonel of the 8th Cavalry and he served with the regiment in the West until 1877 when he was promoted colonel of the 3rd Cavalry.[35] However, by the time of his promotion, Devin was in poor health. After a five month leave of absence, he returned to his regiment at Fort Laramie for three months before departing for home on sick leave in February 1878. Confined to his bed, he died in New York two months later on April 4. The *New York Times*, in writing of Devin's funeral, noted that "General Devin was one of those fearless men who never faltered in his duty, no matter how great the danger was; yet he always had great consideration for the men under his command."[36]

Brigadier General Henry Davies continued in brigade or divisional command until the end of the war and was wounded at Hatcher's Run on February 6, 1865. Following the war, Davies was promoted to major general of volunteers and assigned as commander of the Middle District of

Custer and his wife, Libbie, who died in 1933, are buried in the West Point cemetery. The grave is marked by an obelisk that sits atop a large pedestal. The pedestal was originally designed as the base for the long-gone Custer statue (author's photograph).

Alabama. After several months of occupation duty, Davies resigned his commission and returned to New York to practice law. He served as New York's public administrator from 1866 until 1869, followed by three years service as assistant district attorney for the Southern District of New York. In declining health, he then retired to Fishkill, New York, where he wrote a biography of Sheridan. The biography was published three years after Davies's death in September 1894.[37]

At the beginning of the war, Colonel John Irvin Gregg had accepted appointment as a captain in the newly-formed 6th U.S. Cavalry before transferring to the volunteer ranks as commander of the 16th Pennsylvania. Usually in command of a brigade, Gregg was wounded at Sailor's Creek on April 5, 1865 and captured the following day near Farmville. After the war, Gregg, who was brevetted as a brigadier general in both the volunteers and the regular army and brevetted a major general of volunteers, was appointed colonel of the 8th US Cavalry. Until his retirement in 1879, Gregg served in the West engaging in expeditions against hostile Indians and commanding Fort Union, New Mexico. Upon leaving the army, Gregg settled in Washington, DC, where he died on January 6, 1892. He is buried in Arlington National Cemetery.[38]

Sheridan took twenty-five regiments of cavalry and five batteries of artillery on the Trevilian's Raid. The officers exercising command of the regiments consisted of five captains, four majors, eight lieutenant colonels, and eight colonels, while each of the artillery batteries was commanded by a captain. In the ten months of war remaining after the raid, there were few opportunities for commanders to be promoted into higher grades. However the army did take action to recognize the heroism or meritorious service of its deserving officers. From the end of the war until March 1, 1869, the army brevetted 1367 officers as brigadier general of volunteers. Among those commanding cavalry regiments at Trevilian's, thirteen were so brevetted, with two of the four artillery commanders receiving brevets.

The regimental commanders who received brevets to brigadier general were: Colonel Peter Stagg, 1st Michigan; Colonel Russell A. Alger, 5th Michigan, who was also brevetted to major general of volunteers; Major James H. Kidd, 7th Michigan; Captain Nelson B. Sweitzer, 1st U.S.; Captain Theophilus F. Rodenbough, 2nd U.S., who was also brevetted to brigadier general U.S.; Lieutenant Colonel Samuel E. Chamberlain, 1st Massachusetts; Lieutenant Colonel Matthew H. Avery, 10th New York; Colonel John P. Taylor, 1st Pennsylvania; Colonel William Stedman, 6th Ohio; Colonel Charles H. Smith, 1st Maine, who also received brevets to brigadier general U.S. and major general of both volunteers and US; Colonel Pennock Huey, 8th Pennsylvania; Lieutenant Colonel John K. Robison, 16th Pennsylvania. Colonel William Sackett, who was mortally wounded on the first day's fighting at Trevilian's, also was brevetted to brigadier general. Among the artillery commanders, both Captains Alexander C.M. Pennington and Alanson M. Randol were brevetted to brigadier general of volunteers.

Several other officers who fought at Trevilian's but were not in command positions also received brevets to brigadier general of volunteers after the war. These officers were: Lieutenant Colonel Jonathan P. Cilley, 1st Maine; Major Charles Leiper, 6th Pennsylvania; Lieutenant Colonel George S. Nichols, 9th New York; Major George A. Forsyth, 8th Illinois serving on General Sheridan's Staff; and Major Marcus Reno, 1st U.S. serving on General Torbert's staff.

While a brevet commission did not confer additional military responsibilities or increased pay for those officers so-honored, they were permitted to refer to themselves as generals, and to wear the uniform of a general officer when not on duty.[39]

21. Old Soldiers Fade Away 233

Colonel Russell A. Alger continued to command the 5th Michigan Cavalry until the end of the war. Afterward, he returned to Detroit and made a fortune in the lumber industry. Active in politics, Alger was elected governor of his state in 1884, serving a two-year term from 1885 until 1887.[40] Alger was also active in veterans' affairs. He was elected commander of the Michigan Department of the Grand Army of the Republic in 1888, and elected national commander of the GAR in 1889.

In 1897, President McKinley appointed Alger Secretary of War. In that position, Alger received much of the blame for the army's lack of preparedness for the war with Spain. As a result, McKinley asked for Alger's resignation in 1899.[41] Alger, however, presented his own view of events to the public with the publication of his book, *The Spanish American War*, in 1901.

Alger's travails as a cabinet officer apparently did not diminish his popularity in Michigan. It 1902, Michigan's governor appointed Alger to the U.S. Senate to fulfill the term of Senator James McMillan, who had died in office. In 1903, the Michigan state legislature elected Alger to a full term in the U.S. Senate. Like his predecessor, Alger failed to complete his term, dying while in office on January 24, 1907.

Russell Alger had a very successful life after the war. He made a fortune in the lumber industry, was elected governor of Michigan, and was appointed Secretary of War by President McKinley. Unfortunately, he was blamed for the army's lack of preparedness for the Spanish-American War and forced to resign. He considered his charge at Trevilian Station as the one "brilliant" thing he had done.

Throughout his life, Russell Alger remained justly proud of his exploits at Trevilian's on the morning of June 11, 1864. He once wrote, "If ever I did a brilliant thing in the world, the fight at Trevillian Station was the one."[42]

Immediately after the Trevilian's Raid, James H. Kidd received his promotion to colonel of the 6th Michigan with an effective date of May 19, 1864. Kidd commanded the regiment for most of the remainder of the war, and after Custer was given command of the 3rd Cavalry Division, he was placed in command of the Michigan Brigade. On September 19, 1864, at Winchester, Kidd was wounded in a charge, and that same day, his horse, Billy, was also wounded.[43] To the regret of Kidd and many of his men, the Michigan Brigade remained in the Valley when Sheridan returned to Petersburg, thus missing out on the final campaign of the war.

Many of the men in the Michigan Brigade had terms of service extending late into 1865.

Instead of being mustered out at the end of the war, the brigade was ordered to the Department of the Missouri to campaign against Indians. Naturally, this turn of events was unpopular with both the officers and the men. Colonel Kidd was discharged at Fort Leavenworth, Kansas at the end of his term of service in November 1865.[44]

At home in Iona, Michigan, Kidd became a newspaperman, owning, editing, and publishing the daily and weekly Iona *Sentinel*. He was active in the Masons, Republican politics, the local horse breeders' association, the horticultural society, and various veterans' organizations. Kidd also served in numerous positions in the Michigan National Guard from 1876 until his retirement as a brigadier general in 1911.[45]

For much of his latter life, Kidd worked on writing his memoirs which were published by the *Sentinel* in 1908. The book, *Personal Recollections of a Cavalryman with Custer's Michigan Brigade in the Civil War*, was well regarded at the time of publication and remains popular today.

During a large veterans' parade in Detroit in 1882, Kidd rode the now twenty-six-year-old Billy. Perhaps during the parade, Kidd reflected on the difference between the parade and the charge during the first day at Trevilian's when the horse he was riding for a fellow officer bolted, carrying Kidd into a brief period of Confederate captivity. Billy, a beloved companion, died in 1888 and was buried in Kidd's yard in Iona. Kidd, who died from a stroke in March 1913, outlived his faithful mount by twenty-five years.[46]

Lieutenant Colonel Peter Stagg, 1st Michigan, was promoted to colonel of the regiment on August 17, 1864. Following the Grand Review in Washington on May 25, 1865, Stagg and his men were—like Kidd and the 7th Michigan—sent west to fight hostile Indians. In September 1865, as some of the Wolverines were being mustered out of service, several detachments of the Michigan Brigade were consolidated into the 1st Michigan Veteran Cavalry with Stagg as its commander. Stagg, along with the bulk of his command, was finally mustered out of the service in Utah on March 10, 1866.

At the insistence of Michigan's governor, the state adjutant general conducted an inquiry into the consolidation of men from the regiments of the Michigan Brigade into the 1st Michigan Veteran Cavalry. In his report, the adjutant general concluded that Major General John Pope's order to consolidate the men into a single regiment was contrary to existing War Department regulations and the retention of the officers and men in the service by Major General Grenville Dodge, the department commander, was "an unwarrantable and inexcusable act." Subsequently, the men who were mustered out in March 1866 received $210 each in compensation for travel expenses from Utah to Michigan.[47]

Major Melvin Brewer, continuing in command of the 7th Michigan, was promoted to lieutenant colonel with an effective date of June 6, 1864, only to be again wounded in action at Winchester on September 19, 1864. He died from his wounds on September 25. In his report of the battle, Custer noted that Brewer "fell farthest in advance of those that on that day surrendered their lives in their country's cause."[48] Brewer's color bearer, who was near Brewer when he was shot, recalled the event as "one of the saddest calamities of the war to me."[49]

Colonel Luigi di Cesnola, angry because he considered himself more capable than the officers appointed over him, mustered out of the service with his regiment in September 1864. Initially, he attempted to obtain a senior position with the Veteran Reserve Corps but was not successful in that endeavor. To earn a living, he opened a military school in Manhattan with the intent of training men to become officers in volunteer regiments. However, the end of the war reduced the need for newly trained officers. Consequently, Cesnola sought a patronage position with the government. After meeting with Secretary of State Seward, and with the support of New York's two senators, he was appointed United States consul to Cyprus. After a visit to his family home in Italy, Cesnola arrived in Cyprus on Christmas Day, 1865. From the time of his discharge from the army until his arrival in Cyprus, Cesnola told friends and acquaintances that President Lincoln had promised him promotion to brigadier general, a claim for which no substantiating evidence has been found. Nonetheless, Cesnola began referring to himself as "general" and he was commonly addressed as "General di Cesnola." Once in Cyprus, Cesnola began wearing a uniform with the gold epaulettes of a general officer.[50]

ANOTHER RESTORER OF ANTIQUITIES À LA CESNOLA.

The Luigi di Cesnola libel trial was a major society news event of 1883–1884. The editors of *Punch* used the trial to poke fun at former Assistant Secretary of War Charles A. Dana, then the editor of the *New York Sun*. Dana had supported former New York governor Samuel Tilden for president in 1876, but Tilden was defeated by Rutherford B. Hayes. In this cartoon, Dana is attempting to restore Tilden's reputation by gluing parts on a resurrected statue of Tilden "à la Cesnola" (Library of Congress).

Apparently, di Cesnola's consular duties were not particularly time-consuming or arduous, because during his seven-year tenure he amassed a vast collection of ancient artifacts. In November 1872, Cesnola sold the bulk of his collection to the fledgling New York Metropolitan Museum of Art for $50,000. In the mid–1870s, Cesnola returned to Cyprus as a private citizen and excavated another horde of artifacts, which he—after convoluted negotiations with the British Museum—sold to the Metropolitan Museum for $60,000. In 1879, when the Metropolitan Museum opened its new building on 5th Avenue—prominently displaying di Cesnola's collections—its board of trustees appointed the "general" as the museum's first director.[51]

Cesnola's long tenure—lasting until his death in November 1904—as director of the Metropolitan Museum began with a scandal. In 1880, Gaston Feuardent, a prominent antiquarian and coin collector, accused Cesnola of fraud; specifically alleging that he converted a small statue of one Greek goddess into another, more valuable goddess. Over time, the coin dealer charged that Cesnola had tampered with other artifacts as well. After several rounds of charges and counter-charges, the antiquarian sued Cesnola for libel and defamation. The hearing stretched over nine weeks in late 1883 and early 1884. After twenty-eight hours of deliberation, the jury concluded that Cesnola had not libeled or defamed the antiquarian. However, testimony at the trial indicated that Cesnola had clearly never been a general officer, and that Cesnola and museum employees had been lax in matching up the pieces of various statues.[52]

Although never a general, Cesnola did belatedly receive recognition for his military service. In 1897, the government awarded him the Medal of Honor for his actions at Aldie on June 17, 1863. Two days after attending a dinner for veterans of the 11th Corps, Cesnola took ill and died. Ironically, his obituary in the *New York Times* noted, "At the close of the war President Lincoln promised [Cesnola] a promotion to the grade of Brigadier General, and, though the commission was never made out, owing to the death of the President, he was always greeted with the title promised him."[53]

Lieutenant Colonel James Quigly Anderson remained in command of the 17th Pennsylvania following the Trevilian's Raid. He had been in poor health for some time and shortly after deploying to the Valley with Sheridan he was hospitalized in Washington for more than a month. In January 1865, he was promoted to colonel. Going into the spring campaign his health had declined to the point where he needed the assistance of his faithful orderly to mount his horse. Consequently, Anderson was assigned to less arduous duty at the remount depot at City Point. After Appomattox, Anderson was mustered out of service with the remainder of his regiment and returned home to Beaver County, Pennsylvania, where he was confined to bed until his death from consumption on October 9, 1865. One of the soldiers of the 17th wrote of Anderson, "It is the testimony of his men that, in all the battles in which he was engaged, he not only *commanded*, but *led* them bravely and efficiently."[54]

Alfred Gibbs, 1st New York Dragoons, received a brevet to major, U.S. Army for gallantry at Trevilian's, and he was promoted to Brigadier General of Volunteers effective October 19, 1864, the date of the Battle of Cedar Creek. He commanded the Reserve Brigade during the final campaigns of the Civil War, earning for his service brevets to major general in both volunteer and regular ranks. After six months commanding a brigade in the Department of the Gulf and six months of recruiting duty, he joined the 7th U.S. Cavalry in Kansas in October 1866 as a major. Gibbs died unexpectedly at Fort Leavenworth on December 26, 1868, at the age of forty-four.[55] The cause of his death was listed as "congestion of the brain."[56]

Captain J. Hinckley Clark, 6th Pennsylvania, served with his regiment until the fall of 1864. On September 18, he was transferred to C Company of the regiment, and the following day was mustered out of the service with the company. In March 1865, he was awarded brevets to major of volunteers for gallant and meritorious service at Gettysburg and to lieutenant colonel of volunteers for service for the campaign from the Rapidan to the James.[57]

Captain Nelson Sweitzer left the 1st U.S. Cavalry in November 1864 for appointment as a colonel of volunteers and to take command of the 16th New York Cavalry. Until the end of the war, the regiment was mostly involved in countering Mosby's partisans in Loudoun County. Upon the assassination of President Lincoln, the regiment was deployed to southern Maryland to participate in the hunt for the conspirators.

Appointed major of the 5th U.S. Cavalry, Sweitzer served with that regiment and then with the 2nd U.S. Cavalry in the West until June 1877, when he was promoted to lieutenant colonel of the 8th Cavalry. In the absence of Colonel Devin, the 8th Cavalry's colonel, Sweitzer commanded the regiment and its posts along the Rio Grande River. He was promoted to colonel and took command of the 2nd U.S. Cavalry at Walla Walla, Washington in the spring of 1886, where he retired in 1888. Sweitzer died in Washington, DC, in 1898, and is buried in Arlington National Cemetery.[58]

Theophilus Rodenbough, after recovering from his wound at Trevilian's, returned to command of the 2nd U.S. Cavalry in early September, only to be wounded again on the 19th of that month at Opequon where he lost his right arm. Rodenbough returned to field duty at the end of April 1865 as Colonel of the 18th Pennsylvania Cavalry. After the war, Rodenbough, received a commission as major of the 42nd Infantry and served with the regiment in New York until 1870 when he was retired from the service as a colonel of cavalry for disability due to his wounds. Afterward, Rodenbough worked as deputy commissioner of the Soldiers Home in Washington for a year, and later was employed as chief of the Bureau of Elections in New York City. Today, he is perhaps best known as an author. He edited a history of the 2nd U.S. Cavalry, and the volume on cavalry in the *Photographic History of the Civil War* series. In September 1893, Rodenbough was awarded the Medal of Honor in recognition of his service at Trevilian's. His citation noted that he handled his regiment with great skill and valor and that he was severely wounded. Rodenbough died in 1912 at the age of seventy-four.[59]

Captain Charles Leoser, who was captured shortly after Rodenbough was wounded, was confined at Libby Prison, in Macon, Georgia, and in Charleston, South Carolina. During his captivity he once escaped only to be recaptured, and was exposed to Cholera and Yellow Fever. Leoser was paroled in September 1864 and exchanged in January 1865, upon which he was assigned to duty on the staff of Major General Torbert in Winchester. In October 1865, Leoser resigned his commission and entered the mercantile business, then in 1880 became a publisher.

In 1884 Leoser helped found the Noah L. Farnham Post—named for his commander in the Fire Zouaves—of the Grand Army of the Republic in New York City. Leoser was elected the post's first commander and under his leadership the Post adopted a controversial resolution. The members of the Farnham Post proposed that only Civil War veterans who were prevented from earning a living because of their wounds be entitled to pensions. In response, in 1893 the GAR, which supported a more liberal disability policy, expelled the Farnham Post and rescinded its charter. The post was later readmitted to the GAR after Leoser had resigned from its membership.

Leoser died in New York City in February 1896. His West Point Association of Graduates obituary ends with a cryptic observation: "Often deceived, considering his own word as his bond, he believed that of others to be the same, until sad experience, in some instance, taught him differently."[60]

In August 1864, the army transferred Captain Abraham Arnold from the 5th U.S. Cavalry, which he had commanded at Trevilian's, to West Point for duty as Assistant Instructor of Cavalry. After five years at the academy, he was promoted to major of the 6th U.S. Cavalry and joined his regiment in Texas. For the next thirty years Arnold served continuously in the West and on the Plains, except for six years—1872–1878—during which he was detailed as disbursing officer for the Freedman's Bureau in New Orleans. In 1886 Arnold was promoted to lieutenant colonel of the 1st U.S. Cavalry, and five years later was advanced to colonel of that regiment. At the beginning of the Spanish-American War, Arnold received a commission as brigadier general of volunteers and commanded the 2nd Division of the VII Corps in Cuba. He died on November 23, 1901. According to his obituary, his death was the result of "care and exposure" during the recent war. He was buried in Garrison, New York, on the east bank of the Hudson River opposite West Point.[61]

At the end of September 1864, Samuel Chamberlain, 1st Massachusetts, was promoted to colonel. However, instead of remaining with the regiment he was posted to Annapolis to command the camp for Union parolees, a position he had held earlier from June 1863 through May 1864. In July 1865, he was assigned to the command of the 5th Massachusetts Cavalry, a black unit, and served with the regiment in Texas until the end of November of that year. Chamberlain received a brevet to brigadier general for his gallantry at Samaria Church.[62]

After returning to Massachusetts, Chamberlain served as quartermaster-general for the state militia, and then for almost twenty years was employed as the warden of prisons in Massachusetts and Connecticut. In 1893 he retired to his home near Worcester where he regaled his grandchildren with stories of his exploits in the West. Chamberlain would frequently refer to a manuscript that he had written describing his experiences during the Mexican War, and which he had had richly illustrated with watercolor drawings.[63]

Chamberlain died in 1908 at the age of 78. In the 1940s, his manuscript was found in an antique shop and purchased by a collector who later sold the work to *Life* magazine. In 1956 *Life* published portions of the manuscript in serial form and arranged for its publication, in book form, by Harper with the title *My Confession*. *Life* then donated the manuscript to the museum of the United States Military Academy at West Point.[64]

A month after the battle at Trevilian's, Lieutenant Colonel John Kester, commander of the 1st New Jersey, was promoted to colonel, filling the billet formerly occupied by Percy Wyndham. However, Kester was becoming increasingly incapacitated from injuries he suffered during an engagement at Fauquier Sulphur Springs on October 12, 1863. During that fight, Kester had been thrown to the ground after his horse was struck by a fragment from an artillery shell. Since that time, Kester suffered frequent headaches and complained of deafness. On September 26, 1864, he mustered out of the service and returned home to Philadelphia. Over the ensuing years, his condition continued to deteriorate and he began showing signs of mental illness. In November 1882, Kester, armed with a pistol, was found outside his home hunkering behind furniture he had piled in the street. The former officer claimed that he had been commissioned to "settle all disputes in the Republican party" and threatened to shoot anyone who tried to seize his "fort." A friend tricked Kester into surrendering to the police, and he was committed to the Friends Asylum in nearby Frankford. Kester remained in the asylum until his death in 1904.[65]

Lieutenant Colonel Matthew Henry Avery, 10th New York, continued to serve with his regiment following the Trevilian's Raid. On November 30, 1864, he was promoted to colonel. Later, the 10th was consolidated with the 24th New York to form the 1st New York Provisional Cavalry with Avery serving as its colonel. Avery and the men of the provisional regiment were mustered out of service at Syracuse on August 4, 1865. Avery, the only field grade officer to serve with the 10th New York from its muster-in until muster-out, was brevetted to brigadier general of volunteers for gallantry at Sailor's Creek on April 6, 1865.

After returning to civilian life, Avery moved to Pennsylvania and entered the oil business, despite having lost his voice and being unable to speak above a whisper. He died in Geneva, New York, on September 1, 1881.[66]

Colonel John P. Taylor mustered out with the bulk of the 1st Pennsylvania on August 31, 1864. In his farewell remarks to his regiment, Taylor addressed himself to those soldiers who had reenlisted and were remaining to be consolidated into a battalion:

> Enlisted veterans:—When you were re-enlisting my lips were sealed from encouraging you, because circumstances unavoidable, rendered my remaining with you impossible; let not our leaving discourage you, but go on to greater deeds of valor; be faithful, be obedient, be prompt and cheerful in duty as you always have been, a hopeful country awaits to crown you; and we shall not forget you; we shall continue to breathe the desired hope and christian prayer that you may soon be permitted to return to your homes, when the red-handed monster, *war*—whose pestiferous breath blasts with withering breath everything lovely on earth—may be banished from our distracted land, and peace, sweet peace again returning, shed evermore her Heaven-born blessings on our fair Columbia's soil.

Taylor was brevetted to brigadier general of volunteers effective March 15, 1865, for gallant and meritorious service.[67]

Colonel William Stedman, 6th Ohio Cavalry, mustered out at the end of this term of service on October 6, 1864. Steadman had been an effective and popular commander. One of the men wrote that the regiment had been handicapped until April 1863 when its original colonel resigned, "leaving the way open for Major Stedman who became a real and much loved colonel until his three-year term had expired. He was the only one of his rank ever worthy of the name, in command."[68]

Stedman went home to Randolph, Ohio, taking with him his war horse, Putman, or "Old Put." Several years after the war, Stedman offered a horse—not "old Put"—for sale. A prospective buyer came by and saw Old Put standing in the barn and asked how much Stedman was asking. Stedman replied "$5000," a ridiculously high price. The buyer asked what about that horse made him so valuable. Stedman answered, "The only thing about that horse is that he is going to die mine." Old Put lived to the age of 35.[69]

Steadman became active in Republican politics in Ohio and was appointed by Grant to the position of US Consul in Santiago, Cuba. Stedman arrived in Santiago on June 30, 1869, and died a week later of Yellow Fever. He was fifty-three years old. He was buried in Santiago, where his remains still lie.[70]

Colonel Charles H. Smith continued in command of the 1st Maine Cavalry until the end of the war whereupon he returned home to Maine and was elected to serve in the state senate. Concurrently he studied law and was admitted to the state bar. However, after his wartime experiences, Smith preferred the military life. On July 28, 1866—after communicating his desires to Grant—Smith was appointed as colonel of the 27th Infantry in the regular army.

Smith's heroism and his valuable wartime service were fully recognized by the government. On August 1, 1864, he was brevetted to brigadier general of volunteers for distinguished conduct at Samaria Church. Effective March 13, 1865, he was brevetted major general of volunteers for highly meritorious service. On March 2, 1867, he was brevetted to brigadier general and major general U.S. Army for meritorious service at Sailor's Creek and during the war, respectively. Additionally, in 1895 Smith was awarded the Congressional Medal of Honor for gallantry at Samaria Church.

In 1868, the 27th Infantry was consolidated into the 19th Infantry, and Smith was appointed commander of that regiment, a post he held until his retirement in November 1891. After his retirement, Smith and his family took up residence in Washington where he remained active in veterans' affairs until his death on July 17, 1902. Smith was buried in Arlington National Cemetery.[71]

Less than two weeks after the battle at Trevilian's, Colonel Pennock Huey of the 8th Pennsylvania Cavalry was captured at Samaria Church. He was exchanged late in the year, shortly before he was discharged from the service on January 23, 1865. During the Gettysburg Campaign, Huey had commanded a cavalry brigade, and for his gallantry and meritorious service during the war he received a brevet to brigadier general of volunteers effective March 15, 1865.

On May 2, 1863, during the battle at Chancellorsville, the 8th Pennsylvania was moving down a heavily wooded lane when it found itself between the main body of infantry from Jackson's Corps and the corps' skirmishers. The regiment made a charge to try and cut their way through the Rebels and suffered heavy casualties in the process. Later, appearing before the Joint Committee on the Conduct of the War, Alfred Pleasonton testified, "It was in this battle that, with three regiments of cavalry and twenty-two pieces of artillery, I checked the attack of the rebel general Stonewall Jackson after he had routed the Eleventh Corps." Pleasonton recounted how he went to Major Peter Keenan of the 8th Pennsylvania and said, "Major, you must charge in these woods with your regiment, and hold back the rebels until I get some of these guns into position." For emphasis, Pleasonton added, "You must do it at all cost."[72]

In 1883, Huey published a book entitled *A True History of the Charge of the Eighth Pennsylvania Cavalry at Chancellorsville*. In the book, Huey took issue with accounts of the charge that had been given by General Pleasonton.[73]

In his book, Huey examined commanders' reports and letters sent to him from other participants. Huey refuted Pleasonton's account, noting, "The whole of General Pleasonton's testimony bears improbability on its very face." Huey observed that since the war, people had "adopted, almost invariably the egotistical and unreliable romances of General Alfred Pleasonton."[74] Fortunately, in recent years, historians have recognized Pleasonton's account for what it was: a self-serving fabrication intended by Pleasonton to enhance his reputation.

After the war Huey worked as a merchant and as an agent for the Pennsylvania Canal Company. He died in Bustleton, Pennsylvania, near Philadelphia, on September 28, 1903.

Major Michael Kerwin, who enlisted in the Irish Dragoons, a battalion which formed the nucleus of the 13th Pennsylvania, remained with the regiment until it was mustered out of the service in Raleigh, North Carolina, on July 14, 1865. In the month after the Trevilian's

Raid, Kerwin was promoted to colonel of the regiment and struck by lightning, which may have resulted in a permanent partial loss of hearing. After the war, Kerwin returned home to Marcellus, New York, "a debilitated man of shattered constitution with a nervous affliction." He worked in the coal business and as a railroad contractor before obtaining a clerical position with the New York Post Office. Kerwin died of "Chronic Nephritis" on July 12, 1912.[75]

In October 1864, Alexander C.M. Pennington, who after more than three years of war was still serving as a regular captain of artillery, accepted volunteer appointment as Colonel of the 3rd New Jersey Cavalry, a regiment that had been raised earlier in the year and had taken the field in the late spring. Pennington commanded the regiment through Sheridan's Valley Campaign and during the Appomattox Campaign. After the war and back in the artillery, Pennington served in a variety of assignments in West, South and East. For several months during 1876–1877, he was detailed to duty in South Carolina during the contentious election by which Wade Hampton ousted the carpetbag administration of Daniel Chamberlain. The following year he was posted to Pittsburg in response to labor disturbances on the railroads. Promoted to colonel, he commanded the 2nd Artillery, in which he had served as a battery commander during most of the Civil War. During the Spanish-American War, he was appointed brigadier general of volunteers and assigned to command of Camp Black, a facility on Long Island used to train and muster-in National Guard units. Pennington did not see action during that war, and in 1899 he retired from the army in the grade of brigadier general, regular army. On November 30, 1917, Pennington suffered a heart attack while taking a train to his sister's funeral. He was taken from the train at Newark's Market Street Station, where he died.[76] Pennington was buried in the West Point Cemetery.

Edward Williston continued to serve in the army following the war, exemplifying the adage that promotions in the artillery came slowly. Although brevetted to colonel during the war, he remained a captain until promoted to major of the 3rd Artillery Regiment in 1885, followed by promotions to lieutenant colonel and colonel in 1895 and 1898, respectively. Williston was appointed brigadier general of volunteers during the Spanish-American War in 1898 but served in that capacity for only a year due to the short duration of the war. In 1900 he retired in the grade of colonel. However, Williston did receive recognition, although belatedly, for his service. In 1892 he was awarded the Medal of Honor for his gallantry at Trevilian's twenty-eight years earlier. Additionally, in 1904, four years after his retirement, Congress advanced Williston to the grade brigadier general on the retired list of the regular army. Williston died in 1920 at the age of eighty-three. He is buried at Arlington National Cemetery.[77]

Captain Alanson Randol left the field artillery in August 1864, returning to West Point as a member of the faculty teaching artillery tactics and mathematics. In December he accepted appointment as colonel of the 2nd New York Cavalry, the Harris Light. With his regiment he participated in Sheridan's campaign in the Shenandoah Valley and in the Appomattox Campaign. In July 1865, Randol was mustered out of volunteer service and reverted to captain in the 1st Artillery. Afterward, Randol served in a variety of artillery assignments throughout the country, earning promotion to major in the 3rd Artillery in 1882. Like Alexander Pennington, Randol was detailed to duty in South Carolina in 1876–1877 and to Pennsylvania the following year to cope with the railroad disturbance. In 1882 the army sent Randol to San Francisco where he commanded Fort Winfield Scott—an artillery fort adjacent to The Presidio—and Alcatraz Island. In November 1886, Randol was transferred to Fort Canby, Washington. However, suffering from kidney disease, he left on sick leave after a month. He died at the home of his brother in New Almaden, California, on May 7, 1887.[78]

In the early twentieth century, the army began constructing an extensive system of coast artillery fortification to protect American harbors. Many of the fortifications were named after distinguished artillery officers. In 1922, the army constructed Battery Pennington on Cape Henry, Virginia with four sixteen-inch guns to protect the entrance to the Chesapeake Bay. The battery, now part of Fort Story, was inactivated after World War II. In 1924 the army established Battery Williston as part of the defenses of Pearl Harbor in Hawaii. Armed with two sixteen-inch guns, the battery was inactivated in 1948. From 1900 until 1918, a coast artillery battery near Port Townsend, Washington was named in honor of Randol. Ironically, Pennington, Williston, and Randol, who had very capably commanded horse artillery batteries, were honored by having coast artillery batteries—the heaviest and least mobile of the army's artillery—named after them.

One Union lieutenant went on to a highly distinguished career after the war. Adna R. Chaffee enlisted as private in the 6th U.S. Cavalry in July 1861. By the fall of 1862, he had risen to First Sergeant of Company K, and in May 1863 was commissioned as a second lieutenant. After the war he served in a variety of assignments during campaigns in the West and commanded a brigade at Santiago in the Spanish-American War. In January 1904 he was promoted to the grade of lieutenant general and appointed Army Chief of Staff, the second officer to hold that position.[79]

Sergeant James Henry Avery and his men of the 5th Michigan, having avoided capture and made their way by circuitous route to Washington, expected only a short stay for remounting before returning to their regiment, However, that was not to be. Due to a shortage of horses, remounting was delayed, and on July 4, the men were issued muskets and pressed into infantry service to help repel Early's foray against the capital. Avery and his men were finally issued their horses on September 12. Avery observed that the horses were "all new and vicious ones" and as he was attempting to get his horse to stand still to be fed, the horse kicked at him with both hind feet. The men finally left Giesboro on September 15 and rejoined their regiment on September 21, 102 days after Colonel Alger made his charge of "pardonable zeal" at Trevilian Station.[80]

Avery, although suffering from dysentery, survived the war and returned home to Hopkins, Michigan and farming. Over the years, Avery and his wife, Ellen, had five children, joining a daughter who was born before Avery enlisted. In 1880, Avery was granted a pension of twenty-five dollars per month for disability associated with his dysentery. He died in November 1902.[81]

J.E.B. Stuart's influence over the cavalry of the Army of Northern Virginia ended with his death at Yellow Tavern. However, Stuart's officers and men, other veterans, and private citizens continued to hold fond memories for the fallen cavalier. Well after the war, Virginians honored those memories with monuments.

In June 1888, a simple obelisk was dedicated to J.E.B. Stuart along the Telegraph Road, about 30 feet from where the Confederate commander received his mortal wound on May 11, twenty-four years earlier. The then-governor, Fitzhugh Lee, presided over the ceremony and spoke nearly an hour. In his remarks, Lee praised Stuart as "the ideal of a hero, a born soldier, and a pure Christian." He closed his oration by asking that "the God of battles guard and bless the spot sanctified by blood of a hero, hailed when living as 'The Prince of Cavaliers.'"

In May 1907, an equestrian statue of J.E.B. Stuart was unveiled on Monument Avenue in Richmond with roughly 50,000 people in attendance. On the Avenue, Stuart, Jackson, and Lee are immortalized in bronze, all on horseback. Although he was junior among the three, Stuart would certainly enjoy the company (author's photograph).

Lee then paraphrased Tennyson's ode to another hero, Wellington, by observing that in death, Stuart "wears a truer crown than any man can weave him." Afterward, the band played Dixie, followed—perhaps ironically—by the Star Spangled Banner.[82]

In 1953, the Virginia state government considered a proposal to move the monument about one-half mile from the Telegraph Road to a lot adjacent to U.S. Highway 1. The Sons of Confederate Veterans had recommended the move because there was little traffic on Telegraph Road and they wished to provide opportunity for more people to see and appreciate the monument. The group also complained that the monument site was secluded and at times used as a "lover's lane." Fortunately, the State decided to leave the monument at the spot selected by Stuart's veterans. U.S. Highway 1 near Yellow Tavern today epitomizes the blight of urban sprawl.[83]

In May 1907, an equestrian statue of Stuart, with saber drawn, was dedicated on Richmond's Monument Avenue. The ceremony was attended by a crowd estimated at fifty thousand, with the principle oration delivered by Theodore Garnett, who as a lieutenant had served as Stuart's aide de camp and was present at Yellow Tavern when Stuart received his mortal wound. J.E.B. Stuart's daughter, Virginia Pelham Stuart Waller, who was just seven months old at the time of her father's death, pulled the cord to drop the veil from her father's statue.[84]

Shortly before World War II, the army developed the M-3 Light Tank, several thousand of which were given the British under Lend-Lease. The British named the tank after J.E.B. Stuart, although it was nicknamed the "Honey" because it was easy to operate and maintain. This photograph shows an Australian armor unit training with M-3s. Although the Stuart was the first U.S. designed and manufactured tank to see combat, it was lightly armed and armored and not suitable for modern tank warfare (Library of Congress).

Like Sheridan, Stuart had an army tank named after him. Prior to entry into World War II, the United States provided its M5 light tank, an upgraded M3, to Great Britain under the Lend Lease Program. The British, fittingly, named the tank the Stuart, after America's most famous cavalry commander. However, the U.S. Army never officially adopted the name. While praised for its reliability by British and U.S. soldiers, the Stuart was simply unsuited for tank combat in Europe. With a 37 millimeter cannon as a main gun and only lightly armored, the Stuarts were overmatched by German medium tanks, and consequently relegated to scouting and reconnaissance missions. Stuart tanks proved more useful in the Pacific Theater, since they were easily transportable and faced little threat from Japanese armor. In 1944, the U.S. army began replacing its M3 Stuarts with a more capable light tank.[85] Like Sheridan, J.E.B. Stuart would probably have felt little satisfaction with his armored namesake.

Wade Hampton's career after the battle at Trevilian Station is well known. Following his formal appointment as cavalry corps commander, Hampton continued in command of Lee's cavalry until January 1865 when he was ordered with Butler's Division to South Carolina to counter Sherman's march up the coast from Georgia. On February 15, 1865, Hampton was promoted to Lieutenant General to rank from February 14, an honor not conferred upon Stuart by the Confederate government.[86]

After the war, Hampton returned to Columbia to manage his estates and later entered politics. In 1876 he was elected governor, bringing an end to South Carolina's reconstruction government. In December 1878, the state legislature appointed Hampton to fill a vacancy in the U.S. Senate where he served until 1891. From 1892 until 1897, Hampton served as the U.S. Commissioner of Pacific Railroads. Afterwards, Hampton returned to private life but remained active in Confederate veterans' affairs. In May 1899, Hampton's home, known as Southern Cross, burned, destroying all his books and papers. Well-wishers from across the state contributed to purchase a house in Columbia for the old general. In December 1901, Hampton attended a reunion of South Carolina College where he caught a persistent cold. In April 1902 he became severely ill and died on the 11th of the month.[87]

Hampton was highly successful in all his endeavors—farming, military service, and politics—yet he paid a heavy price. During the war he lost a brother at Brandy Station and a son at Burgess Mill in October 1864. After the war his fortune was gone and his home in ruins. His political movement was defeated and repudiated by "Pitchfork Ben" Tillman who succeeded Hampton as governor. In his later years, Hampton seemed to take most pleasure from hunting and most comfort from the company of former soldiers with whom he had served. Undoubtedly, throughout his life and after, Hampton remained the most beloved Confederate of the Carolinas.

Matthew Calbraith Butler's career paralleled Hampton's. When Hampton was elevated to corps command, he arranged Butler's promotion and appointment to divisional command. Butler went to South Carolina with Hampton in January 1865 and served in the Car-

After the war, Wade Hampton distinguished himself as the governor of South Carolina and in the U.S. Senate. At the time of his death in 1902, Hampton was very likely the most beloved and respected Confederate (Library of Congress).

olinas until the end of the war. Afterward, Butler returned to Edgefield, South Carolina where he resumed farming and the practice of law.

Butler quickly entered politics and was elected to the state legislature in the fall of 1865 where he served until the Republican party took control the government under reconstruction in 1868. In the summer of 1876, Butler wrote to Hampton asking that he run for governor, initiating the Red Shirt Campaign which led to Hampton's election that November. On December 20, 1876, the South Carolina legislature elected Butler to the U.S. Senate.[88] Butler served three terms in Washington. In 1893, Butler ran again for reelection. Although the election was to be decided by vote of the state legislature, Butler and the leader of the party opposing him, "Pitchfork Ben" Tillman, faced each other in a lengthy and heated series of public debates. After a particularly raucous affair at Union, South Carolina on July 31, Butler accosted Tillman on the train to Spartanburg, the site of the next debate. "You put those hoodlums up to howling at me ... you have perpetuated a fraud and a lie. These matters must be settled personally. I'll meet you anywhere." Tillman answered, "You are old, infirm, and one-legged. I won't fight you." Butler replied, "And you're one-eyed." Tillman answered, "That don't hurt my physical power. I'm not afraid of you." Butler got in the last word, "Never mind my infirmities. When you want to fight ... just say so." By that point a crowd had gathered and one of Butler's supporters drew his pistol. Fortunately the train's conductor, claiming that he would lose his job, was able to defuse the situation. In December 1893, the South Carolina legislature elected former governor Tillman as Butler's successor.[89]

Matthew C. Butler served three terms in the U.S. Senate and afterward was appointed major general of volunteers during the Spanish-American War. Butler's son, M. C. "Cabbie" Butler, Jr., graduated from West Point in 1888 and served mostly with the cavalry until he was murdered while on duty along the border between Texas and Mexico (Library of Congress).

After his defeat, Butler spent most of his time in Washington practicing law and representing special interests. As the Spanish-American War began, the nation mobilized volunteer forces and President McKinley offered volunteer commissions at the grade of major general to both Fitz Lee and Joseph Wheeler as part of an effort to gain Southern support for the war. Butler, anxious to regain his reputation, arranged for many old friends, including Hampton, to solicit the president for a like commission. Butler accepted his commission as major general of volunteers on May 31, 1898. His first duty assignment was Camp Alger, named for Russell Alger, former Wolverine and now Secretary of War, near Falls Church, Virginia. Although the war was over before Butler's troops were prepared to deploy, Butler was sent to Cuba where he served in an administrative capacity from September 1898 until January 1899. After three months sitting on a court-martial board hearing charges against the army's Commissary General for buying tainted meat, Butler returned to civilian life.[90]

After leaving the military, Butler spent much time preparing a suit by the Cherokee Nation against the United States Government. The case was finally decided in 1905 with the Cherokees being awarded $5 million. Butler's share of the attorney's fees was $25,000. Shortly afterward he remarried—his first wife died in 1900—and retired to North Augusta, South Carolina. In March 1909, Butler's health began to fail and he became bedridden. After converting to Catholicism, Butler died on April 14. He is buried in Edgefield, South Carolina.[91]

Colonel Benjamin Huger Rutledge continued in command of the 4th South Carolina until the end of the war, occasionally acting in brigade command during the final campaigns in the Carolinas. After the end of hostilities, Rutledge returned to Charleston and resumed the practice of law. In the early 1870s he again was elected commander of the Charleston Light Dragoons, a position he had last held in 1861. The Dragoons, at the time an unofficial "saber club" ostensibly organized to keep the peace, supported the election of Wade Hampton and the Democratic Party's return to power in 1876. Rutledge, who had been returned to the legislature in that election, gave up his leadership in the Dragoons in 1877, replaced by Zimmerman Davis, formerly lieutenant colonel and colonel of the 5th South Carolina. Rutledge, however, remained close to the Dragoons, who were officially reconstituted in the South Carolina militia in 1878. Rutledge presided over the dedication of the monument to the Dragoons in Charleston's Magnolia Gardens cemetery on May 10, 1886. The keynote speaker for the occasion was his former commander, M.C. Butler. Rutledge died in Charleston on April 30, 1893, and is buried in Magnolia Gardens. His obituary referred to him as a "courteous, accomplished, and kindly man."[92]

Colonel John Dunovant, 5th South Carolina, quickly overcame any stigma resulting from being cashiered for drunkenness while in command of the 1st South Carolina Infantry in 1862. Wounded in the hand at Haw's Shop, Dunovant missed Trevilian's, returning to duty on July 8. In August, upon Butler's promotion and assignment to command of Hampton's Division, Dunovant was promoted to brigadier general and given command of Butler's Brigade. On October 1, Dunovant was killed in action while leading a charge on the Vaughn Road near Petersburg. Dunovant was shot in the chest and as he fell from his saddle his foot became stuck in his stirrup. Dunovant's horse bolted and dragged his body into Union lines. Dunovant suffered massive injuries when his head apparently struck a tree root, but Butler, who was present at the time, opined that Dunovant had been killed by the gunshot. Dunovant's remains were returned to South Carolina for burial in his family cemetery near Chester.[93]

In the weeks following the battle at Trevilian's, Colonel Hugh Aiken, 6th South Carolina, received abundant and attentive treatment for the gunshot wound to his chest. After being wounded, Aiken was carried to the rear and placed in an ambulance. Shortly afterward he was captured by Custer's men, and then he was recovered by the Confederates several hours later. After the battle Aiken was taken to the home of a Mr. Hunter in Louisa Courthouse. There he was first joined by his brother, Augustus, who was accompanied by Aiken's servant, Perry. Shortly afterward a second brother, Dr. William Aiken, arrived in Louisa bringing Aiken's wife, Mary. On July 1, Mary took Aiken to her sister's home in Richmond—the sister's husband was Colonel Josiah Gorgas, the Confederacy's Chief of Ordnance. Aiken completed his convalescence as a guest in the Gorgas home.[94]

After completing his recovery, Aiken rejoined his regiment, and in January 1865 returned with Hampton to South Carolina, in an attempt to impede Sherman's progress north from Georgia. On February 27, 1865, Aiken was shot and killed near Cheraw, South Carolina, during a meeting engagement between the men of his regiment and a party of Union troops. Aiken, who was reportedly struck nine times, died in the arms of his nephew before his troopers were forced to abandon his body on the field. Initially, Aiken's remains were placed in a crude coffin and buried in the cemetery of a local church. After the war Aiken's family moved his remains to the family plot in the cemetery of the Presbyterian Church in Winnsboro, South Carolina.

On the field where he fell, Aiken's papers were taken by the Union soldiers who searched his body. Among his papers was a letter he had written to his wife. Years later, General Sherman, who as a lieutenant had met Mary Aiken when she lived in Washington with her father, then a Congressman from Alabama, arranged for the return of the purloined letter to Aiken's widow.[95]

Colonel Gilbert "Gid" Wright continued to effectively command P.M.B. Young's Brigade in Virginia and the Carolinas until the end of the War. Unfortunately, the Confederate War Department never promoted Wright to brigadier, an honor he richly deserved. After the war, Wright returned to his law practice in Albany, Georgia where he served as mayor from 1866 until 1896, and as circuit judge from 1875 until 1880. Then, in failing health, he retired to farming in Monroe County, Georgia, where he died in 1895.[96]

In his later years, Fitz Lee could politely be termed "portly." Note the pin used to hold the knot in Lee's necktie. The pin is a miniature of a cavalry saber (USMA Library).

In January 1856, Lieutenant Colonel William W. Rich, who had been in poor health, resigned his commission and relinquished command of the Phillips Legion. Making his way home to Cassville, Georgia, he was attacked and injured by several marauding recently freed slaves, but survived. After the war, Rich worked as a railroad agent, operated a mercantile store, and served two terms as sheriff of Bartow County. According to family lore, Rich and his wife informally adopted and raised two orphaned black children. Rich's wife died in 1885 and in 1886, he remarried and moved to Gadsden, Alabama, where he opened a charcoal production facility. Rich died at the age of 69 in 1892. His remains were returned to Cassville where he was buried next to his first wife, Bathsheba.[97]

Fitzhugh Lee, if he was disappointed that Hampton was selected to command the Army of Northern Virginia's cavalry corps, never wrote or spoke of it. After Trevilian's, he continued in command of his division. Moving to the Valley to support Jubal Early, he was seriously wounded—a rifle ball struck him in the thigh—on September 19, 1864, during the third battle of Winchester. Carried from the field, Lee required three months of convalescence before returning to duty.[98]

After Wade Hampton returned to South Carolina in January 1865, Lee, as the senior cavalry officer with the Army of Northern Virginia, became the de-facto commander of the cavalry corps. At Appomattox, Lee and several hundred of his men—all that remained of J.E.B. Stuart's once proud legion—evaded capture and crossed the Blue Ridge to Lynchburg. There Lee disbanded his men and returned to Appomattox where he surrendered to Union Major General John Gibbon, whom he had known at West Point. The two spent that evening in the McLean house, and the following morning Lee, in possession of a parole, set out for Richmond and civilian life.[99]

Lee took up farming at Richland, an estate in Stafford County that was owned by his aunt and god-mother, Maria Fitzhugh. Through the hard work of Fitz and his brothers, the farm eventually proved profitable, and in 1871 Lee married Ellen Fowlee. The bride, a seventeen-year-old daughter of an Alexandria doctor, was less than half Lee's age at the time of their marriage. They had seven children, five of whom lived to adulthood. Two sons served

At the outbreak of the Spanish-American War, Fitz Lee was commissioned a major general of volunteers and given command of an infantry corps in Tampa. The war ended before the corps was ready to deploy, but Lee, who had been U.S. Consul in Havana when the *Maine* exploded, was sent to Cuba as part of the military government. This photograph shows Lee, on a gray horse, entering Havana (Library of Congress).

The officers and men of the VII U.S. Corps dedicated a monument to Fitz Lee which stands today in Richmond's Monroe Park (author's photograph).

as officers in the 7th U.S. Cavalry and two of their three daughters married officers in that same regiment.[100]

Lee was active in veterans' affairs. He was a frequent contributor to the *Southern Historical Society Papers* and a sought-after speaker at reunions and gatherings of veterans from both North and South. The culmination of his activities as a former Confederate came in May 1890 when he presided as grand marshal at the ceremonial unveiling of the equestrian statue of Robert E. Lee on Monument Avenue in Richmond. He also authored a biography of his uncle that was well received.[101]

In 1872, Lee entered politics, an arena in which he usually achieved dismal results. In that year he campaigned for Horace Greely for President in opposition to U.S. Grant. Grant won the election easily.[102] In 1874 Lee sought to represent Stafford County in the Virginia General Assembly. Nominated by the Conservative Party, he was defeated in the election. Three years later, he unsuccessfully sought the Conservative nomination for governor. In 1878, the Conservatives nominated Lee for a seat in the U.S. House of Representatives, but he was again defeated. Lowering his sights considerably, Lee ran for a seat in the Virginia

House of Delegates in 1879, but, as in the past, he was not successful. Finally, in 1885, Fitz Lee was elected governor of Virginia as a Democrat. After serving his term—Virginia governors were and are now limited to a single term in office—Lee sought election to the U.S. Senate. Although Lee seemed a shoo-in for the Senate, the Virginia legislature instead selected Thomas S. Martin, a little known but well funded railroad lobbyist with a talent for backroom politics.[103]

Moving away from politics, Lee accepted appointment from the Cleveland administration as revenue collector for southwest Virginia. Afterward he was appointed U.S. Consul-General in Havana, Cuba, a post he held until the eve of the Spanish-American War. Upon the outbreak of hostilities with Spain, the McKinley administration commissioned Lee as major general of Volunteers and he was given command of the troops designated to seize Havana. Although the war ended before Fitz and his federal command deployed, he went to Cuba and served as commander of the district of Havana for two years. Afterward, he was retained in the Army as a brigadier general until March 1901 when he reached retirement age and was retired in that grade.[104] It had been forty years since he had resigned his lieutenant's commission upon Virginia's secession.

Once back in Virginia, Lee was placed in charge of organizing events in celebration of the three hundredth anniversary of Jamestown. While returning from a fund-raising trip to Boston, he suffered a stroke and died in Washington on April 28, 1905. After memorial services in Washington and Richmond, he was buried in Hollywood Cemetery near the grave of his former commander, J.E.B. Stuart.[105] After his death, the veterans of the VII US Corps, the organization commanded by Lee during the Spanish-American War, erected a monument commemorating Lee in Richmond's Monroe Park.

Williams C. Wickham continued serving with the cavalry, either in command of his

After the war, Williams Wickham was employed as president and vice president of the Virginia Central Railroad, today CSX. In 1891, a statue of Wickham by Edward Valentine was dedicated in Richmond's Monroe Park. In 1956, the statue's sword was stolen and has never been recovered (author's photograph).

brigade or Fitz Lee's Division, until October 5, 1864. On that date he resigned his commission in order to take his seat in the Confederate Congress in Richmond. On April 23, 1865, Wickham, who as a delegate to the state's April 1861 convention had voted against the ordinance of secession, announced openly that he supported the Republican Party. This act alienated him from many, if not most, of his former comrades in arms. Nonetheless, Wickham was successful in politics, being elected chairman of the Hanover County board of supervisors in 1871, and state senator in 1881. He held both positions until his death in July 1888. In November 1865, Wickham was elected president of the Virginia Central Railroad, the line he had fought over in June 1864. Wickham began an ambitious program to expand the line west to the Ohio River and east to Norfolk, Virginia. In 1869, a wealthy New York railroad man, Collis P. Huntington, was brought in as president of the newly-named Chesapeake & Ohio, with Wickham holding the office of vice-president until his death. Today the railroad continues in operation as CSX. In 1891, Wickham's supporters dedicated a bronze statue to his memory in Monroe Park, Richmond. The oration at the ceremony was delivered by the general's former commander, Fitzhugh Lee.[106]

On March 20, 1865, Fitzhugh Lee recommended that the Confederate government promote Thomas T. Munford, commander of the 2nd Virginia, to Brigadier General to date from Wickham's resignation.[107] The War Department never acted on the request. At Appomattox Munford commanded Fitz Lee's Division, evaded capture, and disbanded his force at Lynchburg. After the war, Munford initially returned to farming near Lynchburg and in Alabama. He then became vice-president of the Lynchburg Iron, Steel, & Mining Company. Munford also served two terms on the Virginia Military Institute's board of governors and was secretary of the Southern Historical Society. He died in February 1918 in Uniontown, Alabama, and is buried in Spring Hill Cemetery in Lynchburg.[108]

In August 1864, Lunsford Lomax was promoted to major general and assigned to command of a division of five brigades which had formerly operated independently in the Shenandoah and western Virginia. At Woodstock on October 9, he was captured for several hours, but escaped by overpowering his guard. After Lee's surrender, Lomax made his way to North Carolina and surrendered his division with General Johnston at Greensboro. After the war, Lomax returned to Virginia and took up farming. On July 1, 1886, Governor Fitzhugh Lee appointed his former West Point classmate and cavalry subordinate to the presidency of the Virginia Agricultural and Mechanical College in Blacksburg, a land grant college that is today Virginia Tech. Lomax encountered several problems administering the school, including a hazing scandal, and resigned his position in April 1891. Afterward, he worked for the War Department in Washington on the compilation of the *Official Records* and served on the Gettysburg Battlefield Commission. Lomax died in Washington on May 28, 1913, and is buried in Warrenton, Virginia.[109]

Daniel Grimsley, commanding the 6th Virginia, had been recommended for promotion to major in 1863, but the promotion was not confirmed until January 1865 with an effective date of June 4, 1864.[110] Although he was not promoted, Grimsley commanded the regiment much of the time during the final ten months of the war. Afterwards, Grimsley returned to his home in Rappahannock County and studied law under a private tutor. In 1867 he received his law license, moved to Culpeper, and opened a practice. Grimsley was elected to the state senate in 1869 and served in that body until 1879. In 1880, he was appointed judge of the sixth judicial circuit to fill the vacancy created by the death of Judge Henry Shackleford.[111]

However, he was voted out of that position when it came up for election. In 1885 he was elected to the House of Delegates and in 1886 was again elected judge of the sixth circuit, a position he retained for many years. Grimsley authored a small book, *Battles in Culpeper County, Virginia*, which is still in print. He died in February 1910 and is buried in Culpeper's Fairview Cemetery. Grimsley's portrait still hangs in the county courthouse.[112]

Thomas Rosser recovered from his wound at Trevilian's and returned to duty in late August 1864. Almost immediately, he was deeply disappointed when Hampton selected M.C. Butler for divisional command, believing that Hampton, by favoring his fellow South Carolinian—who happened to be senior to Rosser—had done him an injustice. In October, Rosser took the Laurel Brigade to the Shenandoah Valley to support Jubal Early's Army of the Valley. There, Rosser assumed command of Fitz Lee's Division since Lee had been wounded at Winchester. Shortly after arriving, Rosser, the self-styled "Savior of the Valley," was soundly thrashed by Torbert at Tom's Brook. Despite the loss, Rosser was promoted to Major General with a date of rank of November 1, 1864.

In March 1865, Rosser brought his division east to join the Army of Northern Virginia at Petersburg. On April 1, Rosser hosted a shad bake for fellow West Pointers Fitz Lee and George Pickett, resulting in the absence of three division commanders from their posts when the battle at Five Forks began. The Confederate defeat that day prompted Robert E. Lee to begin his withdrawal toward Appomattox. Rosser, who with some of his men had separated from the Army before Lee's surrender, withdrew to Lynchburg where Rosser disbanded them. Rosser returned to his wife's home in Hanover County, where he was captured on May 2.[113]

During the war, Thomas Rosser's rise had been spectacular—from West Point cadet to Confederate major general in less than four years. However, with hostilities over, he found himself unemployed and with limited prospects.

Initially, Rosser went to Lexington, Virginia, to study law. However, he quickly found he was not suited to be an attorney, and accepted a position as a regional representative in the National Express Company, a company that had been formed by former Confederate general Joseph Johnston. Rosser's job was to travel about the South setting up shipping offices. However, the company soon went bankrupt, leaving Rosser again out of work.[114]

Rosser and his wife moved to Baltimore, where Rosser worked for the city's waterworks while Betty Rosser managed a truck farm. While in Baltimore, Rosser accepted a position in a brokerage house, but apparently he never actually worked as a broker.[115] In 1868 Rosser decided to seek his fortune in the railroad business, initially in Pennsylvania, then in the Midwest, and finally in the Pacific Northwest and Canada. Over the next fifteen years, Rosser rose from laborer to construction engineer with the Northern Pacific Railroad.[116]

In 1883, Rosser, who had earned enough money to live comfortably, returned to Virginia and bought a small estate, Rugby, in Charlottesville. Back in his home state, Rosser became active in politics, an endeavor in which he was consistently unsuccessful. In 1892, he sought the Democratic nomination for a seat in the U.S. House of Representatives, but was defeated by the incumbent, Charles T. O'Ferrall, a former captain in the Laurel Brigade. The following year, Rosser again campaigned against O'Ferrall, this time for the Populist Party candidate who opposed O'Ferrall for governor. Rosser traveled the state stumping for his candidate, thereby raising the ire of many of his former comrades. Moreover, he was not successful in his efforts and O'Ferrall was elected governor.[117]

In 1898, the Federal Government commissioned Rosser as a brigadier general of volunteers in the build-up for the war with Spain. However, Rosser, who was in poor health, spent his entire tour in Virginia training an infantry brigade. Neither he nor his men saw action.[118]

In 1905, Rosser made a complete break with most former Confederates by supporting the Republican candidate for president. After the election of Theodore Roosevelt, the new administration rewarded Rosser with an appointment as postmaster of Charlottesville. Unfortunately, Rosser suffered a stroke in 1906, and afterward was unable to speak. Nonetheless, he kept his position as postmaster until his death on March 29, 1910. He is buried in Riverview Cemetery in Charlottesville.[119]

Richard Dulany, colonel of the 7th Virginia commanded the Laurel Brigade until Thomas Rosser completed his convalescence, then again commanded the brigade while Rosser temporarily commanded Fitz Lee's Division. In that capacity, he received his third wound of the war—a gunshot to the left shoulder—at Tom's Brook on October 9, 1864. After several months convalescence, Dulany returned to his regiment. However, no longer fit for field duty, he was ordered to report to Richmond for court-martial duty in February 1865. However, instead, Dulany took leave of absence to continue his recuperation and then offered his resignation, thus missing the final campaign of the war.[120]

After receiving his parole, Dulany resumed farming at Welbourne, the family home in Loudoun County. Unlike many Confederates, most of the Dulany family's business interests survived the war, and Richard Dulany remained a wealthy man. He resumed hosting the annual Upperville Colt and Horse Show, which continues until this day. He also resumed fox

Many of the Confederates who were seriously wounded were taken to the hospital in Gordonsville that occupied the Exchange Hotel which stands immediately adjacent to the Virginia Central line. Today the hotel is operated as a museum (author's photograph).

hunting, and for many years was master of the hunt club that today is known as the Piedmont Fox Hounds.[121]

Dulany was also active in veterans' affairs, and served as a marshal at the unveiling of Lee's statue on Monument Avenue in Richmond in 1890. He considered writing an account of the war, but his efforts were stymied by the loss of his papers. Earlier, he had loaned his war-time papers to Wade Hampton, who had also intended to write a book. Unfortunately, the papers of both former officers were eaten by mice while in Hampton's care.[122]

Richard Dulany, who never remarried after the death of his wife in 1858, died at Welbourne on October 31, 1906, and was buried on the farm. The following week, the Warrenton newspaper published Dulany's obituary. Reflecting on Dulany, the writer observed: "In that Heaven, where he surely is, the other angels may be beating the air with their wings, but the Colonel is on horseback."[123]

Lieutenant Gabriel Manigault, the adjutant of the 4th South Carolina, made the long march into captivity. He was unable to avoid a search upon his arrival at Point Lookout, but managed to conceal his watch in his trousers and paid a guard twenty-five cents "to persuade him not to see anything."[124] Manigault spent virtually the rest of the war as a prisoner, being exchanged in March 1865. After the war he returned home and managed "Silk Hope," the

After the war, the federal government established the National Cemetery system. Approximately 1,300 remains of Union soldiers from Culpeper and surrounding counties were gathered and reinterred in the Culpeper National Cemetery. Included were 115 of the dead from Trevilian Station (author's photograph).

family plantation, until 1873. He then joined the faculty of the College of Charleston as professor of Natural History and Geology and head of the department's museum, a position he held until his death in 1899. Manigault was a noted "gentleman architect" who is credited with designing Charleston's city hall. He also designed the "Manigault House" as a residence for his brother. The house is today owned by the Charleston Museum and is on the National Register of Historic Places. After his death, Manigault's estate sold a portrait of Mr. and Mrs. Ralph Izard, his great-great grand-parents, by John Singleton Copley to the Boston Museum of Fine Arts. The portrait remains in the museum's collection today.

Lieutenant Colonel John Critcher was relieved of command of the 15th Virginia by Lomax shortly before Fitz Lee launched his attack against Custer. However, the stigma of the relief did not apparently affect Critcher's postwar career. In 1869, the Virginia General Assembly elected Critcher as judge of the 8th Judicial Circuit, and in 1871 he was elected to the U.S. House of Representatives from Virginia's 1st Congressional District, serving a single term. He then was elected to the Virginia Senate for one term. In 1879, Critcher moved to Washington, DC, where practiced law for several years. He died in Alexandria, Virginia in 1901.[125]

Colonel Joseph McAllister's remains were reburied in Oakland Cemetery in Louisa Courthouse. The cemetery also contains the remains of at least sixty Confederate dead, most of whom are unknown, their graves marked by a simple rectangular headstone. The inscription on McAllister's headstone, "Dulce pro patria mori," is from the Roman poet Horace and is translated as "It is sweet to die for one's country." The inscription also appears above the entrance to the Amphitheater at Arlington National Cemetery (author's photograph).

Captain James Thomson, who commanded Chew's Battery (the 1st Stuart Horse Artillery) with great *élan* at Trevilian's, was promoted to major and appointed to command of a two-battery horse artillery battalion on March 20, 1865. At the time, the batteries of Thomson's battalion were scattered in the Shenandoah Valley, so he set out for Petersburg on April 1, with the guns to follow. Thomson rejoined Lee's army just in time to begin the retreat. Fighting with the cavalry, Thomson was wounded slightly in the arm at Amelia Springs on April 5. At High Bridge on April 6, Thomson borrowed Rosser's saber—Rosser had also been wounded—and joined Dearing's Brigade in the fighting. Thomson was shot twice—through the neck and in the chest—and fell dead. Thomson and the "Gallant" John Pelham were the only field grade officers serving with Confederate horse artillery to be killed during the war. Thomson was buried next to Turner Ashby and his brother in the Stonewall Cemetery in Winchester.[126]

While it is interesting to read about the postwar lives of participants in the battle, it is important to acknowledge that not all soldiers lived to become old soldiers. Lieutenant Colonel William Carter, shot in the right knee and left on the field on June 11, was found in an abandoned Union aide station on June 13. He was taken to the Confederate hospital in Gordonsville where he succumbed to his wound on July 8. Major Henry B. McClellan, who had been the regimental assistant adjutant general before moving up to Stuart's staff, wrote of Carter: "Always cool and collected, always provident for the wants of his men even to the minutest details, he commanded their confidence and respect. He was frequently in command

The only monument on the Trevilian Station Battlefield was dedicated by the United Daughters of the Confederacy in 1926. It sits on the south side of Highway 22 near where Custer and Rosser fought on June 11, 1864 (author's photograph).

of the regiment and always fought it well." Carter's remains were returned to Nottoway County for burial.[127] Carter was the senior Confederate officer to die from the fighting at Trevilian's.

Private Michael Barr, 5th South Carolina, was also shot in the right knee on June 11. He was evacuated to the Confederate hospital at Charlottesville where his wound became infected. Doctors amputated his leg above the knee and then a second amputation was performed further up the thigh. Barr lingered until August 29. His wife arrived from Leesville, South Carolina, and spent several days nursing her husband before his death. She, with her husband's remains, traveled by railroad flatcar from Charlottesville to Columbia, and by wagon from Columbia to Leesville. There he was buried in the family cemetery.[128]

In 1866 the Federal government enacted into law a bill establishing the system of national cemeteries. Over the next few years, work parties under the auspices of the Army Quartermaster Department fanned out across the South, disinterring deceased Union soldiers and reburying their remains in the nearest national cemetery. The remains of 115 Union cavalrymen—92 of whom were not identified—were removed from the fields and farmyards about Trevilian's and taken to Culpeper Courthouse, and there laid to rest with the dead of Cedar Mountain and the cavalry fight at Brandy Station.[129]

After the war roughly sixty of the Confederate dead were reinterred in Oakland Cemetery in Louisa Courthouse. Most of the Confederate dead remain unknown, their graves identified by plain, unmarked headstones. Lieutenant Colonel Joseph McAllister's remains were also moved to Oakland where he undoubtedly rests with some of his men who died on June 11, 1864.

* * *

In 1926, the Louisa Chapter of the United Daughters of the Confederacy erected a small monument on the Trevilian Station battlefield. The bronze plate on the monument refers to the fighting on June 11 and 12 as the "Greatest All Cavalry Battle of the War" and a "Signal Confederate Victory." It is likely that all Confederate participants, and many Union participants as well, would agree with both assertions.

Appendix A
Order of Battle and Casualties

Accurately determining the strengths of units during any Civil War battle is a challenge, particularly with battles such as Trevilian's, which came in the midst of a lengthy and intense campaign.

During the Civil War, commanders in both the Union and Confederate armies were required to muster their personnel at the end of each even-numbered month. The resulting "muster rolls"—certified by the company and regimental commanders—provided a by-name accounting for the men assigned to the organization, and served as a basis for paying the men who were present or accounted-for. Muster rolls are consequently considered the most accurate record of an organization's personnel status. However, muster rolls are only a "snapshot" of the organization's personnel status on the day the muster was performed. Cavalry regiments which mustered at the end of April—the fourth month of 1864—had significant changes in their present for duty strengths as a result of casualties at Todd's Tavern, Spotsylvania Court House, Yellow Tavern, Haw's Shop, and various other fights at locations throughout central Virginia between the Rappahannock and the James Rivers.

In addition to mustering every other month, each commander was required to report the numerical strength of his unit at the end of each month via a "return" to be filed on the first day of the following month. As with the muster roll, the return provided merely a snapshot of the unit's strength. Unfortunately for historians, musters and the preparation of returns were frequently deferred because of the press of combat, or simply not completed as required. Further, the resulting paper reports were in many instances lost or destroyed.

What is frequently missing from strength reports is information on men who, while present for duty, might be detailed to temporary assignments and were thus not available to their unit. Additionally, within cavalry organizations a man might be present for duty although his horse was dead or otherwise unserviceable. In that regard, in April 1864, as discussed earlier, Captain Frederick Newhall, an assistant inspector general on the cavalry corps staff, called attention to the difference between "paper reports" and the actual state of units after inspecting two of Sheridan's divisions. Determining the difference between paper and reality is a challenge today when estimating the effective strength of both Union and Confederate units.

Sheridan, in his memoirs written in 1888, reported that he took on the raid 6,000 cavalrymen in the 1st and 2nd Divisions. As discussed earlier, it is generally accepted that Sheridan understated his strength, although by how much is subject to question. On the other hand, historians have generally been confident that Hampton—in his division and Fitz Lee's—had approximately 5,000 men at Trevilian's.[1] The numbers provided in June's returns indicate that Sheridan's strength likely ranged between six thousand and eight thousand, depending upon the number of dismounted men who were left behind, and that Hampton had approximately five thousand men available at Trevilian's.

Another way of comparing the relative strengths of the opposing forces is to determine the number of cavalry companies available for battle. At Trevilian's, Sheridan had available 283 cavalry companies while Hampton had 188. While the present-for-duty strength of companies varied, an average company effective strength would be roughly thirty men—perhaps a little more or less. Applying that figure to the number of companies indicates personnel strengths in the 8,000 versus 5,000 range.

A squadron of two companies combined under the command of the senior company commander was the fundamental tactical maneuver unit of the cavalry arm during the Civil War. At Trevilian's, Sheridan could commit 135 squadrons into battle (14 companies, or 7 squadron-equivalents were on other duty at corps, division, and brigade headquarters) while Hampton had available 94 squadrons. Thus, with respect to maneuver units, Sheridan had almost a fifty-percent advantage over Hampton.

Compiling casualties by regiment presents problems similar to those encountered when determining regimental strengths. After each battle or skirmish, commanders were required to prepare "field returns" providing the name and rank of all soldiers killed, wounded, or missing. For wounded, field returns were to list the time, place, and nature of the wound. Field returns were to be completed in sufficient detail to support the just claims of the wounded or the heirs of the dead. Needless to say, many commanders must have found it difficult to compile accurate field returns with the specificity required immediately following a battle, particularly if the fighting extended into the hours of darkness.

While compilation of Civil War casualties is not—and never will be—an exact science, the figures provided in this appendix are probably a reasonable accounting of the human cost of the fighting at Trevilian's on June 11 and 12, 1864.

Union

At Trevilian's, Sheridan had two divisions consisting of twenty-three regiments of cavalry available, with each regiment authorized twelve companies of cavalry. Fifteen companies were detached from their regiments and assigned to duty outside the Cavalry Corps.[2] Two companies were detached from their regiments for other duties within the cavalry corps, and while not available to their parent regiment, were nonetheless available to Sheridan or his division commanders during the battle.

Sheridan took five batteries of horse artillery on the Trevilian's Raid. As was the Union practice, he allocated the batteries to his divisions and they were in-turn allocated to the brigades, with three batteries to Torbert's and two to Gregg's division. Each of the batteries consisted of two sections: one equipped with two 12-pound Light Napoleon smoothbores and the other with two 3-inch Ordnance Rifles.

In his official report, dated June 16, 1864, Sheridan advised General Grant that his command had lost "about" 575 men killed and wounded, of whom 490 were wounded. He also advised that the number of his men captured would not exceed 160, for a total estimate of 735.³ However, when Sheridan's casualties from the two days' fighting at Trevilian's were officially tabulated, they were considerably higher than the figure initially reported. While the total of 572 killed and wounded was very close to the number in Sheridan's official report, a total of 435 men—not 160—were listed as missing.⁴ The missing in Custer's brigade alone, most of whom were presumed captured, almost doubled Sheridan's initial estimate.

The Union casualties shown in the table below are from the *Official Records* unless otherwise noted.⁵

Cavalry Corps, Army of the Potomac
Major General Philip Sheridan

	KIA	WIA	MIA	TOTAL
Cavalry Corps Totals	102	470	435	1007

HEADQUARTERS ESCORT, 6TH U.S. CAVALRY
CAPT IRA W. CLAFLIN

	KIA	WIA	MIA	TOTAL
Headquarters Escort Totals		3	1	4

FIRST CAVALRY DIVISION
BRIGADIER GENERAL ALFRED T.A. TORBERT

	KIA	WIA	MIA	TOTAL
First Division Totals	83	378	376	837

First Brigade, First Division
Brig Gen George A. Custer⁶

Regiment	Commander	KIA	WIA	MIA	TOTAL
Staff⁷				1	1
1st Michigan (-D & G)⁸	LtCol Peter Stagg	12	23	64	99
5th Michigan	Col Russell A. Alger	4	11	136	151
6th Michigan	Maj James H. Kidd	7	22	60	89⁹
7th Michigan	Maj Melvin Brewer (WIA)¹⁰	2¹¹	26¹²	48	76
First Brigade Totals		25	82	309	416

Second Brigade, First Division
Colonel Thomas C. Devin

Regiment	Commander	KIA	WIA	MIA	TOTAL
4th New York	Col Luigi di Cesnola	6	32	6	44¹³
6th New York (-L)¹⁴	Lt Col William H. Crocker	2	11	27	40¹⁵
9th New York	Col William Sackett (MWIA)	4	41	5	50¹⁶
17th Pennsylvania	Lt Col James Q. Anderson	5	19	2	26
Second Brigade Totals		17	103	40	160¹⁷

Reserve (3rd) Brigade, 1st Division
Brigadier General Wesley Merritt

Regiment	Commander	KIA	WIA	MIA	TOTAL
19th New York (10 Companies)[18]	Col Alfred Gibbs	16	61	8	85[19]
6th Pennsylvania (-A)[20]	Capt J. Hinckley Clark[21]	6	56	5	67
1st U.S.	Capt Nelson B. Sweitzer	8	32	5	45[22]
2nd U.S.	Capt Theophilus F. Rodenbough	8	38	5	51[23]
5th U.S. (-A, B, C, D, F, K)[24]	Capt Abraham K. Arnold	3	6	4	13[25]
Reserve Brigade Totals		**41**	**193**	**27**	**261**

SECOND CAVALRY DIVISION
BRIGADIER GENERAL DAVID McM. GREGG

	KIA	WIA	MIA	TOTAL
Second Division Totals	16	81	21	118

First Brigade, Second Division
Brigadier General Henry E. Davies, Jr.

Regiment	Commander	KIA	WIA	MIA	TOTAL
1st Massachusetts (-A, B, C, D)[26]	Lt Col Samuel E. Chamberlain			2	2
1st New Jersey	Lt Col John W. Kester	1	2	3	6
10th New York[27]	Lt Col Matthew Henry Avery	4	16		20
1st Pennsylvania	Col John P. Taylor			1	1
6th Ohio	Col William Stedman				0[28]
First Brigade Totals		**5**	**18**	**6**	**29**

Second Brigade, Second Division
Colonel John Irvin Gregg

Regiment	Commander	KIA	WIA	MIA	TOTAL
1st Maine	Col Charles H. Smith				0[29]
2nd Pennsylvania	Lt Col Joseph P. Brinton	1	5	1	7
4th Pennsylvania (-F)[30]	Lt Col George H. Covode	2	26	3	31
8th Pennsylvania (- A & K)[31]	Col Pennock Huey	5	16	5	26
13th Pennsylvania	Maj Michael Kerwin	1	2	6	9
16th Pennsylvania	Lt Col John K. Robison	2	14		16
Second Brigade Totals		**11**	**63**	**15**	**89**

Horse Artillery Batteries

Battery	Commander	Supporting	KIA	WIA	MIA	TOTAL
2nd U.S., Battery M	Lt Alex. C.M. Pennington	1st Bde, 1st Div (Custer)	2	5	37	44
2nd U.S., Batteries B&L	Lt Edward Heaton	2nd Bde, 1st Div (Devin)				0
2d U.S., Battery D	Lt Edward Williston	3rd Bde, 1st Div (Reserve Brigade) (Merritt)		2		2
2nd U.S. Battery A	Lt W. Neil Dennison[32]	1st Bde, 2nd Div (Davies)				0
1st U.S., Batteries H&I	Capt Alanson Randol	2nd Bde, 2nd Div (Gregg)	1	1		2
Artillery Totals			**3**	**8**	**37**	**48**

Engineers
Captain W.W. Folwell

Unit	KIA	WIA	MIA	TOTAL
I, 50th New York (Pontoon Train with 52 enlisted men)				0

Confederate

Sheridan, in his report dated June 16, 1864, wrote that on June 11 the Confederates had abandoned their dead and most of their wounded on the battlefield, and twenty officers and 500 enlisted men were in Federal hands. Sheridan, in the same report, also claimed that Confederate losses on June 12 were very heavy, and that when he withdrew from the battlefield he took with him 370 prisoners of war, including 20 officers. The difference between the two figures given for the number of Confederates captured is not explained. Presumably some of the prisoners were wounded who were unable to be moved.

Wade Hampton, in his official report dated July 9, 1864, wrote that his division lost 612 men at Trevilian's: 59 killed; 258 wounded; and 295 missing. Fitzhugh Lee did not initially write an official report of the battle. However, in a postwar report for his division, dated December 20, 1866, Lee simply noted that at Trevilian's "My loss had been severe."[33] Given the description of the fighting on June 11 and 12, it seems likely that Lee's division suffered far fewer casualties than did Hampton's, a supposition supported by data from regimental histories.

Unfortunately, if any of the five Confederate brigade commanders or nineteen Confederate regimental and battalion commanders wrote official reports, they were lost and have yet to come to light. Consequently, accurately determining casualties by brigade and regiments is difficult.

The casualty figures for the Confederate corps are a sum of the numbers from Hampton's official report and information from regimental and battery sources for the casualties in Fitz Lee's Division and the artillery. For Hampton's Division, both the figures from Hampton's official report and a tally of the division's regimental figures are provided for information. Overall, the numbers are similar, although the regimental sources reported thirty-one more men killed/mortally wounded. The casualty figures provided for the Confederate regiments are from various sources as noted. Brigade figures are a sum of the casualties of the regiments assigned to the brigade.

Confederate regiments were authorized ten companies of cavalry. Organizations with less than ten companies on the field at Trevilian's are noted, below.

Cavalry Corps—Army of Northern Virginia
Major General Wade Hampton

	KIA	MWIA	WIA	MIA	TOT.
Corps Total	83	8	335	317	743

HAMPTON'S DIVISION
MAJOR GENERAL WADE HAMPTON

Division Total	KIA	MWIA	WIA	MIA	TOT.
From Hampton's Report	59		258	295	612[34]
From Regimental Sources	74	16	220	285	595

Young's Brigade
Colonel G.J. Wright

Regiment	Commander	KIA	MWIA	WIA	MIA	TOT.
7th Georgia	LtCol Joseph L. McAllister (KIA)	21		23	181	225[35]
Cobb's Legion	LtCol Barrington S. King	3	3	5	4	15[36]
Phillips Legion (9 Companies)[37]	LtCol William W. Rich	2	2	9	4	17
Jeff Davis Legion (6 Companies)	LtCol J. Fred. Waring	3		5	8	16[38]
20th Georgia Battalion (7 Companies)	Major Samuel B. Spencer					
Brigade Totals		29	5	42	197	273

Rosser's Brigade
Brigadier General Thomas L. Rosser (WIA)

Regiment	Commander	KIA	MWIA	WIA	MIA	TOT.
7th Virginia	Col Richard H. Dulany			13		13[39]
11th Virginia	Col O.R. Funsten			1		1[40]
12th Virginia	LtCol Thomas B. Massie		1	4		5[41]
35th Virginia Battalion (6 Companies)	LtCol Elijah V. White	1		5		6[42]
Brigade Totals		1	1	23		25

Butler's Brigade
Brigadier General Matthew Calbraith Butler

Regiment	Commander	KIA	MWIA	WIA	MIA	TOT.
4th South Carolina	Col B. Huger Rutledge	14		38	53	105[43]
5th South Carolina	Maj Joseph H. Morgan[44]	9	10	25	7	51[45]
6th South Carolina	Col Hugh K. Aiken (WIA)	21		92	28	141[46]
	Brigade Totals	**44**	**10**	**155**	**88**	**297**

Maryland Line[47]
Colonel Bradley T. Johnson

Regiment	Commander	KIA	MWIA	WIA	MIA	TOT.
1st Maryland (6 Companies)	Col Bradley T. Johnson[48]					
Baltimore Light Artillery	1st Lt William B. Beane[49]					

FITZHUGH LEE'S DIVISION
MAJOR GENERAL FITZHUGH LEE

	KIA	MWIA	WIA	MIA	TOT.
Division Total	**20**	**6**	**67**	**22**	**115**

Lomax's Brigade
Brigadier General Lunsford L. Lomax

Regiment	Commander	KIA	MWIA	WIA	MIA	TOT.
5th Virginia	Capt Reuben Boston	2		6	10	18[50]
6th Virginia	Capt Daniel A. Grimsley[51]	5		13	7	25[52]
15th Virginia	LtCol John Critcher (Relieved)[53]	1		2		3[54]
	Brigade Totals	**8**		**21**	**17**	**46**

Wickham's Brigade
Brigadier General Williams C. Wickham

Regiment	Commander	KIA	MWIA	WIA	MIA	TOT.
1st Virginia	LtCol William A. Morgan			2		2[55]
2nd Virginia	Col Thomas T. Munford	6		17	2	25[56]
3rd Virginia	LtCol William Carter (MWIA)	3	6	16		25[57]
4th Virginia	Unknown[58]	3		5	3	11[59]
	Brigade Totals	**12**	**6**	**40**	**5**	**63**

Appendix A

Stuart Horse Artillery[60]
Major Roger Preston Chew

Battery	Commander	KIA	MWIA	WIA	MIA	TOT.
Hart's[61]	Capt James F. Hart (Chew)	1	2	2		5
Thomson's[62]	Capt James W. Thomson (Chew)	3		8		11
Johnston's	Capt Phillip P. Johnston (Breathed)			1		1
Shoemaker's (-)	Capt John J. Shoemaker (Breathed)			4		4[63]
Battalion (-) Totals		**4**	**2**	**15**		**21**

Summary

The combined casualties of Sheridan's and Hampton's forces during the two-day battle at Trevilian Station were 193 men killed, 805 wounded, and 742 missing or captured, for a total of 1,740. In comparison, during the one-day battle at Brandy Station a year earlier, Pleasonton and Stuart's forces suffered 171 killed, 663 wounded, and 618 missing or captured, about 300 fewer casualties than at Trevilian's. At Trevilian's, between eleven thousand and thirteen thousand cavalrymen were on the field of battle, while at Brandy Station approximately sixteen thousand troopers were engaged. Thus the casualty rate at Trevilian's was significantly higher than at Brandy.

Soldiers on both sides commented on the ferocity of the fighting at Trevilian's. In many ways the action was more characteristic of an infantry fight than a cavalry engagement, a fact that is reflected in the number of casualties and made Trevilian's the bloodiest cavalry battle of the Civil War.[64]

Appendix B
West Pointers at Trevilian Station

At Trevilian's, as at Brandy Station a year earlier, West Point graduates played a prominent role on both the Union and Confederate sides during the battle. At Brandy Station, twenty Military Academy graduates served with Union forces during the battle, while eleven served on the Confederate side. A year later, twenty West Pointers were present with the Union, while only three were present with Confederate forces. However, at Trevilian's all Confederate academy graduates filled senior leadership positions.

Union

During the campaigns of 1864, Military Academy Graduates continued to fill the bulk of the general officer positions in the Cavalry Corps of the Army of the Potomac. Sheridan was an academy graduate, as were his three division commanders, Torbert, Gregg, and James H. Wilson (1860, #1852).[1] Half of the six brigadier general billets in the cavalry corps were also filled by academy graduates: Custer and Merritt in Tolbert's division; Colonel Timothy M. Bryan, Jr. (1855, #1703), in Wilson's division.

However, only four of the twenty-five Union cavalry regiments on the field at Trevilian's were under the command of West Pointers, and only one of those regiments was a volunteer regiment commanded by an officer in the grade of colonel. Interestingly, that commander, Colonel Alfred Gibbs of the 19th New York, was by six years the oldest West Point graduate on the field. As at Brandy Station, the regular cavalry regiments were commanded by junior officers. At Trevilian's, three of the four commanders of regular regiments obtained their commissions from the academy. One of those officers, Captain Nelson Schweitzer, commanding the 1st U.S. Cavalry, was a classmate of Sheridan, both having graduated in 1853.

At least four academy graduates served in staff positions during the battle. Also, two of the five Union artillery battery commanders were West Point graduates.

Union graduates present at Trevilian's are shown in the following table. Graduates in Wilson's division, which did not participate in Sheridan's raid toward Charlottesville, are not shown.[2]

Name	Grade	Duty Position	Class	Cullum #
Gibbs, Alfred	Col	Cdr, 19th N.Y.	1846	1313
Sweitzer, Nelson B.	Capt	Cdr, 1st U.S.	1853	1602
Sheridan, Philip H.	Maj Gen	Cdr, Cavalry Corps	1853	1612
Gordon, George	Capt	AdC to Brig Gen Torbert	1854	1660
Gregg, David McM.	Brig Gen	Cdr, 2d Cav Div	1855	1684
Torbert, A.T.A.	Brig Gen	Cdr, 1st Cav Div	1855	1697
Forsyth, James	Lt Col	CofS, Cav Corps	1856	1738
Claflin, Ira	Capt	Cdr, 6th U.S.	1857	1786
Reno, Marcus	Capt	Act. IG, 1st Cav Div	1857	1779
Arnold, Abraham	Capt	Cdr, 5th U.S.	1859	1845
Randol, Alanson	Capt	Cdr, H&I Btry, 1st U.S. Arty	1860	1855
Merritt, Wesley	Brig Gen	Cdr, 3rd Bde, 1st Cav Div	1860	1868
Pennington, Alex C.M.	Capt	Cdr, M Btry, 2nd U.S. Arty	1860	1864
McQuestern, James[3]	Capt	Act. IG, 3rd Bde 1st Cav Div	May 1861	1926
Leoser, Charles M.[4]	Capt	Co Cdr, 2nd U.S.	May 1861	1907
Custer, George A.	Brig Gen	Cdr, 1st Bde, 1st Cav Div	June 1861	1966
Calef, John A.	1Lt	Sec Cdr, Btry A, 2nd U.S Arty	1862	1988
McIntire, Samuel B.	1Lt	Sec Cdr, Btry B&L, 2nd U.S. Arty	1862	1989
Lester, Charles H.	1Lt	Act. IG, 3rd Bde, 1st Cav Div[5]	1863	2016
Robbins, Kenelm	2Lt	Co. Cdr, 2nd U.S.	1863	2017

Confederate

Upon secession, civilian and military leaders in the South looked to the West Point graduates and former cadets who supported the Confederacy as a cadre for the army's officer corps. Very quickly, men who learned their military skills at the academy on the Hudson filled many general officer and colonel billets within the Confederate army. However, unlike in the North, as the war progressed the South was unable to replace those veteran officers with graduates of more recent classes. The resulting attrition among West Pointers is evident in the cavalry of the Army of Northern Virginia.

At the time of the battle at Brandy Station in June 1863, fifteen academy graduates were assigned to J.E.B. Stuart's cavalry division, with fourteen of those officers present for duty. Of those fourteen officers, eleven were on the field at Brandy Station. In addition to Stuart, three of his brigade commanders—William Jones, Beverly Robertson, and Fitzhugh Lee— were academy graduates, although Lee was incapacitated by a bout of rheumatism on June 9 and did not participate in the fighting. Seven of Stuart's regimental commanders were academy graduates or former cadets. A year later, six West Pointers remained in the Cavalry Corps of the Army of Northern Virginia, of whom five were present for duty. Three of those five, shown below, fought at Trevilian's.

Name	Grade	Duty Position	Class	Cullum #
Lomax, Lunsford	Brig Gen	Cdr, Bde	1856	1731
Lee, Fitzhugh	Maj Gen	Cdr, Div	1856	1755
Rosser, Thomas	Brig Gen	Cdr, Bde	Ex May 1861	

P.M.B. Young (Ex. June 1861), whose brigade was commanded at Trevilian's by Colonel Gid Wright, had been wounded near Ashland on May 30, 1864, and did not return to duty until August. Brigadier General John Chambliss (1853, #1609), commanding a brigade, and Colonel J. Lucius Davis (1833, #722), who command the 10th Virginia Cavalry, served in Rooney Lee's division, which had remained in support of Robert E. Lee's infantry.[6]

Of the nine West Pointers at Brandy Station who no longer served with the cavalry, four were battle losses. Three had been killed serving with the cavalry. Colonel Solomon Williams (1858, #1808), 2nd North Carolina Cavalry, was shot in the forehead on Yew Ridge on June 9, 1863, the senior Confederate killed at Brandy Station. Colonel Charles Collins (1859, #1827), 15th Virginia Cavalry, was killed on May 12, 1864 at Spotsylvania Court House. J.E.B. Stuart (1854, #1643), as described earlier, was mortally wounded at Yellow Tavern on May 11. Brigadier General Lawrence Baker (1851, #1535), who commanded the 1st North Carolina at Brandy before being promoted and given command of the North Carolina brigade, had been incapacitated by wounds since August 1863. Consequently, Baker had been transferred to less arduous duty in the Department of North Carolina and Southern Virginia in the spring of 1864.

In the year since Brandy Station, five West Pointers left the cavalry under other circumstances. After the Gettysburg Campaign, Robert E. Lee, who doubted Brigadier General Beverly Robertson's (1849, #1431) abilities as a combat commander, arranged that officer's transfer to the Department of South Carolina, Georgia, and Florida. In September 1863, Stuart filed court-martial charges against Brigadier General William E. "Grumble" Jones (1848, #1378). The court found Jones guilty, but because the offense—disrespect to a superior—was so trivial in nature, it recommended only a verbal reprimand as punishment. Nonetheless, Robert E. Lee deemed it necessary to transfer Jones to the Department of Southwest Virginia and East Tennessee. Jones was killed at Piedmont on June 5, 1864. Under the grade structure established by the Confederate War Department, Major Robert Beckham (1859, #1830), Stuart's horse artillery commander, was unable to obtain a richly deserved promotion to lieutenant colonel. Consequently, he transferred to the army in Tennessee in February 1864. Beckham was killed at Franklin on November 30, 1864. Lieutenant Colonel William G. Robinson (1858, #1822), who had replaced his classmate, Solomon Williams, in command of the 2nd North Carolina, transferred to the Confederate Navy in May 1864.[7] Finally, Colonel John Logan Black (Ex. 1850), who attended the academy but resigned before graduation, had returned to his home state with his regiment, the 1st South Carolina, in the spring of 1864.

Appendix C
Custer's Captured Wagons

Trevilian Station was not the first instance in which Custer had lost his personal baggage wagon in battle. At Buckland, Virginia, on October 19, 1863, his wagon was seized by the men of Lunsford Lomax's brigade.

At Buckland, Stuart had lured Kilpatrick with Davies's brigade toward Warrenton while Custer lagged behind at Buckland, the site of a bridge over Broad Run. Fitz Lee, moving up from Catlett intended to strike Kilpatrick in the rear as Stuart, with Hampton's Division—Hampton was convalescing from wounds received at Gettysburg—attacked Kilpatrick from the front. At the sound of Lee's guns, Stuart wheeled about and charged up the Warrenton Pike routing Davies's brigade and giving the battle its name, The Buckland Races. In the rear, however, Custer reacted quickly to Lee's flanking movement and put up a spirited defense. He held the bridge until his artillery crossed the creek, and managed to withdraw many of his men to safety across Broad Run as well. Unfortunately, Custer's headquarters wagon with his personal belongings was unable to get across the bridge and was left in Confederate hands.

Writing well after the war, Major W.W. Blackford, Stuart's staff engineer, recalled that the Confederates that day "captured about two hundred fifty prisoners and eight or ten ambulances. Among the latter was one containing Custer's baggage and correspondence." Blackford went on, "Some of the letters to a fair, but frail, friend of Custer's were published in the Richmond papers and afforded some spicy reading although the most spicy parts did not appear."[1]

The previous month, Custer had traveled on convalescent leave—he had been slightly wounded at Culpeper Courthouse on September 13—to Monroe, Michigan. Custer had for some time been enamored with a young woman in Monroe, Elizabeth Bacon, the daughter of Judge Daniel Bacon. Once in Monroe, Custer asked for Judge Bacon's permission to marry Elizabeth. Judge Bacon deferred making a decision and asked that Custer and "Libbie" not correspond while he made up his mind. Custer agreed, but "where there is a will, there is a way."

Instead of corresponding directly, Custer would write to Annette Humphrey, Libbie's best friend, and "Nettie" would read the letter aloud to Libbie. Libbie would then describe how she would respond had she received such a letter, and Nettie would transcribe Libbie's thoughts and send them to Custer. With the convoluted system of communication in place at the time of the Buckland Races, it is unlikely that the letters contained much "spice" and Blackford was probably mistaken regarding their publication.

Eventually Judge Bacon relented and allowed Custer and Libbie to correspond directly. Their romance progressed and the two were married on February 9, 1864.² Thus the circumstances between Custer and Libbie had changed significantly in the eight months since Buckland, and after their marriage the two apparently were quite intimate in their correspondence. With good reason, many officers and men on both sides during the Civil War prudently burned letters from their loved ones before going on campaign. Thus, they avoided the indignity of having strangers possibly read their intimate thoughts should they be killed or captured. Custer, however, apparently chose to preserve his letters from Libbie.

At Trevilian's on the night of June 11, after the fighting for the day had died down, some of Lomax's troopers amused themselves by rummaging through Custer's wagon. Among the trove of baggage, the men discovered several letters written to Custer by Libbie, and the letters provided entertaining reading. Private James Wood, Company F, 7th Virginia, noted in his diary entry for June 11, "The letters showed him [Custer] to be a man of very loose morals."³

Custer was concerned about the loss of the letters and after the battle he wrote to Libbie, commenting: "I regret the loss of your letters more than all else. I enjoyed every word you wrote, but do not relish the idea of others amusing themselves with them, particularly as some of the expressions employed.... Somebody must be more careful hereafter in the use of *double entendu*."⁴ In response, Libbie replied, "I suppose some rebel is devouring my epistles.... Let me unburden my mind about the matter, since your letter implies chiding, tho the slightest and kindliest. No Southerner could say, if they are *gentlemen* that I lacked refinement. There can be nothing low between man and wife if they love each other. What I wrote was holy and sacred. Only cruel people would not understand the spirit in which I wrote it."⁵ In responding to Libbie, Custer wrote that he did not mean to "chide," but only wished to "impress on [her] the need of more prudence in writing." Libbie put the matter to rest in a letter to Custer in July, writing: "I

Custer and his wife, Elizabeth, are shown here shortly after their marriage in February 1864. Libbie's letters to Custer, which were found among Custer's belongings when his wagon was captured on June 11, provided salacious reading for some of the soldiers in Fitz Lee's Division (Library of Congress).

shall not again offend my dear boy's sense of nicety by departing from that delicate propriety which, I believe, was born in me—the lady in me inherited from my mother."[6]

Custer's concern over the privacy of his correspondence with Libbie was well-founded. On July 1, a letter entitled "The Second Virginia Cavalry in the Fights at Trevillian's and Nance's Shop" appeared in the *Richmond Examiner*. After a brief account of the fighting, the letter's author, identified only as "T," wrote that the 2nd Virginia drove back the enemy, "capturing three of Custer's headquarters wagons containing his trunks, clothes, &c.... We have Custer's uniform complete in our regiment, his commission as brigadier, and his letters." Later in the letter "T" elaborated, "Custer had a negress with him as cook, who was placed in one of his best conveyances, driving in state, and had cooking utensils enough to supply a first class hotel. His [Custer's] letters show a depravity in Northern society beyond anything our people could imagine; and if they could be published, they would fully expose the villainy of high officers in Yankee commands, and the condition of affairs at the north." Perhaps— fortunately for Custer's reputation—Libbie's letters were not published with the letter from "T."[7]

Along with the letters, the wagon's captors also found several items of silverware that had apparently been taken by Custer for his personal use. In its June 28, 1864, edition, under the headline, "A MAJOR-GENERAL WHO STEALS SPOONS," the *Richmond Examiner* printed a letter from General Lomax in which he provided a description of each piece of silver found, that it might be returned to its rightful owner: "One silver tea pot; five silver spoons marked 'F'; one pair sugar tongs marked 'H.B.E.L.'; one pair sugar tongs, unmarked." The *Examiner* staff could not resist editorializing over this incident: "From the following letter, it will be seen that not only the private soldiers of the Yankee armies are thieves, but [also] their officers of the highest rank. Thievery runs through them from the highest to the lowest. Here is a Yankee, not a dirty soldier in the ranks, not, what is dirtier, an officer of 'coloured' troops, but a Yankee wearing the epaulettes of a Major-General in the service of the United States, caught with silver spoons in his mess chest, which he had stolen from the tea table of a Virginian lady."[8]

Custer, however, was not the only Union general who apparently stole spoons. Two weeks after the Trevilian's Raid, Fitz Lee's men captured Brigadier General James Wilson's headquarters wagon near Ream's Station. The July 5, 1864, edition of the *Richmond Examiner* printed a letter from Major J.D. Ferguson, Lee's adjutant, informing the paper's readers that in the wagon they found: "One large silver waiter, with heavy beading, One silver plated castor, One silver plated cream pot, Eleven old silver spoons, engraved 'W,' One old silver spoon, engraved 'B,' One double silver plated salt stand, One silver goblet, marked 'Nablett,' One Silver goblet engraved 'St. John's Church, Cumberland Parish, Luneburg county, Virginia.'"[9]

Additionally Ferguson advised, "A light roan gelding, with black mane and tail, both hind feet white—about two years old, and having the appearance of a thoroughbred, was found tied behind General Wilson's headquarters ambulance, and is supposed to have been taken by him and reserved for his own use." Ferguson went on to provide the address of the farm in Powhatan County where the horse had been sent for safe keeping so that its owner might reclaim it.[10]

As with Custer, the *Examiner* staff editorialized regarding Wilson's apparent larcenous behavior, writing, "We supposed this list refers only to what was found in Wilson's 'Headquarters ambulance.' But *all* the marauders should be personally examined, and their stolen goods thus advertised."[11] It is not known whether any of the silver—from either Custer's or Wilson's wagons—was returned to its rightful owner.

Interestingly, the information regarding Custer's wagon in the letter from "T" was provided by a soldier of the 2nd Virginia in Wickham's Brigade, while the inventory of stolen silverware found in Custer's wagon was provided by Brigadier General Lomax. Colonel Thomas Munford claimed that his regiment captured the wagon, while Lunsford Lomax claimed that honor for the 15th Virginia, of his brigade. While the question of which regiment captured the wagon may not be resolved, it ended up in Munford's possession. Captain Jacob S. Green, Custer's assistant adjutant general who was captured at Trevilian's, wrote to Custer from captivity that after the battle he had met Munford, who at the time had charge of Custer's headquarters wagon. Green advised Custer that Munford offered to send him Custer's commission and personal property while Green was in Richmond. However, Green only spent a few days in Richmond before being moved to Charlottesville, and consequently he did not know the whereabouts of Custer's belongings.[12]

Munford later wrote that many of the things Custer lost to the 2nd Virginia at Trevilian's were recaptured by Custer at Tom's Brook in October 1864, where Custer took the headquarters wagons of Munford, Lomax and Rosser.[13] Further, in 1901—well after Custer's death at the Little Bighorn—Munford returned to Libbie several of the personal items that had been captured from Custer at Trevilian's.[14]

Ironically, after Tom's Brook, Custer wrote to Libbie, "Among the papers I captured from the rebels are all of Genl. Mumford's private correspondence (He captured all mine at Trevillian) including his wife's letters. I have them tied in a bundle, neither reading them nor allowing others to do so. I think the relation of husband and wife too sacred to be violated, even in war."[15]

The disposition of Libbie's letters to Custer, as well as correspondence between Munford and his wife, remains unknown.

Appendix D
Edward L. Wells and the Hampton vs. Lee Controversy

In the years following the Battle of Trevilian Station, some participants pondered the apparent lack of coordination between Hampton and Fitzhugh Lee during the first day's fighting on June 11. *Battles and Leaders of the Civil War*, published in 1887, featured an account of Trevilian's by M.C. Butler. In it, Butler wrote that as his men moved forward on the Fredericksburg Road, Hampton said that he expected to hear Fitz Lee's guns on the right at any moment. Butler added that as he deployed his and Wright's regiments, he "paid little attention to my right … as I supposed it was protected by Lee's division" with whom he "expected at every moment to form a juncture."[1]

At about the same time, an article written by Thomas Rosser appeared in the "Annals of the War" series in the *Philadelphia Weekly Times*. In his account of Trevilian's Rosser, wrote

> Up to the time that I was wounded there appeared to have been very little co-operation between General Fitz Lee and General Hampton, and while I am not prepared to say whose fault it was I felt then, and all of us who were in the fight of the 11th felt, that it was very unfortunate that General Lee did not unite with us that day…. After the death of General Stuart no chief of the cavalry was appointed. When the divisions were together General Hampton, who was the senior officer, took command, but I very much question whether General R.E. Lee put the entire cavalry force of his army under General Hampton when he sent it in pursuit of General Sheridan. If he did, I am surprised that Hampton did not bring Fitz Lee to him on the first day's fight at Trevillian.

Rosser went on to praise the manner in which Hampton managed the two divisions—his own and Lee's—on June 12, writing that he "handled them with consummate skill."[2]

Significantly, while both Butler and Rosser noted the lack of cooperation between Hampton and Lee on June 11, neither affixed blame for that deficiency. A decade later, however, circumstances changed. In 1899, Edward L. Wells published *Hampton and His Cavalry in '64*, in which he asserted that Fitz Lee had willfully obstructed Hampton's plan of attack on June 11. At the time, Wells's allegation sparked interest among veterans, and it has influenced scholars' views of the battle ever since. Consequently, it is useful to examine Edward Wells, his motivation, and the accuracy of his allegation.

Wells had a unique background. He was born in New York City in 1839 and graduated from Rutgers University in 1859. For health reasons, in 1860 he temporarily moved to

Charleston, South Carolina, where well-to-do relatives lived. In Charleston, Wells became an ardent secessionist. Nonetheless, he spent the first two years of the war practicing law in New Jersey and New York. However, after the passage of the Union's Conscription Act, Wells booked passage back to Charleston via Nassau. Once in Charleston, he enlisted in the Charleston Light Dragoons and accompanied the 4th South Carolina Cavalry to Virginia in May 1864. Wells was wounded at Trevilian Station and late in the war fought under Hampton's direct command in a notable engagement at Fayetteville, North Carolina, on March 11, 1865.[3]

After the war, Wells settled in Charleston, practiced law, and began writing articles for the *Southern Historical Society Papers* and various newspapers. In 1898, Wells began work on *Hampton and His Cavalry in '64*. In preparing the book, he corresponded extensively with Hampton and relied heavily upon information provided to him by the old general.[4]

The book, when published by B.F. Johnson of Richmond in 1899, was very disparaging of the performance of Fitz Lee and his Virginia division at Trevilian's. Wells wrote that Custer was able to advance into Hampton's rear because the skirmishing between Lee and Custer "was so feebly conducted by the Confederate brigade that Custer drew off down the road" and that "this [Custer's flanking movement] could not have happened if Lee's division had advanced in the manner ordered." Moreover, Wells asserted that the failure of Hampton's plan to destroy Sheridan's force south of the North Anna River on June 11 was "due only" to Fitz Lee's failure to follow orders. Wells went on to write that Fitz Lee's division withdrew to Louisa and was "of no use" during the first day's fighting, leaving Hampton to fight Sheridan's entire force alone. In Wells's view, the only thing that prevented Sheridan's force from "crushing the life out of Hampton's division" was Hampton's superior generalship.[5]

Sales of *Hampton and His Cavalry in '64* were disappointing, despite the announcement by Wells and the publisher that proceeds would go toward purchasing a new house for Hampton, whose home in Columbia, South Carolina, had recently burned.[6] While Wells placed most of the blame for poor sales on the publisher, he opined that the book might have been unpopular because "Virginians do not like the truth told about Fitz Lee."[7]

How much Wells's criticism of Fitz Lee affected the sales of *Hampton and His Cavalry in '64* will never be known. However, some veterans of the cavalry of the Army of Northern Virginia took issue with Wells's views.

On December 31, 1899, a lengthy review of *Hampton and His Cavalry in '64* appeared in the *Richmond Dispatch*. The review, which had appeared earlier in the *Baltimore American*, was written by Bradley T. Johnson who had commanded the 1st Maryland Cavalry which fought with Rosser's Brigade at Trevilian's. Johnson, in the course of his review, laid out Wells's criticism of Lee and added a few observations of his own.

Regarding the events on June 11, Johnson wrote of Hampton's plan: "Fitz. Lee was ordered to move on the road from Louisa Courthouse by Sheridan's left, join Hampton, who would push down the main road, and then Sheridan's army would have been destroyed. But Fitz Lee didn't get there and Sheridan got off." Describing the fighting, Johnson added: "Sheridan was moving up and Hampton proposed to attack him before he got to the railroad—he would strike him below a fork in the road, would draw him on beyond the fork, and he gave Lee directions on how to move down and strike Sheridan on the flank and rear, while hotly engaged with Hampton in his front. Hampton carried out his programme; .... Lee not coming up left a gap between Hampton and himself, and Custer, dare-devil as he was, drove the wedge of his brigade through the interval."[8]

Going beyond the battle at Trevilian's, Johnson provided his general opinion of the book: "The author [Wells] states the facts and we have no right to doubt them, as he wrote from the official records and papers. This book was not written under the direction or with the assistance of General Hampton, though Hampton furnished him with many reports and memoranda he had preserved, but he did not know he [Wells] was going to write this book."[9]

As a separate topic, Johnson also commented on the issue of the chain of command of the cavalry corps. Regarding Robert E. Lee's decision following Stuart's death to have the three cavalry division commanders report to him directly, Johnson wrote: "It is impossible at this late date to explain all the reasons for this conduct. Part of them were the result of jealousy of a South Carolina militia man ranking two Virginia West Pointers. But there must have been something else."[10] He went on to opine that had Hampton been placed in command of the cavalry corps, the fighting at Trevilian's on June 12 would not have occurred because Sheridan's force would have been destroyed on June 11.

A week later, the January 7, 1900, issue of the *Richmond Dispatch* featured a letter in rebuttal to both Well's book and Johnson's review. The letter was written by Griefe T. Cralle, who had served in the 3rd Virginia Cavalry and fought at Trevilian's. Cralle wrote, "It is strange that in reviewing this story General Johnson did not protest against this perversion of the facts of the great cavalry fight at Trevillian Station." Cralle asserted that it was Wickham's charge against Custer that "saved the day" for Hampton, and he pointed out that his regiment's commander during the battle, Lieutenant Colonel William Carter, was mortally wounded on June 11.[11]

Two weeks later, on January 21, 1900, the *Richmond Dispatch* published a rebuttal to Johnson written by Daniel Grimsley who as a captain had commanded the 6th Virginia at Trevilian's.[12] Grimsley, in his critique of Johnson's review, wrote that Johnson "does injustice to Fitz Lee and his command, and violence to the truth of history." Grimsley pointed out that Johnson's description of Hampton's plan differed significantly from Hampton's description of his plan in his official report of the battle. Grimsley went on to point out that Lee's division did participate in the fighting against Custer's brigade on June 11, and that their participation had been also documented in Hampton's report. Grimsley concluded by quoting from Hampton's official report, "Major General Fitzhugh Lee cordially co-operated with me and rendered me valuable assistance."[13]

Also in the January 21 issue of the *Richmond Dispatch*, were letters from Bradley Johnson and Edward Wells, apparently written in response to the criticism they had received from Cralle. Johnson explained that in his review he was not stating his own views, but merely "sticking closely to the chain of events as stated by the author [Wells]." Johnson went on to add that his only opinion in his article was that Rosser's charge ended the battle, and he admitted that he was "utterly wrong" since the hardest fighting took place on the following day, June 12.[14] Wells, in his letter, explained that Fitz Lee's division did not operate "effectually" on Hampton's right and consequently allowed Custer to pass in between the two Confederate divisions. He added that Lee's division was "cut off, isolated, and rendered useless for over twenty-four hours." Wells, in his own defense asserted that "These are the simple facts of the case, and are matter of record."[15]

Over the years, many historians, including most of Hampton's biographers, have incorporated Wells's views regarding the first day at Trevilian's into their work. Consequently, readers today will more likely than not be led to conclude that much of Hampton's difficulty on

June 11 can be attributed to either Fitz Lee's tactical ineptitude, or—even worse—to his willful obstruction of Hampton's plans. According to Wells and others, Lee at Trevilian's was either incompetent or a rogue. Interestingly, most authors fail to fully explore the almost abominable nature of Lee's alleged misconduct directed at Hampton.

Were Lee found to be incapable of effectively maneuvering his division in accordance with his orders, Hampton should have relieved him from command and brought him before a board of inquiry. Moreover, were it determined that Lee intentionally failed to follow orders, he should have faced a general court-martial for misconduct in the face of the enemy, an offense punishable by death. Essentially, if Lee failed to cooperate with Hampton because he was dissatisfied that Hampton had been given command over him, Lee revealed an almost unimaginable degree of moral corruption. Under such circumstances, Lee would have chosen to sacrifice the lives of loyal Confederate soldiers merely to soothe his own hurt feelings and damage his superior's reputation.

In view of the seriousness of Wells's allegations—both stated and implied—against Lee, it is important to review the underlying facts of the matter.

- Hampton described his plan of attack in his official report. That description and the concept set forth by Wells in his book—and later summarized by Johnson—differ significantly.
- Like almost all books of the time, *Hampton and His Cavalry in '64* was not sourced. However, when writing his book, Wells corresponded extensively with Hampton and relied heavily upon information provided by Hampton. At the time Wells and Hampton were collaborating on the book, Hampton was eighty years old and the battle was thirty-four years in the past.[16] It is not clear whether—or how much—age and time had clouded Hampton's memory.
- There is no evidence that Wells contacted Fitz Lee to solicit Lee's recollection of events at Trevilian's.
- Wells, in his rebuttal to Cralle's letter, claimed that Lee's actions on June 11 were "ineffectual." However, he offered no explanation as to what he meant; nor did he provide any evidence to corroborate his assertion.
- In his book, Wells claimed that Lee did not advance in the manner ordered. However, other than Hampton's brief description of his plan in the *Official Records* (described earlier), we have no information regarding how Lee was directed to conduct his advance. We do not know who carried Hampton's orders to Lee, nor do we know what specific instructions Lee was given, if any.
- Wells's claim that Lee's division was pushed back beyond Louisa, isolated, and played no part in the fighting around Trevilian Station on June 11, was factually inaccurate. As acknowledged by Hampton in his official report, Lee withdrew his division to Louisa Courthouse then advanced west along the railroad, striking Custer near Trevilian Station.
- After the publication of the book and the questions over Lee's culpability during the battle surfaced, Wells and Hampton consulted on the matter. By letter dated January 18, 1900, Hampton wrote, "Lee returned to Louisa C.H. just after Rosser's charge, & he did not join me until 2 P.M.— the next day!!" While it may be true that Hampton and Lee did not physically meet until the afternoon of June 12 (Hampton put the time at noon in his official report), Lee's division did "join" in the fighting at Trevilian Station on the afternoon of June 11.[17]
- By letter dated February 22, 1900, Hampton rather cryptically informed Wells, "I really did not know at first how greatly [Lee] had failed on the first day and my regard for Genl. R.E. Lee induced me to omit all mention of misconduct on the part of Fitz."[18] It is unclear how or when Hampton learned that Lee had failed him if he were not aware of those failings on June 11–12, 1864.
- Fitz Lee, who was serving with the U.S. occupation government in Cuba at the time *Hampton and His Cavalry in '64* was published, made no public comment regarding the assertion that he had not followed Hampton's orders at Trevilian's. Likewise, Hampton—who had provided his

views privately to Wells—made no reported public statement on Fitz Lee's performance at Trevilian's. Finally, regarding the events of June 11, Hampton, in his letter to Wells dated January 18, 1900, wrote, "Of course, I shall not say anything about it unless forced to do so."

Both Johnson and Wells wrote in the *Richmond Dispatch* that the events as described in *Hampton and His Cavalry* were facts and not subject to dispute. However, the facts of the matter—as set forth above—raise questions regarding Wells's portrayal of events

Underlying Wells's account, which other authors since have included in their work, is that Fitz Lee was resentful when required to serve under Hampton's command.[19] However, by the rules governing seniority, discussed earlier, Hampton was the senior of the two major generals, and there was no practical manner by which Hampton could have been placed under Fitz Lee's command. Lee, Hampton, and virtually every other general officer in the Confederate army understood the system. Lee had two alternatives if he could not bring himself to willingly and loyally serve under Hampton: resign his commission; or, arrange a transfer, either to the infantry or to another theater. Lee chose to do neither; nor is there any indication he ever considered pursuing either course of action. Lee certainly may have felt some discontent in having to serve under Hampton, but if so, he kept it to himself. Significantly, in the intervening years, no statements by Lee have come to light indicating he was averse to serving under Hampton's command.

The effectiveness, or lack thereof, with which Lee carried out his orders on June 11, 1864, is also subject to question. Lee was ordered to advance up the Marquis Road and attack the enemy at Clayton's Store as Hampton advanced up the Fredericksburg Road to attack the enemy at that same location. Lee's division began its movement north at approximately 3:00 a.m., about two hours before the movement of Hampton's division. About a mile north of Louisa, Wickham's men made contact with Custer's pickets and skirmishing began. We do not know why Lee did not immediately attempt to fight-through Custer's screen and proceed on to Clayton's Store. One can speculate that had he done so—and brought on a decisive engagement—Custer might not have been able to disengage and make his way into Hampton's rear.

At about the time Wickham was skirmishing with Custer, Butler's brigade became heavily engaged about half way between Trevilian Station and Clayton's Store. Lee could certainly hear the sound of the fighting several miles to his west and this may have raised questions in his mind as to what he should do. Hampton's plan—and presumably his orders to Lee—were that the two divisions would together bring on a general engagement with Sheridan's force at Clayton's Store. The circumstances on the ground had obviously rendered that plan invalid. Given the new conditions, Lee had four basic courses of action available: press on to Clayton's store; slide left through the woods to tie in to Hampton's right flank; reverse course and march to the sound of the guns; hold his position and wait for orders. After some time had passed, Lee apparently decided to retrace his steps to Louisa Courthouse and then swing west to Trevilian's where he again made contact with Custer's brigade in the rear of Hampton's division.

The time of Lee's engagement with Custer at Trevilian Station was not recorded. Apparently, Lee's division spent two or more hours on the Marquis Road before Lee determined that there were no significant enemy forces to his front. He thereupon decided to move to Hampton's assistance. Once headed south toward Louisa, Lee's division reportedly went to the trot, an appropriate pace for such a movement. Lee's division made contact with Custer's brigade in Hampton's rear at some time after noon on June 11.

Lee might be faulted for not fighting Custer more aggressively or for not deciding sooner to move to Hampton's assistance. However, the events do not appear sufficiently egregious to substantiate either gross negligence or willful misconduct on Lee's part. In battle, the unforeseen is the norm, not the exception. As an old saying goes, "The best plan only lasts until the first shot is fired." Given the apparent disconnect between the plan as envisioned and the events on the ground, Lee's course of action does not appear unreasonable. On the contrary, in view of the confusion regarding what was occurring on the morning of June 11, it is reasonable to expect Lee to proceed cautiously.

Bradley Johnson asserted in the *Richmond Dispatch* that had Hampton been appointed to corps command immediately after Stuart's death, the second day of Trevilian's would not have been fought because Sheridan would have been crushed on the first day. It is interesting to speculate what would have happened had Robert E. Lee not ordered the commanders of the three cavalry divisions to report directly to him.

If Fitz Lee was resentful that Hampton was his senior, it seems unlikely that Lee's feelings would have been assuaged simply because Hampton was appointed to corps command—the issues of seniority in grade and experience remained unchanged. If Lee considered himself a superior cavalryman to Hampton, it also appears unlikely that his opinion would change because of Hampton's appointment.

It is further unlikely that conferring the mantle of corps command on Hampton would have affected his tactical acumen or his abilities as a leader and fighter in the month between Stuart's death and Trevilian's. The plan of battle he conceived on the evening of June 10 was based upon Hampton's understanding of the enemy and the terrain, and would not likely have been altered because of a change in Hampton's duty position.

However, Hampton, had he been appointed corps commander, would have had more flexibility in exercising command and control over the two divisions which participated in the Trevilian's fight.

It is possible that Hampton would have retained tactical control of his division during the Trevilian's expedition and battle. A precedent had been set by Stuart, who although corps commander, had exercised direct control over Hampton's division during the fighting in the late summer and fall of 1863 while Hampton was convalescing from his Gettysburg wounds.

It seems more likely, however, that Hampton would have relinquished command of his division to Butler—it was well known that Hampton considered his fellow-South Carolinian a highly effective combat commander. However, elevation of Butler to divisional command might actually have weakened the leadership posture within that division. The bulk of Butler's combat experience was gained as commander of the 2nd South Carolina Cavalry. He had been absent from the theater for almost a year while convalescing from his loss of a foot at Brandy Station and on detail organizing the "New Issue" for their movement to Virginia. In Hampton's absence, Butler had commanded Hampton's division at Haw's Shop, his most notable experience at more senior levels of command. Were Butler to move up to division, Colonel Hugh Aiken would likely have moved up to brigade command. Aiken had almost no actual combat experience before coming to Virginia, and no experience at brigade command.

A third—and intriguing—possibility is that as corps commander, Hampton may have chosen to accompany Fitz Lee's division during the attack on the morning of June 11. Such a decision would have been logical if Hampton had more confidence in Butler than in Lee. It is interesting to speculate how different the battle may have unfolded if Hampton and Lee had been together on the Marquis Road when the fighting began.

Finally, one may question Wells's motivation in criticizing Fitzhugh Lee. While it may have been true, as Johnson wrote, that *Hampton and His Cavalry in '64* was not written "under the direction or assistance" of Hampton, it is not necessarily accurate to conclude that Wells was an impartial chronicler of events. In early 1898, Wells wrote to Hampton, "Anything that you may say or write to me will be worked up to the best of my ability in the sense desired by you, but as if coming from me only."[20] Clearly, Wells intended to burnish Hampton's reputation with his book. Since many at the time of the battle and afterward felt that Sheridan got the better of Hampton during the first day's fighting at Trevilian's, perhaps Wells felt it necessary to affix blame elsewhere. Wells, in *Hampton and His Cavalry in '64*, absolved Hampton of any responsibility for Sheridan's success on June 11. Instead, Wells held Fitz Lee entirely responsible for the debacle. Regardless of his motivation, Wells succeeded in firmly establishing his views in the generally accepted history of Trevilian Station.

Perhaps more than any other modern biographer, Manly Wade Wellman, in his 1949 biography of Hampton, bought into Wells's views of Fitz Lee's misconduct at Trevilian's, writing:

> ... [Hampton] and his Georgians and Carolinians wondered if more might not have been done with a more loyal comrade than Fitz Lee. At Trevilian and again at Ream's Station, Fitz had seemed slow and stupid. Butler and one or two others suggested to Hampton that Fitz was jealous, calculating, wishful that Hampton might meet disaster and so be cleared from the way to his own promotion as Stuart's successor. Both Butler and Rosser frankly urged Hampton to ask for a court-martial, but Hampton refused. He, too, mistrusted Fitz Lee, but his admiration for Robert E. Lee was too warm to allow such an accusation of the commander's nephew.[21]

Wellman's source for his information was a pencil manuscript by Hampton's son, Alfred McDuffie Hampton, in typescript by Mary Hampton. The typescript had been forwarded to Wellman by Douglas Southall Freeman. Freeman, however, in *Lee's Lieutenants* expressed a more charitable view of both Fitz Lee's performance and his motivation at Trevilian's: "[Fitz Lee] may have cherished still the ambition to take the place of his beloved Stuart; but if Fitz hoped to outshine Hampton, he was too good a soldier and too honorable a patriot to withhold full support."[22]

The difference in opinion between Wellman and Freeman is telling. In the absence of evidence regarding Fitz Lee's attitude and motivation, historians have drawn their own conclusions which, unfortunately, are now accepted by many as facts.

Chapter Notes

Introduction

1. John Keegan, *The Price of Admiralty: The Evolution of Naval Warfare* (New York: Viking, 1988), 10. Keegan contrasts walking the battlefields of Gettysburg or Waterloo with entering the gun deck of HMS *Victory*, Admiral Nelson's flagship at Trafalgar.
2. Shelby Foote, *The Civil War: A Narrative*, vol. 3, *Red River to Appomattox* (New York: Random House, 1974; reprint, New York: Vintage, 1986), 308.
3. Douglas Southall Freeman, *Lee's Lieutenants*, vol. 3, *Gettysburg to Appomattox* (New York: Charles Scribner's Sons, 1944), 521.
4. Stephen Z. Starr, *The Union Cavalry in the Civil War*, vol. 2, *The War in the East from Gettysburg to Appomattox, 1863–1865* (Baton Rouge: Louisiana State University Press, 1979), 136.
5. Bruce Catton, *Grant Takes Command* (Boston: Little, Brown, 1968), 297.
6. Allan Nevins, *War for the Union, 1864–1865*, vol. 3, *The Organized War* (New York: Charles Scribner's Sons, 1959; reprint, New York: Konecky & Konecky, 2000), 51.

Chapter 1

1. From Colonial times, the area had been a center for smelting iron ore. The original forests had been cut down to feed numerous "furnaces."
2. Margaret Wagner, et al., eds., *Library of Congress Civil War Desk Reference* (New York: Simon & Schuster, 2002), 306.
3. Philip Sheridan, *Personal Memoirs of P.H. Sheridan, General United States Army* (New York: L.C. Webster, 1888; reprint., Da Capo, 1992), 199–200; *OR* 36, II:552; David M. Gregg, "Brevet Major General David McMurtrie Gregg" (Typescript, 1934) in Papers of David McMurtrie Gregg, 1716–1916 (MMC 0539) (Manuscript Collection, Library of Congress, Washington), 260. Lieutenant Colonel Theodore Lyman, of Meade's staff, recorded the incident in his notebook and opined that "Maybe this was the beginning of his [Sheridan's] dislike for Warren and his ill-feeling against Meade" (Theodore Lyman, *Meade's Headquarters, 1863–1865: Letters of Colonel Theodore Lyman from The Wilderness to Appomattox*, edited by George R. Agassiz [Boston: Atlantic Monthly, 1922], 144). Sheridan relieved Warren of his command of the V Corps at Five Forks in April 1865. In 1879, Warren's conduct at Five Forks was examined by a board of inquiry. The board completely exonerated Warren and criticized the manner of his relief from command (Ezra J. Warner, *Generals in Blue* [Baton Rouge: Louisiana State University Press, 1999], 542).
4. Edward Tobie, *Personal Recollections of General Sheridan* (Providence, RI: Snow & Farnum, 1889), 17.
5. Henry B. McClellan, *The Life and Campaigns of Major-General J.E.B. Stuart, Commander of the Cavalry of the Army of Northern Virginia* (New York: Houghton Mifflin, 1885); republished as *I Rode with JEB Stuart: The Life and Campaigns of Major-General J.E.B. Stuart* (Bloomington: University of Indiana Press, 1958); reprint ed. (New York: DaCapo, 1994), 410.
6. Tobie, *Personal Recollections of General Sheridan*, 8. Tobie described Sheridan's order to unsaddle and make camp as "something new and exceeding rare in our experience of raiding."
7. South of the junction with Mountain Road, Telegraph Road was known as the Brook Turnpike. Today, U.S. Highway 1 follows the route of the Brook Turnpike. Interstate 295 now bisects the battlefield, running parallel and to the south of Turner's Run and between Wickham's and Lomax's initial positions. The battlefield is now filled with residential and commercial development.
8. McClellan, *I Rode with JEB Stuart*, 412. McClellan did not return to Yellow Tavern until after the battle had begun. He was delayed when forced to detour to avoid Federal troops who had penetrated across the Brook Turnpike.
9. U.S. War Department, *War of the Rebellion: A Compilation of the Official Records of the Union and Confederate Armies*, 70 vols. in 128 books and index (Washington, D.C.: Government Printing Office, 1880–1901), 36, I:803. Hereafter cited as "*OR.*"
10. Stuart sent his Inspector General, Colonel Walter Jenifer, to Rosser with an ultimatum: either pledge to refrain from drinking alcohol while in Confederate service, or face court-martial. Rosser sent Stuart a letter via Jenifer which convinced the cavalry general that a court-martial would not be necessary (Henry Clay Pate, "Proceedings of the General Court Martial, in the Case of Lieut. Col. H. Clay Pate, 5th Va. Cavalry," [Richmond: Np., 1863]).
11. *Richmond Examiner*, May 17, 1864.
12. Freeman, *Lee's Lieutenants*, 3:420. As noted by Freeman, none of the Union commanders' official reports stated the time that the attack commenced. However, Devin, with a trailing brigade, reported moving through Glenn Allen a few miles east of the battlefield at 11:00 a.m. indicating that the attack likely began after noon.
13. Merritt and Custer both ranked from June 29, 1863, but Merritt's name appeared ahead of Custer's on the promotion order. Thus he was the senior of the two brigadiers.

14. J.H. Kidd, *Personal Recollections of a Cavalryman with Custer's Michigan Cavalry Brigade in the Civil War* (Ionia, MI: Sentinel, 1908), 297.

15. Edward Tobie of the 1st Maine was favorably impressed with Sheridan. After the war he recalled, "So our commander became to us something tangible, something we saw and knew, instead of a mere name, as before" (Tobie, *Personal Recollections of General Sheridan*, 18).

16. Theodore S. Garnett, *Riding with Stuart*, ed. Robert Trout (Shippensburg, PA: White Mane, 1994), 67. Garnett wrote his account of Yellow Tavern roughly thirty years after the war. At the time Garnett delivered Stuart's message to Pate, Lunsford Lomax, the brigade commander, was supervising the fighting from a small hill behind his line. Henry Clay Pate is perhaps better known today for his association with "Bleeding Kansas" than from his service as a regimental commander in the Confederate cavalry. In June 1859, while working as a newspaper editor in Westport, Missouri, Pate led a "company" of pro-slavery men on an expedition into Kansas, ostensibly to capture John Brown. Much to Pate's chagrin, after a brief skirmish near Baldwin, south of Lawrence, he and his men were instead captured by Brown. Pate reported, "I went up to Kansas to take John Brown, and John Brown took me!" The army, at the request of the territorial governor, intervened, the two leaders signed an exchange agreement—Pate and his men for captured Jayhawkers—and the captives were released. Major General E.V. Sumner, then lieutenant colonel of the 2nd US Cavalry, and a detachment of his men arranged the release of Pate and his party. Stuart, then a lieutenant, was present during negotiations and formed an unfavorable opinion of Pate. Later, in justification for recommending Thomas Rosser instead of Pate for regimental command, Stuart wrote to the Confederate Secretary of War, "Henry Clay Pate was no stranger to me. I was somewhat a witness to his redoubtable exploits in Kansas, in the Border Ruffian days, and am confident he could not be a corporal in the Missouri army. I knew he did not possess the rare qualities so essential to a cavalry colonel, which I will not here dilate upon" (Alex G. Hawes, "In Kansas with John Brown," *The Californian* 4 [July 1881], 68–75; Pate, "Proceedings of the General Court Martial," 85). Pate was promoted to colonel and appointed to the command of the 5th Virginia in February 1864 following Rosser's promotion to brigadier general.

17. Gordon C. Rhea, *Battles for Spotsylvania Court House and the Road to Yellow Tavern, May 7–12, 1864* (Baton Rouge: Louisiana State University Press, 1997), 204.

18. John L. Johnson, *The University Memorial: Biographical Sketches of Alumni of the University of Virginia Who Fell in the Confederate War* (Baltimore: Turnbull Brothers, 1871), 590. Pate was initially buried at Dr. Shepherd's, but four days later his body was recovered and taken to Richmond and he was reburied in Hollywood Cemetery. In his official report on the battle of Yellow Tavern, Custer noted that among the dead on the battlefield, his men found the body of "the notorious" Henry Clay Pate (Garnett, *Riding with Stuart*, 67; *Richmond Daily Examiner*, May 17, 1874; *OR*, 36, I:818).

19. James Ewell Brown Stuart, *Letters of Major General James E.B. Stuart*, ed. Adele H. Mitchell (Stuart-Mosby Historical Society, 1990), 394.

20. Sheridan sent Colonel Thomas Devin's cavalry brigade toward Richmond to ensure that no Confederates from the garrison would threaten his rear.

21. Elias W.H. Beck, "Letters of a Civil War Surgeon," *Indiana Magazine of History* 27 (1931), 153. Beck, however, acknowledged that Chapman managed his regiment, the 3rd Indiana well, and that he would fight. Chapman was later promoted to brigadier general and brevetted to major general.

22. Gordon C. Rhea, *Battles for Spotsylvania Court House*, 207. In his official report of the battle, Chapman wrote that the attack—made by the 1st Vermont and one of Custer's regiments—had been proposed by Custer and agreed to by Chapman (*OR* 36, I:898). Lieutenant Colonel Preston was killed near Salem Church on June 3, 1864 (*OR* 36, I:901).

23. The heavy rainfall provided an advantage to the advancing Federals. First, it helped conceal their movement from the defenders. Additionally, some Union regiments were armed with Spencer carbines which fired metal cartridges. The metal cartridges were less susceptible to moisture than the paper cartridges fired by the Confederate troopers with their muzzle loading and breach loading weapons.

24. Gregory W. Urwin, *Custer Victorious: The Civil War Battles of General George Armstrong Custer* (Rutherford, NJ: Farleigh Dickenson University Press, 1983; reprint Lincoln: University of Nebraska Press, 1990), 143.

25. In his report of the battle, Fitz Lee wrote that during the initial Union attack, Stuart oversaw events with Lomax's brigade while Lee positioned himself with Wickham. In the lull between Sheridan's morning and afternoon attacks, Lee and Stuart conferred. Afterward, Stuart remained with Wickham, and Lee moved to Lomax's brigade (Janet Hewett, et al., *Supplement to the Official Records* [Wilmington, NC: Broadfoot, 1995–2000] part 1, vol. 6:792–793).

26. Frank Dorsey, "Gen. J.E.B. Stuart's Last Battle," *Confederate Veteran* 17 (February 1909), 76. To fight dismounted, the men would form "fours." The number one man would dismount and affix the reins of his horse to the bridle of the number two man's horse. The number two man would dismount and affix his horse's reins to the bridle of the number three man's horse. The number three man would dismount and hand his reins to the number four man. The number four man, remaining in the saddle, was responsible for leading the three horses to the rear and bringing them forward again when needed.

27. "The Death of General J.E.B. Stuart," in *Battles and Leaders of the Civil War*, 4 vols., edited by Robert Underwood Johnson and Clarence Clough Buel (New York: E.P. Dutton, 1887–1888; reprint ed., New York: Thomas Yoseloff, 1956), 4:194.

28. Freeman, *Lee's Lieutenants*, 3:425. Freeman wrote that Stuart was armed with his LeMat pistol that day. The LeMat was a unique weapon: its cylinder of pistol ammunition rotated about a barrel loaded with buckshot. However, Jeffry Wert, in his biography of Stuart, wrote that Start was firing his .36 caliber Whitney pistol that day (Jeffry D. Wert, *Cavalryman of the Lost Cause* [New York: Simon & Schuster, 2008], 356).

29. Edward Longacre, "Last Stand of the Last Knight," *Civil War Times Illustrated* 43 (June 2004), 32–33; Freeman, *Lee's Lieutenants*, 3:761. Freeman's account of Stuart's wound was prepared by Lieutenant Colonel I. Ridgeway Trimble, an army medical officer. Whether or not Huff actually fired the shot that killed Stuart is open to question. The identification of Huff as the shooter is based solely upon the assertion to that effect made by his regimental commander, Colonel Russell Alger, in his official report of the battle (*OR*, 36, I:828). At least two other troopers, Private Dunn of the 5th Michigan and Sergeant Bellinger of the 7th Michigan, were identified in other accounts as having fired the fatal shot (Dunn with his carbine instead of his pistol) (Edward Longacre, *Custer and His Wolverines: The Michigan Cavalry*

Brigade, 1861–1865 [New York: Da Capo, 1997], 215). By one account, Major Henry Granger, who led the 7th Michigan and was killed in the afternoon charge toward the Telegraph Road, is credited with downing Stuart with a "snap-shot" over his horse's neck while at the gallop (Urwin, *Custer Victorious*, 144). Asa Isham, an officer in the 7th Michigan who was captured at Yellow Tavern near where the Telegraph Road crossed Turner's Run, opined that Stuart was killed by a mounted or dismounted man in either the 1st or the 7th Michigan, and more likely the latter regiment (Asa B. Isham, *An Historical Sketch of the Seventh Regiment Michigan Volunteer Cavalry From Its Organization, in 1862, to Its Muster Out, in 1865* [New York: Town Topics, 1893], reprint *Seventh Michigan Cavalry of Custer's Wolverine Brigade* [Huntington, WV: Blue Acorn, 2000], 47). Douglas Southall Freeman, who credited Huff, wrote that the range of Huff's shot was "no more than 10 or 15 yards." Edward Longacre concluded that Huff fired from a much longer range, "approximately 40 yards." (In the cited article, Longacre wrote that the range of Huff's shot was four hundred yards, a mistake he corrected in the following issue of the *Civil War Times*.) Even at a range of only forty yards, Huff was either remarkably accurate or remarkably lucky.

30. Hampton H. Smith, *J.E.B. Stuart: A Character Sketch* (Ashland, VA: Np, Nd), 14. Stuart had been wounded once as a first lieutenant—shot in the chest by an Indian in western Kansas in 1857.

31. Dorsey, "Gen. J.E.B. "Stuart's Last Fight," 76.

32. Freeman, *Lee's Lieutenants*, 3:425.

33. McClellan, *I Rode with JEB Stuart*, 415. Faced with losses among his regimental and brigade commanders during the Gettysburg Campaign, Stuart included the following admonition in a general order regarding cavalry tactics: "The position which cavalry officers generally take in battle is a subject requiring immediate correction. Though highly creditable to their gallantry, it is highly derogatory to their discretion and at direct variance with their duty." Stuart went on to advise that squadron commanders lead their men, while more senior commanders position themselves where they can control their entire formation, and to "check any wavering by prompt support; to order squadron commanders successively to the charge; and superintend their rallying and return to action." (*OR*, 27, III:1055.) While this guidance pertained to conducting charges, Stuart clearly believed that the place for senior commanders was not always in the front line. At Yellow Tavern, as in most other battles, Stuart failed to heed his own advice. However, given the desperate nature of the situation at the time, his actions that day are understandable.

34. The torpedoes were apparently not particularly effective, and, much like modern landmines, they did not discriminate between friend and foe. On May 31, a Confederate gunner in Captain Philip P. Johnston's battery, then supporting Fitz Lee's division, spied a wire stretched across the road upon which the battery was traveling. Unaware of its purpose, the gunner pulled the wire and set off a torpedo hidden at the side of the road. The only damage was to the draw-bar between the two lead horses—broken into two pieces as the horses "spooked" at the explosion (Robert Trout, *Galloping Thunder: The Stuart Horse Artillery Battalion* [Mechanicsburg, PA: Stackpole, 2002], 489).

35. Sheridan, *Personal Memoirs*, 206–211.

36. Stuart, *Letters of Major General James E.B. Stuart*, 167; Wert, *Cavalryman of the Lost Cause*, 359. Dr. Brewer was married to Flora Cooke Stuart's sister, Maria.

37. Characteristically, in his account of Stuart's death von Borcke placed himself at the center of events, claiming that Stuart's last coherent words—"My dear Von, I am sinking fast now, but before I die I want you to know that I never loved a man as much as yourself. I pray your life may be long and happy; look after my family after I'm gone, and be the same true friend to my wife and children that you have been to me."—were spoken to him (Heros von Borcke, *Memoirs of the Confederate War for Independence* [Edinburgh: W. Blackwood & Sons, 1866; reprint Nashville, TN: J.S. Sanders, 1999], 443–446). In his diary entry for May 12, John B. Jones, a clerk in the War Department, wrote: "Maj-Gen J.E.B. Stuart was wounded last evening, through the kidney, and now lies in this city, in a dying condition! Our best generals thus fall around us" (John B. Jones, *A Rebel War Clerk's Diary* [Philadelphia: J.B. Lippincott, 1866; reprint, 2 vols. Time-Life, 1982], 2:206).

38. There is some question concerning the interaction of Stuart and Pate on May 11. In its May 17 edition, the *Richmond Examiner* described the meeting between the two officers as having occurred "in the face of the enemy with bullets flying." During the meeting Stuart complimented Pate, after which the two shook hands and "made up their differences and were friends again." Several historians, among them Douglas Southall Freeman (*Lee's Lieutenants*, 421) and Emory Thomas (*Bold Dragoon*, 291), concluded that Stuart, during the face-to-face meeting, personally gave Pate the orders to hold his position. This interpretation of events is contradicted by Stuart's aide de camp, Theodore Garnett, who wrote that he carried Stuart's orders to Pate. Jeffrey Wert, concluded that the meeting between Stuart and Pate was probably apocryphal (*Cavalryman of the Lost Cause*, 353). Significantly, however, several sources indicate that on his deathbed Stuart was effusive in his praise for Pate's conduct on May 11.

39. Freeman, *Lee's Lieutenants*, 3:428–431; McClellan, *I Rode with Jeb Stuart*, 416–417; *Richmond Examiner*, May 14, 1864.

40. McClellan, *I Rode with Jeb Stuart*, 417.

41. Freeman, *Lee's Lieutenants*, 3:432.

42. The following day, May 13, the news of Stuart's death was announced at the headquarters of the Cavalry Corps. Stuart's couriers, affected much like Lee's staff officers, bowed their heads and wept like children (Robert J. Trout, *With Pen and Saber: The Letters and Diaries of J.E.B. Stuart's Staff Officers* [Mechanicsburg, PA: Stackpole, 1995], 254).

43. Robert E. Lee, *Wartime Papers of Robert E. Lee*, 2 vols., ed. Clifford Dowdey (New York: Little, Brown, 1961; reprint Pennington, NJ: Collector's Reprints, 1996), 2:731.

44. *OR*, 36, III:800.

45. *Richmond Examiner*, Richmond, VA: May 14, 1864.

46. St. James Church was located at the corner of 5th and Marshall streets. It is now the site of the Richmond Convention Center.

47. In 1882, Stuart's brother erected a more suitable monument—an obelisk roughly twenty feet tall—over Stuart's grave (Fitzhugh Lee to Elliot Fishburne, August 25, 1882, Papers of Elliot Guthrie Fishburne [MSS 6542], Albert and Shirley Small Special Collections Library, University of Virginia. Charlottesville, VA).

48. *Richmond Examiner*, May 14, 1864; "The Death of Major General J.E.B. Stuart," *Southern Historical Society Papers*, 7 (January-December 1879), 109–110.

49. McClellan, *I Rode with Jeb Stuart*, 416–417. Stuart's spurs were a gift from several of his friends from the St. Louis, Missouri, area where he had once been assigned. The spurs were brought east and presented to Stuart by Mrs. William Fitzhugh Lee, whose husband, the lieutenant colonel of the 33rd Virginia Infantry of the "Stonewall" Brigade,

had been killed at First Manassas (Alexander L. Tinsley, "General Stuart's Spurs" in *Confederate Veteran* 37 [May 1929], 198). Stuart also directed McClellan to send a small Confederate Flag, hidden in the lining of Stuart's plumed hat, to a woman in Charleston, South Carolina.

Chapter 2

1. *OR*, 36, I:1030. Edward "Allegheny" Johnson and George "Maryland" Steuart were taken prisoner, and "the brave" Abner Perrin was killed. Perrin, who had reportedly remarked that he would come out of the battle either "a live major general or a dead brigadier," was shot seven times as he led his brigade forward to contain the Union's early morning attack (Ezra J. Warner, *Confederate Generals in Gray* [Baton Rouge: Louisiana State University Press, 1959], 235). Brigadiers James Walker and Junius Daniel were wounded, with Daniel dying the following day.

2. Unfortunately for historians, Lee left no written record of his thoughts regarding the selection of Stuart's successor. Consequently, much of this discussion is informed speculation.

3. Lee, *Wartime Papers*, 2:490. Unfortunately for the Confederate cause, the problem of finding suitable senior commanders remained a significant challenge for Lee, particularly as the war progressed and casualties among leaders increased.

4. Hampton was promoted to brigadier on May 23, 1862, while Lee was promoted to brigadier on the following July 24.

5. *OR* 27, III:1069.

6. Hampton graduated in 1836. Wigfall graduated the following year. South Carolina College has since become the University of South Carolina.

7. For a more detailed discussion of Hampton's promotion to major general, see Walter B. Cisco, *Wade Hampton: Confederate Warrior, Conservative Statesman* (Washington, D.C.: Brassey's, 2004), 123–125. Wilcox, who was promoted to brigadier effective October 26, 1861, was senior among the four officers while Stephen D. Lee, whose promotion to brigadier was November 6, 1862, was junior. Lee went on to become the youngest lieutenant general in the Confederate Army. He was promoted to that grade on June 23, 1864, and thus at the close of the war was six months senior to Hampton.

8. *OR* 25, II:614–619, 651, 657, 728–730. Hampton's letter to Lee regarding this issue is not included in the *Official Records*. From Lee's response, it appears that Hampton also proposed that more than one horse artillery battalion be allocated to each cavalry brigade, and that Blakely guns be consolidated within one organization. Regarding the former, Lee advised Hampton that he favored placing any additional artillery batteries in an artillery reserve, and he noted the difficulty in providing horses for additional batteries. (A six-piece light artillery battery with six-horse teams required 84 horses; a similarly equipped horse artillery battery required 149 horses [Jennings C. Wise, *The Long Arm of Lee: A History of the Artillery of the Army of Northern Virginia* (Lynchburg, VA: J.P. Bell, Inc., 1915; reprint, 2 vols., Lincoln, NE: University of Nebraska Press, 1991), 1:111]). Regarding consolidation of the Blakely guns, Lee noted that all Blakely ammunition was imported from England, and he believed placing Blakely guns exclusively in one unit would not be prudent.

9. In the early months of 1863, Hampton's brigade was assigned to picket duty along the upper Rappahannock River in Culpeper County. The horses of the brigade became so malnourished that Robert E. Lee determined that the brigade was incapable of fighting effectively. He ordered Hampton to take the brigade farther south into Amherst County to "recruit," replacing them in Culpeper with Fitz Lee's brigade. In fairness, however, Hampton's Carolina regiments were at a disadvantage since their troopers were less able—compared to Virginians—to travel home to obtain remounts.

10. Thomas Rosser and P.M.B. Young were twenty-seven, Lunsford Lomax and M.C. Butler were twenty-eight, and John Chambliss was thirty-one. The only brigadiers approaching Hampton's age were Williams Wickham, who was forty-three, and James B. Gordon, who was forty-one. In comparison, Philip Sheridan was thirty-three years old at the time.

11. Cisco, *Wade Hampton*, 150–151.

12. Throughout 1862 and 1863, a majority of the cavalry regiments in the Army of Northern Virginia were from Virginia. For example, at the time of the Battle of Brandy Station, thirteen of the twenty-two regiments in Stuart's Cavalry Division were Virginian.

13. C. Vann Woodward, ed., *Mary Chesnut's Civil War* (New Haven: Yale University Press, 1981), 588. Hampton complained twice to Mary Chesnut of Lee's remarks, the second time as Mary returned from the Davis residence on the day Jefferson Davis' son, Joe, fell to his death from a ledge on the family's house, perhaps an indication of how bothered Hampton was by Lee's criticism (Ibid., 602).

14. Wert, *Cavalryman of the Lost Cause*, 332–333.

15. Edward Longacre, *Fitz Lee: A Military Biography of Major General Fitzhugh Lee, C.S.A.* (Cambridge, MA: Da Capa, 2005), 24. Lee chased down the Indian warrior, wrestled him to the ground, and shot him in the cheek. An enlisted man following Lee then shot the Indian, killing him.

16. Ibid., 10–11.

17. *OR*, 36, II:1001. The special order also included orders for the consolidation of several infantry brigades that were depleted during the fighting over the previous week.

18. A year earlier at Chancellorsville, Stuart had temporarily taken command of Jackson's Corps after that officer had been mortally wounded on the evening of May 2, 1863. Stuart's performance in temporary command of an infantry corps was noteworthy. While there was speculation that Stuart might be promoted and appointed to infantry corps command following Jackson's death, Stuart correctly discounted that possibility and Lee instead decided to reorganize his army into three infantry corps and promote both A.P. Hill and Richard Ewell to lieutenant general. However, it is interesting to speculate how Lee might have sorted cavalry division command on the eve of the Gettysburg Campaign had Stuart been transferred to the infantry and how changes in cavalry division command may have affected events at Brandy Station and during the invasion of the North (Wert, *Cavalryman of the Lost Cause*, 235).

Chapter 3

1. On May 27, 1863, Stuart submitted two reorganization plans for Lee's consideration, neither of which met with the approval of the commanding general (*OR*, 25, II:836).

2. *OR*, 27, III:1068–1069. Lee, writing to Jefferson Davis on August 1, 1863, proposed to the president that Stuart's cavalry be organized into a corps with two divisions and seven brigades, including that of Brigadier General Albert Jenkins. Each of the brigades, except Jenkins's, would have four regiments. Jenkins's brigade would retain its five regiments which had been raised for local defense. However, after Gettysburg, Jenkins and his men returned to duty in

southwest Virginia and no longer served with the Army of Northern Virginia.

3. In the Confederate army, brigades and divisions were habitually referred to in official correspondence by their commander's name (e.g.: Hampton's Brigade) a convention followed throughout this work. In contrast, in the Union army, divisions and brigades were officially referred to by their numeric designation. For example, Custer's brigade was the 1st Brigade of the 1st Division,

4. In May 1863, Wickham was elected to the Confederate Congress but had not yet left the army to take his seat in Richmond.

5. OR, 27, III:1006. After Gettysburg, the 4th and 5th North Carolina, the two regiments under Robertson's command, together mustered only 300 men.

6. OR 27, III:1069. Stuart and Robert E. Lee both shared the view that Robertson was perhaps a good trainer and administrator, but was a poor combat commander. Robertson remained on duty on the coast of South Carolina and Georgia until the area was evacuated because of Sherman's advance. After the war he lived briefly in Memphis, and then moved to Washington, D.C. where he was employed in real estate. He died on November 12, 1910, at the age of 83, outliving all the general officers serving with Stuart's cavalry at the time except for Lunsford Lomax (Association of Graduates, United States Military Academy, *Annual Reunion* [West Point, NY, 1911], 91–93).

7. By orders dated June 9, 1864, Baker was assigned to command of the Second District in the Department of North Carolina and Southern Virginia with headquarters in Goldsborough, North Carolina, a position he held until the end of the war (OR, 36, III:876). Afterward, he went into farming, and from 1878 until his death in 1907 he was employed as a railroad station agent in Suffolk, Virginia (Warner, *Generals In Gray*, 15; AOG, USMA, *Annual Reunion* [1908], 83).

8. Edward Longacre, *Lee's Cavalrymen: A History of the Mounted Forces of the Army of Northern Virginia* (Mechanicsburg, PA: Stackpole, 2002), 246. Jones was killed in action at Piedmont near Waynesboro on June 5, 1864.

9. Following a successful raid into West Virginia in February 1864, Rosser and his brigade's performance were praised by both JEB Stuart and Robert E. Lee. Stuart, in his endorsement wrote, "The bold and successful enterprise herein reported furnishes additional proofs of General Rosser's merit as a commander, and adds fresh laurels to that veteran brigade so signalized for valor already." Later Rosser began referring to his brigade as the Laurel Brigade and encouraged his men to wear a sprig of laurel on their uniform (OR, 33:45–46; , Millard K Bushong and Dean M. Bushong, *Fightin' Tom Rosser, C.S.A.* [Shippensburg, PA: Beidel, 1983], 75).

10. In his letter to General Samuel Cooper recommending Lee's promotion, Stuart—in addition to effusively praising Lee's valor and capacity as a cavalry commander—proposed creating a division consisting of Chambliss's and Rosser's brigades to create Lee's major general billet (Stuart, *Letters*, 377–378). Upon receiving orders from the War Department to organize Lee's division with Chambliss's and Gordon's brigades, Stuart wrote to the Secretary of War requesting that he reconsider. Stuart pointed out that part of the North Carolina Brigade was detached and not available at the present, that Rosser—by virtue of his seniority—should be the senior brigadier in a division, and that assigning Rosser's brigade to Lee's division would more equally distribute the manpower among the three cavalry divisions (Ibid., 387–388). The elements of the North Carolina Brigade on detached service were directed to return to the Army of Northern Virginia by the War Department on May 2, 1864 (OR, 36, II:941).

11. Letter, Robert E. Lee to Wm. F. Lee, April 24, 1864 (GLC05979), New York: Gilder Lehrman Institute.

12. Walter Clark, ed., *Histories of the Several Regiments and Battalions from North Carolina in the Great War 1861–65: Written by Members of the Respective Commands*, 5 vols. (Raleigh: E.M. Uzzell, Printer and Binder, 1901; reprint ed., Wendell, NC: Broadfoot's Bookmark, 1982), 3:592. This special order is not in the *Official Records*.

13. Since the end of March, Hampton had been in South Carolina arranging for fresh regiments from the Deep South to be sent to the Army of Northern Virginia. He left Columbia on the evening of April 27, and returned to his division headquarters on May 2. On that day, Hampton advised Stuart that he had an effective strength of only 637 men and requested that his division be "concentrated" in preparation for the coming action. On May 5, Hampton informed Robert E. Lee—he "feared Stuart was absent"—that if General Gordon's Brigade were to be reassigned, he would be left 200 men under his command (Rosser's Brigade was still en route from the Shenandoah Valley) (Cisco, *Wade Hampton*, 133–134; OR, 36, III:941, 953–954). It is not clear whether or to what degree Hampton was consulted on the organization of a third division before he returned to Virginia. However, the messages cited above indicate clearly that he wished to forestall the reorganization.

14. OR, 36, II:954. Due in part to Hampton's foot-dragging, Rooney Lee did not receive Gordon's Brigade before the Army of the Potomac crossed the Rapidan River to begin the Overland Campaign. Once Sheridan's Richmond Raid had begun, Stuart directed Gordon to pursue and harass the Union raiding column while he, with Fitz Lee's division, marched rapidly to block Sheridan before he could reach Richmond. Gordon was mortally wounded fighting Sheridan's forces at Meadow Bridge on May 12, 1864, and died in Richmond six days later (Longacre, *Lee's Cavalrymen*, 290).

15. Letter, JEB Stuart to Flora Stuart, September 11, 1863, Richmond (Virginia Historical Society).

16. For example, Emory Thomas wrote: "For his part, Lee seemed to have used the non-promotion to chasten Stuart without injuring him. Stuart had not lost Lee's favor; yet Lee seemed increasingly to assume an avuncular tone in correspondence with his cavalry commander—as though Stuart needed more guidance and instruction" (Emory Thomas, *Bold Dragoon: The Life of J.E.B. Stuart* [New York: Harper & Row, 1986], 261).

17. Freeman, *Lee's Lieutenants*, 2:211–212.

18. OR, 25,II:836.

19. For example, on the bi-monthly strength returns for the January through April 1864, the average aggregate present for duty strength for Ewell's Corps was 19,025, for Hill's Corps it was 21,259, and for the cavalry corps it was 6,488. No returns were provided for Longstreet's Corps, which was on detached service in Tennessee.

20. Naturally, there are trade-offs when modifying the structure of military units. For example, to achieve the combat power of a brigade with five regiments, a commander might have to employ two brigades or a single division. Also, larger units may be better able to maintain their operational capability during sustained operations.

Chapter 4

1. Robert Driver, Jr., *1st Virginia Cavalry* (Lynchburg, VA: H.E. Howard, 1991), 159; Lee A. Wallace, Jr., *A Guide*

to Virginia Military Organizations 1861–1865 (Richmond: Virginia Civil War Commission, 1964), 46–47.

2. Kenneth L. Stiles, *4th Virginia Cavalry* (Lynchburg, VA: H.E. Howard, 1985), 130, 132. It appears that Payne, who was promoted to brigadier general in November 1864, saw very limited duty with the 4th Virginia after his exchange. Randolph was shot in the head and killed at Meadow Bridge on May 12, 1864.

3. Walbrook D. Swank, ed., *Sabers, Saddles and Spurs: Lieutenant Colonel William R. Carter, CSA* (Shippensburg, PA: Burd Street, 1998), 3. During the Bristoe Campaign in October 1863, Owen commanded Wickham's Brigade and Carter commanded the regiment. On May 7, 1864, Owen was shot in the hand at Todd's Tavern. The bullet severed his second finger (Thomas P. Nanzig, *3rd Virginia Cavalry* [Lynchburg, VA: H.E. Howard, 1989], 121).

4. Upon his promotion to brigadier general, Rosser wrote to Lomax recommending that Pate not be advanced to the grade of colonel. However, the board of officers who evaluated Pate considered him qualified and he was duly promoted.

5. Robert Driver, Jr., *5th Virginia Cavalry* (Lynchburg, VA: H.E. Howard, 1997), 55, 242.

6. According to regulations, the promotion should have been made from among the qualified officers of the regiment based upon the recommendation of a board of officers.

7. Michael Musick, *6th Virginia Cavalry* (Lynchburg, VA: H.E. Howard, 1990), 115, 119, 122. Harrison was retired to the Invalid Corps in March 1865. Flournoy was killed at Cold Harbor on May 31, 1864.

8. John Fortier, *15th Virginia Cavalry* (Lynchburg, VA: H.E. Howard, 1993), 120, 127, 129. Critcher was captured as a result of his own poor judgment. He left his regiment purportedly to travel to his home in Westmoreland County to attend a funeral. Unfortunately for Critcher, on May 23 he encountered a Union raiding party and was taken prisoner (Fortier, *15th Virginia Cavalry*, 30–31).

9. Daniel Balfour, *13th Virginia Cavalry* (Lynchburg, VA: H.E. Howard, 1986), 93.

10. Robert K. Krick, *9th Virginia Cavalry* (Lynchburg, VA: H.E. Howard, 1982), 57. Beale was wounded—shot in the leg—on September 13, 1863, near Brandy Station. As a result, he was absent for three months while convalescing. He rejoined his regiment near Charlottesville on Christmas Day (R.L.T. Beale, *History of the Ninth Virginia Cavalry in the War Between the States* [Richmond: B.F. Johnson, 1899], 106–7).

11. Robert Driver, Jr., *10th Virginia Cavalry* (Lynchburg, VA: H.E. Howard, 1992), 100, 107.

12. Neil H. Raiford, *4th North Carolina Cavalry in the Civil War* (Jefferson, NC: McFarland, 2003), 127, 158, 162. Payne had captured a prisoner who was being marched to the rear through the yard of a tannery. The prisoner picked up a carbine lying on the ground and shot Payne's horse. The horse, struggling as it went down, threw Payne into a vat of dye. According to the now-former Yankee prisoner, as he emerged from the dye, Payne "presented a laughable sight."

13. Ibid., 221; Bruce S. Allardice, *Confederate Colonels: A Biographical Registry* (Columbia: University of Missouri Press, 2008), 44, 325. Robinson, who was born in Canada, was a West Point classmate of Solomon Williams, both having graduated in 1859. He was apparently not held in particularly high regard. One officer wrote that Robinson was "incompetent to command cavalry," and that he was "one of the most unprincipled dogs that walk the earth."

14. Chris J. Hartley, *Stuart's Tarheels: James B. Gordon and His North Carolina Cavalry in the Civil War* (Jefferson, NC: McFarland, 2d ed., 2011), 146.

15. Clark, ed. *Histories of the Several Regiments and Battalions from North Carolina*, 3:572; Robert Krick, *Lee's Colonels: A Biographical Registry of the Field Officers of the Army of Northern Virginia*, 4th ed., revised (Dayton: Morningside, 1992), 132; Allardice, *Confederate Colonels*, 270. Stephen Evans is mentioned only once after assuming command in the regimental history contained in Clark's *Histories*. Evans was retired to the Invalid Corps on January 28, 1865. McNeill was killed in action at Chamberlain Run on March 31, 1865.

16. William D. Henderson, *The Road to Bristoe Station: Campaigning with Lee and Meade, August 1–October 20, 1863* (Lynchburg, VA: H.W. Howard, 1987), 158–159; Rufus Barringer, *The First North Carolina. A Famous Cavalry Regiment* (Np. Nd), 7–8; Clark, ed., *Histories of the Several Regiments and Battalions from North Carolina* 3:418. The engagement at Auburn where Ruffin was mortally wounded is sometimes called the Battle of Coffee Hill—Stuart's artillery began the engagement by opened fire on Warren's men as they stacked arms and began brewing their morning coffee. Ruffin fell into Union hands and died on October 18 in Alexandria.

17. Raiford, *4th North Carolina Cavalry*, 92.

18. Dearing, a Virginian, resigned from West Point in April 1861 to accept a commission in the Washington Artillery of New Orleans. After almost three years' service with the artillery, Dearing received a colonel's commission in the cavalry and was assigned to command of a detachment of cavalry in Major General George Pickett's infantry division. Dearing was then promoted to brigadier on April 29, 1864, four days shy of his 24th birthday. Dearing was mortally wounded at High Bridge on April 6, 1865, in a one-on-one gunfight with Union Lieutenant Colonel (brevet brigadier general) Theodore Read. Read was killed in the encounter while Dearing died in Lynchburg on April 22, 1865 (Raiford, *4th North Carolina Cavalry*, 67, 89–90; Warner, *Generals in Gray*, 69–70; Roger D. Hunt and Jack R. Brown, *Brevet Brigadier Generals in Blue* [Gaithersburg, MD: Olde Soldier Books, 1990; revised ed. 1997], 500). Colonel Dennis Ferebee remained in command of the 4th North Carolina until he resigned his commission in March 1865. After the war he served one term as sheriff of Camden County, North Carolina, where he was described as "what a gentleman should be." He died in Camden County in 1878 (Raiford, *4th North Carolina Cavalry*, 92).

19. Richard L. Armstrong, *7th Virginia Cavalry* (Lynchburg, VA: H.E. Howard, 1992), 139.

20. Ibid., 22, 143. The 7th Virginia, when commanded by Brigadier General Turner Ashby, grew to strength of twenty-nine companies, almost three times the size of a standard regiment. Upon Ashby's death, the regiment was split apart. Seven companies were organized into the 17th Battalion Virginia Cavalry with Funsten as its commander. In January and February 1863, the War Department added three companies to the 17th Battalion to form the 11th Regiment Virginia Cavalry (Wallace Jr., *A Guide to Virginia Military Organizations 1861–1865*, 65). As the battalion commander, Funsten was the logical choice for regimental commander, and he desired the appointment. Further, the officers of the regiment signed a petition recommending his appointment. However, since the regiment was newly organized, regulations gave the president of the Confederacy the authority to appoint the commander. Stuart arranged for the appointment of Lomax. Lomax graduated from West Point in 1856, two years behind Stuart, and both

had served together in the 1st US Cavalry in Kansas during the years before the Civil War. At the time of the appointment, Lomax was serving as an inspector general in Tennessee (Richard L. Armstrong, *11th Virginia Cavalry* [Lynchburg, VA: H.E. Howard, 1989], 22; George W. Cullum, *Biographical Register of the Officers and Graduates of the U.S. Military Academy at West Point, N.Y. From its Establishment in 1802, to 1890 with the Early History of the United States Military Academy*, 3 vols., 3rd ed. [New York: Houghton Mifflin, 1891], #1731; Warner, *Generals in Gray*, 191). Shortly after assuming command, Funsten appointed his son, Oliver R. Funsten, Jr., to the position of regimental adjutant in the grade of first lieutenant (Armstrong, *11th Virginia Cavalry*, 143).

21. Dennis E. Frye, *12th Virginia Cavalry*, 2nd ed. (Lynchburg, VA: H.E. Howard, 1988), 134, 149.

22. Wallace, *A Guide to Virginia Military Organizations*, 67; John E. Devine, *35th Battalion Virginia Cavalry* (Lynchburg, VA: H.E. Howard, 1985), 12–13.

23. Donald A. Hopkins, *Horsemen of the Jeff Davis Legion: The Expanded Roster of the Men and Officers of the Jeff Davis Legion, Cavalry* (Shippensburg, PA: White Mane, 1999), 103.

24. Richard M. Coffman, *Going Back the Way They Came: A History of the Phillips Georgia Legion Cavalry Battalion* (Macon, GA: Mercer University Press, 2011), 136; Lt. Col William Wofford Rich, http://www.anglefire.com/ga2/PhillipsLegion/rich/html.

25. Lynwood M. Holland, *Pierce M.B. Young: The Warwick of the South* (Athens: University of Georgia Press, 1964, reprint, 2009), 77–78.

26. Harriet Bey Mesic, *Cobb's Legion Cavalry: A History and Roster of the Ninth Georgia Volunteers in the Civil War* (Jefferson, NC: McFarland, 2009), 215–216.

27. Ibid., 177–178; Bruce S. Allardice, *More Generals in Gray* (Baton Rouge: Louisiana State University Press, 1995), 239.

28. For a succinct discussion of the challenges faced by the Confederate Ordnance Department, see Wagner, et al., eds. *The Library of Congress Civil War Desk Reference*, 489–491.

29. For example, 8,283 smooth-bore flintlock muskets were seized from federal arsenals (*OR*, Series IV, 1:292).

30. Colonel Gorgas, the Confederacy's Chief of Ordnance, estimated that his department had sufficient machinery to manufacture 300 weapons—both rifles and pistols—per day if his department's manpower was increased by 500 or 600 workers (*OR*, Series IV, 3:677).

31. From September 30, 1862, until September 30, 1863, the Confederacy manufactured 28,000 small arms in its arsenals and imported 113,504 small arms from Europe (*OR*, Series IV, 3:296–297). During the period July 1, 1862, until December 31, 1863, also arranged for the shipment of 16,178 cavalry sabers through the blockade. Small arms were just part of the Confederacy's effort to import war materiel from Europe. The Confederate Ordnance Department also purchased and shipped through the Federal blockade artillery pieces, ammunition, powder, saddles, harnesses, and other accoutrement. Also, large quantities of quartermaster stocks—such as clothing and boots—were purchased in Europe and shipped to the South through the blockade (*OR*, Series IV, 2:382–383).

32. During the war, the U.S. Army purchased 10,000 or more breach loading carbines in ten different designs (Burnside, Gallager, Joslyn, Merrill, Maynard, Remington, Sharps, Smith, Spencer, and Starr). The Army also purchased carbines in smaller quantities from nine other manufacturers (Berkeley R. Lewis, "Notes on Ammunition of the American Civil War 1861–1865" [Washington, D.C.: American Ordnance Association, 1959], table: Ordnance and Ordnance Stores Purchased by the Ordnance Department, U.S.A.).

33. For example, Culpeper's Little Fork Rangers, Company D, 4th Virginia, mustered into service on June 30, 1861, with four officers, nine sergeants and corporals, and forty-four privates, of whom only thirty-six had horses at the time. The average appraised value for the officers' horses was $143; the non-commissioned officers' horses appraised at $133; the privates' horses appraised at $120. The most valuable horse, appraised at $190, was owned by eighteen-year-old private James W. McDonald. The least valuable horse, owned by eighteen-year-old private Silas M. Newhouse, was appraised at $75 (Woodford B. Hackley, *The Little Fork Rangers: A Sketch of Company "D" Fourth Virginia Cavalry* [Richmond: Dirtz Printing Co., 1927, reprint, Stephens City, VA: Commercial Press, 1999], 31–20).

34. Those dismounted troopers who were unable to obtain horses were subject to transfer to the infantry.

35. Boteler was a prominent farmer from Shepherdstown, now West Virginia. Upon the secession of Virginia, Boteler resigned from the U.S. House of Representatives, where he was serving his first term. Earlier in the war, he had served as a volunteer aide to Stonewall Jackson. Following Stuart's death, Boteler was commissioned as a colonel and appointed presiding judge of a military court. After the war he returned to Shepherdstown where he was active in business and held several governmental appointments at both the state and federal levels. He died in Shepherdstown in 1892 (Robert Trout, *They Followed the Plume: The Story of J.E.B. Stuart and His Staff* [Mechanicsburg, PA: Stackpole, 1993], 67–72).

36. *OR*, Series IV, 2:718–721.

37. Ibid. Gorgas, in his endorsement, stated that "officers of great experience pronounce in favor of the muzzle loading carbine" and offered to provide a model for Stuart for examination by his officers. Some of Chambliss's criticism—soldiers detailed from their regiments; compensation for lost horses; improved veterinary care—were not within the purview of the Chief of Ordnance.

Chapter 5

1. *OR*, 33:1086. Lee was likely referring to the Rutledge Mounted Riflemen, a South Carolina militia company raised by Captain William Trenholm. That company had been split into a two-company squadron and eventually incorporated into the 7th South Carolina Cavalry. Captain Benjamin H. Rutledge's cavalry company was better known as the Charleston Light Dragoons, a militia company with lineage dating back to before the revolution. At the beginning of 1864, Rutledge assumed command of the newly-formed 4th South Carolina and his former company was under the command of Captain Richard H. Colock. Although well over strength for the first three years of the war, the "Drags" as they were called, had not been split to form additional companies (W. Eric Emerson, *Sons of Privilege: The Charleston Light Dragoons in the Civil War* [Columbia: University of South Carolina Press, 2005], 122–123, 137; Edward L. Wells, *Charleston Light Dragoons* [Charleston, SC: Lucas, Richardson, 1888; reprint, Camden, SC: J.J. Fox, Nd], 4, 28).

2. *OR*, 33:1097–1098. Lee went on to recommend that should the War Department not have authority to correct the conscription abuse problem, it be addressed by the Confederate Congress. The strength figures for the South Carolina regiments were provided to Lee by Hampton. It is likely that the figures were given to Hampton by Butler, who was

in South Carolina at the time recuperating from the loss of his foot at Brandy Station.

3. *OR*, 35, I:627–628.

4. Samuel Cooper, who graduated from West Point in 1815, was appointed Adjutant General of the Regular Army in 1852. Although he was born in New York, he married a Virginian and in March 1861 resigned his regular commission and volunteered his services to the Confederacy. He was the senior general officer serving in the Confederate Army (Warner, *Generals in Gray*, 63–64).

5. In his diary entry for January 26, 1864, John B. Jones, a clerk in the Confederate War Department, recorded: "Gen. Lee recommends the formation of several more brigades of cavalry, mostly from regiments and companies in South Carolina, and to this he anticipates objections on the part of the generals and governors along the Southern seaboard; but he deems it necessary, as the enemy facing him has a vastly superior cavalry force" (Jones, *A Rebel War Clerk's Diary*, 2:135). This entry indicates that it is likely that at some time in late January Lee and Davis discussed swapping worn-out regiments for fresh regiments from the Deep South.

6. *OR*, 35:628–629. The order also established maximum strengths for heavy and light artillery companies.

7. *OR*, 33:1118–1119.

8. *OR*, 33:1125.

9. *OR*, 29, II:862. A Confederate cavalryman whose horse died or went lame could be issued a "horse pass" which allowed him to travel home to secure a new mount, commonly from the soldier's family farm. However, given the distance to South Carolina, Georgia, Alabama, and Mississippi, it was generally impractical to allow soldiers from those states to travel home. Consequently, many of those soldiers were forced to purchase remounts in Virginia. As the war progressed, the supply of horses diminished and prices rose beyond the means of many soldiers. Cavalrymen who were temporarily dismounted remained with their unit, generally aggregated into a "Company Q" within each regiment. Later in the war, it became common to consolidate soldiers without horses in a dismounted battalion within a brigade. Cavalrymen who were permanently dismounted were subject for transfer to the infantry.

10. *OR*, 29, II: 862. Regarding the 5th Georgia, Hampton wrote that "Anderson's regiment desires to come on." Robert H. Anderson, an 1857 graduate of West Point, was at the time commanding the 5th Georgia Cavalry. In the spring of 1863, Anderson wrote to Robert E. Lee advising that his regiment was not needed around Savannah and requesting that the regiment be ordered to join Stuart's division. In his letter to the War Department, Lee opined that the regiment was not needed in Georgia, although he admitted that General Beauregard might disagree. Lee also advised the War Department that if he were not sent to Virginia, Anderson would apply for transfer to Tennessee. Anderson and his regiment were sent to Tennessee in the spring of 1864 to serve in Major General Joseph Wheeler's cavalry division (*OR*, 25, II: 741).

11. *OR*, 29, II:862–863.

12. Charles F. Cauthen, ed., *Family Letters of the Three Wade Hamptons, 1782–1901* (Columbia: University of South Carolina Press, 1953), 100–101.

13. *OR*, 33:1088–1089.

14. *OR*, 33:1140, 1145.

15. *OR*, 33:1153.

16. *OR*, 33:1154.

17. *OR*, 33:1154. It is not clear from the endorsement whether Lee had been informed of Davis' January 22 thoughts on swapping full regiments for "skeletons."

18. *OR*, 33:1163–1164. The *Official Records* do not contain an endorsement from Lee for this communication.

19. *OR*, 33:1155.

20. *OR*, 33:1229–1230. Apparently the name of the general who ordered the brigade to picket the lower Rappahannock was either illegible or missing, and the editors of the *OR* inserted "Lee?" as their best guess. It seems unlikely that Robert E. Lee involved himself in the specific positioning of cavalry brigades. It is more likely that he would defer such decisions to Stuart, the corps commander.

21. *OR*, 35, II:362.

22. David G. Douglas, *A Boot Full of Memories: Captain Leonard Williams, 2nd S.C. Cavalry* (Camden, SC: Gray Fox, 2003), 336, 338.

23. John Logan Black, *Crumbling Defenses*, ed. by Eleanor McSwain (Macon, GA: McSwain, 1960), 71–72. Black attended West Point with the class of 1854 but left before graduating.

24. *OR*, 35, II:364. Jordan graduated second from the bottom in his 1840 class at West Point, where he roomed with William Tecumseh Sherman. He had been wounded at Shiloh while on Joseph Johnston's staff, and was promoted to brigadier general for his gallantry on the field that day. Thus far in the war, nearly all of Jordan's duty had been as a staff officer (Warner, *Generals in Gray*, 167–168).

25. *OR*, 35, II:364.

26. *OR*, 35, II:364–365.

27. *OR*, 33:1232. Special Order Number 65 was based upon recommendations presented to Cooper on March 14 by Major Samuel Melton, one of Cooper's staff officers. For insight into the Adjutant General's understanding of field units distant from Richmond and its internal staff procedures, see *OR* 51, II:835–837. Also in the order, the Holcomb Legion, later the 7th South Carolina, was assigned to the Department of Richmond. The 7th South Carolina served with the Army of Northern Virginia only during the retreat from Richmond to Appomattox. Special Order Number 65 also directed that the Hampton Legion, then an infantry regiment, proceed from East Tennessee, where it was serving with Longstreet's Corps, to Greenville, South Carolina. There the officers and men were to receive twenty-day furloughs for the purpose of obtaining horses for service as mounted infantry. Afterward, the Legion was to march to Richmond for duty on the Peninsula. In making this recommendation to General Cooper, Major Melton wrote of the Hampton Legion's commander: "Colonel [Martin W.] Gary has been in more battles perhaps, than any officer of his grade in the service. He is a thoroughbred fighter, cool and deliberate, with great good sense, and that rare quality which enables him to make men confident and firm under him. We need such a man to meet sudden advances upon the capital with his band of trained veterans—men who have fought often as infantry alone can fight" (*OR*, 51, II:837). Colonel Gary would find opportunity to again show his mettle on June 24 at Samaria Church. After the implementation of Special Order 65, Hart's Battery was the sole element of the original Hampton Legion remaining with the Army of Northern Virginia.

28. The three generals were well acquainted. Bragg, Beauregard, and Jordan had been cadets together at West Point in the classes of 1837, 1838, and 1840 respectively. Jordan had served under Beauregard since First Manassas, and all three served together under Albert Sidney Johnston in Mississippi. At Shiloh, Beauregard was Johnston's deputy commander. Bragg, a corps commander, also acted as Johnston's chief of staff. Jordan served as Johnston's assistant adjutant general. After Johnston's death, Beauregard assumed

command of the Army of Tennessee, only to be removed by Jefferson Davis and be replaced by Bragg two months later. Beauregard, who considered himself wronged, from that time felt great animosity toward Jefferson Davis and perhaps those feelings clouded Jordan's attitude toward Bragg. However, this error by Jordan was not his only—or even most serious—error in judgment with regard to the transfer of cavalry from South Carolina. See Jefferson Davis, *Rise and Fall of the Confederate Government*, 2 vols. (New York: Thomas Yoseloff, 1958), 74–75, for Davis' justification for Beauregard's relief from command.

29. *OR*, 35,II:372–373.
30. *OR*, 35, II:373–374.
31. *OR*, 35, II:379–380.
32. *OR*, 35, II:374–375. There is no indication in the *Official Records* that the telegram was intercepted by the Union. In his diary entry for March 25, 1864, John B. Jones, the War Department clerk, recorded a lengthy account of the Charleston telegraph delivered by Congressman Miles. He wrote that Seddon sent the telegraph to Bragg with a note advising that "the citizens signing it were the most *influential* in the state, etc." and that "Gen. Bragg sent it back [to Miles] with an indignant note." He added that Bragg, in the note, wrote that disclosing military matters "ought not to be suffered to pass without a merited rebuke." He went on to opine that "poor Beauregard" would receive the rebuke because "all the military and civil functionaries near the government partake of something of a dislike for him" (Jones, *A Rebel War Clerk's Diary*, 2:176).
33. *OR*, 33:1243.
34. *OR*, 33:1243–1243.
35. *OR*, 33:1258.
36. *OR*, 33:1258–1259. Colonel Rhett was the son of U.S. Senator Robert B. Rhett. On September 5, 1862, Rhett killed his superior, Colonel William R. Calhoun, a nephew of John C. Calhoun, in a duel. Rhett was cashiered for dueling, but in an ironic twist he was pardoned by Beauregard and promoted to colonel to fill the vacancy created by Calhoun's death (Allardice, *Confederate Colonels*, 87, 321).
37. *OR*, 33:1259.
38. *OR*, 33:1258.
39. *OR*, 33:1258–1260.
40. *OR*, 33:1260. In apparent reference to Congressman Miles's communication, Cooper also directed his staff to "let me have these papers after you have done with them, for submission to the President in the case of General Jordan." On May 4, 1864, Cooper's office relieved Jordan from general staff duty. Under departmental orders issued in Charleston, Jordan was subsequently assigned to command of the Third Military District of South Carolina, a command of roughly 1800 officers and men and 17 pieces of artillery with headquarters at Pocotaglio. After South Carolina was overrun by Sherman, Jordan joined Beauregard in North Carolina where he remained until the end of the war in an unofficial capacity. In 1869, Jordan went to Cuba where he served as commander of the insurrectionists fighting for independence from Spain. That endeavor was unsuccessful and Jordan escaped from Cuba in an open boat with a price on his head. Afterward, Jordan moved to New York where he founded and edited a magazine, the *Financial and Mining Record*. Jordan died in New York City in November 1895 (AOG, USMA, *Annual Reunion* [1896], 77–81).
41. George F. Price, *Across the Continent with the Fifth Cavalry* (New York: Noble, 1883; reprint, New York: Antiquarian, 1959), 466–468. Jenifer attended West Point with the class of 1845, but left before graduation. Nonetheless, he received a commission in the Regiment of Mounted Rifles during the Mexican War. Discharged after the war, Jenifer later received a commission in the 2nd U.S. Cavalry when that regiment was organized in 1855. At the outbreak of the war, Jenifer resigned from the regular army and accepted a commission from the Confederacy. As he traveled south from Carlisle Barracks, he was arrested by Pennsylvania authorities and briefly held in irons. Early in the war he commanded the 8th Virginia Cavalry, but was voted out of his colonel's billet during the reorganization of the army in the spring of 1862. For most the remainder of the war, Jenifer served as an inspector of cavalry in southern Alabama. After the war, Jenifer spent five years in Egypt as inspector of cavalry for the Khedive. He died in Richmond in 1878 of a throat ailment. Jenifer was not highly regarded by many of his contemporaries. Always known for his fine mounts, one officer observed that Jenifer's horses showed more sense than Jenifer did (Ibid.; Allardice, *Confederate Colonels*, 213).

42. In a letter to Colonel Josiah Gorgas, the Confederacy's Chief of Ordnance, dated June 8, 1863, Robert E. Lee wrote that had had been advised by cavalry officers that the saddles manufactured in Richmond ruined the horses' backs. Specifically, he added, "It is the tree of the Richmond saddle that is complained of" (Lee, *Wartime Papers*, 2:504).

43. Nailing iron shoes onto horses' hooves came into regular practice around 1000 A.D., although there is some evidence that the technique was known several hundred years earlier. By the beginning of the Civil War, modern industrial practices were having an effect on horse shoeing practices, at least for the Union forces. In 1834, Henry Burden of Troy, New York, patented a machine for manufacturing horseshoes. During the war, his much improved machine could produce sixty shoes per minute. Machines to manufacture horseshoe nails were developed in 1840. "Burden Shoes" were commonly issued to Federal units, reducing the need for blacksmiths to create shoes one-by-one from iron bar stock using their forges, tongs, and hammers. In contrast, the Confederate War Department awarded contracts to privately owned foundries for the manual production of horseshoes using forge and hammer. During the course of the war the Confederacy purchased 267,000 pounds of horseshoes, which sounds like a significant quantity of shoes. However, a modern shoe for a medium-size horse weighs approximately ¾ pound, or three pounds for a full set of shoes. Since horses require shoeing approximately eight times per year, each horse would consume twenty-four pounds of shoes annually. Thus the shoes purchased in bulk by the War Department would only be sufficient to shoe JEB Stuart's cavalry corps for a year, more or less (Karl D. Butler, *Principles of Horseshoeing II: An Illustrated Textbook of Farrier Science and Craftsmanship* [Laporte, CO: Butler Publishing, 1983], 25; Wagner, et al., eds., *The Library of Congress Civil War Desk Reference*, 490).

44. At the beginning of the Civil War the Confederacy had available several thousand breech loading carbines. Federal arsenals in Southern states held 1881 Hall carbines, which were issued to the regular army beginning in 1833. Also, several Southern states purchased 2,369 Maynard carbines from the Massachusetts factory before the outbreak of hostilities. During the war close to 5,000 Sharps carbines were produced in Richmond and roughly 1,000 Morse carbines were produced in Greenville, South Carolina (Henry Woodhead, ed., *Arms and Equipment of the Confederacy* [Alexandria, VA: Time-Life Books, 1996], 46–48). However, many of the breech-loaders carried by Confederate

cavalrymen were of Union manufacture, either taken from captured Federal troopers or scavenged on battlefields.

45. Wells, *Charleston Light Dragoons*, 14.

46. Cisco, *Wade Hampton*, 133.

47. Carolyn Clay Swiggart, *Shades of Gray: The Clay and McAllister Families of Bryan County, Georgia during the Plantation Years (ca. 1760–1888)* (Darien, CT: Two Bytes, 1999), 62–63. P.M.B. Young, who reviewed the troops in Hampton's absence, rode one of McAllister's horses, a mare named Mina. Mina was apparently a very attractive horse, since McAllister wrote to his sister that "a great many of the girls after the review came up and begged me not to take so pretty a creature to the wars." (Ibid., 63.)

48. *Charleston Light Dragoons*, 32.

49. *Daily South Carolinian*, April 23, 1864.

50. Many riders find riding one horse while leading another—commonly called "ponying"—to be a tiresome activity.

51. Stewart Sifakis, *South Carolina and Georgia*, vol. 9, *Compendium of the Confederate Armies* (New York: Facts on File, 1995), 42.

52. Allardice, *Confederate Colonels*, 331; Samuel J. Martin, *Southern Hero: Matthew Calbraith Butler, Confederate General, Hampton Red Shirt, and U.S. Senator* (Mechanicsburg, PA: Stackpole, 2001), 82.

53. William Stokes, *Saddle Soldiers: The Civil War Correspondence of General William Stokes of the 4th South Carolina Cavalry*, edited by Lloyd Halliburton (Orangeburg, SC: Sandlapper, 1993), 133.

54. Hewett, et al., eds., *Supplement*, I, 6:446–448; Eric W. Emerson, *Sons of Privilege*, 66.

55. Sifakis, *Compendium of the Confederate Armies*, 9:43.

56. Beauregard requested Ferguson's assignment in a letter to the War Department dated October 18, 1862, in which he wrote: "Lieutenant-Colonel Ferguson is a graduate of West Point, a cavalry officer of experience, both of regular and volunteer cavalry; served with distinction at the battle of Manassas and Shiloh; is a citizen and native of this immediate section of South Carolina, and there would seem to be entire propriety in his appointment to the command of South Carolina troops. I have great need of a cavalry officer of his experience, and I regard his appointment as of vital importance to the cavalry arm in this department" (*OR*, 14:644).

57. Warner, *Generals in Gray*, 67; AOG, USMA, *Annual Report* (1917), 99–104.

58. Warner, *Generals in Gray*, 78–79.

59. James Michael Barr, *Let Us Meet in Heaven: The Civil War Letters of James Michael Barr, 5th South Carolina Cavalry*, ed. Thomas D. Mays (Abilene, TX: McWhiney, 2001), 194.

60. Ibid., 203–204.

61. Alfred B. Mulligan, *"My Dear Mother & Sisters": Civil War Letters of Capt. A.B. Mulligan, Co. B 5th South Carolina Cavalry—Butler's Division—Hampton's Corps 1861–1865*, ed. Olin Fulmer Hutchinson, Jr. (Spartanburg, SC: Reprint, 1992), 104–105.

62. Ibid., 108.

63. Ibid., 112, 113, 115.

64. Ibid., 116–117.

65. Ibid., 118.

66. Ibid., 120.

67. Sifakis, *Compendium of the Confederate Armies*, 9:45.

68. *OR*, 28, I:196–197. Colonel Aiken, the regimental commander, reported that two Union bodies were said to be seen floating down the river the following day. He also reported capturing two brass six-pound cannons from the boat that had caught fire and been abandoned.

69. Allardice, *Confederate Colonels*, 39; Josiah Gorgas, *The Journals of Josiah Gorgas, 1857–1878*, ed. Sarah Woolfolk Wiggins (Tuscaloosa: University of Alabama Press, 1995), 255–256.

70. *OR*, 36, III:853.

71. *OR*, 36, III:852–854. The men moving north by train did not travel in a single group because of the limited trains between Greensboro and Richmond. Aiken, on his way north, visited the mounted detachment at Winnsborough, Charlotte, Greensboro, and Danville.

72. Sifakis, *Compendium of the Confederate Armies*, 9:157.

73. Colonel Robert Houston Anderson, an 1857 graduate of West Point, commanded the 5th Cavalry which was transferred to Tennessee where Anderson was promoted to brigadier and appointed to brigade command in July 1864 (Warner, *Generals in Gray*, 9–10).

74. John W. Latty, *Gallant Little 7th: A History of the 7th Georgia Cavalry Regiment* (Wilmington, NC: Broadfoot, 2004), 1–11. The father of Edward Anderson, Jr., who had been elected three times as mayor of Savannah, rose to the grade of colonel of artillery commanding the batteries in Savannah. He then served as commander in Charleston after Savannah was evacuated (Allardice, *Confederate Colonels*, 43).

75. *OR*, 35, I:542. The 21st Georgia Battalion had a strength of 396, The 24th Georgia Battalion had a strength of 298, and the Hardwick Mounted Rifles had a strength of 174.

76. Latty, *Gallant Little 7th*, 24, 46, 56.

77. Ibid., 13–15; Allardice, *Confederate Colonels*, 393.

78. Ibid., 195–201. Captain Bowen, who was born in Rhode Island, was held in confinement at Charleston until the city was captured by Union forces. Afterward, he worked for Federal authorities during reconstruction. As a Republican, he served two terms in the U.S. House of Representatives. In 1875, Bowen was tried for White's murder but acquitted.

79. Swiggart, *Shades of Gray*, 49–56. Fort McAllister is today a Georgia State Park.

80. Ibid., 64–69.

81. Ibid., 71.

82. Sifakis, *Compendium of the Confederate Armies*, 9:162; *OR*, 35, I:542.

83. Hewett, *Supplement*, II, 5:624.

84. Donald A. Hopkins, *The Little Jeff: The Jeff Davis Legion, Cavalry, Army of Northern Virginia* (Shippensburg, PA: White Mane, 1999), 242–243; *OR*, 52, I:925. The orders directing the transfer of Love's Battalion to the Army of Northern Virginia are not in the *Official Records*.

85. *OR*, 51, II:925. By Special Order Number 161, dated July 11, 1864, the War Department assigned Love's Battalion to the Jeff Davis Legion. However, the transfer was not executed until November (*OR*, 40, III:763; Hopkins, *Horsemen of the Jeff Davis Legion*, 105).

86. William H. Locke to My Dear Wife, May 25, 1864, Civil War Letters of William Herrod Locke and William Horatio Thornton, 1859–1866 (Mss 13485), Albert and Shirley Small Special Collections Library, University of Virginia, Charlottesville.

87. Locke to My Dear Wife, May 28, 1864, Locke and Thornton Letters, 1859–1866 (Mss 13485). Locke is in error regarding either the day he arrived in Richmond or the extent of the delay on the rails. He wrote that he arrived in Richmond on Thursday evening, May 26, the day after he wrote to his wife from Greensboro.

88. Richard Coffman, *Going Back the Way They Came*, 126–127. In July, Love's Battalion was transferred to the Jeff Davis Legion.

89. Locke to My Dear Wife, May 29, 1864, Locke and Thornton Letters, 1859–1866 (Mss 13485).
90. Ibid.
91. *OR*, 36, III:808, 841.
92. Ulysses R. Brooks, *Butler and His Cavalry in the War of Secession, 1861–1865* (Columbia, SC: State, 1909; reprint ed., Camden, SC: Gray Fox, Nd), 216; *OR*, 36, III:853.
93. Manigault Diary, 401.

Chapter 6

1. George Gordon Meade, *The Life and Letters of George Gordon Meade, Major-General, United States Army*, 2 vols. (New York: Charles Scribner's Sons, 1913), 2:176.
2. Meade, *Life and Letters*, 2:182–183. In another opinion on Pleasonton's relief, in April 1864, Elizabeth "Libbie" Custer wrote to her mother from Washington that she had heard Pleasonton was removed, "not on account of feelings between him and Genl. Meade," but because Pleasonton's two sisters, who lived in the capital, spoke badly of President Lincoln and Secretary of War Stanton, and people believed they were repeating General Pleasonton's views (Marguerite Merington, ed., *The Custer Story: The Life and Intimate Letters of General Custer and His Wife Elizabeth* [New York: Devin-Adair, 1950], 91).
3. Ulysses S. Grant, *Personal Memoirs of U.S. Grant* (New York: Charles L. Webster, 1885; reprint, New York: Library of America, 1990), 480.
4. Edward Longacre, "Alfred Pleasonton: The Knight of Romance," in *Civil War Times Illustrated* 13 (December 1974): 18–20.
5. Joseph Hergesheimer, *Sheridan: A Military Narrative* (Boston: Houghton Mifflin, 1931), 8–12; Eric J. Wittenberg, *Little Phil: A Reassessment of the Civil War Leadership of Gen. Philip H. Sheridan* (Washington, D.C.: Potomac, 2002), 142–143. It would be natural for Sheridan to claim to be born in the United States given the widespread bias against the foreign-born at the time. Additionally, there was speculation that Sheridan later concealed his Irish birth because he contemplated seeking the nomination for President.
6. Sheridan, *Personal Memoirs*, 6. West Point's official records indicate that on September 9, 1851, Sheridan displayed "Insubordinate Conduct, using highly insulting and disrespectful language to a file closer of his company at drill[, a] Violation of the 134th paragraph of the Academic Regulations." As punishment, by Special Order Number 159, dated October 13, 1851, Sheridan was suspended from the Military Academy until August 28, 1852 (United States Military Academy Records [Records Group 404], Section 105, Registers of Punishments, United States Military Academy Library, West Point, NY). In the mid-1800s it was more common than in more recent years to "turn-back" cadets to a following class for disciplinary or academic reasons. Ten members of the class of 1853—roughly 20 percent of that year's graduates—entered the academy in 1848 with the class of 1852. A century later, only 12 of the 512 members of the class of 1953 came into the academy with the class of 1952. In his memoirs, Sheridan admitted that his actions were improper, despite his belief that Terrill had used an "irritating" tone of voice toward him. William R. Terrill, also a member of the class of 1853, graduated sixteenth of fifty-two. Although admitted to the academy from Virginia, Terrill remained loyal to the Union under an agreement that the War Department not ask him to serve in his home state. Terrill was promoted to brigadier general of volunteers in September 1862, and was mortally wounded at Perryville, Kentucky, a month later (Warner, *Generals in Blue*, 496–497).

7. Cullum, *Biographical Register*, #1612. Commissions for new graduates were dependent upon vacancies within the army's regiments, and sometimes the regiments were at their authorized strength for officers. In such cases, it was common for new academy graduates to initially receive commissions as brevet second lieutenants in their branch of service (e.g.: infantry). As vacancies occurred through the death, retirement, or resignation of more senior officers, the newly-brevetted officers would be promoted to second lieutenant and assigned to regiments with vacant billets.
8. Sheridan, *Personal Memoirs*, 96. Rienzi was wounded several times, but survived the war and lived until 1871. Afterward, Sheridan, who had renamed the horse "Winchester," had the horse's carcass stuffed. In 1923 Rienzi was donated to the Smithsonian where he remains on display in the Museum of American History. Rienzi, Mississippi, is located about eleven miles south of Corinth. Today it has a population of a little more than three hundred. Traditionally, a horse's height is measured in "hands." A hand is equal to four inches.
9. Roy Morris, Jr., *Sheridan: The Life and Wars of General Phil Sheridan* (New York: Crown Books, 1992), 153; Grant, *Personal Memoirs*, 348. In his memoirs, Grant further wrote that the selection of Sheridan relieved Pleasonton, but his decision was not a reflection on Pleasonton's abilities "for I do not know but that he had been as efficient as any other cavalry commander."
10. Sheridan, *Personal Memoirs*, 185. Sheridan selected Forsyth, who until then had been serving as the adjutant general of the regular infantry brigade in the Army of the Cumberland, as his chief of staff because Forsyth had experience with the Army of the Potomac. Forsyth, like Sheridan, was a turn back. He was admitted to West Point in 1851 and graduated five years later with the class of 1856. Forsyth served with the Army of the Potomac from March 1862 until May 1863 and for part of that time was on McClellan's staff. Earlier in his career Forsyth had served under Captain George Pickett during the occupation of the San Juan Islands in Puget Sound (Cullum, *Biographical Register*, #1738).
11. Sheridan, *Personal Memoirs*, 169.
12. Merington, ed., *The Custer Story*, 86.
13. The 1st Corps Chief of Artillery, Colonel Charles Wainwright—the son of a well-to-do farmer in Rhinebeck, New York—upon observing Sheridan in the Wilderness, wrote that "he is very short, close built, with rather a jolly face, but not a great one. He dresses and wears his hair much in the Bowery soap-lock style, and could easily pass himself off for one of the 'b'hoys'" (Charles S. Wainwright, *A Diary of Battle: The Personal, Journals of Colonel Charles S. Wainwright, 1861–1865*, ed. Alan Nevins [New York: Harcourt, Brace & World, 1962], 349). By "b'hoy," Wainwright was referring to young men from the lower echelon of New York society, including Irish immigrants from the Bowery.
14. Edward G. Longacre, *Jersey Cavaliers: A History of the First New Jersey Volunteer Cavalry, 1861–1865* (Hightown, NJ: Longstreet House, 1992), 170–171. During the Gettysburg Campaign, Wyndham was placed in command of the various detachments of cavalry around Washington, numbering more than 3,000 men. Afterwards, Wyndham remained in Washington, initially as commander of the Giesboro cavalry depot, while still encumbering the colonelcy of the 1st New Jersey Cavalry. Wyndham was mustered out of the service on June 5, 1864. Why Wyndham did not return to duty with the 1st New Jersey is unclear. There is speculation that he mismanaged financial accounts while in temporary command of the cavalry depot at Gies-

boro, or that he was he was involved in a plot to kidnap President Lincoln. It seems more likely, absent compelling evidence to the contrary, that he was merely a victim of Alfred Pleasonton's well-known prejudice against foreign-born officers (Ibid.; *Philadelphia Inquirer*, July 29, 1867).

15. In 1866, Whiting was reinstated in the army in the grade of major. He served with the cavalry in the West and was promoted to lieutenant colonel of the 6th Cavalry in 1869. In 1871 the War Department reduced the size of the army, and Whiting, who was excess to the army's needs, was discharged (Cullum, *Biographical Register*, #789).

16. Warner, *Generals in Blue*, 131.

17. Edward Longacre, *Lincoln's Cavalrymen: A History of the Mounted Forces of the Army of the Potomac* (Mechanicsburg, PA: Stockpole, 2000), 245. Sherman, warned of Kilpatrick's failings, reportedly remarked, "I know that Kilpatrick is a hell of a damned fool, but I want that sort of a man to command my cavalry" (Ibid.).

18. Although the Union order of battle in the *Official Records* indicates diCesnola was in command of a brigade at Brandy Station, it is possible that he was not present at that battle. While a June 10, 1863, account in the *New York Times* reported that diCesnola commanded the advance line of skirmishers and that his "cool bravery" set an example for the command, it is important to note that newspaper reporters did not accompany the cavalry on the foray into Culpeper and were thus not present during the battle. Further, diCesnola's regiment did not participate in the battle and he is not mentioned in the official reports or other accounts of the day's fighting.

19. *OR*, 29, I:114.

20. *OR*, 33:891.

21. Initially, Gregg commanded the 3rd Cavalry Division, but after reorganizations, his division was designated the 2nd Cavalry Division because Gregg was junior to Buford but senior to Kilpatrick.

22. Cullum, *Biographical Register*, #1684.

23. Warner, *Generals in Blue*, 666 n. 691; A.D. Slade, *A.T.A. Torbert: Southern Gentleman in Union Blue* (Dayton, OH: Morningside, 1992), 22–23.

24. Warner, *Generals in Blue*, 188, 502.

25. Slade, *A.T.A. Torbert*, 86–87.

26. Major General John Newton commanded the 3rd Division in the VI Corps before taking command of I Corps after the death of John Reynolds at Gettysburg. On July 6, 1863, Newton asked Meade to assign either Brigadier General David Russell or Torbert to command of the 3rd Division, VI Corps. Meade refused the request perhaps indicating that he had reservations about Torbert and/or Russell (*OR*, 27, II:556).

27. It is possible that Wilson was homosexual, which if true—and had become known—would have been highly problematic for the new general. One Grant biographer wrote that "there can be little doubt that Wilson was susceptible to the physical appeal of young men," and concluded that shortly before the war Wilson "engaged in what was almost certainly a homosexual affair" with a writer named Adam Badeau, who later served on Grant's staff as his private secretary (Geoffrey Perret, *Ulysses S. Grant: Soldier & President* [New York: Random House, 1997; reprint, New York: Modern Library, 1999], 292–293). Another Grant biographer more cautiously referred to Badeau as Wilson's "intimate associate" (Brooks Simpson, *Ulysses S. Grant: Triumph Over Adversity, 1822–1865* [New York: Houghton Mifflin, 2000], 279). Wilson, himself, described Badeau as a "modest, slender, and delicate man of agreeable manners and high intelligence," and added that Badeau was frequently his companion (James H. Wilson, *Under the Old Flag*, 2 vols. [New York: D. Appleton, 1912], 1:81). If Wilson and Badeau did have an "intimate" relationship, it was well-concealed from Wilson's military contemporaries. Badeau served for seven years during and after the war as one of General Grant's private secretaries, earning brevets to brigadier general both as a volunteer and in the regular army. After Grant's death, he served as U.S. Consul General in London and then in Havana. (Hunt, *Brevet Brigadier Generals in Blue*, 23).

28. On April 16, 1864, Custer wrote to his wife, Elizabeth, that "everything is satisfactorily arranged now" and that General Torbert, his new commander, was "an old and intimate friend of mine, and a very worthy gentleman." (Merington, ed., *The Custer Story*, 89). It appears that Custer over-stated his familiarity with Torbert, since Torbert graduated from West Point six years earlier than Custer, and the two had not served together thus far during the war.

29. Along with Merritt and Custer, Pleasonton arranged for the promotion of Captain Elon Farnsworth, 8th Illinois Cavalry, to brigadier general effective June 29, 1893. Farnsworth was killed four days later at Gettysburg.

30. John M. Carroll, *Custer in the Civil War: His Unfinished Memoirs* (San Rafael, CA: Presidio, 1977), 102–104, 129–130.

31. Custer's family lived in Ohio, and he was appointed to West Point from that state. However, Custer had attended school while living with an older sister in Monroe, Michigan, and he considered that community as his home. On June 30, 1863, Custer replaced Brigadier General Joseph T. Copland in command of the Michigan Brigade, which was then camped near Gettysburg. Copeland, twenty-six years older than Custer, was relegated to command of the draft rendezvous in Annapolis, and then in Pittsburgh. Afterward he was detailed to command the military prison in Alton, Illinois (Michigan Adjutant General's Office, *Michigan in the War*, revised, compiled by Jno. Robertson [Lansing, MI: W.H. George, 1882], 574–575).

32. Warner, *Generals in Blue*, 113. The Union rout at the Buckland Races was more a result of Kilpatrick's poor tactical judgment than failure on Davies's part.

33. Ibid., 124.

34. Samuel P. Bates, *Martial Deeds of Pennsylvania* (Philadelphia: T.H. Davis, 1876), 851–853.

35. *OR*, 36, I:115; Warner, *Generals in Blue*, 300. Afterwards Bryan was placed in temporary command of detachments from the 18th Pennsylvania and several other regiments which were assigned to support VI Corps (*OR*, 40, I:228). In poor health, Bryan left the Army of the Potomac on sick leave in July 1864. He served as president of a board inspecting wounded enlisted men at military hospitals in Indiana until his discharge for disability in December of that year. As a civilian, Bryan worked as a geologist and scientist until his death in April 1881. West Point Association of Graduate records erroneously indicate that Bryan participated in the Trevilian's Raid (Cullum, *Biographical Register*, #1703).

36. Bates, *Martial Deeds of Pennsylvania*, 664–665. For more information on McIntosh's brother, James, who graduated from West Point in 1849, see James P. Robbins, *Last in Their Class: Custer, Pickett, and the Goats of West Point* (New York: Encounter Books, 2006).

37. Warner, *Generals in Blue*, 80.

38. Beck, "Letters of a Civil War Surgeon," 153.

39. Colonel Gamble, the colonel of the 8th Illinois, was absent on convalescent leave in Washington during November and December 1863. In January and February 1864, he and the bulk of the 8th Illinois Cavalry went home to Illinois

on leave after the majority of the men reenlisted. In March and April, Gamble and the regiment were detailed to Camp Stoneman, adjacent to the Giesboro cavalry depot, for remounting (Longacre, *Lincoln's Cavalrymen*, 227, 298; Abner Hard, *History of the Eighth Cavalry Regiment Illinois Volunteers During the Great Rebellion* [Aurora, IL: Np., 1868; reprint, Dayton, OH: Morningside Bookshop, 1996], 288–293). Gamble, who was born in 1818 and had served in the dragoons during the late 1830s as an enlisted man, at the time was among the oldest cavalry commanders in the Army of the Potomac. At Malvern Hill in the spring of 1862, he had been shot in the chest, and the wound continued to cause him physical problems. By orders dated May 2, 1864, Gamble was transferred from the Army of the Potomac to command of the Cavalry Division, Defenses of Washington. There, he replaced Colonel John McIntosh, freeing McIntosh to return to the Army of the Potomac and replace Colonel Timothy Bryan in command of Wilson's 1st Brigade (*OR*, 37, I:368). Gamble, promoted to brigadier general of volunteers in September 1865, remained in the service as major of the 8th U.S. Cavalry after the war. In 1866, he died of cholera while en route to the West Coast with his regiment. Gamble was buried in Virgin Bay, Nicaragua (Warner, *Generals in Blue*, 165–166).

40. Torbert was afflicted by rheumatism in the spring of 1862. He took furlough to recuperate from that and other illness, perhaps malaria, after the Seven Days campaign, returning to his brigade after Second Manassas. From January until June, 1863, he was on sick leave of absence due to malaria (Slade, *A.T.A. Torbert*, 41–45; Cullum, *Biographical Register*, #1697).

41. Marsena Patrick Journal 1862–1865, Miscellaneous Manuscripts Collection, Library of Congress, entry for June 9, 1863.

42. Warner, *Generals in Blue*, 124.

43. Perhaps the officer most bitter with the promotion of Wilson and his assignment to division command was George A. Custer who was senior in grade but only in brigade command. Following the Wilson-Kautz Raid south of Petersburg in June 1864, which was by all accounts a debacle, Custer wrote to his wife, Libbie: "The papers have no doubt informed you of the disgrace brought upon a *portion* of the Cavalry corps by the upstart and imbecile Wilson.... Here is the result of consigning several thousand cavalry to the charge of an inexperienced and untrained officer. All who knew Genl. W. prophesied a disastrous outcome, but the most charitable never imagined the half of this.... Genl. Grant obtained the confirmation of W's appointment by the Senate, but it will require influence even more powerful to satisfy the people—above all, the Army, that this was a judicious measure, in view of his total ignorance and inexperience of cavalry, because he was a favorite of Genl. Grant.... I hope the authorities have learned from this unnecessary disaster that a man may be a good engineer, but an indifferent cavalry leader.... We also know, the whole Army knows, that it was not the fault of the brave men ... but that the sole blame rests on W. and on those who, knowing his deficiencies placed him in such a position of responsibility" (Merington, ed., *The Custer Story*, 110–111). Doubtless, some experienced cavalry officers felt and perhaps expressed similar feelings when Custer—who had served mostly as an aide de camp—was promoted from first lieutenant to brigadier general in June 1863.

Chapter 7

1. The Confederate government enacted a conscription act in March 1862.

2. *OR*, Series III, 3:414–415. General Order 191 applied to infantrymen, artillerymen, and cavalrymen in volunteer units. General Order Number 190 provided similar incentives for soldiers who reenlisted for five years in regular army regiments.

3. Ibid., 1084.

4. *OR*, 33:347.

5. General Meade noted that the average furlough was thirty-five days in duration (*OR*, 33:347). By November 1864, in all theaters of war, more than 136,000 veteran volunteers had reenlisted (*OR*, Series IV, 4:930).

6. Ella Lonn, *Desertion During the Civil War* (Gloucester, MA: American Historical Association, 1928; reprint, Lincoln: University of Nebraska Press, 1998), 140. Lonn and ther historians have concluded that the offer of large bounties contributed to the desertion problems encountered by the Union army. In that regard, Brigadier General James B. Frye, the Provost Marshal General, in a letter to Senator H.S. Lane dated December 20, 1863, wrote: "We have gradually and very naturally run into the evil system of large bounties, &c. I think the sooner we can extricate ourselves from it the better. It is absurd to try to compensate the soldier fully in money for his services, and it is equally absurd to try to establish or approach an equality between the compensation of the officer and the private" (*OR*, Series III, 3:1177).

7. William C.H. Reeder, *From a True Soldier and Son: The Civil War Letters of William C.H. Reeder*, commentary by Carolyn Reeder and edited by Jack Reeder (Brandy Station, VA: Brandy Station Foundation, 2008), 176–177. Reeder survived the Overland Campaign and with seventy-nine other soldiers of the 20th Indiana was mustered out of federal service on July 29, 1863 (Ibid., 217).

8. Daniel Peck, *Dear Rachel: The Civil War Letters of Daniel Peck* (Ashville, NY: Berrybook, 1993), 68. Daniel Peck, unlike many of his comrades, did not re-enlist. He was seriously wounded at Todd's Tavern on May 8, 1864, and discharged for disability in August 1864.

9. See Gene C. Armistead, *Horses and Mules in the Civil War* (Jefferson, NC: McFarland, 2013), 14–17, for a discussion of graft and mismanagement in the purchase of horses for the Union army.

10. *OR* 23, II:271, 289; *OR*, 25, II:543–544. Brigadier General Rufus Ingalls, the Army of the Potomac's Quartermaster General, generally concurred with Meigs's views regarding the mismanagement of mounts (*OR*, 25, II:547).

11. *OR*, Series III, 3:1041.

12. *OR*, Series III, 3:886. Horses purchased in the West generally cost less than those purchased in the East.

13. Bureaus held functional responsibilities within the War Department in Washington. The Cavalry Bureau joined bureaus directed by the Quartermaster General, Chief of Ordnance, Surgeon General, Commissary General, Paymaster General, Chief Engineer, and the Adjutant General.

14. *OR*, Series III, 3:580, 581.

15. *OR*, Series III, 3:580.

16. Ibid.

17. Starr, *The Union Cavalry in the Civil War*, 2:6. Additionally, there is little indication that the reports were used by the War Department to correct any deficiencies that were surfaced.

18. The Secretary of War decided that the Quartermaster Department would continue to issue horses to units until the Cavalry Bureau was prepared to assume that duty (*OR*, Series III, 3:884).

19. *OR* Series III, 3:886. Initially, the inspectors were assigned at Washington, Chicago, Syracuse, Indianapolis,

and Pittsburg. During 1864, the Quartermaster Department purchased 154,400 cavalry horses (*OR*, Series III, 4:1167). With eleven inspectors assigned to the Cavalry Bureau, the examination of potential cavalry mounts must have been cursory in many instances.

20. Warner, *Generals in Blue*, 165.

21. Henry S. Olcott, "The War's Carnival of Fraud" in *Annals of the War, Written by Leading Participants North and South* (Philadelphia: Times Publishing Co., 1879; reprint, Edison, NJ: Blue & Gray Press, 1996), 713.

22. Ibid.

23. The site of the Giesboro depot is today on Joint Base Anacostia-Bolling, formerly Bolling Air Force Base.

24. Charles D. Rhodes, "The Mounting and Remounting of the Federal Cavalry," in Theophilus F. Rodenbough, *The Cavalry*, vol. 4 of *Photographic History of the Civil War* (New York: Review of Reviews, 1911; reprint, Secaucus, NJ: Blue & Gray Press, 1987), 328.

25. General Stoneman, in a report to Secretary of War E.M. Stanton dated October 15, 1863, noted that after the battle at Gettysburg, the army collected about 5,500 unserviceable horses. Of that number, 2,000 remained alive, 1,000 of which had been returned to cavalry units, with 1,000 still recuperating. Thus, according to Stoneman, 3,500 horses had "died, strayed, or been stolen." Stoneman asserted that the remount depot in Washington could have been paid for by the salvageable portion of the 3,500 horses, had those horses received proper care (*OR*, Series III, 3:861).

26. Starr, *Union Cavalry in the Civil War*, 2:8.

27. *OR*, 29, II:401.

28. Ibid., 448–449.

29. Theophilus F. Rodenbough, *From Everglade to Canyon with the Second United States Cavalry: An Authentic Account of Service in Florida, Mexico, Virginia, and the Indian Country, 1836–1875* (New York: D. Van Norstrand, 1875; reprint, Norman: University of Oklahoma Press, 2000), 301. Instead of remounting the entire brigade, Merritt thought it preferable to consolidate the "worn and tried" horses and materiel and send "skeleton battalions from regiments, or regiments from brigades" to the remount depot, thereby "leavening" the new with the old (Ibid.).

30. Ibid., 418.

31. Ibid., 419–420. Once active campaigning began in May 1864, it soon became more expedient for horses to be sent to the Army of the Potomac in the field than to continue transporting individuals and groups of men from the field to Giesboro for remounting.

32. *OR*, Series III, 3:1042. On April 22, 1864, the War Department issued General Order Number 174. The order allowed dismounted or partially mounted cavalry regiments to be temporarily armed and employed as infantry. It also stated, "Commanders of departments and separate armies are authorized to dismount and employ as infantry any cavalry regiment which has been neglectful of wasteful of its horses, or has proved inefficient in the field, and transfer its horses to others" (*OR*, Series III, 4:241).

33. If Secretary Stanton was anxious to be rid of Stoneman, Stoneman was happy to be rid of the Cavalry Bureau. Shortly before he left Washington, he wrote to a friend, "I am now on my way to the Army in Tennessee. Having thank god got out of the Cavry Bureau and into the field again" (Ben Fuller Fordney, *George Stoneman: A Biography of the Union General* [Jefferson, NC: McFarland, 2008], 86). Stoneman quickly returned to mounted service, commanding a cavalry corps during the Atlanta Campaign. He was captured in July 1864 while conducting a raid to free Union prisoners held at Andersonville, Georgia. After being exchanged, his final operation of the war was another raid, this time from Tennessee into North Carolina to complement Sherman's advance north from Georgia. Following the war, Stoneman was appointed colonel of the 21st Infantry Regiment and served in Arizona until he retired due to disability in 1871. Afterward, Stoneman settled near Los Angeles, California, on a farm he had admired while serving there as a lieutenant in 1847. In 1882, Stoneman reentered public life as Rail Road Commissioner for California, and following year was elected Governor of that state as a Democrat. Stoneman died in September 1894 while visiting at his sister's home in Buffalo, New York. He is buried in Lakewood, New York, near the site of his childhood home (USMA AOG, *Annual Reunion* [1895], 25–36; Warner, *Generals in Blue*, 482).

34. *OR*, III, 4:47. Orders appointing Garrard to the Cavalry Bureau were dated January 2, 1864. Orders relieving him were dated January 26. Garrard ended the war serving in command of an infantry division in the 16th Corps with brevets to major general in both regular and volunteer service. He resigned his commission in November, 1866, and lived in Cincinnati while serving as chairman of the city Platting Commission and member of the city Sewerage Board. He died in Cincinnati in May, 1879 (Cullum, *Biographical Register*, # 1501; USMA AOG, *Annual Reunion* [1879], 95–100).

35. *OR*, 32, II:115–116, 131.

36. *OR*, Series III, 4:47.

37. *OR* 32, II:337. Wilson was much in demand. Major General George Thomas, commanding the Army of the Cumberland, had asked that Grant assign him to his command.

38. Wilson, *Under the Old Flag*, 1:330.

39. *OR*, 33:753, 809, 816.

40. *OR*, Series III, 4:219.

41. Ibid., 229.

42. Ibid. During the remainder of the war, Ekin was promoted to colonel and brevetted to brigadier general. Ekin's most noteworthy service came as a result of his appointment to the board of officers who tried the Lincoln conspirators.

43. Warner, *Generals in Blue*, 162, 196. Upon his promotion to major general in August 1861, Halleck had also been junior to Winfield Scott who retired in October 1861. Fremont resigned his commission in June 1864. McClellan, who was on the army rolls awaiting orders in New York, resigned his commission in November 1864.

44. *OR*, 33:850, 877, 879; Wilson, *Under the Old Flag*, 1:340–341. Grant and Davidson had attended West Point together, Grant graduating in 1843 and Davidson in 1845. Commissioned in the 1st Dragoons, Davidson had seen extensive service on the Plains, in Mexico, and in the Southwest before the beginning of the Civil War. Although from Virginia, then–Captain Davidson remained loyal to the Union. In February 1862 he was appointed Brigadier General of Volunteers and after the Peninsular Campaign, during which he commanded an infantry brigade, he was posted to Missouri. During the war, Davidson was brevetted to Major General in both regular and volunteer ranks. After the war, he rose to grade of colonel and commanded the 2nd Cavalry before his death in June, 1881 (Cullum, *Biographical Register*, #1257).

45. *OR*, 33:930. Kautz took command of a small cavalry division at the time consisting of two brigades of two regiments each.

46. Stephen Z. Starr, "The Inner Life of the First Vermont Cavalry, 1861–1865," *Vermont History* 46 (Summer 1978), 172, 174 n. 52. Unlike many other states, Vermont

actively recruited to fill vacancies in its regiments. Consequently, the 1st Vermont was frequently at greater strength than other regiments in the Cavalry Corps (Starr, *The Union Cavalry in the Civil War*, 2:11, n.24).

47. The terms cartridge and round are today generally used interchangeably and refer to a metal or plastic case containing a projectile, powder charge, and primer. In the Civil War the term cartridge was generally applied to a paper or cloth sleeve containing black powder and a ball. The primer was separate.

48. Roy M. Marcot, *Spencer Repeating Firearms*, (Rochester, NY: Rowe Publications, 1990), 35. In general, many officers and officials in the army's Ordnance Department have over the years resisted adopting innovative technologies with respect to small arms. While a detailed discussion of that topic is beyond the scope of this book, interested readers may refer to the history of the M-14 rifle or the M-16 rifle (*OR*, 45, II:488).

49. Ibid. The army's institutional reluctance to embrace the new technology of the Spencer did not end with the decision to award the December 1861 procurement contract. In 1866 the army organized a board, chaired by Winfield Scott Hancock, to determine what caliber and type of breech loaders should be adopted for infantry muskets and cavalry carbines. Hancock's board found that "the Spencer magazine carbine is the best gun of this kind yet offered." However, the board was unable to decide whether it would be best to have only magazine carbines in cavalry service. In reaching this conclusion, the board considered the greater cost of repeaters, and the "greater inconvenience" of using a "lever-gun" (Marcot, *Spencer Repeating Firearms*, 109). As a point of interest, at the Little Big Horn in 1876, the men of the 7th U.S. Cavalry were armed with the then-standard army cavalry carbine: a Springfield single-shot breech-loader which fired metallic center fire cartridges.

50. Marcot, *Spencer Repeating Firearms*, 48, 62, 80, 94. The figure for Spencers includes both 1860 and 1865 models manufactured by both the Spencer Repeating Rifle Company and the Burnside Rifle Company. In contrast, the army purchased only 1731 of the popular Henry rifles (which were actually the length of Civil War era carbines (Berkeley R. Lewis, "Notes on Cavalry Weapons of the American Civil War 1861–1865," [Washington, D.C.: American Ordnance Association, 1961], 12).

51. Starr, *Union Cavalry in the Civil War*, 2:252.

52. *OR*, 49, II:236.

53. Starr, *Union Cavalry in the Civil War*, 2:252, n. 48.

54. In initial trials conducted by the navy, seven rounds were fired in ten seconds. In subsequent trials conducted by the army, fourteen rounds were fired in 1 minute 7 seconds. However, at such rapid rates the weapon would quickly overheat. During trials conducted by the navy, a sustained rate of fire of 91 rounds in 29 minutes was recorded (Marcot, *Spencer Repeating Firearms*, 29, 75).

55. Private Rufus Peck, 2nd Virginia Cavalry, recalled that after Yellow Tavern, Sheridan's raiders attempted to force a crossing over the Chickahominy River. As the Union troopers waded through the water, they crouched down, leaving only their heads above the surface. Many Confederates on the east bank of the river mistook the Union soldiers for turtles, which were plentiful at the time. According to Peck, about fifty yards from the bank the Union troopers stood and opened fire on the Confederates, an action which was only possible for men armed with weapons using metallic ammunition (Rufus H. Peck, *Reminiscences of a Confederate Soldier of Co. C, 2nd Va. Cavalry* [Fincastle, VA: Np, 1913], 47).

56. *OR*, 45, II:488. For example, before departing for his raid to Selma, Alabama, in March 1865, James Wilson arranged for Spencers to be switched among divisions so that most of the raiders were armed with repeaters (*OR*, 49, I:356).

57. The inspection occurred before the reorganization to accommodate General Wilson's lack of seniority.

58. *OR*, 33:891–893.

Chapter 8

1. Not included in this tally of forces are the 1st West Virginia Cavalry, which had two companies assigned to the cavalry corps, and Orton's company of the District of Columbia cavalry which was also assigned to the cavalry corps.

2. Longacre, *Jersey Cavaliers*, 171.

3. Ibid., 171. Wyndham lacked confidence in Major Myron Beaumont and considered Major Hugh Janeway too young and inexperienced to command a regiment, leading him to recommend that the governor promote Kester, then a captain, to lieutenant colonel. Major Janeway was eventually promoted to colonel after Kester was mustered out of the army on September 1864. Janeway was killed at Amelia Springs, Virginia, in April 1865. Major Myron Beaumont was promoted to colonel after Janeway's death.

4. Cullum, *Biographical Register*, #1859; H.P. Moyer, *History of the Seventeenth Regiment Pennsylvania Volunteer Cavalry, or One Hundred Sixty-Second in the Line of Pennsylvania Volunteer Regiments, War to Suppress the Rebellion, 1861–1865* (Lebanon, PA: Sowers, Nd), 81–2.

5. Samuel P. Bates, *History of Pennsylvania Volunteers, 1861–1865*, 5 vols. (Harrisburg: B Singerly, 1869–1871), II:531. The preceding colonel of the regiment, James K. Kerr, resigned his commission in May 1863.

6. William N. Pickerill, *History of the Third Indiana Cavalry* (Indianapolis: Aetna, 1900), 9, 182. Colonel Chapman continued to encumber the colonel's billet in the 3rd Indiana throughout the Overland Campaign. He was promoted to brigadier general on August 31, 1864 (Ibid., 156).

7. Edward Tobie, *History of the First Maine Cavalry, 1861–1865* (Boston: Emery & Hughes, 1887), 452–453, 513; Torlief S. Holmes, *Horse Soldiers in Blue: First Maine Cavalry* (Gaithersburg, MD: Butternut, 1985), 71, 85.

8. William Hyndman, *History of a Cavalry Company: A Complete Record of Company "A," 4th Penn'a Cavalry* (Philadelphia: Jas. A. Rogers, 1870; reprint, Hightown, NJ: Longstreet House, 1997), 76.

9. Cullum, *Biographical Register*, #1602.

10. Cullum, *Biographical Register*, #1845.

11. Orders from the army's Adjutant General transferred Claflin to the 6th U.S. Cavalry when that regiment was organized in June 1861. However, Claflin did not join his new regiment until April 1862 because he was participating in military operations in New Mexico. Accounts of Val Verde and military records indicate that during the battle, Claflin commanded Company G, 1st U.S. Cavalry (John Taylor, *Bloody Val Verde: A Bloody Battle on the Rio Grande, February 21, 1862* [Albuquerque: University of New Mexico Press, 1995], 128; Cullum, *Biographical Register*, #1786).

12. Cullum, *Biographical Register*, #1786.

13. Rodenbough, ed., *From Everglade to Canyon*, 465–466; Cullum, *Biographical Register*, #1660.

14. Three regiments—the 4th New York, the 8th Pennsylvania, and the 12th Illinois—did not participate in the Battle of Brandy Station. The 3rd West Virginia had two companies assigned to the cavalry corps in June 1863. Those companies returned to their regiment in the Department of West Virginia in November 1863 (Frederick H. Dyer, ed.,

A Compendium of the War of the Rebellion, 3 vols. [Des Moines, IA: Dyer, 1908, reprint, New York: Thomas Yoseloff, 1959], 3:1655). A separate company of District of Columbia volunteer cavalry, Orton's Company, left the cavalry corps in December 1863.

15. Two regiments, the 2nd West Virginia and the 1st Ohio, were assigned to the cavalry corps during the Gettysburg Campaign and reassigned from the cavalry corps before campaigning began in the spring of 1864. Those two regiments are not included in the tabulation of the Cavalry Corps' composition and are not further discussed.

16. The four regiments assigned to Burnside's corps were the 3rd New Jersey, the 22nd New York, the 2nd Ohio, and the 13th Pennsylvania.

17. *OR*, 33:972. Rawlins' memo to Sheridan was dated April 25, 1864. To no avail, on April 26, Sheridan again requested the 8th Illinois be returned (*OR*, 33:985).

18. Abner Hard, *History of the Eighth Cavalry Regiment Illinois Volunteers During the Great Rebellion* (Aurora, IL: Np., 1868; reprint, Dayton, OH: Morningside, 1996), 289–293; Dyer, *Compendium*, 3:1027.

19. Samuel M. Blackwell, Jr., *In the First Line of Battle: The 12th Illinois Cavalry in the Civil War* (DeKalb, IL: Northern Illinois University Press, 2002), 128–128; Dyer, *Compendium*, 3:1029.

20. Daniel C. Toomey and Charles A. Earp, *Marylanders in Blue: The Artillery and the Cavalry* (Baltimore: Toomey, 1999), 104–105. In October 1864, following a request from Brigadier General Kautz, who commanded Butler's cavalry—and much to the pleasure of the Maryland troopers—the War Department remounted the regiment and assigned it to Kautz's division. Lieutenant Colonel Jacob Counselman, a Marylander who received a commission in the artillery when he graduated from West Point in June 1863, was appointed to command of the regiment.

21. Dyer, *Compendium*, 3:1627.

22. Pleasonton to Farnsworth, June 23, 1863, Alfred Pleasonton Papers, Miscellaneous Manuscripts Collection, Library of Congress, Washington, D.C. Stahel, had been promoted to major general of volunteers in March 1863. Farnsworth, the uncle of Elon Farnsworth, had commanded the 8th Illinois earlier in the war. He resigned his commission to resume his seat in the US Congress.

23. Dyer, *Compendium*, 3:1271–1273.

24. Ibid., 1:378; Michigan AGO, *Michigan in the War*, 567.

25. Kidd, *Personal Recollections of a Cavalryman*, 75. The three regiments, although they participated in a few minor scouts and skirmishes, suffered no casualties among their officers until Gettysburg.

26. In 1879, Richard Taylor, who served as a brigadier under Jackson early in the war, wrote an account of the Valley Campaign of the spring of 1862. In his account, Taylor was disparaging toward Nathaniel Banks's cavalry, writing that the troopers' horsemanship was so poor, that they had to be strapped into their saddles. He also claimed that Union cavalrymen, probably out of fear of harm, wore breastplates and other "protective devices." Taylor's account caused some consternation among veterans in Michigan since the 1st Michigan Cavalry had been assigned to Banks's army, prompting publication of accounts refuting Taylor's "violent slander." It seems unlikely that Union cavalrymen strapped themselves into their saddles. In the case of a fall—either due to a horse stumbling or as a result of enemy fire—it is best for a rider to hopefully get his feet out of his stirrups and be thrown clear. It also seems unlikely many—if any—Union cavalrymen wore breastplates. Finally, one former Union cavalry officer pointed out that men from rural areas of the North were as accustomed to riding horses as were their Southern counterparts (Michigan AGO, *Michigan in the War*, 561–563).

27. Dyer, *Compendium*, 3:1269; Michigan AGO, *Michigan in the War*, 565; John Gill, *Reminiscences of Four Years as a Private Soldier in the Confederate Army, 1861–1865* (Baltimore: Sun Printing Office, 1904), 73.

28. Michigan AGO, *Michigan in the War*, 553; Longacre, *Custer and His Wolverines*, 204. Colonel Town resigned his commission in August 1864 and died several months later.

29. Michigan AGO, *Michigan in the War*, 760.

30. Michigan AGO, *Michigan in the War*, 569, 865; James H. Kidd, *One of Custer's Wolverines: The Civil War Letters of Brevet Brigadier General James H. Kidd, 6th Michigan Cavalry*, ed., Eric Wittenberg (Kent, OH: Kent State University Press, 2000), 76, 208 n.63. Colonel George Gray resigned his commission in May 1864.

31. Dyer, *Compendium*, 3:1373–1374.

32. Louis N. Beaudry, *Historic Records of the Fifth New York Cavalry, Ira Harris Guard: Its Organization, Marches, Raids, Scouts, Engagements, and General Services during the Rebellion of 1861–1865* (Albany: S.R. Gray, 1865) 301. Hammond had been wounded—shot in the right hand—in the summer of 1863. On June 1, 1864, he was shot in the leg near Ashland, Virginia. In July 1864 he was promoted to colonel of the regiment, mustering out two months later at the beginning of September.

33. Bates, *History of the Pennsylvania Volunteers, 1861–1865*, 2:320–322.

34. Bates, *Martial Deeds of Pennsylvania*, 801

35. Bates, *History of the Pennsylvania Volunteers, 1861–1865*, 4:1041–1043.

36. "A Genealogy of the Kirk Family by Chas. H. Stubbs, 1872." (http://wc.rootsweb.ancestry.com/cgi-bin/igm.cgi?op'REG&db'kirk-stubbs&id'I0165).

37. George Grenville Benedict, *Vermont in the Civil War*, 2 vols. (Burlington: Free Press Association, 1888), 2:632; Joseph D. Collea, Jr., *The First Vermont Cavalry in the Civil War: A History* (Jefferson, NC: McFarland, 2010), 222–223.

38. Dyer, *Compendium*, 3:1655.

39. Ibid., 1006; W.A. Croffut and John M. Morris, *The Military and Civil History of Connecticut during the War of 1861–65*, 3d ed. (New York: Ledyard Bill, 1869), 495–96. Blakeslee is probably best known today as the developer of the "Blakeslee Box," which held up to ten metal tubes, each with a capacity of seven rounds of ammunition for the Spencer rifle/carbine. Using a filled tube, a cavalry man could more quickly reload his weapon's magazine. Eventually, the Ordnance Department purchased 33,000 Blakeslee Boxes, all but 1,000 of which were issued to cavalry troopers (Randy Steffen, "The Blakeslee Quickloader for the Spencer Rifle Gave the Union Army its First Modern Firepower," *Civil War Times Illustrated* 1 [October 1962], 35).

40. James R. Bowen, *Regimental History of the First New York Dragoons (Originally the 130th N.Y. Vol. Infantry) During Three Years of Service in the Great Civil War* (The Author, 1900), 7, 89.

41. Ibid., 97.

Chapter 9

1. With regard to Cold Harbor, in his memoirs Grant wrote: "I have always regretted that the last assault at Cold Harbor was ever made.... no advantage whatever was gained to compensate for the heavy loss we sustained" (Grant, *Personal Memoirs*, 433).

2. As it turned out, the Army of the Potomac's engi-

neers built two pontoon bridges to effect the movement to the south side of the James: the bridge across the Chickahominy River was one thousand seven hundred feet long, and the bridge over the James was two thousand feet long. Troops and equipment were also shuttled across the river on ferry-boats (Meade, *Life and Letters*, 2:203).

3. Ulysses S. Grant, *The Papers of Ulysses S. Grant*, vol. 11, June 1-August 15, 1864, edited by John Y. Simon (Carbondale: Southern Illinois University Press, 1984), 16.

4. *OR*, 36, III:598–599.

5. *OR*, 36, III:603, 629.

6. *OR*, 36, III:599.

7. *OR*, 36, 3:629. In his instructions, Meade made no mention of the option for Sheridan to foray to the south and destroy the James River Canal. Sheridan was well aware of the nature of the terrain in central Virginia. Before the raid was contemplated, he had on June 3 requested a pontoon train of 12 boats be assigned to his command (*OR*, 36, III:558).

8. Also on June 6, Grant dispatched a party of scouts to the Valley with written instructions for Hunter. The scouts expected to find Hunter at Staunton, but upon crossing the Blue Ridge, they discovered that Hunter had already moved up the Valley toward Lynchburg. Consequently, the scouts returned to the Army of the Potomac without delivering Grant's message (James Rodney Woods, "Civil War Memoirs," Maud Wood Park Papers [MMC 1938], Washington, Library of Congress). Woods had formerly served as a private in the 6th U.S. Cavalry (Donald C. Caughey and Jimmy J. Jones, *The 6th United States Cavalry in the Civil War: A History and Roster* [Jefferson, NC: McFarland, 2013], 247).

9. James A. Johnston II, *Virginia Railroads in the Civil War* (Chapel Hill: University of North Carolina Press, 1961), 4, 10, 13–14, 258 n. 27; J.C. Swayze, *Hill & Swayze's Confederate States Rail-road & Steam-boat Guide, Containing the Time-Tables, Fares, Connections and Distances on all the Rail-roads of the Confederate States; also, the Connecting Lines of Rail-roads, Steam-boats and Stages. And will be Accompanied by a Complete Guide to the Principal Hotels, with a Large Variety of Valuable Information, Collected, Compiled, and Arranged by J.C. Swayze* (Griffin, GA: Hill & Swayze, Publishers, 1862), 30; W.G. Ryckman, "The Battle of Trevilians, Miscellaneous Commentary," *Louisa County Historical Magazine* 35 (Spring 2004), 29. Business at Trevilian Station had decreased during the course of the war. In May 1864, only nineteen passengers had arrived at Trevilian Station and station manager J.H. Whitlock had sold only forty-five departure tickets. (Ibid.)

10. Johnston II, *Virginia Railroads in the Civil War*, 17, 18.

11. McClellan, *I Rode with Jeb Stuart*, 410; Freeman, *Lee's Lieutenants*, 3:416.

12. General Grant, aware that iron rails were in critically short supply in the South, directed that repair work on railroads north of the James River be halted and that Union construction crews lay no track that might be salvaged by the Confederates after he moved the Army of the Potomac to the south side of the James (*OR*, 36, I:91).

13. Johnston II, *Virginia Railroads in the Civil War*, 9, 13–14, 258 n. 26 & 28, 299 n. 46.

14. *OR*, 25, 1:1063.

15. *OR* 25, I:1089

16. *OR*, 36, I:806, 854–855, 882–883.

17. It is not clear whether Sheridan was aware of the army's pending move to the south side of the James. While it may earlier have become apparent to senior commanders that such a move was planned, the orders to begin the operation were not issued until June 11 for execution on the evening of June 12 (*OR*, 36, III:745, 747–749).

18. *OR*, 36, III:569.

19. *OR*, 36, III:590. Sheridan considered it an "error" that the army was mounting new recruits while veterans remained dismounted. On June 7, Sheridan advised the Cavalry Bureau that most of the new regiments and recruits mounted at the cavalry depot at Port Royal were dismounted as soon as they reported to the Army of the Potomac's Cavalry Corps (*OR*, 36, III:661, 689).

20. *OR*, 36, III:661. Sheridan established a camp at White House for collecting cavalry returning to the Army of the Potomac from remount depots, accepting shipments of horses from the Cavalry Bureau, and remounting veterans.

21. Grant, *Personal Memoirs*, 410–411; *OR*, 36, II:811.

22. *OR*, 36, I:813; Wainwright, *A Diary of Battle*, 374–375.

23. *OR*, 36, I: 285. The two horse artillery brigades consisted of 43 officers, 1,714 enlisted men, and 2,064 horses at the beginning of the campaign. Of the batteries accompanying Sheridan on the raid, Pennington's, Heaton's and Denison's batteries were initially equipped with six rifled guns each. Williston's and Randol's batteries were initially equipped with four Napoleons each.

24. *OR*, 36, I:289.

25. Ibid. Battery G, 1st U.S. Artillery moved to Washington on June 18. Battery G, 2nd U.S. Artillery was dismounted on June 2 and ordered to Washington. Battery A, 4th U.S. Artillery was dismounted and sent to Washington on June 4. The 6th Battery Independent New York Light Artillery reported to the defenses of Washington in June with the date not specified (Dyer, *Compendium*, 3:1695, 1699, 1703, 1397).

26. *OR*, 36, I:315. Captain Folwell's company consisted of fifty-two men and his train carried eight canvas pontoons and two trestles.

27. *OR*, 14:365–366.

28. *OR*, 25, I:1069–1070.

29. *OR*, 29, II:420–422. In summary, General Orders No. 100 allowed each division headquarters two wagons and each brigade headquarters one wagon for baggage and camp equipage. The division and brigade headquarters were also allowed two wagons and one wagon, respectively, in the supply train for stores "not provided hereto." Regiments were allowed baggage wagons based upon their strength, ranging from 6 wagons for a regiment of 1,000 men down to 3 wagons for a regiment of less than 300 men. With a strength of roughly 6,000 men, the ordnance train would be allowed 30 wagons for small arms ammunition and 16 wagons for artillery ammunition. The supply train would have an allowance of approximately eighty wagons, carrying mostly rations, plus sixty wagons—thirty per division—carrying forage for the horses. A few wagons were allocated for medical stores, armorer tools, and pioneer equipment.

30. *OR*, 34, II:422; U.S. War Department, *Revised Regulations for the Army of the United States, 1861* (Philadelphia: J.G.L. Brown, 1861; reprint ed., Harrisburg, PA: National Historical Society, 1980), 166. Meade's order was specific: "When the army is on the march…. The wagons will carry only the marching ration (10 pounds average to each animal per day)."

31. *OR*, 36, I:795; Sheridan, *Personal Memoirs*, 227; *New York Herald*, June 21, 1864.

32. The Medical Director of the Army of the Potomac reported that on May 31, the Ambulance corps had allocated in support of the Cavalry Corps 77 ambulances, 4 Autenrieth medical wagons, and 58 army wagons (*OR*, 36, I:266).

33. *OR*, 36, I:795; Sheridan, *Personal Memoirs*, 227; Henry R. Pyne, *Ride to War: The History of the First New Jersey Cavalry*, edited by Earl S. Miers (New Brunswick: Rutgers University Press, 1961), 217; Hyndman, *History of a Cavalry Company*, 124. Although Sheridan wrote in his memoirs that unserviceable horses and dismounted men had been sent to the White House depot several days earlier, both Pyne and Hyndman indicate that further culling of weak horses took place the day before the raid began. This is consistent with Sheridan's message to the Cavalry Bureau Inspector General on June 7 that he had "every prospect of having all dismounted men with the trains sent to the White House" (*OR* 36, III:690).

34. Pyne, *Ride to War*, 217.

35. B.J. Haden, *Reminiscences of J.E.B. Stuart's Cavalry* (Charlottesville: Progress, 1909), 22; Henry St. George T. Brooke, "Autobiography" (25146-Typescript), Richmond, Library of Virginia, 37–38.

36. Pyne, *Ride to War*, 217.

Chapter 10

1. *OR*, 36, I:315.

2. Union cavalry regulations specified that horses were to cover a mile in 16 minutes at the walk, in 8 minutes at the trot, and in 6 minutes at the gallop (Phillip St. George Cooke, *Cavalry Tactics: or, Regulations for the Instruction, Formations and Movements of the Cavalry of the Army and Volunteers of the United States* (Philadelphia: J.B. Lippincott, 1862; reprint, Union City, TN, Pioneer Press, 1997), 177).

3. Ibid., 180.

4. The U.S. Army's field manual on foot marches says, "An accordion effect in marching is caused by changes in the rate of march and most often occurs as lead elements of a unit ascend or descend terrain, or pass through critical points along the march route. A change in the rate of march increases as it passes down the column, so that the rear elements must either double time to maintain the distance or be left far behind. Thus, a minor change of rate at the head of the column becomes magnified by the time it reaches the tail of the column" (Headquarters, Department of the Army, *Field Manual 21–18, Foot Marches* [1 June 1990], 4–9, 4–10).

5. Isham, *An Historical Sketch*, 172–173. Today when trotting long distances, most riders "post": flexing their legs to rise and fall with the movement of the horse. Posting was developed in the 1700s by the young men in England who rode horses drawing mail (Royal Post) carriages over long distances. Posting is generally considered comfortable for riders and less fatiguing for horses. However, during the Civil War, only a few, mostly European-trained, riders posted at the trot. Instead, the army's cavalry manual charged instructors—when training new recruits to ride at the trot—to instruct recruits to "understand that it is in remaining well seated, and in relaxing measurably, all the parts of the body, especially the thighs and legs, that they can acquire the necessary ease and solidity" (Cooke, *Cavalry Tactics*, 84). With many horses, trying to "sit" a trot can be a bone-jarring experience for the rider, particularly over long distances.

6. The regiment found the Confederate hospital later that day. Wounded Confederates who were unable to be moved were paroled. Wounded—both Union and Confederate—who could be moved were taken with the regiment as it marched south to link-up with Sheridan's main body. The 17th Pennsylvania arrived at the Trevilian battlefield on the afternoon of June 11 (Moyer, *History of the Seventeenth Regiment Pennsylvania Volunteer Cavalry*, 84). Moyer was the bugler of Company E.

7. *OR* 36, I:784, 840, 868; 36, III:716. The area through which Sheridan's troopers marched is today rural and in many places appears much as it did in 1864. Today at New Castle Ferry the land on both sides of the Pamunkey River is devoted to agriculture. Aylett remains an unincorporated community in King William County where US Highway 360 crosses the Mattaponi River. Polecat Station, a water and wood stop near where the Richmond, Fredericksburg, and Potomac crossed Polecat Creek, no longer exists. Penola, a small community where county route 601 crosses the CSX track is the approximate site of Polecat Station. Chilesburg, in the southeastern corner of Caroline County, is at the intersection of county routes 639 and 738, and consists of a convenience store and a farm supply center. New Market no longer exists. Partlow, an unincorporated community in southeastern Spotsylvania County is near where New Market was located. In 1971 the North Anna River was dammed, creating Lake Anna to provide cooling water for a nuclear power plant. Carpenter's Ford and most other crossing sites between Louisa and Spotsylvania County are today well under water. The distances cited are based upon map reconnaissance and while reasonably accurate, are not exact. It is reasonable to expect recorded mileages to vary among regiments based upon the routes traveled and the location of camps which may have extended several miles, or more, depending upon water sources and the availability of grass for grazing. The itinerary of the 8th Pennsylvania recorded the following distances for the march: June 7—18 miles; June 8—24 miles; June 9—32 miles; June 10—21 miles, for a total of 95 miles. How that daily mileage was determined is not known. However the distances cited for the 8th Pennsylvania for June 8 and 9 appear excessive (*OR*, 36, I:868).

8. *OR*, 25, I:1060, 1063–1064, 1099. In May 1863, General Stoneman dispatched Captain Richard S.C. Lord with the 1st U.S. Cavalry to destroy Carr's Bridge on the road between Frederickshall and Fredericksburg. Other bridges were destroyed by the raiders to cover their withdrawal to the north.

9. Bowen, *Regimental History of the First New York Dragoons*, 188.

10. Noble D. Preston, "Trevilian Station. The Most Stubborn Cavalry Fight of the War," *National Tribune*, January 5, 1888. Preston went on to add that "any fowl or porker that could survive the administration of the two armies that had overrun the country, was too tough for mastication."

11. Hyndman, *History of a Cavalry Company*, 125–126.

12. In contrast, the execution of six of Mosby's Rangers in September 1864, and Mosby's hanging of three Federal soldiers in retaliation were widely publicized.

13. Tobie, *History of the First Maine Cavalry*, 283.

14. Hyndman, *History of a Cavalry Company*, 125.

15. Preston, "Trevilian Station," *National Tribune*, January 5, 1888.

16. Eustace C. Moncure, "Reminiscences of the Civil War," Personal Papers Collection (32349, Typescript) (Richmond: Library of Virginia), 13–14.

17. Brooks, *Butler and His Cavalry*, 106–107.

18. Thomas Nelson Conrad, *The Rebel Scout: A Thrilling History of Scouting Life in the Southern Army* (Washington, D.C.: National, 1904; reprint, Westminster, MD: Heritage, 2009), 49; Thomas L. Rosser, *Riding with Rosser*, ed., S. Roger Keller (Shippensburg, PA: Burd Street, 1997), 36–37.

19. Edward L. Wells, *Hampton and His Cavalry in '64* (Richmond, VA: B.F. Johnson, 1899; reprint, Richmond,

VA: Owen, 1991), 187–188. Fitz Lee, in his report which was written in December 1866, recounted that information regarding Sheridan's movement was received on June 6 (Hewett, et al., eds., *Supplement to the Official Records*, 6, 36:800). No explanation is given for why, if information regarding the Federal movement was received by the Confederates on either June 6 or 7, the Confederate pursuit did not begin until June 9.

20. Wells, *Hampton and His Cavalry in '64*, 188; Brooks, *Butler and His Cavalry*, 238.

21. *OR*, 36, III:883–884. Earlier in the war, Cooke had served in various positions on JEB Stuart's staff.

22. Hewett, et al., eds., *Supplement*, 6, 36:784.

23. Today the Green Spring Valley is designated a national historic landmark district by the National Park Service.

24. The tavern, a large, two-story frame building on a brick foundation, was established in 1822 on property owned by James Woods. Nearby was a two-story frame house. The property with tavern and house changed hands several times before being purchased by William A. Netherland at the beginning of the Civil War ("Netherlands House and Tavern," *Louisa County Historical Magazine* 11 [Winter 1979], 28–29).

25. *OR*, 36, III:735; *OR*, 36, I:735, 840, 858. Today the site of Clayton's Store is a crossroads near the hamlet of Oakland (Virginia Department of Conservation and Recreation, *A Feasibility Study for the Establishment of a Trevilian Station Battlefield State Park* [Richmond: Commonwealth of Virginia, 2001], 12).

26. Possibly part of Davies's brigade camped for the evening on the north side of the North Anna. In a diary entry for June 10, Corporal Robert Boyce, Company K, 1st Pennsylvania Cavalry, wrote that his regiment "encamped on a branch of the North Anna River about ten miles from Louisa Court House." Further, in a post-war manuscript, Thompson A. Snyder, Company D, 1st Pennsylvania Cavalry, recorded that the regiment crossed the North Anna on the June 11 (Robert Boyce, "Civil War Diary: January 1864-December 1864." [Andrew Knez, Jr., Pittsburgh, PA]; Thompson A. Snyder, "Recollections of Four Years with the Union Cavalry," Typescript [Andrew Knez, Jr., Pittsburg, PA, 1927], 37).

27. *OR*, 36, III:735–736. The time on Sheridan's orders to Gregg was 8:00 p.m. and the *Official Records* do not contain similar correspondence from Sheridan to Torbert. The Orange and Alexandria Railroad crosses South Fork Creek and Cuffy's Creek between Gordonsville and Lindsay, the first station south of Gordonsville.

Chapter 11

1. Coffman, *Going Back the Way They Came*, 81. Arthur Clayton died in 1832 (Ibid., 81, n. 32).

2. *OR*, 36, I:807. Torbert wrote that this was the first enemy "seen" thus far in the raid.

3. The Marquis Road is named for the Marquis de Lafayette, who in June 1781 reopened the back country road to move his troops into a position to prevent Lord Cornwallis from seizing Continental Army stores located in Charlottesville (Virginia Department of Highways).

4. *OR*, 36, I:1095.

5. Supporting distance may vary based upon the movement rates of the supporting units, terrain, and meteorological conditions. Today a commander would likely develop a plan of attack with control measures such as phase lines and checkpoints that would allow him to monitor the movement of his units and synchronize their introduction into battle. Such measures were not used during the Civil War.

6. Since no written orders from Hampton to Lee have been found, it seems likely that Hampton's orders were given to Lee verbally. The person who carried the orders to Lee remains unknown.

7. Meteorological data, U.S. Naval Observatory, Astronomical Applications Department, Washington, D.C.

8. Alternatively, Lee may have sent a staff officer to Hampton to inquire about orders for the following day. Were that the case, the time required for Lee to receive his orders would have likely been reduced since his staff officer would presumably have known the way back to Lee's headquarters.

9. In recent times, there is a rule of thumb that each echelon of command should take about one-third of the time available for its internal planning, leaving two-thirds available to subordinate echelons. Thus, today a brigade commander with nine hours to plan an attack might take three hours to develop his plans and issue orders to his battalion commanders. The battalion commanders then might take about two hours to plan and issue orders to their company commanders, leaving about four hours to the company commanders to plan, issue orders to their platoon leaders, and move their companies into position for the attack. However, today military operations are characterized—at least at the lower echelons—by more thorough and complex planning than operations during the Civil War. As mentioned, it is more likely that Lee's regimental commanders were simply given an order of march, and told to have their men ready to move at a specific time.

10. Mathew C. Butler, "The Cavalry Fight at Trevilian Station" in *Battles and Leaders of the Civil War* (New York: Thomas Yoseloff, Inc., 1956), 4: 237.

11. Brooks, *Butler and His Cavalry*, 239.

12. Sunrise on June 11, 1864, in Louisa County came at 4:48 a.m. Sufficient light for military operations would have been available by the beginning of civil twilight—commonly referred to as dawn—at 4:17 a.m., and enough light for Rosser to easily ride his horse would have been available at the beginning of morning nautical twilight about one-half hour earlier. (Nautical twilight is "the illumination level at which the horizon is still visible even on a Moonless night.") Consequently, Rosser probably departed from his camp sometime around 4:00 a.m. (U.S. Naval Observatory, Astronomical Applications Department, Washington, D.C.).

13. Brooks, *Butler and His Cavalry*, 239–240.

14. Butler, "The Cavalry Fight at Trevilian Station," 4:237.

15. Ibid., 4:240.

16. Hewitt, et al., eds., *Supplement*, 6, 36:815. The information on Lee's movement start-time is from a memorandum prepared in December 1866 by Lee's assistant adjutant general, Major James D. Ferguson.

17. Gabriel Manigault, "Autobiography, 1887–1897," Manigault Family Papers #484, Southern Historical Collection, Wilson Library, University of North Carolina, Chapel Hill, 422. Butler, in his account of the battle, mistakenly wrote that Captain Mulligan's squadron was assigned to the 4th South Carolina (Butler, "The Cavalry Fight at Trevilian Station," 4:237). Manigault correctly noted that Mulligan was from Dunovant's Regiment, the 5th South Carolina Cavalry (Manigault, "Autobiography," 422).

18. Butler, "The Cavalry Fight at Trevilian Station," 4:237. Butler wrote that his intent in ordering Snowden to charge was to "develop the force in front of us."

19. Manigault, "Autobiography," 423.

20. Johnson, *University Memorial*, 407. Later that morn-

ing Palmer was briefly captured, but after coming under fire from Confederate artillery, was recovered by the Confederates. Although his wound initially showed signs of healing, Palmer died of infection on June 28, 1864. He was buried in the University of Virginia burying ground. The *University Memorial* mistakenly describes the events surrounding Palmer's wounding as having occurred in May 1863 in action against Stoneman's raiders. However, Palmer is correctly identified as a Trevilian's casualty in a letter dated July 25, 1864, by Captain James Lipscomb, Butler's assistant adjutant general (Hewett, et al., eds., *Supplement*, 3, 95, 587).

21. Brooks, *Butler and His Cavalry*, 191, 236. Captain Calhoun was the grandson of the Southern statesman of the same name. His squadron made two mounted charges during the day's fighting.

22. Manigault, "Autobiography," 423. The horse Butler was riding belonged to Private James Adger of the Charleston Light Dragoons.

23. U.R. Brooks, "Memories of Battles," *Confederate Veteran*, XXII, 9 (September 1914), 408. In contrast, Brooks wrote that Hampton never cursed when ordering his men into battle. Brooks's brother, Winfield Butler Brooks, a private in company B, 6th South Carolina, was killed in action at Trevilian's (*Recollections and Reminiscences: 1861–1865 Through World War I*, 12 vols. [South Carolina Division, United Daughters of the Confederacy, 1992–2002], 3:546).

24. *OR*, 36, I:808. Torbert's official report of the battle was dated July 4, 1864. Custer made no mention of Torbert's orders in his own report.

25. Bowen, *Regimental History of the First New York Dragoons*, 7, 89, 97, 197.

26. Eli H. Lawyer, "Sheridan's Trevillian Raid: Incidents on that Expedition as Told by One of the 2nd Cav. Boys," in *National Tribune*, April 13, 1911. The similarity between Stephen Palmer's account of the Confederate charge through the woods and Lawyer's account of Rodenbough's wounding is interesting. However, according to Lawyer, the Confederate who wounded Rodenbough was himself wounded in the fray and captured. The wounded and captured Confederate informed Lawyer that he was seventeen years old. Palmer was twenty-three years old at the time of the battle (Johnson, *University Memorial*, 407).

27. *OR*, 36,I:849.

28. For a discussion of the effects of isolation on individual soldiers and small-unit cohesion, see S.L.A. Marshall's *Men Against Fire: The Problem of Battle Command in Future War* (Gloucester, MA: Peter Smith, 1978). Although somewhat dated—Marshall conducted his research during World War II—his insights regarding the behavior of soldiers and the performance of small units in battle endure.

29. Charles McK. Leoser, "Personal Recollections—Prison Life," in Theophilus F. Rodenbough, *From Everglade to Canyon in the 2nd United States Cavalry: An Authentic Account of Service in Florida, Mexico, Virginia, and the Indian Country, 1836–1875* (New York: D. Van Norstrand, 1875; reprint ed., Norman: University of Oklahoma Press, 2000), 315–318. Leoser claimed that his horse was worn out and died within two hours after he gave it up, thus "impoverishing the Confederate States to that extent." Thus far in the war, Leoser had a varied career. At the beginning of the conflict, he had been detailed to Washington to drill the 11th New York Infantry, better known as the "Fire Zouaves." He had been appointed lieutenant colonel of that regiment upon the death of Colonel Elmer E. Ellsworth—generally regarded as the war's first casualty—in Alexandria in May 1861. Leoser was promoted to colonel of the regiment following the death of Colonel Noah L. Farnham at First Manassas in July 1861. In April 1862, he resigned his volunteer commission and returned to duty with the 2nd U.S. where he quickly impressed his contemporaries with his demeanor. Today Leoser would be called "unflappable." Within his regiment, his friends referred to him as "the cool captain" (USMA AOG, *Annual Reunion* [1896], 125–129; Theophilus F. Rodenbough, ed., *The Army of the United States: Historical Sketches of Staff and Line with Portraits of Generals in Chief* [New York: Maynard, Merrill, 1896], 179).

30. Brooks, *Butler and His Cavalry*, 243. In reality, Butler's response was not particularly helpful to Rutledge. To "flank back," presented Rutledge with two feasible options, both of which were risky. He could shift his entire line to the right, preventing the enemy from flanking him, but at the same time opening a gap on his left between the 4th South Carolina and the 5th South Carolina. Potentially, that gap could be exploited by Merritt. Alternatively, Rutledge could extend his line to the right, thinning his forces all along his front. However, by doing so, his entire line would be weakened. Butler's guidance to "flank back" may have been given in jest. In the account in *Butler and His Cavalry*, the following day Butler and Rutledge laughed about the exchange of messages. Rutledge's immediate reaction to Butler's terse retort was not recorded, but may have been perceived by Rutledge as a slight. Gabriel Manigault, Rutledge's adjutant, felt that Butler did not hold Rutledge in high regard. During an engagement on Old Church Road two days after Haw's Shop, Butler while deploying his forces, ignored Rutledge, the senior colonel present. Manigault wrote that "this was the first act of hostility by Butler toward Rutledge and it was persisted until the end of the war" (Manigault, "Autobiography," 409). Rutledge later confided to Manigault that a disparaging comment he had made in private about Butler's generalship—"if that [fight on the Old Church Road] was war, then Jomini was a fool"—had been relayed to Butler and was the source of Butler's animosity (Manigault "Autobiography," 412). Antoine Henry Jomini's *The Art of War* was published in France in 1838. Based upon Napoleon's campaigns, Jomini's writings had been widely studied in both Europe and the United States. An English translation was published by the United States Military Academy in 1862.

31. Brooks, *Butler and His Cavalry*, 243.

32. John Bausketт, "The Fight at Louisa Court House and Trevellion," *Louisa County Historical Magazine* 30 (Spring 1999), 20–21.

33. Ibid., 21.

34. Manigault, "Autobiography," 423.

35. Ibid., 424.

36. Ibid., 424–426.

37. Ibid., 426.

38. Ibid.

39. Ibid., 428.

40. Bowen, *Regimental History of the First New York Dragoons*, 187–188. During the Civil War, infantry and cavalrymen were generally uncomfortable with friendly artillery firing over their heads. The technology for fusing projectiles was rudimentary and setting fuses correctly depended entirely upon the skill of gunners in estimating ranges to targets. "Short rounds," exploding over the heads of friendly troops were not uncommon and could be lethal. Additionally, with rifled cannons, a sabot, which was frequently used to impart spin on a projectile, would detach from its projectile upon leaving the muzzle of the cannon. Fragments of the sabot would travel some distance downrange potentially injuring any friendly troopers who might be struck.

41. At least one man in the regiment blamed Thorp's

capture on the regulars of the 2nd U.S. He wrote: "He [Thorp] would probably not have been captured had the United States regulars of our brigade done their duty and kept up on the line of battle; instead, they played us the same old trick as at Manassas, Cold Harbor, and on other occasions—slunk back to the rear, out of the reach of bullets, leaving a gap in the line, enabling the Johnnies to swing around and gobble up a man worth more to the Union cause than their entire pusillanimous crowd." It is unlikely that "pusillanimous" conduct on the part of the regulars resulted in Thorp's capture. The 6th Pennsylvania Cavalry, a volunteer regiment, occupied position on the left flank of the 1st New York Dragoons. Later that day, Thorp was briefly freed by the men of Custer's brigade only to be quickly captured again by the Confederates. He remained a prisoner of war until the end of the war (Bowen, *Regimental History of the First New York Dragoons*, 187, 288; *OR*, 36, I:849).

42. Bowen, *Regimental History of the First New York Dragoons*, 188. In this instance, "sanguinary" is defined as "accompanied by much bloodshed," differing from "sanguine" which generally means "confidently hopeful."

43. When the regiment was organized in the fall of 1861, the men were initially armed with nine-foot lances. The regiment's commander, Richard Rush and the then–Army of the Potomac Commander, George B. McClellan, were West Point classmates. McClellan, who had been very favorably impressed by the French military during an inspection tour in Europe in 1855, arranged for the regiment to be outfitted in the style of French cavalry. The lances proved useless in Virginia and unpopular among the men, and in May 1863 the lances were turned in and replaced with carbines.

44. The situation in the 6th Pennsylvania reveals how difficult regimental succession of command could be during the Civil War. The regiment had been without either a colonel or lieutenant colonel since the spring of 1863 when the regiment's colonel, Richard Rush, who was in ill health, was transferred to the Reserve Corps in Washington. The lieutenant colonel of the regiment, C. Ross Smith, was at the time detailed to the Cavalry Corps staff. Consequently, command was exercised by the regiment's senior major. Upon Rush's resignation in September 1863, Smith was promoted to colonel. However, Smith remained on detail and was never mustered-in the more senior grade. At the same time, Smith continued to encumber the regiment's lieutenant colonel billet until he was discharged at the end of his three-year term of service in September 1864. Majors thus continued in command of the regiment during that time. At the beginning of the Overland Campaign, the regiment's senior major, William P.C. Treichel, was absent on sick leave and the Lancers were commanded by Major James Barr. Barr was wounded—pistol ball in the face—at Todd's Tavern, and commanded devolved upon Captain Charles Leiper. Leiper was seriously wounded at Old Church on May 30, leading to Captain Clark, the next senior officer who commanded Company M, being designated the regiment's commander. After the Trevilian's Raid, Treichel returned briefly to the regiment only to be medically discharged on July 14, 1864. Leiper returned to duty in August 1864 and by the end of the war had been promoted in succession to major, lieutenant colonel, and colonel of the 6th Pennsylvania. Leiper also earned a brevet to brigadier general of volunteers (S.L. Gracey, *Annals of the Sixth Pennsylvania Cavalry* [Philadelphia: E.H. Butler, 1868; reprint, Lancaster, OH: Vanberg, 1996], 235–236, 254, 265; Bates, *History of Pennsylvania Volunteers, 1861–1865* [1871], 2:753).

45. Cullum, *Biographical Register*, #1602; USMA AOG, *Annual Reunion* (1898), 47–50.

Chapter 12

1. Warner, *Generals in Blue*, 124. At the time of the battle, Devin was forty-one years old, Merritt had just turned thirty, and Custer was twenty-four. Torbert was within three weeks of his thirty-first birthday.

2. On June 10, the 17th Pennsylvania found the Confederate hospital near Spotsylvania Courthouse. Lieutenant Colonel James Q. Anderson, the regiment's commander, demanded a surrender from the hospital officials. After that formality, Confederates who could not be moved were paroled. All casualties—both Union and Confederate—who could be moved were taken with the regiment as it made a forced march to rejoin Sheridan's main body. Marching through the night, the Pennsylvanians were harassed by bushwhackers, but no casualties were reported. The 17th Pennsylvania arrived near the battlefield on the afternoon of June 11 and although placed in support of Devin's brigade, it was not engaged (Moyer, *History of the Seventeenth Regiment Pennsylvania Volunteer Cavalry*, 84–85).

3. Neither Torbert nor Merritt in their reports describe in detail the repositioning of Merritt's regiments as Devin moved up. However, close comparison of Merritt's description of his deployment with Devin's description of his initial array indicates that Merritt must have shifted his regiments to his right. As a result, the 1st New York Dragoons, which had been on Merritt's right, became his left-flank regiment which was tied-in with the 9th New York of Devin's brigade (*OR* 36, I:849, 840–841). This repositioning to the west would presumably have been made on Torbert's orders. Torbert, an experienced infantry commander would have known that management of the fighting in the woods would be made significantly more difficult were regiments of two brigades intermingled. Later in the afternoon as the Union forces occupied terrain about the station, Devin confirmed that Merritt still was on his right, or to the west (*OR*, 36, I:841).

4. The 9th New York got off to a troubled start after it mustered into service and arrived in Washington on November 29, 1861. In early 1862, the War Department had been unable to mount the newly-organized regiment due to a shortage of horses. During the Peninsular Campaign, four companies of the regiment were detailed to service with the artillery while eight companies were issued muskets and served as infantry. This caused much resentment among the men and prompted a near-mutiny. The regiment was sent from the Peninsula to Washington to await a decision by the War Department on whether regiment would be mounted or the men discharged and allowed to return home. At the end of June the regiment was finally mounted, ending talk of possibly mustering out. After that inauspicious start, the regiment had served credibly since taking the field with Pope's Army of Virginia in mid–July 1862 (Newel Cheney, *History of the Ninth Regiment New York Volunteer Cavalry, War of 1861 to 1865* [Jamestown, NY: Martin Mertz, 1900; reprint, Ashville, NY: Berrybook, 1998], 23, 29–49).

5. Maps depicting the June 11 fighting along the Fredericksburg Road usually place Devin's brigade to the right of Merritt's brigade, contrary to the description provided here. The map accompanying Theophilus Rodenbough's account of Trevilian's in *Battles and Leaders* depicts Devin on the right, Merritt in the center, and John I. Gregg on the left and most accounts since have followed suit. In evaluating the accuracy of Rodenbough's map, it is important to note that Rodenbough was wounded early in the action that day, likely before Devin's brigade came up. Further, Rodenbough

did not discuss the disposition of the three brigades in the text of his *Battles and Leaders* article. Also, Rodenbough's account originally appeared in *Century Magazine* before the War Department's publication of the *Official Records*. Consequently, Rodenbough may have not had ready access to the various commanders' official reports of the action when he composed his piece. Devin, in his report of the battle, made clear that his brigade was on Merritt's left. "The Ninth New York deployed and advanced on the right of the main road, connecting on its right with the First New York Dragoons, and on the left with a small detachment of the Second Regulars (30 men). I was now ordered to send in the Fourth New York on the left of General Merritt's line. The regiment was deployed connecting on the right with the First Regulars and on the left with Colonel Gregg's brigade. The First Regulars being soon after withdrawn from the left [of the 9th New York], the Fourth New York was ordered to move to the right and connect with the road.... The two regiments of my brigade, Fourth and Ninth New York, now being formed on each side of the road, I assumed command at that point and advanced the line" (*OR*, 36, I:840–841).

6. *OR* 36, I:841. One of the twelve companies of the 6th New York is not accounted for in this disposition.

7. Gary R. Baker, *Cadets in Gray: The Story of the Cadets of the South Carolina Military Academy and the Cadet Rangers in the Civil War* (Columbia, SC: Palmetto Bookworks, 1989) 97; Gorgas, *The Journals of Josiah Gorgas*, 117; Brooks, *Butler and His Cavalry*, 548. Shortly before Trevilian's, the regiment's lieutenant colonel, Lovick P. Miller, had been detailed by Butler to duty at the brigade's "dead line camp" near Richmond. The dead line camp held men physically unfit for field duty, men who were dismounted, and men with unserviceable horses. Butler placed Miller in charge of the camp with orders to "break it up." Miller organized most of the men into a dismounted battalion and sent them to rejoin the brigade upon its return from the raid. He also forced shirkers to either return to duty with their regiments or be admitted to hospital. Finally, Miller arranged for better care for unfit horses (Brooks, *Butler and His Cavalry*, 341–343).

8. Barr, *Let Us Meet in Heaven*, 236. John Wesley Barr was one of James Barr's older brothers.

9. Ibid., 242, 246.

10. Stanton P. Allen, *Down in Dixie: Life in a Cavalry Regiment in the War Days from the Wilderness to Appomattox* (Boston: D. Lothrop, 1893), 362. Very late in the day, another of Davies's regiments, the 1st New Jersey, participated with Gregg's brigade in an attack that closed out the action on June 11 (*OR*, 36, I:855, 858, 862).

11. In their official reports, Colonel John I. Gregg and his regimental commanders failed to describe their deployment. Gregg's single comment on the day's fighting was "[June] 11th, engaged all day with the enemy at Trevilian Station" (*OR*, 36, I:862). The itinerary of the 8th Pennsylvania hints that the regiment was on the left of the brigade line: "... regiment moved to the left, dismounted, and to the advance, driving the enemy half a mile" (*OR*, 36, I:868). Samuel Bates, in his summary of the history of the 4th Pennsylvania Cavalry, wrote that later in the day the 4th and 2nd Pennsylvania regiments came upon the rear of a body of Confederates, whom they attacked. The 4th then became separated in thick woods with a squadron under Colonel Covode "taking the right of the First Division," and the remainder of the regiment under Major W.N. Biddle "moving to the center of the brigade and holding the line near the railroad." In actuality, the "right of the First Division was likely almost a mile to the west of the 4th Pennsylvania (Bates, *History of Pennsylvania Volunteers*, 2:529).

12. Tobie, *History of the First Maine Cavalry*, 283–286.
13. *OR*, 36: I:807–808.
14. *OR*, 36, I:868.
15. Cheney, *History of the Ninth New York Cavalry*, 184. In Cheney's account, the regiment was mounted in the rear on the road when the order came to make their attack. Given the redeployment of Merritt's regiments earlier, it seems more likely that the 9th New York would have already dismounted and deployed.

Chapter 13

1. William O. Lee, *Personal and Historical Sketches and Facial History of and by Members of the Seventh Regiment Michigan Volunteer Cavalry, 1862–1865* (Detroit: 7th Michigan Cavalry Association, Nd), 82, 230, 239. Major Brewer had just been transferred from the 1st Michigan to the 7th Michigan to replace Major Henry Granger, who had been killed at Yellow Tavern. Brewer was promoted to lieutenant colonel effective June 6, 1864, but never mustered-in at that grade. He was mortally wounded at Winchester on September 19, 1864, and died the following week (Isham, *An Historical Sketch*, 50, 89–90).

2. Robert T. Hubard, Jr., *The Civil War Memoirs of a Confederate Cavalryman*, ed. Thomas P. Nanzig (Tuscaloosa: University of Alabama Press, 2007), 170–171. Robert T. Hubard, Jr., graduated from Hampden-Sydney College and was studying law at the University of Virginia upon the outbreak of the war. Hubard enlisted as a private in the 3rd Virginia in May 1861, was later promoted to lieutenant and appointed regimental adjutant. He was wounded at Five Forks on April 1, 1865 (Ibid., xii-xiii). Shoemaker's Battery supported Wickham's Brigade. In Captain Shoemaker's words, "one section of my battery was engaged in the morning in shelling the woods near Louisa courthouse" (Hewett, et al., *Supplement*, 6, 36:825).

3. In a letter to his wife, dated June 21, 1864, Custer proudly informed Libbie, "As usual, the Michigan Brigade was detached from the main body, for the purpose of turning the enemy flank and, if possible, attacking him in the rear" (Merington, ed., *The Custer Story*, 104).

4. Hubard, Jr., *The Civil War Memoirs of a Confederate Cavalryman*, 171.

5. *OR*, 36, I:831. Colonel George Gray, the former commander of the 6th Michigan, had recently resigned his commission. Shortly before departing on the Trevilian's Raid, Custer sent a letter to Michigan Governor Austin Blair recommending he appoint Kidd to fill the vacant colonel's billet. To the letter, Custer appended a petition recommending Kidd's promotion which had been signed by all the officers of the 6th Michigan. Concurrently, Gray interceded personally on Kidd's behalf with Governor Blair, who was attending the Republican Party Convention in Baltimore (Kidd, *One of Custer's Wolverines*, 90–92).

6. Lee, *Personal and Historical Sketches*, 230. Although he does not explicitly say so, if Smith did not detect the departure of the main body of the regiment and had to run to catch up, it is likely the men of Company F were also left behind when the regiment moved out.

7. Custer reported that Wickham's men followed his brigade "but did not press my rear very close." However, Fitz Lee reported that he "quickly retrac[ed] his steps" instead of following the Michigan Brigade on the track through the woods. Since no contact on the track through the woods was reported, it is likely that Wickham did not follow Custer (*OR*, 36, I:823, Hewett, et al. eds., *Supplement*, 6, 36:800).

8. Kidd, *Personal Recollections*, 352.

9. Ibid. According to the drill manual, on the march, a "four" required ten feet of what today is termed "road space." Consequently, the column of a regiment with four hundred men would extend one thousand feet, not counting intervals between units. A regiment moving in a column of twos or single file would be proportionally longer, and the longer the column, the more time required to deploy the regiment in preparation for a charge. The appropriate interval between platoons varied based upon the strength of the platoon. This was necessary to allow space for the platoons to move from a column into line to either the right or left. Specifically, platoon guides were to maintain a distance from the platoon to the front equivalent to the frontage of their platoon (Cooke, *Cavalry Tactics*, 180).

10. OR, 36, I:823; Urwin, *Custer Victorious*, 155.

11. Hewett, et al. eds., *Supplement*, 6, 36:821. During the day's fighting, Hart's Battery suffered four casualties. Lieutenant William T. Adams was seriously wounded and three men were killed (U.R. Brooks, *Stories of the Confederacy* [Columbia, SC: State, 1912], 267).

12. OR, 36, I:830.

13. OR, 36, I:823, 830–831. Custer excused Alger's disobedience, writing in his official report that the colonel "acting under the impulses of pardonable zeal, did not halt at the station as the order required, but advanced more than a mile hoping to increase his captures." In his official report of the action, Alger made no mention of the order to halt his regiment at the station, and later Alger did not publicly dispute Custer's account. However, forty-two years after the fight at Trevilian's, J.K. Lowden, who had served in Company D of the 5th Michigan and had been captured at Trevilian's, wrote rather obliquely about the genesis of the charge in a *National Tribune* article. "One day in 1890 it came in my way to find out the inwardness of the matter, and I freely acknowledge that it came as the light of revelation across midnight darkness why we [the 5th Michigan] were so placed at Trevilian. Now I firmly believe, and know, that Col. Alger was—by the act of another, and not by a pardonable zeal or by his own volition—placed by positive orders from his superior in a spot where his regiment must suffer a loss of one-half its strength." Admittedly, Lowden—loyal to Alger and having been captured—was not impartial in the matter. He concluded his article with a tribute to Colonel Alger, "whose name is emblazoned in gold on the heart of every one of Michigan's 5th Cavalry…" (J.K. Lowden, "A Gallant Record: Michigan's 5th Cav. In the Latter Period of the War," *National Tribune*, July 30, 1896). Unfortunately, Lowden provided little specific information regarding the source of his information that a superior officer—presumably Custer—ordered the 5th Michigan to charge beyond the railroad station. Consequently it is difficult to assess the veracity of his assertion. Interestingly, Major Kidd later wrote that his orders at Trevilian's were to change and that "Nothing was said about stopping" (Kidd, *Personal Recollections*, 354).

14. Wiley C. Howard, *Sketch of Cobb Legion Cavalry and Some Incidents and Scenes Remembered: Presented and Read under appointment of Atlanta Camp 159, United Confederate Veterans*, August 19, 1901 (Np. Nd), 15–16. Before the war, Howard, who had three brothers serving in the Cobb's Legion, attended the University of Georgia where he studied law. On August 1, 1864, Howard was elected lieutenant of Company C. After the war he practiced law and then worked as a bill collector. He died on April 29, 1930 (Mesic, *Cobb's Legion Cavalry*, 243).

15. Kidd, *Personal Recollections*, 353.

16. Ibid.

17. Ibid., 354–355.

18. Kidd, *Personal Recollections*, 357.

19. In his official report, Alger claimed that in the charge the 5th Michigan captured 800 prisoners, 1,500 horses, 1 stand of colors, 6 caissons, 40 ambulances, and 50 army wagons. He noted that many of the prisoners, rather than surrendering their weapons, broke their arms upon being captured (OR, 36, I:830). Alger and the 5th Michigan were certainly successful in capturing many men, horses, and much equipment. However, it seems unlikely that either Alger or any of his subordinate officers could make an accurate inventory of the captures since they quickly came under Confederate attack and were driven back in some disorder.

20. OR, 36, I:830.

21. OR, 36, I:831.

22. OR, 36, I:831; Avery wrote that as the group with Alger was charging through Confederate lines, someone ordered counter-march and the group split apart with some of the men—including Avery—falling back. Remaining behind with Avery, who also had charge of several captured Confederates, were six sergeants, two or three corporals, and about fifteen men representing every company in the regiment (Avery, *Under Custer's Command*, 89).

Chapter 14

1. Thomas L. Rosser, "The Battle of Trevilian Station, VA., June 11 and 12, 1864," in *Confederate Soldier in the Civil War 1861–1865* 1 (July 5, 1897), 260.

2. Butler, "The Cavalry Fight at Trevilian Station," 237.

3. Brooks, *Butler and His Cavalry*, 245. Using today's tactics, a commander would likely designate a portion of his command to act as a security force—sometimes called a Detachment Left in Contact (DLIC)—to cover the withdrawal of his main body while deceiving the enemy regarding the operation. Once the main body had moved to the rear, the security force might then break contact and withdraw. Alternatively, the security force might delay the enemy by fighting from successive positions as it maneuvered to the rear (Headquarters, Department of the Army, *Field Manual 3-90: Tactics* [Washington, 2001], sections 11–65 thru 11–91; Headquarters, Department of the Army, *Field Manual 71-3: The Armor and Mechanized Infantry Brigade* [Washington, 1996], Chapter 6, Section 4).

4. Butler, "The Cavalry Fight at Trevilian Station," 237.

5. OR, 36, I:807.

6. Rosser, "The Battle of Trevilian Station," 260.

7. Kidd, *Personal Recollections*, 357–358.

8. Ibid, 358.

9. OR, 36, I:823.

10. Rosser, "The Battle of Trevilian Station," 260. Since Rosser's brigade was moving in column on the road, it is likely that it took some time to bring a sizeable amount of force to bear on Custer's brigade.

11. Rosser resigned from the Class of 1861 shortly before its graduation in May of that year. Custer was a year behind Rosser in the Class of 1862 which graduated in June 1861, one year early because of the war.

12. William N. McDonald, *A History of the Laurel Brigade, Originally the Ashby Cavalry of the Army of Northern Virginia and Chew's Battery* (Baltimore: Sun Job Office, 1907; reprint, Baltimore: Johns Hopkins University Press, 2002), 252; Merington, ed., *The Custer Story*, 105; Rosser, "The Battle of Trevilian Station," 260. U.R. Brooks identified Custer's color bearer as Sergeant John Nash and also claimed he was shot by Major Conrad (Brooks, *Butler and*

His Cavalry, 244). In his account of the death of his color bearer in a letter to Libbie on June 21, 1864, Custer inexplicably identified his color bearer as a Sergeant Mashon who "was struck while gallantly carrying his flag at the head of a charge." However, in his official report, Custer eulogized Sergeant Belloir, writing: "With unfeigned sorrow I am called upon to record the death of one of the 'bravest of the brave,' Sergt. Mitchell Belloir of the First Michigan Cavalry, who has been my color bearer since the organization of this brigade. Sergt. Mitchell Belloir received his death-wound while nobly discharging his duty to his flag and to his country. He was killed in the advance while gallantly cheering the men forward to victory" (*OR*, 36:824). Other sources indicate that Major Holmes Conrad was appointed assistant chief of staff to Brigadier General John Imboden on June 9, 1864, and did not join Rosser until about October of that year. Robert Krick, *Staff Officers in Gray: A Biographical Register of the Staff Officers in the Army of Northern Virginia* (Chapel Hill: University of North Carolina Press, 2003), 102. However, Conrad's participation in the Overland Campaign with the Laurel Brigade is documented on several instances in McDonald's *History of the Laurel Brigade*. It thus appears likely that Conrad was detailed to duty with Rosser, although orders formally assigning him to the Laurel Brigade were prepared and issued—today referred to as being "cut"—later.

13. Frank M. Myers, *The Comanches: A History of White's Battalion, Virginia Cavalry, Laurel Brigade, Hampton's Div., A.N.V., C.S.A.* (Baltimore, MD: Kelly, Piet, 1871; reprint, Alexandria, VA: Stonewall House, 1985).

14. Isham, *An Historical Sketch*, 56–57.

15. *OR*, 36, I:823–824.

16. *OR*, 36, I:823. Estimates of the numbers of horses, men, and wagons captured vary. In a letter to his wife, Elizabeth dated June 21, 1864, Custer claimed that his brigade captured "over 1500 horses with saddles, complete; 6 caissons of artillery filled with ammunition; 250 wagons and several hundred prisoners" (Merington, ed., *The Custer Story*, 104). Alger put his captures at "800 prisoners, 1,500 horses, 1 stand of colors, 6 caissons, 40 ambulances, and 50 army wagons" (*OR*, 36, I:830).

17. Lee, *Personal and Historical Sketches*, 230.

18. *OR*, 36, I:824.

19. Mark S. Stowe, *Company B, 6th Michigan Cavalry* (Grand Rapids, MI: Stowe, 2002), 39–41. Obviously, Captain Powers did not receive the due process one would expect under similar circumstances today, and he probably did not receive the due process set forth in regulations at that time. One may fairly question Custer's motivation in this matter: an attempt to affix responsibility for the losses on the failure of a subordinate. Also, one might ask, "Given the circumstances, where could Powers have positioned baggage train, prisoners, and captured materiel to prevent recapture by the Confederates?" However, to be fair, it is possible that Custer—in the heat of battle—did not recall a request to move the trains. Interestingly, James Kidd made no mention of Powers's "cowardice and treachery," his capture, or his dismissal in his *Personal Recollections*.

20. Rodenbough, "Sheridan's Trevilian Raid," 233.

21. Brooks, *Butler and His Cavalry*, 187–188, 191. Writing to a cousin in July 14, 1864, R.G. Maynard, a courier for Butler, cited Calhoun's actions at Trevilian's: "*In the fight at 'Trevillian' Station' Captain Calhoun led two very gallant charges which reflected such a lustre on his military capacities that he was complimented on the field by General Hampton*" [emphasis in original] (Ibid., 194).

22. Hewett, et. al., *Supplement*, 6, 36:784.

23. A mural at the Citadel depicting Hampton leading Rangers in the charge commemorates the event.

24. Brooks, *Butler and His Cavalry*, 194–195, 244–245; Bauskett, "The Fights at Louisa Courthouse and Trevellion," 22–23; Isham, *An Historical Sketch*, 57. The wartime history of Hampton and Hart's Battery were closely entwined. In 1861, Hampton had purchased and imported from England three Blakely guns for the Washington Artillery Battery of the Hampton Legion. Hart initially served as first lieutenant of the battery. The battery, later commanded by Hart, habitually supported Hampton's Brigade of cavalry. Moses Humphrey was wounded at Trevilian's, and wounded a second time at Monroe's Crossroads in March 1865. He died of his wounds on April 30, 1865 (Research Online, http://www.researchonline.net/sccw/rosters/6thcavf.htm).

25. Brooks, *Butler and His Cavalry*, 245–246. It was initially believed that Buchanan was mortally wounded, but he survived. After the war he represented his Georgia district in the United States Congress.

26. Andrew Butler, called either "Pick" or "Tall Pick," was commissioned in the 1st South Carolina Infantry before being appointed to Butler's staff in 1864. In September 1864 he became a volunteer aide de camp to General Dunovant, but was captured on the 30th of that month and spent the remainder of the war in a federal prison camp (Krick, *Staff Officers in Gray*, 89).

27. Hubard, *Civil War Memories*, 171.

28. An incident in 1862 was indicative of Critcher's ineffectiveness as a combat leader. As Major General George McClellan withdrew from the Peninsula, Critcher was ordered to take his battalion—the 15th Virginia Regiment had not yet been organized—to Fredericksburg. Critcher set a few pickets forward at the Rappahannock River while most of his men bedded down for the night in the city. Shortly before daylight, one of the pickets galloped up Princess Anne Street toward Critcher's headquarters shouting, "Run for your lives! The Yankees are coming!" Critcher's entire command panicked and fled. The event was described by an officer from another cavalry battalion: "Many of them mounted their horses with only halters on and rode off, leaving everything, even their headquarters flag…. Major Critcher's men came straggling in after many days, and were very much ashamed that they had allowed themselves to be stampeded by one of their men before they had even seen the enemy" (Horatio C. Haggard, "Cavalry Fight at Fredericksburg," *Confederate Veteran* 21 [June 1913], 295). Obviously, in this incident Lieutenant Colonel Critcher failed to ensure adequate security, and then lost control of his command.

29. Before he was captured, Critcher had temporarily commanded the regiment in the absence of the commander, Colonel William Ball who was on lengthy sick leave. Upon Ball's resignation in February 1864, Major Charles Collins had been promoted to colonel over the more-senior Critcher who was still in Union captivity. Even though exchanged, Critcher did not return to duty with the regiment until after the death of Colonel Collins, who was killed at Todd's Tavern on May 7, 1864 (John Fortier, *15th Virginia Cavalry*, 127).

30. Fortier, *15th Virginia Cavalry*, 75–76; Hewett, et al., eds., *Supplement*, 6, 36:815. Naturally, Critcher was bitter about his relief and submitted his resignation from the army the following day, writing, "Having enlisted and mustered into the service nearly half the Regt., and having commanded it for nearly twelve months, I was informed yesterday on the battlefield in the presence of my Regt. that it was placed under the command of another. Under such circum-

stances, my honor and self respect require that I promptly and unconditionally, but respectfully, resign my commission, which I do accordingly to take effect from this date." Part of Critcher's pique may have resulted from the fact that he was replaced by an officer junior in grade. In his endorsement of Critcher's resignation, Lomax commented—perhaps as a face-saving measure for the relieved Critcher—that "I consider Lt. Col. Critcher a gallant officer and regret to lose his services entirely from the command." Nonetheless, Lomax recommended that the resignation be accepted, which it was the following week. Critcher left the division for home immediately after submitting his resignation. Lee's adjutant, Major James Ferguson, suspected that there would be some "trouble" resulting from the relief, but apparently none materialized (Hewett, et al., eds., *Supplement*, 6, 36:816–817). Major Mason's appointment to command also met with disapproval from Captain John Cooper, who had temporarily commanded the regiment from after Collins's death until Critcher's return to duty. Cooper also submitted his resignation, but it was not accepted. Cooper remained on duty with the regiment until he was captured at Luray on September 24, 1864 (Fortier, *15th Virginia Cavalry*, 75–76, 128, 129).

31. How the baggage train came to be positioned to the east of Custer's perimeter is not is not well documented. It appears most likely that when Custer summoned his trailing regiments forward, the trains moved with them, prompting the interaction in the perimeter between Custer and the "muddled officer" described earlier. However, it is possible that when the trailing regiments moved forward, the trains remained behind so as not to become engaged in the fight around the depot and to the west.

32. Arlene Reynolds, ed., *The Civil War Memories of Elizabeth Bacon Custer* (Austin: University of Texas Press, 1994), 45. Custer hired Eliza as a cook while camped at Amissville in August 1863. Eliza, a slave, had lived on a nearby farm in Rappahannock County (T.J. Stiles, *Custer's Trials* [New York: Alfred A. Knopf, 2015], 117).

33. Beverley K. Whittle to Father, July 13, 1864, Papers of Beverley Kennon Whittle (Mss 7973), Albert and Shirley Small Special Collections Library, University of Virginia, Charlottesville.

34. Merington, *The Custer Story*, 104.

35. Ibid. It is somewhat surprising given the restrictions imposed by Sheridan regarding the number of wagons accompanying the raiding party, that Custer took his personal wagon loaded with baggage that was clearly not mission-essential. On the surface, it appears that Custer's wagon may have been in violation of army regulations, which in its section on Baggage Trains, states: "The General commanding the army and the Generals of Division will not permit any general or staff officer, or regiment under their orders, or any person whatsoever, attached to their command, to have more than the authorized amount or means of transportation. For this purpose they will themselves make, and cause to be made, frequent reviews and inspections of the trains. They will see that no trooper is employed to lead a private horse, no soldier to drive a private vehicle, and that no trooper is put on foot to lend his horse to an officer. They will not permit the wagons of the artillery or of the train to be loaded with anything foreign to their proper service, nor any public horse, for any occasion, to be harnessed to a private carriage" (U.S. War Department, *Revised Regulations*, paragraph 779).

36. Conrad, *The Rebel Scout*, 50–51. Conrad identified the artillery officer as Major Thompson, mistaking both the spelling of Thomson's name and his grade. Captain Thomson was promoted to major on February 18, 1865 (Robert J. Trout, *"The Hoss": Officer Biographies and Rosters of the Stuart Horse Artillery Battalion* [Richmond: JEBFLO, 2003], 59).

37. Johnson, *University Memorial*, 742–743. Boston had already experienced Union captivity once, which likely provided the impetus behind his escape. At Aldie, Virginia, on June 17, 1863, Thomas Rosser, the then-commander of the 5th Virginia, ordered Reuben Boston's squadron to dismount and fight in a hay field beyond supporting distance of the rest of the regiment. Boston and his men then came under attack from two Union regiments. Wounded, unsupported, and almost out of ammunition, Boston surrendered his men. Until his exchange in March 1864, Boston was held at Johnson Island and Point Lookout (Ibid.; Driver, Jr. *5th Virginia Cavalry*, 54–55, 186).

38. Thomas D. Gold, *History of Clarke County, Virginia, and Its Connection with the War Between the States* (Berryville, VA: Np., 1914), 288–289; Leroy E. Williams, "Charge of the Clarke Cavalry at Trevelyan Station," *Southern Bivouac* 3 (Sep 1884-May 1885), 218–219. The charge was made by about thirty men of Company D, the Clarke County Cavalry, and a "small remnant" of Company H, The Wise Dragoons of Fauquier County. Gold wrote that Captain Joseph Kennerly of Company D led the charge and reported that company's casualties as three killed and five wounded. In the withdrawal, Leroy Williams was shot through the hand and lung, fell from his horse, and was left on the field. Taken prisoner, Williams was well treated by Custer's men. He was carried to a spot with shade, given water and coffee, and during the night given a blanket with which to keep warm. Around midnight, a few officers passed by and hearing the groans of the wounded prisoners, offered the Confederates some apple brandy, which Williams believed saved his life. Williams concluded his *Southern Bivouac* article with praise for the men from Michigan: "I say, from the bottom of my heart, God bless Custer's men for their great kindness and humanity to me!"

39. Rodenbough, "Sheridan's Trevilian Raid," 233.

40. *New York Herald*, June 21, 1864.

41. Lee, *Personal and Historical Sketches*, 230–231.

42. *OR*, 36, I:824. Custer did not mention the recovery of Pennington's gun in his letter to Libbie describing the battle.

43. *OR*, 36, I:808. Since Torbert did not personally witness Custer in action, it is possible that he heard this account from Custer.

44. Merington, ed., *The Custer Story*, 104.

45. Urwin, *Custer Victorious*, 162–163; *New York Herald*, June 21, 1864. Initially, Dana was commissioned second lieutenant in Company E, 8th Illinois Cavalry. He advanced to captain in command of Company L before he resigned his commission in July 1862 to accept appointment in the adjutant general's corps in which he eventually was promoted to lieutenant colonel (Hard, *History of the Eighth Cavalry*, 330, 336, 340).

Chapter 15

1. *OR*, 36, I:807–808, 841, 849–850.
2. Sanford, *Fighting Rebels and Redskins*, 243–244.
3. Ibid., 245.
4. Analysis of the terrain reveals that the Fredericksburg Road runs north-south along a ridge line. To the east the ground drops in elevation by fifty feet to a stream, South Fork, which runs generally parallel to the Fredericksburg Road at a distance of about 750 yards from the road. To the

west and south of the stream the ground rises fifty feet to the ridge line upon which the railroad and the Gordonsville Road run east-west and then southeast-northwest. It appears likely that both the 1st U.S. and the 9th New York, as they emerged from the woods, oriented their advance on the terrain—specifically the high ground to their right front which was occupied by Confederates, than on keeping their left flank anchored on the Fredericksburg Road.

5. *OR*, 36, 1:841. The misdirected regiment from Gregg's brigade was not identified.

6. Ibid.; Hall, *History of the Sixth New York Cavalry*, 197. The actual positioning of the 6th New York is not specified in the *OR*, or in the accounts by Hillman Hall or Alonzo Foster. However, according to Hall, "The Sixth and Ninth New York then made a charge near the station, capturing about 100 prisoners.... About noon we were ordered to the right to the station." Thus it appears more likely that the 6th New York was on the left of the 9th New York rather than the right.

7. Although not documented in the *OR*, the unidentified regiment from Gregg's brigade may have participated in the advance with Devin's regiments.

8. Brooks, *Butler and His Cavalry*, 246. The identity of Lieutenant Long is unclear. Brooks was a member of the 6th South Carolina and would presumably not err when identifying an officer of that regiment, but the regimental records do not reveal an officer named Long (although several privates were so-named). However, the rolls of the 4th South Carolina contain a Henry A. Long who was promoted to 3rd Lieutenant in 1863 (John Rigdon, *Historical Sketch and Roster: The SC 4th Cavalry Regiment* [Powder Springs, GA: Eastern Digital Resources, 2004], 110). It therefore seems likely that the provost guard was from the 4th South Carolina, not the 6th South Carolina.

9. Letter, Luigi diCesnola to George Wood, Esq., June 24, 1864, Spencer/Wood Family Papers of the Jonathan Drayton Papers (William L. Clement Library, University of Michigan, Ann Arbor). In the letter, diCesnola asserted that Torbert in his official report "suppressed" everything concerning the seizure of the station by the 4th New York. However, diCesnola did not provide a reason why Torbert would slight the performance of the 4th New York.

10. Cheney, *History of the Ninth New York*, 185. Corporal Nelson Taylor, Company I, 9th New York, claimed in a letter that he personally captured the battle flag which he found in a loaded ammunition wagon that had broken down during the Confederate flight (Nelson Taylor, *Saddle and Saber: The Letters of the Civil War Cavalryman Corporal Nelson Taylor*, ed. Gray Nelson Taylor [Bowie, MD: Heritage, 1993], 159).

11. Pat Jones, "Mother's Race across the Battlefield" in *Louisa Historical Magazine* 35 (Spring 2004), 38–39. At the time, the two major crops in central Virginia were corn, which was used mostly to feed livestock, and wheat, which was ground into flour to feed people. While horses can eat wheat flour, it is highly unusual. It would seem more likely that should Union soldiers—who were on short rations—find flour, they would have made bread or hoe cakes to feed themselves. Years later, a man named H.C. Orme from Phoenix, Arizona visited Louisa. He identified himself as the captain who had escorted Lucy to safety and recalled that he had aided "a very pretty lady, and a very pretty baby." Afterwards he was contacted by Lucy, who had moved to Waynesboro, Virginia, and she was presumably able to thank him for his concern for her safety during the war. A soldier named H.C. Orme is not listed in the National Park Service's Civil War Soldiers and Sailors Database, nor does the database contain a soldier named Orme assigned to a unit present at Trevilian's. Additionally, the name H.C. Orme is not found in the *Official Records*.

12. Major Avery had been promoted to lieutenant colonel on April 19, 1864, to date from June 11, 1863, but never mustered in at that grade. Nonetheless, he was promoted to colonel on November 30, 1864, effective November 29. He mustered in as colonel on December 28, 1864 (Preston, *History of the Tenth New York Cavalry*, 269, 271).

13. There are at least five accounts of this engagement, all of which differ in the details. Noble Preston provided an account as the author of *History of the Tenth New York Cavalry*, along with personal recollections by the regimental adjutant, Captain George Kennedy, the commander of Company L, Captain George Vanderbilt, and Lieutenant J.M. Reynolds of Company G. Preston also provided a personal and more detailed account in the *National Tribune* (Preston, *History of the Tenth New York Cavalry*, 197–204, 388, 469; *National Tribune*, January 5, 1888).

14. *National Tribune*, January 5, 1888.

15. Preston, *History of the Tenth New York Cavalry*, 198. Writing in the *National Tribune*, Preston gave a different and more detailed account of how the 10th New York's charge was initiated. Preston wrote that when Gregg's brigade launched their attack, the men of the 10th began firing at the Rebels from the cover of the rail fence, and that the Rebels began to return fire. Preston, who was in the center of the line, made his way to the right and finding Avery, urged him to charge. Avery responded that since it appeared Gregg's attack had failed, "It would be a very foolish thing for me to try it with one regiment. But I have no orders and I would not undertake so important a movement without authority." Despite Preston's urging, Avery was reluctant to attack and expressed concern that he might be "cashiered" should the attack fail. After Preston offered to personally accept responsibility for ordering the charge, Avery relented by saying, "All right; you may do as you please," upon which Preston moved to the center and ordered the attack (*National Tribune*, January 5, 1888). It is difficult to determine the accuracy of Preston's account of his conversation since it is not corroborated by others and it is not the account he included in his *History of the Tenth New York Cavalry*. Moreover, there is an old army adage that "A commander is responsible for all his unit does or fails to do." Avery, a superior officer, could not absolve himself of personal responsibility by allowing Preston, a junior officer, to make a critical decision in his stead. Despite any issues over the accuracy of Preston's account, there is no question regarding his bravery on June 11, 1864, when he led the men of the 10th New York over the rail fence. In November 1899, Preston was awarded the Medal of Honor for his actions that day, the citation reading: "Voluntarily led a charge in which he was severely wounded."

16. Preston, *History of the Tenth New York Cavalry*, 199. Pearsons was carried to the rear where he died. Sergeant Hubert Farnsworth wrote to Pearsons's sister advising her of her brother's death. He informed her that "he suffered a good deal but he bore up with it bravely and met his fate bravely and like a true soldier. He was liked by the Officers and men." Pearsons was buried under the shade of an oak tree in a well marked location. After the war, Pearsons's remains were reinterred in Culpeper National Cemetery (David B. Russell, ed., *Tough & Hearty: Kimball Pearsons, Civil War Cavalryman, Company L, Tenth Regiment of Cavalry, New York State Volunteers* [Westminster, MD: Heritage, 2012], 259–260; 262).

17. Swiggart, *Shades of Gray*, 73. The information on the death of McAllister is contained in a memorandum written

by Major Anderson after the battle (Anderson escaped from the federals later on June 11). In it he noted that Lieutenant Colonel McAllister's death was described to him by a private who was next to McAllister when he fell. Anderson also wrote that McAllister was buried about one and one-half miles from Trevilian Station between the station and Louisa Court House.

18. Upon the murder of Colonel W.P. White, the 7th Georgia's first commanding officer, the promotions of McAllister, Anderson and Russell would have been expected. However, the Confederate army policy stipulated that promotion to fill vacant field grade positions would be made from within a regiment based upon the recommendations of a board of officers. Doubtless, with the 7th's move to Virginia and its introduction into combat almost immediately upon its arrival there, a board had not been convened and the three officers had not been promoted. Anderson was promoted from major to colonel in December 1864.

19. Latty, *The Gallant Little 7th*, 100–101. According to Latty, many more men of the 7th were captured but managed to escape or were recovered by the Confederates as Sheridan began his withdrawal on the night of June 12–13.

20. Ibid., 104. The officer identified by Private Brooks as Captain Bostie was Captain Samuel D. Bostick, the commander of Company D. According to M.C. Butler, it is likely that Captain Bostic is the officer who later confronted Major General Judson Kilpatrick as Butler's division overran Kilpatrick's camp at Monroe's Crossroads on the morning of March 19, 1865. Bostic rode up to Kilpatrick, who was clad in his nightgown and slippers, and demanded to know who was in charge. Thinking quickly, Kilpatrick pointed to a fleeing Union soldier and said, "There he goes on that black horse." Bostick wheeled his horse about and gave chase as Kilpatrick sneaked into the bushes to hide (Brooks, *Butler and His Cavalry*, 444).

21. Swank, *Battle of Trevilian Station*, 110.

22. Given the inaccuracy in Civil War artillery fusing, men were generally reluctant to have friendly artillery fire over their heads.

23. Preston, *History of the Tenth New York Cavalry*, 204. For his heroism, Farnsworth was promoted to lieutenant, and in April 1898 he was awarded the Medal of Honor for his gallantry on June 11, 1864.

24. Tobie, *History of the First Maine Cavalry*, 283–284.

25. Ibid., 285–286.

26. Ibid., 286, 496. On Stoneman's Raid in May 1863, Trask had been captured at Louisa Court House. He was exchanged in September 1863.

27. Kidd, *Personal Recollections*, 360.

28. Margaret Ann Vogtsberger, *The Dulanys of Welbourne: A Family in Mosby's Confederacy* (Berryville, VA: Rockbridge, 1995), 219. Colonel Dulany mentioned Rosser's order in a letter to his father dated September 5, 1864.

29. Hewett, et al., eds., *Supplement*, 6, 36:825; Henry H. Matthews, "The Pelham-Breathed Battery," in *Memoirs of the Stuart Horse Artillery Battalion*, edited by Robert Trout (Knoxville: University of Tennessee Press, 2010), 2–131; Trout, *Galloping Thunder*, 497–498.

30. Hubbard, Jr., *Civil War Memories*, 173–174; Nanzig, *3rd Virginia Cavalry*, 54–55, 100. Carrington had been captured at Aldie on June 17, 1863, and held until he was exchanged in March of 1864.

31. *OR*, 36, 1:855, 858, 862; Pyne, *Ride to War*, 221. Davies reported that his brigade was not engaged as a brigade, although three of his regiments were involved in the fighting on June 11.

32. *OR*, 36, I:824.

33. *OR*, 36, I:808. The accompanying table listed the division's casualties by brigade for the period May 26–June 26. Total casualties—officers and men killed, wounded, and missing—for Torbert's division were as 1248. Torbert's figures for the Confederates captured—totaling 437—appear reasonably accurate and is consistent with the body of the report for his losses at Trevilian's.

34. Ibid.

Chapter 16

1. Hall, *History of the Sixth New York Cavalry*, 197–198; Brooks, *Butler and His Cavalry*, 238. Army Regulations permitted some flexibility with respect to care of the horses. Specifically, the guidance relating to bivouacs stated that "The horses of each platoon are placed in a single row, and fastened [to pickets firmly planted in the ground] as prescribed for camps; near the enemy they remain saddled all night, with slackened girths.... The distance from the enemy decides the manner in which the horses are to be fed and led to water. When permitted to unsaddle, the saddles are to be placed to the rear of the horses" (U.S. War Department, *Revised Regulations*, paragraphs 540, 546; Confederate States War Department, *Regulations for the Army of the Confederate States, 1863* [Richmond: J.W. Randolph, 1863; reprint, Evansville, IN: Crescent City Sutler, Nd.], paragraphs 528, 534). The Confederate regulations on this topic are a verbatim copy of the Union regulations.

2. According to the drill manuals, when taking horses to water, the rider was to remove his horse's bridle with curb bit and replace it with a more comfortable watering bridle with snaffle bit. The curb bit features shanks to which the reins are affixed, providing leverage to allow the rider to better control his horse, particularly when holding the reins in one hand while in battle. With the snaffle bit, which has no shanks, the reins are affixed to metal rings at the ends of the bit.

3. Because of their digestive system, horses can subsist better on hay than on grain. As was customary, neither Sheridan's nor Hampton's forces had transported any hay, frequently referred to as "long forage."

4. Brooks, *Butler and His Cavalry*, 213.

5. Tobie, *History of the First Maine Cavalry*, 236.

6. "Some of the Experiences of J.V. Baxley, a Confederate Veteran, as told by him," in *Recollections and Reminiscences 1861–1865 through World War I* (South Carolina Division, United Daughters of the Confederacy), I:98–99.

7. Ibid., 247.

8. Preston, *History of the Tenth Regiment of Cavalry*, 209–210. Chaplain Bradley, writing from memory, mistakenly wrote that the following morning, after "The day broke gloriously" the regiment began its return march.

9. During the Civil War, Union surgeons reported 29,980 amputations, although the number of amputations performed was certainly greater since for the first eighteen months of the war, few reports were made to the Office of the Surgeon General and hospital records were "found to be very meager." The mortality rates varied by procedure. Soldiers whose legs were amputated at the hip suffered a mortality rate of 83.3 percent while for those whose legs were amputated in the thigh, the mortality rate dropped to 54.2 percent. Survival rates among those whose arms were amputated were significantly better. The mortality rate for those who lost their arm at the shoulder was 29.1 percent while those whose arms were amputated in the forearm had a rate of 14.0 percent (U.S. Surgeon General's Office, *Medical*

and Surgical History of the War of the Rebellion (1861–1865), 3 vols. in 6 parts [Washington, D.C.: Government Printing Office], II, 3:877–878).

10. Bowen, *History of the First New York Dragoons*, 189. The nature of Civil War wounds were to a large degree a result of weapons and ammunition in use at the time. In simple terms, Civil War firearms fired large lead bullets at relatively low velocity. When striking a human body, and particularly a bone, the bullets deformed and dissipated most of their kinetic energy on the soldier who had been struck. Today's smaller, metal-jacketed bullets traveling at high velocity are more likely to pass through a human body. For comparison, a .58 caliber a rifle musket fired a 500 grain lead bullet at a muzzle velocity of 914 feet per second, while a modern M16A2 fires a 5.56 millimeter (.223 caliber) 62 grain metal-jacketed lead bullet at a muzzle velocity of 3100 feet per second (Claude E. Fuller, *The Rifled Musket* (New York: Bonanza, 1958), 51; U.S. Department of the Army, *Field Manual 3-22.9, Rifle Marksmanship* (Washington, D.C., April 2003), 2–1, 2–27.

11. *National Tribune*, January 5, 1888. The sub-heading of Preston's article in the National Tribune was erroneously "End of a Virginian" although Major Russell was from Georgia. The death of Russell was also included in Preston's account of the battle that was published in the *Philadelphia Times* in 1880. Major Russell's sister received a copy of the article and wrote to Preston thanking him for providing more definite information on her loved-one's last moments (Preston, *History of the Tenth Regiment of Cavalry*, 203).

12. Nancy S. Pate, "Old Trevilian Home," in U.S. Works Progress Administration, "Virginia Historical Inventory" (Richmond: Library of Virginia, 1937).

13. Rodenbough, *From Everglade to Canyon*, 318. The following morning Leoser was taken to see Thomas Rosser, his West Point classmate, who was being treated for the wound to his leg. Leoser recalled that he was "very cordially greeted" and at Rosser's insistence was given a drink of whisky by one of the surgeons (Ibid., 319).

14. Manigault, "Autobiography," 429; *Charleston Daily Courier*, June 24, 1864.

15. Manigault, "Autobiography," 428.

16. Swank, *Battle of Trevilian Station*, 108.

17. Avery, *Under Custer's Command*, 90.

Chapter 17

1. George M. Neese, Diary Entry for June 12, 1864, Papers, 1859–1921, Personal Papers Collection (13994). Library of Virginia, Richmond.

2. It is not clear which brigades and regiments were detailed to destroy the railroad. Within the 1st Division, Torbert wrote that on the morning of June 12, his division began destroying the railroad and Colonel Devin wrote that his brigade was engaged in the destruction of the railroad until noon. Neither Custer nor Merritt commented in their reports on their brigades' activities that morning. David McM. Gregg made no mention of troops from his division being detailed to the destruction of the railroad, but Colonel Henry Davies wrote that his men "Marched to the station and assisted in destroying the railroad." Colonel John I. Gregg, on the other hand, recorded tersely, "12th in camp." However, 16th Pennsylvania, one of Colonel Gregg's regiments, did participate in the destruction of the railroad. From the conflicting reports, it appears that some regiments were allowed to rest on the morning of June 12 (*OR* 36, I:808, 842, 858, 863, 870).

3. James C. Mohr, ed., *Cormany Diaries: A Northern Family in the Civil War* (Pittsburgh: University of Pittsburgh Press, 1982), 434–435. Cormany had been promoted to second lieutenant from sergeant on June 8, 1864, while the regiment was on the march to Trevilian's. Two months later, on August 16 on the Charles City Road, Cormany ordered his men to fire on a Confederate officer who had mistakenly approached their line. As the officer wheeled to flee, he was hit twice and fell from the saddle, dead. Cormany quickly learned that the officer was Brigadier General John Chambliss. Cormany took from the body Chambliss's saber with belt and his smoking pipe. Four days later, Cormany met informally between lines with several Confederate pickets. One recognized Chambliss's saber and said he knew the general and his family. Cormany gave the picket the general's pipe and asked that it be returned to the general's wife with the message: "Tell Mrs C. you saw the officer who gave the order to fire—and had the general not been more brave than judicious he might have escaped, by surrendering—as my men were too near for him to expect to escape (Ibid., 465–466, 469–470).

4. Allen, *Down in Dixie*, 365. This measure of railroad destruction was favored by Sherman during his march through Georgia.

5. Ryckman, *The Battle of Trevilians: Miscellaneous Commentary*, 5. Edward Wells was dismissive of the Union effort to destroy the railroad, writing that "Nothing of importance had been accomplished by them thus far, for they had torn up only a hundred feet or so of railroad track at Trevilian station, which could be restored easily without any interruption of consequence to the road (Wells, *Hampton and His Cavalry in '64*, 203). This is a significant understatement of the damage done to the Virginia Central. While one must be cautious when speculating on a writer's intent, it is possible that Wells was attempting to burnish Hampton's reputation as discussed in Appendix D.

6. Sanford, *Fighting Rebels and Redskins*, 244–245; Preston, *History of the Tenth New York Cavalry*, 205. After the war, Ogden's remains were recovered by his cousin, Ranald MacKenzie, and reinterred in the burying ground at Newport, Rhode Island. MacKenzie graduated first in his West Point Class of 1862 and by the end of the war was brigadier general of volunteers in command of a cavalry division. Considered one of the most promising officers in the army, MacKenzie served with distinction after the war commanding a cavalry regiment in campaigns against the Indians. Promoted to brigadier general in 1882, he was retired in 1884 due to disability from wounds. He died in New York in 1889 (Cullum, *Biographical Register*, #1957; Warner, *Generals in Blue*, 301–302).

7. Swank, *Battle of Trevilian Station*, 122.

8. Howard, *Sketch of Cobb Legion Cavalry*, 16–17. On June 13, Jubal Early and his corps passed through Trevilian's on the way to Lynchburg to counter Hunter. Early was dismissive of the hasty defenses prepared by Hampton's men, referring to them as "nothing more than rails put up in a manner in which cavalry were accustomed to arrange them to prevent a charge." Early was apparently attempting to discredit Sheridan's assertion that his men on June 12 faced infantry protected by "well-constructed rifle-pits," so it is quite possible that Hampton's defensive works were a little more substantial than as described by Early (Jubal Early, *Autobiographical Sketch and Narrative of the War Between the States; With Notes by R.H. Early* [Philadelphia: J.B. Lippincott, 1912], 372).

9. Swank, *Battle of Trevilian Station*, 122–123.

10. Significantly, because of the ballistic characteristics of the rifle musket—the ball traveled in a parabolic arc—

aimed fire from a weapon sighted at 300 yards would pass over the heads of advancing enemy soldiers as they moved through the center of the field described (Earl J. Hess, *The Rifle Musket in the Civil War: Reality and Myth* [Lawrence: University Press of Kansas, 2008], 92–93).

11. Both Dunovant and Aiken were senior to Rutledge. Dunovant had been promoted to colonel shortly after the secession of South Carolina. Aiken was promoted to colonel on November 1, 1862, while Rutledge's date of rank in that grade was December 16, 1862 (Allardice, *Confederate Colonels*, 39, 331; Allardice, *More Generals in Gray*, 78).

12. Hampton, in his official report wrote that Lee's division arrived at 12:00 noon. Lee did not record his time of arrival. However Lee's adjutant, Major James Ferguson, reported that the division arrived about 10:00 a.m. Ferguson had left the division after dark on June 11 with orders to proceed through Lastley's Church, which was about two miles south of Trevilian's, and from there "to make [his] way to General Hampton's headquarters and spend the night." While the purpose of Ferguson's movement in advance of the division is not known, it is likely he provided Hampton with a report on the status of the division after the day's fighting. He also may have been briefed by Hampton on the plans for June 12's fight (Hewett, et al., eds., *Supplement*, 6, 36:816).

13. *OR*, 36, I:1095; Hewett, et al., eds., *Supplement*, 6, 36:801; Trout, *Memoirs of the Stuart Horse Artillery Battalion: Moorman's and Hart's Batteries*, 92.

14. *OR* 36, I:785, 808, 824, 850. This account conforms to Sheridan's version of events as laid out in his official report dated June 16, 1863. Differences between that report and his report dated May 13, 1866, are discussed in Chapter 20.

15. Kidd, writing well after the war, did not describe the spot at which he was directed to halt.

16. It seems likely that Avery observed Fitz Lee's division moving into position to the rear of Butler and Wright's brigades.

17. *OR*, 36, I:824; Kidd, *Personal Recollections*, 361–362. Inexplicably, Custer in his official report and Kidd in his *Personal Recollections*, differ completely in their description of the deployment of the brigade's regiments. Kidd wrote that the 6th was put in on the right of the road (which parallels the railroad) and the 7th was put in on the left. Custer wrote that "the Sixth was put in on the left of the railroad and the Seventh on the right." Custer's disposition is used in this account.

18. *OR*, 36, I:824; Kidd, *Personal Recollections*, 361–362.

19. Isham, *An Historical Sketch*, 60.

20. Swank, *Battle of Trevilian Station*, 124.

21. *OR*, 36, I:850. Other than writing that the 6th Pennsylvania was on the extreme right of his line, Merritt did not describe the order or alignment of his regiments as they deployed.

22. *OR*, 36, I:808–809. In his official report, Torbert mistakenly wrote that Custer's brigade was sent in on the Gordonsville Road while Merritt, on the extreme right was to "if possible, turn the enemy's right." Merritt attacked on Butler's left.

23. *OR*, 36, I:824, 850.

24. *OR*, 36, I:850. Merritt here indirectly criticized Custer for not attacking vigorously. In defense of the Michigan Brigade, Major James Kidd later wrote: "[The Michigan Brigade] began the fight and stayed in it till the end. Harder fighting has rarely been done than that which fell to the Michigan men in that battle. Several attempts were made to drive the enemy from their front. The First Michigan especially made a charge across an open field in the face of a terrible fire from behind breastworks, going half way across before they were repulsed. When the first Michigan could not stand, before a storm of bullets, no other regiment in the cavalry corps need try. That is a certainty" (Kidd, *Personal Recollections*, 363).

25. Hubard, Jr., *Civil War Memories*, 174–175. Johnston's Battery, sometimes called the 2nd Stuart Horse Artillery, had been organized by Captain John Pelham and later was commanded by James Breathed after Pelham was elevated to battalion command.

26. Ibid., 175. Hubard implied that because of the heavy fire, Munford was not particularly anxious to move his regiment up on the right where they would likely be more exposed.

27. Ibid., 176. It is difficult to determine exactly how many assaults were made by Torbert's forces against Hampton's lines, or in what strength those assaults were made. Some Confederates recalled seven charges, others recall three. In his report, Hampton wrote that after beating back an initial heavy attack, "the enemy made a succession of determined assaults, all of which were handsomely repulsed" (*OR*, 36, I:1096).

28. Bowen, *History of the First New York Dragoons*, 193–194, 441. Stockweather was captured by the Confederates and the next day turned over to the 1st New York Dragoons' assistant surgeon who had been left to care for federal soldiers who were too seriously wounded to transport. Although severely wounded, Stockweather survived. He was paroled and exchanged in December 1864, and mustered out with his company in June 1865.

29. *OR 36*, I:808–809, 842.

30. *OR*, 36, I:850.

31. Thomson's Battery was formed in November 1861 in the Shenandoah Valley. It was frequently called the Ashby Battery after Brigadier General Turner Ashby. Its first Commander was Roger Preston Chew. Chew and Thomson were both graduates of the Virginia Military Institute (Wise, *The Long Arm of Lee*, 1:162).

32. George M. Neese, *Three Years in the Confederate Horse Artillery* (New York: Neale, 1911; reprint ed., Clearwater, SC: Eastern Digital Resources, 2003), 353.

33. Ibid.

34. Charles W. McVicar, Diary, 1862–1865, Personal Papers Collection (29971, Typescript, Library of Virginia, Richmond), 43; Butler, "The Cavalry Fight at Trevilian Station, 238. John "Jap" Pierce was sent to Charlottesville, "where the ladies will take special care of him," for medical treatment. He returned to duty, was captured in October 1864 and spent the remainder of the war as a prisoner at Point Lookout (McVicar, Diary 1862–1865, 43; Trout, *"The Hoss,"* 55).

35. McVicar, Diary, 1862–1865, 43–44.

36. Neese, *Three Years in the Confederate Horse Artillery*, 354.

37. Ibid., 354–355. In a letter to *The Shenandoah Valley*, the New Market, Virginia, newspaper, Neese explained that he kept his diary in small books which he sent home for safe keeping when full, adding, "When I transcribed it [the diary] into ink I wrote out some of the incidents from personal recollection—occurrences that I wished to remember more distinctly and all their environments in days and years to come." In his original diary Neese did not record being sent to take over as gunner of the number two gun. While Neese wrote of firing on the house, he did not mention Butler's order to "Fire that house." However, Neese assured the newspaper's readers that his accounts of battles were "all rather under than overdrawn" (Neese, Papers, 1859–1921).

McVicar, in his diary, described firing on the house claiming that the order was given by Fitz Lee. McVicar made no mention of Neese's role in firing on the house (McVicar, *Diary 1862–1865*, 44).

38. *OR*, 36:I:850–851; Rodenbough, *From Everglade to Canyon*, 303.

39. Brooks, *Butler and His Cavalry*, 213–214, 250. Nealy Grant survived the war. He died in Chester County, South Carolina, in September 1907 at the age of eighty-seven.

40. Hewett, et al., eds., *Supplement*, 6, 36:825. When the expedition began, Shoemaker had left one gun behind on picket duty at Long Bridge. On June 12, Shoemaker had initially been directed to place Lieutenant Charles Phelps's section of two guns in support of Butler. Presumably Shoemaker had regained control of Phelps's section; Fitz Lee wrote that Lomax's Brigade was accompanied by a battery under Major Breathed, who was in overall command of the two batteries supporting Lee's Division.

41. Hall, *History of the Sixth New York Cavalry*, 198.

42. DiCesnola to George Wood, Esq., July 7, 1864, Spencer/Wood Family Papers of the Jonathan Drayton Papers (William L. Clement Library, University of Michigan, Ann Arbor).

43. Musick, *6th Virginia Cavalry*, 82.

44. Hall, *Sixth New York Cavalry*, 198–199.

45. DiCesnola to George Wood, Esq., July 7, 1864. DiCesnola wrote that he took into action 180 men, the remainder of the regiment holding horses, and that in less than 2 hours he had 52 "*hors de combat*." Alonzo Foster, in his history of the 6th New York, explained the action differently. He wrote that the 4th New York fell back to the rear of the 6th New York allowing the 6th to be flanked on both right and left. As the 6th fell back they were mistakenly taken under fire from soldiers of the 4th New York "and it was with much difficulty that we made them understand that we wore blue jackets instead of gray coats." After sorting things out with the 4th, the 6th withdrew some distance to high ground skirted by a small stream (Alonzo Foster, *Reminiscences and Record of the 6th New York V.V. Cavalry*, 61–62). Merritt also later wrote that the 4th New York had "by mistake" withdrawn, although he did not mention that matter in his official report (Rodenbough, *From Everglade to Canyon*, 303). It seems more likely that as Lee began his attack against the 6th New York's right flank, the officers of the 6th reoriented their men to meet that threat. Consequently, the 4th New York, which had been to the left of the 6th, was then in the rear of the 6th. If diCesnola adjusted his line to face the new threat based upon the sounds of the fighting off to his right, the fire of his men would have been into the rear of the 6th New York. Since the fighting took place in partially wooded terrain as darkness fell, incidents of friendly fire would not be unexpected.

46. Hewett, et al., eds., *Supplement*, 6, 36:501. Apparently there were also some instances of friendly fire on the Confederate side with men from Wickham's Brigade firing into Lomax's Brigade in the darkness. However, it is not likely that such fratricide was a significant factor in causing Lee to suspend his attack (Musick, *6th Virginia Cavalry*, 82).

47. *OR*, 36, I:809. No infantry were sent to reinforce Hampton. It is not clear how Torbert mistakenly determined he was facing infantry as well as cavalry. As an experienced infantryman, Torbert was certainly aware that Hampton's soldiers were for the most part armed with muzzle loading rifles.

48. Coffman, *Going Back the Way They Came*, 84–85.

49. Isham, *An Historical Sketch*, 62.

Chapter 18

1. Fighting a pitched battle starting mid-afternoon on June 12 is inconsistent with Sheridan's later statement that Torbert's movement was a reconnaissance to secure the road to Mallory's Ford as withdrawal route.

2. *OR*, 36, I:785, 809.

3. Ibid. Regarding the horses, Sheridan noted that for the entire two days of fighting, the animals were without forage and the surrounding country "afforded nothing but grazing of very inferior quality, and generally at such points that were inaccessible to us."

4. *OR*, 42, I:627–628. The Autenrieth was a type of light medical wagon that was adopted and issued during the last year of the war.

5. Sheridan, *Personal Memoir*, 227. There were several types of ambulances used by the Union Army during the war, including one designed by Major General William Rosecrans. Most ambulances could carry four patients on stretchers or eight to ten patients on seats (Surgeon General, *Medical and Surgical History*, II, 3: 944–947).

6. *OR*, 36, I:797; *OR*, 42, I:627; Cheney, *History of the Ninth New York Cavalry*, 187–188; Hewett, et. al., eds., *Supplement*, 6:651. Surgeon Pease, 10th New York Cavalry, who was acting as Corps Surgeon, wrote that to move the wounded he had available—in addition to the ambulances—thirty army wagons and twelve ammunition wagons. This number appears reasonable since consumption of supplies and expenditure of ammunition would have emptied a fair number of wagons. The hospital for the 2nd Division was staffed by two assistant surgeons, one hospital steward, and seven attendants. In his report, Sheridan wrote that "the surgeons left in charge were not well treated by the enemy and that the hospitals were robbed of liquors and stores."

7. Preston, *History of the Tenth New York Cavalry*, 202.

8. Ibid., 203–204. Preston added that General Sheridan had given up his "private ambulance" for use by Preston and Lieutenant P.D. Mason, an artillery officer. The reason for the haste was not explained. Other accounts of the withdrawal do not provide insight into the need to hurry the evacuation of the wounded. Also unexplained is why the ambulance was allocated to the two officers when it had capacity for several more patients. On the evening of June 18, after arriving at West Point, Surgeon Pease removed the ball from Preston's hip and the next day he was sent by boat to Washington.

9. Manigault, "Autobiography," 430.

10. The number of Union prisoners is not particularly well documented and provides an example of the difficulty in accurately determining Civil War casualties. Hampton reported that during the two days' fighting and the pursuit of the raiders, his force captured 570 Union soldiers, in addition to 125 who were wounded and left on the battlefield (*OR*, 36, I:1096). Sheridan, in his initial report dated June 16, 1864, wrote, "My loss in captured will not exceed 160. These were principally in the Fifth Michigan Cavalry" (*OR*, 36, I:785). Additionally, Sheridan, in his subsequent report dated May 13, 1866, wrote that he left behind ninety nontransportable wounded (*OR*, 36, I:797). Those were likely not included with the 160 figure Sheridan provided earlier and would thus raise the total captured to 250. However, the returns for the fighting at "Trevilian Station and Newark (or Mallory's Cross Roads), June 11–12, 1864," show a total of 8 officers and 427 enlisted men missing (*OR*, 36, I:186–187). Since some of the wounded were not immediately taken to Richmond and some of the missing were either dead or attempting to make their way back to Union lines,

the number of Union prisoners marched to the rear under guard was probably between 200 and 300.

11. Rodenbough, *From Everglade to Canyon*, 320.

12. Ibid., 321.

13. Ibid., 321–322.

14. Bradley T. Johnson, "Maryland" in *Confederate Military History*, 11:1–184, edited by Clement A. Evans (Atlanta, GA: Confederate Publishing Co., 1899, reprint, Secaucus, NJ: Blue and Grey, 1980), 123–124. There is scant documentation on Johnson's plan to capture Lincoln. Johnson wrote of it in *Confederate Military History*, but it is not mentioned by Early in his *Autobiographical Sketch*, not is it discussed in the various biographies of Hampton. There are several obvious difficulties with Johnson's plan: the raiding party lacked sufficient strength to fight through opposition that might be encountered either en route to Washington or on the return; there was no—in today's terms—"actionable intelligence" regarding Lincoln's whereabouts, activities, or security measures; finally, there were little, in any, provisions made for the logistical support of the raiding party. Moreover, one may question whether Hampton, a major general commanding a division—would approve a raid with a strategic objective that was well beyond the scope of his responsibilities. While it is possible that records do not exist because of the need for secrecy, one may question the accuracy of Johnson's recollection of events after the passage of thirty-five years.

15. McVicar, *Diary*, 46–47.

16. Latty, *Gallant Little 7th*, 105; Swank, *Battle of Trevilian Station*, 111.

17. *OR*, 36, I:1096. Hampton did not explain how he offered battle with a river between Sheridan and his division. While one might say that the Confederates "pursued" Sheridan, they did not actually conduct a "pursuit." In military terms, a pursuit is an offensive operation that is conducted against a retreating enemy with the objective of destroying the opposing force. Pursuing commanders conduct various maneuvers to intercept, capture, or destroy the enemy. Pursuits test the audacity and endurance of both leaders and the men under their command (U.S. Department of the Army, *Field Manual 100-5, Operations*, 7–9, 7–10). Perhaps the best example of an effective pursuit during the Civil War was Sheridan's of Lee from Petersburg to Appomattox in April 1865.

18. *OR*, 36, III:599.

19. Avery, *Under Custer's Command*, 90–91.

20. *OR*, 36, I:797. Sheridan wrote that earlier he intended to march on the Catharpin Road after crossing the North Anna at Mallory's Ford, "which would have saved much time and distance." However the way was blocked by Hampton. While the Catharpin Road may have been a better road for movement of a large body of cavalry, a review of maps of the era indicates that the distance marched would have been longer, not shorter, had Sheridan marched west to cross the North Anna at Mallory's Ford.

21. Sheridan, *Personal Memoirs*, 232; *OR*, 36, I:798.

22. Preston, *History of the Tenth New York Cavalry*, 203.

23. Earlier in the war, Sheridan might have elected to parole the prisoners on the battlefield. However, on July 3, 1863, the federal War Department published General Orders Number 207 which specified that all paroles must be made in compliance with the "Dix-Hill Cartel," named for Major Generals John Dix and D.H. Hill who negotiated the exchange agreement in July 1862. According to the agreement, all prisoners in the East were to be delivered to Aiken's Landing, on the James River about thirty miles downstream from Richmond. There, the prisoners would be exchanged or paroled if there were not sufficient prisoners on either side. The only exception permitted by General Order 207, was "the case of commanders of two opposing armies, who are authorized to exchange prisoners or to release them on parole at other points mutually agreed upon by said commanders" (*OR*, Series II, 6:78). Thus, since neither Sheridan nor Hampton was an army commander, an exchange on the battlefield was not permitted. By mid–1864, the exchange system had broken down over disagreements regarding the treatment of black Union soldiers captured by the Confederacy. Additionally, many leaders in the North had privately come to the conclusion that since the conflict had become one of attrition and since the Union possessed greater manpower resources, that the exchange system was more advantageous to the South than the North. In that regard, on August 18, 1864, Grant wrote to Major General Benjamin Butler, who had been appointed Commissioner of Exchange, with his views on the matter. "It is hard on our men held in Southern prisons not to exchange them, but it is humanity to those left in the ranks to fight our battles. Every man we hold, when released on parole or otherwise, becomes an active soldier against us at once either directly or indirectly. If we commence a system of exchange which liberates all prisoners taken, we will have to fight on until the whole South is exterminated. If we hold those caught they amount to no more than dead men. At this particular time to release all rebel prisoners [in the] North would insure Sherman's defeat and would compromise our safety here" (*OR*, Series II, 7:606–607). For a comprehensive discussion of issues related to prisoner exchange from a distinctly Southern Perspective, see Robert Ould, "The Exchange of Prisoners" in *Annals of the War*, 32–59.

24. Manigault, "Autobiography," 432.

25. Swank, *Battle of Trevilian Station*, 108–109. Rucker, unlike most Virginia cavalrymen, had been conscripted in the spring of 1864. After his capture he spent the rest of the war as a prisoner at Johnson Island (Musick, *6th Virginia Cavalry*, 151).

26. Cheney, *History of the Ninth New York Cavalry*, 188.

27. Tobie, *History of the First Maine Cavalry*, 289; Hyndman, *History of a Cavalry Company*, 126–127; Gracey, *Annals of the Sixth Pennsylvania Cavalry*, 263; Benjamin W. Crowninshield, *A History of the First Regiment of Massachusetts Cavalry Volunteers* (Boston: Houghton, Mifflin, 1991; reprint, Baltimore: Butternut and Blue, 1995), 223.

28. Tobie, *History of the First Maine Cavalry*, 289.

29. Crowninshield, *First Massachusetts Cavalry*, 224.

30. Brooks, *Butler and His Cavalry*, 267, 253. Since Hampton's Division was marching parallel to Sheridan's corps with a river in between, it is not exactly clear how Brooks and Davis became knowledgeable regarding the extent of the dead horses. Presumably, scouts brought word of what became a shocking and much discussed matter among Confederate cavalrymen.

31. Myers, *The Comanches*, 306.

32. William Locke to My Dear Wife, June 18, 1864, Civil War Letters of William Herrod Locke, Mss 13485.

33. Hewett, et al., eds., *Supplement*, 6, 36:802. Horses can suffer from a condition named Exertional Myopathy, more commonly known as Tying-up Syndrome. It was originally called "Monday morning disease" because it frequently occurred when horses began heavy work after a weekend's rest. The syndrome, which generally occurs in horses that are being fed grain, is brought on by an accumulation of glycogen that causes the horse's major muscles to become stiff and painful. A horse that is tying-up will exhibit an increased heart-rate, sweat profusely, and perhaps—

because of pain—stand completely still and refuse to move. It is possible that some of the Union horses which were destroyed had become incapacitated by Tying-up (James M. Griffin and Tom Gore, *Horse Owner's Veterinary Handbook*, 2d ed. [New York: Howell Book House, 1989], 5–7. Syndrome).

34. Brooks, *Butler and His Cavalry*, 392, 395, 397. Brooks's rebuttal to Rodenbough, which ran for ten pages, was added as an appendix to the book.

35. See Armistead, *Horses and Mules in the Civil War*, Chapter 5, for a discussion of the privations suffered by horses and mules.

36. Ibid., 341–343, 380.

37. R.H. Peck, *Reminiscences of a Confederate Soldier of Co. C, 2nd Va. Cavalry* (Fincastle, VA: Np., 1913), 49–50. The battle began as Peck got underway and he was captured by Custer's men and freed by Rosser's. After starting out a second time, he had ridden about one-half mile when he "met a nice sorrel horse, galloping saddled and bridled, but no rider." Peck caught the horse and took it with him. Arriving at the horse hospital, Peck left his condemned horse and rode the sorrel back to his command. He then rode the sorrel on horse-pass to his home in Fincastle to pick up a better horse he had at home. Fincastle is a small town in Botetourt County about fifteen miles north of Roanoke, Virginia.

38. Charles Minor Blackford and Susan Leigh Blackford, *Letters from Lee's Army*., ed. Charles Minor Blackford III (New York: Charles Scribner's Sons, 1947; reprint, Lincoln: University of Nebraska Press, 1998), 264.

39. Conrad, *The Rebel Scout*, 50. The events described likely occurred in King & Queen County, not King William County. Conrad identified the woman as a Mrs. Haines.

40. Ibid. Conrad described Old Whitie as a sorrel with four white feet and a white "forefront," which would likely today be called a blaze on the horse's face. Old Whitie was "observant of bypaths and mountainways, and never lost his head. He did not seem the slightest disturbed by pistol shots, musket fire, or artillery roar. I could ride him about twilight through swamps, thickets, and undergrowths, and upon returning he would not miss his way though the night were starless and the return a labyrinth." Conrad claimed that John Wilkes Booth rode Old Whitie part of the way en route to the barn where he was surrounded and killed (Ibid., 65, 69).

41. William L. Wilson, *A Borderland Confederate*, edited by Festus P. Summers (Pittsburgh: University of Pittsburgh Press, 1962), 81–82. Wilson, a graduate of Columbia College, today George Washington University, was the regimental sergeant major. After the war, Wilson obtained a law degree from Columbia and returned to Charlestown, West Virginia, where he practiced. He served in the U.S. House of Representatives from 1883 to 1894. Afterwards, he served as U.S. Postmaster General from 1895 to 1897. From then until his death in October 1900, he was president of Washington & Lee University in Lexington, Virginia (Frye, *12th Virginia Cavalry*, 179).

42. OR, 36, III:778, 780.

43. Avery, *Under Custer's Command*, 92–95.

44. OR, 36, I:798, 842–843.

Chapter 19

1. Upon arriving at White House on June 20, Sheridan notified Meade of his arrival, and of his need for ammunition and supplies "of all kinds," noting that "I find little subsistence and forage here, but they can be obtained at Fort Monroe, and I shall take the necessary means to obtain the same" (OR, 36, III:784).

2. OR, 36, III:784–785. Abercrombie, who graduated from West Point in 1822, had a distinguished career before the war, rising to the grade of colonel and appointment to command of the 7th Infantry in February, 1861. Much older than other officers of his grade in volunteer service, since the fall of 1862 he had been assigned to the Defenses of Washington and to duty on various military commissions. During the Overland Campaign, he commanded depots around Fredericksburg before taking command at White House in early June. He mustered out of volunteer service immediately after leaving White House and retired from the regular army in March 1865. George Washington Getty graduated from West Point with the class of 1840 and was commissioned in the artillery. Promoted to brigadier general of volunteers in the spring of 1862, he commanded a division in the Wilderness where he was severely wounded and earned a brevet to colonel in the regular army (Cullum, *Biographical Register*, #322, #1031).

3. Sheridan, *Personal Memoirs*, 237.

4. Hewlett, et al., eds., *Supplement*, 6, 36:803.

5. Brooks, *Butler and His Cavalry*, 268.

6. Cheney, *History of the Ninth New York Cavalry*, 190.

7. OR 36, I:859.

8. OR, 36, I:810.

9. OR, 36, I:843, 187. The 4th New York, which escorted the pontoon train from Dunkirk to White House, rejoined the brigade in camp that afternoon.

10. OR, 36, I:855.

11. Tobie, *History of the First Maine Cavalry*, 292.

12. Lloyd, *History of the First Pennsylvania Volunteers*, 100. OR, 36, I:859.

13. OR, 36, I:855, 187.

14. Merington, *The Custer Story*, 103; OR, 36, I:187.

15. John Locke to My Dear Wife, June 22, 1863, Civil War Letters of William Herrod Locke, Mss 13485. In the same letter, Locke commented on the condition of the command. "I do hope and trust we'll go up nearer Richmond and have a few days where we can rest for both our men & horses are broke down & worn out."

16. OR, 36, III:786–787.

17. OR, 36, III:789.

18. OR, 25, II:561. An army wagon drawn by a six-horse team required about twelve yards of road space.

19. OR, 36, III:794.

20. Mary B. Daughtry, *Gray Cavalier: The Life and Wars of General W.H.F. "Rooney" Lee* (Cambridge, MA: DaCapo, 2002), 186–187.

21. Mohr, *The Cormany Diaries*, 437. Lieutenant Samuel Cormany reported that destroying the bridge and wharf was a hot and dusty job. Nonetheless, the Pennsylvanians worked quickly and marched from the depot at 9:00 a.m.

22. OR, 36, I:844; Cheney, *History of the Ninth New York Cavalry*, 190–191.

23. OR, 36, I:844. Devin reported that this action occurred on the morning of June 23, while Torbert reported Devin was "strongly attacked" late that afternoon. It appears that Torbert was in error with regard to the time. Torbert complimented Devin, writing in his report that "the colonel held his ground with his usual stubbornness, and finally drove the enemy from his front (Ibid., 810).

24. OR, 36, I:855, 859, 863.

25. OR, 36, I:798–799.

26. OR, 36, III:790. There is nothing in the *Official Records* to indicate why these instructions were not issued on June 21 when Meade first surfaced the potential problem with using the bridge at Deep Bottom.

27. *OR*, 36, III:791; Crowinshield, *First Regiment Massachusetts Cavalry*, 225.

28. *OR*, 36, I:1096. Gary was promoted to brigadier general effective May 19, 1864. However he did not receive notice of his promotion until June 26 (Stephen Elliott Welch, *Stephen Elliot Welch of the Hampton Legion*, edited by John Michael Priest [Shippensburg, PA: Burd Street, 1994], 37).

29. Allardice, *More Generals in Gray*, 102.

30. *OR*, 33:1232.

31. Wallace, Jr., *A Guide to Virginia Military Organizations*, 82–83; Allardice, *Confederate Colonels*, 325. James Dearing's regiment of Confederate States Cavalry had been broken up upon Dearing's promotion to Brigadier General. This made the two Georgia companies available for reassignment to the 24th Virginia, bringing it up to regimental strength. Robins Air Force Base in Georgia is named after Brigadier General Augustine W. Robins, the son of Colonel William Robins.

32. Elijah White and the 35th Virginia had been dispatched to King William County to round up any stragglers from Sheridan's march. Consequently the battalion, which found no stragglers, was not present at Samaria Church (Myers, *The Comanches*, 307).

33. *OR*, 36, I:855. Gregg's division was habitually supported by two artillery batteries. Captain Alanson Randol's H&I Batteries, 1st U.S. Artillery supported Gregg's brigade while W. Neil Dennision's A Battery, 2nd U.S. supported Davies's brigade. The role played by Dennison's battery during the Trevilian's Raid is elusive. The battery is only mentioned once in the *Official Records*, that being the tabulation of the casualties at Samaria Church, where the battery lost one man killed and one wounded (*OR*, 36, I:187). Dennison, the son of Ohio governor William Dennison, Jr., is mentioned three times in the *Official Records*, but those entries shed little light on the activities of the battery. Torbert wrote that "I cannot speak too highly of the Horse Artillery (three batteries) commanded by Lieutenants Williston, Pennington, and Heaton, serving with the division, and part of the time Lieutenants Dennison and Randol, for they always used their guns to the advantage of everyone, except the enemy" (*OR*, 36, I: 810). Merritt wrote that "our standard is high, but Williston and Dennison have always come up to our expectations, if not exceeded them" (*OR*, 36, I:851). Gregg, in his report concluded: "Light Batteries H and I, first U.S. Artillery, Captain A.M. Randol and Lieutenant Dennison commanding" were present with his division from May 31 until July 7, 1864 (*OR*, 36, I:856). It may be that on June 12, Dennison's battery supported Merritt for part of the afternoon.

34. G.W. Beale, *A Lieutenant of Cavalry in Lee's Army* (Boston: Gorham, 1918; reprint, Baltimore: Butternut & Blue, 1994), 162.

35. Brooks, "Memories of Battles," 409.

36. Ibid.

37. Brooks, *Butler and His Cavalry*, 269–270. In his account of this incident in *Confederate Veteran*, Brooks wrote, "How vividly this pathetic scene seems to me, which was truly depressing." At the beginning of July, George Covode's father, John Covode—a prominent politician and member of Congress—seeking his son's body, arrived in the 4th Pennsylvania's camp on the south bank of the James River. A request to send a small party across the river into enemy lines was forwarded up the chain of command and approved by Sheridan. That night a lieutenant and four sergeants were transported across the James to search for Covode's remains. The small party evaded Confederate pickets and made their way to Samaria Church. With the help of an old black man living nearby, they found Covode's body buried in a shallow grave. The following night, the lieutenant led a party of thirty men with two ambulances back to the Samaria Church to retrieve the body. The colonel's remains were taken home by his father and reburied in Ligonier, Pennsylvania (William E. Doster, ed., *A Brief History of the Fourth Pennsylvania Veteran Cavalry, Embracing Organization, Reunions, Dedication of Monument at Gettysburg and Address of General W.E. Doster, Venango County Battalion, Reminiscences, Etc.* [Pittsburgh, PA: Ewens & Eberle, Book and Job Printers, 1891, reprint ed., Hightstown, NJ: Longstreet House, 1997], 28–31). The lieutenant identified Covode by his "peculiarly formed teeth" and his flannel underwear (Covode's uniform had been removed). In another account of this incident, a captain in the 4th Pennsylvania later wrote that Covode had been "stripped entirely naked" and left to die in the open. Further, the captain wrote that it appeared the Confederates had mutilated Covode's body. In view of the other accounts, this information does not appear likely (Hyndman, *History of a Cavalry Company*, 131).

38. Beale, *History of the Ninth Virginia Cavalry*, 131. Davis died in hospital in Richmond the following day (Driver, Jr., *10th Virginia Cavalry*, 108).

39. DeWitt Clinton Gallaher, *A Diary Depicting the Experiences of DeWitt Clinton Gallaher in the War* (Reorganized Co. E, 1st Va. Cav., 1961), 6–7. Gallaher, Coiner, and Kerr were all from Waynesboro, Virginia (Driver, Jr., *1st Virginia Cavalry*, 162, 176, 194).

40. Crowinshield, *First Regiment of Massachusetts Cavalry*, 226. Regarding the condition of the men, Gregg, in his report, wrote that "the intense heat prostrated many men and produced some deaths" (*OR*, 36, I:856).

41. *OR*, 36, I:856.

42. *OR*, 36, I:856; 1097; Wittenberg, *Glory Enough for All*, 297–298, n. 121. In his official report, Hampton wrote that he had not received reports of losses from other commands.

43. Sheridan, *Personal Memoirs*, 236.

44. *OR*, 36, III:792; 794. By message at 10:30 on June 26, Grant advised Meade, who had been "out of the loop" on the alarm over Gregg's losses, that Sheridan "is now safe in as comfortable a place as he can be for recruiting his men and horses" (Ibid.).

45. *OR*, 36, I:810, 859, 863; *OR*, 36, III:793, 797, 799.

Chapter 20

1. *OR*, 36, I:784–786. There quickly appeared some skepticism to Sheridan's claims. In his diary entry for June 24, Lieutenant Colonel Theodore Lyman, a volunteer aide de camp to General Meade, recorded in his diary: "His [Sheridan's] expedition and attempt to reach Hunter was entirely foiled. At Trevilian Station he had a very severe action, and, though he gained advantages the first day, the enemy (Hampton) turned the breastwork system against him, and stopped the whole advance (Theodore Lyman, *Meade's Army: The Private Notebooks of Lt. Col Theodore Lyman*, edited by David W. Lowe [Kent, OH: Kent State University Press, 2007], 226). Lieutenant Colonel Lyman, whose father had been mayor of Boston, graduated from Harvard in 1855. The following year he went to Florida to collect specimens for Harvard's newly-opened Museum of Comparative Zoology. There he met First Lieutenant George Meade who as a Corps of Engineers officer was supervising lighthouse construction along the coast (Lyman, *Meade's Army*, 5).

2. *OR*, 36, I:1095.

3. *OR*, 36, I:1095–1098.
4. *OR*, 36, I:22.
5. F.C. Newhall, *The Battle of Beverly Ford* in *Annals of the War, Written by Leading Participants North and South* (Philadelphia: Times Publishing Co., 1879; reprint ed., Edison, NJ: Blue & Gray Press, 1996), 137. A reconnaissance in force is conducted to gather intelligence on enemy locations, dispositions, strengths, and intentions. A unit conducting a reconnaissance in force is given sufficient strength and is organized so that, if necessary, it can fight the enemy to gather the desired information (U.S. Department of the Army. *Field Manual 100–5, Operations*, 7–4).
6. *OR*, 36, I:795. Sheridan's report was dated May 13, 1866.
7. *OR*, 36, I:802.
8. *OR* 36, I:797. There is no mention of Mallory's Ford in the reports of other senior Union officers of the Cavalry Corps. General Torbert wrote that his orders on the afternoon of June 12 were "to reconnoiter the enemy's position on the Charlottesville and Gordonsville Roads" (*OR*, 36, I:808).
9. *OR*, 36, I:785.
10. *OR*, 36, I:796.
11. *OR*, 36, I:785, 796.
12. Sheridan, *Personal Memoirs*, 225–226.
13. *New York Times*, June 20, 1864. The *New York Times* also published Sheridan's June 16 report in its June 19 issue.
14. The *Times* staff did have some limited information regarding the raid's objectives. The June 15 edition included the following: "A dispatch from Washington announces that no positive information had been received from Gen. SHERIDAN, who started on a great raid on Thursday last. He headed for Charlottesville, and it was understood that after visiting that place he would move upon Lynchburg."
15. *OR*, 36, III:599.
16. Sheridan, *Personal Memoirs*, 226.
17. *OR*, 27, I:951, 1045.
18. *OR* 36, I:26.
19. It is difficult to determine the exact distances since we do not know the specific locations of Sheridan's camp sites or the exact routes the corps followed as it made its way to Trevilian's. Based upon available records and map reconnaissance, the following distances seem reasonable approximations: Day 1 (Newcastle Ferry–Herring Creek via Ayletts)—16 miles; Day 2 (Herring Creek–Athens via Polecat Station)—18 miles; Day 3 (Athens–North East Creek via Chilesburg)—17 miles; Day 4 (North East Creek–Louisa County via Good Hope Church)—21 miles.
20. In modern tactical terms, Hampton, who was not aware of the disposition of the Union force, was conducting a "movement to contact" which would end with an anticipated "meeting engagement" after which he would launch a "hasty attack" to overwhelm the enemy. From Sheridan's perspective, however, the situation was different. Sheridan was unaware of Hampton's presence and he did not anticipate meeting Hampton on the Fredericksburg Road. As the U.S. Army's Field Manual 100–5, *Operations* notes: "Sometimes a meeting engagement occurs by chance wherever the opposing forces meet. This is not a preferred operation or one that intelligence assets should allow to happen. Rather, commanders seek to surprise the enemy whenever possible." Unsaid is the concept that commanders should also seek to avoid being surprised (U.S. Department of the Army, *FM 100–5, Operations*, 7–4, 7–5).
21. *OR*, 36, I:785, 797, 808–809.
22. Sheridan, *Personal Memoirs*, 230–231. Sheridan did not specify when he made the decision.

23. Allen, *Down in Dixie*, 366.
24. Presumably, the 6th U.S., which was assigned as Sheridan's escort, was not included in Sheridan's total for the two divisions.
25. Sheridan, *Personal Memoirs*, 227.
26. Rodenbough, "Sheridan's Trevilian Raid," 4:233; Butler, "The Cavalry fight at Trevilian Station," 4:239; Brooks, *Butler and His Cavalry*, 564; Jerry Meyers, "Trevilian!," *Louisa County Historical Magazine* 30 (Spring 1999), 31; Eric J. Wittenberg, *Glory Enough for All: Sheridan's Second Raid and the Battle of Trevilian Station* (Washington, D.C.: Brassey's, 2002), 34 n.96.
27. At the same time, Grant was obviously considering initiating operations against the Weldon Railroad once the Army of the Potomac had crossed the James.
28. Grant apparently had some concerns that Hunter might be defeated should he overextend himself by advancing up the Valley to Lynchburg. There was good basis for Grant's concern. After advancing to Lynchburg, Hunter withdrew precipitously into West Virginia, opening the Valley to Early's expedition against Washington. In any event, Moving Hunter to Richmond may have presented problems, at least initially. Hunter, while serving as a paymaster in the grade of major at Fort Leavenworth, had ingratiated himself with Lincoln immediately after the election of 1860, and he was subsequently detailed to the President elect's escort from Springfield to Washington. In May 1861, Hunter was promoted colonel of the newly organized 6th U.S. Cavalry. He was promoted to brigadier general of volunteers in May 1861 and to major general of volunteers in August 1862. Consequently, Hunter was senior to Meade on both the regular rolls (colonel and major, respectively) and fifteen months senior to Meade in the ranks of the volunteers. Meade was promoted from major to major general in the regular army on August 18, 1864, thus becoming senior to Hunter (Cullum, *Biographical Register*, #310, #804).
29. *Richmond Examiner*, Richmond, VA, June 27, 1864.
30. Crowninshield, *First Regiments Massachusetts Cavalry*, 226–227.
31. Ibid., 228–229. In his book, the quote reads "honors were about easy." Since honors won in battle are not generally considered easy, and that Sheridan enjoyed success one day and Hampton the other, it is likely Crowninshield meant to write that the "honors were about even."
32. Coffman, *Going Back the Way They Came*, 88.
33. Soldiers at the time and scholars since have noted that Hampton generally fought dismounted. Some have indicated that Hampton preferred dismounted combat and resorted to mounted charges only as a "last resort" (Rod Andrew, Jr., *Wade Hampton*, 216). However, it appears more likely that Hampton's tactics were driven primarily by the situation he faced, not by personal preference. Then, as now, commanders dispose their forces for battle based upon an analysis of factors such as their mission, enemy forces, friendly troops, terrain and weather, and time available. These factors are usually referred to today by the acronym METT-T. (U.S. Department of the Army, *Field Manual 100–5, Operations*, Glossary–5). Interestingly, Douglas Southall Freeman wrote to the commandant of the Army War College in May 1935 asking for the "Time at which the employment of dismounted cavalry began in the war between the States." In his letter, Freeman also wrote that "Stuart's biographers leave one to infer that he initiated the tactics of dismounted combat." Drawing heavily from George T. Denison (*Modern Cavalry: Its Organisation, Armament, and Employment in War* [London: Thomas Bosworth, 1868]), the War College staff replied that cavalry had fought dismounted on

many occasions since early Greek and Roman times, that Stuart was likely the first cavalry commander to dismount and fight on foot on the Peninsula on June 27, 1862, but more credit is due to Generals John Hunt Morgan and Nathan Bedford Forrest for developing a system of tactics for employing cavalry as mounted riflemen. Hampton is not mentioned in the War College response.

34. Vogtsberger, *The Dulanys of Welbourne*, 219. Dranesville was a small battle in Northern Virginia on December 20, 1861. Stuart attacked a Union force without proper reconnaissance and took heavy casualties.

35. B.J. Haden, *Reminiscences of J.E.B. Stuart's Cavalry*, 33. Haden's view, shown here in its entirety, is sometimes much abbreviated.

36. Myers, *The Comanches*, 291.

37. Freeman, *Lee's Lieutenants*, 3:550–551.

38. Lee, *Wartime Papers*, 2:813.

39. *OR*, 42, II:1171.

Chapter 21

1. After his death in 1878, Sheridan had Rienzi's skin preserved and mounted. He then presented the stuffed horse to the Military Service Institution, a museum on Governor's Island, New York. In its June 10, 1900 issue, the *New York Times* lamented that Rienzi, "one of the most valued trophies in the museum," had been crated up and placed in storage because the army's Ordnance Department needed more room after the beginning of the Spanish-American War. Fortunately for those interested in Civil War history, Rienzi was later transferred to the Smithsonian's collection and placed on display in the National Museum of American History, where it remains today ("Indian and War Trophies," *New York Times*, June 10, 1900; Smithsonian Institution, "'Winchester.' General Philip H. Sheridan's War Horse," http://www.si.edu/Encyclopedia_SI/nmah/horse.htm).

2. Roy Morris, Jr., *Sheridan*, 261; Cullum, *Biographical Register*, #1612.

3. Cullum, *Biographical Register*, #1612.

4. Morris, Jr., *Sheridan*, 328.

5. Sheridan, *Personal Memoirs*, 187; Morris, Jr., *Sheridan*, 388–389.

6. Morris, Jr., *Sheridan*, 390–391.

7. Ibid., 389.

8. Encyclopedia of Chicago, "Fort Sheridan," http://www.encyclopedia.chicagohistory.org/pages/478.html. Fort Sheridan was closed as a result of decisions resulting from the Base Realignment and Closure Act that had been passed by Congress and signed into law in October 1988, one hundred years after Sheridan's death.

9. Army Historical Foundation, "M551 Sheridan Light Tank." https://armyhistory.org/m551-sheridan-light-tank/.

10. Morris, Jr., *Sheridan*, 393.

11. Sheridan, *Personal Memoirs*, 345.

12. Slade, *A.T.A. Torbert*, 186–187. The War Department's decision for Torbert to revert to his permanent grade after the reorganization of 1866 was unprecedented in light of his Civil War service (Warner, *Generals in Blue*, 666 n 692).

13. Slade, *A.T.A. Torbert*, 190–191. It is not known how or when Torbert met Mary Currey.

14. *New York Times*, September 3–6, 1880. The *Vera Cruz* was first suspected lost when mail bags it carried washed ashore on the Florida coast. The steamer was a substantial ship with a displacement of 1,874 tons, a length of 296 feet, and a beam of 37 feet. The bulk of its cargo was 1,000 barrels of potatoes. It also carried 11,187 gallons of petroleum. According to one of the crewmen, General Torbert was alive when washed ashore, only to die shortly afterward. Torbert's head was bruised where it had apparently been struck by pieces of wreckage.

15. *New York Times*, September 30, 1880. The *Times* reported that Torbert's wooden casket was so heavy that a dozen sailors were required to handle it. When opened the remains might be identified, the casket was found to contain a zinc case. The zinc case was embedded with a thick layer of charcoal, which "was deemed inadvisable to remove." Consequently, the casket was reassembled without the remains being formally identified.

16. Slade, *A.T.A. Torbert*, 213–214.

17. Cullum, *Biographical Register*, #1684. See Edward G. Longacre, *Lincoln's Cavalrymen*, pages 322–323 for a discussion of the possible reasons behind Gregg's decision to leave the army when victory was evidently near at hand.

18. AOG USMA, *Annual Report*, 1917, 52–53.

19. AOG USMA, *Annual Report* (West Point, NY: 1931), 79.

20. Foote, *The Civil War: A Narrative*, 3:1009.

21. Wilson, *Under the Old Flag*, 2:519–521.

22. Ibid., 2:521.

23. Ibid., 2:523.

24. Ibid., 2:536; Cullum, *Biographical Register*, #1852. The retirement of Wilson, Fitzhugh Lee, and Joseph Wheeler required special approval from Congress since none of those officers met the time-in-service requirements established by regulation.

25. Cullum, *Biographical Register*, #1852.

26. Ibid., #1868; #1966.

27. Ibid., #1868; Don E. Alberts, *Brandy Station to Manila Bay: A Biography of General Wesley Merritt* (Austin, TX: Presidial, 1980) 276–278, 281–283.

28. *New York Times*, May 24, 1898. Alberts in *Brandy Station to Manila Bay* gives Laura Williams' age as twenty-seven at the time of her marriage to Merritt (319).

29. *New York Times*, June 18, 1893, December 4, 1910.

30. Alberts, *Brandy Station to Manila Bay*, 323–330; AOG USMA, *Annual Reunion*, 1911. 109–110; *New York Times*, December 7, 1910. By order of the academy superintendent, all officers assigned to West Point, with the exception of one duty officer and one medical doctor, attended Merritt's funeral.

31. Elizabeth Custer to My Dear General Sherman, undated, Custer Mss, Special Collections Department, United States Military Academy Library, West Point, NY.

32. Secretary of War Robert T. Lincoln to Brigadier General Oliver O. Howard, January 5, 1885, Custer File, Special Collections Department, United States Military Academy Library, West Point, NY.

33. Elisabeth Custer to Brigadier General Albert L. Mills, June 18, 1906, Custer File, Special Collections Department, United States Military Academy Library, West Point, NY.

34. James S. Robbins, *Last in Their Class: Custer, Pickett and the Goats of West Point* (New York: Encounter, 2006), 407–408.

35. Warner, *Generals in Blue*, 124.

36. *New York Times*, April 5, 1878, April 7, 1878.

37. Warner, *Generals in Blue*, 113; Henry E. Davies, *General Sheridan* (New York: D. Appleton, 1897), v-vi.

38. Bates, *Martial Deeds of Pennsylvania*, 853–1854; Arlington Cemetery.net.

39. In 1870, an act of Congress prohibited officers on duty from referring to themselves by a senior brevetted grade or wearing the uniform of a senior brevetted grade.

40. From statehood in 1837 until 1966, Michigan's governor served a two-year term.

41. The troops sent to fight in Cuba faced many problems, perhaps the least of which was their Spanish adversaries. The army issued soldiers wool uniforms, despite the certainty of tropical heat in Cuba. Many soldiers were armed with obsolete weapons. The quartermaster department reportedly provided tainted meat in its rations. While these problems cannot be fully blamed on Alger, he can be fairly criticized for his selection of corpulent, fellow Michigan man, William R. Shafter to lead the expeditionary forces in Cuba. As Alger's replacement, McKinley appointed the highly competent Elihu Root as Secretary of War.

42. Russell Alger to W.E. Baker, August 28, 1888, Russell A. Alger Papers, William L. Clement Library, University of Michigan, Ann Arbor. MI.

43. Wittenberg, *One of Custer's Wolverines*, 107.

44. Ibid., 169.

45. Ibid., 175–178.

46. Ibid., 176.

47. Michigan AGO, *Michigan in the War*, 611–613.

48. Isham, *An Historical Sketch*, 69–70, 89.

49. Lee, *Personal and Historical Sketches*, 169.

50. Elizabeth McFadden, *The Glitter and the Gold: A Spirited Account of the Metropolitan Museum of Art's First Director, the Audacious and High-handed Luigi Palma di Cesnola* (New York: Dial, 1971), 71, 7, 75, 77–78, 79, 84.

51. Ibid., 137–138, 174–175, 184.

52. Ibid., 190, 208, 226–227, 229. Much of the testimony at the hearing involved repairs and restorations that were made to various pieces in the collection.

53. *New York Times*, November 22, 1904.

54. Bates, *Martial Deeds of Pennsylvania*, 601–602; Moyer, *History of the Seventeenth Regiment Pennsylvania Volunteer Cavalry*, 82–83.

55. Cullum, *Biographical Register*, # 1312.

56. Warner, *Generals in Blue*, 173.

57. Gracey, *Annals of the Sixth Pennsylvania Cavalry*, 309–310

58. AOG USMA, *Annual Reunion*, 1898, 47–51.

59. Rodenbough, ed., *From Everglade to Canyon*, 465; *New York Times*, December 20, 1912; U.S. Army Center for Military History, Medal of Honor citations, http://www.army.mil/cmh pg/Moh1.htm.

60. AOG USMA, *Annual Reunion*, 1896, 132–136.

61. Cullum, *Biographical Register*, #1845; AOG USMA, *Annual Reunion*, 1902, 113–115.

62. Crowninshield, *First Regiment of Massachusetts Cavalry*, 240, 317.

63. "His Successes in Later Life," *Life* 41 (August 7, 1956), 86.

64. Ibid.

65. Kester, *Cavalryman in Blue*, 89, 152, 160 175, 178.

66. Preston, *History of the Tenth New York Cavalry*, 269–270.

67. Lloyd, *History of the First Reg't Pennsylvania Reserve Cavalry*, 122; Bates, *Martial Deeds of Pennsylvania*, 929–930.

68. William G. Burnett, *Better a Patriot Soldier's Grave: The History of the Sixth Ohio Volunteer Cavalry* (N.p., 1982), 69.

69. Richard J. Staats, *Life and Times of Colonel William Stedman of the 6th Ohio Cavalry*, Volume 4, *Grassroots History of the American Civil War* (Bowie, MD: Heritage, 2003), 360–361.

70. Ibid., 336–337, 371.

71. Holmes, *Horse Soldiers in Blue*, 227–8.

72. Pennock Huey, *A True History of the Charge of the 8th Pennsylvania Cavalry at Chancellorsville* (Philadelphia: Porter & Coates, 1883), 25.

73. Hunt, *Brevet Brigadier Generals in Blue*, 302.

74. Ibid., 6, 42.

75. Harold Hand, Jr., *One Good Regiment: The 13th Pennsylvania Cavalry in the Civil War, 1861–1865* (Victoria, B.C.: Trafford, 2000), 4, 222, 230, 252. Kerwin, Irish-born and Catholic, divorced his first wife, Mary, in 1875. In 1896, he married again. His second wife was Catherine C. Burke, the widow of a veteran.

76. Cullum, *Biographical Register*, #1864; AOG USMA, *Annual Report* (1918), 70–71; *New York Times*, December 1, 1917.

77. Cathie Morgan, "The Unknown Hero from the Class of '56," in *The Rattle* 87 (Spring 2007), 6–7; U.S. Army Center for Military History, Medal of Honor citations, http://www.army.mil/cmh pg/Moh1.htm; Theta Chi Fraternity, "For Distinguished Gallantry," http://thetachi.org/news/2013/12/general/for-distinguished-gallantry/.

78. AOG USMA, *Annual Reunion* 1887, 70; Cullum, *Biographical Register*, #1855.

79. William Gardner Bell, *Commanding Generals and Chiefs of Staff, 1775–1991: Portraits & Biographical Sketches of the United States Army's Senior Officer* (Washington, D.C.: Center for Military History, United States Army, 1983), 94; William H. Carter, *Life of Lieutenant General Chaffee* (Chicago: University of Chicago Press, 1917), 25–43. Chaffee's son, Adna R. Chaffee, Jr., was also a career cavalry officer who rose to the grade of major general. Adna Chaffee, Jr. is frequently credited as being the father of the army's modern armor force. The Chaffee light tank and Fort Chaffee, Arkansas are named in his honor (Charles G. Mettier, "Adna Romanza Chaffee," *Assembly* 1 [April 1942], 13–15).

80. Avery, *Under Custer's Command*, 97, 107.

81. Ibid., 5.

82. *Daily Times*, Richmond, VA, June 18, 1888.

83. Virginia Commission to Study the Location of the J.E.B. Stuart Monument, "Location of the J.E.B. Stuart Monument: Report of [to] the Governor and General Assembly of Virginia," Richmond: Commonwealth of Virginia Division of Purchasing and Printing, 1953.

84. Garnett, *Riding with Stuart*, 89–91; *Riding with Stuart* includes a transcript of Garnett's oration, originally published by the Neale Publishing Company in December 1907.

85. Army Historical Foundation, "M551 Sheridan Light Tank," https://armyhistory.org/m551-sheridan-light-tank/.

86. Warner, *Generals in Gray*, 123.

87. Robert K. Ackerman, *Wade Hampton III* (Columbia: University of South Carolina Press, 2007), 267–291. The position of Commissioner of Pacific Railroads was an unofficial sinecure for senior Confederate officers. Earlier Joseph Johnston held the position and James Longstreet was appointed after Hampton.

88. Samuel J. Martin, *Southern Hero: Matthew Calbraith Butler, Confederate General, Hampton Red Shirt, and U.S. Senator* (Mechanicsburg, PA: Stackpole, 2001), 211–212, 219–220. At the time the situation in Columbia was very chaotic. The Republican administration of Daniel Chamberlain had not conceded defeat and both Democratic and Republican legislatures were competing for control.

89. Ibid., 282–283.

90. Ibid., 289–299. In a nuanced decision, the Quartermaster General, Brigadier General Charles Egan, was acquitted of buying tainted beef but censured for buying inedible meat. During his short tenure in volunteer service, Butler arranged for his son, M.C. Butler, Jr., who graduated from West Point in 1888, to serve on his staff as a major of

volunteers. The younger Butler's Association of Graduates obituary begins: "While at the height of his career, in perfect health, without a known enemy in the world, and without a word of warning, 'Cabbie' was struck down by the hand of an assassin while on border duty at Alpine, Texas, July 20, 1916" (AOG USMA, *Annual Report* [1917], 49–50).

91. Martin, *Southern Hero*, 301, 305, 307–308.

92. Emerson, *Sons of Privilege*, 109, 112–113; Allardice, *Confederate Colonels*, 331; Krick, *Lee's Colonels*, 330. In 1923, Peter Poinsett, Rutledge's slave, sought and received a pension for his service in Virginia in 1864–1865 (Emerson, *Sons of Privilege*, 109).

93. Warner, *Generals in Gray*, 78–79; Robert S. Seigler, *South Carolina's Military Organizations During the War Between the States*, vol. 2, *The Low Country and Pee Dee* (Charleston: History Press, 2008), 228.

94. Gorgas, *The Journals of Josiah Gorgas*, 117–121.

95. Ibid., 156, 255, 256. Mary Aiken's father was John Gayle who, although born in South Carolina, had served as governor of Alabama from 1831 until 1835 and as a congressman from Alabama in the U.S. House of Representatives from 1847 until 1849. William Sherman passed Hugh Aiken's letter to his brother, U.S. Senator John Sherman, who gave the letter to Congressman D. Wyatt Aiken, Hugh Aiken's younger brother. D. Wyatt Aiken commanded the 7th South Carolina Infantry in 1862 and 1863 before being assigned to administrative duties due to wounds received at Antietam. He served in the U.S. House of Representatives from 1877–1887 (J. Keith Jones, *The Boys of Diamond Hill: The Lives and Civil War Letters of the Boyd Family of Abbeville County, South Carolina* [Jefferson, NC: McFarland, 2011], 58, 103–4; Allardice, *Confederate Colonels*, 38).

96. Bruce S. Allardice, *More Generals in Gray* (Baton Rouge: Louisiana State University Press, 1995), 239–240.

97. Coffman, *Going Back the Way They Came*, 95–96, 136; Lt. Col William Wofford Rich, http://www.anglefire.com/ga2/PhillipsLegion/rich.html.

98. Longacre, *Fitz Lee*, 177.

99. Ibid., 188–189. Gibbon later wrote that in their discussions, Lee said that he concluded that with Robert E. Lee's surrender, further resistance was futile. In another account, however, while in Lynchburg Lee learned that he and his command were included in the terms of surrender negotiated between his uncle and U.S. Grant, thus requiring him to return to Appomattox (AOG USMA, *Annual Reunion* [1905], 101).

100. Longacre, *Fitzhugh Lee*, 193; AOG USMA, *Annual Reunion* (1905), 109. Lee eventually inherited Richland from his aunt.

101. Longacre, *Fitzhugh Lee*, 196.

102. Grant won with 56 percent of the popular vote. Greeley died before the Electoral College met to cast their ballots.

103. Longacre, *Fitz Lee*, 198–201, 208.

104. Ibid., 216–217.

105. Ibid., 218.

106. Jedediah Hotchkiss, *Virginia*, vol. 3, *Confederate Military History*, edited by Clement A. Evans (Atlanta, GA: Confederate Publishing Co., 1899, reprint, ed., Secaucus, NJ, Blue and Grey, Nd), 685–689. President Rutherford Hayes offered Wickham an appointment as Secretary of the Navy, which Wickham declined.

107. Fitzhugh Lee letter, March 20, 1865, Papers of Thomas Lafayette Rosser (Mss 1171). Albert and Shirley Small Special Collections Library, University of Virginia, Charlottesville, VA.

108. Allardice, *More Generals in Gray*, 171–172. Munford's failure to obtain promotion to brigadier general is somewhat a mystery. He was generally considered a reliable and capable commander. At the grade of colonel, he was senior to all but one of the seven brigadier generals who commander cavalry brigades in 1864. (Ibid.)

109. Hotchkiss, *Virginia*, 628–630; Warner, *Generals in Gray*, 190–191; Patrick Carlton "Confederates in the Collegium: The Influence of J.E.B. Stuart's Leadership on the Development of Virginia Tech," (Blacksburg: University Archives of Virginia Tech, http://spec.lib.vt.edu/arc/125th/confeds/confeds.htm; Duncan L. Kinnear, "The Lomax Administration 1886–1891" in *A Short History of Virginia Tech 1850–1974* [Blacksburg: Special Collections, University Libraries], http://spec.lib.vt.edu/archives/125th/kinnear/lomax.htm).

110. Musick, *6th Virginia Cavalry*, 120.

111. Daniel A. Grimsley, *Battles in Culpeper County, Virginia, 1861–1865* (Culpeper: Raleigh Travers Green, 1900; reprint ed., Orange, VA: Green, N.d.), 1. There had been speculation that Judge Shackleford's daughter, Lucy, was romantically linked to Major John Pelham. Pelham died of his wounds in the Shackleford residence in Culpeper on the night of March 17, 1863. Lucy eventually married a Union cavalry officer.

112. Ibid.; Musick, *6th Virginia Cavalry*, 120.

113. Mildred K. and Dean M. Bushong, *Fighting Tom Rosser, C.S.A.* (Shippensburg, PA: Beidel Printing House, 1983), 183.

114. Beane, "Thomas Lafayette Rosser," 54.

115. Ibid., 55.

116. Ibid., 56–66. Shortly after returning to Charlottesville, an amusing tiff arose between Rosser and his former adversary, Philip Sheridan. A newspaper reported that Sheridan planned to visit the Shenandoah Valley to see if it had recovered from the destruction he had wrought there during the war. Rosser took offense, and wrote critically of Sheridan and his plan to visit the Valley. As could be expected, Rosser was supported in the South and ridiculed in the North. The issue quickly blew over, but afterward both Rosser and Sheridan remained bitter toward one another.

117. Ibid., 71–2. On October 18, 1893, at Hanover Courthouse, Rosser debated then–Democratic governor Fitz Lee, who supported O'Ferrall.

118. Ibid., 79–80. After the war, Rosser became a proponent of American colonization of Cuba, but the idea never caught on.

119. Ibid., 81.

120. Armstrong, *7th Virginia Cavalry*,139; Allardice, *Confederate Colonels*, 134–135; Vogtsberger, *The Dulanys of Welbourne*, 278.

121. Vogtsberger, *The Dulanys of Welbourne*, 279.

122. Ibid., 283.

123. Ibid., 285.

124. Manigault, Autobiography, 436. Ricekingdom.com, "Biographical Dictionary of Postbellum Rice Culture," http://ricekingdom.com/planters.html; College of Charleston, "College of Charleston Archive: About the Collection Archive," http://speccoll.cofc.edu/findingaids/archives.html?referrer' webcluster&; Charleston Museum, "The Joseph Manigault House," http://charlestonmuseum.org/joseph-manigault-house; Boston Museum of Fine Arts, "Mr. & Mrs. Ralph Izard (Alice Delancey)," http://www.mfa.org/collections/object/mr-and-mrs-ralph-izard-alice-delancey.

125. S. Bassett French, "Biographical Sketches," Papers of S. Bassett French (21332, Misc. Reels 4117–4120), Library of Virginia, Richmond.

126. Trout, *Galloping Thunder*, 630–635–641; Trout, *The Hoss*, 254–6. Pelham was mortally wounded fighting with the cavalry at Kelly's Ford on March 17, 1863.

127. Nanzig, *3rd Virginia Cavalry*, 54, 100.

128. Mays, *Let Us Meet in Heaven*, 258–260.

129. Quartermaster General's Office, *Roll of Honor (No. XV.): Names of Soldiers Who Died in Defence of the American Union, Interred in the National Cemeteries at Antietam (Maryland,) and at Arlington (Additional,) Culpeper Court-House, Cold Harbor, Winchester, Staunton, and Various Scattered Localities in Virginia* (Washington, D.C.: U.S. Government Printing Office, 1868; reprint ed., Baltimore, MD: Genealogical Publishing, Inc., 1994), 117–148. The initial burial sites for many of the Union dead are familiar from accounts of the battle: thirty-three from Charles Trevilian's farm; seventeen from J.B. Bibb's farm; nine from G. Ogg's farm; six from A. Nutherlin's [Netherland's] farm. In addition to battle casualties, many of the dead buried in Culpeper National Cemetery succumbed to disease during the Army of the Potomac's encampment around Brandy Station in the winter of 1863–1864.

Appendix A

1. *OR* 40, II:542, 707. The Union Cavalry Corps listed 15,209 enlisted men present for duty on April 30, 1864. In the Army of the Potomac's return dated June 1, 1864, the Union Cavalry Corps' present for duty strength was given as 12,420 officers and men in its three divisions. In its June 30, 1864, return, the corps' present for duty strength was given as 13,350 officers and men in three divisions. (*OR*, 36, I:209; *OR*, 40, II:542) As of June 30, Hampton's and Fitz Lee Fitz's divisions reported a combined strength of 4830 officers and men (40, III:762).

2. A considerable number of cavalry regiments assigned to the Army of the Potomac were not available to Sheridan for the march toward Charlottesville and the ensuing fight at Trevilian's. Wilson's Division of eight regiments remained on duty with Meade's infantry corps. Burnside's IX Corps, operating separately against Richmond, had four cavalry regiments assigned. One additional cavalry regiment, the 24th New York, was dismounted and assigned, along with two heavy artillery regiments, to fight in a provisional infantry brigade in the IX Corps. Another dismounted regiment, the 21st Pennsylvania, joined the Army of the Potomac on June 1 and was assigned to an infantry brigade in the V Corps. The 3rd Pennsylvania was detailed to duty at Army Headquarters. Additionally, two fresh regiments, the 13th Ohio and the 25th New York, were dismounted and left at White House landing. The horses of those regiments were distributed to the men in veteran regiments. The 13th Ohio served dismounted with the IX Corps before joining the cavalry corps in December 1964. The 25th New York was briefly assigned to the Army to the Potomac provost guard and the defenses of Washington before joining Sheridan in the Valley in August 1864 (*OR* 36, I:106, 114, 115, Dyer, *Compendium*, 3:1382, 1579–1478).

3. *OR*, 36, I:785.

4. *OR*, 36, I:186–187. Hampton, in his official report of the battle, reported capturing about 125 wounded "on the ground and in temporary hospitals." He also reported capturing an additional 570 Union troopers, for a total of 695. The number of Union soldiers reported captured by Hampton appears high when compared to the number reported by Sheridan.

5. *OR*, 36, I:186–188. The union casualties in the tables are for the fighting on June 11–12. They do not include 83 casualties at White House on June 21, 339 casualties at Saint Mary's Church on June 24, and 83 casualties incurred during minor skirmishes, for a total of 1512 casualties during the course of the raid (150 killed, 738 wounded, and 624 captured).

6. Writing well after the war, J.H. Kidd, using records from the Michigan Adjutant General's Office, compiled the Michigan Brigade's casualties for the two-day fight at Trevilian's. According to Kidd, the 1st Michigan had thirteen killed or died of wounds and thirty-nine captured, of whom twelve died in captivity. The 5th Michigan had 8 killed and 102 captured, of whom 33 died in captivity. The 6th Michigan had seventeen killed or died of wounds and fifty-eight captured, of whom twenty-four died in captivity. The 7th Michigan had three killed and forty-three captured, of whom fourteen died in captivity. Thus Kidd estimated the casualties for the Michigan Brigade at 41 killed and 242 captured. Kidd did not provide an estimate for the wounded, noting that the reports of the regimental commanders were "very deficient in that particular" (Kidd, *Personal Recollections*, 364–366). However, later in his book, Kidd identified by name a total of fifty-eight officers and men who were killed in action at Trevilian's or died of wounds suffered during the battle. The number of named by regiment were: 1st Michigan—three officers and eleven enlisted; 5th Michigan—fifteen enlisted; 6th Michigan—twenty enlisted; 7th Michigan—nine enlisted (Ibid., 543–576). The difference between the numbers provided by Kidd and those reported in the *Official Records* is indicative of the difficulty in accurately determining Civil War casualties.

7. The sole staff casualty listed was Captain Jacob L. Greene, the brigade assistant adjutant general and a friend of Custer's from Monroe, Michigan, who was captured. One of Custer's staff officers, Lieutenant Richard Bayliss, was wounded in the shoulder and Custer's color bearer, Sergeant Mitchell Belloir was killed. Bayliss and Belloir, while not included in the brigade staff casualties, might be included among the regimental figures (*OR*, 36, I:824).

8. Company D was detached to the Provost Guard in Alexandria, VA, from November 1862 until the end of the war (Michigan AGO, *Michigan in the War*, 566). Company G was detached for duty at Headquarters, V Corps (Hewett, et al., eds., *Supplement*, II, 29:681–682).

9. In contrast to both the *Official Records* and the Michigan AGO, and the data in his *Personal Recollections*, in a letter to his parents dated June 21, 1864, Major Kidd wrote that at Trevilian Station his regiment lost 7 killed, 23 wounded, and 75 missing—a total of 105 (Kidd, *One of Custer's Wolverines*, 95).

10. The colonel of the 7th Michigan, William D. Mann, resigned his commission in March 1864. The lieutenant colonel of the regiment, Allyn C. Litchfield, was captured on March 1, 1864, during the Dahlgren Raid. The senior major of the regiment, Henry W. Granger, was killed at Yellow Tavern. As the Trevilian Raid began, Major Brewer was transferred from the 1st Michigan to the 7th Michigan and nominated for promotion to lieutenant colonel, to date from June 6, 1864. Brewer was senior in grade to the other major in the regiment, Alexander Walker, and thus was in command during the battle at Trevilian's (Isham, *An Historical Sketch*, 95, 94, 93, 98; Kidd, *Personal Recollections*, 343).

11. In his history of the 7th Michigan, Lee recorded three men killed at Trevilian Station (Lee, *Personal and Historical Sketches*, vii).

12. This figure does not include Major Brewer, the sole officer among the regiment's casualties.

13. In letters to the father of a captain who had been

killed, Colonel diCesnola wrote that the 4th New York had suffered seven killed and wounded on June 11 and fourteen killed and thirty-seven wounded on June 12 (Luigi diCesnola to W.N. Wood, June 24 and July 7, 1864, Luigi diCesnola Papers [Ms-68], Rauner Special Collections Library, Dartmouth College, Hanover, NH). The regimental quartermaster, Alexander Newburger, who had not accompanied the regiment on the raid, rejoined the unit when it arrived at White House. In his diary entry for June 12, 1864, Newburger recorded that at Trevilian's the regiment lost six officers and seventy-three men killed, wounded, and missing (Alexander Newburger, Diary, 1864–1865 [Microfilm 16992–1P] [Manuscript Collection, Library of Congress, Washington], 67).

14. Company L was detached to Colonel Devin's Headquarters (Hewett, et al., eds., *Supplement*, II, 41:343).

15. Hillman Hall recorded the regiment's casualties on June 11 and 12 as nine killed or mortally wounded, one officer and eight men wounded, and twenty-five men missing for a total of forty-three casualties (Hall, *History of the Sixth New York Cavalry*, 27).

16. Newel Cheney later wrote that at Trevilian's the regiment suffered more casualties than in any engagement during the war. According to Cheney's by-name tabulation, on June 11–12, the 9th New York lost eight killed and seven mortally wounded, including Colonel Sackett. The regiment also had thirty-three men wounded, of whom two were captured. Three unwounded soldiers were captured, one of whom had volunteered to stay behind to tend to Colonel Sackett. Thus, according to Cheney, the 9th New York lost fifty-one men over the two-day's fight (Cheney, *History of the Ninth New York Cavalry*, 187–188).

17. In his official report, Devin wrote that his brigade's casualties at Trevilian's were one officer killed and five wounded; eighteen enlisted men killed and sixty-two wounded; and fifteen men missing. Thus Devin's casualty count totals 101, or 59 less than as indicated in the Army of the Potomac's consolidated return. Additionally, Devin did not account for the mortally wounded William Sackett in his report.

18. Unlike standard Union Cavalry Regiments, the 1st New York Dragoons was organized with only ten companies.

19. Other accounts differ. A regimental history published shortly after the war stated that the regiment suffered eighty-eight "killed and wounded" during the battle. However, annotations to the regimental roster identified eighteen killed, six mortally wounded, twenty wounded, and three missing/captured for a total of forty-seven casualties not including officers (*Regimental History of the First New York Dragoons with a List of Names, Post-Office Address, Casualties of Officers and Men, ...* [Washington, D.C.: Gibson Brothers, 1865], 13). Bowen, in his more lengthy account published well after the war, stated that the regiment lost eighty-six in killed, wounded, and captured. However the accompanying roster identifies seventeen men killed, four mortally wounded, twenty-seven wounded, and four captured (one of whom was also wounded). Thus according to Bowen's roster, the regiment suffered fifty-two casualties at Trevilian's. Lieutenant Colonel Thorp, who was captured was not identified as a casualty (Bowen, *Regimental History of the First New York Dragoons*, 189). William F. Fox, in his tabulations for *Three Hundred Fighting Regiments*, wrote that at Trevilian's the regiment lost sixteen killed, sixty-one wounded, and eight missing for a total of eighty-five (William F. Fox, *Regimental Losses in the American Civil War: 1861–1865* [Albany, NY: Albany, 1889], 183).

20. Company A was detached to General Torbert's headquarters (Hewett, et al., eds., *Supplement*, II, 56:791).

21. The *OR* lists Major W.P.C. Treichel as in command of the regiment. However, Treichel was absent on sick leave until after the Trevilian Raid (Gracey, *Annals of the Sixth Pennsylvania Cavalry* [1996], 260).

22. In an 1896 historical sketch of the 1st U.S. Cavalry, Captain R.P.P. Wainwright listed two officers killed and one wounded, three enlisted men killed with twenty-nine wounded or missing, for total of thirty-five casualties at Trevilian's (Theophilus F. Rodenbough, ed., *The Army of the United States: Historical Sketches of Staff and Line with Portraits of Generals in Chief* [New York: Maynard, Merrill, 1896], 161).

23. The casualty figures cited in the *OR* conform fairly closely to those later tabulated by the regimental commander, Theophilus Rodenbough, who was wounded on June 11. Rodenbough later wrote that the regiment lost one lieutenant, Michael Lawless, and seven enlisted men killed, two officers and thrity-four enlisted men wounded, and one officer and four enlisted men missing, for a total of forty-nine (Rodenbough, ed., *From Everglade to Canyon*, 314).

24. F. Price, *Across the Continent with the Fifth Cavalry*, 121, 123. Companies A and D were on detached duty at Point Lookout, MD, and Companies B, C, F, and K were detached to Headquarters, Army of the Potomac as General Grant's escort.

25. George Price's casualty figures differ from those in the *OR*. He wrote that one lieutenant, Joseph Henley, and three men were killed at Trevilian's, along with twenty-three horses, and that six men were wounded and two captured (Price, *Across the Continent with the Fifth Cavalry*, 123, 124, 656).

26. *OR*, 36, I: 106. Companies C and D, under the command of Captain Charles Francis Adams, Jr., were detached to Army Headquarters from April 1864 until the end of the war. During the Trevilian Raid, Companies A and B, under the command of Captain Benjamin Crowninshield, were detached and left behind to guard wagon trains at White House on the Pamunkey. Absent the detachments, and after suffering significant casualties during May, the 1st Massachusetts had only 160 officers and men present at Trevilian Station (Crowninshield, *First Regiment, Massachusetts Cavalry*, 200, 223, 227).

27. Eighty men of the 10th New York, who were at White House Landing when Sheridan's movement to Trevilian's began, were temporarily attached to Wilson's Division and did not participate in the raid. The detachment from the 10th New York was under the command of Captain Aaron T. Bliss, the commander of Company D (Warren W. Irish, "Getting Back to the Army: How 80 of the 10th N.J. [sic] Cav. Came to be with Gen. Wilson on his Raid in June 1864, *National Tribune*, February 1, 1900).

28. A history of the 6th Ohio indicates that two men were wounded on June 11 (William G. Burnett, *Better a Patriot Soldier's Grave: The History of the Sixth Ohio Volunteer Cavalry* [Np., 1982], 46).

29. In his regimental history, Tobie reported that four men were wounded on June 11. He also reported that two men were captured on June 10 (Tobie, *History of the First Maine Cavalry*, 689).

30. Company F was dismounted and awaiting horses at Camp Stoneman at the Giesboro remount depot in the District of Columbia (Hewett, et al., eds., *Supplement*, II, 56:689).

31. *OR*, 36, I:126; Hewett, et al., eds., *Supplement*, II, 57:99. Company A was assigned to Headquarters, VI Corps.

Company K was initially detailed to picket duty, then detached to Headquarters, II Corps.

32. At the beginning of the Overland Campaign, Lieutenant Dennison commanded Battery G, 2nd U.S. Artillery. That horse battery was dismounted on June 2 and transferred to the defenses of Washington. Dennison was reassigned to command of Battery A, 2nd U.S., replacing Lieutenant Robert Clarke (*OR*, 36, I:209; Dyer, *Compendium*, III:1697).

33. Janet Hewett, et al., eds., *Supplement*, 6, 36:801.

34. *OR*, 36, I:1096.

35. Latty, *Gallant Little 7th*, 95, 97, 100. The number of prisoners is probably understated. Latty's number—181—is derived from federal records of men of the 7th Georgia who were imprisoned in the North after the battle. Some men who were captured may have either escaped or died before arriving at a Northern prison camp.

36. Mesic, *Cobb's Legion Cavalry*, 120, 124. Among the killed was Lieutenant Henry Francis Jones, the regimental adjutant.

37. The Phillips Legion had six companies assigned. Love's Battalion, the 4th Battalion Alabama Cavalry which consisted of three companies, was attached to the Phillips Legion during the battle. The companies of the Phillips Legion suffered eight casualties: one killed; two mortally wounded; three wounded; two captured, one of whom died in captivity (Coffman, *Going Back the Way They Came*, roster information). Love's Battalion suffered nine casualties: one killed; six wounded (including two with amputated legs); two captured. The battalion was later assigned permanently to the Jeff Davis Legion (Hopkins, *Horsemen of the Jeff Davis Legion*, 117–137).

38. Hopkins, *The Little Jeff*, 210.

39. Armstrong, *7th Virginia Cavalry*, 69. Armstrong identified eight men wounded on June 11, and five wounded on June 12.

40. Armstrong, *11th Virginia Cavalry*, 75. Armstrong identified one man wounded on June 11.

41. Frye, *12th Virginia Cavalry*, 69.

42. Devine, *35th Battalion Virginia Cavalry*, personnel information; Myers, *The Comanches*, 299–300.

43. Wittenberg, *Glory Enough for All*, 353. An accurate accounting of the casualties of the 4th South Carolina at Trevilian's is difficult. Captain James Lipscomb, Butler's adjutant, in a letter dated July 25, 1864, tallied the brigade's casualties from its arrival in Virginia through July 13. He documented 273 casualties in the 4th South Carolina by name: 43 killed; 12 mortally wounded; 93 wounded; 109 missing or captured; 3 mortally wounded and captured; 13 wounded and captured (Hewett, et al., eds., *Supplement*, 3, 95:586–589). In his letters home, William Stokes, the lieutenant colonel of the regiment, informed his wife of the casualties resulting from each engagement: Haw's Shop—125 killed-wounded-missing; near Cold Harbor—54 killed-wounded-missing; Samaria Church—2 killed and 5 or 6 wounded. For Trevilian's, Stokes wrote: "The Regt lost about one hundred, killed, wounded, and missing in the two engagements, mostly captured." Stokes later added that on June 12, the regiment only lost one man killed and "about" two wounded (Stokes, *Saddle Soldiers*, 140–151). Stokes's numbers conform closely to the figures provided by Lipscomb, indicating that Stokes's estimate of "about one hundred" casualties at Trevilian's is fairly accurate. That is also generally consistent with Mr. Bryce Suderow's casualty figures in Wittenberg's *Glory Enough For All*. Wittenberg characterized Suderow's work as "groundbreaking" (Wittenberg, *Glory Enough for All*, xxi). Unfortunately it lacks citation.

As previously discussed, the regimental adjutant, Lieutenant Gabriel Manigault, who was captured, compiled a list of fifty-seven men who had been taken prisoner and noted that there were other prisoners who were wounded whose names he could not obtain (Manigault, "Autobiography," 429; *Charleston Daily Courier*, June 24, 1864). Some of the men Manigault listed as captured may have been recovered by the Confederates on June 12 and 13.

44. Colonel John Dunovant, the regimental commander, was absent recuperating from wounds received at Haw's Shop on May 28 (Brooks, *Butler and His Cavalry*, 241).

45. John Rigdon, *Historical Sketch and Roster: The SC 5th Cavalry Regiment* (Powder Springs, GA: Eastern Digital Resources, 2004), roster information. This information is fairly consistent with that cited by Ulysses R. Brooks, a veteran of the battle, who later wrote that the regiment lost six killed, forty-one wounded, and eight captured at Trevilian's, for a total of fifty-five (Brooks, *Butler and His Cavalry*, 241, 252). Brooks' brother, Whitfield Butler Brooks, was among those of the regiment killed in action at Trevilian's on June 12, 1864.

46. *Charleston Mercury*, June 23, 1864. Of the ninety-two wounded, twenty-three men were listed as being severely wounded while forty men were listed as only slightly wounded.

47. Review of muster roll information in Driver's *First and Second Maryland Cavalry, C.S.A.* and Trout's *The Hoss* does not reveal any casualties within the 1st Maryland or the Baltimore Light Artillery, respectively, at Trevilian Station. However, review of personnel data for the Baltimore Light Artillery, also known as the 2nd Maryland Artillery, reveals one man who may have been wounded at Trevilian's. Private Adam F. Schaffer was admitted to Chimborazo Hospital in Richmond with a wound on his right leg on June 17, 1864. He was returned to duty three days later. The battle in which Schaffer received his wound was not indicated (Trout, *The Hoss*, 219).

48. The commander of the 1st Maryland, Lieutenant Colonel Ridgely Brown, was killed in action during an engagement near Ashland, Virginia on June 1. The regiment's major, Robert C. Smith, was still recovering from wounds received at Greenland Gap, West Virginia a year earlier. Colonel Bradley Johnson, the commander of the Maryland Line, elected to exercise direct command of the 1st Maryland rather than allowing the regiment to be led by the senior captain present (Driver, Jr., *First and Second Maryland Cavalry, C.S.A*, 83).

49. The captain of the battery, Wiley H. Griffin, had been captured at Yellow Tavern on May 11. He remained a prisoner until the end of the war. Griffin was among the "Immortal 600" who were held on Morris Island under the line of fire of Confederate batteries at Charleston, South Carolina (Trout, *The Hoss*, 203). Beane's tenure in command was brief. He was relieved and placed under arrest by Jubal Early on August 22, 1864 for failing to confiscate shoes from a factory in Maryland (Ibid., 204; Trout, *Galloping Thunder*, 742, n.4.)

50. Driver, Jr., *5th Virginia Cavalry*, 118.

51. Musick, *6th Virginia Cavalry*, 60.

52. Ibid., 63.

53. As previously discussed, Major Robert F. Mason, who served as quartermaster on Fitzhugh Lee's staff, was placed in command of the 15th Virginia for the duration of the battle (Fortier, *15th Virginia Cavalry*, 75).

54. Fortier, *15th Virginia Cavalry*, 75. The sole soldier reported killed during the battle was Private David Powers. Powers, who was serving a sentence of confinement to camp

and forfeiture of pay for deserting his post while on picket, was reportedly shot accidentally by one of the men of the regiment "while coming out of a skirmish" (Ibid., 75, 156).

55. Driver, Jr., *1st Virginia Cavalry*, personnel data.

56. Driver, Jr., *2nd Virginia Cavalry*, 179.

57. Nanzig, *3rd Virginia Cavalry*, 64.

58. It is unclear who was in command of the 4th Virginia at Trevilian's. The regiment had no field grade officers present for duty at the time of the battle. The regiment's colonel, William H.F. Payne, had been wounded and captured during the Gettysburg Campaign. Although he had been exchanged in May 1864, he remained absent recuperating from his wounds. Payne, who was promoted to brigadier general on November 1, 1864, never returned to duty with the regiment. The regiment's lieutenant colonel and acting commander, Robert Randolph, was killed at Meadow Bridge on May 12, 1864. This situation prompted Lomax to write to the Secretary or War on June 21, 1864, "Lt Col Randolph 4th Va Cavalry was killed on the 12th of May leaving the Regiment without any field officers. I made application for promotions but have had no response. I respectfully ask that Major W.B. Woolridge, 4th Virginia Cavalry, be appointed Lt. Col. And that Capt Charles Old, Co E. 4th Virginia Cavalry (the ranking Capt with the exception of Capt McKinney, Co B, who has applied to be retired) may be made major of the regiment" (4th Virginia Cavalry Compiled Service Records). The major of the regiment, William B. Wooldridge, had been shot in the knee at Spotsylvania three days earlier. As a result of his wound, Wooldridge's leg was amputated, leaving him incapacitated for several months. Wooldridge was promoted to lieutenant colonel and then colonel while recuperating. After returning to duty, he commanded the regiment until Appomattox (Stiles, *4th Virginia Cavalry*, 130, 132, 144). In the absence of field grade officers, it is possible that the 4th Virginia was commanded at Trevilian's by the senior captain present. The senior captain in the regiment, Phillip McKinney, mentioned above, had been seriously wounded at Brandy Station and did not return to active service. In the spring of 1864 he applied for medical retirement that he might take a seat in the Virginia Legislature. In 1889, McKinney was elected governor of Virginia, serving from 1890 until 1894. The two senior captains in the regiment were Mordecai Strother, commanding Company B, and Charles Old, commanding Company E. Both had been elected captain during the army's reorganization in April 1862 and were apparently capable officers. Old, who had been wounded at Todd's Tavern and may have been convalescing during Travilian's, was promoted to major in October 1864. In February 1865, Fitz Lee recommended Strother for promotion to lieutenant colonel, but the promotion was not approved before the war's end. It is also possible that the 4th Virginia was temporarily commanded by an officer not assigned to the regiment. R.L.T. Beal, colonel of the 9th Virginia, wrote that in June 1864, Major Thomas Waller, of Beal's regiment, had been detailed to temporary command of another, unspecified, regiment (Beale, *History of the Ninth Virginia Cavalry*, 129). The fact that the two regiments—the 9th Virginia and the 4th Virginia—were in different divisions would not necessarily impede such a detail. Similarly, in early 1863 W.H.F. Payne, then a lieutenant colonel, was detailed from the 4th Virginia in Fitz Lee's brigade, to temporary command of the 2nd North Carolina in Rooney Lee's brigade. Unfortunately, documentary evidence shedding light on the command of the 4th Virginia at Trevilian's is lacking. If Major Waller was in temporary command of the 4th Virginia, he did not sign any documents that made their way into that regiment's extant records. It is also possible that Major Waller had been appointed to temporary command of the 13th Virginia which was assigned to Chambliss's Brigade. The 13th Virginia was also suffering from a shortage of field grade officers in May and June 1864.

59. Stiles, *4th Virginia Cavalry*, personnel data.

60. Artillery casualties, unless otherwise noted, are from the personnel data in Trout's *The Hoss*.

61. The strength of Hart's Battery on June 8 was 112 men (*OR*, 36, III:883–884).

62. The strength of Thomson's Battery on June 8 was ninety-eight men (Ibid.).

63. Hewett, et al., eds., *Supplement*, 6, 36:825. Shoemaker's official report was dated September 1, 1864. However, writing well after the war, Shoemaker recorded that his battery suffered five casualties: three severely wounded and two seriously wounded and captured (Shoemaker, *Shoemaker's Battery*, 72). Lewis Nunnelee, in his history of Shoemaker's Battery, wrote that the two captured men assigned to the battery, John Everett, and Madison Porter, were detailed as a hospital steward and hospital wagon driver, respectively. Everett was wounded—saber blow to the wrist—and captured. Porter, although not wounded, was also captured. Both were freed by advancing Confederates shortly afterward. Everett was wearing a fine broad-brimmed cap when captured, which was taken from him by a Yankee. The Yankee was in-turn captured, and Everett was able to liberate his cap (Lewis T. Nunnelee, "History of a Famous Company...," in *Memoirs of the Stuart Horse Artillery Battalion: Moorman's and Hart's Batteries*, ed., Robert Trout [Knoxville: University of Tennessee Press, 2010], 91–92).

64. The National Park Service lists a greater number of casualties for the Battle at Selma, Alabama, which was fought on April 2, 1865. However, unlike Trevilian's, that battle was a lopsided victory for the Union. Major General James's Wilson's cavalry suffered just 319 casualties. The Confederates lost approximately 2700 men, most of whom surrendered when Wilson's raiders penetrated Selma's fortification and overran the city.

Appendix B

1. Unless otherwise noted, the source for the information in this appendix is George W. Cullum, *Biographical Register of the Officers and Graduates of the U.S. Military Academy at West Point, N.Y. From its Establishment in 1802, to 1890 with the Early History of the United States Military Academy*, 3 vols., 3rd ed. (New York: Houghton Mifflin and Co., 1891). Cullum consecutively numbered each graduate, a practice that has been followed by the USMA Association of Graduates to this day. Graduation class and "Cullum numbers," are provided for the graduates mentioned in this appendix, either in the table, for those who fought in the battle, or in parentheses after their names for those who were not present at Trevilian's. For example, Wilson graduated with the class of 1860 and his Cullum number is 1852.

2. Wilson's *aide de camp*, Lieutenant Eugene B. Beaumont, was a West Point graduate (May 1861, #1919). On July 20, 1863, Lieutenant Henry Noyes (June 1861, #1955) replaced Beaumont as Wilson's aide. Two West Point graduates commissioned in the artillery served with batteries that habitually supported Wilson's division: John Egan (1862, #1982) and Thomas Ward (1863, #2010).

3. Captain McQuestern was killed in action at Opequon near Winchester on September 19, 1864.

4. The USMA Association of Graduates incorrectly

spells Leoser's name "Loeser" in its current *Register of Graduates.*

5. During the Trevilian's Raid, Lieutenant Lester was transferred to command of a company in his regiment, the 2nd US Cavalry, on June 18, 1864. During the Army of the Potomac's winter encampment in Culpeper, November 1863-May 1864, Lester made the acquaintance of Lucy Shackleford whose uncle, Muscoe, had graduated from West Point in 1836 and been mortally wounded at Molino Del Rey in 1847. Reportedly, earlier in the war Lucy had been courted by Major John Pelham, JEB Stuart's artillery commander. Pelham died in the Shackleford residence in Culpeper Courthouse on the night of March 17, 1863. Lester and Lucy were married in the spring of 1869 (Association of Graduates, *Annual Reunion*, June 12, 1900).

6. Chambliss was killed in action on the Charles City Road on August 16, 1864. Davis, upset that he was not promoted to brigadier general, resigned his commission in January 1865.

7. Louis Manarin, *The Cavalry*, vol. 2 of *North Carolina Troops 1861–1865, A Roster...* (Raleigh, NC: North Carolina State Department of Archives and History, 1968), 104.

Appendix C

1. William W. Blackford, *War Years with JEB Stuart* (New York: Charles Scribner's Sons, 1945; reprint ed., Baton Rouge: Louisiana State University Press, 1993), 242.

2. Merington, ed., *The Custer Story*, 62–72. Custer, who knew Annett Humphrey from his time spent in Monroe, corresponded with her before he began seriously courting Libbie. Judge Bacon lifted his ban on direct communication between Custer and Libbie on about November 1, 1863.

3. James Wood, "Diary, Jan. 9-July 31, 1864," Personal Papers Collection (25506), Library of Virginia, Richmond.

4. Merington, ed., *The Custer Story*, 105.

5. Ibid., 105–6.

6. Ibid., 112.

7. *Richmond Examiner*, July 1, 1864. While most Custer biographers ascribe to the fact that some of Libbie's letters were published in the Richmond newspapers, there is little actual evidence on the issue. A perusal of Richmond newspapers commonly available to scholars today does not reveal any of such letters in print. Further, Custer biographers have not quoted from any of Libbie's letters, the content of which would certainly be of interest to their readers. Finally, biographers have not cited the newspapers which supposedly carried the letters. It seems more likely that the publication of Libbie's intimate letters to her husband is more Custer lore than historical fact.

8. Ibid., June 28, 1864. Reportedly, Lomax later sent the silver to an attorney in Richmond who was to arrange for it to be identified and claimed (W. Gordon McCabe, "Defense of Petersburg," *Southern Historical Society* 2 [Jul-Dec 1876], 276n).

9. *Richmond Examiner*, July 5, 1864. Wilson's wagon contained more than just silver. Among other things, the Virginians found an envelope containing several *cartes de visite*, including Wilson's sister, General Grant, other officers, "and one of a young saucy looking negro woman very finely dressed" (Robert T. Hubard, Notebook of Robert Thruston Hubard [Mss 10522, Notebook with typescript], Albert and Shirley Small Special Collections Library, University of Virginia, Charlottesville, 105).

10. *Richmond Examiner*, July 5, 1864.

11. Ibid.,

12. Jacob S. Green to George A. Custer, September 29, 1864, Letter to George Armstrong Custer (Mss 10450), Albert and Shirley Small Special Collections Library, University of Virginia, Charlottesville.

13. Thomas T. Munford, "Reminiscences of Cavalry Operations: Operations under Rosser," *Southern Historical Society* 13 (1885), 134. Custer, writing to Libbie after his victory at Tom's Brook, informed Libbie that as he wrote, he was "arrayed in Genl. Rosser's coat." At that battle, Custer also captured Rosser's pet squirrel (Merington, ed., *The Custer Story*, 122–123).

14. Eric J. Wittenberg, *Glory Enough for All: Sheridan's Second Raid and the Battle of Trevilian Station* (Washington, D.C.: Brassey's, 2002), 129, n 79.

15. Merington, ed., *The Custer Story*, 123.

Appendix D

1. Butler, "The Cavalry Fight at Trevilian Station," 4:237.

2. Thomas L. Rosser, Papers of Thomas Lafayette Rosser and the Rosser, Gordon, and Winston Families (Mss 1171) (Albert and Shirley Small Special Collections Library, University of Virginia, Charlottesville). Thomas Rosser's scrapbook contains a copy of the article cut from the *Philadelphia Weekly Times*.

3. A. Wilson Greene, "Introduction" to Edward L. Wells, *Hampton and His Cavalry in '64* (Richmond, VA: B.F. Johnson, 1899; reprint ed., Richmond, VA: Owen, 1991). The pages in Greene's Introduction are not numbered. On the morning of March 11, Hampton, accompanied by a handful of scouts—including Wells—rode into Fayetteville hoping to find breakfast. A squadron of Union cavalry rode into town from the opposite direction. Hampton ordered his men to charge, and the Rebels chased the Yankees up one street and down another. The federals finally withdrew, leaving behind thirteen killed and twelve captured. The loss to the Confederates was one horse killed (Cisco, *Wade Hampton*, 157–158).

4. Greene, "Introduction" to Wells, *Hampton and His Cavalry.*

5. Wells, *Hampton and His Cavalry*, 198–201.

6. By the end of 1899, 1891 copies of the book had sold, leaving 350–400 unsold. There was no second edition, as had been proposed by Wells. (Greene, "Introduction" to Wells, *Hampton and His Cavalry.*)

7. Greene, "Introduction" to Wells, *Hampton and His Cavalry.* Wells also believed that others may have been unhappy with his criticism of Major General Joseph Wheeler's performance during the fighting in North Carolina in the spring of 1865.

8. Bradley T. Johnson, "The Bold Horsemen," *Richmond Dispatch*, December 31, 1899.

9. Johnson, "The Bold Horsemen."

10. Johnson, "The Bold Horsemen." Regarding this statement, Johnson was factually inaccurate. By army policy, Rooney Lee had been prohibited from receiving an appointment to West Point since his older brother, Custis, was enrolled as a cadet. Instead, Rooney attended Harvard.

11. *Richmond Dispatch*, January 7, 1900. Cralle's letter was dated January 2, 1900.

12. Lunsford Lomax forwarded Grimsley's rebuttal to the *Richmond Dispatch* by letter dated January 17, 1900. Lomax was Grimsley's brigade commander at Trevilian's.

13. Daniel A. Grimsley, "Trevillian's Again," *Richmond Dispatch*, January 21, 1900. Grimsley slightly misquoted Hampton, who in his report wrote that "Maj. Gen. Fitzhugh

Lee cooperated with me heartily and rendered valuable assistance." (*OR*, 36, I:1097.)

14. *Richmond Dispatch*, January 21, 1900. No date was indicated for the "card" Johnson sent to the *Dispatch* with his comments. Wells's letter was dated January 12, 1900.

15. Ibid.

16. Hampton was born on March 28, 1818, in Charleston.

17. *OR*, 36, I:1095.

18. Greene, "Introduction," *Hampton and His Cavalry*.

19. For example, Edward Longacre, in his biography of Lee, wrote that for Lee, "the thought of serving under Hampton was depressing..." (Longacre, *Fitz Lee*, 161). Longacre also wrote that Lee's tardiness on June 11 was regarded by Hampton's staff officers as "proof of [Lee's] unwillingness to support any superior other than J.E.B. Stuart" (*Lee's Cavalrymen*, 300).

20. Greene, "Introduction to Wells," *Hampton and His Cavalry*.

21. Manly Wade Wellman, *Giant in Gray: A Biography of Wade Hampton of South Carolina* (New York: Charles Scribner's Sons, 1949; reprint ed., Dayton, OH: Morningside, 1988), 151.

22. Freeman, *Lee's Lieutenants*, 3:523.

Bibliography

With few exceptions, sources listed in this bibliography are limited to those cited in endnotes. Sources which I consulted and found to contain little or no useful information are not included. Many books that are in the public domain can now be found in their original form as electronic files on the Internet. One can anticipate that, over time, more resources will become available online. In light of this trend, I have not in this bibliography differentiated between published sources and sources available both in print and online. However, sources that I found available only online are listed separately at the end of the bibliography.

Books, Articles, and Other Published Sources

Ackerman, Robert K. *Wade Hampton III*. Columbia: University of South Carolina Press, 2007.

Alberts, Don E. *Brandy Station to Manila Bay: A Biography of General Wesley Merritt*. Austin, TX: Presidial, 1980.

Alexander, Edward Porter. *Fighting for the Confederacy: The Personal Recollections of General Edward Porter Alexander*. Edited by Gary W. Gallagher. Chapel Hill, NC: University of North Carolina Press, 1989.

Allardice, Bruce S. *Confederate Colonels: A Biographical Registry*. Columbia: University of Missouri Press, 2008.

———. *More Generals in Gray*. Baton Rouge: Louisiana State University Press, 1995.

Allen, Stanton P. *Down in Dixie: Life in a Cavalry Regiment in the War Days from the Wilderness to Appomattox*. Boston: D. Lothrop, 1893.

Andrew, Rod, Jr. *Wade Hampton: Confederate Warrior to Southern Redeemer*. Chapel Hill: University of North Carolina Press, 2008.

Armistead, Gene C. *Horses and Mules in the Civil War*. Jefferson, NC: McFarland, 2013.

Armstrong, Richard L. *11th Virginia Cavalry*. Lynchburg, VA: H. E. Howard, 1989.

———. *7th Virginia Cavalry*. Lynchburg, VA: H. E. Howard, 1992.

Association of Graduates, United States Military Academy. *Annual Report*. West Point, NY. The *Annual Report*, which was published from 1917 until 1941, contains much of the information that had been included in the *Annual Reunion*, below. This resource is available online from the USMA Library at http://www.library.usma.edu/archives/archives.asp.

———. *Annual Reunion*. West Point, NY. This resource, which was published between 1870 and 1916, includes many obituaries of USMA graduates from the Civil War era. It is available online from the USMA Library at http://www.library.usma.edu/archives/archives.asp.

———. *Register of Graduates*. West Point, NY. The *Register of Graduates*, presently published annually, contains career information on more recent USMA graduates, and abbreviated information from Cullum's *Biographical Register*, below.

Avery, James Henry. *Under Custer's Command: The Civil War Journal of James Henry Avery*. Compiled by Carla J. Husby; edited by Eric J. Wittenberg. Washington, D.C.: Brassey's, 2000.

Avirett, James B. *The Memoirs of General Turner Ashby and his Compeers*. Baltimore: Selby & Dulany, 1867. Reprint. Gaithersburg, MD: Olde Soldier, 1987.

Baker, Gary R. *Cadets in Gray: The Story of the Cadets of the South Carolina Military Academy and the Cadet Rangers in the Civil War*. Columbia, SC: Palmetto Bookworks, 1989.

Balfour, Daniel T. *13th Virginia Cavalry*. 2d ed. Lynchburg, VA: H.E. Howard, 1986.

Barr, James Michael. *Let Us Meet in Heaven: The Civil War Letters of James Michael Barr, 5th South Carolina Cavalry*. Edited by Thomas D. Mays. Abilene, TX: McWhiney, 2001.

Barringer, Rufus. *The First North Carolina. A Famous Cavalry Regiment*. N.p., N.d.

Bates, Samuel P. *History of Pennsylvania Volunteers, 1861–1865*. 5 vols. Harrisburg, PA: B. Singerly, 1869–1871.

———. *Martial Deeds of Pennsylvania*. Philadelphia: T. H. Davis, 1876.

Bauskett, John. "The Fight at Louisa Court House and Trevellion." *Louisa County Historical Magazine* 30 (Spring 1999), 17–28.

Baylor, George. *Bull Run to Bull Run, or Four Years in the Army of Northern Virginia*. Richmond: B. F. Johnson, 1900. Reprint. Whitefish, MT: Kessinger, N.d.

Beach, William H. *The First New York Lincoln Cavalry, April 19, 1861 to July 7, 1865*. New York: Lincoln Cavalry Association, 1902.

Beale, G. W. *A Lieutenant of Cavalry in Lee's Army*. Boston: Gorham, 1918. Reprint. Baltimore: Butternut & Blue, 1994.

Beale, R. L. T. *History of the Ninth Virginia Cavalry in the War Between the States*. Richmond: B.F. Johnson, 1899.

Beaudry, Louis N. *Historic Records of the Fifth New York Cavalry, Ira Harris Guard: Its Organization, Marches, Raids,*

Scouts, Engagements, and General Services during the Rebellion of 1861–1865. Albany: S.R. Gray, 1865.

Beck, Elias W. H. "Letters of a Civil War Surgeon." *Indiana Magazine of History* 27 (1931): 132–163.

Bell, William Gardner. *Commanding Generals and Chiefs of Staff, 1775–1991: Portraits & Biographical Sketches of the United States Army's Senior Officer.* Washington, D.C.: Center of Military History, United States Army, 1983.

Benedict, George Grenville. *Vermont in the Civil War.* 2 vols. Burlington: Free Press Association, 1888.

Beyer, Walter F., and Oscar F. Keydel, eds. *Deeds of Valor: How America's Civil War Heroes Won the Congressional Medal of Honor.* 2 vols. Detroit: Perrien-Keydel, 1912. Reprint. New York: Smithmark, 2000.

Black, John Logan. *Crumbling Defenses.* Edited by Eleanor McSwain. Macon, GA: McSwain, 1960.

Black, Robert C., III. *Railroads of the Confederacy.* Chapel Hill: University of North Carolina Press, 1952.

Blackford, Charles M. "The Campaign and Battle of Lynchburg." *Southern Historical Society Papers* 30 (1902): 279–332.

Blackford, Charles Minor, and Susan Leigh Blackford. *Letters from Lee's Army.* Edited by Charles Minor Blackford III. New York: Charles Scribner's Sons, 1947. Reprint. Lincoln: University of Nebraska Press, 1998.

Blackford, William W. *War Years with JEB Stuart.* New York: Charles Scribner's Sons, 1945. Reprint. Baton Rouge: Louisiana State University Press, 1993.

Blackwell, Samuel M., Jr. *In the First Line of Battle: The 12th Illinois Cavalry in the Civil War.* DeKalb: Northern Illinois University Press, 2002.

Booth, George W. *Personal Reminiscences of a Maryland Soldier in the War Between the States, 1861–1865.* Baltimore: Fleet, McGinley, 1898.

Bowen, James R. *Regimental History of the First New York Dragoons (Originally the 130th N.Y. Vol. Infantry) During Three Years of Service in the Great Civil War.* The Author, 1900.

_____. *Regimental History of the First New York Dragoons, with Lists of Names, Post-Office Address, Casualties of Officers and Men, and Number of Prisoners, Trophies, &c. Captured, from Organization to Muster-Out.* Washington, D.C.: Gibson Brothers, 1865.

Boylston, Ray. *Butler's Brigade: That Fighting Civil War Cavalry Brigade from South Carolina.* Raleigh, NC: Jarrett Press & Publications, 1989.

Bradwell, I. J. "Sheridan and Trevillian Station." *Confederate Veteran* 37 (December 1929): 452–455.

Bridges, David P. *Fighting with JEB Stuart: Major James Breathed and the Confederate Horse Artillery.* Arlington, VA: Breathed, Bridges, Best, 2006.

Brooks, Ulysses R. *Butler and His Cavalry in the War of Secession, 1861–1865.* Columbia, SC: State, 1909. Reprint. Camden SC: Gray Fox, N.d.

_____. "Memories of Battles." *Confederate Veteran* 22 (September 1914): 408–4099.

_____. *Stories of the Confederacy.* Columbia, SC: State, 1912.

Burnett, William G. *Better a Patriot Soldier's Grave: The History of the Sixth Ohio Volunteer Cavalry.* N.p., 1982.

Burns, Vincent L. *The Fifth New York Cavalry in the Civil War.* Jefferson, NC: McFarland, 2014.

Burr, Frank A., and Richard J. Hinton. *"Little Phil" and His Troopers: The Life of Gen. Philip H. Sheridan. Its Romance and Reality: How an Humble Lad Reached the Head of an Army.* Providence: J. A. & R. A. Reid, 1888.

Bushong, Millard K., and Dean M. Bushong. *Fightin' Tom Rosser, C.S.A.* Shippensburg, PA: Beidel, 1983.

Butler, Karl Douglas. *Principles of Horseshoeing II: An Illustrated Textbook of Farrier Science and Craftsmanship.* Laporte, CO: Butler, 1983.

Butler, M. C. "The Cavalry Fight at Trevilian Station." In *Battles and Leaders of the Civil War.* Edited by Robert Underwood Johnson and Clarence Clough Buel, 4:237–239. New York: Century, 1888. Reprint. New York: Castle Books, 1956.

Calvert, Mary R. *First Maine Cavalry.* Monmouth, ME: Monmouth, 1997.

Carroll, John M. *Custer in the Civil War: His Unfinished Memoirs.* San Rafael, CA: Presidio, 1977.

Carter, William H. *From Yorktown to Santiago with the Sixth U.S. Cavalry.* Baltimore: Lord Baltimore, 1900. Reprint. Austin: State House, 1989.

_____. *Life of Lieutenant General Chaffee.* Chicago: University of Chicago Press, 1917.

Carter, William R. *Sabres, Saddles, and Spurs.* Edited by Walbrook D. Swank. Shippensburg, PA: Burd Street, 1998.

Catton, Bruce. *Grant Takes Command.* Boston: Little, Brown, 1968.

Caughey, Donald C., and Jimmy J. Jones. *The 6th United States Cavalry in the Civil War: A History and Roster.* Jefferson, NC: McFarland, 2013.

Cauthen, Charles F., ed. *Family Letters of the Three Wade Hamptons, 1782–1901.* Columbia: University of South Carolina Press, 1953.

Chamberlain, Samuel E. *My Confession.* New York: Harper & Brothers, 1956.

Cheney, Newel. *History of the Ninth Regiment New York Volunteer Cavalry, War of 1861 to 1865.* Jamestown, NY: Martin Mertz, 1900. Reprint. Ashville, NY: Berrybook, 1998.

Chesnut, Mary. *A Dairy from Dixie.* Edited by Isabella D. Martin and Myrta Lockett Avary. New York: Portland House, 1905. Reprint. New York: Random House Value, 1997.

Cisco, Walter Brian. *Wade Hampton: Confederate Warrior, Conservative Statesman.* Washington, D.C.: Brassey's, 2004.

Clark, Walter, ed. *Histories of the Several Regiments and Battalions from North Carolina in the Great War 1861–65: Written by Members of the Respective Commands.* 5 vols. Raleigh: E. M. Uzzell, 1901. Reprint. Wendell, NC: Broadfoot's Bookmark, 1982.

Coffey, David. *Sheridan's Lieutenants: Phil Sheridan, His Generals, and the Final Year of the Civil War.* Lanham, MD: Rowman & Littlefield, 2005.

Coffman, Richard M. *Going Back the Way They Came: A History of the Phillips Georgia Legion Cavalry Battalion.* Macon, GA: Mercer University Press, 2011.

Collea, Joseph D., Jr. *The First Vermont Cavalry in the Civil War: A History.* Jefferson, NC: McFarland, 2010.

Confederate States War Department. *Regulations for the Army of the Confederate States, 1863.* Richmond: J. W. Randolph, 1863. Reprint. Evansville, IN: Crescent City Sutler, N.d.

Conrad, Thomas Nelson. *The Rebel Scout: A Thrilling History of Scouting Life in the Southern Army.* Washington, D.C.: National, 1904. Reprint. Westminster, MD: Heritage, 2009.

Cook, Pattie G. P. *Louisa and Louisa County.* Dover, NH: Arcadia, 1997.

_____. *Wartime Letters of Louisa County, Virginia: The Cooke Family Papers 1859–1866.* Athens, GA: Iberian, 1997.

Cooke, Phillip St. George. *Cavalry Tactics: or, Regulations for the Instruction, Formations and Movements of the Cavalry of the Army and Volunteers of the United States.* Philadelphia: J. B. Lippincott, 1862. Reprint. Union City, TN: Pioneer Press, 1997.

Corson, William C. *Dear Jennie: A Collection of Love Letters from a Confederate Soldier to His Fiancée During the Period 1861–1865*. Edited by Blake W. Corson, Jr. Richmond, Dietz: 1982.

Croffut, W. A., and John M. Morris. *The Military and Civil History of Connecticut during the War of 1861–65*, 3d ed. New York: Ledyard Bill, 1869.

Crowninshield, Benjamin W. *A History of the First Regiment of Massachusetts Cavalry Volunteers*. Boston: Houghton, Mifflin, 1891. Reprint. Baltimore: Butternut and Blue, 1995.

Cullum, George W. *Biographical Register of the Officers and Graduates of the U.S. Military Academy at West Point, N. Y. From its Establishment in 1802, to 1890 with the Early History of the United States Military Academy*. New York: Houghton Mifflin, 1891. Cullum's *Biographical Register* was initially published in 1891 and updated every ten years thereafter until 1950. Graduates are listed in "Cullum Number" order in all editions. This resource is available online from the USMA Library at http://www.library.usma.edu/archives/special.asp.

Daughtry, Mary B. *Gray Cavalier: The Life and Wars of General W. H. F. "Rooney" Lee*. Cambridge, MA: DaCapo, 2002.

Davies, Henry E. *General Sheridan*. New York: D. Appleton, 1897.

Davis, Burke. *JEB Stuart: The Last Cavalier*. New York: Reinhart, 1957. Reprint. New York: Fairfax, 1988.

"The Death of General J.E.B. Stuart." In *Battles and Leaders of the Civil War*, 194. Edited by Robert Underwood Johnson and Clarence Clough Buel. New York: Century, 1888. Reprint. New York: Castle Books, 1956.

"The Death of Major General J.E.B. Stuart." *Southern Historical Society Papers* 7 (1879): 107–110.

Deck, D. M. "Captured at Trevilian Station." *Confederate Veteran* 24 (January 1916): 123–124.

Denison, George T. *Modern Cavalry: Its Organisation, Armament, and Employment in War*. London: Thomas Bosworth, 1868.

Devine, John E. *35th Battalion Virginia Cavalry*. Lynchburg, VA: H. E. Howard, 1985.

Dorsey, Frank. "Fatal Shot of 'JEB' Stuart." *Confederate Veteran* 11 (August 1903): 347.

Dorsey, Frank. "Gen. J.E.B. Stuart's Last Battle." *Confederate Veteran* 17 (February 1909): 76–77.

Doster, William E., ed. *A Brief History of the Fourth Pennsylvania Veteran Cavalry, Embracing Organization, Reunions, Dedication of Monument at Gettysburg and Address of General W. E. Doster, Venango County Battalion, Reminiscences, Etc.* Pittsburgh: Ewens & Eberle, 1891. Reprint. Hightstown, NJ: Longstreet, 1997.

Douglas, David G. *A Boot Full of Memories: Captain Leonard Williams, 2nd S.C. Cavalry*. Camden, SC: Gray Fox, 2003. This book contains the wartime letters Captain Williams wrote to his wife woven into a fictional narrative.

Dowdey, Clifford. *Lee's Last Campaign: The Story of Lee and His Men Against Grant—1864*. Boston: Little, Brown, 1960.

Driver, Robert J., Jr. *First and Second Maryland Cavalry, C.S.A*. Charlottesville, VA: Rockbridge, 1999.

_____. *1st Virginia Cavalry*. Lynchburg, VA: H. E. Howard, 1991.

_____. *2nd Virginia Cavalry*. Lynchburg, VA: H. E. Howard, 1995.

_____. *5th Virginia Cavalry*. Lynchburg, VA: H. E. Howard, 1997.

Duncan, Alexander McC. *Roll of Officers and Members of the Georgia Hussars and of the Cavalry Companies, of which the Hussars are a Continuation, with Historical Sketch Relating Facts Showing the Origin and Necessity of Rangers, or Mounted Men in the Colony of Georgia from the Date of Its Founding*. Savannah, GA: Morning News, 1906.

Dyer, Frederick H., ed. *A Compendium of the War of the Rebellion*. 3 vols. Des Moines, IA: Dyer, 1980. Reprint. New York: Thomas Yoseloff, 1959.

Early, Jubal. *Autobiographical Sketch and Narrative of the War Between the States; With Notes by R.H. Early*. Philadelphia: J. B. Lippincott, 1912.

Edmonds, Amanda V. *Journal of Amanda Virginia Edmonds: Lass of Mosby's Confederacy, 1857–1867*. Edited by Nancy Chappelear Baird. Stephens City, VA: Commercial, 1984.

Emerson, W. Eric. *Sons of Privilege: The Charleston Light Dragoons in the Civil War*. Columbia: University of South Carolina Press, 2005.

First Maine Cavalry Association. *Record of Proceedings at the First Annual Reunion Held in the City of Augusta, September 26th, 1872*. Augusta, ME: Sprague, Owen & Nash, 1872.

First Maine Cavalry Association. *Record of Proceedings at the Second Annual Reunion Held in the City of Bangor, 1873*. Augusta: ME: Sprague, Owen & Nash, 1874.

Foote, Shelby. *The Civil War: A Narrative*. 3 vols. New York: Random House, 1974. Reprint (paperback). New York: Vintage, 1986.

Fordney, Ben Fuller. *George Stoneman: A Biography of the Union General*. Jefferson, NC: McFarland, 2008.

Fortier, John. *15th Virginia Cavalry*. Lynchburg, VA: H. E. Howard, 1993.

Foster, Alonzo. *Reminiscences and Record of the 6th New York V. V. Cavalry*. N.p., 1892. Reprint. Salem, MA: Higginson, 1998.

Foster, John Y. *New Jersey and the Rebellion: History of the Services of the Troops and People of New Jersey in the Aid of the Union Cause*. Newark, NJ: Martin R. Dennis, 1868.

Fox, William R. *Regimental Losses in the American Civil War: 1861–1865*. Albany, NY: Albany, 1889.

Freeman, Douglas Southall. *Lee's Dispatches: Unpublished Letters of General Robert E. Lee, C.S.A, to Jefferson Davis and the War Department of the Confederate States of America*. New York: G.P. Putnam's Sons, 1915.

_____. *Lee's Lieutenants*. 3 vols. New York: Charles Scribner's Sons, 1944.

_____. *R. E. Lee*. 4 vols. New York: Charles Scribner's Sons, 1949.

Frye, Dennis, E. *12th Virginia Cavalry*, 2d ed. Lynchburg, VA: H.E. Howard, 1988.

Fuller, Claud E. *The Breech-Loader in the Service, 1816–1917: A History of All Standard and Experimental U.S. Breechloading and Magazine Shoulder Arms*. New Milford, CT: N. Flayderman, 1965.

_____. *The Rifled Musket*. New York: Bonanza, 1958.

Fuller, Claud E., and Richard D. Steuart. *Firearms of the Confederacy*. Huntington, WV: Standard Publications, 1944. Reprint. Birmingham, AL: Odysseus Editions, 1996.

Gallaher, DeWitt Clinton. *A Diary Depicting the Experiences of DeWitt Clinton Gallaher in the War*. Reorganized Co. E, 1st Va. Cav., 1961.

Garnett, Theodore Stanford. *Riding with Stuart: Reminiscences of an Aide-de-Camp*. Edited by Robert J. Trout. Shippensburg, PA: White Mane, 1994.

Gibbons, J. R. "Concerning the Death of General J. E. B. Stuart." *Confederate Veteran* 20 (March 1912): 120.

Gill, John. *Reminiscences of Four Years as a Private Soldier in the Confederate Army, 1861–1865*. Baltimore: Sun, 1904.

Glatthaar, Joseph T. *General Lee's Army: From Victory to Collapse*. New York: Free Press, 2008.

Gold, Thomas D. *History of Clarke County, Virginia, and Its*

Connection with the War Between the States. Berryville, VA: N.p., 1914.

Gorgas, Josiah. *The Journals of Josiah Gorgas, 1857–1878.* Edited by Sarah Woolfolk Wiggins. Tuscaloosa: University of Alabama Press, 1995.

Gracey, S. L. *Annals of the Sixth Pennsylvania Cavalry.* Philadelphia: E. H. Butler, 1868. Reprint. Lancaster, OH: Vanberg, 1996.

Grant, Ulysses S. *The Papers of Ulysses S. Grant.* 30 vols. Edited by John Y. Simon. Carbondale: Southern Illinois University Press, 1984.

_____. *Personal Memoirs of U. S. Grant.* New York: Charles L. Webster, 1885. Reprint. New York: Library of America, 1990.

Gray, Alonzo. *Cavalry Tactics as Illustrated by the War of the Rebellion, Together with Many Interesting Facts Important for Cavalry to Know.* Fort Leavenworth, KS: U.S. Cavalry Association, 1910.

Griffin, James M., and Tom Gore. *Horse Owner's Veterinary Handbook.* 2d. ed. New York: Howell Book House, 1989.

Grimsley, Daniel A. *Battles in Culpeper County, Virginia, 1861–1865.* Culpeper: Raleigh Travers Green, 1900. Reprint. Orange, VA: Green, N.d.

_____. "Trevilians Again: Another Account of the Great Cavalry Fight." *Richmond Dispatch.* Richmond, VA, January 21, 1901.

Hackley, Woodford B. *The Little Fork Rangers: A Sketch of Company "D" Fourth Virginia Cavalry.* Richmond: Dietz, 1927. Reprint. Stephens City, VA: Commercial Press, Inc., 1999.

Haden, B. J. "Stuart's Death Wound." *Confederate Veteran* 22 (August 1914): 352.

Haggard, Horation C. "Cavalry Fight at Fredericksburg." *Confederate Veteran* 21 (June 1913): 295.

Hall, Hillman A. *History of the Sixth New York Cavalry (Second Ira Harris Guard), Second Brigade—First Division—Cavalry Corps, Army of the Potomac, 1861–1865, Compiled from Letters, Diaries, Recollections, and Official Records.* Worcester, MA: Blanchard, 1908.

Hand, Harold, Jr. *One Good Regiment: The 13th Pennsylvania Cavalry in the Civil War, 1861–1865.* Victoria, B.C.: Trafford, 2000.

Hard, Abner. *History of the Eighth Cavalry Regiment Illinois Volunteers During the Great Rebellion.* Aurora, IL: N.p., 1868. Reprint. Dayton, OH: Morningside, 1996.

Harris, Malcom. *History of Louisa County, Virginia.* Richmond: Dietz, 1936.

Harris, Samuel. *Personal Reminiscences of Samuel Harris (1897).* Chicago: Rogerson, 1897. Reprint. Whitefish, MT: Kessinger, N.d.

Hartley, Chris J. *Stuart's Tarheels: James B. Gordon and His North Carolina Cavalry in the Civil War.* Jefferson, NC: McFarland, 2d ed., 2011.

Hatch, Thom. *Glorious War: The Civil War Adventures of George Armstrong Custer.* New York: St. Martin's, 2013.

Hawes, Alex G. "In Kansas with John Brown." *The Californian* 4 (July 1881): 68–75.

Helm, Lewis. *Black Horse Cavalry: Defend Our Beloved Homeland.* Falls Church, VA: Higher Education Publications, 2004.

Henderson, William D. *The Road to Bristoe Station: Campaigning with Lee and Meade, August 1–October 20, 1863.* Lynchburg, VA: H.E. Howard, 1987.

Henrico County Civil War Centennial Commission. "Rededication Ceremony, Honoring General J.E.B. Stuart, on the One Hundredth Anniversary of his Mortal Wounding, Memorial Site, Telegraph Road, Henrico County, Virginia, May 9, 1964, 3 P.M." Richmond: N.p., 1964.

Hergesheimer, Joseph. *Sheridan: A Military Narrative.* Boston: Houghton Mifflin, 1931.

Hess, Earl J. *The Rifle Musket in the Civil War: Reality and Myth.* Lawrence: University Press of Kansas, 2008.

Hewett, Janet, et al., eds. *Supplement to the Official Records of the Union and Confederate Armies.* Wilmington, NC: Broadfoot, 1995–2000.

Hill, Mrs. J. Murray. "A Tribute to J. Murray Vest." *Louisa Historical Magazine* 35 (Spring 2004): 47–55.

"His [Samuel E. Chamberlain's] Successes in Later Life." *Life* 41 (August 6, 1956): 86.

Holland, Lynwood M. *Pierce M. B. Young: The Warwick of the South.* Athens: University of Georgia Press, 1964, Reprint, paperback. 2009.

Holmes, Torlief S. *Horse Soldiers in Blue: First Maine Cavalry.* Gaithersburg, MD: Butternut, 1985.

Hopkins, Donald A. *Horsemen of the Jeff Davis Legion: The Expanded Roster of the Men and Officers of the Jeff Davis Legion, Cavalry.* Shippensburg, PA: White Mane, 1999.

_____. *The Little Jeff: The Jeff Davis Legion, Cavalry, Army of Northern Virginia.* Shippensburg, PA: White Mane, 1999.

Hopkins, Luther, W. *From Bull Run to Appomattox: A Boy's View.* Baltimore, MD: Fleet-McGinley, 1908. Reprint. Clearwater, SC: Eastern Digital Resources, 2003.

Hotchkiss, Jedediah. *Virginia.* Vol. 3, *Confederate Military History.* Edited by Clement A. Evans. Atlanta, GA: Confederate Publishing Co., 1899. Reprint. Secaucus, NJ: Blue and Grey, 1980.

Howard, Wiley C. *Sketch of Cobb Legion Cavalry and Some Incidents and Scenes Remembered: Presented and Read under appointment of Atlanta Camp 159, United Confederate Veterans, August 19, 1901.* N.p. N.d.

Hubard, Robert T. *The Civil War Memoirs of a Virginia Cavalryman.* Edited by Thomas P. Nanzig. Tuscaloosa: University of Alabama Press, 2007.

Hudgins, Robert Scott, II. *Recollections of an Old Dominion Dragoon: The Civil War Experiences of Sgt. Robert S. Hudgins II, Co. B, 3d Virginia Cavalry.* Edited by Garland C. Hudgins and Richard B. Kleese. Orange, VA: Publisher's, 1993.

Huey, Pennock. *A True History of the Charge of the 8th Pennsylvania Cavalry at Chancellorsville.* Philadelphia: Porter & Coates, 1883.

Humpreys, Andrew A. *The Virginia Campaign of '64 and '65: The Army of the Potomac and the Army of the James.* New York: Charles Scribner's Sons, 1883.

Humphreys, Henry H. *A Critical Examination [In Part] of Pennypacker's Life of General George G. Meade.* Tivoli, NY: Frank O. Green, 1901. Henry Humphrey is the son of Major General Andrew A. Humphrey.

Hunt, Roger D., and Jack R. Brown. *Brevet Brigadier Generals in Blue.* Gaithersburg, MD: Olde Soldier Books, 1990; revised ed. 1997.

Hutton, Andrew P. "Paladin of the Republic: Military Pragmatism and Elastic Ethics made Philip H. Sheridan the Perfect Soldier for an Expansionist Nation." *MHQ: The Journal of Military History* 4 (Spring 1992): 82–91.

Hyde, Bill. *The Union Generals Speak: The Meade Hearings of the Battle of Gettysburg.* Baton Rouge: Louisiana State University Press, 2003.

Hyndman, William. *History of a Cavalry Company: Complete Record of Company "A," 4th Penn'a Cavalry.* Philadelphia:

Jas. A. Rogers, 1870. Reprint. Hightown, NJ: Longstreet, 1997.
Isham, Asa B. *An Historical Sketch of the Seventh Regiment Michigan Volunteer Cavalry from Its Organization, in 1862, to Its Muster Out, in 1865*. New York: Town Topics, 1893. Reprinted as *Seventh Michigan Cavalry of Custer's Wolverine Brigade*. Huntington, WV: Blue Acorn, 2000.
Johnson, Bradley T. "The Bold Horsemen: An Interesting Book on Hampton and His Cavalry." *Richmond Dispatch*. Richmond, VA, December 31, 1899.
_____. *Maryland*. Vol 11, *Confederate Military History*. Edited by Clement A. Evans. Atlanta, GA: Confederate Publishing Co., 1899. Reprint, 13 vols. Secaucus, NJ: Blue and Grey, 1980.
Johnson, John L. *The University Memorial: Biographical Sketches of Alumni of the University of Virginia Who Fell in the Confederate War*. Baltimore: Turnbull Brothers, 1871.
Johnston, James A., II. *Virginia Railroads in the Civil War*. Chapel Hill: University of North Carolina Press, 1961.
Jones, J. Keith. *The Boys of Diamond Hill: The Lives and Civil War Letters of the Boyd Family of Abbeville County, South Carolina*. Jefferson, NC: McFarland, 2011.
Jones, John B. *A Rebel War Clerk's Diary*. 2 vols. Philadelphia: J. B. Lippincott, 1866. Reprint. Time-Life, 1982.
Jones, Virgil Carrington (Pat). "Mother's Race Across Battlefield is Recalled." *Louisa Historical Magazine* 35 (Spring 2004): 35–40.
Keegan, John. *The Price of Admiralty: The Evolution of Naval Warfare*. New York: Viking, 1988.
Kester, Donald E. *Cavalryman in Blue: Colonel John Wood Kester of the First New Jersey Cavalry in the Civil War*. Hightown, NJ: Longstreet, 1997.
Kidd, James H. *One of Custer's Wolverines: The Civil War Letters of Brevet Brigadier General James H. Kidd, 6th Michigan Cavalry*. Edited by Eric Wittenberg. Kent, OH: Kent State University Press, 2000.
_____. *Personal Recollections of a Cavalryman with Custer's Michigan Cavalry Brigade in the Civil War*. Ionia, MI: Sentinel, 1908.
King, Curtis S., William Glenn Robertson, and Stephen E. Clay. *Staff Ride Handbook for the Overland Campaign, Virginia, 4 May to 15 June 1864: A Study in Operational Command*. Fort Leavenworth, KS: Combat Studies Institute Press, N.d.
Krick, Robert. *Lee's Colonels: A Biographical Registry of the Field Officers of the Army of Northern Virginia*. 4th ed., revised. Dayton: Morningside, 1992.
_____. *9th Virginia Cavalry*, 4th ed. Lynchburg, VA: H.E. Howard, 1982.
_____. *Staff Officers in Gray: A Biographical Register of the Staff Officers in the Army of Northern Virginia*. Chapel Hill: University of North Carolina Press, 2003.
Latty, John W. *Gallant Little 7th: A History of the 7th Georgia Cavalry Regiment*. Wilmington, NC: Broadfoot, 2004.
Lawyer, Eli H. "Sheridan's Trevillian Raid: Incidents on that Expedition as Told by One of the 2nd Cav. Boys." *National Tribune*. April 13, 1911.
Lee, Robert E. *Wartime Papers* 2 vols. Edited by Clifford Dowdey. New York: Little, Brown, 1961. Reprint. Pennington, NJ: Collectors Reprints, 1996.
Lee, William O. *Personal and Historical Sketches and Facial History of and by Members of the Seventh Regiment Michigan Volunteer Cavalry, 1862–1865*. Detroit: 7th Michigan Cavalry Association, N.d.
Lewis, Berkeley R. "Notes on Ammunition of the American Civil War 1861–1865." Washington, D.C.: American Ordnance Association, 1959.

_____. "Notes on Cavalry Weapons of the American Civil War 1861–1865." Washington, D.C.: American Ordnance Association, 1961.
Lloyd, William Penn. *History of the First Reg't Pennsylvania Reserve Cavalry, from Its Organization, August, 1861, to September, 1864, with List of Names of All Officers and Enlisted Men*. Philadelphia: King & Baird, 1864.
Lomax, Mrs. Lunsford. "The Death of Stuart." *Confederate Veteran* 15 (August 1907): 362. This account, written by the wife of Brigadier General Lunsford Lomax, was originally published in the *Philadelphia Weekly Times*.
Longacre, Edward. *Custer and His Wolverines: The Michigan Cavalry Brigade, 1861–1865*. New York: DaCapo, 1997.
_____. *Fitz Lee: A Military Biography of Major General Fitzhugh Lee, C.S.A*. New York: DaCapo, 2005.
_____. *From Union Stars to Top Hat: A Biography of the Extraordinary General James Harrison Wilson*. Harrisonburg, PA: Stackpole, 1972.
_____. *Gentleman and Soldier: The Extraordinary Life of Wade Hampton*. Nashville, TN: Rutledge Hill, 2003.
_____. *Jersey Cavaliers: A History of the First New Jersey Volunteer Cavalry, 1861–1865*. Hightown, NJ: Longstreet House, 1992.
_____. "Last Stand of the Last Knight." *Civil War Times* 43 (June 2004): 24–33.
_____. *Lee's Cavalrymen: A History of the Mounted Forces of the Army of Northern Virginia*. Mechanicsburg, PA: Stackpole, 2000.
_____. *Lincoln's Cavalrymen: A History of the Mounted Forces of the Army of the Potomac*. Mechanicsburg, PA: Stackpole, 2000.
_____. "The Long Run for Trevilian Station." *Civil War Times Illustrated* 18 (November 1979): 28–39.
_____. *Mounted Raids of the Civil War*. Lincoln, University of Nebraska Press, 1994.
Lonn, Ella. *Desertion During the Civil War*. Gloucester, MA: American Historical Association, 1928. Reprint. Lincoln: University of Nebraska Press, 1998.
Lyman, Theodore. *Meade's Army: The Private Notebooks of Lt. Col. Theodore Lyman*. Edited by David W. Lowe. Kent, OH: Kent State University Press, 2007.
_____. *Meade's Headquarters, 1863–1865: Letters of Colonel Theodore Lyman from The Wilderness to Appomattox*. Edited by George R. Agassiz. Boston: Atlantic Monthly, 1922.
Manarin, Louis H. *The Cavalry*. Vol. 2, *North Carolina Troops 1861–1865, A Roster*. Raleigh, NC: North Carolina State Department of Archives and History, 1968.
Marcot, Roy M. *Spencer Repeating Firearms*. Rochester, NY: Rowe, 1990.
Martin, Samuel J. *Southern Hero: Matthew Calbraith Butler, Confederate General, Hampton Red Shirt, and U.S. Senator*. Mechanicsburg, PA: Stackpole, 2001.
McCabe, W. Gordon. "Defense of Petersburg." *Southern Historical Society Papers* 2 (Jul-Dec 1876), 257–306.
McClellan, George B. *The Civil War Papers of George B. McClellan: Selected Correspondence 1861–1865*. Edited by Stephen W. Sears. New York: Ticknor & Fields, 1989.
McClellan, Henry B. *The Life and Campaigns of Major-General J.E.B. Stuart, Commander of the Cavalry of the Army of Northern Virginia*. New York: Houghton Mifflin, 1885. Republished as *I Rode with Jeb Stuart: The Life and Campaigns of Major-General J.E.B. Stuart*. Bloomington: University of Indiana Press, 1958. Reprint. New York: DaCapo, 1994.
_____. *The Life, Character and Campaigns of Major-General J.E.B. Stuart: Address by Major H. B. McClellan of Sayre*

Institute, Ky., before the Virginia Division of the Army of Northern Virginia at their Annual Meeting held in the Capitol in Richmond, VA., Oct 27th, 1880. Richmond: William Ellis Jones, 1880.

McCormick, Cyrus. "How Gallant Stuart Met His Death." *Confederate Veteran* 37 (February 1931): 98–101.

McDonald, William N. *A History of the Laurel Brigade, Originally the Ashby Cavalry of the Army of Northern Virginia and Chew's Battery*. Baltimore: Sun Job Office, 1907. Reprint. Baltimore: Johns Hopkins University Press, 2002.

McFadden, Elizabeth. *The Glitter and the Gold: A Spirited Account of the Metropolitan Museum of Art's First Director, the Audacious and High-handed Luigi Palma di Cesnola*. New York: Dial, 1971.

McKinney, Edward P. *Life in Tent and Field, 1861–1865*. Boston: Gorham, 1922.

Meade, George Gordon. *The Life and Letters of George Gordon Meade, Major-General, United States Army*. 2 vols. New York: Charles Scribner's Sons, 1913. Meade's son, George Meade, is credited with writing and compiling this book, and Meade's grandson, George Gordon Meade, is credited with editing the book.

Merington, Marguerite, ed. *The Custer Story: The Life and Intimate Letters of General Custer and His Wife Elizabeth*. New York: Devin-Adair, 1950.

Mesic, Harriet Bey. *Cobb's Legion Cavalry: A History and Roster of the Ninth Georgia Volunteers in the Civil War*. Jefferson, NC: McFarland, 2009.

Mettier, Charles G. "Adna Romanza Chaffee." *Assembly* 1 (April 1942): 13–15.

Meyers, Jerry. "Trevilian!" *Louisa County Historical Magazine* 30 (Spring 1999): 29–50.

Michigan Adjutant General's Office. *Michigan in the War*. Revised ed. Compiled by Jno. Robertson. Lansing, MI: W.H. George, 1882.

Mohr, James C., ed. *The Cormany Diaries: A Northern Family in the Civil War*. Pittsburgh, PA: University of Pittsburgh Press, 1982.

Monaghan, Jay. "Custer's 'Last Stand'—Trevilian Station, 1864." In *The Custer Reader*. Edited by Paul Andrew Hutton. Lincoln: University of Nebraska Press, 1992.

Moore, Robert H., II. *Chew's Ashby, Shoemaker's Lynchburg, and the Newtown Artillery*. Lynchburg, VA: H. E. Howard, 1995.

_____. *The 1st and 2nd Stuart Horse Artillery*. Lynchburg, VA: H. E. Howard, 1985.

Morgan, Cathie. "The Unknown Hero from the Class of '56." *The Rattle* 87 (Spring 2007): 6–7. This resource is available online at http://www.thetachi.org/clientuploads/Rattle/_Spring percent202007.pdf.

Morris, Roy Jr. *Sheridan: The Life and Wars of General Phil Sheridan*. New York: Crown, 1992.

Moyer, H. P. *History of the Seventeenth Regiment Pennsylvania Volunteer Cavalry, or One Hundred Sixty-Second in the Line of Pennsylvania Volunteer Regiments, War to Suppress the Rebellion, 1861–1865*. Lebanon, PA: Sowers, N.d.

Mulligan, Alfred B. *"My Dear Mother & Sisters": Civil War Letters of Capt. A. B. Mulligan, Co. B 5th South Carolina Cavalry—Butler's Division—Hampton's Corps 1861–1865*. Edited by Olin Fulmer Hutchinson, Jr. Spartanburg, SC: Reprint, 1992.

Munford, Thomas T. "Reminiscences of Cavalry Operations: Operations under Rosser." *Southern Historical Society Papers* 13 (1885): 133–148.

Musick, Michael P. *6th Virginia Cavalry*. Lynchburg, VA: H.E. Howard, 1990.

Myers, Frank M. *The Comanches: A History of White's Battalion, Virginia Cavalry, Laurel Brigade, Hampton's Div.*, A. N. V., C. S. A. Baltimore, MD: Kelly, Piet, 1871; Reprint. Alexandria, VA: Stonewall House, 1985.

Naisawald, L. VanLoan. "Stuart as a Cavalryman's Cavalryman." *Civil War Times Illustrated* 1 (February 1963): 6–8, 42–47.

Neese, George M. *Three Years in the Confederate Horse Artillery*. New York: Neale, 1911. Reprint. Clearwater, SC: Eastern Digital Resources, 2003.

Nelson, Horatio. *"If I am killed on this trip, I want my horse kept for my brother": The Diary of the Last Weeks in the Life of a Confederate Cavalryman*. Manassas, VA: Manassas Chapter, United Daughters of the Confederacy, 1980.

"Netherlands, House and Tavern." *Louisa County Historical Magazine* 11 (Winter 1979): 25–30. *Louisa County Historical Magazine* reprinted this article in volume 35 (Spring 2004), 41–46.

Nevins, Allan. *War for the Union*. 4 vols. New York: Charles Scribner's Sons, 1959. Reprint. New York: Konecky & Konecky, 2000.

Newhall, F. C. *The Battle of Beverly Ford*. In *Annals of the War, Written by Leading Participants North and South*. Philadelphia: Times Publishing Co., 1879. Reprint. Edison, NJ: Blue & Gray Press, 1996.

_____. *With Sheridan in the Final Campaign against Lee*. Edited by Eric. J. Wittenberg. Baton Rouge: Louisiana State University Press, 2002. Newhall initially published this book anonymously (Philadelphia: J. B. Lippincott, 1866).

Nichols, James L. *General Fitzhugh Lee—A Biography*. Lynchburg, VA: H.E. Howard, 1989.

O'Ferrall, Charles T. *Forty Years of Active Service*. New York: Neale, 1904.

Olcott, Henry S. "The War's Carnival of Fraud" in *Annals of the War, Written by Leading Participants North and South*. Philadelphia: Times Publishing Co., 1879. Reprint. Edison, NJ: Blue & Gray Press, 1996.

Oliver, J. R. "J. E. B. Stuart's Fate at Yellow Tavern." *Confederate Veteran* 19 (November 1911): 531.

Ould, Robert. "The Exchange of Prisoners" in *Annals of the War, Written by Leading Participants North and South*. Philadelphia: Times Publishing Co., 1879. Reprint. Edison, NJ: Blue & Gray Press, 1996.

Parker, Robert W. *Lee's Last Casualty: The Life and Letters of Sgt. Robert W. Parker, Second Virginia Cavalry*. Edited by Catherine M. Wright. Knoxville: University of Tennessee Press, 2008.

Pate, Henry Clay. *American Vade Mecum: or The Companion of Youth*. Cincinnati, OH: Morgan, 1852.

_____. "Proceedings of the General Court Martial, in the Case of Lieut. Col. H. Clay Pate, 5th Va. Cavalry." Richmond: N.p., 1863.

Peck, Daniel. *Dear Rachel: The Civil War Letters of Daniel Peck*. Edited by Martha G. Stanford. Ashville, NY: Berrybook, 1993.

Peck, R. H. *Reminiscences of a Confederate Soldier of Co. C, 2nd Va. Cavalry*. Fincastle, VA: N.p., 1913.

Pennypacker, Isaac R. *General Meade*. New York: D. Appleton, 1901.

Perret, Geoffrey. *Ulysses S. Grant: Soldier & President*. New York: Random House, 1997. Reprint. New York: Modern Library, 1999.

Pickerill, William N. *History of the Third Indiana Cavalry*. Indianapolis, IN: Aetna, 1900.

Preston, Noble D. *History of the Tenth Regiment of Cavalry New York State Volunteers, August, 1861, to August, 1865*. New York: D. Appleton and Co., 1892.

_____. "Trevilian Station: The Most Stubborn Cavalry Fight of the War." *National Tribune*. January 5, 1881.

Price, George F. *Across the Continent with the Fifth Cavalry*. New York: Noble, 1883. Reprint. New York: Antiquarian, 1959.

Pyne, Henry R. *Ride to War: The History of the First New Jersey Cavalry*. Edited by Earl S. Miers. New Brunswick: Rutgers University Press, 1961.

Quartermaster General's Office. *Roll of Honor (No. XV.): Names of Soldiers Who Died in Defence of the American Union, Interred in the National Cemeteries at Antietam (Maryland,) and at Arlington, (Additional,) Culpeper Court-House, Cold Harbor, Winchester, Staunton, and Various Scattered Localities in Virginia*. Washington, D.C.: U.S. Government Printing Office, 1868. Reprint. Baltimore, MD: Genealogical Publishing, 1994.

Raiford, Neil H. *4th North Carolina Cavalry in the Civil War*. Jefferson, NC: McFarland, 2003.

Ramsdell, Charles W. "General Robert E. Lee's Horse Supply, 1862–1865." *American Historical Review* 35 (July 1930): 758–777. This article is available on the Internet at http://penelope.uchicago.edu/Thayer/E/Journals/AHR/35/4/Lees¬_Horse_Supply*.html

Recollections and Reminiscences: 1861–1865 Through World War I. 12 vols. South Carolina Division, United Daughters of the Confederacy, 1992–2002.

Reeder, William C. H. *From a True Soldier and Son: The Civil War Letters of William C. H. Reeder*. Commentary by Carolyn Reeder. Edited by Jack Reeder. Brandy Station, VA: Brandy Station Foundation, 2008.

Regimental History of the First New York Dragoons with a List of Names, Post-Office Address, Casualties of Officers and Men, ... Washington, D.C.: Gibson Brothers, 1865.

Reid, Whitelaw. *Ohio in the War: Her Statesmen, Generals, and Soldiers* 2 vols. Cincinnati: Robert Clarke, 1895.

Rhea, Gordon C. *Battle of the Wilderness, May 5–6, 1864*. Baton Rouge: Louisiana State University Press, 1994.

_____. *Battles for Spotsylvania Courthouse and the Road to Yellow Tavern, May 7–12, 1864*. Baton Rouge: Louisiana State University Press, 1997.

_____. *Cold Harbor: Grant and Lee, May 26-June 3, 1863*. Baton Rouge: Louisiana State University Press, 2002.

_____. *To the North Anna River: Grant and Lee, May 13–25, 1864*. Baton Rouge: University of Louisiana Press, 2000.

Reynolds, Arlene, ed. *The Civil War Memories of Elizabeth Bacon Custer*. Austin: University of Texas Press, 1994.

Rigdon, John. *Historical Sketch and Roster: The SC 4th Cavalry Regiment*. Powder Springs, GA: Eastern Digital Resources, 2004.

_____. *Historical Sketch and Roster: The SC 5th Cavalry Regiment*. Powder Springs, GA: Eastern Digital Resources, 2004.

_____. *Historical Sketch and Roster: The SC 6th Cavalry Regiment*. Powder Springs, GA: Eastern Digital Resources, 2004.

Robbins, James P. *Last in Their Class: Custer, Pickett, and the Goats of West Point*. New York: Encounter, 2006.

_____. *The Real Custer: From Boy General to Tragic Hero*. Washington, D.C.: Regnery, 2014.

Rodenbough, Theophilus F., ed. *The Army of the United States: Historical Sketches of Staff and Line with Portraits of Generals in Chief*. New York: Maynard, Merrill, 1896.

_____. *The Cavalry*. Vol.4 of *Photographic History of the Civil War*. New York: Review of Reviews, 1911. Reprint. Secaucus, NJ: Blue & Gray Press, 1987.

_____. *From Everglade to Canyon with the Second United States Cavalry: An Authentic Account of Service in Florida, Mexico, Virginia, and the Indian Country, 1836–1875*. New York: D. Van Norstrand, 1875. Reprint. Norman: University of Oklahoma Press, 2000.

_____. "Sheridan's Trevilian Raid." In *Battles and Leaders of the Civil War*. 4 vols. Edited by Robert Underwood Johnson and Clarence Clough Buel, 4:233–236. New York: Century, 1888. Reprint. New York: Castle Books, 1956.

Roemer, J. *Cavalry; Its History, Management, and Uses in War*. New York: D. Van Nostrand, 1863.

Rosser, Thomas L. "The Battle of Trevilian Station, VA., June 11 and 12, 1864" in *Confederate Soldier in the Civil War 1861–1865* 1 (July 5, 1897): 260.

_____. *The Cavalry, A.N.V.: Address by Gen T.L. Rosser at the Annual Reunion of the Association of the Maryland Line, Academy of Music, Baltimore, MD., February 22, 1889*. Baltimore: Sun, 1889.

_____. *Riding with Rosser*. Edited by S. Roger Keller. Shippensburg, PA: Burd Street, 1997.

Russell, David B., ed. *Tough & Hearty: Kimball Pearsons, Civil War Cavalryman, Company L, 10th Regiment of Cavalry, New York State Volunteers*. Westminster, MD: Heritage, 2012.

Ryckman, W. G. "The Battle of Trevilians, Miscellaneous Commentary." *Louisa County Historical Magazine* 7 (Summer 1975): 2–9. *Louisa County Historical Magazine* reprinted this article in Vol. 35 (Spring 2004): 27–34.

_____. "Clash of Cavalry at Trevilians." *Virginia Magazine of History and Biography* 75 (October 1967): 443–459.

Sanford, George B. *Fighting Rebels and Redskins*. Edited by E. R. Hagemann. Norman: University of Oklahoma Press, 1969.

Sauerberger, Dona B., and Thomas L. Bayard, eds. *I Seat Myself to Write You a Few Lines: Civil War Letters from Thomas Lucas and Family*. Bowie, MD: Heritage Books, 2002.

Schiller, Laurence D. *Of Sabres and Carbines: The Emergence of the Federal Dragoon. A Scholarly Monograph*. Saline, MI: McNaughton and Gunn, 2001.

Shannon, Fred Albert. *Organization and Administration of the Union Army, 1861–1865*. 2 vols. Cleveland: Arthur H. Hicks, 1928.

Sheridan, Philip. *Personal Memoirs of P. H. Sheridan*. New York: Charles Webster, 1888. Reprint. New York: DaCapo, 1992.

Shoemaker, John J. *Shoemaker's Battery, Stuart Horse Artillery, Pelham's Battalion, afterwards Commanded by Col. R. P. Chew, Army of Northern Virginia*. Memphis, TN: S. C. Toof. Reprint. Gaithersburg, MD: Butternut Press, 1983.

Siegler, Robert S. *South Carolina's Military Organizations During the War Between the States*. 3 vols. Charleston: History, 2008.

Sifakis, Stewart. *South Carolina and Georgia*. Vol, 9, *Compendium of the Confederate Armies*. New York: Facts on File, 1995.

Simpson, Brooks D. *Ulysses S. Grant: Triumph Over Adversity, 1822–1865*. New York: Houghton Mifflin, 2000.

Slade, A. D. *A. T. A. Torbert: Southern Gentleman in Union Blue*. Dayton, OH: Morningside, 1992.

Smith, Hampton H. *J.E.B. Stuart: A Character Sketch*. Ashland, VA: N.p, N.d.

Smith, Thomas W. *We Have It Damn Hard Out Here: The Civil War Letters of Sergeant Thomas W. Smith, 6th Pennsylvania Cavalry*. Edited by Eric J. Wittenberg. Kent, OH: Kent State University Press, 1999.

Spratt, Thomas M. *Virginia's Civil War Casualties: A Roster*. 6 vols. Athens, GA: New Papyrus, 2004.

Staats, Richard J. *Life and Times of Colonel William Stedman of the 6th Ohio Cavalry,* Volume 4, *Grassroots History of the American Civil War.* Bowie, MD: Heritage, 2003.

Starr, Stephen Z. "The Inner Life of the First Vermont Cavalry, 1861–1865." *Vermont History* 46 (Summer 1978): 157–174.

_____. *The Union Cavalry in the Civil War.* 3 vols. Baton Rouge: Louisiana State University Press, 1979.

Steffan, Randy. "The Blakeslee Quickloader for the Spencer Rifle Gave the Union Army Its First Modern Firepower." *Civil War Times Illustrated* 1 (October 1962): 35–37.

Stiles, Kenneth. *4th Virginia Cavalry,* 2d ed. Lynchburg, VA: H.E. Howard, 1985.

Stiles, T.J. *Custer's Trials.* New York: Alfred A. Knopf, 2015.

Stokes, William. *Saddle Soldiers: The Civil War Correspondence of General William Stokes of the 4th South Carolina Cavalry.* Edited by Lloyd Haliburton. Orangeburg, SC: Sandlapper, 1993.

Stowe, Mark S. *Company B, 6th Michigan Cavalry.* Grand Rapids, MI: Stowe, 2002.

Stuart, James Ewell Brown. *Letters of Major General James E. B. Stuart.* Edited by Adele H. Mitchell. Richmond: Stuart-Mosby Historical Society, 1990.

Swank, Walbrook D. *Battle of Trevilian Station: The Civil War's Greatest and Bloodiest All Cavalry Battle.* Shippensburg, PA: Burd Street, 1994.

_____. *Confederate Letters and Diaries, 1861–1865.* 3d ed. Shippensburg, PA: Burd Street Press, 1992.

Swayze, J. C. *Hill & Swayze's Confederate States Rail-road & Steam-boat Guide, Containing the Time-Tables, Fares, Connections and Distances on all the Rail-roads of the Confederate States; also, the Connecting Lines of Rail-roads, Steamboats and Stages. And will be Accompanied by a Complete Guide to the Principal Hotels, with a Large Variety of Valuable Information, Collected, Compiled, and Arranged by J. C. Swayze.* Griffin, GA: Hill & Swayze, Publishers, 1862. This resource is available from Documenting the American South Collection, Academic Affairs Library, University of North Carolina, Chapel Hill, NC. http://docsouth.unc.edu/imls/swayze/menu.html.

Swiggart, Carolyn Clay. *Shades of Gray: The Clay and McAllister Families of Bryan County, Georgia during the Plantation Years (ca. 1760–1888).* Darien, CT: Two Bytes, 1999.

Taylor, John. *Bloody Val Verde: A Bloody Battle on the Rio Grande, February 21, 1862.* Albuquerque: University of New Mexico Press, 1995.

Taylor, Nelson. *Saddle and Saber: The Letters of the Civil War Cavalryman Corporal Nelson Taylor.* Edited by Gray Nelson Taylor. Bowie, MD: Heritage, 1993.

Thomas, Emory M. *Bold Dragoon: The Life of J.E.B. Stuart.* New York: Harper & Row, 1986.

Thomas, Hampton S. *Some Personal Reminiscences of Service in the Cavalry of the Army of the Potomac.* Philadelphia: L. R. Hamersly, 1889.

Thomason, John. *JEB Stuart.* New York: Charles Scribner's Sons, 1930.

Tinsley, Alexander L. "General Stuart's Spurs." *Confederate Veteran* 37 (May 1929): 198.

Tobie, Edward. *History of the First Maine Cavalry, 1861–1865.* Boston: Emery & Hughes, 1887. Reprint. Gaithersburg, MD: Ron R. Van Sickle, 1987.

_____. *Personal Recollections of General Sheridan.* Providence, RI: Snow & Farnum, 1889.

Toomey, Daniel C., and Charles A. Earp. *Marylanders in Blue: The Artillery and the Cavalry.* Baltimore, MD: Toomey, 1999.

Treasured Reminiscences Collected by the John K. McIver Chapter, United Daughters of the Confederacy; Including Accounts of the 1st, 6th, 8th, 9th, and 21st Regiments, South Carolina Volunteer Infantry, the 6th South Carolina Cavalry Regiment, and the 1st, 15th and Pee Dee Volunteer Artillery Battalions, Confederate States Army, 1861–1865. Columbia, S.C.: State, 1911. Reprint. University, AL: Confederate Publishing Co.

Trout, Robert J. *Galloping Thunder: The Stuart Horse Artillery Battalion.* Mechanicsburg, PA: Stackpole, 2002.

_____. *"The Hoss": Officer Biographies and Rosters of the Stuart Horse Artillery Battalion.* Richmond: JEBFLO, 2003.

_____, ed. *Memoirs of the Stuart Horse Artillery Battalion: Breathed's and McGregor's Batteries.* Knoxville: University of Tennessee Press, 2010.

_____, ed. *Memoirs of the Stuart Horse Artillery Battalion: Moorman's and Hart's Batteries.* Knoxville: University of Tennessee Press, 2008.

_____. *They Followed the Plume: The Story of J.E.B. Stuart and His Staff.* Mechanicsburg, PA: Stackpole, 1993.

_____. *With Pen & Saber: The Letters and Diaries of J.E.B. Stuart's Staff Officers.* Mechanicsburg, PA: Stackpole, 1995.

Tyler, Lyon Gardiner, ed. *Encyclopedia of Virginia Biography.* 5 vols. New York: Lewis Historical, 1915.

Urwin, Gregory, J. W. "Custer: The Civil War Years." In *The Custer Reader.* Edited by Paul Andrew Hutton. Lincoln: University of Nebraska Press, 1992.

_____. *Custer Victorious: The Civil War Battles of General George Armstrong Custer.* Rutherford, NJ: Fairleigh Dickenson University Press, 1983. Reprint. Lincoln: University of Nebraska Press, 1990.

U.S. Department of the Army. *Field Manual 3-21.20, The Infantry Battalion.* Washington, D.C.: U.S. Government Printing Office, December 2006.

_____. *Field Manual 3-22.9, Rifle Marksmanship.* Washington, D.C.: U.S. Government Printing Office, April 2003.

_____. *Field Manual 3-90, Tactics.* Washington, D.C.: U.S. Government Printing Office, July 2001.

_____. *Field Manual 5-33, Terrain Analysis.* Washington, D.C.: U.S. Government Printing Office, July 1990.

_____. *Field Manual 21-18, Foot Marches.* Washington, D.C.: U.S. Government Printing Office, July 1990.

_____. *Field Manual 71-3, Armor and Mechanized Infantry Brigade.* Washington, D.C.: U.S. Government Printing Office, July 1996

_____. *Field Manual 100-5, Operations.* Washington, D.C.: U.S. Government Printing Office, June 1993.

U.S. Surgeon General's Office. *Medical and Surgical History of the War of the Rebellion (1861–1865).* 3vols. in 6 parts. Washington, D.C.: Government Printing Office, 1875–1885.

U.S. War Department. *Atlas to Accompany the Official Records of the Union and Confederate Armies.* Washington, D.C.: Government Printing Office, 1891–1895. Reprinted as *The Official Military Atlas of the Civil War.* New York: Gramercy, 1983.

_____. *Revised Regulations for the Army of the United States, 1861.* Philadelphia: J. G. L. Brown, 1861. Reprint. Harrisburg, PA: National Historical Society, 1980.

_____. *War of the Rebellion: A Compilation of the Official Records of the Union and Confederate Armies.* 70 vols. in 128 books and index. Washington, D.C.: Government Printing Office, 1880–1901. Unless otherwise noted, all citations are from Series I (Reports and Correspondence Relating to Operations in the Field).

VanDiver, F. E. "Notes on an Engagement at Green Springs, Near Trevillian Station, Virginia, June 1864." *William & Mary Quarterly,* Second Series, 23 (April 1943): 160–161.

Virginia Commission to Study the Location of the J.E.B. Stuart Monument. *Location of the J.E.B. Stuart Monument: Report of [to] the Governor and General Assembly of Virginia.* Richmond: Commonwealth of Virginia Division of Purchasing and Printing, 1953.

Virginia Department of Conservation and Recreation. *A Feasibility Study for the Establishment of a Trevilian Station Battlefield State Park.* Richmond: Commonwealth of Virginia, 2001.

Vogtsberger, Margaret Ann. *The Dulanys of Welbourne: A Family in Mosby's Confederacy.* Berryville, VA: Rockbridge, 1995.

von Borcke, Heros. *Memoirs of the Confederate War for Independence.* 2 vols. Edinburgh, UK: W. Blackwood and Sons, 1866. Reprint (1 vol., paperback). Nashville: J. S. Sanders, 1999.

Wagner, Margaret E., et al., eds. *The Library of Congress Civil War Desk Reference.* New York: Simon & Schuster, 2002.

Wainwright, Charles S. *A Dairy of Battle: The Personal Journals of Colonel Charles S. Wainwright, 1861–1865.* Edited by Alan Nevins. New York: Harcourt, Brace, & World, 1962.

Wallace, Lee A., Jr. *A Guide to Virginia Military Organizations 1861–1865.* Richmond: Virginia Civil War Commission, 1964. This work was later published by H. E. Howard, Lynchburg, VA.

Warner, Ezra J. *Generals in Blue.* Baton Rouge: Louisiana State University Press, 1999.

———. *Generals in Gray.* Baton Rouge: Louisiana State University Press, 1999.

Watson, Thomas J. "Was with 'JEB' Stuart When He Was Shot." *Confederate Veteran* 11 (December 1903): 553.

Weigley, Russell F. "David McMurtrie Gregg." *Civil War Times Illustrated* 1 (November 1962): 10–13, 28–30.

Welch, Stephen Elliott. *Stephen Elliot Welch of the Hampton Legion.* Edited by John Michael Priest. Shippensburg, PA: Burd Street, 1994.

Wellman, Manly Wade. *Giant in Gray: A Biography of Wade Hampton of South Carolina.* New York: Charles Scribner's Sons, 1949. Reprint. Dayton, OH: Morningside, 1988.

Wells, Edward L. *Hampton and His Cavalry in '64.* Richmond, VA: B. F. Johnson, 1899. Reprint. Richmond, VA: Owen, 1991.

———. *A Sketch of the Charleston Light Dragoons.* Charleston, SC: Lucas, Richardson, 1888. Reprint. Camden, SC: J.J. Fox, N.d.

———. "Hampton at Fayetteville." *Southern Historical Society Papers* 13 (January-December 1885): 144–148.

Wert, Jeffry D. *Cavalryman of the Lost Cause: A Biography of J.E.B. Stuart.* New York: Simon & Schuster, 2008.

———. *Custer: The Controversial Life of George Armstrong Custer.* New York: Simon & Schuster, 1996.

Williams, Leroy E. "Charge of the Clarke Cavalry at Trevelyan Station." *Southern Bivouac* 3 (Sep 1884-May 1885): 217–219.

Williamson, Mary L. *The Life of J.E.B. Stuart.* Richmond: B.F. Johnson, 1914.

Wilson, William L. *A Borderland Confederate.* Edited by Festus P. Summers. Pittsburgh: University of Pittsburgh Press, 1962.

Wise, Jennings C. *The Long Arm of Lee: A History of the Artillery of the Army of Northern Virginia.* Lynchburg, VA: J. P. Bell, 1915. Reprint (2 vols.). Lincoln: University of Nebraska Press, 1991.

Wittenberg, Eric J. *Glory Enough for All: Sheridan's Second Raid and the Battle of Trevilian Station.* Washington, D.C.: Brassey's, 2002.

———. *Little Phil: A Reassessment of the Civil War Leadership of Gen. Philip H. Sheridan.* Washington, D.C.: Potomac, 2002.

Whittaker, Frederick. *A Complete Life of Gen. George A. Custer, Major General of Volunteers, Brevet Major General U.S. Army, and Lieutenant-Colonel Seventh U. S. Cavalry.* New York: Sheldon, 1876.

Wilson, James H. *Under the Old Flag.* 2 vols. New York: D. Appleton, 1912.

Woodhead, Henry, ed. *Arms and Equipment of the Confederacy.* Alexandria, VA: Time-Life Books, 1996.

Woodward, C. Vann, ed. *Mary Chesnut's Civil War.* New Haven, CT: Yale University Press, 1982.

Woodward, W. E. *Meet General Grant.* New York: Literary Guild, 1928. Reprint. New York: Liveright, 1965.

"The Wounding and Death of General J.E.B. Stuart—Several Errors Corrected." *Southern Historical Society Papers* 7 (January-December 1879): 140–144.

Manuscripts and Other Unpublished Sources

Alger, Russell A. Papers. William L. Clement Library, University of Michigan, Ann Arbor.

Anderson, Carter S. "Train Running for the Confederacy." (Manuscript) Albert and Shirley Small Special Collections Library, University of Virginia, Charlottesville. This manuscript consists of eleven articles originally published in *Locomotive Engineering* in the 1890s.

Beane, Thomas O. Master's thesis. "Thomas Lafayette Rosser: Soldier, Railroad Builder, Politician, Businessman (1836–1910)." University of Virginia, Charlottesville, 1957.

Boyce, Robert. "Civil War Diary: January 1864-December 1864." Andrew Knez, Jr., Pittsburgh, PA.

Brooke, Henry St. George T. "Autobiography" (25146-Typescript). Richmond, Library of Virginia.

Byars, A. H. Letter, May 17, 1864. Personal Papers Collection (38883). Library of Virginia, Richmond. A transcript of this letter is available at the Valley of the Shadow Project http://valley.lib.virginia.edu/papers/A0318.

Carter, William R. Diary and Letters. Carter Family Papers, 1817–1892 (#33886). Library of Virginia, Richmond. This diary, edited by Walbrook D. Swank, is published as *Sabres, Saddles, and Spurs*, Shippensburg, PA: Burd Street Press, 1998.

Clarke, George Philip. Diary, 1863–1865. Personal Papers Collection (34036, Typescript). Library of Virginia, Richmond.

Compiled Service Records, National Archives, Washington, D.C. Compiled Service Records for personnel who served in Virginia units are also available on microfilm at the Library of Virginia, Richmond.

Cullum, George W. Files. West Point, NY: United States Military Academy Library.

Custer, George A. Letters (SPEC Mss). West Point, NY: United States Military Academy Library.

Davis, Richard T. Letters. Davis-Preston-Saunders Papers (Mss 4951). Albert and Shirley Small Special Collections Library, University of Virginia, Charlottesville.

di Cesnola, Luigi Palma. Letters. Luigi diCesnola Papers (Ms-68). Rauner Special Collections Library, Dartmouth College, Hanover, NH.

———. Letters. Spencer/Wood Family Papers of the of the Jonathan Drayton Papers. William L. Clement Library, University of Michigan, Ann Arbor.

Donahue, John C. Civil War Diary, 1861 April – 1865 Feb

1 (Microfilm, Misc Reel 519) Library of Virginia, Richmond.

Fishburne, Elliot G. Papers of Elliot Guthrie Fishburne (Mss 6542). Albert and Shirley Small Special Collections Library, University of Virginia. Charlottesville.

Folwell, William Watts. Civil War Diary (Typescript). Archives, University of Minnesota Library, Minneapolis. This diary is available on the Internet at http://umedia.lib.umn.edu/node/697406?mode=basic.

Freeman, Douglas Southall. Letters. Papers of Douglas Southall Freeman (#5220). Albert and Shirley Small Special Collections Library, University of Virginia, Charlottesville, VA.

French, S. Bassett. "Biographical Sketches." Papers of S. Bassett French (21332, Misc. Reels 4117–4120), Library of Virginia, Richmond.

Gallaher, William B. Papers of this Waynesboro, Va. Resident, 1861–1961 (Mss 6543). Albert and Shirley Small Special Collections Library, University of Virginia. Charlottesville.

Garnett, Theodore S. Notebook and Journal. Papers of the Garnett Family, 1812–1913 (Mss 35-45-b). Albert and Shirley Small Special Collections Library, University of Virginia, Charlottesville.

Greene, Jacob S. Letter to George Armstrong Custer (Mss 10450). Albert and Shirley Small Special Collections Library, University of Virginia, Charlottesville.

Gregg, David M. "Brevet Major General David McMurtrie Gregg" (Typescript, 1934) in Papers of David McMurtrie Gregg, 1716–1916 (MMC 0539). Manuscript Collection, Library of Congress, Washington.

Hawse, Jasper. "Diary of Jasper Hawse, 1861–1864" (Mss 5188). Albert and Shirley Small Special Collections Library, University of Virginia, Charlottesville. An edited typescript of this diary, prepared by Patrick Bowmaster, a student at Virginia Tech, is available, as is an unedited typescript at the Handley Library, Winchester, VA.

Hubard, Robert T. Notebook of Robert Thruston Hubard (Mss 10522, Notebook with typescript). Albert and Shirley Small Special Collections Library, University of Virginia, Charlottesville. This memoir is published as *The Civil War Memoirs of a Virginia Cavalryman*, edited by Thomas P. Nanzig, Tuscaloosa: University of Alabama Press, 2007.

Lee, Fitzhugh. Correspondence of Fitzhugh Lee 1863–1888 (Mss 7841). Albert and Shirley Small Special Collections Library, University of Virginia, Charlottesville.

Lee, Fitzhugh. Letters. Fitzhugh Lee Papers, 1731–1952 (Microfilm #1829–1931). Albert and Shirley Small Special Collections Library, University of Virginia, Charlottesville.

Lee, Robert E. Letter to William Fitzhugh (Rooney) Lee (GLC05979). Gilder Lehrman Institute, New York.

Locke, William H. Civil War Letters of William Herrod Locke and William Horatio Thornton, 1859–1866 (Mss 13485). Albert and Shirley Small Special Collections Library, University of Virginia, Charlottesville.

Manigault, Gabriel E. Autobiography, 1887–1897, Manigault Family Papers #484, Southern Historical Collection. Wilson Library, University of North Carolina, Chapel Hill.

McVicar, Charles W. Diary, 1862–1865. Personal Papers Collection (29971, Typescript). Library of Virginia, Richmond.

Moncure, Eustis. C. "Reminiscenses of the Civil War." Personal Papers Collection (32349, Typescript). Library of Virginia, Richmond.

Neese, George M. Papers, 1859–1921. Personal Papers Collection (13994). Library of Virginia, Richmond.

Newburger, Alexander. Diary, 1864–1865 (Microfilm 16992–1P). Manuscript Collection, Library of Congress, Washington.

Pate, Nancy S. "Old Trevilian Home." U.S. Works Progress Administration. "Virginia Historical Inventory." Richmond: Library of Virginia. 1937.

———. "Trevilians." U.S. Works Progress Administration. "Virginia Historical Inventory." Richmond: Library of Virginia. 1937.

Patrick, Marsena. Journal 1862–1865. Miscellaneous Manuscripts Collection, Library of Congress, Washington.

Pinckney, Thomas. "My Reminiscences of The War and Reconstruction Times" (Mss 11112, Proof sheets). Albert and Shirley Small Special Collections Library, University of Virginia, Charlottesville.

Rosser, Thomas L. Papers of Thomas Lafayette Rosser and the Rosser, Gordon, and Winston Families (Mss 1171). Albert and Shirley Small Special Collections Library, University of Virginia, Charlottesville.

Snyder, Thomas A. "Recollections of Four Years with the Union Cavalry, 1861–1865." (Typescript). Andy Knez, Pittsburg, PA, 1927.

Stokes, William. "A Brief Account of His War Record" (Mss 7896, Pocket diary and typescript). Albert and Shirley Small Special Collections Library, University of Virginia. Charlottesville.

Stuart, JEB. Letters to his wife, Flora Cooke Stuart (Mss 7442). Albert and Shirley Small Special Collections Library, University of Virginia. Charlottesville.

United States National Archives and Records Administration. Records Group 404 (U.S. Military Academy Records). West Point, NY: United States Military Academy Library.

Virginia Department of Confederate Military Records, 1859–1996, (Subseries 2: Cavalry), (#27684). Library of Virginia, Richmond.

Waring, Joseph Frederick. Transcript of Diary in Joseph Frederick Waring Papers (#1664Z), Southern Historical Collection. Wilson Library, University of North Carolina, Chapel Hill. This resource is also available online at http://www2.lib.unc.edu/mss/inv/w/Waring,Joseph_Frederick.html#.

Whittle, Beverley K. Papers of Beverley Kennon Whittle (Mss 7973). Albert and Shirley Small Special Collections Library, University of Virginia. Charlottesville.

Whitehead, Irving. "Campaigns of Munford and the 2d Virginia Cavalry (Mss 910, Microfilm)." Albert and Shirley Small Special Collections Library, University of Virginia. Charlottesville.

Wood, James Rodney. "Civil War Memoir" in Papers of Maud Wood Park, 1844–1955 (0448E), Manuscript Collection, Library of Congress, Washington.

Wood, James Ward. "Diary, Jan. 9-July 31, 1864." Personal Papers Collection (25506). Library of Virginia, Richmond.

Woods, Micajah. "Complete Roll of the Members of the Albemarle Light Horse" (Mss 10689-b). Albert and Shirley Small Special Collections Library, University of Virginia. Charlottesville.

———. "Scrapbook of Micajah Woods—1895 (Mss 1379). Albert and Shirley Small Special Collections Library, University of Virginia, Charlottesville, VA.

Young, George C. Letters. Civil War Correspondence of George C. and I. A. Young (Mss 3676). Albert and Shirley Small Special Collections Library, University of Virginia, Charlottesville, VA.

Newspapers

Charleston Daily Courier, Charleston, SC. June 14, 1864; June 17, 1864; June 21, 1864, June 24, 1864.
Charleston Mercury. Charleston, SC. June 15, 1864; June 21, 1864; June 22, 1864; June 23, 1864; June 25, 1864.
Confederate Union. Milledgeville, GA. June 28, 1864.
Daily Richmond Enquirer Richmond, VA: June 11, 1864; June 13, 1864; June 16, 1864.
Daily South Carolinian., Columbia, SC: May 10, 1863; April 23, 1864; June 22, 1864; June 24, 1864.
Edgefield Advertiser, Edgefield, SC: June 22, 1864; June 29, 1864; July 13, 1864; July 27, 1864.
Lynchburg Virginian, Lynchburg, VA: June 10, 1864; June 13, 1864; June 23, 1864.
National Tribune, Washington, D.C.: May 8, 1884; January 5, 1888; February 2, 1888; February 9, 1888; May 3, 1888; May 10, 1888; June 28, 1888; August 31, 1893; June 21, 1894; July 30, 1896; March 24, 1898; February 1, 1900; August 30, 1900; November 21, 1901; August 4, 1910; April 13, 1911.
New York Daily Herald, New York: June 21, 1864.
New York Times, New York: June 10, 1863; May 16, 1864; June 15, 1864; June 16, 1864; June 18, 1864; June 19, 1864; June 20, 1864; March 11, 1865; April 5, 1878; April 7, 1878; September 3–6, 1880; September 30, 1880; May 24, 1898; June 10, 1900; April 12, 1902; November 22, 1904; December 4, 1910; December 7, 1910; December 20, 1912; December 1, 1917.
New York Tribune, New York: June 11, 1864; June 20, 1864.
Richmond Daily Dispatch, Richmond, VA: June 10, 1864; June 11, 1864; June 13, 1864; June 14, 1864; June 16, 1864; June 17, 1864; June 18, 1864; June 20, 1864; June 21, 1864; June 22, 1864; June 23, 1864; June 24, 1864. Issues of this newspaper from November 1860 through December 1865 are available online at the University of Richmond, http://imls.richmond.edu/d/ddr/.
Richmond Daily Examiner, Richmond, VA: May 12, 1864; May 13, 1864; May 14, 1864; May 17, 1864; June 15, 1864; June 27, 1864; June 28, 1864.
Richmond Daily Times, Richmond, VA: June 19, 1888.
Richmond Dispatch, Richmond, VA: December 31, 1899; January 7, 1900; January 21, 1900.
Richmond Times Dispatch, Richmond, VA: August 23, 1914; August 1, 1915.
Richmond Whig, Richmond, VA: June 10, 1864; June 11, 1864; June 12, 1864; June 14, 1864.
Washington Bee, Washington, D.C.: May 27, 1893.

Online Resources

Army Historical Foundation. "M551 Sheridan Light Tank." https://armyhistory.org/m551-sheridan-light-tank/
"Biographical Dictionary of Post Bellum Rice Culture." Ricekingdom.com. http://ricekingdom.com/planters.html
Carlton, Patrick. "Confederates in the Collegium: The Influence of J.E.B. Stuart's Leadership on the Development of Virginia Tech." Blacksburg: University Archives of Virginia Tech. (http://spec.lib.vt.edu/arc/125th/confeds/confeds.htm
"College of Charleston Archive: About the Collection Archive." College of Charleston. http://speccoll.cofc.edu/findingaids/archives.html?referrer=webcluster&
Encyclopedia of Chicago. "Fort Sheridan." http://www.encyclopedia.chicagohistory.org/pages/478.html.
"For Distinguished Gallantry." Theta Chi Fraternity. http://thetachi.org/news/2013/12/general/for-distinguished-gallantry/
"A Genealogy of the Kirk Family by Chas. H. Stubbs, 1872." http://wc.rootsweb.ancestry.com/cgi-bin/igm.cgi?op=REG&db=kirk-stubbs&id=I0165
"Joseph Manigault House." Charleston Museum. http://charlestonmuseum.org/joseph-manigault-house
Kinnear, Duncan L. "The Lomax Administration 1886–1891" in *A Short History of Virginia Tech 1850–1974*. Blacksburg: Special Collections, University Libraries. http://spec.lib.vt.edu/archives/125th/kinnear/lomax.htm
"Lt. Col William Wofford Rich." http://www.anglefire.com/ga2/PhillipsLegion/rich.html
"Medal of Honor Citations." U.S. Army Center for Military History. http://www.army.mil/cmh pg/Moh1.htm
"Mr. & Mrs Ralph Izard (Alice Delancey)." Boston Museum of Fine Arts. http://www.mfa.org/collections/object/mr-and-mrs-ralph-izard-alice-delancey
Mollan, Mark C. "The Army Medal of Honor: The First Fifty-five Years." Washington, D.C.: U.S. National Archives and Records Administration. http://www.archives.gov/publications/prologue/2001/summer/medal-of-honor-1.html
"South Carolina 6th Cavalry Regiment Companies B and F." Research Online. http://www.researchonline.net/sccw/rosters/6thcavb.htm
"Sunrise & Sunset Data." U.S. Naval Observatory. http://aa.usno.navy.mil/
"Virginia Historical Inventory." Library of Virginia, Richmond, VA. http://www.lva.lib.va.us/whatwehave/map/vhiabout.htm
"'Winchester.' General Philip H. Sheridan's War Horse." Smithsonian Institution. http://www.si.edu/Encyclopedia_SI/nmah/horse.htm

Index

Page numbers in **_bold italics_** indicate pages with illustrations

Aaron (servant of Noble Preston) 172
Abercrombie, J.J. 200; military career 314*n*2
Adams, Charles Francis, Jr. 321*n*26
Adams, William T. 305*n*11
Aiken, D. Wyatt 319*n*95
Aiken, Hugh K. 47, 48, 56, 57, 60, 129, 130, 131, 265, 288, 292*n*68, 272*n*71, 311*n*11, 319*n*95; convalescence and later death of 247–248; wounding of 136; 146, 179
Aiken, Mary (Mrs. Hugh Aiken) 248, 319*n*95
Aiken's Landing, Virginia 313*n*23
Aiken's Partisan Rangers *see* Confederate Regiments, Battalions, and Companies, South Carolina, 16th Battalion South Carolina Cavalry
Alabama 4, 36, 41, 57, 59, 127, 227, 232, 248, 252, 290*n*9, 291*n*41, 297*n*56, 319*n*95, 323*n*64
Albany, Georgia 37, 248
Albemarle County, Virginia 37, 196
Alcatraz Island, California 241
Aldie, Virginia 32, 67, 68, 94, 95, 236, 307*n*37, 309*n*30
Alexandria, Virginia 105, 106, 198, 249, 256, 288*n*16, 302*n*29, 320*n*8
Alger, Russell 99, 100, ***140***, 141, 147, 148, 151, 152, 174, 216, 232, 242, 246, 261, 284*n*28, 305*n*13, 305*n*19, 305*n*22, 318*n*41; charge at Trevilians 142–144; later career ***233***; questions regarding Custer's orders 142, 216, 305*n*13
Alton, Illinois 98, 294*n*31
Amelia Springs, Virginia 256, 287*n*8
American Bible Society 35
Amherst College 58
Amherst County, Virginia 286*n*9
Amputations 165, 172, 258, 322*n*37, 323*n*58; mortality rates resulting from 309*n*9
Anderson, Edward C. 292*n*74
Anderson, Edward "Ned" C., Jr. 57, 58, 120, 164, 309*n*17, 309*n*18
Anderson, James Q. 95; later career 236; 261, 303*n*2

Anderson, Robert H. 57, 290*n*10, 292*n*73
Andersonville, Georgia 296*n*33
Andrews, Clinton M. 34
Antietam, Maryland 67, 74, 101, 319*n*95
Antietam Campaign 71, 95
Appomattox, Virginia 223, 231, 236, 241, 249, 252, 253, 290*n*27, 313*n*17, 319*n*99, 323*n*54
Arkansas 74, 318*n*79
Arlington National Cemetery 225, 232, 237, 240, 241, 256
Army of Northern Virginia 1, 3, 4, 16, 17, 20, 21, 22, 23, 24, 25, 26, 27, 28, 30, 32, 37, 41, 43, 44, 47, 49, 50, 60, 104, 108, 204, 220, 221, 222, 242, 248, 249, 253, 264, 268, 276, 286*n*12, 286–287*n*2, 287*n*10, 287*n*13, 290*n*27, 292*n*84
Army of Tennessee 290–291*n*28
Army of the Cumberland 87, 293*n*10, 296*n*37
Army of the James 90, 97
Army of the Potomac 3, 7, 8, 15, 32, 63, 64, 65, 66, 67, 70, 71, 78, 80, 81, 84, 86, 87, 88, 90, 91, 94, 95, 96, 97, 99, 101, 104, 105, 106, 107, 109, 110, 112, 114, 132, 134, 188, 192, 195, 196, 199, 204, 210, 214, 215, 218, 220, 225, 267, 287*n*14, 293*n*10, 294*n*35, 294–295*n*39, 295*n*10, 296*n*34, 298–299*n*2, 299*n*8, 299–300*n*32, 303*n*43, 316*n*27, 320*n*129, 320*n*1, 320*n*2, 321*n*17, 324*n*5
Army of Virginia (Pope's Army) 100, 101, 303*n*4
Arnold, Abraham 96, 238, 262, 268
Arthur, President Chester A. ***224***
Artillery: fusing problems 302*n*40; heavy artillery 320*n*2; Union reorganization of 110–111, 299*n*23, 299*n*24; *see also* Blakely rifled gun; 3-Inch Ordnance Rifle; 12-pound Napoleon
Artillery regiments and batteries:
1st United States Artillery, Battery G 299*n*25
2nd United States Artillery, Battery G 299*n*25, 322*n*32

2nd United States Artillery Regiment 241
3rd New Jersey Light Artillery 204
3rd United States Artillery Regiment 242
4th United States Artillery, Battery A 299*n*25
6th Battery, New York Independent Light Artillery 299*n*25
Baltimore Light Artillery (2nd Maryland Light Artillery) 265, 322*n*47, 322*n*49
Dennison's (2nd United States Artillery, Battery A) 263, 299*n*23, 315*n*33; *see also* Dennison, W. Neil
Hart's Battery (Washington Artillery, South Carolina) 21, 119, 142, 153, 154, 166, 266, 290*n*27, 305*n*11, 306*n*24, 323*n*61; *see also* Hart, James
Heaton's (2nd United States Artillery, Batteries B&L) 135, 161, 182, 263, 299*n*23; *see also* Heaton, Edward
Johnston's Battery (2nd Stuart Horse Artillery) 166, 181, 266, 285*n*34, 311*n*25; *see also* Johnston, Phillip
Pennington's (2nd United States Artillery Battery M) 149, 153, 156, 184, 263, 299*n*23; *see also* Pennington, Alexander C.M
Pulaski Light Artillery 59
Randol's Battery (1st United States Artillery, Batteries H & I) 137, 165, 263, 299*n*23, 315*n*33; *see also* Randol, Alanson
Shoemaker's Battery 166, 185, 266, 304*n*2; *see also* Shoemaker, John J
Thomson's Battery 119, 191, 266, 311*n*31, 323*n*62; action on June 12, 1864, 183–184; *see also* Thomson, James W
Washington Artillery, New Orleans 288*n*18
Williston's (2nd United States Artillery, Battery D) 128, 132, 181, 263, 299*n*23; *see also* Williston, Edward

339

340   Index

Association of Graduates, United States Military Academy 228, 323n1
Atlanta, Georgia 172
Auburn, Virginia 35, 288n16
Augusta, Georgia 58
Autenrieth wagon 189, 299n32, 312n4
Averell, William Woods 24
Avery, Ellen (Mrs. James Henry Avery) 242
Avery, James Henry 144, 174, 192, 198, 242, 305n22
Avery, Martin 147, 148, 180, 311n16
Avery, Matthew Henry **161**, 162, 163, 164, 172, 232, 239, 308n12, 308n15
Aylett, Virginia 11, 118, 300n7, 316n19

B.F. Johnson (publisher) 276
Bacon, Judge Daniel 271, 272, 324n2
Badeau, Adam 294n27
Baggs, William 180
Baker, Cecil 209
Baker, Laurence 27, 28, 35, 269, 207n7
Baker's Brigade *see* North Carolina Brigade
Baldwin, Kansas 284n16
Ball, William 33, 306n29
Baltimore, Maryland 97, 101, 253, 304n5
Baltimore American 276
Baltimore Crossroads, Virginia 203
Baltimore Store, Virginia 204
Banks, Nathaniel 99, 100, 298n26
Barr, James Michael 55, 136, 258, 303n44
Barr, John Wesley 136, 304n8
Barton Haxall's farm, Virginia 191
Bartow County, Georgia 248
Base Realignment and Closure Act 317n8
Battery Pennington, Virginia 242
Battery Williston, Hawaii 242
Battles and Leaders of the Civil War 135, 275, 303–304n4
Battles in Culpeper County, Virginia 253
Bauskett, John 129, 130, 153, 154
Baxley, J.V. 170, 171
Bayliss, Richard 320n7
Beale, R.L.T. 33, **34**, 184, 207, 209, 288n10
Beane, William B. 265, 322n49
Beaumont, Eugene B. 323n2
Beaumont, Myron 297n3
Beauregard, P.G.T. 35, 42, 43, 214, 291n36, 291n40, 292n56; opposition to transfer of the "New Issue" 46–51, 57, 290n10, 291n28, 291n32; relations with Jefferson Davis 290–291n4
Beaver County, Pennsylvania 236
Beaver Dam Station, Virginia 15, 106, 108, 120
Beckham, Robert 269

Belle Plain, Virginia 97, 110
Bellinger, Sergeant 284n29
Belloir, Mitchell 148, 150, 306n12, 320n7
Benny Havens tavern, New York 24
Beverly Ford Road, Virginia 33, 67, 75
Bibb, J.B. 320n129
Bibb's Crossroads, Virginia 121, 125
Biddle, W.N. 304n11
Billy (horse) 233, 234
Birge, Manning D. 144, 147
Birney, David B. 63
Black, John Logan 47, 48, 269, 290n24
Black Creek 203, 204
Black Stock, South Carolina 61
Blackford, Susan Leigh 196
Blackford, W.W. 271
Blacksburg, Virginia 252
Blackshears, Georgia 59
Blacksmiths 40, 43, 51, 57, 84, 156, 291n43
Bladensburg, Maryland 100
Blair, Governor Austin 304n5
Blakely rifled gun 21, 119, 286n8, 306n24
Blakeslee, Erastus 101, 298n39
Blakeslee Box 298n39
Bleeding Kansas 284n16
Bliss Aaron T. 321n27
Bloody Angle, Spotsylvania 15
Bolling Air Force Base (Joint Base Anacostia-Bolling) 296n23
Boonesville, Mississippi 99
Booth, John Wilkes 314n40
Border Ruffian 32, 284n16
Borglum, Gutzon 224, 225
Bostic, Samuel D. 164, 309n20
Boston, Massachusetts 79, 251, 315n1
Boston, Reuben 156, 265, 307n37
Boston Museum of Fine Arts 256
Boteler, Alexander R. 39, 40, 289n35
Botetourt County, Virginia 314n37
Bottoms Bridge, Virginia 109
Bowen, C.C. 58, 292
Bowen, James 172, 321n19
Boxer Rebellion 227
Boyce, Robert 301n26
Boyd, William 140
Bradley, Joseph H. 171, 173, 176, 309n8
Bragg, Braxton 9, 11, 48, 49, 60, 61, 65, 290–291n28, 291n32
Brandy Station, Virginia 1, 3, 4, 5, 6, 16, 20, 27, 28, 30, 32, 33, 34, 35, 36, 53, 63, 67, 69, 71, 73, 74, 75, 77, 78, 94, 95, 96, 97, 101, 102, 137, 212, 213, 215, 217, 220, 245, 258, 266, 280, 286n12, 286n18, 288n10, 289–290n2, 294n18, 297n14, 320n129, 323n58; West Pointers at 267, 268, 269
Breathed, James **166**, 266, 311n25, 312n49

Breckinridge, John C. 214, 215
Brewer, Dr. Charles 15, 16, 285n36; residence of **16**
Brewer, Maria Cooke 285n36
Brewer, Melvin 139, 140, 157, 234, 304n1, 320n10, 320n12
Brewster 144
Brinton, Joseph P. 100, 262
Brinton, William P. 100
Bristoe, Virginia 177
Bristoe Campaign 33, 35, 85, 288
Britain, British 52, 69, 108, 244
British Museum, London 236
Broad Run 271
Broderick, Virgil 94
Brodhead, Thornton R. 99
Brook Turnpike 9, 283n7, 283n8
Brooks, Noble 164, 191, 309n20
Brooks, U.R. 127, 195, 302n23, 305n2, 308n8, 313n30, 314n34, 315n37, 322n45
Brooks, Winfield Butler 302n23
Brown, Eliza *see* Eliza
Brown, John 12, 284n16
Brown, Ridgely 322n48
Bruington, Virginia 198
Bryan, Thomas 100
Bryan, Timothy 74, 75, 267, 294n35, 294–295n39
Buck Chile's, Virginia 121, 139
Buckland, Virginia 271, 272
Buckland Races 73, 77, 271, 294n32
Buffalo, New York 296n33
Buford, John 33, 67, 68, 71, 74, 75, 109, 294n21
Burden, Henry 291n43
Bureau of Elections, New York City 237
Burgess, Anthony Beale 184, 191
Burgess Mill, Virginia 245
Burkesville (Burkeville), Virginia 59, 61, 204
Burnside, Ambrose 97, 102, 298n16, 320n2
Burnside carbine 37, 91, 289n32
Burnside Rifle Company 297n50
Bustleton, Pennsylvania 240
Butler, Andrew Pickens 194, 306n26
Butler, Benjamin 9, 15, 56, 90, 210, 298, 313n13
Butler, Matthew C. 26, 28, 36, 43, 46, 48, **53**, 54, 60, 123, 125, 126, 127, 128, 129, 130, 131, 132, 134, 136, 137, 138, 145, 146, 147, 148, 152, 153, 154, 156, 161, 166, 173, 178, 179, 181, 183, 184, 185, 196, 201, 207, 208, 216, 217, 218, 244, 253, 275, 280, 281, 286n10, 289n2, 301n17, 301n18, 301–302n20, 302n22, 302n30, 304n7, 306n21, 309n20, 311n16, 311n22, 311n37, 312n40, 318–319n90, 322n43; later career 245, **246**, 247
Butler, Matthew C., Jr. 318–319n90
Butler and His Cavalry 195
Butler's Brigade 30, 31, 36, 38, 42, 44, 45, 46, 47, 49, 120, 125, 131,

Index

140, 142, 143, 152, 154, 166, 169, 176, 178, 179, 185, 247, 265, 279
Calef, John A. 268
Calhoun, John C. 126, 146, 152, 302n11, 306n21
Calhoun, Senator John C. 36, 302n11
Calhoun, William R. 291n36
California 65, 70, 242, 296,n33
Camden, South Carolina 54
Camden County, North Carolina 288n18
Cameron, Simon 91
Camp Alger, Virginia 246
Camp Black, New York 241
Camp Stoneman, D.C. 294–295n39, 321n30
Canada 253, 289n13
Cape Henry, Virginia 242
Carolinas 22, 104, 227, 245, 247, 248
Caroline County, Virginia 300n7
Carpenter's Ford 116, 120, 190, 300n7
Carrington, Henry, Jr. 167, 309n30
Carr's Bridge, Virginia 300n8
Carter, Richard Welby 32
Carter, William R. 32, 155, 167, 257, 258, 265, 277, 288n3
Carthage, Kendall 184
Carver, Lucius **152**, 154
Casey, Silas 98, 99
Caskie, Robert 34
Cassville, Georgia 248
Catawba River 58
Catharpin Road 192, 313n20
Catholic, Catholicism 247, 318n75
Cating, Lieutenant 182
Catton, Bruce 6
Cavalry Bureau 72, 77, 80, 296n34, 299n19, 299n20, 300n33; organization of 81–90, 295n12, 295n18, 295–296n19, 296n33
Cavalry Corps: Army of Northern Virginia organization of 31–32; Army of the Potomac organization of 102–103
Cedar Creek, Virginia 223, 224, 225, 231, 236
Cedar Mountain 95, 258
Century Magazine 218, 303–304n5
Chadbourne, Paul 213
Chaffee, Adna R. 242, 318n79
Chaffee, Adna R., Jr. 318n79
Chamberlain, Governor Daniel 24, 318n88
Chamberlain, Samuel E. 232, 238, 262
Chamberlain Run 288
Chambliss, John 28, 29, 31, 33, **38**, 204, 205, 207, 208, 209, 210, 269, 286n10, 287n10, 324n6; death of 310n3; views on Confederate cavalry deficiencies 39–40, 289n37
Chambliss's Brigade 29, 31, 33, 204, 205, 207, 323n58
Chancellorsville, Virginia 18, 24, 81, 82, 108, 240, 286n18

Chantilly, Virginia 100
Chapman, George H. 12, 75, **76**, 95, 284n21, 284n22, 297n6
Charles City Courthouse, Virginia 205, 210
Charles City Road 38, 310n3, 324n6
Charleston, South Carolina 48, 50, 51, 52, 54, 237, 247, 256, 276, 285–286n49, 291n32, 291n40, 292n74, 292n78, 322n49, 325n16
Charleston Daily Courier 176
Charleston Museum 256
Charlestown, West Virginia 314n41
Charlotte, North Carolina 53, 58, 61
Charlottesville, Virginia 35, 37, 106, 107, 108, 175, 176, 188, 190, 196, 212, 213, 214, 215, 217, 219, 253, 254, 258, 267, 274, 288n10, 292n71, 301n3, 311n34, 316n14, 319n116, 320n2
Charlottesville Road 171, 316n8
Chattanooga, Tennessee 65, 71
Cheek, W.H. 35
Cheraw, South Carolina 247
Cherokee Nation 246
Chesapeake & Ohio Railroad (CSX) 252
Chesapeake Bay 242
Chesnut, Mary 286n13
Chester, South Carolina 61, 247
Chester County, South Carolina 312n39
Chesterfield, Virginia 15
Chew, Roger P. 119, 153, 184, 266
Cheyenne Indians 15
Chicago, Illinois 97, 223, 224, 230, 295
Chickahominy River 15, 106, 204, 205, 213, 215, 297n55, 298–299n2
Chilesburg, Virginia 116, 300n10, 316n18
Chimborazo Hospital, Richmond 322n47
Cholera 237, 294–295n39
Christian 16, 239, 242
Christianville, Virginia 59
Cilley, Jonathan 203, 232
Cincinnati (horse) **105**
Cincinnati, Ohio 83, 296n34
City Point, Virginia 106, 200, 201
Civil War: A Narrative 5
Claflin, Ira 96, 261, 268, 297n11
Clark, Joseph Hinckley 132, 237, 262, 303n44
Clarke, Dr. Henry K. 172
Clarke, Robert **153**, 322n32
Clark's Ferry, Virginia 61
Clayton, Arthur 122, 301n1
Clayton's Store, Virginia 121, 122, 123, 125, 127, 139, 140, 154, 216, 279, 301n25
Clement, William 209
Cleveland, President Grover 224, 251
Coffee Hill, battle of 288
Coiner, Phil 209, 315n39
Cold Harbor, Virginia 59, 104, 105, 109, 214, 218, 288n7, 298n1

College of Charleston 256
Collins, Charles R. 33, 269, 306n29, 306–307n30
Colock, Richard H. 289n1
Columbia, South Carolina 47–58, 61, 151, 244, 245, 258, 276, 287n13, 318n88
Columbia College, D.C. 314n41
Columbia River 71
Columbus, Georgia 227
Columbus, Ohio 91
Company Q 4, 38, 290n9
Confederate Regiments, Battalions, and Companies: (*see also* artillery regiments and batteries)
Alabama
  4th Battalion Alabama Cavalry (Love's Battalion) 59, 60, 195, 204, 292n84, 292n85, 292n88, 322n37
Georgia
  5th Georgia Cavalry 44, 57, 290n10
  7th Georgia Cavalry 31, 52, 57, 58, 59, 120, 129, 164, 166, 172, 264, 292n74, 309n18, 322n35
  10th Georgia Infantry 59
  20th Battalion Georgia Partisan Rangers (Millen's Battalion) 31, 48, 59, 61, 129, 264
  21st Battalion Georgia Cavalry (White's Battalion) 57
  24th Battalion Georgia Cavalry 57
  Cobb's Legion Cavalry 27, 30, 31, 36, 43, 120, 143, 164, 191, 264, 305n14
  Georgia Hussars 36
  Hardwick Mounted Rifles 57, 58, 292n75
  Phillips Legion Cavalry 30, 31, 36, 43, 60, 154, 187, 207, 220, 248, 264, 322n37
Maryland
  1st Maryland Cavalry 31, 146, 170, 190, 191, 265, 276, 322n47, 322n48
Mississippi
  Jeff Davis Legion Cavalry 30, 31, 36, 43, 44, 143, 152, 207, 264, 292n85, 292n88, 322n37
North Carolina
  1st North Carolina Cavalry 26, 27, 28, 30, 31, 35, 269
  2nd North Carolina Cavalry 27, 30, 31, 34, 269, 323n58
  4th North Carolina Cavalry 30, 35, 287n5, 288n12, 288n18
  5th North Carolina Cavalry 27, 30, 31, 34, 35, 287n5
South Carolina
  1st South Carolina Cavalry 30, 43, 47, 48, 50, 52, 53, 269
  1st South Carolina Infantry 247, 306n26
  2nd South Carolina Cavalry 22, 30, 43, 47, 48, 50, 52, 53, 280
  3rd South Carolina Cavalry 42
  4th South Carolina Cavalry 31, 42, 47, 48, 50, 52, 53, 54, 61, 125, 126, 129, 131, 146, 152, 174, 178, 181,

206, 247, 255, 265, 276, 289n1, 301n17, 302n30, 308n8, 322n43
5th South Carolina Cavalry 31, 42, 47, 48, 50, 54, 55, 61, 125, 129, 136, 146, 162, 178, 195, 201, 206, 247, 258, 265, 301n17, 302n30
6th South Carolina Cavalry 31, 42, 47, 48, 50, 56, 57, 61, 130, 136, 146, 153, 161, 170, 171, 178, 206, 247, 265, 302n23, 308n8
7th South Carolina Cavalry (Holcomb Legion) 48, 289n1, 290n27
7th South Carolina Infantry 319n95
10th Battalion South Carolina Cavalry 53
12th Battalion South Carolina Cavalry 53
14th Battalion South Carolina Cavalry 54
16th Battalion South Carolina Cavalry (Aiken's Partisan Rangers) 56
17th Battalion South Carolina Cavalry 54
Boykin's Company, Cavalry 47
Cadet Rangers 130, 153
Charleston Light Dragoons (the Drags) 52, 54, 247, 276, 289n1
McGee's Company, Cavalry 47
Rutledge Cavalry (Rutledge Mounted Riflemen) 41, 289n1
Trenholm's Company, Cavalry 47, 48, 289n1
Tucker's Company, Cavalry 47
Wallace's Company, Cavalry 47
Virginia
 1st Virginia Cavalry 9, 12, 13, 24, 30, 31, 32, 209, 221, 265
 2nd Virginia Cavalry 30, 31, 32, 33, 155, 156, 167, 181, 196, 252, 265, 273, 274, 297n55
 3rd Virginia Cavalry 30, 31, 32, 119, 140, 155, 156, 166, 167, 181, 265, 304n2
 4th Virginia Cavalry 22, 26, 30, 31, 32, 34, 139, 155, 166, 167, 265, 288n2, 289n33, 323n58
 5th Virginia Cavalry 10, 11, 12, 26, 28, 30, 31, 32, 156, 265, 284n16, 307n37
 6th Virginia Cavalry 11, 26, 30, 31, 33, 156, 174, 186, 193, 252, 265, 277
 7th Virginia Cavalry 30, 31, 35, 166, 254, 264, 272, 288n20
 8th Virginia Cavalry 291n41
 9th Virginia Cavalry 30, 31, 33, 34, 118, 207, 209, 323n58
 10th Virginia Cavalry 30, 31, 34, 207, 209, 269
 11th Virginia Cavalry 26, 30, 31, 36, 149, 264
 12th Virginia Cavalry 30, 31, 35, 36, 146, 156, 198, 207, 264
 13th Virginia Cavalry 28, 30, 31, 33, 207, 209, 323n58
 15th Virginia Cavalry 30, 31, 33, 139, 154, 155, 256, 265, 269, 274, 306n28
 17th Battalion Virginia Cavalry 288n20
 24th Virginia Cavalry 207, 209, 315n31
 33rd Virginia Infantry 285–286n49
 35th Battalion Virginia Cavalry (the Comanches) 30, 31, 35, 36, 146, 149, 150, 195, 221, 264, 315n321
 Black Horse Troop 32
 Little Fork Rangers 289n33
 White's Rebels 36
 Wise Dragoons 307n38
Conrad, Holmes 150, 305–306n12
Conrad, Thomas 119, 156, 196–198, 307n36, 314n39, 314n40
Conservative Party (Virginia) 250
Continental Army 301n3
Cooke, John Esten 119, 301n21
Cooper, John 307n30
Cooper, Samuel 42–51, 287n10, 290n27, 291n40; service in regular army 290n5
Copeland, Joseph T. **98**
Copley, John Singleton 256
Cormany, Samuel 175, 310n3, 314n21
Cornwallis, Lord 301n3
Council, Mrs. 198
Counselman, Jacob 298n20
Covode, George 95, 96, 315n37, 304n11; death of **208**
Covode, John 315n37
Cralle, Griefe T. 277, 278, 324n11
Crawford, James 184
Critcher, John R. 33, 265, 288n8, 306n28, 306n29; later career 256; relief of 154–155, 306–307n30
Crocker, William H. 182, 261
Crowninshield, Benjamin 220, 316n31, 321n26
Cuba 226, 227, 238, 246, 278, 291n40, 318n41, 319n119; see also Havana; Santiago
Cuffy's Creek 121, 301n27
Cullum, George W. 6, 66, 268, 269, 323n1
Culpeper County, Virginia 5, 7, 13, 24, 66, 68, 72, 80, 101, 155, 198, 213, 215, 223, 252, 253, 255, 286n9, 289n33, 294n18, 324n5
Culpeper Courthouse, Virginia 258, 271, 319n111, 324n5
Culpeper National Cemetery **255**, 308n16, 320n129
Cumberland Landing, Virginia 203
Custer, Elizabeth Bacon "Libbie" (Mrs. George A. Custer) 13, 67, 158, 204, 229, 293n2, 294n28, 295n43, 304n3, 305–306n12, 306n16, 307n42; letters to George A. 271, **272**, 273, 274, 324n2, 324n7, 324n13; opinion on Custer statue 230, 231
Custer, George A. 3, 10, 11, 12, **13**, 67, 72, 73, 75, 77, 85, 86, 98, 99, 100, 114, 117, 121, 128, 134, 135, 137, 138, 139, 140, 141, 142, 143, 144, 145, 159, 161, 162, 166, 167, 168, 169, 173, 178, 179, 180, 181, 182, 187, 203, 204, 213, 218, 225, 228, 229, 233, 234, 247, 256, 257, 261, 263, 267, 268, 276, 277, 278, 279, 283n13, 284n18, 284n22, 287n3, 294n28, 294n29, 294n31; on Wilson 295n43; 302n24, 302–303n41, 303n1, 304n3, 304n5, 304n7; orders to Alger 305n13; 305n22, 305n11, 310n2, 311n17, 311n22, 311n24, 314n37, 320n7; first last stand 146–158, 305n16, 305–306n12, 306n16, 306n19, 307n31, 307n35, 307n38, 307n42, 307n45; letters from Libbie 271, 272, 274, 324n2, 324n7, 324n13; monument at West Point **229**, 230–**231**; photo of Custer and Libbie **272**
Custis, Martha 197
Cyprus: diCesnola as consul to 235–236

Dahlgren Raid 63, 68, 101, 320n10
Daily South Carolinian 52
Dana, Amasa E. 158, 159
Dana, Charles 87, **235**, 307n45
Daniel, Junius 286n1
Danville, Virginia 53, 59, 61, 204, 292n71
Davidson, John W. 90, 296n44
Davies, Henry **72**, 73, 74, **77**, 94, 121, 137, 153, 162, 163, 167, 179, 202, 203, 204, 205, 208, 218, 262, 263, 271, 294n32, 301n26, 304n10, 309n31, 310n17, 315n33; later career 231–232
Davis, Benjamin Franklin "Grimes" 67, 68, 74, 75
Davis, J. Lucius, Jr. 209, 315n38
Davis, James Lucius 34, 269, 324n6
Davis, Jefferson 15, 17, 19, 20, 21, 23, 24, 26, 27, 41, **42**, 43, 47, 48, 49, 221, 222, 227, 286n13, 286ch3n2, 290n5, 290n17, 290–291n28
Davis, Joe 286n13
Davis, Zimmerman 195, 247, 313n30
Dearing, James 35, 56, 256; career of 288n18; 315n31
Deep Bottom, Virginia 200, 204, 205, **206**, 314n26
The Deep South 35, 37, 41, 42, 46, 47, 61, 287n13, 290n5
Delaware 70, 225, 226
Deloney, William G. 36
Democratic Party 247, 251, 253, 296n33, 318n88, 319n116
Dennison, W. Neil **153**, 263, 315n15, 322n32
Dennison, Governor William, Jr. 315n33
Department of Florida 71
Department of Mississippi 92
Department of North Carolina & Southern Virginia 269, 287n7

Department of Ohio 83
Department of Richmond 290n27
Department of South Carolina, Georgia & Florida 42, 47, 269
Department of Southwestern Virginia & East Tennessee 28, 269
Department of the Gulf 213, 236
Department of the Missouri 223, 234
Department of West Virginia 106, 297n14
Department of Western Virginia 67
Detachment Left in Contact 305n3
Detroit, Michigan 98, 99, 233, 234
Devin, Thomas C. 10, 67, **73**, 74, 75, 93, 116, 121, 127, 128, 134, 135, 136, 137, 147, 148, 151, 157, 158, 159, 160, 161, 166, 168, 169, 179, 182, 185, 203, 205, 225, 237, 261, 263, 283n12, 284n20, 303n1, 303n2, 303n3, 303–304n5, 308n7, 310n2, 314n23, 321n14, 321n17; later career 231
DiCesnola, Luigi Palma 67, 68, 94, 161, 162, 182, 185, 186, 205, **235**, 236, 231, 294n18, 308n9, 312n45, 320–321n13; later career 234
District of Columbia 97, 297n1, 297–298n14, 321n30
District of West Tennessee 97
Division of the Missouri 223, 334
Dix, John 313n23
Dix-Hill Cartel 313n23
"Dixie" 243
Dodge, Grenville 234
Donohoe, John C. 186
Dorsey, Gus W. 13
Douthat's Landing (Wharf), Virginia 200, 206, 210, 211
Douty, Calvin 94, 95
Dover Mills, Virginia 196
Drake, James 32
Dranesville, Virginia 221, 317n34
Duffié, Alfred Napoleon 67, 69, 74, 77
Dulany, Richard 35, 36, 166, 176, 178, 207, 220, 264, 309n28; later career 254–255
Dunkirk, Virginia 199, 314n9
Dunn, Private 284n29
Dunovant, John 47, 48, **54**, 55, 179, 301n17, 306n26, 311n11, 322n44; death of 247

Early, Jubal 191, 212, 223, 248, 253, 310n8, 322n49
The East 70, 96, 97, 295n12, 313n23
The Eastern Theater 79, 84, 89
Eastport, Maine 95
Edgefield, South Carolina 245, 247
Edisto River 56
Egan, John 323n2
Egypt 291n41
Ekin, James A. **89**, 90, 296n42
El Salvador 226
XI Corps 236
Eliza 155, 307n32
Ellis's Ford, Virginia 198

Ellsworth, Elmer E. 302n29
Enfield rifle 52, 61, 91, 218
Evans, Peter 34, 35
Evans, Stephen B. 35, 288n15
Everett, John 323n63
Ewell, Richard 29, 215, 286n18
Ewell's Corps 214, 287n19

Fairview Cemetery, Culpeper 253
Falls Church, Virginia 246
Farnham, Noah L. 237, 302n29
Farnsworth, Charles 101
Farnsworth, Elon 100, 294n29, 298n22
Farnsworth, Hubert E. 164, 308n16, 309n23
Farnsworth, John 98, 298n22
Fauquier County, Virginia 32, 307n38
Fauquier Sulphur Springs, Virginia 238
Fayetteville, North Carolina 37, 276, 324n3
Ferebee, Dennis 35, 288n18
Ferguson, James D. 273, 301n16, 306–307n30, 311n12
Ferguson, Samuel W. 54, 55, 292n56
Ferguson, Thomas B. 57, 60, 61, 130, 136, 153
Feuardent, Gaston 236
V Corps 8, 71, 283n3, 320n2, 320n8
Financial and Mining Record 291n41
Fincastle, Virginia 314n37
1st Brigade, 1st Division *see* Michigan Brigade
I Corps 293n13, 294n26
1st Georgia Infantry (Mexican War) 36
First Manassas, Battle of 73, 285–286n49, 290n28, 292n56, 302n29
Fish, William 101
Fisher's Hill, Virginia 228
Fishkill, New York 232
Fitz Lee's Brigade 30, 286n9, 323n58
Fitz Lee's Division 9, 11, 30, 31, 32, 37, 44, 119, 120, 121, 122, 123, 125, 139, 145, 156, 166, 171, 179, 191, 201, 204, 215, 216, 252, 253, 254, 263, 265, 272, 275, 276, 277, 278, 279, 280, 285n34, 287n10, 287n14, 311n12, 311n16, 312n40
Fitzhugh, Maria 249
Five Forks, Virginia 253, 283n3, 304n2
Fleet, Dr. 198
Fleetwood Hill, Virginia 5, 67, 68, 69, 94, 95, 217
Florida 48, 70, 71, 75, 226, 315n1, 317n14
Flournoy, Cabel 33, 288n7
Fluvanna County, Virginia 190
Folwell, W.W. 111, 112, 113, 115, 199, 263, 299n26
Fontaine, Edmund 15, 108
Fontaine, Dr. John 15
Foote, Shelby 5
Forge Bridge, Virginia 213

Forrest, Nathan Bedford 220, 227
Forsyth, George 200, 232
Forsyth, James W. **66**, 268, 293n10
Fort Canby, Washington 241
Fort Chaffee, Arkansas 318n79
Fort Leavenworth, Kansas 223, 228, 234, 236, 316n28
Fort McAllister, Georgia 58, 292n79
Fort Monroe, Virginia 314n1
Fort Sheridan, Illinois 224, 317n8
Fort Union, New Mexico 232
Fort Vancouver, Washington 71
Fort Winfield Scott, California 241
Foster, Alonzo 308n6, 312n45
Fowlee, Ellen (Mrs. Fitzhugh Lee) 249
Frankford, Pennsylvania 239
Franklin, William B. 66
Frederick, Maryland 95
Fredericksburg, Virginia 7, 44, 66, 300n8, 306n28, 314n2
Fredericksburg Road 122, 123, 125, 126, 127, 134, 136, 137, 138, 140, 146, 152, 155, 159, 160, 161, 216, 218, 275, 279, 303n5, 307–308n4, 316n20; wooded terrain along **127**
Frederickshall, Virginia 300n8
Freeman, Douglas Southall 5, 221, 281, 283n12, 284n28, 284–285n29; query to Army War College regarding dismounted cavalry 316–317n33
Fremont, John C. 89, 296n43
Friends Asylum, Pennsylvania 239
Frye, James B. 295n6
Funsten, Oliver O., Jr. 288–289n20
Funsten, Oliver R. 36, 264, 288–289n20

Gadsden, Alabama 248
Gaines Mill, Virginia 96
Gallager carbine 289n32
Gallaher, DeWitt Clinton 209
Galveston, Texas 227
Gamble, William 75, 83; career 294–295n39
Garnette, Theodore 243, 284n16, 285n38, 318n84
Garrard, Kenner 87; later career 296n34
Garrison, New York 238
Gary, Martin 206, 207, 208, 210, 290n27, 315n28
Gary's Brigade 206, 207
General Order Number 14 24
General Order Number 25 43, 50
General Order Number 100 113, 299n29
General Order Number 153 112
General Order Number 162 88, 89
General Order Number 174 296n32
General Order Number 191 79, 295n2
General Order Number 207 315n23
General Order Number 236 81–82, 84
General Order Number 237 82

General Order Number 376 80
Geneva, New York 239
Georgetown, South Carolina 58
Georgia 4, 22, 35, 36, 41, 42, 43, 44, 45, 46, 47, 53, 57, 59, 60, 71, 127, 227, 244, 247, 269, 287n6, 290n9, 290n10, 296n33, 306n25, 310n11, 310n4
Getty, G.W. *200*, 204, 205, 314n2
Gettysburg, Gettysburg Campaign 4, 21, 26, 27, 29, 32, 34, 35, 44, 63, 64, 73, 75, 81, 83, 91, 95, 96, 97, 98, 99, 100, 101, 102, 237, 240, 269, 271, 280, 283n1, 285n33, 286n18, 286–287n2, 287n5, 293n14, 294n26, 294n29, 294n31, 296n25, 298n15, 298n25, 323n58
Gettysburg Battlefield Commission 252
Gibbon, John 249, 319n99
Gibbs, Alfred 10, 101, *126*, 128, 132, 262, 267, 268; later career 236
Giesboro Depot, D.C. 67, 80, *84*, *85*, 86, 90, 97, 198, 242, 293n14, 294–295n39, 296n23, 296n31, 321n30
Glenn Allen, Virginia 12
Goldsboro, North Carolina 56, 287n7
Good Hope Church, Virginia 116, 316n19
Gordon, David S. 128
Gordon, George A. 96, 268
Gordon, James B. 9, 28, 29, 34, 35, 286n10, 287n14
Gordon's Brigade *see* North Carolina Brigade
Gordonsville, Virginia 106, 107, 108, 109, 116, 120, 121, 123, 147, 154, 167, 171, 176, 179, 186, 188, 190, 191, 212, 213, 214, 215, 216, 217, 219, 257, 301n27, 307–308n4; Exchange Hotel hospital in *254*
Gordonsville Road, Virginia 128, 142, 143, 146, 149, 155, 167, 171, 176, 182, 208, 213, 217, 311n22, 316n8
Gorgas, Josiah 40, 57, 247, 289n30, 289n37, 291n42
Governor's Island, New York 317n1
Grand Army of the Republic (GAR) 233, 237
Grand Review 223, 234
Granger, Henry W. 12, 100, 284–285n29, 304n1, 320n10
Grant, Nealy 185, 312n39
Grant, Ulysses S. 1, 7, 8, 18, 63, 65, 66, 68, 70, 71, 72, 77, 78, 87, 88, 89, 90, 97, 102, 104, *105*, 106, 107, 108, 109, 110, 192, 198, 204, 205, 210, 211, 212, 213, 214, 215, 217, 219, 220, 223, 226, 227, 239, 240, 250, 260, 293n9, 294n27, 295n43, 296n37, 296n44, 298n1, 299n8, 299n12, 313n23, 315n44, 316n27, 316n28, 319n99, 319n102, 321n24, 324n9
Grant Takes Command 6

Gray, George 110, 298n3, 304n5
Great Ogeechee River 58
Greely, Horace 250
Green, John Shackelford 33
Green Farm, Virginia 71
Green Spring Valley, Virginia 120, 123, 125, 301n23
Greene, A. Wilson 6
Greene, Jacob S. 274, 320n7
Greenland Gap, West Virginia 35, 322n48
Greensboro, North Carolina 53, 54, 59, 60, 61, 252, 292n71, 292n87
Greenville, South Carolina 290n27, 291n44
Gregg, David McMurtrie 11, 67, *68*, 69, 70, 73, 74, *77*, 100, 109, 110, 111, 114, 115, 121, 137, 159, 164, 167, 171, 172, 175, 179, 189, 198, 201, 202, 203, 204, 260, 262, 267, 268, 294n21, 301n27, 310n2, 315n33, 315n40, 315n44, 317n17; at Samaria Church 205–210, 215, 217, 219; later career 226–227
Gregg, John Irwin 67, 74, 137, 138, 147, 148, 159, 160, 161, 162, 163, 164, 166, 167, 202, 205, 208, 218, 225, 262, 303–304n5, 304n10, 304n11, 308n5, 308n7, 308n15, 310n2, 315n33; later career 232
Griffin, Whiley H. 322n49
Grimes, Eli 58
Grimsley, Daniel 156, 265, 277, 324n12; later career 252–253
Gwathmey, Temple 198

Haden, Jerry: comparison of Hampton to Stuart 221, 317n35
Hagerstown, Maryland 34
Hall, Hillman 308n6, 321n15
Hall, John 161
Hall carbine 291n44
Halleck, Henry 65, 66, 81, 86, 87, *88*, 89, 90, 97, 105, 108, 296n43
Halsey, F. Lindsay 142
Hammond, John 100, 298n32
Hampton, Alfred McDuffie 281
Hampton, Mary 281
Hampton, Wade 3, 4, 5, 6, 19, *20*, 21, 22, 23, 24, 26, 29, 30, 31, 35, 41, 43, 44, 45, 46, 47, 49, 50, 51, 52, 53, 57, 62, 68, 118, 119, 120, 121, 122, 123, 124, 125, 127, 129, 130, 133, 137, 139, 140, 141, 142, 143, 144, 146, 147, 148, 150, 151, 152, 153, 154, 155, 156, 157, 159, 161, 164, 165, 167, 169, 170, 171, 173, 176, 177, 178, 179, 181, 182, 185, 186, 188, 190, 191, 192, 193, 196, 199, 201, 204, 205, 206, 207, 208, 209, 210, 212, 213, 215, 216, 217, 21, 241, 246, 247, 248, 253, 255, 260, 263, 266, 271, 286n4, 286n6-n10, 286n13, 287n13, 287n14, 289n2, 290n10, 292n47, 301n6, 301n8, 302n23, 306n23, 306n24, 310n5, 310n8, 311n12, 311n27, 312n47, 312n10,

313n14, 313n17, 313n20, 313n23, 315n42, 315n1, 316n20, 316n31, 318n87, 320n4; comparison with Stuart 220–221; Hampton-Lee controversy 275–281, 324n3, 324–325n13, 325n16, 325n19; later career 244–*245*; preference for fighting dismounted 316–317n37; selection for corps command 221–222
Hampton and His Cavalry in '64 6, 275, 276, 278, 279, 281
Hampton Legion 21, 53, 206, 207, 290n27, 306n24
Hampton-Sydney College 304n2
Hampton's Brigade 21, 26, 30, 286n9, 287n3, 306n24
Hampton's Division 31, 35, 36, 42, 44, 47, 62, 119, 120, 123, 137, 138, 139, 140, 152, 165, 169, 170, 216, 217, 247, 263, 264, 271, 276, 279, 280, 313n30
Hampton's position on June 12, 1864 *178*, *179*
Hancock, Winfield Scott 297n49
Hanover, Pennsylvania 32, 34, 95
Hanover County, Virginia 109, 114, 119, 252, 253
Hanover Courthouse, Virginia 319n117
Hanover Junction, Virginia 56, 60, 106, 107, 108, 214
Hansell, Charles 176
Hare, John 184
Harmon, Asher 36
Harpers Ferry, West Virginia 37
Harrison, Julien 33, 288n7
Hart, James 119, 142, 266, 306n24
Hastings, H.S. 141, 142
Hatcher's Run, Virginia 231
Haupt, Herman 105
Havana, Cuba 249, 251, 294n27
Haw's Shop, Virginia 61, 109, 126, 129, 131, 221, 247, 259, 280, 302n30, 322n43, 322n44
Haynes, Mrs. Captain 198
Hays, President Rutherford 226
Heaton, Edward 263, 315n33
Henry rifle 297n50
Heth, Henry 75
High Bridge, Virginia 256, 288n18
High Point, North Carolina 61
Hill, Ambrose Powell 29, 286n18
Hill, D.H. 313n23
Hill, Mr. 198
Hill's Corps 287n19
Hines, John 164
Holcomb Legion *see* Confederate Regiments, Battalions, and Companies, South Carolina, 7th South Carolina Cavalry
Hollywood Cemetery, Richmond 17, 251, 284n18
Hood, John Bell 18, 227
Hooker, Joseph 24, 64, 101, 104, 213
Hopkins, Michigan 242
Horse shoes, manufacture of 291n43

Horses *see* Billy; Cincinnati; Jeff Davis; Jim; Morgan (breed); Mina; Old Blue; Old Pete; Old Whitie; Putman (Old Put); Rienzi (Winchester)
Howard, Wiley 143, 305n14
Hubard, Robert T., Jr. 140, 181, 304n2, 311n26
Hudson River 226, 229, 230, 238, 268
Huey, Pennock 232, 262; later career 240
Huff, John 13, 284–285n29
Hughson, Lucy Dettor 162
Hughson, Otis 162
Humphrey, Annette 271, 324n2
Humphrey, Moses 130, 153, 154, 306n24
Humphreys, A.A. 64
Hungary 97
Hunt, Henry **109**, 110
Hunt, Lieutenant 131
Hunter, David 99, 106, **107**, 108, 191, 212, 213, 214, 219, 299n8, 310n8, 315n1, 316n28
Hunter, Mr. 247
Huntington, Colis P. 252
Hunton, Eppa 11

Immortal 600 322n49
Indian Territories 228
Ingalls, Rufus 105, 205, 210, 211, 295n10
Invalid Corps 288n7, 288n15
Iona, Michigan 234
Ireland 65
Irwinville, Georgia 227
Isham, Asa 115, 284–285n29
IX Corps 97, 103, 320n2
Izard, Mr. and Mrs. Ralph 256

Jack's Shop, Virginia 36
Jackson, Thomas J. 16, 24, 243, 289n35
Jackson's Corps 240, 286n18
Jackson's River 108
Jacksonville, Georgia 48
James River 9, 15, 35, 56, 68, 104, 106, 107, 190, 196, 205, 211, 213, 214, 217, 219, 259, 299n12, 313n23, 315n37
James River Canal 190, 219, 299n7
Jamestown, Virginia 251
Janeway, Hugh 167, 297n3
Jeff Davis (horse) 55, 136
Jefferson County, West Virginia 198
Jeffords, Robert 55, 56
Jenifer, Walter 51, 283n10; career 291n41
Jenifer saddle 51
Jenkins, Albert 286n2
Jim (horse) 136
Johnson, Bradley 190, 191, 265, 276, 277, 278, 279, 280, 281, 313n14, 322n48, 324n10, 325n14
Johnson, Edward "Allegany" 286n1
Johnson's Island, Ohio 154, 307n37, 313n25

Johnston, Joseph 44, 252, 253, 290n24, 290n28, 318n87
Johnston, Phillip 266
Joint Committee on the Conduct of the War 63, 240
Jomini, Antoine Henry 302n30
Jones, John B. 285n37, 290n5, 291n32
Jones, Willliam E. "Grumble" 33, 35, 106, 268, 269, 287n8; relief of 28
Jones' Bridge, Virginia 204, 205
Jones's Brigade 28, 30
Jordan, Thomas 43, 48, 49, 50, 51; early career 290n24, 290–291n28; later career 291n40
Josiah Gorgas 40, 57, 247, 289n3, 289n37, 291n42
Joslyn carbine 93, 289n32
Journal of Military Service 195

Kansas 12, 15, 16, 64, 223, 228, 234, 236, 284n16, 285n30, 288–289n20
Kautz, August 70, 84, 90, 227, 295n43, 296n45, 298n20
Keegan, John 4, 283n1
Keenan, Peter 240
Kellogg, Francis W. 98
Kellogg, Josiah 95
Kelly's Ford, Virginia 24, 69, 95, 320
Kennedy, Dolf 118, 119
Kennedy, George 308n13
Kennerly, Joseph 307n38
Kentucky 65
Kerr, James K. 297n5
Kerr, Jim 209, 315n39
Kerwin, Michael 240, 241, 262, 318n75
Kester, John 94, 167, 262, 297n3; later mental illness 238–239
Keysville, Virginia 61
Khedive of Egypt 291n41
Kidd, James H. 100, 166, 180, 232, 304n5, 305n13, 306n19, 311n15, 311n17, 311n24, 320n6, 320n9; charge at Trevilians 141–148; later career 233–234
Kilpatrick, Judson 63, 67, 68, 72, 73, 77, 78, 85, 86, 93, 99, 100, 227, 271, 294n17, 294n21, 294n32, 309n20
King, Barrington S. 43, 264
King & Queen County, Virginia 192, 198, 199, 314n39
King William County, Virginia 115, 197, 198, 199, 300n7, 314n39, 315n32

Lafayette, Marquis de 301n3
Lane, Senator H.S. 295n6
Lastley's Church, Virginia 311n12
Laurel Brigade *see* Rosser's Brigade
Laurel Grove, Virginia 61
Lawless, Michael 321n23
Lawrence, Kansas 284n16
Lawyer, Eli H. 302n26
Lee, Fitzhugh 3, 4, 5, 6, 9, 12, 13, 20, 21, 22, 26, 29, 44, 70, 122, 123, 125, 140, 154, 155, 165, 166, 167, 169, 171, 179, 181, 185, 186, 192, 193, 195, 196, 201, 207, 208, 209, 213, 220, 242, 243, 246, 252, 253, 256, 260, 263, 265, 268, 269, 271, 273, 284n25, 286n4, 300–301n19, 301n6, 301n8, 301n9, 301n12, 304n7, 306–307n30, 311n12, 311–312n37, 312n40, 312n45, 312n46, 319n117, 322n53, 323n58; early career **23**, 24, 286n15; later career **248, 249, 250,** 251, 317n24, 319n99, 319n100; Lee-Hampton controversy 275–281, 324–325n13, 325n19; *see also* Fitz Lee's Brigade; Fitz Lee's Division
Lee, George Washington Custis **19**, 23, 324n10
Lee, Robert E. 4, 5, 7, 8, 15, 16, 17, 18, **19**, 20, 21, 22, 23, 24, 25, 26, 27, 28, 29, 30, 35, 36, 37, 40, 41, 42, 43, 44, 45, 46, 47, 49, 59, 60, 63, 64, 104, 106, 108, 109, 119, 122, 204, 213, 214, 215, 217, 219, 221, 222, 223, 243, 244, 252, 253, 255, 256, 269, 277, 280, 281, 285n42, 286n2, 286n3, 286n8, 286n9, 286n13, 286n18, 286ch3n1, 287n6, 287n9, 287n13, 287n16, 289n1, 289n2, 290n5, 290n10, 290n17, 290n18, 290n20, 291n42, 313n17, 319n99
Lee, Steven D. 21, 220, 286n7
Lee, Mrs. William Fitzhugh 285n49
Lee, William H. F. "Rooney" 4, 20, 22, 27, **28**, 29, 33, 34, 197, 287n10, 287n14, 324n10; *see also* Rooney Lee's Brigade, Rooney Lee's Division
Lee's Lieutenants 5, 281
Leesville, South Carolina 258
Leiper, Charles 132, 232, 303n44
LeMat pistol 284n28
Lend-Lease Program 244
Leoser, Charle McK. 128, 129, 173, 190, 268, 310n13, 323–324n4; earlier career 302n29; later career 237–238
Lester, Charles H. 268, 324n5
Lexington, North Carolina 61
Lexington, Virginia 214, 253, 314n41
Libby Prison, Richmond 67, 94, 101, 237
Life (magazine) 238
Ligonier, Pennsylvania 208, 315n37
Lincoln, President Abraham 66, 67, 99, 104, 107, 191, 235, 236, 237, 293n3, 293–294n14, 313n14, 316n28
Lincoln, Todd **224**
Lindsay, Virginia 301n27
Linney, Mr. 109
Lipscomb, James 301–302n20, 322n43
Lisbon, Portugal 226
Litchfield, Allyn C. 320n10
Little Bighorn 297n49
Liverman (Hampton's Scout) 118
Locke, William H. 60, 195, 204, 292n87, 314n15

Index

Lomax, Lunsford 11, 26, 36, 123, 156, 185, 186, 269, 272, 273, 274, 283n7, 284n16, 284n25, 286n10, 287n6, 288n4, 288–289n20, 323n58, 324n8, 324n12; later career 252; relief of Lt. Col. John Critcher 154–155, 306–307n30
Lomax's Brigade 9, 10, 22, 30, 31, 139, 154, 155, 167, 181, 185, 186, 205, 207, 265, 271, 284n25, 312n40, 312n46
Long, Lieutenant (Henry A.) 161, 308n8
Long Island, New York 241
Longacre, Edward 284–285n29, 317n17, 325n19
Longstreet, James 29, 196, 318n87
Longstreet's Corps 287n19, 290n27
Lord, Richard S.C. 300n8
Loudoun County, Virginia 36, 237, 254
Louisa County, Virginia 5, 6, 116, 119, 120, 122, 155, 162, 163, 171, 173, 190, 196, 198, 215, 216, 300n7, 301n12, 308n11, 316n16
Louisa Courthouse, Virginia 9, 109, 116, 120, 121, 123, 125, 128, 137, 139, 142, 144, 154, 155, 167, 170, 171, 175, 179, 212, 247, 256, 258, 276, 278, 279, 302n26, 304n2, 308–309n17, 309n26
Louisiana 97, 223
Louisville, Kentucky 84
Love, Andrew P. 59
Love's Battalion *see* Confederate Regiments, Battalions, and Companies, Alabama, 4th Battalion Alabama Cavalry
Lowden, J.K. 305–306n13
Lyman, Theodore 283n3, 315n1
Lynchburg, Virginia 106, 107, 108, 191, 196, 204, 213, 214, 215, 219, 249, 252, 253, 288n18, 299n8, 310n8, 316n14, 316n28, 319n99
Lynchburg Iron, Steel, & Mining Company 252
Lyon, Lieutenant 157

Macon, Georgia 60, 227, 237
Madison Courthouse, Virginia 191
Magnolia Gardens 247
Mallory's Cross Roads 121, 312–313n10
Mallory's Ford, Virginia 213, 217, 312n1, 313n20, 316n8
Malvern Hill, Virginia 294–295n39
Manassas 101
Manhattan, New York 234
Manigault, Gabriel 126, 127, 129, 130, 179, 190, 193, 301n17, 322n43; Butler's view toward Rutledge 302n30; later career 255–256; observes Regulars in action on June 11, 1864, 131
Manila, Philippine Islands 228, 230
Mann, William D. 100, 320n10
Marcellus, New York 241

Marion County, Indiana 76
Market Street Station, Newark, New Jersey 241
Marquis Road 121, 122, 123, 128, 134, 137, 139, 140, 279, 280, 301n3
Marsh, Elias J. 189
Marshall, S.L.A. 302n28
Mashon, Sergeant 305–306n12
Mason, P.D. 312n8
Mason, Robert 155, 306–307n30, 322n53
Masons (Freemasonry) 234
Massachusetts 65, 74, 95, 194, 238, 291n44
Massie, Thomas 36, 264
Mattaponi River 116, 194, 198, 199, 300n27
Matthews County, Virginia 46
Maynard, R.G. 306n21
Maynard carbine 37, 289n32, 291n44
McAllister, Emma 58
McAllister, Joseph L. 52, 57, 129, 164, 192, 258, 264, 292n47, 208309n17, 309n18; diary of march to Virginia 58–59; grave of **256**
McClellan, George B. 51, 71, 78, 89, 96, 112, 132, 197, 236, 293n10, 296n43, 303n43, 306n28
McClellan, Henry B. 9, 11, 257, 283n8, 286–287n49
McClellan saddle 39, 40, 51, 142
McClure, William 95
McDonald, James W. 289n33
McDonald, William N. 305–306n12
McGuire, Captain 130
McIntire, Samuel B. 268
McIntosh, James 294n36
McIntosh, John B. **74**, 75, 78, 294–295n39
McKinley, President William 233, 246, 251, 318n41
McKinney, Phillip 323n58
McLean House, Appomattox 249
McNeil, James H. 35, 288n15
McPherson's Ridge 75
McQuestern, James 268, 323n3
McVicar, Charles 184, 191, 311–312n37
Meade, George Gordon **8**, 13, 15, 63, 64, 66, 71, 78, 80, 85, 86, 106, 107, 108, 110, 111, 112, 113, 192, 200, 201, 204, 212, 214, 215, 226, 283n3, 288n16, 293n1, 293n2, 294n26, 295n5, 299n7, 299n30, 314n1, 314n26, 315n44, 315n1, 316n28, 320n2
Meadow Bridge, Virginia 287n14, 288n2, 323n58
Mechanicsville, Virginia 121, 176, 179
Medal of Honor 68, 99, 183, 236, 237, 240, 241, 308n17, 309n23
Meigs, Montgomery 81, 105, 295
Melton, Samuel 290n27
Memphis, Tennessee 287n6
Memphis & Charleston Railroad 91

Merrill carbine 289n32
Merritt, Wesley 9, 10, 11, **71**, 72, 73, 77, 86, 94, 121, 127, 128, 132, 134, 135, 137, 140, 147, 148, 151, 157, 158, 159, 161, 166, 168, 169, 179, 180, 181, 182, 183, 184, 185, 186, 203, 216, 218, 225, 230, 262, 263, 267, 268, 283–284n13, 294n29, 296n29, 302n30, 303n1, 303n3, 304n15, 310n2, 311n21, 311n22, 311n24, 312n4, 317n28, 317n30; later career **228**; on artillery support 315n33; positioning of units on June 11, 1864, 303–304n5
Metropolitan Museum of Art, New York 236
Mexican War 36, 54, 55, 74, 75, 101, 126, 137, 238, 291n41
Mexico 21, 226, 246, 296n44
Meyers, Jerry 218
Michigan Brigade 12, 72, 73, 98, 99, 128, 145, 152, 158, 233, 234, 294n31, 304n3, 304n7, 311n24, 320n6
Michigan Department of the Grand Army of the Republic 233
Middle District of Alabama 231
Middleburg, Virginia 15, 35, 67, 69
Middlesex County, Virginia 46
The Midwest 253
Miles, William Porcher 48
Milford, Deleware 226
Military Order of the Loyal Legion of the United States (MOLLUS) 227
Military Service Institute 317n1
Millen, John M. 47, 48, 59, 129
Miller, Cal 184
Miller, Lovick P. 57, 61, 304n7
Mina (horse) 292n47
Missionary Ridge, Tennessee 65, 67
Mississippi 21, 22, 23, 36, 41, 42, 44, 54, 65, 92, 97, 99, 127, 290n9, 290n28, 293n8
Missouri 32, 63, 64, 65, 99, 223, 234, 284n16, 296n49
Moncure, E.C. 118
Monroe County, Georgia 248
Monroe, Michigan 271, 294n31, 320n7, 324appcn2
Monroe Park, Richmond 250, 251, 252
Monroe's Crossroads, North Carolina 306n4, 309n20
Monument Avenue, Richmond 243, 250, 255
Moore, "Little Jimmy" 11
Moore, T.W.C. 66
Morgan (breed of horse) 65
Morgan, John Hunt 220, 316–317n33
Morgan, Joseph H. 265
Morgan, William A. 265
Morris Island, South Carolina 322n49
Morse carbine 291n44
Mosby, John 97, 100, 101, 237, 300
Mountain Road 9, 283n7
Mrs. Watson's farm, Virginia 179

Mulligan, Alfred B. 125, 130, 301*n*17; move to Virginia 55, 56
Munford, Thomas T. 32, **33**, 155, 179, 181, 182, 265, 274, 311*n*26; later career 252, 319*n*108
Munford's Bridge, Virginia 179, 182
My Confession 238
Myers, Frank 194, 221

Nablett 273
Nagasaki, Japan 227
Nash, John 305*n*12
Nashville, Tennessee 87, 227
Nassau, Bahamas 276
National Express Company 253
National Tribune 305*n*13, 308*n*15, 310*n*11
Natural Bridge, Virginia 230
Neese, George 183, 184, 311–312*n*37
Netherland, William A. 301*n*24
Netherlands Tavern, Virginia 120, 123, **124**, 216, 301*n*24
Nevins, Allan 6
New Almaden, California 242
New Castle Ferry, Virginia 109, 111, 112, 114, 116, 118, 170, 215, 219, 300*n*7
New Jersey 70, 94, 225, 276
New Market, Shenandoah County, Virginia 311*n*37
New Market, Spotsylvania County, Virginia 116, 117, 300*n*7
New Mexico 70, 96, 297*n*11
New Orleans, Louisiana 213, 238, 288*n*18
New York 65, 73, 235
New York City 72, 73, 79, 132, 226, 227, 230, 231, 232, 237, 238, 252, 275, 276, 291, 296*n*43, 310*n*6
New York Herald 157, 158
New York Sun **235**
New York Times 214, 226, 231, 236, 241, 294*n*18, 317*n*1, 317*n*15
Newark, New Jersey 241
Newark, Virginia *see* Mallory's Cross roads
Newburger, Alexander 320–321*n*13
Newhall, Frederick C. 93, 259
Newhouse, Silas M. 298*n*33
New's Ferry, Virginia 61
Newton, John 294*n*36
Nicewander, George 184
Nichols, George S. 160, 232
Noah J. Farnham Post, GAR 237
Nonquitt, Massachusetts 224
Norfolk, Virginia 252
The North 38, 56, 90, 108, 268, 286*n*18, 298*n*26, 313*n*23, 319*n*116, 322*n*35
North Anna River 25, 112, 116, 117, 120, 121, 122, 190, 191, 192, 213, 215, 216, 276, 300*n*7, 313*n*20
North Augusta, South Carolina 246
North Carolina 27, 34, 54, 55, 56, 252, 291*n*40, 296*n*33, 324*n*7
North Carolina Brigade 27, 29, 30, 31, 34, 35, 44, 269, 287*n*10, 287*n*13, 287*n*14
Northeast Creek 116
Northern Pacific Railroad 253
Nottoway County, Virginia 32, 258
Noyes, Henry 323*n*2
Nunnelee, Lewis 23*n*63

Oakland, Virginia 301*n*25
Oakland Cemetery, Louisa Courthouse **256**, 258
O'Ferrall, Charles T. 253, 319*n*117
Official Records 47, 91, 252, 261, 277, 278, 286*n*8, 287*n*12, 290*n*18, 291*n*32, 292*n*89, 294*n*18, 301*n*27, 303–304*n*5, 308*n*11, 315*n*33, 320*n*6, 320*n*9
Ogden, Frederick C. 160, 176, 310*n*6
Ogg, G. 320*n*129
Ogg House **178**
Ohio River 252*n*129
Oklahoma 228
Oklahoma Land Rush 228
Olcott, Henry S. 83
Old, Charles 323*n*58
Old Blue (horse) 128
Old Church, Virginia 109, 132, 303*n*44
Old Church Road 302*n*30
Old Pete (horse) 136
Old Stage Road, Virginia 121
Old Whitie (horse) 188, 314*n*40
Opequon Creek 237, 323*n*3
Orange & Alexandria Railroad 106, 107, 108, 177
Orange County, Virginia 7, 116, 190
Ordnance Department: Confederate 37, 39, 52, 289*n*23, 289*n*31; federal 83, 92, 297*n*48, 298*n*39
Oregon 65
Orme, H.C. 308*n*11
Osband, E. D. 91
Overland Campaign 5, 7, 13, 69, 102, 103, 104, 110, 219, 287*n*14, 295*n*7, 297*n*6, 303*n*44, 305–306*n*12, 314*n*2, 322*n*32
Owen, Thomas 32, 288*n*3

Pacific Northwest 65, 70, 132, 253
Pacific Theater (World War II) **244**
Palmer, Dr. Benjamin 53
Palmer, Stephen 126, 301–302*n*20, 302*n*26
Palmetto Regiment (Mexican War) 55
Pamunkey River 105, 107, 109, 111, 114, 115, 116, 118, 192, 195, 197, 198, 199, **201**, 202, 205, 300*n*7, 321*n*26
Paris, France 226, 230
Pate, Henry Clay 10, 11, **12**, 15, 32, 33, 156, 284*n*16, 284*n*18, 285*n*38, 288*n*4
Patton, William 95
Payne, William H.F 32, 34, 288*n*2, 288*n*12, 323*n*58
Pea Ridge, Arkansas 74, 75
Pearl Harbor, Hawaii 242
Pearsons, Kimball 164
Peck, Daniel 81, 295*n*8
Peck, Rufus 196, 297*n*55, 314*n*37
Peking, China 227, 228
Pelham, John 21, 257, 311*n*25, 319*n*111, 320*n*126, 324*n*5
Pendleton, William Nelson 21, 24, 119
Pennington, Alexander C.M. 141, 143, 149, 151, 152, **153**, 155, 156, 157, 166, 232, 263, 268, 307*n*42, 315*n*33; later career 241
Pennington's Battery 149, 153, 156, 184, 299*n*23
Pennsylvania Canal Company 240
Pennsylvania Militia (pre Civil War) 74, 137
Penola, Virginia 300*n*7
Peralta, New Mexico 96
Perrin, Abner 286*n*1
Personal Recollections of a Cavalryman {ellip} 234, 311*n*17, 320*n*9
Petersburg, Virginia 54, 56, 204, 213, 214, 226, 227, 233, 247, 253, 256, 95*n*43, 319*n*17
Philadelphia 100, 226, 238, 240
Philadelphia Weekly Times 275, 310*n*11
Philippine Islands 230
Phillips, Reuben 184
Phoenix, Arizona 308*n*11
Photographic History of the Civil War 237
Pickens, Governor Francis W. 55
Pickett, George 253, 295*n*10
Pickett's Division 188, 212, 214, 215, 288*n*11
Piedmont Fox Hounds 255
Pierce, John "Jap" 184, 311*n*34
Pitkin, P.P. 105
Pitts, Fred 13
Pittsburg 74, 98, 241, 294*n*31, 295–296*n*19
Pleasonton, Alfred 3, 4, 11, 89, 94, 97, 98, 99, 102, 212, 216, 215; on charge of the 8th Pennsylvania at Chancellorsville 240; as corps commander 63, **64**, 65; 66, 67, 68, 71, 72, 73, 75, 81, 85; 266, 293–294*n*14, 294*n*29; relief from command 63, 293*n*2, 293*n*9; view on remount depots 86–87
Poinsett, Peter 319*n*92
Point Lookout, Maryland 255, 307*n*37, 311*n*34, 321*n*24
Pole Cat Station, Virginia 116
Pon Pon River 56
Pond, Thos. G. 180
Pontoon bridging 104, 106, 107, **111**, **112**, 113, 115, 121, 200, **201**, 205, **206**, 263, 295–296*n*2, 299*n*7, 299*n*26, 314*n*9
Pope, John 66, 69, 234
Populist Party 253
Port Townsend, Washington 242
Portage, New York 101

Porter, Madison 323n63
Powers, Daniel 151, 306n19
Powers, David 322–323n54
Prague, Czech Republic 227
The Presidio, California 241
Preston, Addison W. 12, 101, 284n22
Preston, J.S. 41, 42
Preston, Noble 117, 118, 300n10; leads charge 163, 308n13, 308n15; treatment and evacuation for wound 172–173, 189, 310n11, 312n8
Price, George 321n25
Price, Richard B. 100
The Price of Admiralty 4
Princess Anne Street, Fredericksburg 306n28
Prisoner exchange system 313n23
Puerto Rico 227
Puget Sound 293n10
Putman, "Old Put" (horse) 239

Raleigh, North Carolina 240
Randol, Alanson: later career 232, 241–242, 263, 268, 315n33
Randolph, Ohio 239
Randolph, Robert Lee 32, 288n2, 323n58
Rapidan River 7, 101, 104, 198, 237, 287n14
Rappahannock River 4, 5, 7, 16, 44, 46, 47, 198, 259, 286n9, 290n20, 306n28
Rawlins, John A. 97, 294n17
Read, Theodore 288n18
Reading, Pennsylvania 227
Ream's Station 273, 281
Red Shirt Campaign 245
Reeder, William C.H. 81, 295n7
Reidsville, North Carolina 61
Reily, Frank 184
Remington carbine 289n32
Reno, Marcus 232, 268
Republican Party 83, 283, 234, 238, 239, 245, 252, 254, 292n78, 304n5, 318n88
Reserve Brigade 67, 71, 73, 75, 77, 86, 93, 101, 102, 103, 109, 127, 159, 168, 179, 181, 236, 262, 263
Reynolds, J.M. 308n13
Reynolds, John 294n6
Rheinbeck, New York 293n13
Rhett, Alfred M. 50, 291n36
Rhett, Senator Robert B. 291n36
Rich, Bathsheba (Mrs. William Rich) 248
Rich, William W. 36, 60, 154, 187, 264; later career 248
Richmond 7, 8, 9, 11, 14, 15, 16, 17, 19, 25, 34, 35, 48, 49, 51, 53, 54, 56, 57, 59, 60, 61, 63, 68, 70, 104, 106, 107, 108, 109, 110, 136, 161, 176, 187, 190, 196, 204, 206, 207, 210, 213, 214, 215, 219, 223, 227, 243, 247, 249, 251, 252, 254, 271, 274, 276, 284n18, 284n20, 285n46, 287n4, 287n14, 290n27, 291n41,
291n42, 291n44, 292n71, 292n87, 304n7, 312n10, 313n23, 314n15, 315n38, 316n28, 320n2, 324n7, 324n8
Richmond & Danville Railroad 204
Richmond & York River Railroad 202
Richmond Arsenal 37
Richmond Dispatch 276, 277, 279, 280
Richmond Examiner 16, 220, 273, 285n38
Richmond, Fredericksburg & Potomac Railroad 108, 116, 300n7
Richmond Sharps carbine 37, 39, 291n44
Rienzi (horse) 65, 223, 225, 293n8, 317n1
Rienzi, Mississippi 293n8
Ripley, James 91
Rivanna River 106, 107, 175, 188, 212, 214, 219
Riverview Cemetery, Charlottesville 254
Robbins, Kinelm 268
Robertson, Beverly **27**, 30, 268, 269, 287n5; later career 287n6
Robertson, James M. 110, 111
Robertson's Brigade 30
Robins, Augustine W. 315n31
Robins, William T. 207, 209, 315n31
Robins Air Force Base, Georgia 315n31
Robinson, William G. 34, 269, 288n13
Robison, John K. 232, 262
Rock Hill, South Carolina 55, 58, 61
Rockfish Gap, Virginia 215
Rodenbough, Theophilus 96, 128, 135, 195, 218, 262, 302n26, 303–304n5, 314n34, 321n23; later career 232–233
Rooney Lee's Brigade 27, 28, 30, 39
Rooney Lee's Division 31, 33, 34, 35, 119, 269
Roosevelt, President Theodore 254
Root, Elihu 318n41
Rosecrans, William 312n5
Rosser, Betty Winston (Mrs. Thomas Rosser) 114
Rosser, Thomas 33, 114, 119, 123, 125, **147**, **148**, 149, 150, 152, 155, 166, 167, 169, 213, 216, 217, 223, 256, 257, 264, 269, 274, 283n10, 286n9, 287n9, 287n10, 288n4, 301n12, 305n11, 305–306n12, 307n37, 239n28, 310n113, 319n117, 324n13; controversy with H.C. Pate 10, 32, 284n16; Hampton-Lee controversy 275–281; later career 253–254, 319n116
Rosser's Brigade 31, 35, 37, 44, 114, 120, 145, 146, 162, 170, 176, 207, 264, 276, 287n9, 287n10, 287n13, 305n10
Rucker, Samuel Burns, Sr. 174, 193, 194, 313n25
Ruffin, Thomas 35, 288n16
Rugby, Charlottesville, Virginia 253
Rush, Richard 303n43
Rush's Lancers *see* Union Regiments, Battalions, and Companies, Pennsylvania, 6th Pennsylvania Cavalry
Russell, David 294n26
Russell, Whiteford 164, 172, 173, 309n18, 310n11
Rutgers University 275
Rutledge, Benjamin Huger 47, 48, 53, 54, 125, 129, 179, 317n11, 319n92; early career 289n1; later career 247; 265; relationship with Butler 302n30

Sackett, William 134, **136**, 137, 138, 160, 162, 232, 261, 321n16, 321n17
Sailor's Creek, Virginia 232, 239, 240
Saint James Church, Brandy Station 5
St. James Episcopal Church, Richmond 17, 285n46
"St. John's Church, Cumberland Parish, Luneburg County, Virginia" 273
St. Louis, Missouri 84, 285n49
St. Mary's Church, Virginia 205, 320n5; *see also* Samaria Church, Virginia
Saint Patrick's Day 74
Saint Peter's Church, Virginia 203, 204
Sale, John B. 60
Salisbury, North Carolina 58, 61
Samaria Church, Virginia 68, 200, 205, 206, 207, 208, 210, 213, 221, 238, 240, 290n27, 315n32, 315n33, 315n37, 322n43; *see also* St. Mary's Church, Virginia
San Francisco 227, 241
San Juan Islands, Washington 293n10
Sanford, George B. 159, 160
Santiago, Cuba 239, 242
Sawyer, Edward 90, 100, 101
Schaffer, Adam F. 322n97
Scott, Hugh 118, 119
Scott, Winfield 296n43
Scottsdale, Virginia 219
II Corps 321–322n31
Second Manassas 74, 95, 96, 99, 100, 295n40, 302–303n41
Seddon, Secretary James A. 40, 42, 43, 46, 47, 49, 291n32
Selma, Alabama 220, 227, 297n56, 323n64
Seminole Indians 71
Sentinel 234
Seven Days Campaign 295
VII Corps 238, 250
Seward, Secretary William H. 235
Shackleford, Henry 252, 319n111
Shackleford, Lucy 319n111, 324n5
Shackleford, Muscoe 324n5
Shafter, William R. 318n41

Sharps carbine 37, 61, 39, 91, 289n3; see also Richmond Sharps carbine
Shelmire, John 94
Shenandoah Valley 37, 44, 99, 100, 107, 108, 118, 148, 191, 213, 215, 219, 223, 225, 227, 230, 241, 252, 253, 256, 287n13, 311n31, 319n116
The Shenandoah Valley 311n37
Shepherd, Dr. 11, 284n18
Shepherdstown, West Virginia 17, 285n35
Sheridan, Michael V. 66, **224**
Sheridan, Phillip 1, 3, 4, 5, 6, 7, 8, 9, 10, 11, 12, 13, 15, 23, 63, 64, 67, 68, 69, 70, 71, 73, 75, **77**, 78, 91, 96, 97, 99, 102, 106, 107, 108, 109, 110, 111, 113, 114, 115, 116, 117, 118, 119, 120, 121, 122, 125, 132, 136, 137, 139, 152, 156, 159, 167, 169, 171, 175, 176, 179, 186, 188, 189, 190, 191, 192, 193, 194, 195, 196, 197, 198, 199, 200, 201, 202, 204, 205, 206, 208, 210, 211, 212, 213, 214, 215, 216, 217, 220, 226, 227, 232, 233, 236, 241, 244, 259, 260, 261, 263, 266, 267, 268, 275, 276, 277, 279, 280, 281, 283n3, 283n6, 284n15, 284n20, 284n25, 286n10, 287n14, 293n8, 293n9, 293n10, 293n13, 297n55, 298n17, 299n7, 299n17, 299n19, 299n20, 299n23, 300n33, 300n6, 300n7, 300-301n19, 301n27, 303n2, 307n35, 309n19, 309n3, 310n8, 311n14, 312n1, 312n3, 312n6, 312n8, 312n10, 313n17, 313n20, 313n23, 313n30, 314n1, 315n32, 315n37, 315n44, 315n1, 316n6, 316n13, 316n14, 316n19, 316n22, 316n24, 316n31, 317n1, 317n8, 319n116, 320n2, 320n4, 321n27; early career 65–66, 293n5, 293n6; later career 223, **224**, **225**; estimate of strength on Trevilians raid 218–219
Sheridan Circle, Washington, D.C. **225**
Sheridan Tank (M551 Armored Reconnaissance Assault Vehicle) 224
Sherman, Senator John 319n95
Sherman, Willliam T. 68, 175, 195, 223, 227, 229, 230, 244, 247, 248, 287n6, 290n24, 291n40, 294n17, 296n34, 310n4, 313n23, 319n95
Shiloh, Tennessee 290n24, 290n28, 292n56
Shoemaker, John J. 186, 266, 304n2, 312n40, 323n63
Sickles, Daniel 226
Silk Hope, South Carolina 255
Simon (slave of A. B. Mulligan) 56
VI Corps 71, 294n26, 294n35, 321n31
Small Arms: ballistics/wounding effects 310ch16n10, 310–311ch17n10; see also Burnside carbine; Enfield rifle; Gallager

carbine; Joslyn carbine; LeMat pistol; Maynard carbine; Merrill carbine; Morse carbine, Richmond Sharps carbine, Sharps carbine; Smith carbine; Spencer carbine and rifle; Springfield rifle, Starr carbine; Whitney pistol
Smith, C. S. Ross 303n44
Smith, Charles 94, 95, 118, **165**, 203, 232, 262; later career 239–240
Smith, Harmon 141, 151, 157, 304n6
Smith, Mrs. 198
Smith, Robert C. 322n48
Smith, William F. "Baldy" 226
Smith carbine 93, 289n32
Smith's Store, Virginia 207
Smithsonian Institution 223, 225, 293n8, 317n1
Snowden, J.S. 125, 301n18
Snyder, Thompson A. 301n26
Soldiers Home, Washington, D.C. 191, 237
Sons of Confederate Veterans 243
The South 4, 37, 38, 51, 104, 120, 180, 196, 208, 253, 258, 268, 289n31, 290n5, 299n12, 302n21, 313n23, 319¬n116
South Anna River 179, 182
South Carolina 4, 21, 22, 26, 27, 29, 35, 36, 37, 41, 42, 43, 44, 45, 46, 47, 48, 49, 53, 54, 56, 57, 58, 60, 61, 62, 71, 241, 244, 245, 246, 247, 248, 277, 287n6, 287n13, 289–290n2, 290n5, 290n9, 290–291n28, 291n40, 292n56, 311n11, 319n95
South Carolina College 21, 245, 286n6
South Carolina Soldiers Home, Richmond 56
South Fork 307–308n4
South Fork Creek 121, 301n27
Southern District of New York 232
Southern Historical Society Papers 250, 276
Southern Historical Society 252
Southside Railroad 204
The Southwest 132, 296n44
Spanish-American War 227, 228, 230, 233, 238, 241, 242, 246, **249**, 251, 317n1
Spartanburg, South Carolina 246
Spencer, Christopher M. 90, 91
Spencer, Samuel 129, 264
Spencer carbine and rifle 167, 195, 284n23, 289n32, 297n49, 297n54, 297n56, 298n39; advantages of 90–92, 297n50
Spotswood Hotel, Richmond 56
Spotsylvania Battle/Battlefield 18, 104, 110, 221, 323n58; exposed remains on 194
Spotsylvania County, Virginia 104, 109, 116, 117, 134, 182, 192, 194, 300n7
Spotsylvania Court House, Virginia 7, 15, 25, 116, 194, 259, 269, 303n2
Spring Hill Cemetery, Lynchburg 252

Springfield, Illinois 316
Springfield, Massachusetts 95
Springfield rifle 297n49
Stafford County, Virginia 188, 249, 250
Stagg, Peter 99, 140, 232, 261; later career 234
Stahel, Julius 97, 98, **99**, 101, 298n22
Stanton, Secretary Edwin M. 63, 82, 87, 293n2, 296n25, 296n33
"Star Spangled Banner" 243
Starr carbine 289n32
Starr, Stephen Z. 5
Statesburg, South Carolina 53
Staunton, Virginia 106, 107, 108, 214, 215, 219, 299n8
Staunton River 61
Stedman, William 94, 232, 262; later career 239
Steuart, George "Maryland" 286n1
Stevensburg, Virginia 22, 26, 33, 198
Stevensville, Virginia 198
Stockweather, George 181, 311n28
Stokes, William 54, 322n43
Stoneman, George **82**, as chief of the Cavalry Bureau 81–87, 296n25; later career 296n33
Stoneman's Raid 95, 108, 112, 116, 300n8, 301–302n20, 309n26
Stonewall Brigade 285n49
Stonewall Cemetery, Winchester 257
Stranahan, F. Stewart 142
Strathy Hall, Georgia 58
Strother, Mordecai 323n58
Stuart, Flora Cooke (Mrs. J.E.B. Stuart) 15, 29, 285n36
Stuart, J.E.B. 3, 4, 8, 9, **10**, 12, 18, 19, 20, 21, 22, 23, 24, 26, 32, 33, 35, 36, 37, 39, 40, 41, 62, 66, 73, 77, 87, 94, 99, 101, 108, 131, 196, 209, 213, 215, 219, 285n47, 244, 249, 251, 257, 266, 268, 269, 271, 275, 277, 280, 281, 284n28, 285n42, 285n49, 286n2, 286n18, 286ch3n1, 287n7, 287n10, 288n20, 289n35, 289n37, 290n20; comparison with Hampton 220–221; 222, 316–317n33; considered for promotion to lieutenant general 29–30, 287n16; frictions with Generals Robertson and Jones 27–28, 287n6; funeral of **17**; monuments to **14**, 242–**243**; relationship with Henry Clay Pate 10–11, 283n10, 284n16, 285n38; response to Hampton's concerns regarding unit strengths 43–47, 287n13, 287n14; wounding and death of 13–15, 284n25, 284n29, 285n33, 285n37
Stuart Light Tank (M3/5) **244**
Suderow, Bruce A 218, 322n43
Suffolk, Virginia 101, 287n7
Sumner, Edwin V. 284n16
Sweitzer, Nelson 96, 132, 160, 232, 262, 268; later career 237
Syracuse, New York 239, 295–296n19

Tampa, Florida 75, 249
Taylor, Dr. B.W. 208
Taylor, John P. 94, 232, 239, 262
Taylor, Nelson 308n10
Taylor, Richard 298n26
Taylor, Walter 19
Telegraph Road 9, 10, 11, 12, 242, 243, 283n7, 284–285n29; monument to Stuart on 14
Tennessee 55, 65, 66, 68, 82, 87, 95, 206, 227, 269, 287n19, 288–289n26, 290n10, 290n27, 292n73, 296n33
Tennyson, Alfred Lord 243
Terrill, William R. 65, 293n6
Texas 21, 23, 24, 65, 70, 149, 223, 238, 246, 318–39n90
3rd Brigade, 1st Division *see* Reserve Brigade
Third Military District of South Carolina 291n40
Thomas, Emory 287n16
Thomas, George 227, 296n37
Thomson, James W. 153, 156, 184, 307n36; death of 256–257
Thorp, Thomas J. 132, 302–303n41, 321n19
3-Inch Ordnance Rifle 110, 151, **153**, 260
Tidball, Charles **153**
Tilden, Samuel **235**
Tillman, Benjamin "Pitchfork Ben" 245, 246
Tobie, Edward 283n6, 284n15, 321n29
Todd's Tavern, Virginia 8, 259, 288n3, 295n8, 303n44, 306n29, 323n58
Tom's Brook, Virginia 253, 254, 274, 324n13
Torbert, A.T.A. 5, 9, **69**, 70, 71, 72, 73, 74, 75, **77**, 96, 109, 111, 112, 114, 115, 116, 121, 122, 127, 128, 131, 133, 134, 135, 137, 139, 140, 146, 147, 157, 158, 159, 160, 162, 165, 166, 167, 168, 171, 179, 180, 181, 182, 185, 186, 188, 202, 203, 204, 205, 211, 213, 216, 217, 218, 219, 232, 237, 253, 260, 261, 267, 268, 294n26, 294n28, 295n40, 301n27, 301n1, 302n24, 303n1, 303n3, 307n43, 308n9, 309n33, 310n2, 311n22, 311n27, 311n47, 312n1, 314n23, 315n33, 316n8, 317n12, 317n14, 317n15, 321n20; later career and death of 225–**226**
Torbert, Mary Elizabeth Curry (Mrs. A.T.A. Torbert) 226
Totopotomy River 109
Town, Charles H. 99, 298n28
Trask, Thomas 165, 309n26
Trenholm, William 289n1
Trevilian, Charles Goodall 6, 320n129; home of **173**
Trevilian Station: depot in 2015 **141**
Trimble, I. Ridgway 284n29
Trinity Church, New York City 226

Troy, New York 79, 291n43
True History of the Charge of the Eighth Pennsylvania Cavalry 240
Tunstall's Station, Virginia 202, 203, 204
Turner's Run 9, 11, 283ch1n7, 284–285n29
XXII Corps 97, 98
12-pound Napoleon 110, 111, 151, 260, 299n23
Tying-up syndrome 313–314n33

Union, South Carolina 245
Union Cavalry in the Civil War 5
Union Regiments, Battalions, and Companies: (*see also* artillery regiments and batteries)
Federal
 1st United States Cavalry (1st Dragoons) 15, 83, 96, 102, 103, 128, 134, 159, 160, 176, 232, 237, 238, 262, 267, 268, 296n44, 297n11, 300n8, 307–308n4, 321n22
 1st United States Infantry 65
 2nd United States Cavalry 23, 73, 96, 102, 103, 111, 128, 129, 132, 134, 141, 181, 182, 218, 232, 237, 262, 268, 291n41, 302n29, 302–303n41, 315n33
 3rd United States Cavalry, (Regiment of Mounted Rifles) 96, 291n41
 4th United States Infantry 65
 5th United States Cavalry 71, 75, 96, 102, 103, 128, 132, 237, 238, 262, 268
 6th United States Cavalry 70, 74, 90, 96, 102, 103, 137, 232, 238, 242, 261, 268, 297n11, 299n8, 316n24, 316n28
 7th United States Cavalry 236, 250, 297n49
 8th United States Cavalry 294–295n38
 9th United States Cavalry 228
 10th United States Infantry 55
 11th United States Infantry 137
 21st United States Infantry 296
 27th United States Infantry 240
 28th United States Colored Troops 204, 205
 35th United States Infantry 227
Connecticut
 1st Connecticut Cavalry 93, 101, 103
District of Columbia
 Orton's Company 297n1, 297–298n14
Illinois
 8th Illinois Cavalry 83, 97, 102, 200, 232, 294n29, 294n39, 298n17, 298n22, 307n45
 12th Illinois Cavalry 97, 102, 297n14
Indiana
 3rd Indiana Cavalry 75, 95, 102, 103, 284n21, 297n6

 9th Indiana Cavalry 95
 20th Indiana Infantry 81, 295n7
Maine
 1st Maine Cavalry 94, 95, 102, 103, 117, 137, 164, 165, 170, 194, 203, 232, 239, 262, 284n15
Maryland
 1st Maryland Cavalry 97, 102, 288n20
Massachusetts
 1st Massachusetts Cavalry 194, 206, 209, 220, 232, 238, 262, 321n26
 5th Massachusetts Cavalry 238
Michigan
 1st Michigan Cavalry 98, 99, 102, 103, 140, 141, 145, 149, 232, 234, 261, 298n26, 304n1, 320n6, 320n10
 2nd Michigan Cavalry 65, 99
 5th Michigan Cavalry 13, 91, 98, 99, 100, 102, 103, 140, 141, 142, 144, 147, 148, 151, 174, 180, 192, 198, 232, 233, 242, 261, 284n29, 305n13, 305n19, 320n6
 6th Michigan Cavalry 98, 100, 102, 103, 141, 144, 145, 147, 151, 166, 180, 233, 261, 304n5, 320n6
 7th Michigan Cavalry 12, 85, 98, 100, 102, 103, 115, 139, 141, 145, 147, 149, 151, 154, 157, 167, 180, 181, 232, 234, 261, 284–285n29, 304n1, 320n6, 320n10, 320n11
New Jersey
 1st New Jersey Cavalry 70, 94, 102, 103, 167, 203, 238, 262, 293n14, 304n10
 3rd New Jersey Cavalry 103, 241, 298n16
New York
 1st New York Cavalry 73
 1st New York Dragoons (19th New York Cavalry; 130th New York Infantry) 93, 101, 103, 117, 126, 128, 132, 134, 172, 181, 236, 262, 267, 302–303n41, 303n3, 311n28, 321n18
 1st New York Provisional Cavalry 239
 2nd New York Cavalry (Harris Light) 72, 73, 102, 103, 241
 4th New York Cavalry 67, 68, 94, 102, 103, 134, 135, 159, 160, 161, 182, 184, 185, 186, 199, 205, 239, 261, 297n14, 308n9, 312n45, 314n9, 320–321n13
 5th New York Cavalry 100, 102, 103
 6th New York Cavalry 73, 80, 102, 103, 134, 135, 160, 170, 182, 185, 186, 203, 205, 261, 304n6, 308n6, 312n45
 8th New York Cavalry 102, 103
 9th New York Cavalry 81, 102, 103, 134, 135, 136, 137, 159, 160, 161, 162, 182, 202, 203, 205, 232, 261, 303n3, 303n4, 303–304n5,

Index

304n15, 307–308n4, 308n6, 308n10, 321n6
10th New York Cavalry 102, 103, 117, 137, 161, 162, 163, 164, 167, 171, 172, 176, 186, 189, 232, 239, 262, 308n15, 312n6, 321n27
11th New York Infantry (Fire Zouaves) 302n29
16th New York Cavalry 237
22nd New York Cavalry 103, 298n16
24th New York Cavalry 320n2
25th New York Cavalry 204, 320n2
50th New York Engineers 112, 263
Ohio
  1st Ohio Cavalry 298n15
  2nd Ohio Cavalry 103, 298n16
  6th Ohio Cavalry 94, 102, 103, 232, 239, 262, 321n28
  13th Ohio Mounted Infantry 110, 204, 320n2
Pennsylvania
  1st Pennsylvania Cavalry 94, 102, 103, 203, 204, 232, 239, 262, 301n26
  2nd Pennsylvania Cavalry 100, 102, 103, 262, 304n11
  3rd Pennsylvania Cavalry 75, 97, 102, 320n2
  4thPennsylvania Cavalry 95, 96, 102, 103, 194, 208, 262, 304n11, 315n37
  6th Pennsylvania Cavalry (Rush's Lancers) 74, 93, 102, 103, 128, 132, 181, 182, 194, 232, 237, 262, 302–303n41, 303n43, 303n44, 311n21
  8th Pennsylvania Cavalry 70, 102, 103, 232, 240, 262, 297n14, 300n14, 300n7, 304n11
  13th Pennsylvania Cavalry 240, 103, 262, 298n16
  16th Pennsylvania Cavalry 74, 102, 103, 137, 175, 232, 262, 310n2
  17th Pennsylvania Cavalry 95, 102, 103, 116, 134, 182, 186, 203, 205, 236, 261, 300n6, 303n2
  18th Pennsylvania Cavalry 74, 102, 103, 237, 294n35
  21st Pennsylvania Cavalry 320n2
  Irish Dragoons 240
Rhode Island
  1st Rhode Island Cavalry 67, 97, 102
Vermont
  1st Vermont Cavalry 12, 90, 100, 102, 103, 284n22, 297–298n46
West Virginia
  1st West Virginia Cavalry 101, 102, 297n1
  2nd West Virginia Cavalry 298n15
  3rd West Virginia Cavalry 297n14
Uniontown, Alabama 252
United Daughters of the Confederacy: monument on Trevilians Battlefield 257–258
University of South Carolina 286n6
Upperville, Virginia 35, 95

Upperville Colt & Horse Show 254
U.S. Army War College 316–317n33
U.S. Commissioner of Pacific Railroads 245, 318n87
U.S. Highway 1 243, 283n7
U.S. House of Representatives 250, 253, 256, 289n35, 292n78, 314n41, 319n95
U.S. Military Academy 6, 66, 71, 238, 267; Sheridan's suspension from 293n6; commissions upon graduation from 293n7; 302n30; *see also* West Point, New York
U.S. Senate 233, 245, 246, 251
Utah 70, 234

Val Verde, New Mexico 96, 297n11
Valentine, Edward **251**
Vanderbilt, George 164, 309n13
Vaughn Road, Virginia 297
Vera Cruz 226, 317n14
Veteran Reserve Corps 234, 303n44
Vicksburg, Mississippi 71
HMS *Victory* 283n1
Vinton, Harvey 143, 144
Virgin Bay, Nicaragua 294–295n39
Virginia Agricultural and Mechanical College 252
Virginia Central Railroad 6, 15, 106, 106, 107, 119, 212, 213, 219, 251, 254, 310n5; damage to on June 12, 1864 175, **176**, **177**; history of and capacity in 1864 108–109
Virginia Military Institute 252, 311n31
Virginia Tech 252
Von Borcke, Heros 15, 285n37

Wainwright, Charles 293n13
Wainwright, R.P.P. 321n22
Walker, Alexander 157, 320n10
Walker, James 286n1
Walkerton Mills, Virginia 198
Walla Walla, Washington 257
Waller, Thomas 323n58
Waller, Virginia Pelham Stuart 243
War Department: Confederate 21, 22, 26, 27, 28, 29, 33, 37, 38, 41, 43, 47, 48, 49, 50, 51, 54, 57, 59, 62, 248, 252, 269, 285n37, 287n10, 288n20, 289n2, 290n5, 290n10, 291n32, 291n43, 292n56, 292n85; federal 4, 63, 67, 79, 80, 81, 82, 83, 84, 88, 90, 97, 98, 99, 101, 126, 207, 218, 225, 226, 227, 234, 252, 293n6, 294n15, 295n13, 295n17, 296n32, 298n20, 303n4, 303–304n5, 313n23, 317n12
War for the Union 6
Ward, Thomas 323n2
Waring, J. Frederick 36, 120, 152, 153, 264
Warren, Gouverneur 8, 35, 283n3, 288n16
Warren County, Virginia 36
Warrenton, Virginia 64, 252, 255, 271

Warrenton Pike 271
Washington (state) 65, 71
Washington, George 197
Washington, D.C. 9, 35, 36, 63, 67, 72, 74, 80, 81, 82, 84, 85, 87, 88, 89, 94, 97, 98, 99, 100, 101, 105, 108, 111, 119, 191, 198, 200, 212, 223, 225, 227, 232, 234, 236, 237, 240, 242, 245, 246, 248, 251, 252, 256, 287n6, 293n2, 293n14, 294–295n39, 285n13, 295n19, 296n25, 296n33, 299n25, 302n29, 303n44, 303n4, 312n8, 313n14, 314n2, 316n14, 316n28, 320n2, 322n32
Washington & Lee University 314n41
Waterloo, Battle of 4, 283n1
Waycross, Georgia 59
Waynesboro, Virginia 106, 191, 287n8, 308n11, 315n39
Weir, H.C. 163
Welbourne, Virginia 254, 255
Weldon, North Carolina 44, 56
Weldon Railroad 176, 316n27
Wellford Farm (Farley) 71
Wellington, Duke of 4, 243
Wellman, Manly Wade 20, 281
Wells, Edward L. 6, 275, 276, 277, 278, 279, 281, 310n5, 324n3, 324n7, 325n14
Wert, Jeffrey 284n28, 285n38
The West 21, 23, 55, 87, 232, 237, 238, 242, 294n15, 295n12
West Point, New York 6, 19, 21, 22, 23, 24, 54, 65, 66, 70, 71, 74, 75, 87, 90, 96, 101, 107, 114, 132, 147, 149, 165, 226, 228, 229, 230, 231, 238, 241, 246, 249, 252, 253, 267, 268, 269, 277, 288n13, 288n18, 288–289n20, 290n4, 290n10, 290n23, 290n24, 290n28, 291n41, 292n56, 292n73, 293n6, 293n10, 294n28, 294n31, 294n35, 294n36, 296n44, 298n20, 303n43, 310n13, 310n6, 312n8, 314n2, 317n30, 318n90, 323n2, 324appBn5, 324appDn10
West Point, Virginia 107, 192, 198, 199, 312n8
West Virginia 44, 101, 287n9, 316n28
Westmoreland County, Virginia 154, 288n8
Westport, Missouri 284n16
West's Mill, Virginia 179
Wheeler, Joseph 55, 246, 290n10, 317n24, 324n7
White, Elijah 32, 36, **149**, 150, 315n32, 221, 264, 315n32
White, Stanford 230, 231
White, William P. 47, 48, 57, 58, 282n78, 309n18
White House on the Pamunkey 105, 113, 195, **197**, 198, 199, 200, **201**, 203, 204, 213, 219, 299n20, 300n33, 314n1, 314n2, 314n9, 320n2, 320n5, 320–321n13, 321n26, 321n27
Whiting, Charles J. 67, 77, 294n15
Whitlock, J.H. 299n9

Whitney pistol 284n28
Whittle, Beverly K. 155
Wickham, Williams 26, 32, 33, 123, **139**, 140, 167, 181, 182, 185, 207, 210, 265, 277, 279, 283n7, 284n25, 286n10, 287n4, 304n7, 319n106; later career **251**–252
Wickham's Brigade 9, 11, 12, 30, 31, 32, 139, 154, 155, 181, 182, 197, 203, 205, 274, 289n3, 304n2, 312n46
Wigfall, Senator Louis 21, 286n7
Wilcox, Cadmus 21, 286n7
Wilcox's Landing 205
Wilderness 7, 8, 24, 104, 110, 116, 293, 314
Williams, Laura (Mrs. Wesley Merritt) 230, 317n28
Williams, Leonard 47
Williams, Leroy 307n38
Williams, Solomon 34, 269, 288n13
Williston, Edward **183**, 184, 188, 263, 315n33; later career 241–242
Willstown Bluff, South Carolina 56
Wilson, James 11, **70**, 73, 74, 75, 76, 77, 78, 89, 90, 100, 109, **176**, 204, 220, 226, 267, 268, 296n 37, 297n56, 317n24, 320n2, 321n27, 323n64, 323n1, 323n2; at Cavalry Bureau 87–88; captured wagon 273–274, 324n9; Custer's opinion of 295n43; early career 71–72; later career 227–228; on Spencer carbines 91–92
Wilson, William 198, 314n41
Wilson-Kautz Raid 70, 295n43
Wilson's Wharf, Virginia 205
Winchester (horse) *see* Rienzi
Winchester, Virginia 74, 184, 223, 228, 233, 234, 237, 248, 253, 257, 304n1, 323n3
Winnsboro, South Carolina 61, 248, 292n71
Witcomb, Henry D. 108
Wood, James 272
Woodlawn, Virginia 121
Woods, James 301n4
Woodstock, Virginia 252
Woodville, North Carolina 35
Woolridge, W. B. 323n58
Worcester, Massachusetts 238
Wright, Captain 182
Wright, Gilbert "Gid" 36, 37, 120, 123, 127, 129, 130, 139, 143, 145, 146, 148, 152, 166, 169, 176, 178, 207, 216, 217, 264, 269, 274, 311n16; later career 248
Wyndham, Sir Percy 67, 69, 78, 94, 100, 238, 293n14, 297n3

Yale University 54, 160
Yellow Fever 237, 239
Yellow Tavern 3, 4, 7, 9, 12, 13, 14, 15, 156, 219, 242, 243, 259, 269, 283n8, 284n16, 284n18, 284–285n29, 285n33, 297n55, 304n1, 320n10, 322n49
Yellowstone **224**
Yew Ridge, Virginia 33, 73, 269
Young, P.M.B. 27, 36, 44, **45**, 46, 53, 60, 269, 286n10, 292n47
Young's Brigade 31, 36, 59, 120, 127, 129, 130, 146, 147, 148, 152, 176, 207, 248, 264
Young's Mill, Virginia 116

Zimmerman, George 156

www.ingramcontent.com/pod-product-compliance
Lightning Source LLC
Chambersburg PA
CBHW081536300426
44116CB00015B/2655